Contemporary Peacemaking

Also by John Darby and Roger Mac Ginty

THE MANAGEMENT OF PEACE PROCESSES (*eds*)
GUNS AND GOVERNMENT: The Management of the Northern Ireland Peace Process
CONTEMPORARY PEACEMAKING: Conflict, Violence and Peace Processes (*eds*)

Contemporary Peacemaking

Conflict, Peace Processes and Post-war Reconstruction

Second Edition

Edited by

John Darby
Professor of Comparative Ethnic Studies
University of Notre Dame, USA

and

Roger Mac Ginty
Senior Lecturer, Post-war Reconstruction and Development Unit, Department of Politics
University of York, UK

Second edition published in 2008 by
PALGRAVE MACMILLAN
Palgrave Macmillan in the UK is an imprint of Macmillan Publishers Limited,
registered in England, company number 785998, of Houndmills, Basingstoke,
Hampshire RG21 6XS.

Palgrave Macmillan in the US is a division of St. Martin's Press LLC,
175 Fifth Avenue, New York, NY 10010.

Palgrave Macmillan is the global academic imprint of the above companies
and has companies and representatives throughout the world.

Palgrave® and Macmillan® are registered trademarks in the United States,
the United Kingdom, Europe and other countries.

ISBN-13: 978–0–230–21020–2 hardback
ISBN-10: 0–230–21020–1 hardback
ISBN-13: 978–0–230–21021–9 paperback
ISBN-10: 0–230–21021–X paperback

This book is printed on paper suitable for recycling and made from fully
managed and sustained forest sources. Logging, pulping and manufacturing
processes are expected to conform to the environmental regulations of
the country of origin.

A catalogue record for this book is available from the British Library.

A catalog record for this book is available from the Library of Congress.

Printed and bound in Great Britain by
CPI Antony Rowe, Chippenham and Eastbourne

Contents

List of Tables   viii

List of Abbreviations   ix

Acknowledgements   xiii

Notes on Contributors   xiv

Introduction: What Peace? What Process?   1
John Darby and Roger Mac Ginty

Part I   Preparing for Peace: An Introduction
John Darby and Roger Mac Ginty

1   Explaining the Conflict Potential of Ethnicity   11
Crawford Young

2   The Timing of Peace Initiatives: Hurting Stalemates and
Ripe Moments   22
I. William Zartman

3   Cultivating Peace: A Practitioner's View of Deadly
Conflict and Negotiation   36
John Paul Lederach

4   New Contexts for Political Solutions: Redefining
Minority Nationalisms in Northern Ireland, the Basque
Country, and Corsica   45
John Loughlin

Part II   Negotiations: An Introduction
John Darby and Roger Mac Ginty

5   Negotiations and Peace Processes   63
Adrian Guelke

6   Rules and Procedures for Negotiated Peacemaking   78
Pierre du Toit

7   Mediation and the Ending of Conflicts   94
Christopher Mitchell

8 Women, Gender and Peacemaking in Civil Wars   105
   Antonia Potter

9 Traditional and Indigenous Approaches to
   Peacemaking   120
   Roger Mac Ginty

10 The Role of the News Media in Peace Negotiations:
    Variations over Time and Circumstance   131
    Gadi Wolfsfeld

**Part III   Violence and Peace Processes:
An Introduction**

John Darby and Roger Mac Ginty

11 Peace Processes and the Challenges of Violence   147
    Stephen John Stedman

12 Reframing the Spoiler Debate in Peace Processes   159
    Marie-Joëlle Zahar

13 Post-Agreement Demobilization, Disarmament, and
    Reconstruction: Towards a New Approach   178
    Virginia Gamba

Part IV   Peace Accords: An Introduction

John Darby and Roger Mac Ginty

14 Power Sharing after Civil Wars: Matching
    Problems to Solutions   195
    Timothy D. Sisk

15 Negotiating Human Rights   210
    Christine Bell

16 Democratic Validation   230
    Ben Reilly

17 Territorial Options   242
    Yash Ghai

**Part V Peace Accord Implementation and Post-war
Reconstruction: An Introduction**

John Darby and Roger Mac Ginty

18 The UN and Liberal Peacebuilding: Consensus and
Challenges   257
Oliver Richmond

19 From Peace to Democratization: Lessons from
Central America   271
Cynthia J. Arnson and Dinorah Azpuru

20 Casting Long Shadows: War, Peace, and
Extra-Legal Economies   289
Carolyn Nordstrom

21 Military and Police Reform after Civil Wars   300
William D. Stanley and Charles T. Call

22 Refugees and IDPs in Peacemaking Processes   313
Karen Jacobsen, Helen Young, and Abdalmonim Osman

23 Negotiating Justice: The Challenge of Addressing Past
Human Rights Violations   328
Priscilla Hayner

24 Borrowing and Lending in Peace Processes   339
John Darby

Conclusion: Peace Processes, Present, and Future   352
John Darby and Roger Mac Ginty

Bibliography   373

Index   395

List of Tables

4.1	Changing paradigms of state–society relationships 1945–2000	49
12.1	Stedman's typology of spoilers	160
14.1	Consociational power sharing	202
14.2	Integrative power sharing	204
21.1	Security arrangements and peace-plan implementation	301
21.2	Post-civil war police reforms	306
22.1	Top five refugee camp populations in 2005	316
22.2	Top five IDP populations assisted by UNHCR, 2005	317

List of Abbreviations

AG	Administrator General
ANC	African National Congress
APSA	African Peace and Security Agenda
ARENA	National Republican Alliance
ASEAN	The Association of Southeast Asian Nations
AU	African Union
BiH	Bosnia Herzegovina
CDG	Chicken Dilemma game
CEDAW	Convention on the Elimination of All forms of Discrimination against Women
CEH	Historical Clarification Committee
CIVPOL	United Nations Civilian Police
CODESA	Congress for a Democratic South Africa
COPAZ	National Commission for the Consolidation of Peace
DDR	Demobilization, Disarmament and Reintegration
DDRR	Demobilization, Disarmament, Reintegration and Reconstruction
DFID	Department for International Development
DPA	Darfur Peace Agreement
DPA	Dayton Peace Agreement
DRC	Democratic Republic of Congo
DTA	Democratic Turnhalle Alliance
DUP	Democratic Unionist Party
EAC	East African Community
EC	European Community
ECCAS	Economic Community of Central African States
ECOWAS	Economic Community of West African States
ETA	Euskadi ta Askatasuna/Basque Homeland and Freedom
EU	European Union
FARC	Revolutionary Armed Forces of Colombia
FLNC	Front de Libération Nationale de la Corse
FMLN	Farabundo Marti National Liberation Front
FRELIMO	Front for the Liberation of Mozambique
FRG	Guatemalan Republican Front
FSM	Federated States of Micronesia
FUNCINPEC	Front for an Independent, Neutral, Peaceful and Cooperative Cambodia

GAL	Grupos Antiterroristas de Liberación – Anti-terrorist Liberation Groups
GANA	Great National Alliance
GCE	Spanish Civil Guard
HB	Herri Batasuna
HSIC	Head of State Implementation Committee
ICC	International Criminal Court
ICCPR	International Covenant on Civil and Political Rights
ICJ	International Court of Justice
IDP	Internally Displaced Person
IDMC	Internal Displacement Monitoring Center
IGAD	Intergovernmental Authority on Development
IEC	Independent Electoral Commission
IFI	International Financial Institutions
IFOR	Implementation Force
IFP	Inkatha Freedom Party
IICD	Independent International Commission on Decommissioning
ILO	International Labour Organization
INGOs	International Non Government Organisations
IMF	International Monetary Fund
IRA	Irish Republican Army
ISDSC	Inter-State Defense and Security Committee
KLA	Kosovo Liberation Army
LAPD	Los Angeles Police Department
LRA	Lord's Resistance Army
LTTE	Liberation Tigers of Tamil Eelam
MEO	Mutually Enticing Opportunities
MHS	Mutually Hurting Stalemate
MILF	Moro Islamic Liberation Front
MINUGUA	United Nations Verification in Guatemala
MPLA	Popular Movement for the Liberation of Angola
MPNP	Multi Party Negotiating Process
NATO	North Atlantic Treaty Organisation
NCA	Norwegian Church Aid
NEPAD	New Partnership for Africa's Development
NP	National Party
NYPD	New York Police Department
OAS	Organisation of American States
OAU	Organisation of African Unity
OMT	Organização da Mulher Timor
ONUSAL	United Nations Mission in El Salvador

OSCE	Organisation for Security and Cooperation in Europe
PCRD	Post Conflict Reconstruction and Development
PDG	Prisoners' Dilemma game
PLO	Palestine Liberation Organisation
PMA	Ambulatory Military Police
PMC	Politics-Media Cycle
PMP	Politics-Media-Politics
PNC	National Civilian Police
PNG	Papua New Guinea
PNV	Partido Nacionalista Vasco
PPA	Peace Processes Archive
PUP	Progressive Unionist Party
REC	Regional Economic Communities
REMHI	Recovery of Historical Memory
RUC	Royal Ulster Constabulary
RUF	Revolutionary United Front
SADC	Southern African Development Community
SAG	South African Government
SALW	Small Arms and Light Weapons
SARPCCO	Southern African Regional Police Chiefs Coordinating Committee
SAT	Superintendency of Tax Administration
SCR	Security Council Resolution
SDLP	Social Democratic and Labour Party
SIDDR	Stockholm Initiative on Disarmament, Demobilization and Reintegration
SLM	Sudan Liberation Movement
SOC	State of Cambodia
SRSG	Special Representative of the Secretary General
SWAPO	South West Africa People's Organization
TEC	Transitional Executive Council
TRC	Truth and Reconciliation Commission
TULF	Tamil United Liberation Front
UCDP	Uppsala Conflict Data Project
UDA	Ulster Defence Association
UKUP	United Kingdom Unionist Party
UNAMA	United Nations Assistance Mission in Afghanistan
UNAVEM	United Nations Angola Verification Mission
UNDP	United Nations Development Programme
UNHCR	United Nations High Commission for Refugees
UNIFEM	The United Nations Development Fund for Women
UNITA	National Union for Total Independence of Angola

UNMIBH	United Nations Mission on Bosnia and Herzegovina
UNMIK	United Nations Interim Administration in Kosovo
UNSG	United Nations Secretary General
UNTAC	United Nations Transitional Authority in Cambodia
UNTAG	United Nations Transition Assistance Group
UNTAET	United Nations Transitional Administration in East Timor
URNG	Unidad Revolucionaria Nacional Guatemalteca/Guatemalan National Revolutionary Unit
USAID	United States Agency for International Development
USIP	United States Institute of Peace
WCG	Western Contact Group
WO	Way Out

Acknowledgements

We would like to acknowledge the help and encouragement of Alison Howson, Amy Lankester-Owen, and Gemma D'Arcy Hughes from Palgrave Macmillan. Our main thanks, of course, are due to the contributing authors.

Notes on Contributors

Cynthia J. Arnson is Director of the Latin American Program of the Woodrow Wilson International Center for Scholars. She is editor of *Comparative Peace Processes in Latin America*, co-editor of *Rethinking the Economics of War: The Intersection of Need, Creed, and Greed*, and author of *Crossroads: Congress, the President, and Central America, 1976–1993*.

Dinorah Azpuru is assistant professor in the Department of Political Science, Wichita State University. Her areas of expertise are comparative politics, Latin American politics, democratization and peacebuilding. She has published extensively on those subjects.

Christine Bell is Professor of International Law and Co-Director of the Transitional Justice Institute, University of Ulster. She is author of *Peace Agreements and Human Rights*, and a report published by the International Council on Human Rights Policy entitled *Negotiating Justice? Human Rights and Peace Agreements*.

Charles T. Call is Assistant Professor of International Relations in the School of International Service at American University. His publications secure *Constructing Security and Justice after War* and *Building States to Build Peace* and numerous articles on post-conflict peacebuilding and security reforms.

John Darby is Professor of Comparative Ethnic Studies at the Kroc Institute in the University of Notre Dame, where he is establishing a Peace Accords Matrix (PAM). He was founding director of INCORE at the University of Ulster. His recent books include *The Management of Peace Processes*; *Guns and Government* (both with Roger Mac Ginty); *The Effects of Violence on Peace Processes*; *Violence and Reconstruction*; and *Peacebuilding after Peace Accords* (with Tristan Anne Borer and Siobhan McEvoy-Levy).

Virginia Gamba is Director of Safer Africa. She specializes in global security issues with a particular reference to arms management and disarmament, micro-development and security, civil–military integration, and defence restructuring. She is author of *Signals of War* (with L. Freedman), *Governing Arms* and the UNIDIR collection on *The Management of Arms during Peace Processes*.

Yash Ghai was formerly professor of public law at the University of Hong Kong. He is the head of the Constitution Advisory Support Unit, UNDP in Kathmandu assisting with the constitution making process in Nepal. He was Chair of the Constitution of Kenya Review Commission (2000–2002) and of the Kenya Constitutional Conference (equivalent to a constituent assembly) from 2002–2004. His publications include *Autonomy and Ethnicity: Negotiating Competing Claims in Multi-Ethnic States* and *Hong Kong's New Constitutional Order: Resumption of Chinese Sovereignty and the Basic Law.*

Adrian Guelke is Professor of Comparative Politics and Director of the Centre for the Study of Ethnic Conflict at Queen's University, Belfast. Recent books include *Terrorism and Global Disorder, Rethinking the Rise and Fall of Apartheid, Democracy and Ethnic Conflict*, and *A Farewell to Arms?: Beyond the Good Friday Agreement.*

Priscilla Hayner co-founded the International Center for Transitional Justice and is director of its Geneva office and Peace and Justice Program. She has written widely on truth commissions. She previously served as programme officer for the Joyce Mertz-Gilmore Foundation and consultant to the Ford Foundation and the United Nations.

Karen Jacobsen is a faculty member in the School of Nutrition and Science Policy, Tufts University and is based at the Feinstein International Center, where she leads the Refugees and Forced Migration Program. Her current research focuses on urban refugees and IDPs, and on remittances and livelihood interventions in conflict-affected areas. Her last book was *The Economic Life of Refugees.*

John Paul Lederach is Professor of International Peacebuilding in the Joan B. Kroc Institute for International Peace Studies at the University of Notre Dame and a Distinguished Scholar at Eastern Mennonite University's Conflict Transformation Program. He works extensively as a practitioner in conciliation processes, active in Latin America, Africa, and Central Asia.

John Loughlin is Professor of European Politics at Cardiff University. His recent books include *Subnational Government: the French Experience* (with M. Bogdani), *Albania and the European Union* (edited with D. Hanley), *Spanish Political Parties* (with M. Keating and K. Deschouwer), *Culture, Institutions and Regional Development.*

Roger Mac Ginty is a senior lecturer at the Post-war Reconstruction and Development Unit, Department of Politics, University of York. He has been principal investigator on a number of Economic and Social Research Council projects and directed the Chevening Programme on conflict resolution at York. His books include *The Management of Peace Processes, Guns and Government* (both with John Darby) and *No War, No Peace: The Rejuvenation of Stalled Peace Processes and Peace Accords.*

Christopher Mitchell is Emeritus Professor of Conflict Research in the Institute for Conflict Analysis and Resolution, George Mason University, Virginia. He is the author of *Gestures of Conciliation* and has edited *Zones of Peace* with Landon Hancock. He has worked as a mediator or facilitator on conflicts in Europe, Africa, and the Middle East.

Carolyn Nordstrom is Professor of Anthropology at the University of Notre Dame. Her principal research interests are political violence, extra-legal economies, globalization, and gender. Her publications include *Global Outlaws: Crime, Money and Power in the Contemporary World* and *Shadows of War: Violence, Power, and International Profiteering in the Twenty-First Century.* She was recently awarded John D. and Catherine T. MacArthur and John Guggenheim Fellowships.

Abdalmonim Osman studied veterinary science in Khartoum and Edinburgh, and is currently studying livelihoods and conflict in Darfur as part of his PhD research at the Feinstein International Center, Tufts University.

Antonia Potter is a project manager at the Centre for Humanitarian Dialogue in Geneva who specializes on gender and mediation issues. She is author of *We the Women: Why Conflict Mediation Is Not Just a Job for Men.*

Ben Reilly is Director of the Centre for Democratic Institutions at the Australian National University, and has previously worked for the United Nations, International IDEA, and the Australian government. He has advised many governments and international organizations on issues of democratization, and conflict management, and published six books and over 40 journal articles on these subjects. His latest book is *Democracy and Diversity: Political Engineering in the Asia-Pacific.*

Oliver Richmond is professor in the School of International Relations, University of St. Andrews. He is also director of the Centre for Peace and Conflict Studies. He is currently working on a major research project on Liberal Peace Transitions and a book entitled, *Peace in IR Theory.* His publications include *The Transformation of Peace* and *Maintaining Order, Making Peace.*

Timothy D. Sisk is associate professor in the Graduate School of International Studies, University of Denver, where he also serves as faculty in the Master of Arts Program in Conflict Resolution. He is currently finishing a book titled *Bargaining with Bullets: Political Violence and Peace Processes.* Sisk is the author of six books and many articles, including *Democracy, Conflict and Human Security* (with Judith Large), *Democratization in South Africa,* and *Power Sharing and International Mediation in Ethnic Conflicts.*

William D. Stanley is Professor of Political Science at the University of New Mexico. A specialist on Central America, he is author of one book and numerous articles and chapters on international peacekeeping, political violence, and its prevention. His work emphazises the reform of judicial, police, and military institutions.

Stephen John Stedman is senior research scholar at the Center for International Security and Cooperation at Stanford University. He was research director of the UN High-Level Panel on Threats, Challenges, and Change.

Pierre du Toit is Professor in the Department of Political Science at the University of Stellenbosch, South Africa. He is the recipient of a Fulbright New Century Scholars Award for 2002/2003. His latest book is *South Africa's Brittle Peace – The Problem of Post-Settlement Violence.*

Gadi Wolfsfeld is professor in the Department of Political Science, Hebrew University of Jerusalem. His research deals with the role of the news media in political conflicts and peace processes. He is author of *Media and Political Conflict: News from the Middle East.*

Crawford Young is Rupert Emerson and H. Edwin Young Professor of Political Science at the University of Wisconsin-Madison. His major books include *Politics in the Congo, The Politics of Cultural Pluralism, Ideology and Development in Africa, The Rise and Decline of the Zairian State,* and *The African Colonial State in Comparative Perspective.* A former president of the African Studies Association, he is a fellow of the American Academy of Arts and Sciences.

Helen Young is a faculty member in the School of Nutrition and Science Policy, Tufts University, and is based at the Feinstein International Center. Her current research analyses the impact of conflict on livelihoods, trade, and remittances in Darfur and the implications for humanitarian programmes, peace, and recovery. She is co-editor of the journal *Disasters,* and her study of Darfur, *Livelihoods under Siege,* was published in 2005.

Marie-Joëlle Zahar is an associate professor of Political Science at the Universite de Montreal. She specializes in the politics of non-state actors engaged in civil conflicts. She has published articles in *International Peacekeeping* and the *International Journal,* and has contributed chapters to several edited books on conflict resolution and peace implementation.

I. William Zartman is the Jacob Blaustein Professor of International Organizations and Conflict Resolution and Director of the Conflict management Program at the Paul H. Nitze School of Advanced International Studies, Johns Hopkins University, Washington, DC. He has contributed to the field of negotiation analysis, editing and co-authoring almost twenty books including *Getting in: Mediators' Entry into the Settlement of African Conflicts, Peacemaking in International Conflict: Methods and Techniques,* and *Cowardly Lions: Missed Opportunities to Prevent Deadly Conflict and State Collapse.*

Introduction: What Peace?
What Process?

John Darby and Roger Mac Ginty

Just as the past two decades has seen a significant number of civil wars, it has also seen a significant number of peace processes, peace agreements, post-war reconstruction programmes, and efforts to reach intergroup reconciliation. Many international organizations, governments, militant groups, NGOs, and communities have gained vast experience of making, keeping, and building peace. Much of this experience has come the hard way: through trial and error, fire brigade-style emergency reactions, or because – forced into a corner – they had little choice but to strive for accommodation with an opponent. But some of this experience has been able to build on lessons learned from other peace processes. Political parties, government officials, and United Nations personnel in Nepal, for example, were keen students of the ways in which peace agreements were reached and implemented in other locations. Peacemaking processes cannot be lifted wholesale like templates and applied to other locations; the variations in civil war contexts are too great. Quite simply, some peacemaking environments are more benign than others. But the very fact that peacemaking efforts are underway in one location may encourage peacemaking in another. Techniques used in one location may be investigated and adapted for use in another location.

This book brings together both scholars and practitioners with expertise on peacemaking in an attempt to distil the key lessons from peace processes since 1990. Rather than taking a case study approach, whereby each chapter focuses on an individual peace process, the book is organized around the main themes or stages found in many peace processes. This thematic approach allows for the easier identification of transferable lessons between peace processes and means that contributors have been able to draw on multiple examples. Five key themes or stages in a peace process are identified: preparing for peace, negotiations, violence, peace accords, and post-accord peacebuilding and reconstruction. While this is a comprehensive framework and helps us conceptualize peace processes for the purposes of this book, real world peace processes defy neat categorization. Indeed, there is no such thing as a typical peace process that follows a precisely linear path from tentative pre-negotiation contacts to full-scale negotiations, agreement, and implementation. Instead, the reality of peace processes is often a stop-go dynamic and a complex choreography of the sequencing of initiatives and concessions to suit local circumstances.

Mirroring the five themes or stages, the book is organized into five sections. Each section begins with a brief introduction of the main issues and contains chapters relevant to the theme or stage of the peace process. Some issues, such as gender or indigenous approaches to peacemaking, are cross-cutting and potentially have relevance to all stages of a peacemaking process. The book is deliberately comparative and draws on examples that are often overlooked in other studies of peacemaking. This is the second edition of the book, allowing contributors to update their chapters in the light of the changing pattern and context of peacemaking, and in the light of changing academic debates.[1] Perhaps the most significant contextual change since the publication of the first edition has been the post-9/11 'war on terror' and the rush by some governments and international organizations to classify militant opponents as 'terrorists'. In some cases, for example the Philippines, the space for inclusive approaches to peacemaking has narrowed noticeably. Yet there have been other, more positive, changes such as more sophisticated and patient efforts by the international community to introduce democracy in post-civil war societies or the increasing recognition that sustainable development is the key to sustainable peace.

The second edition of the book has also allowed the introduction of new chapters in recognition of the growing complexity of peacemaking and its linkage with other issues such as globalization or international campaigns to reduce poverty. Thus this edition includes new chapters on the international structures of peacemaking, gender, traditional peacemaking techniques, refugees and the internally displaced, the political economy of peacemaking, and peacebuilding. The additional and revised chapters have allowed a greater focus on the post-peace accord phase of peacemaking. Several hundred peace accords have been reached over the past two decades.[2] Yet the mere reaching of an accord brings no guarantee of its implementation. Indeed, the implementation and reconstruction phases of a peace process are often the site of further conflict. The concluding chapter ends with a set of propositions designed to help policymakers and those involved in peacemaking. These propositions have been fully revised from the first edition.

What is a peace process?

The use of the term 'peace process' may be recent but the concept is as old as war. Sophisticated conventions on ceasefires and peace negotiations were already well established and accepted when the Iliad was composed. Harold Saunders has described the gestation of the term:

> In the early years of Secretary of State Henry Kissinger's 1974 shuttle diplomacy in the Middle East, those of us flying with him first used the phrase 'negotiating process' to describe our mediation of a series of interim agreements. Soon, however, we realized that the phrase was too narrow, because our stated purpose was for each interim agreement to change the surrounding political environment and make possible a further step. We coined the phrase 'peace process' to capture the experience of this series of mediated agreements embedded in a larger political process.[3]

The popularity of the term, and the processes themselves, increased markedly during the 1990s, although the extensive set of variables involved during the peace processes greatly complicates the task of defining them. Despite this, 'peace process' has become a convenient term to describe persistent peace initiatives that develop beyond initial statements of intent and involve the main antagonists in a protracted conflict. They are likely to be more significant than an isolated peace proposal. Instead a peace process will have certain robust and systemic qualities enabling it to withstand some of the pressures hurled against it, and to develop beyond initial statements of intent made by the main actors. The extensive set of variables involved in peace processes greatly complicates the task of definition. Peace initiatives can be formal or informal, public or private, subject to popular endorsement or restricted to elite-level agreement. They can be sponsored by the United Nations or other external parties, or can spring from internal sources. All peace processes are fragile, and most fail sooner rather than later. The task of the implementation of any accord is highly dependent on the political will of the parties and on the international political and economic context.

We suggested in an earlier work in 2000 that five essential criteria are required for a successful peace accord: that the protagonists are willing to negotiate in good faith; that the key actors are included in the process; that the negotiations address the central issues in dispute; that force is not used to achieve objectives; and that the negotiators are committed to a sustained process. We continued:

> Outside these general principles, peace processes follow greatly varied directions. Pre-negotiation contacts may be used to test the ground, and may involve external or internal mediators. The official process usually begins with a public announcement and often with a ceasefire. Once started, the rules and sequence of negotiation are determined by negotiators who, by definition, have little experience of negotiation. It is not essential to start with a defined constitutional or political outcome for the process, but a

peace process cannot be regarded as completed unless a political and constitutional framework has been agreed. Even if it is, the detailed implementation presents other opportunities for failure. Throughout, the process is likely to run into periods, sometimes extensive, of stalemate. The ultimate test of its durability is its ability to retain all of its key characteristics and to leave open the possibility of restoring momentum.[4]

A peace accord will not mark a definitive endpoint in a long-running, complex civil war. Instead the conflict will continue to have to be managed through the implementation and institutionalization of the accord. Post-war reconstruction is part of a peace process. The pace, format, and priorities of the reconstruction process are likely to have important bearings on the quality and longevity of the peace. Reconstruction does not merely concern the repair of physical damage. Instead, it extends to the rebuilding of fractured relationships and communities.

Just as many civil wars have transnational and international characteristics, most peacemaking processes have significant cross-border dimensions. Regional neighbours may regard a peace process as an opportunity to stabilize the region or as a threat to a profitable *status quo*. Importantly, political actors in a civil war country may be prone to a series of external events and processes over which they have no control. The election of a new US President, a new mandate for an international organization, or a downturn in a commodity price may produce a new set of circumstances that spell success or failure for a peace process.

Academic and policy-related studies of peace processes have tended to concentrate on a relatively narrow range of cases, with the highest volume of publications on Northern Ireland, the Israeli-Palestinian 'Oslo process', and South Africa's transition. Other peace processes, for example in Mindanao, Guinea-Bissau, or southern Sudan have received considerably less attention. A growing number of comparative studies have been published, and efforts have been made to identify the conditions that favour or hinder the implementation of peace accords.[5] Sub-fields of specialist academic interest have grown around certain issues (such as spoiler groups, truth recovery and demobilization, disarmament and reintegration). Other issues, however, have received relatively scant attention. For example, the differing impacts of peace processes on men and women are under-researched as are the economics of war and peacemaking – two issues dealt with in this book.

The critical view of peace processes

Many peace processes in last two decades have allowed antagonists to reach an accommodation and end violent conflict. Moreover, many peace processes have been accompanied by humanitarian and reconstruction programmes that have made real improvements to the lives of millions. Yet critical analyses of contemporary peace processes have identified a series of shortcomings with the structures and methods of peacemaking.[6] Three main criticisms are worth illuminating. The first criticism is that many contemporary peace processes fail to address the underlying causes of conflict. Instead, they concentrate on the manifestations of conflicts. Ministering to conflict manifestations often has the capacity to make a qualitative difference to people's lives (e.g., through the repatriation of refugees or the reconstruction of homes) but without dealing with underlying conflict causes, the conflict may be stored for future generations. Internationally supported efforts to deal with conflict manifestations are often reduced to technocratic interventions (such as the reform of government institutions under the 'good governance' agenda) but are less well-equipped to deal with behaviour and perceptions. This affective dimension of conflict, and the related attitudes of hatred, prejudice, grievance, fear, and insecurity, holds the key to the transformation of violent conflict and yet is often overlooked by technocratic interventions.

A second criticism of contemporary peacemaking is that it is often a creature of the international community and their co-opted national elites and has limited connection with the bulk of citizens in the war-affected state. There can be little doubt that international actors often have the skills and resources required to encourage local actors to reach and implement a peace accord. Yet, in some cases, international actors have sought to make peace deals that have little community acceptance. While the top-down peace may be celebrated in diplomatic capitals it may struggle to be regarded as anything other than a foreign imposition. Scholars from the critical perspective have also noted how internationally supported peace-support interventions (often called 'the liberal peace') reflect Western political, economic, and cultural norms in their peacebuilding and reconstruction activities.[7] Thus, democratization programmes, human rights legislation, new constitutions, and economic reform may conform to Western expectations but overlook indigenous norms. Many international peace-support interventions are little short of comprehensive state-building programmes, but the state is rebuilt in a Western image.

A key element of Western-supported peace and reconstruction interventions is the acceptance of neo-liberal economic norms. Thus peacebuilding is often accompanied by marketization, privatization, the formalization of the economy, the cutting of the public sector, and the opening up of the economy to international economic forces. Indeed, international reconstruction assistance is usually explicitly linked to an acceptance of World Bank and International Monetary Fund stipulations. The role of the market in post-peace accord societies is decidedly mixed. In a significant number of cases 'peace' has been accompanied by mass unemployment, a brain-drain, aid dependency, rural-urban migration, and the failure of the economy to find a model for sustainable development in the context of unrestrained international market forces. This is perhaps one of the most persistent and wicked problems associated with contemporary peace processes: how can the benefits of peace be made real and shared as widely as possible when international economic structures condemn citizens in many post-peace accord societies to long-term poverty?

A third criticism of contemporary peacemaking is that it often reinforces power-holders and replicates exclusive patterns of social and political relations. Peace processes have a strong tendency to entrench the legitimacy and position of antagonists. Those who held the guns or the dominant position on the battlefield when a ceasefire was called become negotiating (and possibly government) partners regardless of their authority to represent their community. Other voices, often those without firepower, tend to go unheard. This might help explain why many peace processes are overwhelmingly male. While the transition from militant group to political party is to be encouraged, the structure of many peace processes prevents the break-up of the 'civil war cartel' and the development of political parties not based on exclusive ethnic programmes. So while the means of the conflict may change, the basic outlines of the conflict remain in place. Moreover, in many peace processes, participants have been unwilling or unable to challenge prevailing patterns of social and political organization. Although violence ends, patterns of land ownership, patriarchy, and political participation remain unchanged. As a result, the 'peace' is essentially conservative rather than transformative.

In a number of cases, peace processes have become protracted, freezing rather than transforming the conflict. At certain times, peace processes in the Middle East, Basque Country, Colombia, Sri Lanka, and Northern Ireland have had this frozen character. Peace process participations recognize the benefits of the existence of a peace process (e.g., a respite from violence and greater opportunities to attract external aid) but are not motivated to pursue the peace process to a conclusion such as a comprehensive peace accord. These 'no war, no peace' situations are often attended by the rhetoric of peace and can attract considerable international support (often in terms of peacebuilding and reconstruction resources) but they can engender popular cynicism in the civil war country.[8] No war, no peace situations may also be found in post-peace accord societies in which an accord has been reached, but participants adopt a tardy or selective attitude to its implementation. The result may be a grudging co-existence between former antagonists rather than a comprehensive attempt to deal with grievances.

The continued need for peace processes

Despite the possible pitfalls, the promise held out by peace processes is enormous. There is a chance that a successful peace process will create the political space to enable the antagonists to enter into a serious dialogue that will address the underlying causes of the conflict. Moreover, the potential benefits stemming from the *process* of making peace are not to be underestimated. A peace process holds out the prospect of reducing the costs of an ongoing conflict, whether the costs are measured in terms of human lives, quality of life opportunities, or squandered economic potential. It is in the realm of humanitarian benefits that peace processes can have most impact. Seemingly prosaic details such as fewer checkpoints or easier access to markets and schools constitute the real peace dividend.

The need for peace processes remains strong. Although the 'insurgencies' of Iraq and Afghanistan and the 'war on terror' have dominated Western media headlines in the years since 9/11, ethnonational tensions and civil wars remain a persistent problem. Their capacity to spark complex political and humanitarian emergencies remains undiminished. Moreover, the fact that civil wars tend to last for many years and have substantial cross-border dimensions means that they will require repeated attention from international actors. Some of the key questions facing those interested in contemporary peace and conflict include:

- how to satisfy demands for, and resistance to, autonomy and separation;
- how to accommodate the needs of minorities, and the insecurities of the majorities, in deeply divided societies;
- how to identify, or cultivate, moments in which political rather than military initiatives might be fruitful;
- how to deal with violence deliberately targeted at derailing peace initiatives;
- how to deal with former combatants and their weapons;
- how to reconcile a society with its fraught past;
- how to realize a peace dividend in terms of jobs, housing, and sustainable development?

This book attempts to deal with these issues.

Notes

1. The first edition was J. Darby & R. Mac Ginty (eds), *Contemporary Peacemaking: Conflict, Violence and Peace Processes* (Basingstoke: Palgrave Macmillan, 2003).
2. Many of these have been minor agreements or part agreements. In the autumn of each year the *Journal of Peace Research* usually publishes an update from the Uppsala Conflict Data Program which lists peace accords in the previous 12 months.
3. H. Saunders, *A Public Peace Process: Sustained Dialogue to Transform Racial and Ethnic Conflicts* (Basingstoke: Palgrave, 2001), p. xx.
4. J. Darby & R. Mac Ginty, *The Management of Peace Processes* (London: Macmillan, 2000), p. 8.

5. See, for example, N. Ball, 'The Challenges of Rebuilding War-Torn Societies', in C.A. Crocker, F.O. Hampson, & P. All (eds), *Turbulent Peace: The Challenges of Managing International Conflict* (Washington DC: United States Institute of Peace Press, 2001), pp. 719–736.

6. Critical studies of peacemaking include D. Chandler, *Faking Democracy* (London: Pluto, 2002) and D. Chandler, *From Kosovo to Kabul: Human Rights and International Intervention* (London: Pluto, 2002); M. Pugh, *War Economies in Their Regional Context: The Challenge of Transformation* (Boulder CO: Lynne Rienner); R. Paris, *At War's End* (Cambridge: Cambridge University Press, 2004); O. Richmond, *The Transformation of Peace* (Basingstoke: Palgrave, 2005); and R. Mac Ginty, *No War, No Peace: The Rejuvenation of Stalled Peace Processes and Peace Accords* (Basingstoke: Palgrave, 2006).

7. See the works of historian Michael Howard for discussion of the creation of peace in the likeness of the victor: *War and the Liberal Conscience* (London: Temple Smith, 1978) and *The Invention of Peace: Reflections on War and International Order* (New Haven CT: Yale University Press, 2000).

8. 'No war, no peace' situations are discussed in more detail in R. Mac Ginty (2006), op. cit.

Part I

Preparing for Peace: An Introduction

John Darby and Roger Mac Ginty

Peace processes do not emerge from a vacuum. They require conscious decisions, initial steps, fresh analyses, and risk taking. Altered local and international circumstances, both contrived and fortuitous, can also play a role. What seems essential from the outset is a clear conflict analysis in which the causes, manifestations, and costs of the conflict can be reviewed. The immediacy of violence and recrimination, and in-group pressure mean that this is not always possible. The tendency of 'ethnic conflict' to adopt peculiar dynamics and forms of violence that demand tailored responses further complicates matters. But ethnic conflicts are not ancient, tribal, or biologically determined. They are usually driven by modern, rational causes, and their management requires equally modern, rational approaches.

Preparations for a peace process are necessarily delicate and often proceed against a backdrop of continuing violence and instability. Often it is easier to continue the conflict than to investigate the possibilities of peace and the accompanying accusations of treachery. Those moments that bear the possibility for positive engagement with antagonists are often fleeting and require 'cultivation'. Events beyond the control of any of the immediate participants in the conflict often have a decisive influence in tipping a conflict towards a more or less violent trajectory. System level change, in the form of changing economic, ideological, or strategic fortunes can have a major impact in creating the conditions whereby a sustainable peace process can develop.

Ultimately, the pre-negotiation phase of a peace process requires faith. It is nothing less than a high-risk gamble to ascertain the seriousness of other conflict participants. The chances of collapse in the early stages are high and are increased by the distrust, secrecy, and involvement of third parties that characterizes initial exchanges. Parties may offer or demand signals of good faith. Termed 'confidence-building measures' these vary from public statements of intent to the release of prisoners or ceasefires. The aim of the initial phase of a peace process is to create the environment in which serious interparty negotiations can start.

1
Explaining the Conflict Potential of Ethnicity

Crawford Young

Characteristics of ethnicity

Ethnicity, as collective phenomenon and form of identity, has in the contemporary world a singular capacity for social mobilization. Although it is not inherently conflictual, ethnicity has psychological properties and discursive resources which have the potential to decant into violence. No other form of social identity, in the early twenty-first century, has a comparable power, save for the closely related forms of collective affiliation, race, and religion. Social class, however significant a political vector, lacks in most settings the clarity of boundaries, the primordial dimensions, and affective resonance evident in ethnicity. Other forms of social categorization, such as occupation, gender, political affiliation, or the many other kinds one might list, although frequently a basis for competition and conflict, fall far short of the potential volatility of ethnic consciousness. The task of this chapter is to unravel the distinctive properties of ethnicity which explain this phenomenon.

Instances of conflict pitting human groups bearing different ethnonyms extend far back into the mists of the past in all parts of the world. Indeed, some authors assert that a prehistoric competence in recognizing and utilizing group solidarity was a key to survival in the early years of the species, embedding a genetic propensity to within-group kin-like altruism, and distrust tinged with fear towards the out-group 'other'.[1] Others trace 'ethnie' as a state-forming force back more than two millennia.[2] But the scale and salience of ethnic conflict has increased in recent decades. There is surely significance in the recent origins of the term 'ethnicity', which the linguistic custodians of the *Oxford English Dictionary* had yet to uncover in the 1933 edition, acknowledging its currency only in the 1972 supplement.[3] Equally significant is the contemporary coinage (1944) of the term 'genocide', a word precipitated by the Holocaust. In its original usage, configured by the Nazi effort to exterminate Jews (and Roma), genocide meant the deliberate policy of a state to liquidate an entire people. By extension, genocide has come to include lethal assaults by one people upon another, with an intention of their physical elimination. Emblematic of the political force of ethnicity is the frequency of genocidal events and allegations in the 1990s: Bosnia, Rwanda, Burundi and Kosovo.

Once given lexical recognition, ethnicity has been defined in diverse ways, usually in terms of some of its attributes: mythical kinship, ancestry, language, shared values, common culture, and the like. I prefer conceptualizing ethnicity in terms of three prime components. First, ethnos is rooted in a variable array of shared properties. Language is often a core element, but not always (Hutu and Tutsi in Rwanda and Burundi share the same language; Serbian and Croatian are mainly distinguished by the script). The metaphor of fictive kinship is usually present, joined to a mythology of shared ancestry. Common cultural practices and symbols help define group identity. Sometimes the group is defined by a particular economic or social niche.

Equally important are the other two attributes. The shared culture becomes a visible ingredient in identity when it is joined to active collective consciousness. This in turn is contingent upon 'the other'. A group achieves consciousness not only in terms of the culture they share but also whom they do not. The boundary which demarcates 'we' and 'they' is critical in giving social meaning to the collective self.[4]

Ethnicity and nationalism

Grasping the conflict potential of ethnicity requires exploring its relationship to nationalism. Whether one traces its origin to sixteenth-century England (e.g., Greenfeld) or the French Revolution (e.g., Hobsbawm), nationalism is a distinctly modern ideology which links an assertion of collective identity, initially ethnic, to a particular set of political claims.[5] The nation achieves fulfilment through possession of its own state. This vocation rests upon two master precepts: popular sovereignty, and the doctrine of self-determination. The former locates the ultimate source of legitimation not in the institutions of rule, much less in a monarch, but in the citizenry collectivized as a 'people'. The latter asserts a right of a 'people', originally understood as an ethnic collectivity, to have their own state, or at least autonomous self-rule.

Nationalism as an ideology also elevates the mythologies associated with ethnicity to new levels of intensity. By joining the intrinsic solidarities of ethnicity to the institutional resources of a state, nationalism ratchets up the stakes of potential conflict any number of notches. Nationalism, runs the epigram, is ethnicity with an army and a navy. The most aggressive forms of nationalism, in the contemporary world, are those with an explicit ethnic content: ethnonationalism, a term given currency by Walker Connor.[6]

We need to underline at once that nationalism and ethnicity are not identical terms. The most crucial distinction between ethnicity and nationalism lies in the nature of the political claims advanced. Of the thousands of ethnic groups in the world, only a modest minority assert a demand for full sovereignty. There is, of course, always the possibility that ethnic consciousness may mutate into ethnonationalism, but there is no inevitable progression.

Conversely, not all nationalism is ethnic; it can be grounded in shared political values (civic nationalism), a given territory, or a shared history of colonial oppression. However, the sharpness of the distinction between civic and ethnic nationalism drawn by some authors (e.g., Greenfeld) has been subject to effective critique.[7] Even in the swathe of countries from the Atlantic to the Pacific in Europe, the northern part of the Eurasian land mass, and parts of Southeast Asia where the dominant ethnic group gives its name to the state, there is a discernable spectrum in the degree to which the discourse of nationalism is exclusively ethnic, or reflects shared political values (the republican virtues of liberty, equality, and fraternity of the French Revolution, or the 'constitutional patriotism' of post-war Germany). Western hemisphere nationalisms originated in a territorialized rendition of the creole or settler independence elites needing to demarcate their identity from that of the former colonial ruler.[8] Most African and Asian nationalisms imagined a community from culturally diverse populations whose shared historical experience was colonial oppression. To transform from ideology of anti-colonial revolt to doctrine of post-colonial state legitimation, such a nationalism was compelled to assert an exclusively territorial referent and deny any ethnic attachments.

Thus, ethnicity and nationalism are overlapping but distinct terms. But their area of intersection as well as the zones of differentiation assume in the nineteenth and especially the twentieth centuries a new importance for some other reasons. Here we need to note the marriage through hyphenation of state and nation. The great imperial multi-national states (Austro–Hungarian, Ottoman, and most recently the Soviet) shattered before the force of ethnonationalism in the wake of lost wars, hot or cold, and the overseas empires dissolved under the impact of anti-colonial nationalism and a newly hostile international environment. In the wake of this epic transformation of the world state system, the ideology of nationalism, however defined, silently permeated reason of state.[9] The imperative of legitimation compelled states to represent themselves at least as nations in formation, and to deploy the considerable didactic capacities of the state to 'nation-building'.

The nationalizing of the state posed the issue of inclusion with a novel intensity. In the substantial number of states where a 'titular nation' named the country, cultural communities who fell outside the reach of this dominant identity became 'national minorities', a category whose juridical personality first achieved international recognition after World War I. Even when 'nation' was a more political or territorial idea than ethnic, patterns of exclusion were frequent (indigenous or African diaspora peoples in Western hemisphere states).

Further intensifying the conflict potential of cultural pluralism was the vast expansion in the role of the twentieth-century state. The fraction of total resources subject to allocation through the public domain rose sharply through the emergence of the welfare state, costly technological innovations in the military field, and the enlargement of the administrative reach of the state. Despite the modest retrenchments associated with the rise of market liberalism in the 1980s, the group stakes in access to and control of state power are immensely greater than in previous centuries.

This leads to two basic premises regarding the contemporary political landscape. First, the politics of cultural pluralism are framed by the state system. Conflict and competition between ethnic groups, virtually without exception, occurs within the political arena enclosed by the territorial boundaries of a nation-state. Second, the overwhelming majority of the nearly two hundred nation-state entities, defined by United Nations membership, are culturally plural. Even with an only moderately rigorous definition of homogeneity, one is hard pressed to identify more than a dozen countries devoid of cultural plurality.

The variable conflict potential of ethnicity

With the context of ethnicity thus described, we may now return to explaining its conflict potential. Critical to an understanding of its mobilizational force is a recognition that ethnicity is highly variable along two dimensions. First, at a group level, ethnicity is not constantly activated. In any given social space there is likely to be some multiplicity of ethnic groups; most of the time, even though some consciousness of difference is present, interaction is civil and ethnicity quiescent. Social capital may accumulate primarily within groups, but everyday transactions involve no discernable tension.

The texture of group relationships varies widely. In some settings, such as that of the Swedish minority in Finland, cultural rights are well assured, political tensions are minimal, and intermarriage frequent. In others, a long-standing pattern of everyday frictions, and endemic political competition, keep ethnicity foregrounded, as in the relationships between Flemings and Walloons in Belgium. In still others, an ineradicable memory of conquest and subordination continuously reinscribe difference in social and political life, as with francophone Quebec or Chechens in the Russian Federation. In yet other instances, the stigmatization and marginalization by dominant components of society forces consciousness into a ghetto escapable only through identity denial or assertion (Ainu in Japan, Roma in Europe). Territorially concentrated groups, which have the possibility of a self-determination claim, are differently positioned than those which are geographically dispersed. The ethnic consciousness of those who have voluntarily migrated differs fundamentally from that of national minorities with a strong sense of territorial attachment and linguistic distinctiveness; these contrasts give rise to very different ethnic claims[10] and make intergenerational dilution a possible, even likely outcome. These enduring patternings of group relationships all shape the intensity of ethnicity.

Second, one must recollect that ultimately ethnicity is experienced and performed at an individual level. Here as well the range of possible variation is very wide. The daily life of a given individual may have a low level of interactions defined by ethnic content; equally variable is the degree to which the 'other' is encountered in situations evoking threat or antagonism. Ethnic consciousness is reinforced or attenuated by the frequency of identity performance, through participation in rituals or routines defined by ethnicity (a rite of passage, a religious ceremony, even a meal). The individual member of the Arab minority in Israel finds identity constantly imposed by the manifold differences in citizenship status, and the ebb and flow of confrontation and crisis between Israel, the nascent state of Palestine, and the Arab world more broadly. It is frequently performed in diverse protest actions. However, ethnic Americans of European ancestry, as Mary Waters[11] engagingly shows, find ethnicity an option, to be ignored or employed dependent on context and situation; for many, ethnicity is a very weakly held identity, further attenuated for many by multiple ancestries. Where large numbers of ethnic subjects hold only a feeble level of communal consciousness, and participate only sporadically or not at all in rituals of identity, the mobilization potential of ethnicity is far less than for a group such as Palestinian Arabs in Israel or Palestine.

Analytical approaches to ethnicity

In recent years, ethnicity has frequently been analysed in terms of three dimensions: the primordial, the instrumental, and the constructivist.[12] These three faces of cultural pluralism can provide a useful framework for illuminating the aspects of ethnicity which explain its exceptional potential for conflictual mobilization. The three are distinguishable only analytically; in real world social action they are interwoven.

The primordial dimension of ethnicity calls attention to its affective properties. For those whose ethnic moorings are robust, the consciousness of cultural identity is deeply embedded in the constitution of the self. The solitary individual bereft of anchorings in some web of cultural affinity and solidarity is unusual. Although ethnicity is not the only available such relationship, it enjoys an unusually broad array of discursive resources in framing identity: name, language, narratives of shared ancestry, cultural practices, common symbols. There is force to the primordialist arguments of Harold Isaacs that ethnic identity serves basic human needs for a safe place of ultimate belonging.[13]

The social psychology of identity provides important clues to the puzzle of the social force of ethnicity.[14] The child acquires early from the socializing influence of family, school, and play group a cognitive capacity to recognize difference and to derive expectations of nurture from 'we' or danger from 'they'.[15] The perceptual representation of the ethnic 'we' is normally laden with positive symbols, and not infrequently with some sense of past harm rendered by some ethnic other. Ethnicity beyond the boundary of the collective self is often subject to negative stereotyping; the universal phenomenon of the ethnic joke could not subsist but for the widely shared attribution of particular characteristics to ethnic populations, usually at least mildly pejorative. The negative stereotype quickly mutates into apprehensions of hostile behaviour on the part of the ethnic other. Fear is a singularly powerful emotional field. Its nature and impact are well captured by the words of a Northern Nigerian delegate to constitutional talks on the eve of the Nigerian civil war:

> We all have our fears of one another. Some fear that the opportunities in their own areas are limited and they would therefore wish to expand and venture unhampered in other parts. Some fear the sheer weight of number of other parts which they feel could be used to the detriment of their own interests. Some fear the sheer weight of skills and the aggressive drive of other groups which they feel has to be regulated if they are not to be left as the economic, social, and possibly political, under-dogs in their own areas of origin in the very near future. These fears may be real or imagined; they may be reasonable or petty. Whether they are genuine or not, they have to be taken account of because they influence to a considerable degree the actions of the groups towards one another and, more important perhaps, the daily actions of the individual in each group towards individuals from other groups.[16]

The emotive properties of ethnicity and the cognitive frames it provides lend themselves to the historicization of the collective self. Ethnicity frequently invokes the language and symbols of kinship.[17] By historical legerdemain, imagined kinship becomes shared ancestry. Identity in the process acquires a potent narrative.

The instrumental dimension of ethnicity captures its utilization as a weapon in social competition.[18] The ethnic politician is a familiar figure in contemporary politics, using the group as a vote bank in electoral competition. Particularly in urban settings, the social competition for scarce resources – employment, housing – readily translates into ethnic mobilization. Nigerian popular imagery expresses metaphorically the instrumental aspect of ethnicity; politics, runs the aphorism, is about cutting the national cake. The resources of the country, in this colourful portrait, are sweet to the taste, and divisible into slices. The relative size of the servings will be visible to all; elementary justice requires equal slices, but the ethnic partisanship of the power-holder who holds the knife makes likely unequal portions.

The instrumental use of ethnicity has feedback consequences. The more ethnic mobilization is deployed as a political weapon, the more the ethnic other is compelled to respond by counter-mobilization. This readily decants into a cycle of outbidding, which deepens the politization of identity and sharpens antagonisms, a possible dynamic identified long ago by Rabushka and Shepsle, armed with rational choice theory.[19] In turn, its repeated instrumental use tends to inscribe it more deeply in the popular consciousness.

Practitioners of rational choice theory such as Russell Hardin also persuasively argue that the prior existence of group consciousness means that 'self-interest can often successfully be matched with group interest'.[20] Moreover, mobilized ethnicity provides its leaders with effective resources for both summoning and enforcing solidarity. The large flow of funds from the Tamil diaspora to the insurgent 'Tigers' in Sri Lanka is assured not only by the dictates of ethnic solidarity but also by the capacity of Tiger representatives abroad to identify, monitor and discipline reluctant diasporic Tamils.

Finally, a full grasp of ethnicity requires attention to the processes by which identity is socially constructed. Ultimately all forms of identity are social constructs, products of human creativity. Examination of the dynamics of ethnogenesis in any given group illuminates the nature of the discursive resources of the group. Crucial is the role of cultural entrepreneurs who codify and standardize a language, equipping it with a written form, create an ethnos-centred historical narrative, populated with internal heroes and external villains, and build a literary tradition.

The constructivist focus reveals the uneven degree of mobilization potential among ethnic communities. Some have only a weak ideology of the collective self; in the absence of such discursive capacity, activation is much more difficult. An extensively elaborated theorization of the group as speakers of a prestigious language, holders of a deep and heroic historical legend, and possessors of a rich cultural tradition constitutes ethnicity ripe for mobilization.

The dynamic of ethnic conflict

With ethnicity thus assembled, we can begin to appreciate its primal force in some conflict situations. When antagonism between groups, or state repressive action directed at an ethnic community, reaches a threshold of mutual threat, then the emotional dimensions of ethnic consciousness can take command. The other can come to pose a mortal threat to one's very existence; in the genocidal confrontations in Rwanda, Burundi, and former Yugoslavia in the 1990s this clearly became the case. Along with fear came the longing for revenge. In polarized moments, selective perception is general. The atrocities committed towards the ethnic in-group are instantly perceived and indeed exaggerated in the rumours which flood an environment of violent confrontation. The harms which may have been inflicted upon the ethnic other recede into the remote recesses of awareness. Thus a passion for vengeance takes hold; this punitive impulse is entirely separated from any need to identify perpetrators. Any random members of the ethnic other are suitable victims for retribution.

In such situations, the ethnic other becomes dehumanized and demonized. As a source of boundless evil, and a mortal threat to the ethnic self, moral inhibitions dissolve and unspeakable violence can occur: the widespread use of machetes in the mass killings in Rwanda, or the large-scale rape accompanying these deadly episodes, whose purpose was much less sexual gratification than ritualized humiliation and moral destruction of the ethnic other. Indeed, the singular bestiality often associated with ethnic violence further escalates the fears and animosities. Such eruptions of inter-group hostility are inscribed in historical memory and are not readily dissolved. Control of political power becomes a matter of life or death. Should power be the exclusive possession of one's ethnic adversaries, one is fated to unlimited insecurity (among several studies on Rwanda, see Prunier; on Burundi see Lemarchand).[21]

Comparative study of *The Deadly Ethnic Riot* reveals a common set of patterns reflecting the pathologies described above.[22] The riot differs from the genocidal struggles in Rwanda, Burundi, or Bosnia in its relatively brief duration and often the greater spontaneity. However, in regions such as South Asia where communal violence has become an institutionalized part of the landscape, riots accumulate specialized personnel, readily available for participation, and what Brass[23] terms as 'fire-tenders', who have an interest in sustaining communal tensions. In turn, individual episodes are easily converted into grand narratives of communal conflict, by the press or by the state authorities.

Our discussion has focused upon ethnicity. One may note that much of the analysis would also apply to the sometimes overlapping but analytically distinct forms of identity constituted by race and religion. Race is defined by a social definition of phenotype, a construction originating in the imposition of hierarchy upon differentiated populations coerced into unfree labour, and permeated with stigmatization of the subordinated as inferior. Thus, in contrast to ethnicity which is an asserted form of consciousness, race categories were assigned by the dominant.[24] Though racial solidarity comes to be asserted by the oppressed categories, accompanied by claims of collective worth contesting the stigmatization, its discursive sources are quite different.[25]

Religious identity is also a distinct domain of cultural identity, overlapping with ethnicity in some instances where religion demarcates a group also possessing ethnic characteristics and self-consciousness (e.g., Jews or Armenians). Since community is defined by theology, elaborated in sacred texts, affiliation comports very distinctive obligations. The world religions possess sophisticated institutional structures for their perpetuation and reproduction, as well as anointed specialists for their leadership. The divine nature of their calling opens them to struggle over doctrine and frequent sectarian splintering. As the frequency of communal riots pitting Hindus against Muslims in India attests, religion can also serve as a mobilizing idiom for violent confrontation. In the early modern age, religion was the prime source of communal conflict, tamed only in the Western state by secularization and religious toleration.

Concluding reflections

In this chapter, I have endeavoured to explain the conflict potential of ethnicity. In closing, one must return to the variability in degree to which ethnic groups in presence within a nation-state arena have constantly conflictual relations. In the great majority of cases, conflict which exceeds the bounds of the civil is unusual. Further, there is evidence that, with a greater acknowledgement throughout the world that cultural pluralism is 'normal', and not a threat to the polity requiring erasure or repression through exclusionary 'nation-building' projects, one may discern a global process of political learning in the accommodation of cultural diversity.[26] A large repertoire of policy options for this purpose is available: decentralization, asymmetric federalism, electoral systems, affirmative action, legal pluralism, among others. Ted Gurr in a quantitative survey of ethnic conflicts concludes that they have significantly diminished in number in the 1990s; a counterintuitive finding he attributes in part to political learning.[27]

A modicum of political learning occurs at the level of the international community and a doctrine of humanitarian intervention to halt ethnic violence takes form. The education process is marked with failures, as in the early stages of a Bosnia intervention, and more disastrously in Rwanda, where the United States and France in particular pursued policies which exacerbated the calamity.[28] But an acceptance of a global responsibility to contain ethnic violence, however difficult its implementation, is an important development.

But these encouraging developments do not eliminate the possible perils of ethnicity which escapes the bounds of civility. Insensitive policies and ethnic extremists can form a lethal cocktail. A sustained and robust commitment to conflict containment and resolution will remain indispensable to a peaceful world.

Notes

1. P.R. Shaw, *Genetic Seeds of Warfare: Evolution, Nationalism, and Patriotism* (Boston: Unwin Hyman, 1989).
2. A.D. Smith, *The Ethnic Origin of Nations* (Oxford: Basil Blackwell, 1986).
3. N. Glazer & D.P. Moynihan (eds), *Ethnicity: Theory and Experience* (Cambridge MA: Harvard University Press, 1975) p. 1.
4. F. Barth (ed.), *Ethnic Groups and Boundaries* (Boston: Little, Brown and Company, 1976).
5. L. Greenfeld, *Nationalism: Five Roads to Modernity* (Cambridge MA: Harvard University Press, 1992) and E.J. Hobsbahm, *Nations and Nationalism since 1780* (Cambridge: Cambridge University Press, 1990).
6. W. Connor, *Ethnonationalism: The Quest for Understanding* (Princeton NJ: Princeton University Press, 1994).
7. Greenfield (1992), op. cit.; B. Yack, 'The Myth of the Civic Nation', in R. Beiner (ed.), *Theorizing Nationalism* (Albany NY: State University of New York Press, 1999) pp. 103–118.
8. B. Anderson, *Imagined Communities: Reflections on the Origin and Spread of Nationalism* (Cambridge: Cambridge University Press, 1983).
9. C. Young, *The African Colonial State in Comparative Perspective* (New Haven CT: Yale University Press, 1994).
10. W. Kymlicka, *Multicultural Citizenship: A Liberal Theory of Minority Rights* (Oxford: Oxford University Press, 1995).
11. M. Waters, *Ethnic Options: Choosing Identities in America* (Cambridge MA: Harvard University Press, 1990).
12. S. Cornell & D. Hartmann, *Ethnicity and Race: Making Identities in a Changing World* (Thousand Oaks CA: Pine Forge Press, 1998) and C. Young (ed.), *The Rising Tide of Cultural Pluralism* (Madison WI: University of Wisconsin Press, 1993).
13. H.R. Isaacs, *Idols of the Tribe: Group Identity and Political Change* (New York: Harper & Row, 1975).
14. D. Chirot & M.E.P. Seligman (eds), *Ethnopolitical Warfare: Causes, Consequences, and Possible Solutions* (Washington DC: American Psychological Association, 2001).
15. L.A. Hirshfeld, *Race in the Making: Cognition, Culture, and the Child's Construction of Human Kinds* (Cambridge: MIT Press, 1996).
16. C. Young, *The Politics of Cultural Pluralism* (Madison WI: University of Wisconsin Press, 1976), pp. 467–468.
17. D.L. Horowitz, *Ethnic Groups in Conflict* (Berkeley CA: University of California Press, 1985).
18. S. Olzack & J. Nagel (eds), *Competitive Ethnic Relations* (Orlando FL: Academic Press, 1986).
19. A. Rabushka & K.A. Shepsle, *Politics in Plural Society: A Theory of Political Instability* (Columbus OH: Charles E. Merrill Publishing Company, 1972).
20. R. Hardin, *One for All: The Logic of Group Conflict* (Princeton NJ: Princeton University Press, 1995), p. 5.
21. On Rwanda see G. Prunier, *The Rwanda Crisis: History of a Genocide* (New York: Columbia University Press, 1995) and on Burundi see R. Lemarchand, *Burundi: Ethnocide as Discourse and Practice* (Washington DC: Woodrow Wilson Center Press, 1994).
22. D.L. Horowitz, *The Deadly Ethnic Riot* (Berkeley CA: University of California Press, 2001).

23. P.R. Brass, *Theft of an Idol: Text and Context in the Representation of Collective Violence* (Princeton NJ: Princeton University Press, 1997).

24. Cornell & Hartmann (1998), op. cit., pp. 31–35.

25. A.W. Marx, *Making Race and Nation: A Comparison of South Africa, the United States and Brazil* (Cambridge: Cambridge University Press, 1998) and M. Omi & H. Winant, *Racial Formation in the United States from the 1960s to the 1990s* (New York: Routledge, 1994).

26. C. Young (ed.), *Ethnic Diversity and Public Policy: A Comparative Inquiry* (Basingstoke: Macmillan, 1998) and C. Young (ed.), *The Accommodation of Cultural Diversity: Case Studies* (Basingstoke: Macmillan, 1999).

27. T.R. Gurr, 'Ethnic warfare on the wane', *Foreign Affairs*, 79, 3 (May/June 2000) pp. 52–64.

28. S. Power, 'Bystanders to genocide', *Atlantic Monthly*, 288, 2 (September 2001) pp. 84–108 and Prunier (1995), op. cit.

2
The Timing of Peace Initiatives: Hurting Stalemates and Ripe Moments

I. William Zartman

While most studies on peaceful settlement of disputes see the substance of the proposals for a solution as the key to a successful resolution of conflict, a growing focus of attention shows that a second and equally necessary key lies in the timing of efforts for resolution.[1] Parties resolve their conflict only when they are ready to do so – when alternative, usually unilateral, means of achieving a satisfactory result are blocked and the parties feel that they are in an uncomfortable and costly predicament. At that ripe moment, they are more likely to grab on to proposals that usually have been in the air for a long time and that appear attractive only now.

The idea of a ripe moment lies at the fingertips of diplomats. 'Ripeness of time is one of the absolute essences of diplomacy', wrote John Campbell.[2] 'You have to do the right thing at the right time' without indicating specific causes. Henry Kissinger did better, recognizing that 'stalemate is the most propitious condition for settlement'.[3] Conversely, practitioners often are heard to say that certain mediation initiatives are not advisable because the conflict is not ripe just yet. In mid-1992, in the midst of ongoing conflict, the Iranian deputy foreign minister noted, 'The situation in Azerbaijan is not ripe for such moves for mediation.'[4]

The concept of a ripe moment centres on the parties' perception of a Mutually Hurting Stalemate (MHS), optimally associated with an impending, past or recently avoided catastrophe.[5] The concept is based on the notion that when the parties find themselves locked in a conflict from which they cannot escalate to victory and this deadlock is painful to both of them (although not necessarily in equal degree or for the same reasons), they seek an alternative policy or Way Out (WO). The catastrophe provides a deadline or a lesson indicating that pain can be sharply increased if something is not done about it now; catastrophe is a useful extension of MHS but is not necessary either to its definition or to its existence. Using different images, the stalemate has been termed the Plateau, a flat and unending terrain without relief, and the catastrophe the Precipice, the point where things suddenly and predictably get worse. If the notion of mutual blockage is too static to be realistic, the concept may be stated dynamically as a moment when the upper hand slips and the lower hand rises, both parties moving towards equality, with both movements carrying pain for the parties.[6] The notion of the MHS is important because, unlike some current discussions of 'readiness', it tells *why* parties are ready to envisage settlement.

The MHS is grounded in cost-benefit analysis, fully consistent with public choice notions of rationality[7] and war termination and negotiation,[8] which assume that a party will pick the alternative which it prefers, and that a decision to change is induced by increasing pain associated with the present (conflictual) course.[9] In game theoretic terms, it marks the transformation of the situation in the parties' perception from a prisoners' dilemma game (PDG) into a chicken dilemma game (CDG)[10] or, in other terms, the realization that the status quo or no negotiation (DD, the southeast corner) is a negative-sum situation, and that to avoid the zero-sum outcomes now considered impossible (CD and DC, the northeast and southwest corners) the positive-sum outcome (CC, the northwest corner) must be explored.

Ripeness is necessarily a perceptual event, although as with any subjective perception, there are likely to be objective referents to be perceived. These can be highlighted by a mediator or an opposing party if they are not immediately recognized by the party itself, and resisted so long as the conflicting party refuses or is otherwise able to block out their perception. However, it is the perception of the objective condition, not the condition itself that makes for a MHS. If the parties do not recognize 'clear evidence' (in someone else's view) that they are in an impasse, a MHS has not (yet) occurred, and if they do perceive themselves to be in such a situation, no matter how flimsy the 'evidence', the MHS is present.

The other element necessary for a ripe moment is less complex and also perceptional: a WO. Parties do not have to be able to identify a specific solution, only a sense that a negotiated solution is possible for the searching and that the other party shares that sense and the willingness to search too. Without a sense of a WO, the push associated with the MHS would leave the parties with nowhere to go. Spokespersons often indicate whether they do or do not feel that a deal can be made with the other side and that requirement (i.e., the sense that concessions will be reciprocated, not just banked) exists, particularly when there is a change in that judgement.[11]

Ripeness is only a condition, necessary but not sufficient for the initiation of negotiations. It is not self-fulfilling or self-implementing. It must be seized, either directly by the parties or, if not, through the persuasion of a mediator.

Thus, it is not identical to its results, which are not part of its definition, and is therefore not tautological. Not all ripe moments are so seized and turned into negotiations, hence the importance of specifying the meaning and evidence of ripeness so as to indicate when conflicting or third parties can fruitfully initiate negotiations.[12] Although ripeness theory is not predictive in the sense that it can tell when a given situation will become ripe, it is predictive in the sense of identifying the elements necessary (even if not sufficient) for the productive inauguration of negotiations. This type of analytical prediction is the best that can be obtained in social science, where stronger predictions could only be ventured by eliminating free choice (including the human possibility of blindness, mistakes, and creativity). As such, it is of great prescriptive value to policy makers seeking to know when and how to begin a peace process.

Finding a ripe moment requires research and intelligence studies to identify the objective and subjective elements. Subjective expressions of pain, impasse, and inability to bear the cost of further escalation, related to objective evidence of stalemate, data on numbers, nature of casualties and material costs, and/or other such indicators of MHS, along with expressions of a sense of a WO, can be researched on a regular basis in a conflict to establish whether ripeness exists. Researchers would look for evidence, for example, whether the fluid military balance in conflict – such as mountainous Karabagh, or the Sudanese or Sri Lankan civil wars, for example – has given rise at any time to a perception of MHS by the parties, and to a perception by authoritative spokespersons that the parties are ready to seek a solution to the conflict, or, to the contrary, whether indications reinforce the conclusion that any mediation is bound to fail because one or both parties believe in the possibility or necessity of escalating out of the current impasse to achieve a decisive military victory. Research and intelligence would seek to learn why Bosnia in the war-torn summer of 1994 was not ripe for a negotiated settlement and mediation would fail, and why it was in November 1995 and mediation could encourage that condition to move towards an agreement.[13] Similarly, research would indicate that there was no chance of mediating a settlement in the Ethiopia–Eritrean conflict in the early 1980s, early or mid-1990s, or in the Sudanese conflicts in the 1990s or the early 2000s, the skills of President Carter and other mediators notwithstanding, because the components of ripeness were not present.[14]

While ripeness has not always been seized upon to open negotiations there have been occasions when it has come into play, as identified by both analysts and practitioners. A number of studies beyond the original examination[15] have used and tested the notion of ripeness with regard to negotiations in Zimbabwe, Namibia and Angola, Eritrea, South Africa, Philippines, Cyprus, Iran–Iraq, Israel, Mozambique, among others.[16] Touval's work on the Middle East was particularly important in launching the idea.[17] In general, these studies have found the concept applicable and useful as an explanation for the successful initiation of negotiations or their failure, while in some cases proposing refinements to the concept.

The most important refinements carry the theory onto a second level of questions about the effects of each side's pluralized politics on both the perceptions and uses of ripeness. What kinds of internal political conditions are helpful both for perceiving ripeness and for turning that perception into the initiation of promising negotiations? The careful case study by Stephen J. Stedman of the negotiations for Rhodesian's independence as Zimbabwe and by Lieberfield of Middle East and South African negotiations takes the concept into the complexities of internal dynamics.[18] Stedman specifies that some but not all parties must perceive the hurting stalemate, that patrons rather than parties may be the agents of perception, that the military in each party is the crucial element in perceiving the stalemate, and that the WO is as important an ingredient as the stalemate in that all parties may well see victory in the alternative outcome prepared by negotiation (although some parties will be proven wrong in that perception).[19] They also highlight the potential of leadership change for the subjective perception of a MHS where it had not been seen previously in the same objective circumstances, and of threats to incumbent leadership from domestic rivals – rather than from the enemy – as the source of impending catastrophe.

The original formulation of the theory added a third element to the definition of ripeness, the presence of a valid spokesperson for each side.[20] As a structural element, it is of a different order than the other two defining perceptual elements. Nonetheless, it remains of second-level importance, as Stedman and Lieberfield have pointed out. The presence of strong leadership recognized as representative of each party and that can deliver that party's compliance to the agreement is a necessary (while alone insufficient) condition for productive negotiations to begin, or indeed to end successfully.

Diplomatic memoirs have explicitly referred to ripeness by its MHS component. Chester A. Crocker, US Assistant Secretary of State for Africa between 1981 and 1989, patiently mediated an agreement for the withdrawal of Cuban troops from Angola and of South African troops from Namibia, then to become independent. For years a MHS, and hence productive negotiations, had eluded the parties. 'The second half of 1987 was…the moment when the situation "ripened"'.[21] Military escalations on both sides and bloody confrontations in southeastern Angola beginning in November 1987 and in southwestern Angola in May 1988 ended in a draw.

By late June 1988, the…Techipa-Calueque clashes in southwestern Angola confirmed a precarious military stalemate. That stalemate was both the reflection and the cause of underlying political decisions. By early May, my colleagues and I convened representatives of Angola, Cuba, and South Africa in London for face-to-face, tripartite talks. The political decisions leading to the London meeting formed a distinct sequence, paralleling military events on the ground, like planets moving one by one into a certain alignment.[22]

In his conclusion, Crocker identifies specific signs of ripeness, while qualifying that 'correct timing is a matter of feel and instinct'.[23] The American mediation involved building diplomatic moves that paralleled the growing awareness of the parties, observed by the mediator, of the hurting stalemate in which they found themselves.[24]

Alvaro de Soto, Assistant Secretary-General for Political Affairs at the United Nations (UN), also endorsed the necessity of ripeness in his mission to mediate a peace in El Salvador. After chronicling a series of failed initiatives, he points to the importance of the Farabundo Martí National Liberation Front's (FMLN) November 1989 offensive, the largest of the wars, which penetrated the main cities including the capital but failed to dislodge the government.

> The silver lining was that it was, almost literally, a defining moment – the point at which it became possible to seriously envisage a negotiation. The offensive showed the FMLN that they could not spark a popular uprising,...The offensive also showed the rightist elements in government, and elites in general, that the armed forces could not defend them, let alone crush the insurgents...Neither side could defeat the other. As the dust settled, the notion that the conflict could not be solved by military means, and that its persistence was causing pain that could no longer be endured, began to take shape. The offensive codified the existence of a mutually hurting stalemate. The conflict was ripe for a negotiated solution.[25]

In Yugoslavia, Secretary of State James Baker looked for a ripe moment during his quick trip to Belgrade in June 1991 and reported the same day to President George Bush that he did not find it: 'My gut feeling is that we won't produce a serious dialogue on the future of Yugoslavia until all the parties have a greater sense of urgency and danger.'[26] Richard Holbrooke calls this 'a crucial misreading', and had his own image of the MHS (or the upper hand slipping and the underdog rising), 'The best time to hit a serve is when the ball is suspended in the air, neither rising nor falling. We felt this equilibrium had arrived, or was about to, on the battlefield [in October 1995].'[27] He saw a better moment created by the Croatian Krajina offensive in August 1995.[28] It took the offensive, coupled with the North Atlantic Treaty Organisation (NATO) bombing, to create a MHS composed of a temporary Serb setback and a temporary and unsustainable Croat advance to instil a perception of the ripe moment in the mind of Bosnian President Izetbegovic. A State Department official stated, 'Events on the ground have made it propitious to try again to get the negotiations started. The Serbs are on the run a bit. That won't last forever. So we are taking the obvious major step.'[29]

In his parting report as Under-Secretary-General of the UN, Marrack Goulding specifically cited the literature on ripeness in discussing the selection of conflicts to be handled by an overburdened UN.

> Not all conflicts are 'ripe' for action by the United Nations (or any other third party)...It therefore behooves the Secretary-General to be selective and to recommend action only in situations where he judges that the investment of scarce resources is likely to produce a good return (in terms of preventing, managing and resolving conflict).[30]

Some practitioners have given a more nuanced endorsement of the concept, although not all have read the conceptual fine print carefully. Itamar Rabinovich, the careful historian and skilful ambassador in the failed negotiations between Israel and Syria, terms the concept 'a very useful analytical tool...but...less valuable as an operational tool', but he expects that 'ripeness will account for the success of negotiations' rather than simply provide a necessary but insufficient condition for their initiation.[31]

Others have also missed the point. John Paul Lederach, a good analyst and Track 2 practitioner, confuses the mediator's hopes with the protagonists' 'unripe' perceptions; he misses the value of the theory in alerting the mediator with the difficulties of instilling a perception (as Holbrooke did), grasping a moment (as deSoto did), or pursuing a long-term change once the negotiation/mediation process is begun (as Crocker did). Happily, Lederach then turns around and provides a good understanding of the ripening process, as discussed below.[32]

Resistant reactions

Ripeness is not just waiting for the apple to fall. One complication with the notion of a hurting stalemate arises when increased pain increases resistance rather than reducing it (it must be remembered that while ripeness is a necessary precondition for negotiation, not all ripeness leads to negotiation). Although this may be considered 'bad', irrational, or even adolescent behaviour, it is a common reaction and one that may be natural and functional. Reinforcement is the normal response to opposition: 'don't give up without a fight', 'no gain without pain', 'hold the course, whatever the cost', 'when the going gets tough, the tough get going', and 'if at first you don't succeed, try, try again'. [33] The imposition of pain to a present course in conflict is not likely to lead to a search for alternative measures without first being tested. The theory itself considers this by referring to the parties' perception that they cannot escalate an exit from their stalemate, implying efforts to break out before giving in (without being able to predict when the shift will take place). It often takes quite a while for parties wholly committed to a struggle to see that they are stuck in a stalemate and need to seek others ways to get out of it.

Furthermore, pressure on a party in conflict often leads to the psychological reaction of worsening the image of the opponent, a natural tendency that is often decried as lessening chances of reconciliation but which has the functional advantage of justifying resistance. Particular types of adversaries such as 'true believers', 'warriors', or 'hardliners' are unlikely to be led to compromise by increased pain; instead, pain is likely to justify renewed struggle. [34] Justified struggles call for greater sacrifices, which absorb increased pain and strengthen determination. The cycle is functional and self-protecting. To this type of reaction, it is the release of pain or an admission of pain on the other side which justifies relaxation; when the opponent admits the error of its ways, the true believer can claim the vindication of its efforts which permits a management of the conflict. [35] Yet escalation can lead to the perception of ripeness, when it shows that the cycle has reached its end and has actually produced awareness of the MHS. [36]

Implications

Inescapable as it may be, the most unfortunate implications of the notion of a hurting stalemate lie in its dependence on conflict. In itself, the concept explains the difficulty of achieving pre-emptive conflict resolution and preventive diplomacy, even though nothing in the definition of the MHS requires it to take place at the height of the conflict or at a high level of violence. The internal (and unmediated) negotiations in South Africa between 1990 and 1994 stand out as a striking case of negotiations opened (and pursued) on the basis of a MHS perceived by both sides aware of impending catastrophe, not of present casualties. [37] However, the greater the objective evidence, the greater the subjective perception of the stalemate and its pain is likely to be, and this evidence is more likely to come late, when all other courses of action and possibilities of escalation have been exhausted. In notable cases, a long period of conflict is required before the MHS sinks in. [38] Yet given the infinite number of potential conflicts which have not reached 'the heights', evidence would suggest that perception of an MHS occurs either (and optimally) at a low level of conflict, where it is relatively easy to begin problem-solving in most cases, or, in salient cases, at rather high levels of conflict. Thus, conflicts not treated 'early' appear to require a high level of intensity for a MHS perception to kick in and negotiations towards a solution to begin. To ripen for resolution at least those conflicts that have not been managed early, one must raise the level of conflict until a stalemate is reached, and then further until it begins to hurt, and then still more, to ensure the perception of pain, and then still more yet, to create the perception of an impending catastrophe as well. The ripe moment becomes the godchild of brinkmanship.

As the notion of ripeness implies, MHS can be a very fleeting opportunity, a moment to be seized lest it pass, or it can be of a long duration, waiting to be noticed and acted upon by mediators. The moment was brief in Bosnia but longer in Angola. In fact, failure to seize the moment often hastens its passing, as parties lose faith in the possibility of a negotiated WO or regain hope in the possibility of unilateral escalation. Worse yet, when a moment of joint perception of a hurting stalemate passes without producing any results, parties frequently fall back on their previous perceptions that the other side will never be ready and the only course left is to hope and fight for a total realization of one's goals, no matter how long it takes: 'Nothing is acceptable but a Palestinian/ Israeli state with Jerusalem as its capital.' By the same token, the possibility of long duration often dulls the urgency of rapid seizure.

Another set of implications comes from the fact that the theory only addresses the opening of negotiations, as noted at the outset and often missed by the critics. Now that the initiation of negotiation is theoretically explained, people would like to see a further theory that explains the successful conclusion of negotiations once opened. Can ripeness be extended in some way to cover the entire process, or does successful conclusion of negotiations require a different explanatory logic?

Practitioners and students of conflict management would also like to think that there could be a more positive prelude to negotiation, through the pull of an attractive outcome without the push of a MHS. Real cases are rare, as explained by prospect theory that shows prevented losses are valued more than possible gains.[39] However, one case is the opening of the Madrid Peace Process on the Middle East in 1992 and another is the negotiation of the Jordan–Israel peace treaty of October 1994;[40] still another may be boundary disputes which are overcome by the prospects of mutual development in the region.[41] However, the mechanisms are still unclear, in part because the cases are so few. As in other ripe moments, these occasions provided an opportunity for improvement, but from a tiring rather than a painful deadlock.[42] In some views, the attraction lies in a possibility of winning more cheaply than by conflict (paradoxically, a shared perception), or else a possibility of sharing power that did not exist before.[43] In other views, enticement comes in the form of a new ingredient, the chance for improved relations with the mediating third party.[44] In other instances, the opportunity for a settlement grows more attractive because the issue of the conflict becomes depassé, no longer justifying the bad relations with the other party or the mediator that it imposed. Such openings might be termed as mutually enticing opportunity (MEO), admittedly a title not as catchy as MHS and a concept not as well researched (or practiced). Few examples have been found in reality.

Nevertheless, MEO is important in the broader negotiation process and has its place in extending ripeness theory. At most, ripeness theory can reach beyond the decision to negotiate into the negotiations themselves by indicating that the perception of ripeness has to continue during the negotiations if the parties are not to re-evaluate their positions and drop out, in the revived hopes of being able to find a unilateral solution through escalation. But negotiations completed under the shadow – or the push – of a MHS alone are likely to be unstable and unlikely to lead to a more enduring settlement. As Ohlson and Pruitt have pointed out, that is the function of the MEO.[45] The negotiators must provide or be provided prospects for a more attractive future to pull them out of their conflict, once a MHS has pushed them into negotiations. The seeds of the pull factor begin with the WO that the parties vaguely perceive as part of the initial ripeness, but that general sense of possibility needs to be developed and fleshed out into the vehicle for an agreement, a formula for settlement, and a prospect of reconciliation that the negotiating parties design during negotiations. When a MEO is not developed in the negotiations, they remain truncated and unstable, even if they reach a conflict management agreement to suspend violence, as in the 1984 and 1999 Lusaka agreements or the 1994 Karabakh ceasefire.[46]

Unripeness should not constitute an excuse for second or third parties' inaction, even if one or both of the conflicting parties are mired in their hopes of escalation and victory. Crocker states very forcefully (in boldface in the original) that 'the absence of "ripeness" does not tell us to walk away and do nothing. Rather, it helps us to identify obstacles and suggests ways of handling them and managing the problem until resolution becomes possible'.[47] Crocker's own experience indicates, before and above all, the importance of being present and available to the contestants while waiting for the moment to ripen, so as to be able to seize it when it occurs. In the absence of a promising situation, either the 'second' party that is alone in feeling the hurt and perceiving the stalemate or the third party has a choice: either to ripen or to position.

Crocker and others list a number of important insights for positioning:[48]

- give the parties some fresh ideas to shake them up;
- keep new ideas flexible to avoid getting bogged down in details;
- establish basic principles to form building blocks of a settlement;
- become an indispensable channel for negotiation;

- establish an acceptable mechanism for negotiation and for registering an agreement; and
- cultivate long-term relationships.

Other strategies include preliminary explorations of items identified with pre-negotiations[49] (Stein et al. 1992):

- identify the parties necessary to a settlement;
- identify the issues to be resolved, and separate out issues not resolvable in the conflict;
- air alternatives to the current conflict course;
- establish contacts and bridges between the parties;
- clarify costs and risks involved in seeking settlement;
- establish requitement; and
- assure support for a settlement policy within each party's domestic constituency.

Since ripeness results from a combination of objective and subjective elements, both need attention. If some objective elements are present, persuasion is the obvious diplomatic challenge. Such was the message of Kissinger in the Sinai withdrawal negotiations and Crocker in the Angolan negotiations, among many others, emphasizing the absence of real alternatives (stalemate) and the high cost of the current conflict course (pain).[50] If there is no objective indicator to which to refer, ripening may involve a much more active engagement of the mediator, moving that role from communication and formulation to manipulation.[51] As a manipulator, the mediator either increases the size of the stakes, attracting the parties to share in a pot that otherwise would have been too small, or limits the actions of the parties in conflict, providing objective elements for the stalemate. Such actions are delicate and dangerous but on occasion necessary. The US massive aid incentives to Israel and Egypt to negotiate a second Sinai withdrawal in 1975, NATO bombing of Serb positions in Bosnia in 1995 to create a hurting stalemate, or American arming of Israel during the October war in 1973 or of Morocco (after two years of moratorium) in 1981 to keep those parties in the conflict, respectively, among many others, are typical examples of the mediator acting as a manipulator to bring about a stalemate.

Practitioners need to employ all their skills and apply all the concepts of negotiation and mediation to take advantage of the necessary but insufficient condition in order to turn it into a successful peacemaking process when it exists, or to help produce it or stand ready to act on it when it does not as yet.

Notes

1. I.W. Zartman, 'Ripeness: The Hurting Stalemate and Beyond', in P. Stern & D. Druckman (eds), *International Conflict Resolution after the Cold War* (Washington DC: National Academy Press, 2000).
2. J. Campbell, *Successful Negotiation: Trieste* (Princeton NJ: Princeton University Press, 1976), p. 73.
3. H. Kissinger, *New York Times* (12 October 1974).
4. Agence France Presse (17 May 1992).
5. I.W. Zartman & M. Berman, *The Practical Negotiator* (New Haven CT: Yale University Press, 1982), pp. 66–78; I.W. Zartman, 'The Strategy of Preventive Diplomacy in Third World Conflicts', in A. George (ed.), *Managing US-Soviet Rivalry* (Boulder CO: Westview, 1983); S. Touval & I.W. Zartman (eds), *International Mediation in Theory and Reality* (Boulder CO: Westview, 1985), pp. 11, 258–260; I.W. Zartman, *Ripe for Resolution* (New York: Oxford University Press, 1985/1989).
6. The same logic has been identified in regard to domestic elite settlements, produced by costly and inconclusive conflict; 'Precisely because no single faction has been a clear winner and all factions have more nearly been losers, elites are disposed to compromise if at all possible' (M. Burton & J. Higley, 'Elite Settlement', *American Sociological Review,* LII 2 (1992) pp. 295–307 at p. 298.
7. A. Sen, *Collective Choice and Social Welfare* (San Francisco: Aldine, 1970); K. Arrow, *Social Change and Individual Values* (New Haven CT: Yale University Press, 1963); M. Olson, *The Logic of Collective Action* (New York: Schocken 1965).
8. S. Brams, *Negotiation Games* (New York: Routledge, 1990); Q. Wright, 'The escalation of conflict', *Journal of Conflict Resolution,* IX, 4 (1965) pp. 434–449.
9. Timing can refer to many things other than costs and benefits, including domestic political schedules, generational socialization, and attitudinal maturation, among others. For an excellent analysis based on the first, see W.B. Quandt, *Camp David* (Washington DC: Brookings, 1986); on the second, see R. Samuels et al., *Political Generations and Political Development* (Boston: Lexington, 1977). These are perfectly valid approaches, but ultimately they can be reduced to cost/benefits, calculated or affected by different referents. To note this is not to deny their separate value, but simply to justify the conceptual focus used here.
10. S. Brams, *Superpower Games* (New Haven CT: Yale University Press, 1985); J. Goldstein, *The Game of Chicken in International Relations: An Underappreciated Model* (Washington DC: School of International Service, American University, 1998).
11. I.W. Zartman & J. Aurik, 'Power Strategies in De-Escalation', in L. Kriesberg & J. Thornson (eds), *Timing the De-Escalation of International Conflicts* (Syracuse NY: Syracuse University Press, 1991).
12. At the outset, confusion may arise from the fact that not all 'negotiations' appear to be the result of a ripe moment. Negotiation may be a tactical interlude, a breather for rest and rearmament, a sop to external pressure, without any intent of opening a sincere search for a joint outcome (F.C. Ikle, *How Nations Negotiate* (New York: Harper & Row, 1964)). Thus the need for quotation marks, or for some elusive modifier such as 'serious' or 'sincere' negotiations. It is difficult at the outset to determine whether negotiations are indeed serious or sincere, and indeed 'true' and 'false' motives may be indistinguishably mixed in the minds of the actors themselves at the beginning. Yet it is the outset which is the subject of the theory. The best that

can be done is to note that many theories contain a reference to a 'false' event or an event in appearance only, to distinguish it from an event that has a defined purpose. Indeed, a sense of ripeness may be required to turn negotiations for side effects into negotiations to resolve conflict.

13. Touval, S. 'Coercive Mediation on the Road to Geneva', in S. Touval & I.W. Zartman (eds), 'Negotiations in the Former Soviet Union and Former Yugoslavia', *International Negotiation*, 1, 3 (1996) pp. 547–570; J. Goodby, 'When war won out: Bosnian peace plans before Dayton', *International Negotiation*, 1, 3 (1996) pp. 501–523; R. Holbrooke *To End a War* (New York: Random House, 1998).

14. M. Ottaway, 'Eritrea and Ethiopia: Negotiations in a Transitional Conflict', and F. Deng, 'Negotiating a Hidden Agenda: Sudan's Conflict of Identities', both in I.W. Zartman (ed.), *Elusive Peace: Negotiating an End to Civil Wars* (Washington DC: Brookings, 1995).

15. Zartman & Berman (1982), op. cit.; S Touval, *The Peace Brokers* (Princeton NJ: Princeton University Press, 1982); Zartman (1983), op. cit.; Touval & Zartman (1985), op. cit.; Zartman (1985/1989), op. cit.; I.W. Zartman, 'Ripening Conflict, Ripe Moment, Formula and Mediation', in D. BenDahmane & J. McDonald (eds), *Perspectives on Negotiation* (Washington DC: Government Printing Office, 1986); Zartman & Aurik (1991), op. cit.

16. Touval (1996), op. cit.; R. Haas, *Conflicts Unending* (Yale: Yale University Press, 1990); S. Stedman, *Peacemaking in Civil War* (Boulder CO: Lynne Rienner, 1991); T. Sisk, *Democratization in South Africa: The Elusive Social Contract* (Princeton NJ: Princeton University Press, 1995); I.W. Zartman (ed.), *Elusive Peace: Negotiating to End Civil War* (Washington DC: Brookings, 1995); D. Druckman & J. Green, 'Playing Two Games', in I.W. Zartman (1995) (ed.) op. cit.; T. Norlen, *A Study of the Ripe Moment for Conflict Resolution and its Applicability to two periods in the Israeli-Palestinian Conflict* (Uppsala: Uppsala University Conflict Resolution Program, 1995); F.O. Hampson, *Nurturing Peace* (Washington DC: US Institute of Peace Press, 1996); J. Goodby (1996), op. cit.; T. Ali & R. Matthews (eds), *Civil Wars in Africa* (Montreal: McGill-Queens University Press, 1999); M. Sala, 'Creating the "ripe moment" in the East Timor conflict', *Journal of Peace Research*, XXXIV, 4 (1997) pp. 449–466; D.G. Pruitt (ed.), 'The Oslo negotiations', *International Negotiation*, II, 2 (1997); K. Agerstam & C. Jönson, '(Un)ending Conflict', *Millennium*, XXXVI, 3 (1997) 771–794; C.A. Crocker, F.O. Hampson, & P. Aall (eds), *Herding Cats: The Management of Complex International Mediation* (Washington DC: US Institute of Peace Press, 1999); M. Mooradian & D. Druckman, 'Hurting stalemate or mediation? The conflict over Nagorno-Marabakh, 1990–1995', *Journal of Peace Research*, XXXVI, 6 (1999) pp. 709–727.

17. S. Touval, *The Peace Brokers* (Princeton NJ: Princeton University Press, 1982), especially. pp. 228–232, 328.

18. Stedman (1991), op. cit.; D. Lieberfield, *Talking with the Enemy* (New York: Praeger, 1999) and 'Conflict "ripeness" revisited', *Negotiation Journal*, XV, 1 (1999) pp. 63–82.

19. Stedman (1991), op. cit., passim, chapter. 7 especially. pp. 238, 241–242.

20. Zartman (1989), op. cit.

21. C.A. Crocker, *High Noon in Southern Africa* (New York: Norton, 1992) p. 363.

22. Ibid., p. 373.

23. Ibid., p. 481.

24. Ibid., chapter 16.

25. A. deSoto, 'Multiparty Mediation: El Salvador', in C.A Crocker, F.O Hampson, & P. Aall (eds) (1999), op. cit., p. 356.
26. J. Baker & T. de Franck, *The Politics of Diplomacy* (New York: Putnam, 1995).
27. Holbrooke (1998), op. cit., p. 27, 193.
28. Ibid., p. 73.
29. *New York Times* (9 Aug l995) A7.
30. M. Goulding, *Enhancing the United Nations' Effectiveness in Peace and Security* (New York: UN Secretariat, Report to the Secretary-General, 30 June 1997) p. 20.
31. I. Rabinovich, *The Brink of Peace: The Israeli-Syrian Negotiations* (Princeton NJ: Princeton University Press, 1998) p. 251.
32. J.P. Lederach, 'Cultivating Peace', in J. Darby & R. Mac Ginty (eds), *Contemporary Peacemaking* (New York: Palgrave, 2003) pp. 32–37.
33. D.G. Pruitt & S. Kim, *Social Conflict* (New York: McGraw-Hill, 2003).
34. E. Hoffer, *The True Believer* (New York: Harper, 1951); H. Nicolson, *Diplomacy* (New York: Oxford University Press, 1960); G. Snyder & P. Diesing, *Conflict Among Nations* (Princeton NJ: Princeton University Press, 1977); Pruitt & Kim(2003), op. cit.
35. R.L. Moses, *Freeing the Hostages* (Pittsburgh PA: University of Pittsburgh Press, 1996).
36. I.W. Zartman & G.O. Faure (eds), *Escalation and International Negotiation* (Cambridge: Cambridge University Press, 2005).
37. T. Ohlson & S.J. Stedman, *The New is Not Yet Born* (Washington DC: Brookings, 1994); Sisk (1995), op. cit.; Zartman (1995), op. cit.; Lieberfield (1999), op. cit.
38. J. Stein & L. Pauly (eds), *Choosing to cooperate: How states avoid loss* (Baltimore: The John Hopkins University Press, 1992).
39. D. Kahneman & A. Tversky, 'Prospect theory: An analysis of decisions under risk', *Econometrica,* IIIL, 3 (1979) pp. 263–291.
40. Baker & de Frank (1995), op. cit.; Pruitt (1997), op. cit.
41. K.Å. Nordquist, 'Boundary Disputes: Drawing the Line', in I.W. Zartman (ed.), *Preventive Diplomacy: Avoiding Conflict Escalation* (Lanham MD: Rowman & Littlefield, 2000).
42. C. Mitchell, 'Cutting Losses', Working Paper 9, Institute for Conflict Analysis & Resolution, George Mason University, appearing in a shorter version in *Paradigms: Kent Journal of International Relations* IX, 2 (1995) p. 3; Zartman (1995), op. cit.
43. Mitchell (1995), op. cit., p. 7.
44. Touval & Zartman (1985), op. cit.; H. Saunders, Guidelines B, Unpublished manuscript (1991).
45. T. Ohlson, *Power Politics and Peace Politics* (Uppsala: University of Uppsala, Department of Peace and Conflict Research) Report 50 (1998); D. Pruitt with P. Olczak, 'Approaches to Resolving Seemingly Intractable Conflict', in B. Bunker & J. Rubin (eds), *Conflict, Cooperation and Justice* (San Francisco CA: Jossey-Bass, 1995).
46. Zartman (1989), op. cit.; Mooradian & Druckman (1999), op. cit.
47. Crocker (1992), op. cit., p. 471.
48. Ibid., pp. 471–472; Haas (1990), op. cit.; Goulding (1997), op. cit.; Lederach (2003), op. cit.
49. Stein & Pauly (1992), op. cit.

50. M. Golan, *The Secret Conversations of Henry Kissinger* (New York: Bantam, 1976) p. 52; Crocker (1992), op. cit., pp. 381–382.
51. Touval & Zartman (1985), op. cit.; S. Touval, 'Mediators' Leverage', National Academy of Sciences, Commission on Conflict Resolution, 1999; D. Rothchild, *Managing Ethnic Conflict in Africa* (Washington DC: Brookings 1997).

3

Cultivating Peace: A Practitioner's View of Deadly Conflict and Negotiation

John Paul Lederach

Introduction

'So do you think it may be possible to move toward dialogue, maybe initial, off record contacts to see what obstacles or possibilities exist for a negotiated process to end the conflict?' The question posed by our peace research team to the representatives of the Basque separatist movement was genuine though intuitively we knew the response. The heads shook slowly and the inevitable short answer emerged, 'No. It is going to be a hard two years,' followed by a much more detailed justification and rationale.

The year of this conversation could have been 1991 prior to the Barcelona Olympic Games, or 1994 following the Olympics. On the other hand, it could have been January 2001, for the answer was much the same. The counterpart could just as well have been representatives of the Spanish Government rather than the separatists. For that matter, the conversation could have taken place in Northern Ireland, Somalia, or Colombia. In protracted conflict, the horizon of expectation is not the rise of peaceful change. The horizon is the regeneration of violence, steady and sure as the rising sun.

The conversation, much repeated in my experience as a conciliator, poses a dilemma that I often hear framed as a significant doubt and question from students in seminars and journalists in interviews. Is it possible to negotiate while the fighting is still raging, and when, for all practical purposes, neither side is expecting or even preparing for any significant change in the cycle of deadly conflict?

In this chapter, I will formulate some initial responses to that question from the standpoint and perspective of a practitioner. Theoretically, the field abounds with suggestions. Most well known is the idea of 'ripeness' first articulated by Zartman in his important book *Ripe for Resolution*.[1] Since 1995 research and writing have focused on lessons gained from peace processes and the question of timing.[2] The arguments have suggested that negotiations, and in particular mediation and conciliation, need to read a situation with a capacity to determine whether the timing is right for nudging the conflict from violence to dialogue, and more specifically to agreements that end the open violence. Conditions, patterns, and criteria have emerged to further develop this capacity, but in the end the metaphor created by 'ripeness' points towards a single important premise: change from cycles of deadly violence to negotiation is possible only when the conflict and its perpetrating actors have reached a certain maturation point; then conciliation and negotiation efforts can be introduced with greater effectiveness and success.

This chapter is not aimed at refuting the important research gained from the studies of peace processes in reference to criteria and patterns for successful intervention and negotiation in deadly conflict. I will provide a critique of the guiding metaphor – ripeness – and propose a re-orientation of the practice of developing negotiated peace processes with particular reference to time periods prior to and following the opening of formal talks. These are reflections that emerge from my own direct experiences and I believe that while they provide an alternative view to the metaphor of ripeness they are complementary to the existing body of literature.

A critique of ripeness

I start with three observations as to why I have found ripeness a limited metaphor for practice and then suggest several alternative metaphors or guiding perspectives in reference to how practitioners might align their work when faced with the question of whether it is possible to work for peace and negotiations when fighting is still raging. Let me start with what I consider to be a few of the practical limitations of ripeness.

Ripeness is a rear-view mirror

From the standpoint of practice ripeness theory and approaches present an awkward challenge and paradox. On the one hand, much of this theoretical emphasis has been pursued in order to create a 'predictive' capacity useful to conciliators and mediators as they engage with people involved in negotiation processes. Such a capacity offers the promise that if, as practitioners, we can recognize factors, conditions, and characteristics of negotiation situations in settings of violent conflict we can effectively increase our capacity to achieve a settlement, or inversely, to know when it is not effective to proceed with the effort. In other words, ripeness proposes to provide a predictive capacity. This is a forward-looking skill orientation, one that assumes linearity of process capable of foretelling outcomes from conditions. To draw the metaphor, ripeness should serve as a large windshield in a car providing a clear and expansive view of what is coming on the horizon such that the driver can adjust the manoeuvres to match the challenges of the approaching road.

However on the other side of the paradox, as I look back across my practical experience, unlike what the metaphor suggests, peacebuilding generally, and negotiations in particular, have not entailed a 'ripeness' process where I have watched the process develop, like the seasonal maturation of an apple moving from blossom to red, juicy, and ready to eat fruit. In fact, more often than not the opposite has been true. I have only recognized the keys to transformative change in retrospect and in differing ways in each context. For example, on several occasions in the Miskito/Sandinista negotiations the times when all the conditions pointed to successfully opening the talks were precisely the moments when all our efforts as conciliations failed. They were, in fact called off at least three times, and once within a day of starting. On the other hand, when they finally opened, what appeared to be a long drawn out entry in the airport where nearly everything fell apart again and seemed to point to a complete lack of ripeness, the talks that followed lasted about a week and were highly successful. 'Who would have known?' we commented time and again to ourselves.

To draw out the metaphor, 'ripeness' (as in recognizing that potential for change happened) was more like a rear-view mirror than a windshield. The roadway of protracted conflict, it seems, may be more akin to dynamic, nearly amoeba-like spaces than the linear and predictable development of fruit. Moreover, herein lies the limitation. Ripeness may be most useful in retrospective (as we look back we can account for things in our interpretation of the history), but is extremely weak in its predictive capacity from the standpoint of a practitioner and in fact may provide us with lens that are not helpful for adapting constructively to the pathways of peacebuilding.

Repeatedly, in situations as varied as Northern Ireland, the Basque Country, or the negotiations between the Philippine government and the communist insurgency, the moments when I thought there was the greatest potential for a significant move forward have been stagnant and even counterproductive. For a practitioner these periods create an emotional roller coaster. The predictive view suggests significant change is near. Then just when hopes are high, everything collapses leading to a deep sense of despair, and often urgent, at times inappropriate responses to save the moment. Other times, exactly when all the predictive characteristics pointed to complete stagnation and even highly escalated cycles of violence, turned out to be the periods when by way of some unexpected suggestion or event, a significant move forward was created.

These experiences have led me towards an attitude not driven by a predictive lens of visible factors but rather towards the development of lens that do not focus excessively on what appear at any given moment to be the limitations of temporal conditions. In protracted conflict, temporal conditions are ephemeral and nonlinear, requiring paradoxical intentionality: a set of mediative attitudes that keeps your feet on the ground (a realist view of the situation) and your head in the clouds (a hope driven idealist view of the possible). Therefore, rather than orienting my action around predictive ripeness, I find the opposite is increasingly true in my work. I am carefully cautious when all appears ripe for settlement and innoculatingly naive when all appears hopelessly lost in the grip of calamity.

Ripeness is in the eye of the beholder

Among the many things I have learnt in the school of hard knocks of protracted conflict is a simple idea with wide-ranging implications: the prevailing system is set up to create a permanently emerging crisis. This essentially has to do with time and response. I find that in situations with a long history of social division and violence the focus of attention is on the immediate situation and the crisis, event, or impending disaster that just happened. This is accompanied with the common view that once this 'crisis' is dealt with we can move onto the deeper and longer range concerns and needs. The tendency across the board is to be driven by the crisis. This I have found particularly true of people who are directly involved on one side or the other of the conflict, and as such there is a prevailing attitude that the situation is not ripe. In other words, ripeness is more often than not something perceived by outsiders with the luxury of dispassionate facts and factors. In the midst of week-to-week and month-to-month emergencies, people rarely see their situations as 'ripe' for peace. Ripeness is in the eye of the beholder and few who live in the settings have the luxury of such vision.

This leads to practical and attitudinal dilemmas for the peacebuilder. The most critical shift required is to understand the process not as linear but *circular and linear*. Ripeness, however, depends exclusively on a linear metaphor of time and change. Circular and linear can be visualized like a horizontal spiral where there is circular movement creating at any given moment forward, upward, backward, and downward movements *and* the whole of the circles is moving forward across time. These actually are the temporal experiences from within the situation that I have commonly experienced: things feel like they may be moving forward, then a crisis comes and it feels like everything has come to a standstill. At other times, it can easily feel like it is moving backwards, or even collapsing. This is the immediate time circle, and it is continuous, a permanent feature of the system. The challenge is how to visualize the possibility of sustaining an overall forward movement over time visible in the lens of decades not months. This requires a capacity to envision a long-term process and recognize opportunities for constructive change in the midst of crisis. In other words, it is a shift towards being crisis-responsive rather than crisis-driven. The key attitude and skill shift is that of adaptation of process that assumes and takes account of constant crisis rather than a linear view of maturation that assumes step-wise progression to resolution.

Ripeness sees mediator action as cherry picking

When I played basketball many years ago, our coach had a phrase with which he provoked us whenever we missed an easy shot, 'I can't believe you missed that cherry picker.' Essentially, it meant that a lot of work had gone into place and then just when everything was right and a give-away opportunity was presented, the basket was missed.

There are times when I have the impression that the metaphor of ripeness leads towards an emphasis on mediator action as if it were 'cherry picking'. The impression emerges from two understandings about mediation that I believe have significant limitations and implications.

The first commonly held belief is that mediation lies primarily in the person, and often the personality of the mediator-as-the-actor rather than mediation-as-process with multiple roles, functions, and activities carried out by a wide array of people.[3] Particularly critical to our discussion here is the idea that the mediator comes from outside the setting and outside the relationships in conflict, or what I have referred to as the 'outside-neutral' view of mediator role.[4] When the mediator provides an outside and neutral role in many cases they are 'in' and 'out' of the setting in terms of their actual physical presence. Ripeness is oriented towards providing terms of reference for this kind of action such that the mediator can gauge when it is most effective to push for agreement or renewed negotiation. What the ripeness metaphor does not provide is a sense of the long-term nature of the process, the building and sustaining of the relationships, nor the multiplicity of roles, activities, and functions that may be necessary to make a sustained dialogue and change in the relationships possible.

The second commonly held belief is that the success of mediation is primarily judged by whether it produced an agreement rather than whether it helped create a space for constructive change in people, perceptions, and relationships that are not always captured in the confines of a written negotiated document. Ripeness suggests the cherry is the agreement and that picking the cherry is like a mediation harvest. In my practical experience in conciliation work, this tends to promote a measuring stick of success based on what is often the least important element for gauging the sustainability of the change process necessary actually to create the transformation from deadly conflict to respect, cooperation, and increased peaceful interdependence. It is not a metaphor that provides a vision of cultivating the soil, planting the seeds, or nourishing the seedling in the face of winds, burning sun, or icy storms, all of which speak to process, relationship, and sustainability rather than a momentary action.

Alternative metaphors to ripeness

What I just outlined suggests that from the standpoint of practice the ripeness metaphor has some limitations when applied to contexts of protracted deadly conflict. The metaphor suggests a focus on content and agreement making rather than being relationship and change-oriented. It places emphasis on the mediator's action and perception rather than on the mediation-as-process with multiple sets of action and people. It tends to have a short-term view of action in mind aimed at intense action in specific timeframes (harvest) but not necessarily the slower and painstaking process of preparing and sustaining process. This suggests a need for additional and complimentary metaphors emerging from and oriented towards the experience of practice. As I reflect on my own experience several come to mind.

Cultivation: the building of long-term authentic relationships

Since the early 1990s, my efforts at peacebuilding and conciliation have led me to the metaphor of cultivator more than harvester, towards nourishment of soil and plant more than picking the fruit. The images that accompany this complementary metaphor suggest an organic connection to context, the building of relationships, and a commitment to process over time. Each of the images provides an avenue towards answering the question posed at the beginning of the chapter: is it possible to pursue negotiations while deadly conflict is raging?

The cultivation metaphor suggests that a deep respect for and connection to the context is critical for sustaining a change process that is moving from deadly expressions of conflict to increased justice and peace in relationships. The context of protracted deadly conflict, like soil, is the people, commonly shared geographies but often sharply differing views of history, rights and responsibilities, and the formation of perception and understandings based on cultural meaning structures. Cultivation is recognizing that ultimately the change process must be taken up, embraced and sustained by people in these contexts. The cultivator, as a connected but outside element in the system, approaches this soil with a great deal of respect, the suspension of quick judgement in favour of the wisdom of adaptation, and an orientation towards supporting the change process through highs and lows, ebbs and flows of violence and thawing of tensions, whether or not the situation appears ripe. The cultivator gives attention to the well-being of the eco-system not just the quick production of a given fruit.

A relationship-centric orientation naturally emerges from the metaphor. This is built on a genuine concern for relationships, not an instrumentalist approach to people in order to achieve an external goal. This suggests a criterion of authenticity, which cannot be overstated from the perspective of cultivation. A relationship-centric orientation keeps the focus on people, realities of histories, and perceptions as the source that generates and regenerates cycles of deadly conflict. The contentious content of specific agreements is often symbolic of this deeper level. In essence, you can resolve an issue but you till the soils of relationships if you are interested in sustained transformation and systemic health.

Both of the above images require a long-term commitment. I think this may be the single most important lesson learnt over the years, a shift from thinking about negotiations as a 'ripe' moment in time to an understanding of the preparation and support for a change process over a much longer period.[5] It requires you to shift from thinking in weeks and months to thinking in decades. If you have ever talked with a farmer about their land, you will hear them talking about years – decades and even a lifetime of relationship to the soil and the climate.

Accompaniment: the pace of presence

To understand accompaniment as a metaphor of peacebuilding and conciliation it is useful to break it down to its Latin origins. The word is built on two primary concepts *'com'* or with – and *'pani'* or bread. A literal translation would be 'with bread'. In other words, this is a table metaphor. To accompany is to sit and share bread with another. In my mind, there are a number of important images this metaphor places before us as practical guidelines.

First, sharing a table provides a sense of intimacy, of being inside a shared space of humanity with another. This takes us back to our earlier idea of relationship. Nevertheless, it goes further because the image suggests presence with another, a quality of what I once called 'alongsideness'.[6] This of course is very much a part of the image that the word 'accompany' creates; we walk alongside the journey of another. The image it suggests is a respect for the journey of others. It represents presence with others as they travel on their way.

The second intriguing aspect of this image is the idea of pace. When it is the journey of the other, the pace is not forced or prescribed from outside, but must, if it is to be authentic, be directed from sources of leading that come from within. In reference to peacebuilding this poses numerous difficult dilemmas, for more often than not the pace of moving from deadly cycles of conflict to more constructive, mutually beneficial and respectful cycles is extremely slow. In addition, much of peacebuilding from outside is oriented towards getting that movement to happen more rapidly. However, if movement or compromise happens because one is obligated or forced, then the change is rarely authentic and sustainable, and plants the seeds of renewed destructive conflict that sprout later. This becomes even more complex when the accompaniment is with people across the lines of division, and when slowness towards change means a great deal of suffering for many people.

Ripeness seems to answer this dilemma by suggesting that if we read the situation correctly we can determine when the greatest potential for change could happen and can then push for this change to take place. Accompaniment suggests an ongoing presence motivated by an interest in supporting a sustainable change process built on making opportunity available for genuine change motivated from within but not under obligation or external time frames. If we were to put this in detail that is more concrete it would suggest that conciliation work is not about moving in and out of a situation according to a measure of the potential for success. Rather, the activities of conciliation are about ongoing presence, a constancy of availability and a regularity of connection.

Naïveté: the art of the possible

Naïveté in the world of *real politik* is generally seen as foolishness, gullibility, and weakness of understanding about the true character of politics, power relationships, and even basic human nature. Those who are naïve are those with a Pollyannaish attitude who make things worse and are usually taken advantage of and eaten up in the process. Applied to peacebuilding, this is a common critique of those who pursue peace, particularly at times when things appear to be falling apart and getting worse.

When I look back at my own experiences, I should like to suggest the inverse may be true, that the key to significant change came not when I was capable of producing a hard, factual, objective view of a situation and the predictable outcomes. Rather it seemed to come from a kind of naïveté that suspended the lens of presented reality and with a commonsensical approach asked questions and pursued ideas that seemed out of line with reality as presented.

Paradoxically, naïveté cuts in both directions. It is equally naïve for the little boy alongside the parade to point a finger and say out loud, 'the emperor has no clothes' (which is exactly what I felt when the Dayton Peace Accords were hatched) or the sustaining of hope and pursuing of a 'couple of ideas' as I heard from Irish colleagues when on numerous occasions the bombs in the ceasefire period seemed to bring everything to a halt.

For my own edification as a peacebuilder, I have come to embrace the utility of naïveté as the art of the possible. Naïveté does not take what is presented on the surface and generally accepted as final truth as the primary measuring stick of how things work, are held together, or fall apart. Naïveté is unafraid of being perceived as stupid and has the courage to raise basic questions, both of optimism when all seems impossible and of common sense realism when everybody expects peace to happen because a paper was signed. In both instances, the art is in seeking a way to reach towards a deeper source of what is possible and needed to keep a constructive change process alive and healthy.

Epilogue

Therefore, what do I say when the journalist asks, 'And do you really believe it is possible to talk about negotiation and peace when war is raging?' I say hope is not negotiated. It is kept alive by people who understand the depth of suffering and know the cost of keeping a horizon of change as a possibility for their children and grandchildren. Quick fixes to a long-standing violent conflict are like growing a garden with no understanding of seeds, soils, and sweat. This conflict traces back across decades even generations. It will take that long to sort out.

Journalists generally do not quote me in their papers. Soundbites about ripeness, people coming to their senses, and the need for realism and pressure seem to find their way to print more often. However, I believe in cultivation. Cultivation as a metaphor suggests that the core of the peacebuilding work – fostering and sustaining committed, authentic relationships across the lines of conflict over time – does not rise and fall with the temporal vicissitudes of the conflict cycles. It answers the question – is it possible to pursue peace when things are bad – with a resounding 'Yes!' Just as it also suggests that when things are suddenly headed towards an agreement the work is hardly over. It has only begun.

Notes

1. I.W. Zartman, *Ripe for Resolution: Conflict and Intervention in Africa* (New York: Oxford University Press, 1985/1989).
2. See, for example, L. Kriesberg & S.J. Thorson (eds), *Timing the De-escalation of International Conflicts* (Syracuse NY: Syracuse University Press, 1991).
3. C. Mitchell, 'External Peace-Making Initiatives and Intranational Conflict', in M.I. Midlarsky (ed.), *The Internationalization of Communal Strife* (New York: Routledge, 1992).
4. P. Wehr & J.P. Lederach, 'Mediating in Central America', *Journal of Peace Research*, 28, 1 (February 1991) 86–98.
5. J.P. Lederach, *Building Peace: Sustainable Reconciliation in Divided Societies* (Washington DC: United States Institute of Peace, 1997).
6. J.P. Lederach, 'Qualities of Practice for Reconciliation', in R. Helmick (ed.), *Reconciliation* (New York: Templeton Press, 2001).

4

New Contexts for Political Solutions: Redefining Minority Nationalisms in Northern Ireland, the Basque Country, and Corsica

John Loughlin

Introduction

Ethnic and minority nationalist conflicts, and the peace processes that attempt to end them, always occur within specific geo-political or regional contexts and can be fully understood only by being situated within these contexts. Although it might be possible to compare conflicts and peace processes and to draw lessons from them across these different contexts, it remains that our analysis should start within them. Furthermore, the regional contexts themselves have been dramatically changing and whether these changes are leading to convergence or divergence remains to be seen. This chapter illustrates these general remarks through an examination of three case studies in Western Europe. Its central argument is that significant political changes, both at the regional level of the European Union (EU) and within the EU member states, have profoundly affected the nature of these struggles and have opened up new opportunities for a peaceful resolution of the conflicts, although the peace processes themselves have been very long and distinctly jagged in their outcomes.

The nation-state and minority nationalism

Nationalism is a complex phenomenon capable of several definitions. At least two are relevant to this chapter: the 'majority' nationalism of those countries which have become 'fully-fledged' nation-states (the United Kingdom, France, and Spain) and the 'minority' nationalism of territorially based groups within these states which have aspired to nation-state status (Northern Irish Catholics, Corsicans, and Spanish Basques). Both types of nationalism appeal to the normative principle of the 'nation-state', that is, that nations ought to have states and that states ought to be co-terminus with nations.[1]

In practice, there has been a wide variation both in terms of the application of the principle and in the institutional expression given to liberal democratic nation-states (from simple unitary states to more complex regionalized and federal states).[2] Furthermore, even in a country such as France, allegedly the 'nation-state' par excellence, there has never been a perfect match between 'state' and 'nation' with cultural and linguistic minorities contesting their belonging to the French 'nation'.[3] It is, *a fortiori*, difficult to apply the 'nation-state' model to either the United Kingdom or Spain, which are more properly categorized as 'Union' states.[4] In the United Kingdom, it is highly problematic whether there exists an overarching (British) 'nation' co-terminous with the United Kingdom 'state', given that England, Scotland and Wales, and, before 1921, Ireland, were constitutionally accepted as the constituent nations of the kingdom. The British 'state',[5] too, is far from homogeneously unified but consists rather of a heterogeneous and asymmetrical collection of administrative arrangements which differed across the different territories of the United Kingdom. Spain, too, has never been a completely united or unitary state although from the nineteenth century onwards, and certainly during the Franco-dictatorship, Spanish elites aspired to the French Jacobin model. This aspiration, however, was frustrated by the existence of Catalonia, the Basque Country, and Galicia.[6] When Spain made the transition to democracy in 1976–1978, political decentralization and, in particular, the recognition of the national rights of the three historic nations of Catalonia, the Basque Country, and Galicia[7] were key elements of the democratization process. Nevertheless, despite the innovative character of the Spanish 'autonomic state', the 1978 Constitution still remained somewhat confused and ambiguous about the relationship between the Spanish 'nation' and the 'nationalities' and 'regions'.[8]

Besides these ambiguities in defining and giving constitutional and legal expression to the nation-state idea, as illustrated by these three country case studies, the concept and political programme deriving from it have also been strongly contested by various ideologies and political movements such as federalists, regionalists, and advocates of a united Europe. In France, the United Kingdom, and Spain, minority nationalists challenged their respective nation-states in a variety of ways. Ideologically, they refused to recognize the legitimacy of the state's presence in their territories, arguing that this had come about by conquest. Each group generated an alternative 'founding myth' of their 'nation': in Northern Ireland, it was the physical force tradition which had expressed itself in various nineteenth-century rebellions but especially the 1916 Easter Rising and the first Dáil of 1919; in the Basque Country, it was the existence of a 'unique' people whose ethnic origins were shrouded in mystery; in Corsica it was the short-lived republic of Pascal Paoli (1749–1769) which had been inspired by Rousseau's writings. The nationalists rejected both the symbols and the institutions of the nation-state of which they were part. However, their most serious challenge, through the setting up of secret armies, was to the state's monopoly of the use of force. In each case, the circumstances surrounding the violence and the forms it took differed. In Northern Ireland, the Provisional Irish Republican Army (IRA) could draw on a long tradition of political violence going back to the nineteenth century. In the Basque Country, the adoption of violent tactics happened only in the 1960s with the formation of Euskadi ta Askatasuna (ETA or 'Basque Homeland and Freedom') but they developed against the background of the appalling violence of the Spanish Civil War (1936–1939).[9] In Corsica, it was only in 1962 that the first bombings took place in protest at French governmental policies on the island.[10] Various clandestine groups appeared in the 1960s and 1970s which, in 1976, coalesced into the Front de Libération Nationale de la Corse (FLNC). However, Corsicans could also call on the mythical violence of the vendetta or the tradition of banditry, somewhat romanticized by authors such as Mérimée and Flaubert.

Whatever the historical or cultural origins of the tradition of violence, its contemporary expression and patterns of development were similar in each of the three cases: a cycle of violence, state repression, and further violence. Although the violent separatists were a minority in each region, their actions were sufficient to influence and even dominate the political agenda and to prevent solutions to their regions' problems arrived at by the national govern-ments and other regional groups. Furthermore, agents close to the state often retaliated with violence, thus further undermining the legitimacy of the state in the eyes of more moderate regionalists or nationalists.[11] The impunity with which these anti-nationalist forces operated damaged trust in the judiciary and the police in all three cases, thus unintentionally playing into the hands of the separatists. Finally, these 'wars' all had the effect of producing large num-bers of prisoners, regarded as 'criminals' by the state and its supporters and as 'prisoners of war' or 'political prisoners' by the separatists and their supporters. Prisoners' issues became a fundamental element of the separatists' campaigns and the prisoners themselves in all three cases were granted legitimacy by their movements as a result of the sacrifice which they had made for the 'cause'.[12]

By the 1980s, the violent conflicts in all three regions seemed insoluble as the protagonists were opposed not only in their sets of demands but also in their very conception of the nature of the problems. At root were two basically similar but conflicting sets of claims about nationhood, sovereignty, legiti-macy, and control of the means of coercion over the same piece of territory. It is remarkable, then, given the complexities of the different conflicts, that break-throughs became possible in all three cases in the 1990s, even if these are still experiencing great difficulties and, in the case of the Basque Country, seem to have been reversed, at least for the moment. The remainder of this chapter will attempt to explain the context which made these breakthroughs possible.

A new geo-political context

A series of developments from the early 1980s changed the context in which these conflicts were being fought out. We have dealt with this elsewhere[13] but it is worthwhile to draw attention briefly to the following. Since 1945, advanced capitalist states have, to use Thomas Kuhn's phrase, gone through at least two and perhaps three 'paradigm shifts'. The first paradigm is what we called the 'Welfare State' model which was adopted by most Western states from the early 1950s until the late 1970s/early 1980s. This was replaced by a 'neo-liberal' paradigm, associated with the ideas of the 'New Right' and politicians such as Ronald Reagan and Margaret Thatcher, and which spread across Western states in the 1980s and 1990s. Today, we seem to be witnessing what may be called the 'post-Welfare State' paradigm which combines some aspects of the Welfare State model with the neo-liberal approach. This 'Third Way' mix has been tried in different proportions in different countries by the centre-Left (Blair in the United Kingdom, Jospin in France, and Schroeder in Germany) and the centre-Right (Aznar in Spain).[14]

Each of these paradigms conceives the relationship between the state, the economy, society and culture/values in a distinct manner. They also conceptualize the relationship between the state and sub-national authorities, including regions and 'stateless nations' in a particular way. The shift refers to a fundamental re-ordering of these relationships and a reconceptualization of central–local relations. The evolution of our three case studies might also be understood in the context of the evolution of the three paradigms as a way of clarifying some of their most salient features and of understanding how solutions now seem to be within their grasp.

In the welfare state paradigm, economies and states were in full expansion to provide and manage sets of needs and demands emanating from society. In order to meet these needs and demands, welfare states were bureaucratic, top-down, and centralizing. Territorial politics and policy were conceived in *national* terms. Regional policy, for example, was conceived as the territorial expression of social policy and both regional and social policies were aimed at integrating the weaker individuals and territories into the national society. In many respects, the welfare state model represents not only the epitome of the nation-state idea but also perhaps its limits.[15] By concentrating on *national* goals, it tended to exclude other perspectives such as those that might be found at the regional or local levels. The regional development programmes were often formulated and carried out by national elites with only token representation and even exclusion of regional and local elites. During this period, regional languages and cultures were regarded as obstacles to economic and social development. At most, they were relegated to quaint folkloric customs that might have a role in amusing tourists. The notion of

Table 4.1 Changing paradigms of the state–society relationships 1945–2000

	Economy	State features	Society	Culture/values
The 'expansive' welfare state	Fordist production methods; heavy industries: coal and steel; geographical factors of production important; Keynesian approaches of macro-economic management; nationalisation; full employment goal; rise in incomes and living standards; top-down regional policy; founding of EEC	equality of opportunity; government intervention; progressive income tax; citizens' right to services and expanding definition of 'needs'; centralisation and bureaucratisation of public administration; managerialism in public sector; fiscal overload (1970s); crisis of ungovernability.	freedom of the individual; urbanisation; sexual 'revolution'; expansive definition of human 'rights'; growing importance of mass media; mass travel and tourism; secularisation; student revolutions and 'youth' culture; social engagement.	new values based on freedom and choice; new lifestyles (clothing, living patterns); cosmopolitan culture; *regional cultures devalued – reduced to 'folklore' for tourists*; *regionalist reactions to revalidate their cultures*; *regional culture seen (by elites) as obstacle to regional development*
The 'conctracting' neo-liberal state	post-Fordist; deregulation and privatisation; new technologies and systems of communication; new (non-geographical) factors of production; predominance of service industries; *globalisation and 'glocalisation'*; *bottom-up models of regional development*; importance of knowledge:	the 'hollow', 'elusive', 'anorexic', state; no government intervention; reduction of taxation; privatisation; deregulation; cutting back of services; decentralisation; regionalisation; 'New Public Management'; 'marketisation' of public services citizens as consumers	'no such thing as society' (Thatcher); individualism; glorification of greed; decline of notions of 'common good' and community; *fragmentation of communities*; creation of an underclass in cities; increasing gap between poor and rich (individual and geographical);	the neo-liberal project = propagation of values; rich less willing to pay for welfare services through taxation; reactions to this – e.g. election of Blair, Jospin; 'remoralisation' in Britain; culture as variable in economic development; *new appreciation of and opportunities for regional cultures*; *Europe of the Cultures 2002 (Flanders)*

Continued

Table 4.1 Continued

	Economy	State features	Society	Culture/values
	the 'learning' and innovative region. accelerated European integration (1985–)			
The 'commmunitarian/ social' state	acceptance of capitalism and the market; low taxation; end of class struggle; innovative entrepreneurship; social dimension and institutional economics; role for trade unions and local authorities; *economic regionalism*;	claims to pursue equality of opportunity and social justice but through competition; concept of the *enabling* state; no return to the old Welfare State; slimming down of bureaucracy; new public-private partnership; decentralisation and devolution; revalidation of local authorities and rebuilding local democracy and sense of citizenship; pro-European.	perhaps limits to individualisation and fragmentation; remoralisation of society; concept of community – communitarianism; new approach to law and order issues – zero tolerance.	acceptance of individualistic trends; toleration of different life-styles; new concepts of human rights; *revalidation of regional and local cultures*; personalism.

national minorities or at least of separatist nationalism was anathema within this paradigm.

France, the United Kingdom, and Spain (even at the time of Franco) all adopted versions of this model despite their very different political systems. In both France and the United Kingdom, there was an overall increase in the standard of living and social benefits available to many citizens. In Spain, during the last years of Francoism, there was a modernizing, technocratic elite, close to the Catholic organization Opus Dei, who tried to put into effect similar approaches, although the country as a whole remained quite poor by West European standards. Whatever the circumstances, in all three countries the arrival of welfare states affected the three regions under consideration in a number of ways. In all three cases, there appeared new political movements which mobilized important sections of the population: in Northern Ireland, the Civil Rights Movement demanded equal treatment for Catholics on the basis of their membership of the United Kingdom; in Corsica (as in other French regions such as Brittany and the French Basque Country), regionalists demanded equal treatment with the French mainland on the basis of their French citizenship; in the Basque Country, moderate nationalists demanded recognition of their language and culture. In all three cases, however, these movements were really coalitions of disparate groups. The demands of the component groups within the coalitions were still couched in 'stato-national' terms ranging from the full implementation of their rights as citizens of that state, to complete separatism but in the form of setting miniature 'nation-states'. The national governments also responded to these demands in similar fashion: at first with repression and then (at least in the United Kingdom and France) with concessions which were usually too little too late. A cycle of violence, repression, and further violence was initiated accompanied by an increasing radicalization of the demands made by some elements of the coalition, thus provoking further violence and repression. This led to the disintegration of the coalitions into moderate and radical factions, with the latter gradually increasing the intransigent nature of their demands. These radical demands and the equally intransigent responses of the national governments were so irreconcilable that solutions seemed impossible to reach. National governments claimed absolute sovereignty over the territories in which the conflicts were happening and the nationalist movements made the same claim. Both resorted to coercion or violence to back up their claims. In all three regions, significant sections of the population withdrew their consent to be governed.[16]

Did the European Community (EC) play a role during this period in either the exacerbation or calming of these conflicts? The answer is that 'Europe' was a dimension which tended to be in the background even if it was not altogether absent. During the welfare state period of state development, the EC was reduced to the role of attempting to complete the Common Market and ensuring harmonization of trade activities across states. The dominant mode of European politics and policy-making was then definitely intergovernmental, that is, firmly based on the predominance of the national governments.[17] At the same time, some moderate regionalists were also European federalists while European federalists, such as the European Federalist Movement, were also sympathetic to regionalism. The more hard-line minority nationalists, however, such as ETA, the FLNC and Sinn Féin (even before the split into Officials and Provisionals) were opposed to European integration. This opposition had two main sources. Some espoused a Marxist analysis which saw the EC as a capitalist 'rich men's club'. Others opposed it because they saw it as a threat to the nationalist idea as such and therefore to what might emerge as their own mini-nation-states. In other words, their opposition mirrored that of nationalists such as De Gaulle and, later, Mrs Thatcher and Tory Eurosceptics.

The Welfare State model of the state entered into crisis at the end of the 1970s and became unable to provide the range of benefits to citizens on which it had been premised. This crisis was probably part of a wider crisis of the capitalist system, which had been based on 'Fordist' methods of production and the smokestack industries of coal and steel. While capitalism successfully renewed itself through the development of new technologies and globalization, the political and administrative systems of Western European states were still based on the old Welfare State model and were much slower to change. Furthermore, these states found themselves increasingly facing stiff economic competition from the United States and Japan, who had been more successful in adapting themselves to the new economic realities. Western states responded to these challenges in two fashions. First, they adopted, in different ways, what we have called the 'neo-liberal' paradigm to restructure their states.[18] Second, and related to this, they decided that they could achieve more by collaboration rather than as single, small or medium-sized countries. As a result, and with the encouragement of other elites such as the European Round Table of Industrialists, they 'relaunched' the process of European integration in the early 1980s. When he became President of the European Commission in 1985, Jacques Delors took up this challenge and decided that European integration would be pushed forward through the Single European Act and the implementation of the Single Market in 1992. Thus, 'Europe' became an increasingly important variable in a growing range of policy sectors, including regional policy. It was during this period of state and economic restructuring that the notion of a 'Europe of the Regions', an old federalist idea, was resurrected by the German Länder in order to advance both the cause of a federalist Europe and to enhance the position of sub-national authorities generally.[19]

Although not intended by neo-liberals such as Mrs Thatcher when she signed the Single European Act in 1986, these political and institutional developments had enormous consequences for both the institutions and policies of the EC which would become the EU and for the position of nation-states and their regions. First, the notion of national 'sovereignty' was further transformed. This had already changed from being the absolute exercise of power by national governments over fixed territories to being 'pooled' over an increasing range of areas. Decisions were increasingly taken in 'Brussels' and incorporated into national law by member state parliaments. Second, the institutions of the Union, especially the European Commission and the European Court of Justice, were immensely strengthened even if the Council of Ministers, which allegedly represents the principle of 'national interest' probably continued to be the most important EU institution.[20] Third, regions and local authorities were given a new lease of life both because of the massive increase in funding for the enhanced Structural and Cohesion Funds, operated through the new principles of partnership and subsidiarity, but also through the setting up of the Committee of the Regions by the Treaty of Maastricht.[21] What occurred here is neither the disappearance of the nation-state (the old dream of regionalists and European federalists) nor the creation of a European federation along the lines of a Europe of the Regions.[22] Rather, what has emerged is a new system of European governance (rather than government), in which the European institutions, national governments, and sub-national authorities have distinct and new roles. This new and evolving system of governance has both state-like and federal-like features without itself being either a state or a federation. This was an entirely new climate in which sub-national authorities operated and both the prospects of increased funding and the lessening of national government hegemony led to a vast mobilization of regions and local governments across Europe. Minority nationalist movements who had previously been opposed to European integration now came to see some merits and windows of opportunity for their political aims, which they now began to formulate as 'independence in Europe', although refusing to see themselves as simply 'regions'.

With the election of Clinton and his programme of 'reinventing government' in the United States and a succession of centre-Left leaders such as Blair, Jospin, and Schröder in Europe, the dominance of the 'neo-liberal' paradigm seems to be giving way to a new formulation of the role of the state and its relationship with civil society. We have called this the 'post-Welfare State' since, unlike neo-liberalism, it allows the state a positive role in economic and social processes but one that is based, unlike the Welfare State, on 'partnership', 'subsidiarity', and mobilization 'from below' while accepting some of the key features of neo-liberalism such as the market and competition. In other words, the post-Welfare state attempts to combine neo-liberalism with some of the traditional values of 'social democracy', without returning to the Welfare State model. These approaches might also be found in the debate about the future model of the European Union and the alleged contrast between an 'Anglo-Saxon' model, based on market-type approaches to policy, and a 'Continental

European' model, which more resembles the German 'social market' approach. These issues were an important factor, especially in the French referendum on the European Constitutional Treaty which failed to be approved in 2005. What is striking today is not the complete replacement of the old Welfare State model with a neo-liberal model of the state but the co-existence of the two models both in the wider European scene and within particular states. This has led to a complexity that is new and which underlies the current preoccupation with 'governance', which means the governing of complexity.

The transformation of the state, European integration, and minority nationalist conflict

These developments have provided a new context in which the violent conflicts in Northern Ireland, the Basque Country, and Corsica have been played out, although, once again, each case is very different from the others. First, they permit new ways of defining the nature of the problems themselves. Whereas, previously, the conflicts revolved irreconcilably around claims of national sovereignty, the redefinition of the latter allows the protagonists to reformulate their claims in a different kind of way. The pooling of national sovereignty at the European level means that it has been relativized. What, then, is the sense in engaging in violent conflict to assert one's 'sovereign' rights? In the case of Northern Ireland, this was at least one strand of the complex process that began with the 1985 Anglo-Irish Agreement and led into the Good Friday Agreement.[23] In Corsica, too, the wider transformation of the European system of governance allowed politicians and activists from different parts of the political spectrum, as well as French national politicians, to redefine the nature of the Corsican problem. This came to be seen, less as a problem of 'internal colonialism' as Corsican nationalists had defined it, or as a merely backward French region as state elites saw it, and more as a 'European island region' in the Western Mediterranean. In other words, the definition now transcended the boundaries of the French state.[24] In the Basque Country, a peace process was launched in the 1990s, mainly by the moderate Partido Nacionalista Vasco (PNV) Basque Government which was partly inspired by the Northern Ireland peace process and partly by the wider developments at the level of Europe.[25]

The second positive development is that the emerging European system of governance provides a new forum within which new identities, or new combinations of complex identities, may be formed which do not threaten the national or regional identities of the various protagonists of the conflict. In this way, what were previously zero-sum relationships between say Irish, Northern Irish, Ulster, or British identities which became intensified and solidified as a result of the conflict could now be expressed in a very different manner because there was an even wider overarching identity which was 'European'.

This is the case even if, as most attitude surveys suggest, the protagonists do not (yet) feel a strong European identity.[26] Nevertheless, 'Europe' provides a new frame of reference and, as we have seen, a new set of opportunities for political action for regions and local authorities. Political elites in British, French, and Spanish regions, as well as elsewhere in Europe, have seized these new realities as tools in a vast process of regional mobilization to assert and promote the interests of their regions in the new Europe. Regional identity and culture, in the new paradigm of the post-Welfare state, are no longer considered an obstacle to regional economic development but may be, on the contrary, an asset, with regions such as Catalonia and Flanders serving as models in this regard.[27] These opportunities and the mobilizations stimulated by them have, to some extent, taken the sting out of identity conflicts and permit minority groups to develop a new self-confidence and pride in themselves. The existence of bodies such as the Committee of the Regions and the European Parliament and interregional associations such as the Assembly of European Regions, gives them new fora to express their identities thus reducing the temptation to use the weapon of political violence. Of course, not all minority nationalists are convinced by these developments but these are increasingly reduced to a hard-core, isolated, largely, from the wider population which had hitherto given them support.

Finally, the new European context and the changing nature of nation-states present a challenge to those minority nationalist movements who had opposed European integration and had tried to set up their own mini-nation-states. It is increasingly recognized by these groups that the goal of complete independence is unrealistic. This has now been reformulated as 'independence within Europe'. 'Europe' and the slogan 'Europe of the Regions' have been used by minority nationalists as a way of repositioning themselves towards, and putting pressure on, their own national governments. This is seen strikingly in the case of the Catalan and Scottish nationalists but it may also be found in our three case studies. Furthermore, often national governments and regions collaborate in seeking greater funding opportunities from the EU, leading to a new type of relationship between them. Thus, the ideological basis of minority nationalism is changing and this makes the conflicts much less of a zero-sum game.

Most of the leading protagonists of peace in our three regions have been national and regional politicians deeply imbued with this European perspective. On the regional level the following may be found: John Hume and the Social Democratic and Labour Party (SDLP) in Northern Ireland; the PNV in the Basque Country; and Claude Olivesi (Socialist Party) and Paul Giacobbi (Left Radical Party) in Corsica. On the national levels: the pro-European Tony Blair, and Lionel Jospin, played important roles in the Northern Irish and Corsican peace processes respectively; while in Spain, the process was more difficult as Aznar, while Prime Minister, had not yet made the link between his

Europeanism and the Basque peace process. Zapatero, on the other hand, has shown a much more open-minded attitude to Spanish national sovereignty as is shown by his willingness to accommodate some of the demands of Catalan nationalists for national recognition and his re-opening of negotiations with the hard-line Basque separatists. Unfortunately, the Basque ceasefire has broken down, mainly because of the instransigence of the Basque terrorists. This is not surprising since what we have been arguing is that the changed *context* has made it easier to negotiate issues of sovereignty. This does not mean that all parties have completely bought into the new paradigm. We have seen how Aznar refused to do so as did the Basque separatists. It is also true that Sinn Féin remains somewhat Eurosceptic but, for the moment, they seem to have decided on a new pragmatism which tones down their previous intransigent republicanism and accepts the opportunities of the new European context.

Conclusion

These remarks should not be taken to imply that the transition from armed struggle to non-violent political action in our three regions has gone smoothly. Indeed, in Northern Ireland, it is over 17 years since the Anglo-Irish Agreement was signed and 12 years since the first IRA ceasefire in 1994 and peace is not yet definitively installed. In Corsica, the process has been much more rapid but scarcely less rocky. In the Basque Country, after a shaky beginning, the ETA ceasefire broke down and violence had even intensified before being resumed under Zapatero, only to break down again.[28] Nevertheless, in all three cases a huge amount of progress has been achieved. Northern Ireland has new institutions, in part modelled on the institutions of the EC, in part on the Nordic Council, which have functioned sporadically but now (in 2007) seem on the verge of coming into operation once again. These institutions may be regarded as a kind of laboratory for testing some of the propositions concerning the emergence of a new kind of state dealt with in this chapter. The IRA has now dismantled its weapons arsenal and is actually disbanding as an organization. Some of the Loyalist groups are still engaged in violence and there is the threat from dissident groups such as the 'Real' IRA but these have little support in the wider population. In Corsica, the French government came to an agreement with the majority of the Corsican political class with regard to radical institutional reforms of the island's status and the ceasefire by the main groups is still holding. The Bill giving effect to these reforms was successfully voted in by the French Parliament in June 2001. Unfortunately, a referendum on the reforms held on the island in July 2003 failed by a whisker to be approved by the island's population with 50.99 per cent voting NO and 49 per cent voting YES with a turnout of 60 per cent of the electorate. In this case, the political elites in favour of the change failed to convince a majority of the population of its merits as the latter remain wedded to the old paradigm of (French) national sovereignty. In the Basque Country, despite the difficulties and the breakdown of the ceasefires, there is nevertheless a new awareness of the possibility of peace and moderate Basques are still pursuing this goal.

Nevertheless, difficulties remain. In all three cases, it would not be an exaggeration to say that these are caused by factions or individuals who have not managed to adapt to the contemporary political realities outlined in this chapter. In Northern Ireland, unionists have undergone a traumatic challenge to their traditional identity as 'British', and an important minority, particularly Ian Paisley's Democratic Unionist Party and also supporters of the more moderate Ulster Unionist Party, tried to resist the changes. Nevertheless, as we have seen, this now seems to have changed, as at least important elements within the Democratic Unionist Party (DUP), including perhaps Paisley himself, seem ready to share power with Sinn Féin, as these are the two largest parties within Northern Ireland. In Corsica, while the majority of the political class, both nationalist and non-nationalist, have adapted, an important faction have resisted. The former French Minister of the Interior, Jean-Pierre Chevènement, vigorously opposed any concessions to Corsican autonomy and eventually resigned in protest at the deal that was struck in the end between the then Prime Minister, Lionel Jospin and the Corsican Assembly. In the Basque Country, the hardliners were not only the radical nationalists ETA/Herri Batasuna (HB) but also the former Spanish Prime Minister Aznar. As we have seen, Zapatero has been more flexible but peace is still some way off. However, in all three countries, there is a wide-ranging debate, at least among academics and politicians, if not the general public, on the meaning of nationhood and nationalism, regionalism, and identity in the context of a changing nation-state and increasing European integration. This debate opens the possibility of a new form of civic republicanism and the discussion of the place of minority groups in European society in which political violence is abandoned as a method of making claims to be replaced, hopefully, by rational and peaceful discussion.

Notes

1. P. Alter, *Nationalism*, 2nd edn (London: Edward Arnold, 1994).
2. J. Loughlin, *Subnational Democracy in the European Union: Challenges and Opportunities* (Oxford: Oxford University Press, 2001).
3. J. Loughlin, *Regionalism and Ethnic Nationalism in France: A Case Study of Corsica* (Florence: European University Institute, 1989).
4. D. Urwin, 'Territorial Structures and Political Developments in the United Kingdom', in S. Rokkan & D. Urwin (eds), *The Politics of Territorial Identity* (London: Sage Publications, 1982) and L. Moreno, *Federalizing the Spanish State* (London: Frank Cass, 2000).

5. It is a moot point as to whether the United Kingdom even possesses a 'state', at least in the sense in which this word is understood in the countries of continental Europe, which possess l'Etat, lo Stato, el Estado, etc. In the United Kingdom and, in the Anglo-Saxon tradition in general, we refer more to 'government' or, perhaps, to the 'Crown' (United Kingdom) or the 'Constitution' rather than the state.

6. D. Conversi, *The Basques, the Catalans and Spain: Alternative Routes to Nationalist Mobilisation* (London: Hurst, 1997) and Moreno (2000), op. cit.

7. Galicia did not have the same degree of nationalist mobilization as the other two regions and, in fact, was quite pro-Franco. Nevertheless, it received the same favourable treatment of recognition after the transition to democracy.

8. The Constitution defines Spain (including the Catalans, Basques and Galicians) as a unitary and indivisible 'nation' within which exist 'nationalities' and 'regions', without specifying which is which.

9. F. Letamendia, *Historia del nacionalismo vasco y de ETA*. 3 Vols. (San Sebastien: R&B Ediciones, 1994).

10. Loughlin (1989), op. cit.

11. In Northern Ireland, various branches of the British security forces carried out clandestine activities against republicans and often assisted loyalist groups in their attacks on the Catholic community, as a recent report by the police ombudsman, Nuala O'Loan into the murder of Raymond McCord by the UVF, has clearly demonstrated. In the Basque Country, the GAL (Anti-terrorist Liberation Groups – *Grupos Antiterroristas de Liberación*) a secret police group operating with the connivance of parts of the Spanish government, carried out assassinations of nationalists, sometimes on French soil. In Corsica, there were suspicions that nationalists were attacked and sometimes killed by *'barbouzes'*, secret militias opposed to nationalism.

12. In Northern Ireland, the death of Bobby Sands on hunger strike consolidated this aspect of the struggle.

13. J. Loughlin, 'The "transformation' of governance: New directions in policy and politics', *Australian Journal of Politics and History*, 50, 1 (March 2004) pp. 8–22.

14. A. Giddens, *The Third Way: A Renewal of Social Democracy* (Malden MA: Polity Press, 1998).

15. It represents its epitome of the nation-state as a democratic system because it attempted to develop the notion of 'social' citizenship as opposed to purely formal 'political' citizenship. It represents its limits because the Welfare State, in the end, failed to deliver on this promise and, instead, became an excessively centralized and bureaucratic system from which the majority of citizens were excluded.

16. This is especially true of Northern Ireland the Basque Country. In Corsica, only a small minority withdrew their consent.

17. It would take us too far outside the scope of this paper to deal with this issue. Suffice it to say that it was in the 1960s that General De Gaulle, as President of France (1962–1969) who left his mark by asserting the notion of a *Europe des Patries* rather than a supranational or federal Europe.

18. We speak here of the neo-liberal paradigm but it is important to remember that this is not a completely coherent model, was not fully implemented even in the United Kingdom, and took several different expressions depending on which country it was applied to. Nevertheless, there are a number of broad ideas which its adherents promoted: less and even no state intervention in the economy and society; the centrality of entrepreneurship; the predominance of markets as a mechanism for the allocation of value; competition; etc.

19. J. Loughlin, 'The "Europe of the regions" and the federalization of Europe', *Publius: The Journal of Federalism* (Fall 1996). The original idea of a 'Europe of the Regions' as a form of European federation involving the abolition of the nation-state was developed by European federalists such as Denis de Rougement in 'Vers une fédération des régions' [1968], *Œuvres complètes*, Tome III (2): Ecrits sur l'Europe (Paris: La Différence, 1994), pp. 210–223 & Guy Héraud, *L'Europe des Ethnies* (Paris: Presses d'Europe. 1964).

20. It could be argued that despite its role of representing 'national interests', the Council has become, in effect, a supranational institution, since, in an increasing number of policy areas, its decisions over-ride the decisions of individual national governments. Furthermore, national governments increasingly frame their so-called 'national interests' in 'European' terms, that is, they arrive at meetings of the Council of Ministers with proposals couched in terms that are likely to be acceptable to their colleagues.

21. J. Loughlin & D.L. Seiler, 'Le comité des Régions et la supranationalité en Europe', *Etudes Internationales* (Décembre 1999).

22. Loughlin (1996), op. cit.

23. Ironically, the process was launched by two rather traditional nationalists: Charles Haughey and Margaret Thatcher. In the case of the latter, however, it is doubtful whether she fully grasped the consequences of the agreements she was entering into, just as she failed to grasp the full consequences of signing the Single European Act. John Hume probably played an important role in the background of these developments as did senior British and Irish Civil Servants working in the European Community.

24. J. Loughlin, C. Olivesi, & F. Daftary (eds), *Autonomies Insularies: vers une politique de difference pour la Corse?* (Ajaccio: Editions Albiana, 1999).

25. F. Letamendia & J. Loughlin, 'Peace in the Basque Country and Corsica', in M. Cox, A. Guelke, & F. Stephen (eds), *A Farewell to Arms? From 'Long War' to Long Peace in Northern Ireland* (Manchester: Manchester University Press, 2000).

26. It is interesting that those with the strongest European identity are those sections of the population that are most highly educated and found in the higher social groups, in other words, among social elites. But it is precisely these elites who must be the bearers either of a nationalist project or the main protagonists in a peace process.

27. See M. Keating, J. Loughlin, & K. Deschouwer, *Culture, Institutions and Regional Development: A Study of Eight European Regions* (Cheltenham: Edward Elgar, 2003).

28. Loughlin & Letamendia (2000), op. cit.

Part II

Negotiations: An Introduction

John Darby and Roger Mac Ginty

Many attempted peace initiatives fail to reach the negotiation stage. Indeed, the conditions laid down for entry to negotiations are often the main stumbling block. In a perfect world, negotiations provide a forum for antagonists to reach a comprehensive set of compromises in a stable environment. The reality is often complicated by suspicion, continuing violence or tension, and politicking within camps. Moreover, the high-stakes nature of negotiations, involving the possibility of gains or losses over power and resources, means that the location, timetable, participant list, chair, and status of any negotiations is likely to cause as much conflict as the issues on the agenda.

Although desirable, trust between negotiating partners is not essential. Instead it is important that they trust the ability of the negotiations, whether embodied by the chair or guaranteed by third parties, to deliver and implement a peace accord. To this end, ground rules for negotiation, procedures for 'trouble-shooting' or addressing impasses, and techniques to ease communication become important. In some circumstances, face-to-face negotiations prove impossible, requiring the involvement of mediators. The media is a potential complicating factor. On the one hand negotiations may prosper away from the glare of publicity. On the other, secret negotiations can generate suspicion and cause confusion, something that may have severe implications if a subsequent peace accord is dependent on public support.

Ultimately it is the quality of the negotiations that matters, and whether they tackle the core issues of the conflict, include the main participants of the conflict, and have sufficient local and international backing to implement any agreement.

5
Negotiations and Peace Processes

Adrian Guelke

The connection between negotiations and peace processes rests on two apparently straightforward and seemingly persuasive propositions. They are that tangible evidence of a commitment to peace on the part of the major combatants is needed to create the right climate for negotiations to end violent political conflict and that the pursuit of a negotiated settlement is needed to sustain any peace process. They imply a more or less symbiotic relationship between negotiations and peace processes. It is a small step from these propositions to argue that the way to peace itself lies through negotiations culminating in a political settlement. However, not merely are political settlements frequently challenged by violence but the two propositions themselves are more problematic than they appear at first sight. Thus, in practice, the circumstances in which parties are willing to enter into negotiations vary widely. What is acceptable in one political context may prove insufficient in another. As far as the assumed relationship between political settlements and peace is concerned, even the converse relationship does not necessarily hold. The consequence of failure of the parties to reach a negotiated settlement may not be the renewed outbreak of violent conflict, as the case of Cyprus's long, largely bloodless conflict since partition in 1974 underlines.

The failure of negotiations to end protracted violent political conflicts is typically attributed to a variety of factors, including most commonly the pursuit of irreconcilable aims by the major antagonists, obdurate political leadership, and the stage of the conflict. The obverse of these propositions is that successful negotiation depends on a readiness of the parties to compromise, political leadership capable of developing a relationship with the other side, and the right timing. In particular, numerous writers have focused on the process of refining the positions of the parties so as to achieve an outcome that meets the aspirations of all of the parties.[1] In the language of conflict resolution, this is referred to as a 'win-win' solution or slightly more realistically as a positive sum solution that is, a formula that gives more to the parties than a simple splitting of the difference between their positions. Other studies have focused on the importance of developing trust between those engaged in the negotiations, on breaking down what is sometimes labelled the psychological dimension of the conflict.[2] Finally, the issue of timing has received considerable attention, most notably in the writings of William Zartman and his very widely quoted notion of ripeness allied to that of a Mutually Hurting Stalemate (MHS).[3]

What these approaches have in common is their rationalistic view of the process of negotiations and the positive value they place on the objective of a negotiated settlement. From this perspective, negotiations are seen as a learning process and their success depends on a maturing of the views of the protagonists during the conflict that opens the way first to mediation, then to direct engagement with their enemies, and finally to a settlement. A remark typifying such a perspective was made by the deputy leader of the Social Democratic and Labour Party, Seamus Mallon, in relation to the Good Friday Agreement in Northern Ireland. He described the settlement as 'Sunningdale for slow learners'. This was a reference to the Sunningdale Agreement of December 1973, which was opposed at the time by both the Republican movement and a majority of Unionists. Another implication of this perspective is that there is a sharp distinction to be drawn between negotiation and coercion. (However, on this point there are important differences among writers whose approach to negotiations can be categorized as fundamentally rationalistic. Thus, Zartman accords a much greater role both to power politics in establishing the context for negotiation and to the use of incentives in the case of mediation than do the followers of John Burton to either.) Even if it is accepted that a consequence of the breakdown of negotiations may be further violence, the readiness of the parties to settle their differences by negotiations is regarded as an indicator of their peaceful intentions. Further, the process of negotiations itself is frequently accompanied by a suspension of hostilities in the form of ceasefires and the like.

However, it is possible to present the process of negotiations, not as separate from coercion, but as integral to it. This realpolitik, as opposed to conflict resolution, model of negotiations is encapsulated in the realist precept of 'negotiations from strength' and in a catch-phrase of South African policy during the 1980s, 'thump and talk'. Since the end of the Cold War, another concept has encapsulated the link between the use of force and negotiations. That is the concept of coercive diplomacy. The term has been used within the discipline of International Relations to apply to the use of the threat of military force to persuade another state to cease action perceived by its adversary as aggressive. From the perspective of peace processes, this is a somewhat narrow definition since it excludes the use of other means such as economic sanctions to persuade parties to comply with the wishes of the international community for a negotiated settlement. Robert Art has described this broader pattern of pressures as 'coercive attempts'.[4] As is also true of coercive diplomacy narrowly defined the record of coercive attempts as a means to create durable political settlements has been a decidedly mixed one. The Arusha accords on Rwanda in 1993 stands out as having had especially disastrous results, though it is open to argument as to how far any responsibility for the genocide that followed should be attributed to the nature of the negotiations that preceded the outbreak of violence. In the case of the Sudanese peace agreement of January 2005, it is arguable that the price of forcing the Sudanese government to come to terms with rebels in the South of the country was the crisis in Darfur.

The most eloquent advocacy of negotiations not as an alternative to power politics but their continuation by other means is to be found in Henry Kissinger's memoirs.[5] In *The White House Years* Kissinger strongly criticized American foreign policy during the 1950s when it was the policy of the government to eschew negotiations with the Soviet Union. He argued that the failure of the United States to engage the Soviet Union in negotiations resulted in missed opportunities to capitalize on the relative weakness of the Soviet Union. In particular, the existing division of Europe remained frozen in place when a more dynamic policy might have forced the Soviet Union into making concessions to the West. Kissinger blamed the notions that trust was necessary to negotiations and that friendship was a necessary component of negotiations for the attitude taken by both American government and public to the question. He used the case of the Korean War to underline his argument.

> Our perception of power and diplomacy as distinct and separate phases of foreign policy prevented us from negotiating to settle the Korean War after the landing at Inchon when we were in the strongest military position; it tempted us to escalate our aims. A year later it also caused us to stop military operations except of a purely defensive nature the moment negotiations got under way, thus removing the enemy's major incentive for a rapid diplomatic settlement. We acted as if the process of negotiation operated on its own inherent logic independent of the military balance – indeed, that military pressures might jeopardize the negotiations by antagonizing our adversary or demonstrating bad faith. Not surprisingly, a stalemate of nearly two years' duration followed, during which our casualties equalled those we had endured when hostilities were unconstrained. Treating force and diplomacy as discrete phenomena caused our power to lack purpose and our negotiations to lack force.[6]

The gulf between this position and that of Burtonian, Mark Hoffman, could hardly be greater. Hoffman defines conflict resolution as follows: 'the attainment of a non-hierarchical, non-coercive integrative solution that is derived from the parties themselves through a process of analytic problem-solving'.[7]

Another position exists. It is possible to argue that in some situations negotiations are undesirable in principle. In particular, it is frequently asserted that governments should not negotiate with terrorists, especially in the context of demands backed up by threats to the lives of hostages. In the course of World War II, the Allies ruled out any possibility of negotiations with the Axis powers by committing themselves to the objective of unconditional surrender. The nature of the regimes the Allies faced meant that this approach encountered little criticism. While these might be seen as exceptional cases, it is possible to extend this approach to apply to almost any conflict and it is important to consider this perspective since its influence among communities or societies resisting change is often very considerable. Parties in internal conflicts frequently argue the case for 'victory before peace', a slogan used by the followers of Ian Paisley in 1976 when they protested against the Peace People, a movement formed to demand an end to political violence in Northern Ireland.

A common theme of opponents of peace processes is that they entail the appeasement of evil groups whose demands ought to be resisted. Opposition to peace processes usually includes the demand that there should be no negotiations with any groups which have not completely and fully repudiated violence, or, if such negotiations have already begun, that they should be ended forthwith. One reason why such demands are made so fervently is the belief that the initiation of negotiations with such groups, regardless of the outcome of any talks, confers a measure of legitimacy upon them that is not warranted. In general, opposition to peace processes comes from groups that are part of the conflict, since outsiders commonly have an interest in a settlement if one can be achieved and typically are not imbued with the same degree of self-righteousness as those caught up in a violent conflict. However, unusually, American foreign policy under the Bush administration has been strongly influenced by a disdain for peace processes in principle among some of its neo-conservative supporters.[8]

It might fairly be suggested that the two models of negotiations described above apply in different contexts, in particular, that the realpolitik model of negotiations is most appropriate to the realm of international relations, the conflict resolution model to that of domestic politics. In support of this proposition, it is evidently the case that the settlement of international disputes through negotiations or the achievement of other objectives through negotiations, such as arms control, does not require the parties to abandon an overall relationship of antagonism. That was apparent during the period of super-power détente in the 1970s and 1980s. A contemporary example is that negotiations, admittedly conducted through the good offices of third parties, between Israel and Hezbollah over prisoner swaps and the like, have not fundamentally reduced their mutual antipathy. By contrast, in a domestic context, without an abatement of the power struggle between the parties, the prospects for the survival of a negotiated political settlement are likely to be poor.

However, the distinction between the two contexts can be overdrawn. Thus, Anwar Sadat's initiative in going to Jerusalem in 1977 was credited with achieving a vital psychological breakthrough in the Arab–Israeli conflict. The continuing influence of this example on international relations of the Middle East was reflected in debate during 2000 on whether a symbolic gesture on behalf of either of the parties might have contributed to a breakthrough in relations between Israel and Syria.[9] The agreement reached between representatives of the United States, South Vietnam, North Vietnam, and the Viet Cong on a ceasefire and elections, though directed at the domestic political context of the future government of South Vietnam, fits the realpolitik model of negotiations much better than the conflict resolution model. The same is true of the Dayton Agreement of December 1995 on Bosnia. The former barely provided the decent interval the Americans were seeking to effect their withdrawal; the latter still remains critically dependent on the presence of external forces more than a decade later.

In the case of failed settlements, there is often plenty of room for argument over whether power politics or a failure to address the root causes of the conflict sufficiently comprehensively or inclusively is to be blamed. In practice, most settlements achieved through a process of negotiation both entail the application of agreed normative political principles and reflect the balance of power among the parties. But while the existing balance of forces in any conflict places limits on what can be achieved through negotiations and while, conversely, a change in the balance of forces may make a settlement possible in a previously intractable conflict, settlements that do not rest on some normative foundation that is separate from the power political considerations are unlikely to prove durable. The point is well made by Ramsbotham, Woodhouse, and Miall: 'Good settlements should not only bridge the opposing interests, but also represent norms that are public goods for the wider community in which the conflict is situated.'[10] Of course, a commitment to some normative element, such as power sharing, may be made in bad faith by one or more of the parties, so the mere existence of normative elements as part of a negotiated settlement does not guarantee their success, as the examples of Rwanda and Sierra Leone in the 1990s underline. However, such failures do not provide grounds for discounting the significance of the normative dimension to political settlements capable of establishing durable peace. Nevertheless, a peace process may never reach this stage. Accusations of bad faith are most commonly made in relation to failure to sustain ceasefires and to end violence. In such cases, the peace process may breakdown before a full political settlement can even be achieved, as the examples of the Israeli–Palestinian conflict and the civil war in Sri Lanka have shown.

Common reasons why people resort to violence in the first place are the perception that they will continue to be denied justice under the existing political system, or, alternatively, that rebellion threatens a valued way of life. Certainly, calculation of the consequences of the use of violence plays a part, but it is secondary to the normative considerations. This is also evident in the phases that typically accompany the negotiated settlement of a violent political conflict within a polity. In difficult cases at least seven phases of the process can be identified. They are

1. the pre-talks phase;
2. an era of secret talks;
3. the opening of multilateral talks;
4. negotiating to a settlement;
5. gaining endorsement;
6. implementing its provisions; and
7. the institutionalization of the new dispensation.

Each phase will be analysed briefly below.

Pre-talks

The unwillingness of both parties to the conflict to enter into negotiations in the early stages of a conflict may be explained by the belief of both parties in their ability to achieve their aims through other means, typically physical coercion. It is based on this assumption that Zartman argues that ripeness, entailing the perception by the parties of the existence of a MHS, is a necessary condition for the initiation of meaningful negotiations. However, the symmetrical avoidance of negotiations by both sides tends to be exaggerated in the literature. External backers of insurgents may insist on their sides being willing to enter into negotiations. Thus, the front-line states supporting the African National Congress (ANC) and other liberation movements in southern Africa insisted that the 1969 Lusaka Manifesto should contain an offer to Pretoria of a willingness to settle the issues causing conflict in the region by negotiations. A motive for insurgents to seek negotiations at the outset of the conflict is that it gives them a measure of legitimacy, by underscoring both the political nature of their demands and by the implication that the conflict cannot be ended without their participation in a settlement. From a very different perspective, a government may calculate that it is better to engage insurgents in negotiations at an early stage in order to be able to deal with their demands from a position of relative strength. (In the conflict between Israel and neighbouring Arab states – admittedly a conflict in which the parties were governments – the stance of the Israeli government for many years was that there should be bilateral negotiations between the parties, based on the belief that such a context was favourable to Israel.)

Of course, for agreement to be reached on the initiation of negotiations the desire of the parties to negotiate has to coincide and their very different motives for entering into talks may tend to militate against such a coincidence. Further, negotiations which take place soon after the eruption of a conflict rarely, if ever, produce positive results. Zartman acknowledges the possibility that negotiations may take place for what he calls tactical reasons, but he argues that a crucial ingredient for serious talks will generally be absent, the intent of the parties to arrive at a joint outcome. However, even tactical negotiations are relatively uncommon in the early stages of a conflict and may not even occur as the conflict matures. This is because characteristic of the initial phases of conflict is mobilization by the parties of their supporters behind mutually exclusive objectives and the demonization of the other side. The persistence and seeming permanence of such factors tend to be features of the most intractable conflicts. It was well described by Meron Benvenisti in 1990 in the case of the conflict between Israelis and Palestinians:

> There is a perpetual conflict, not necessarily violent, between the Jewish majority group that seeks to maintain its superiority, and the Arab minority group (Israeli Arabs and Palestinians in the territories) that seeks to free itself from majority tyranny. The majority community perceives the struggle as one of 'law and order'. The minority community, which does not regard the regime as legitimate, seeks to destroy it. Both communities deny each other's standing as a legitimate collective entity. Hence, the Arabs define Zionism (the expression of the collective aspirations of the Jewish people) as racism – ergo illegitimate. The Israelis, in their turn, define Palestinian nationalism as Palestine Liberation Organisation (PLO) terrorism – ergo illegitimate. The delegitimisation is vital for both sides, for it enables them to believe in the exclusivity of their claim and in the absolute justice of their position.[11]

While the destructiveness of the conflict may seem an unavoidable cost to the antagonists themselves, external parties may be less sanguine than the combatants about the consequences of the conflict's persistence. Mediation may be pursued at this or any other phase of the conflict by such parties. For the reasons alluded to, it is unlikely to prove fruitful. A common way for governments at the centre of conflicts to deflect pressure from external parties for a resolution is the promotion of an alternative partner to that of its principal antagonist. In many conflicts, the search for a 'moderate' alternative turns out to be a chimera. However, it is by no means always the case that the insurgents represent the majority of those on behalf of whom they have taken up arms. Thus, throughout Northern Ireland's troubles it was clear that the Republican movement represented a minority of the Catholic population of the province, notwithstanding the fact that Sinn Féin has subsequently secured the support of a majority of Catholic voters.

Secret talks

Both the desire not to accord legitimacy to the other side and the fear of the reaction of supporters provide two reasons why the first stage in a peace process tends to take the form of secret talks between the main combatants or those who conceive themselves as such. A further reason for secrecy is their exploratory nature. By this point, the parties usually have not committed themselves irrevocably to a negotiated settlement as a way out of conflict. That is reflected in the absence of a truce or ceasefires. Communication through a third party or contact at the level of officials in the case of the government side is common in this phase. To begin with, both the fact that talks between the parties have taken place and the content of the talks tend to be hidden from public view. However, what distinguishes this phase from the previous one is that by this point there is usually a strong desire by both parties simultaneously for an exit from the conflict.

In the later stage of this phase, the general public is likely to become aware that secret talks between the parties have been taking place, though without learning a great deal about the content of the talks. How the public reacts to this knowledge has an important bearing on whether the parties proceed further along the path of negotiations. In situations where the public's overriding concern is that there should be an end to violence, there may be a very positive response to the revelation of secret talks since it can be taken for granted that a central objective of talks between the parties will be to establish the terms for an end to the violence. Where ending violence is not quite so high a priority for the whole of the society, fears about the political compromises discussed in secret between the parties may produce a strongly negative reaction, at least from a section of public opinion.

Multilateral talks

Formal, multilateral negotiations are a necessary phase in practically any peace process. Formality is necessary to provide a public assurance of the commitment of the parties to the successful outcome of the process. How inclusive the process is of significant strands of political opinion has a strong bearing on perceptions of its legitimacy, both internally and externally. Even when the process is largely being driven forward by two parties within a multilateral framework, they will often take great pains to ensure the participation of minor parties in the settlement, as in the case of South Africa, where the National Party government and the ANC amended the transitional constitution in the run-up to the 1994 elections so as to facilitate the participation of the Inkatha Freedom Party and the extreme right Freedom Front. Another consideration is that few conflicts are so simple that the two sides which engaged in secret talks to end the violence are also in a position to construct a comprehensive political settlement that will command widespread acceptance. Other parties need to be drawn into the process if the objective is to achieve a lasting settlement and, in fact, some of them may have to be involved even to achieve the minimal objective of sustaining a temporary truce.

Symbolic issues loom large in formal, multilateral negotiations. Arguments over representation, the venue, procedures, and the agenda may delay the tackling of substantive questions. The initiation of negotiations on the future of South Vietnam in the early 1970s became deadlocked on how the parties should be represented at the talks which famously took the form of an argument over the shape of the table at which the negotiations were to take place. The unwillingness of certain parties to engage in face to face talks may require the mechanism of proximity talks, in which a third party shuttles between two delegations, as occurred at Dayton. Further, it is often the case that much of the real business of the negotiations is conducted outside of the structures of the multilateral negotiations. In particular, the crucial compromises between the main political parties frequently take place in secret talks, the existence of which only becomes apparent when they seek endorsement of these agreements in meetings of the multilateral negotiations. The need to establish as wide support as possible for any agreement rules out the option of bypassing a multilateral process altogether. However, while formal, multilateral negotiations are usually a necessary condition for the creation of lasting political settlements, they are not a sufficient condition.

Settlement

The existence of inclusive negotiations by no means guarantees movement towards a political settlement. Indeed, particularly if there is little likelihood, in the absence of a settlement, of a return to violent conflict on a scale unacceptable to both sides, the process itself may come to be seen as almost a substitute for a settlement, an attitude encapsulated in a long-standing Turkish Cypriot aphorism that 'no solution is a solution'. However, it is worth noting that this attitude lost popular support among Turkish Cypriots as Cyprus was about to join the European Union in 2005. Even if the two sides do in fact passionately share the desire for an end to the conflict through a negotiated settlement, this may prove beyond their capabilities. Just as parties miscalculate what they might achieve through coercion, they can also miscalculate what they can achieve through negotiations. What each side requires as a minimum to be able to present a settlement as legitimate to its supporters may not be reconcilable.

In the case of Cyprus, the United Nations has been seeking for many years to reconcile Greek Cypriot insistence on freedom of movement within the island and the right of refugees to return to their homes with Turkish Cypriot demands for a territorial dimension to guarantees for their community's security, through the formula of a bi-zonal, bi-communal federation. The detailed plan that the United Nations developed to this end was rejected by the Greek Cypriots in a referendum in 2005.

External parties may play a role in bridging the gulf between the principal antagonists, particularly where they have their own interests in wishing to see the conflict ended, such as the capacity for the conflict to affect the stability of an entire region. Thus, during the Lancaster House negotiations on the future of Zimbabwe–Rhodesia, promises of large-scale financial assistance for the purchase of land were made by the British and American governments to the Patriotic Front to persuade the alliance of the main African nationalist parties to accept provisions in the constitution safeguarding white farmers against the expropriation of their land. While they played an important role in the negotiations, the promises were never fulfilled on the scale envisaged during the talks. This case also illustrates well the problem of enforcing such promises once the conflict is over and the interests that impelled the external parties to make their promises are no longer threatened.

An important strategic choice in negotiations towards a settlement is whether the parties should seek to arrive at a comprehensive and detailed blueprint for the future government of the entity in question or simply the outline of a settlement. These represent opposite ends of a spectrum. Commonly, settlements fall between these two extremes. A related issue is whether the parties should set a time limit to negotiations. An advantage of the detailed approach is that the settlement is less likely to unravel as a result of disagreements over the interpretation of its provisions. A disadvantage is that the time needed to reach such a settlement may threaten the peace process itself by causing one or other of the parties to suspect that the purpose of the talks is not to reach a settlement, but to use the truce that accompanies the talks to bring about a shift in the balance of power between the two sides.

Endorsement

Elections usually constitute an important element in the negotiated settlement of peace processes. They provide an obvious way of legitimizing a new dispensation. Even agreements that are the product of power politics such as the 1970s agreement on the future of South Vietnam may pay lip service to the principle, though the actual holding of elections may prove another matter. Elections to a new legislature and of a new President may perform the dual function of providing retrospective endorsement of the settlement and its partial implementation. This is what happened in South Africa in 1994. However, in some settlements, there is special provision for the separate endorsement of the settlement by referendum, as in the case of Northern Ireland's Good Friday Agreement of 1998. The Good Friday Agreement provided for the simultaneous holding of referendums on the settlement in Northern Ireland and the Republic of Ireland.

This approach had a number of advantages in the particular context of the Irish question. The promise by the British government that any settlement coming out of the multi-party negotiations would be put to the Northern Irish electorate provided a means of allaying Protestant fears as to the purpose of the talks. The simultaneous holding of referendums in Northern Ireland and the Republic of Ireland provided a means of addressing the issue of Irish self-determination. The position taken by nationalists since Northern Ireland had come into existence in 1920 was that the province was not a legitimate political entity. This was because partition had been imposed against the wishes of a majority of the population of the island of Ireland as a whole. The 1998 settlement committed Irish nationalists to accept the existence of two jurisdictions on the island, at least for the time being, while the referendums undercut the position of fundamentalists who asserted that partition continued to be illegitimate. There was also a practical dimension to the holding of the referendum in the Republic: it provided the authority for the changes to the Irish constitution which the government had negotiated as a part of the settlement. Another instance of the use of referendums to underwrite a settlement was the series of referendums that accompanied the negotiation of Commonwealth status for Puerto Rico in the 1950s. However, neither these nor subsequent referendums have entirely succeeded in quelling international and internal criticism of Puerto Rico's status as semi-colonial.

Implementation

The less detailed the terms of the negotiated settlement, the greater the difficulties are likely to be at the stage of implementation. A continuing process of negotiations leading to a series of new agreements will be needed to put flesh on the bare bones of the original settlement. It is at this stage that disputes over the interpretation of the settlement are likely to arise. Overcoming these obstacles may present a much larger challenge for the parties and external mediators than arriving at the broad outlines of a settlement had been. Indeed, the reason for confining the original agreement to an outline is most likely to have been the perceived gulf between the parties on the substantive issues. The obvious example in this context is the Declaration of Principles agreed between the government of Israel and the PLO in September 1993. In this case, the parties acknowledged that what they agreed fell far short of a final settlement and that was reflected in their agreeing to a timeframe for the negotiation of a final settlement, though this proved unsustainable almost from the outset.

The process of implementation itself may have a profound effect on how a particular political settlement turns out because of its impact on the balance of power among the parties. Elections usually constitute an early element in the implementation of a settlement. How the parties fare in such elections will almost inevitably have a very large bearing on their influence on the rest of the process. South Africa provides a case in point. As Christopher Saunders has noted, interpretations of the country's transition tend to vary with when they were written, with later authors viewing the process in the light of the ANC's overwhelming electoral predominance and the influence it had on the shape of the final constitution agreed in 1996. By contrast, authors who wrote about the settlement before its implementation tended to portray it as a compromise between the forces of African and Afrikaner nationalism.[12]

Shifts in the balance of forces during the implementation stage may consolidate the settlement by making it apparent that one side has won. Indeed, from this vantage point, a negotiated settlement may come to be seen less as entailing the creation of a 'win-win' solution in which the political aspirations of both sides are accommodated as a process enabling a formerly political dominant group to surrender its position gracefully. In this context, the settlement may simply be transitional to more fundamental change. That possibility may have a significant influence on both sides during the course of the negotiations, the hope of one and the fear of the other. More generally, the normative rationale of the settlement may be undermined by the actual balance of forces in the situation which results in the settlement being implemented in a way that falls far short of what one side or the other and perhaps the outside world sees as legitimate. Thus, Palestinian critics of Arafat such as Edward Said argued that the PLO was simply in too weak a position to secure a legitimate outcome to the Israeli–Palestinian conflict at the time of the Oslo peace process.[13]

Institutionalization

The final stage in any settlement is the point at which it becomes apparent that the new order has taken root and the change that has come with it is seen to be irreversible. A necessary condition for institutionalization is that the settlement is perceived as legitimate internationally, a perception that will itself in part depend on internal reaction to the settlement. Should internal opponents of a settlement be able to sustain an insurgency against the government, a question mark is likely to exist over the legitimacy of the new dispensation even if it meets other tests of legitimacy. Conversely, the appearance of stability and peace may persuade international opinion of the legitimacy of a new political dispensation even if it does not accord fully with international norms of governance. Nevertheless, the issue of legitimacy remains of greater importance than whether the government is seen to accord with the balance of power within the society in question. The durability of even the most powerful government will be in doubt if it does not appear to command widespread acceptance among the people it rules.

That is why in reaching agreement on a new dispensation, parties find that addressing fundamental principles of what constitutes legitimate governance in a divided society is as important, if not more, than constructing arrangements that reflect existing power realities. Of course, international norms as to what constitutes good governance are not unchanging and a settlement that reflects the norms which existed at the time it was reached may be undermined by their subsequent evolution and reinterpretation. By contrast, changes in norms may facilitate a settlement by altering the frame of reference. Thus, a looser interpretation of sovereignty within the context of European integration helped to make possible the compromises on cross-border bodies and the British–Irish Council in the Good Friday Agreement.

Of course, what might appear to some to be a ground-breaking settlement involving the creation of novel political structures to accommodate the different parties may appear to others to be a desperate attempt to reconcile mutually incompatible positions and far from being politically principled to rest on the unstable foundations of the existing balance of power among the parties. Similarly, it is difficult to know where to place the blame when such a settlement breaks down. Almost inevitably, the judgement that a new political dispensation has become institutionalized tends to be a retrospective one. As far as negotiations are concerned, institutionalization forms the point at which politics starts to be conducted in terms of the acceptance of agreed rules, superseding negotiations on what rules should be.

Conclusion

The seven phases of negotiations described above are not intended to provide a rigid model of how all negotiations to end violent conflicts either are or should be conducted. Further, the order of the different phases is not meant to imply a strict separation in time among these phases. In practice, different phases overlap and what are presented above as discreet processes may be collapsed into one another, so that, for example, endorsement is often a part of the implementation process. Further, developments entirely outside the realm of politics may profoundly affect the course of a conflict. A good example is the impact of the Indian Ocean tsunami of 2004 in bringing an end to the conflict in Aceh in Indonesia. While primacy has been given to the role of current norms in the negotiation of the settlement of violent political conflicts, the realm of power politics cannot simply be set aside. At every stage in the process, the parties are likely to consider the implications of any development for the balance of forces in the society. The fear of negotiations as a one-way street is by no means confined to international politics. In domestic politics, it tends to take the form of the suspicion that the other side is pursuing a hidden agenda and that its engagement in negotiations is tactical. Indeed, even the acceptance of a settlement may be perceived as tactical that is designed to extract benefits that will shift the balance of forces in the party's favour, while seeking to evade any obligations that place it at a disadvantage.

Precisely because of these possibilities, issues of trust and good faith have an importance in negotiations to end violent political conflicts that they do not have in limited international negotiations between adversaries where the complications are often largely technical in character. Situations in which mistrust results in the failure of the first serious effort to resolve the conflict are likely to be especially intractable because of the memory of the previous failure. While there is not an automatic incompatibility between negotiations and the continued use of violence, in practice, suspension of hostilities is typically a precondition for the initiation of negotiations or, at the very least, the first item on the agenda if negotiations start in the absence of ceasefires. Just as a shifting balance of power may affect the durability of any negotiated settlement, so too may changes in norms. Thus, much greater importance is attached these days to the recognition of minority rights than was the case in the aftermath of World War II. Further, for good or ill, regional ethno-nationalisms are credited with much greater legitimacy than before the end of the Cold War, with a consequent softening of the international community's hostility towards secession. In fact, the current fluidity in the interpretation of key international norms such as self-determination make it peculiarly hard to predict the outcome of current peace processes and whether the settlements that emerge from negotiations among parties will prove durable. At the same time, since the events of 9/11, it has become more tempting for governments to deny the need for any negotiations with insurgents by the simple expedient of declaring that the conflict is part of the global war against terrorism, a stance whose credibility depends in part on the nature of the groups engaged in violence against the state.

Notes

1. See, for example, J. Burton, *Deviance, Terrorism and War: The Process of Solving Unsolved Social and Political Problems* (New York: St. Martin's Press, 1979) and R. Fisher & W. Ury, *Getting to Yes* (New York: Bantam, 1991).
2. J.P. Lederach, *Building Peace* (Washington DC: United States Institute of Peace, 1997).
3. I.W. Zartman, 'Ripeness: The Hurting Stalemate and Beyond', Paper presented to the International Political Science World Congress (Quebec City: August 2000).
4. R.J. Art & P.M. Cronin (eds), *The United States and Coercive Diplomacy* (Washington DC: United States Institute of Peace, 2003), p. 7.
5. H. Kissinger, *The White House Years* (London: Weidenfeld & Nicolson, 1979).

6. Ibid., pp. 63–64.
7. M. Hoffman, 'Third Party Mediation and Conflict Resolution in the Post-Cold War World', in J. Baylis & N.J. Rengger (eds), *Dilemmas of World Politics* (Oxford: Clarendon Press, 1992), p. 265.
8. See, for example, M.A. Ledeen, 'Why Peace Processes Do Not Work: A Machiavellian View', in L.S. Germani & D.R. Kaarthikeyan (eds), *Pathways Out of Terrorism and Insurgency: The Dynamics of Terrorist Violence and Peace Processes* (New Delhi: New Dawn Press, 2005), pp. 50–54.
9. S. Al-Azm, 'The view from Damascus ... continued', *New York Review of Books*, XLVII, 13 (10 August 2000).
10. H. Miall, O. Ramsbotham & T. Woodhouse, *Contemporary Conflict Resolution* (Cambridge: Polity Press, 2005), p. 175.
11. M. Benvenisti, 'The Peace Process and Intercommunal Strife', in H. Giliomee & J. Gagiano (eds), *The Elusive Search for Peace: South Africa, Israel and Northern Ireland* (Cape Town: Oxford University Press, 1990), p. 123.
12. C. Saunders, 'Of treks, transitions and transitology', *South African Historical Journal*, 40 (May 1999).
13. E.W. Said, *Peace and Its Discontents* (London: Vintage, 1995).

6
Rules and Procedures for Negotiated Peacemaking

Pierre du Toit

Introduction

Rules and procedures provide structure to the process of negotiating for peace. Some rules, such as time frames and deadlines, are primarily intended to provide a formal structure for the *process* of negotiations, while others, such as pre-set constitutional guidelines aim to shape the *outcome* of the negotiating process. Often this seemingly neat distinction becomes blurred, as when tight deadlines affect the thoroughness with which negotiators deal with the details of a constitutional settlement. The aim of this chapter is to consider the impact of the structuring of peace processes through such rules and procedures, with special emphasis on the role of time frames and deadlines. The following questions will be taken up:

- Who makes the rules and procedures? Participants or external third parties?
- Do these rules and procedures apply to the process or to the outcome of peacemaking, and what effect, if any, do they have on each other?
- Who acts as the enforcement agency, ensuring that the rules and procedures are upheld?

The two primary cases which are selected for comparative insights are South Africa and Namibia. Comparability is enhanced by virtue of both countries being considered as very successful cases of democratic transition and hence of peacemaking. Both are African states and both experienced a long period of colonial rule, one German, the other British. Colonial rule ended in white minority government in both of them, where authority was asserted by coercion and resisted by revolt, thus producing violent transitions. Peacemaking and democratic transition, although analytically distinct, went together. These two cases were also both among the very earliest post-Cold War transitions.

Significant differences allow us to make measurable comparisons. The character of white minority rule differed sharply between the two cases. In South Africa, the ruling minority was an indigenous one, entrenching its position through the policies of apartheid, based on racial division and exclusion. This same power elite ruled over Namibia, a position achieved in World War I, when they invaded the then German colony and were awarded a trusteeship by the League of Nations. Although this mandate was not recognized by the United Nations (UN), the successor to the League, the apartheid rulers of South Africa extended this style of domination over the territory, in the face of worldwide opposition and condemnation. This was instrumental in shaping the single outstanding contrast in the peace processes in the two cases. The Namibian conflict became hugely internationalized, resulting in the eventual peace process being shaped by rules and procedures which were drawn up and laid down entirely by outsiders, acting as *third parties*. South Africa, being a sovereign state, allowed the peacemakers to choose whether to engage third parties in setting rules and procedures. They decided to do these themselves. The contrast between the two cases is almost extreme, but the outcomes for them almost identical in that they both led to successful peace settlements.

Time frames and deadlines

Negotiators usually have three ways of responding to offers: accept, refuse, or continue to talk in order to improve subsequent offers. This last option is affected by deadlines. A deadline is a mechanism for imposing time costs on negotiators. It is a jointly recognized ultimatum, tied to a particular calendar date which, upon expiry, sets the incurring of costs into operation. Time frames are subsets within this ultimatum, consisting of the requirement that specific targets be met within a particular chronological sequence. Deadlines convert proposals into final offers, potential sanctions into actual costs, and turn the alternative to negotiated settlements into reality. As they face a deadline, the options narrow down to two: agree to the proposal, or refuse, take it or leave it.[1]

Deadlines have two dimensions: reasonableness and seriousness.[2] The *reasonableness* requirement holds that enough time must be made available to find a quality settlement, that is, one that deals effectively with the basic issues of conflict. When this is not met, and negotiators are forced into rushing a decision, agreements of poor quality may result. Problems of *ownership* may arise when large concessions made under pressure leave one party alienated from the outcome and unable to justify it to their own audiences. They then have every incentive to disown the agreement later, or to actively undermine it. Problems of *detail* may also crop up. If some matters cannot be dealt with adequately because of time pressure, and remain unclarified, unresolved, and/or are carried over to new negotiating arenas in this form, problems may re-emerge.

Seriousness refers to the extent to which the deadline puts pressure on the negotiators to conclude a settlement. Pressure can only result from credible sanctions behind the deadline. Data from experimental settings confirm that impending deadlines induce negotiators to increase the rate of concessions made, thus facilitating movement towards agreement.[3] The implied negative sanction here is that if a party were not to concede, and no settlement is forthcoming, then it may end up being labelled as a *spoiler*. However, when parties anticipate that deadlock or breakdown due to their inability to meet a deadline is imminent and inevitable, then a deadline may produce a hardening effect.[4] Parties adopt a tough position for if and when negotiations fail, so that they can appear to look strong in the eyes of their home audiences. This allows them to claim that they did not capitulate under undue pressure, and that they did not sacrifice vital interests 'just to get a settlement'.

Rule making by outsiders: Namibia

The German colony of South West Africa was established in 1884, after the Berlin Conference in which Africa was carved up into colonial domains by the European powers. The then Union of South Africa invaded the territory in 1915, as part of its contribution to World War I, and as reward for its efforts the League of Nations granted a 'C' class mandate over the territory to the Union. This stipulated that the area be governed as an integral part of the country, extending its own laws over the mandated people and territory.[5]

This became a highly internationalized issue once South Africa, under its defunct mandate, proceeded to implement its racial policies in the occupied territory. In 1950, the International Court of Justice (ICJ) ruled that South Africa could not retain control over the territory under the new UN mandate system; in 1966, the UN General Assembly voted to assume control over the administration of the territory; and in 1971, the ICJ ruled South Africa's continued occupation of Namibia as illegal. South Africa resisted these international pressures, as well as those emerging from within Namibia in the shape of nationalist movements, led by the South West African People's Organization (SWAPO).

The escalation to violent confrontation was again influenced by international forces. In 1966, SWAPO decided to take up arms against South Africa's occupation of the territory. In 1975, Angola's independence dramatically changed the military context. The Popular Movement for the Liberation of Angola (MPLA), with Soviet backing, seized power and a civil war against its rivals, led by the National Union for the Total Independence of Angola (UNITA) ensued. South Africa's African National Congress (ANC) and SWAPO, both with Soviet backing, relocated their military bases to southern Angola, strategically well-placed close to the northern Namibian border. War escalated when the South African forces invaded Angola with two objectives: to destroy SWAPO military bases and to aid UNITA in its fight against the MPLA government. Cuba eventually entered in direct military support of the MPLA, while the United States of America acted in providing logistical support to UNITA.

Peacemakers entered into this complex conflict arena in two ways. First, the UN Security Council passed Resolution 385 in 1976 and Resolution 435 in 1978, setting out rules, procedures, and a time frame for the independence of Namibia. Second, the informal Western Contact Group (WCG) comprising the United States of America, Britain, France, Canada, and Western Germany was set up with the objective of facilitating the implementation of these resolutions. As the name suggests, their primary task was to engage with the recalcitrant South Africans to get them to accede to the UN peace plan.[6] This they did, most visibly by exercising their veto in the Security Council when South Africa refused to accept Resolution 385. At the same time, the South Africans were facilitating the establishment of internal political parties with interests more to their own liking, such as being outside the orbit of Soviet influence, not promoting socialist economic plans, and not considering an independent Namibia as a military base for the ANC. The WCG did produce a plan for Namibian independence by early 1978, which was approved by the Security Council, and came to be the core of the eventual UN plan.

The key ingredients of the UN plan, as far as rules and procedures go, were the following:

- A time frame allowing the setting up of a UN force responsible for the sequential implementation of a ceasefire, followed by the demobilization of military forces, then the holding of an election, the drafting of a constitution, and culminating in independence;
- the demobilization did not make provision for a *de facto* condition of dual power, that is 'liberated areas' under effective SWAPO control within Namibia. The SWAPO forces were to assemble in Angola and Zambia;
- the elections would be run by the incumbent South African administration through the office of the administrator-general, whose activities would be 'supervised and monitored' by the UN. For this purposes a designated UN military force, UN Transition Assistance Group (UNTAG), would be assembled;
- Starting with its recognition as the 'sole and authentic representative' of the Namibian populace, SWAPO would lose its UN privileges and hence, UN funding;
- elections would be held for a Constituent Assembly, not for an independent government. This assembly would have to draft a constitution which, once enacted, would provide the framework within which a government would be established, based on the results of the election;
- The principles on which this constitution would have to be based are prescribed to the political parties. The final constitution would need the approval of two-thirds of the Assembly's members;

- the deadline for the implementation of Resolution 435 was set at 23 October 1978.

With this set of overarching rules the crucial question of who would be the enforcement agency in control the peace process was settled. In the words of one set of analysts: 'the plan brokered by the WCG downplayed the role of the UN in the transition to that of linesman, with South Africa, itself a protagonist, as stage manager'.[7] These rules also reflected the interests of the WCG themselves, with South Africa being their least disliked option as a decolonizing agent.[8]

The implementation of this peace plan was thwarted for about 11 years, coming into effect only on 1 February 1989. Why such a comprehensive collapse of a UN Security Council deadline? Primarily because of a lack of consensus within the ranks of the international actors comprising the collective third party intervenor (i.e., the WCG) about how to proceed. Both South Africa and SWAPO agreed with great reluctance, and under pressure from their backers to accept Resolution 435, and then only in principle. Part of the international community's problem was agreeing how to deal with South Africa's apparent stalling tactics. These tactics evolved from the rules and procedures set out in the UN plan. For the South Africans to shape the peace process to their liking, they had to ensure that in the eventual election SWAPO did not get two-thirds of the vote. This required credible electoral opposition from domestic parties with interests close to the South African position. This in turn required time to build, as there were no such parties in the early 1980s. They bought this time by, amongst other things, escalating the military conflict in Southern Angola. This strategy bore fruit once the United States of America entered the conflict arena and succeeded in linking the Namibian peace process to the withdrawal of Cuban forces from Angola.[9] France objected to this linkage, and eventually withdrew from the WCG in December 1983.

The linkage strategy was effective but costly. Military conflict escalated to full conventional warfare, culminating with the battles at Lomba and Cuito Cuanavale in 1987, by which time a Mutually Hurting Stalemate (MHS) had set in.[10] Two other factors conducive to peacemaking also came into effect at that stage. Gorbachev's initiatives in the Soviet Union had by that time contributed to a considerable thawing of the Cold War, and the South Africans had, in their view, established a credible set of electoral opponents to take on SWAPO in an election.

The result was another set of peace agreements, all concluded in 1988, setting further rules and procedures for the peace process, with yet more specific time frames and deadlines. These included:

- The Geneva Protocol of 5 August 1988, signed by South Africa, Cuba, and Angola, stipulating, amongst other things, that, in preparation for a ceasefire SWAPO forces would be withdrawn to north of the 16th parallel within southern Angola, the complete withdrawal of South African forces from Namibia, and of Cuban forces from Angola, all according to specified dates, as well as a new date for the implementation of Resolution 435;

- the Brazzaville Accord of 13 December 1988, drawn up between the same three parties, revised these target dates, and set the deadline for the implementation of Resolution 435 at 1 April 1989;

- the bilateral agreement between Cuba and Angola of 22 December 1988, setting a time frame for the withdrawal of Cuban troops, starting on 1 April 1989 and to be concluded on 1 July 1991;

- the Tripartite Agreement of 22 December 1988 between South Africa, Cuba, and Angola, reaffirming all the above, and calling on the UN Security Council to implement Resolution 435 on 1 April 1989.

The official implementation of the UN plan started on 1 February 1989. Three aspects of the transition/peace process, all bearing on the rules of the transition, are worth noting here. The first is the military invasion by SWAPO on 1 April 1989, the day of the commencement of the ceasefire. The second is the element of what Cliffe et al. have called 'structural intimidation' by the South African government in its management of the process. The third notable feature was the huge momentum which carried the process through to its successful conclusion.

1 April was a crucial deadline, the date set for the commencement of the ceasefire, ending all hostilities, and setting in motion the phased withdrawal of foreign military forces from the conflict arena. The UNTAG forces were required to monitor this process. However, by the due date less than 1000 of the 4560 military personnel had arrived, and only 12 of the 500 police monitors were deployed.[11] The UNTAG were thus vastly unprepared for the invasion by about 1600 SWAPO soldiers on 1 April. The UN responded to the crisis by authorizing the re-mobilization of some of the internal military units created by the South Africans in the territory. These units effectively dealt with the invaders in the ensuing battles, which stretched over nine days, resulting in a further death toll of close to 300 soldiers (about 250 from SWAPO and 35–40 from the domestic units). The peace process was salvaged when SWAPO retreated in accordance with the Mount Etjo Agreement of 9 April, but the actual implementation of the process was only resumed in mid-May.[12]

The rules and procedures for the transition gave South Africa, through its administrative bureau of the Administrator-General (AG), the opportunity to wield the power of incumbency. As the effective host of the peace process, subject only to monitoring by UNTAG, the AG had to draw up the detailed rules and procedures governing the election and had access to the officials who were implementing these, most notably the local police force, which was the remaining coercive unit after the effective containment of SWAPO units and repatriation of South African forces. This provided opportunities for 'structural intimidation' in various forms, ranging from clandestine financing of anti-SWAPO political parties by the South African government, control over the media, dirty tricks to harass SWAPO, and to boost the Democratic Turnhalle Alliance (DTA), which was the primary electoral opponent of SWAPO, pressure on farm workers and employees by their employers to vote against SWAPO, and so on. A climate of violence also persisted, with intermittent shootings, beatings, and kidnappings taking place.[13]

Despite all of these, the most striking overall feature of the peace process, once set in motion, was its almost inexorable momentum. Having been created, structured, sponsored, and endorsed by the most influential actors in both the regional and international community, the process was virtually unstoppable. Despite the 1 April ceasefire breakdown and despite the electoral climate of intimidation, the elections went smoothly, the result was declared free and fair, and the parties duly assembled to draft a constitution within the laid down perimeters. Such was the momentum that it took them only 80 days to complete this process, leaving the details mostly to a trio of constitutional experts![14] On 21 March 1990, Namibia became independent.

Rule making by insiders: South Africa

In the South African transition, rules and procedures relevant to the *process* also had a remarkable impact on events. First, South Africans reached early agreement that they would establish these rules themselves, without the intervention of outsiders.[15] Second, the substance of these rules was a source of intense disagreement; they became the single largest issue of contention in the constitutional negotiations and provided the source of the breakdown in the talks in mid-1992. Third, only after this matter was resolved did the peace process gain momentum towards a successful settlement.

The public peace process got under way in early 1990 when State President FW de Klerk rescinded the banning on the African nationalist movements such as the ANC and its allies, and unconditionally released Nelson Mandela from serving a term of life imprisonment for high treason. This was preceded by about five years of secret negotiations between Mandela and various state agencies. The 1990 and most of 1991 were spent in negotiating various non-aggression pacts aimed at curtailing public violence (in the absence of a cease-fire to end an undeclared war), and in sorting out pre-conditions to formal constitutional talks, such as the release of political prisoners.

Formal negotiations on a democratic constitution were instituted in December 1991 with the multi-party Congress for a Democratic South Africa (CODESA). One of the vital issues at stake was the rules and procedures for the democratic transition. From the outset the ANC and the National Party (NP) government were, for tactical reasons, at loggerheads about the nature of the transition. The ANC, keen to utilize its expected electoral strength from among the black electorate, wanted an elected constitutional body to draft a new constitution within a very short time frame. The NP government, anticipating their own minority position after any electoral contest, wanted a multi-party conference, such as CODESA, to negotiate a constitution under which elections would take place. This body would then rule, within an almost unspecified time frame, while a final constitution is enacted. They calculated that their interests could in this way be written into a constitutional form *before* the electoral power of the ANC could be brought to bear on the process. In this way, each one wanted to set rules and procedures allowing itself to control the process to its own advantage.

At CODESA five working committees were established. Working Groups 2 and 3 were assigned to deal with rules and procedures for the transition. Here the tactical differences between the major protagonists came to a head. The parties agreed that an interim parliament had to be set up to govern during the transition. They also agreed that this elected interim body had to be set up in terms of constitutional principles negotiated by CODESA and that it would serve as a constitutional assembly which had to negotiate a 'final' constitution. They could not agree, however, on the proportion of votes required to ratify such a final constitution. The NP wanted a white minority veto, either in a direct form or indirectly, by way of very high decision-making percentages. In Working Group 2, for example, they insisted that the powers and functions of regions be protected by a 75 per cent majority vote requirement. At this, the ANC balked along with a dispute about majorities built into a deadlock-breaking mechanism.[16] At the end of May 1992 the ANC declared CODESA a failure, and on 16 June started with its mass action campaign, aimed at putting pressure on the NP government to relent. The next day the Boipatong massacre took place thus renewing the cycle of public violence.

This contest over rules and procedures was not just about a *de facto* white minority veto, expressed in tangible constitutional procedures. It was also about the intangible matters of the power relationship between the major contenders and about the nature of the negotiating process. The question of who set the rules and following from that, who controls the peace process was fundamentally about power. As one analyst noted, at CODESA both the ANC and the NP thought that they were going to talk their opponents into their own agenda for change, set on their own terms.[17] Neither was prepared to accept the other as a negotiating partner of equal strength and standing, and both thought of the negotiating process as one of talking the opponent into defeat.

The campaign of mass mobilization beyond the negotiating table produced a series of violent confrontations culminating in the Bisho massacre of 7 September 1992. Huge international pressure was brought to bear on the ANC and NP government to return to the table. This bore fruit and on 26 September the Record of Understanding, a bilateral agreement between the two parties, was signed. This was essentially an agreement on rules for guiding the transition.[18] It was agreed that

- there would be a constitution-making body which had to be democratically elected;
- this body would function as a single body for this purpose;
- it would be bound by constitutional principles set by a multi-party conference preceding the election of the constitution-making body;
- it would work within a fixed time frame;
- this body would have adequate deadlock-breaking mechanisms for dealing with differences on substantive constitutional matters;
- it would arrive at its decisions democratically with certain yet to be agreed on majorities;
- it would be elected within an agreed predetermined time period.

During the transitional period, this constitution-making body would

- act as an interim parliament;
- with an executive which would be a government of national unity;
- with a constitution providing for both national and regional levels of government.

With this, the two heavyweights came to terms on rules for the transition. From there on the process rapidly gained momentum. In November 1992, the ANC announced that it was prepared to engage in executive power sharing during the transition, and in the same month State President De Klerk produced a timetable for the transition, starting with a reconvened multi-party conference in March 1993 and culminating in elections for the Government of National Unity in March or April 1994.[19] With a few changes, this time frame came to be implemented, with the historic elections taking place over three days, starting on 26 April 1994.

Settling on rules and procedures for the transition in this way also had its costs. The most important was that this bilateral agreement between the NP and the ANC alienated the third heavyweight in the arena, the Inkatha Freedom Party (IFP). Shortly after the release of the Record of Understanding, the IFP announced their withdrawal from the negotiating process.[20] They stayed outside and proceeded to play a very high-risk game of brinkmanship, along with their right-wing allies up until the very end, declaring their willingness to take part in the election only six days before balloting started.

Nonetheless, the NP and ANC, having learnt the hard way that deadlocks over matters of detail can lead to a breakdown in the entire peace process, proceeded with great caution. The reconvened Multi-Party Negotiating Process (MPNP) functioned with the aid of some innovative informal deadlock-breaking rules and procedures to facilitate the process *within* the agreed upon negotiating arena. These included the rule of 'sufficient consensus', which held that proposals which carried the joint support of the NP and ANC were carried despite objections by any number of smaller parties. Their objections would be registered, debated and considered, but could not thwart the adoption of the proposals.[21] Another procedure was the so-called 'channel', an informal sub-committee of the planning committee of the MPNP, comprised of three, and later two, members who met every day to anticipate deadlocks, and to devise pre-emptive strategies for overcoming them. Finally, the device of *bosberade*, informal bilateral summits, held at luxury resorts in the African bush veld, running parallel to the formal negotiating process, helped to smooth formal proceedings.[22]

The deadline posed by the 26 April 1994 date for the election also influenced the transition process. Having decided early on at CODESA to utilize outsiders only as observers at the eventual elections, the South Africans had to find their own internal umpire to act as enforcement agent for the transition. This took the form of newly created institutions, the most important being the Transitional Executive Council (TEC) and the Independent Electoral Commission (IEC). The first was to serve as a multi-party executive authority during the run up to the election, while the latter had to serve as the actual administrative body for the conduct of the election. The IEC was only established during December 1993, and was given a bare four months to create an entirely new institution that comprised of close to 300,000 employees. They had to execute a triple function: administer the election, monitor it, and provide for adjudication of conflicts. In the end, they succumbed under time pressure and the result was an election that was much flawed in meeting its procedural requirements. In the end, the peace process was salvaged by the major stakeholders, who negotiated informally to accept the declared result as legitimate, thus ensuring a successful conclusion to South Africa's messy miracle.[23]

Comparative insights

Ownership

The Namibian rules and procedures for peacemaking had a crucial flaw. They were drawn up by third parties alone. Not a single domestic stakeholder (i.e., a political party which would be represented in parliament after independence) was a signatory to any of these agreements. This was especially relevant to the case of SWAPO, which was required to remove its armed units to above the

16th parallel within Angola, prior to the 1 April 1989 ceasefire. This status of being a non-signatory arguably created a lack of a sense of ownership in the organization, and has been said to account for their military invasion on the day of the ceasefire, in direct violation of the standing agreements.[24] Likewise, the withdrawal of the IFP from the constitutional negotiations in South Africa in late 1992 can also be taken back to the fact that they were not party to the agreement contained in the Record of Understanding.

Seriousness

In the Namibian case, disagreement within the ranks of the collective third party, the Western Contact Group, affected their ability to implement rules, and especially to apply the sanctions required to come into effect with the failure to meet the deadline of implementing Resolution 435. In the South African case, all the parties held to the deadline set by the election date of 26 April 1994, again with the exception of the IFP and its right-wing allies in the Freedom Alliance. The latter pursued a strategy of what can be called in retrospect, *brinkmanship*, joining the elections at the very last moment. However, had they pushed harder and boycotted the election, the result would have been judged as *spoiling*. The fact that they stood down at the very last moment is an indication of the seriousness with which other parties took the deadline – they refused to postpone the election date at the demands of the Freedom Alliance.

Reasonableness

The election deadline in South Africa did create problems of reasonableness. Within the pre-set time frame the Independent Electoral Commission just did not have adequate time to set up a competent administrative machinery with which to run the election. When they duly failed, it was only the pragmatism of the major electoral contestants themselves, who negotiated to accept the election result that saved the day.

Control

Both the Namibian and South African cases show that the rules governing the peace process provide the key to control of the process and hold huge potential power implications. The party that can shape the rules can control the process and is provided with an opportunity to bring to bear whatever sources of power it has at its disposal to maximum effect. This was in essence what the contest between the ANC and NP was about, and was also at the heart of the South African government's strategy in Namibia.

Momentum

Once the major powers in a conflict arena have reached basic agreement on the rules and procedures to govern a peace process, and once such a process has been set in motion, it can rapidly generate substantial momentum. Both cases confirm this proposition. In neither case did potentially major crises divert the peace process. The 1 April 1989 invasion by SWAPO was arguably the most direct threat to the transition, but was effectively contained by the parties driving the peace process. In South Africa, the assassination of Chris Hani, general secretary of the South African Communist Party on 10 April 1993 became the single most important crisis which the MPNP had to overcome. With the adept leadership of Mandela in particular, it did so without faltering.

Conclusion

Rules and procedures shape the arena within which negotiators cooperate and compete with each other on their way to searching for amicable settlements. The negotiations over such rules and procedures are as decisive to the outcome as the negotiations *within* the stage set by these rules and procedures. Rule setting by outsiders can be equally successful to those set by the protagonists themselves, as this comparative overview shows, but both ways of establishing the negotiating arena need to demonstrate an awareness of problems of ownership, reasonableness, and seriousness that may arise. Both cases also show that once the playing field has been accepted as being level by the major players, then such agreement on rules can generate momentum towards successful peacemaking.

Rules and procedures: from peace talks to the 'peace dividend'

With the implementation of peace accords, rules and procedures remain important, as the peace process merges into the public policy process. The consolidation of a peace process is, however, not just an everyday, ordinary policy matter, and issues of reasonableness, ownership, and seriousness, as they apply to rules that set time frames and deadlines, remain. Likewise, procedures remain crucial, but they change from mere devices for shaping a process for establishing constitutional rules into constitutional rules themselves, for shaping subsequent public policy. The South African case, with a wealth of data at our disposal, provides a clear example.

The ANC won the inaugural election in 1994 with the slogan 'A Better Life for All'. They continued to win every subsequent election (1999, 2004) with ever-greater margins using the very same slogan. To the extent that they meet this vast promise, one can argue that the peace dividend is being delivered. The nature of the peace dividend has never been in doubt: it has to address the needs of the poor, and those dispossessed under the racial policies of apartheid. The ANC published a comprehensive policy document, the Reconstruction and Development Programme (RDP) in 1994, detailing a set of service delivery targets embedded in a macro-economic policy of growth *through* redistribution. The immediate time frame was five years.

The 1996 constitution set the rules and procedures in terms of which such delivery had to be executed. Some of the most important rules were contained in the human rights charter, especially section 9, the equality clause. Specific procedures for redistribution of wealth were contained in enabling legislation such as the Employment Equity Act of 1998 detailing affirmative action policies, and the Restitution of Land Rights (amendment) Act of 2004.

Nelson Mandela, as the country's first democratic President, presided over the RDP, which did not meet its stated targets within its five year time frame. Economic growth was sluggish, state capacity was weak, and direct foreign investment hardly materialized. Thabo Mbeki succeeded Mandela in 1999, and launched a new macro-economic policy, GEAR (Growth, Employment, and Redistribution) that is, growth *followed* by redistribution. This entailed a more concerted wooing of foreign investment and eventually yielded higher growth levels, peaking in 2005 with real growth in GDP of 4.5 per cent.

This overall increase in wealth over a decade has accrued differentially to South Africa's 40 million inhabitants (in 1995). Winners include the many poor people who were the beneficiaries of

- piped water that had been extended to 9 million more people since 1994;
- 1.6 million new dwellings erected in cities in the first ten years of democracy;
- social grants for the needy, which reached 7 million by 2005;
- the electrification of an additional 4 million households by 2004.[25]

At the high end of the living scale new winners also emerged.

- The economic elite became fully multi-racial. In 1998, only 1.3 per cent of Africans were in the ranks of 'High' income earners, along with 4.8 per cent of coloureds, 13 per cent of Indians and 30.8 per cent of whites. By 2004, this had increased to 5 per cent of Africans in this category, 7.5 per cent of coloureds, no less than 27.2 per cent of Indians, and 34.5 per cent of whites. This upward mobility extends into the ranks of the super-rich, where according to one report: by 2005, about 30 per cent of the 3000 people worth more than R50 million each were black.
- The same applies to the expanding middle class. The upward movement of the Indian population group is striking. In terms of average household income, they are the most affluent racial group in South Africa today, having overtaken white households in 1999 already.[26]

Yet despite these tangible advances in eliminating poverty and the historic racial divisions in wealth, some problems remain and others have deepened.

Those who have not benefited from the peace dividend include:

- The unemployed. In early 2005, the unemployment rate stood at 27 per cent according to a strict definition (that excludes those who have given up on actively searching for jobs) and 41 per cent in terms of an expanded definition (that includes the above category). Using the strict definition, this amounts to more than 4.2 million economically active unemployed South Africans.
- The destitute. While some citizens have moved upward into the ranks of the middle class, others appear to be spiralling downward. In 1996, there were 1.89 million South Africans living on less than $1-per-day, constituting about 4.5 per cent of the population. By 2004, this had increased to 3.1 million, about 9.1 per cent of the population. Had the government not instituted an extend programme of social grants (see above) this number would have been significantly higher. Overall, in 2005 there were about 23.5 million South Africans still living in relative poverty.[27]

Taken together, the gap between those who benefited from the peace dividend and those who did not can be expressed in the growing income inequality between the have's and have not's. The national Gini co-efficient which stood at 0.60 in 1996, increased to 0.65 by 2005.[28]

This visible gap between the winners and losers in the newly democratized South Africa has led to increasing tension between the ruling ANC and its alliance partners, the South African Communist Party, and the Congress of South African Trade Unions (COSATU) Trade Union Federation, both of who champion the poor, and accuse the ruling party of self-enrichment at the expense of the poor, their historical support base. The visible descent into destitution by so many South Africans has led to demands for more extensive redistributive policies, which in turn puts increasing strain on the negotiated rules and procedures for implementing the peace dividend. This tension is coalescing into two distinct positions, where according to one view, in order to retain the new order's essential democratic quality, the process of redistribution must be conducted within the core, defining characteristics of the new regime, and that includes human rights stipulations and the rule of law. Against this another view is emerging that holds that the essence of democracy is not captured in rules of procedure, but in outcomes, and that maintaining the rule of law without adequate redistribution of resources to the deprived and the poor would be essentially 'undemocratic'.

The test of the 'elongated' peace process in South Africa is to reconcile these views. Once again, the question of reasonableness will be of critical importance. The question is what constitutes a fair, reasonable time frame within which to uplift 20 million poverty-stricken people, given the vagaries of the current global political economy? The matter of ownership is also decisive. Can the ruling party alone set rules, time frames, and attendant policies of development with which to deliver the peace dividend, or is national consensus needed into which all stakeholders can buy into?

Notes

1. I.W. Zartman & M.R. Berman, *The Practical Negotiator* (New Haven CT: Yale University Press, 1982) pp. 191–192.
2. Ibid., pp. 193–197.
3. A.E. Roth, J.K. Murnighan, & F. Schoumaker, 'The deadline effect in bargaining: Some experimental evidence', *The American Economic Review*, 78 (September 1988) pp. 806–823; S. Ghee-Son Lim & J.K. Murnighan, 'Phases, deadlines and the bargaining process', *Organizational Behaviour and Human Decision Processes*, 58 (1994) pp. 153–171.
4. Zartman & Berman, op. cit., pp. 195–196.
5. J. Barber & J. Barratt, *South Africa's Foreign Policy – The Search for Status and Security 1945–1988* (Johannesburg: Southern, 1990), p. 22.
6. The plan came to be centered on the contents of three documents, the so called Western Settlement Plan, drawn up by the WCG and approved by the Security Council as Document S/12636, of April 1978; Resolution 435 of 1978, and the Supplement to this resolution, Security Council Document S/15287, titled 'Constitutional Principles', of 1982. See L. Cliffe, et al., *The Transition to Independence in Namibia* (Boulder CO: Lynne Rienner, 1994), pp. 239–246. Resolution 385, calling for South Africa's withdrawal from Namibia, is an essential precursor to this plan.
7. Ibid., p. 69.
8. V. Jabri, *Mediating Conflict – Decision-making and Western Intervention in Namibia* (Manchester NH: Manchester University Press, 1990); Cliffe, et al. (1994), op. cit., pp. 68–69.
9. C.A. Crocker, *High Noon in Southern Africa – Making Peace in a Rough Neighborhood* (Johannesburg: Jonathan Ball, 1992).
10. According to Crocker this stalemate was the decisive catalyst in moving the regional powers to search for a peaceful settlement. See Crocker (1992), op. cit., p. 486. For a review of the different assessments of the significance of the Cuito Cuanavale confrontation see W. Breytenbach, 'Cuito Cuanavale revisited: Same outcomes, different consequences', *Africa Insight*, 27, 1 (1997) pp. 54–62.
11. Cliffe, et al. (1994), op. cit., p. 84.
12. For a number of different viewpoints on this controversial incident and its implications for both the Namibian and South African peace processes consult A. Seegers, *The Military in the Making of Modern South Africa* (London: I.B. Tauris, 1996), pp. 261–265; Cliffe, et al. (1994), op. cit., pp. 84–94; and J. Geldenhuys, *A General's Story – From an Era of War and Peace* (Johannesburg: Jonathan Ball, 1995), pp. 265–274.
13. Cliffe, et al. (1994), op. cit., pp. 81–83, 94–113.
14. L. Doubell, 'SWAPO in Office', in Colin Leys & J.S. Saul (eds), *Namibia's Liberation Struggle – The Two-Edged Sword* (London: James Currey, 1995), pp. 171–195, at 176; Cliffe, et al. (1994), op. cit., pp. 199–214.

15. This is not to say that outside forces did not impact on the South African process. Influence from outsiders was pervasive but indirect. At no stage did effective decision-making pass into the hands of foreign actors. See D. Geldenhuys, *Foreign Political Engagement – Remaking States in the Post-Cold War World* (London: Macmillan, 1998), pp. 73–99.
16. C. Cooper et al., *Race Relations Survey 1992/93* (Johannesburg: South African Institute of Race Relations, 1993) pp. 503, 504.
17. S. Friedman (ed.), *The Long Journey – South Africa's Quest for a Negotiated Settlement* (Johannesburg: Ravan Press, 1993), p. 174.
18. B.W. Kruger, Prenegotiation in South Africa (1985–1993) – A Phaseological Analysis of the Transitional Negotiations, Unpublished MA thesis (University of Stellenbosch, 1998), pp. 178–179; T.D. Sisk, *Democratization in South Africa – The Elusive Social Contract* (Princeton NJ: Princeton University Press, 1995), pp. 219, 220; Cooper et al. (1993), op. cit., pp. 35–36.
19. Cooper et al. Ibid., pp. 38–39.
20. Ibid., p. 36.
21. D. Atkinson, 'Brokering a Miracle? The Multiparty Negotiating Forum', in S. Friedman & D. Atkinson (eds), *South African Review: 7 The Small Miracle – South Africa's Negotiated Settlement* (Johannesburg: Ravan Press, 1994), pp. 13–43, at p. 22.
22. P. du Toit, 'South Africa: In Search of Post-Settlement Peace', in J. Darby & R. Mac Ginty (eds), *The Management of Peace Processes* (London: Macmillan, 2000), pp. 16–60, at pp. 29, 30.
23. S. Friedman & L. Stack, 'The Magic Moment – The 1994 Election', in Friedman & Atkinson (eds) (1994), pp. 301–330.
24. Cliffe, et al. (1994), op. cit., pp. 53, 54, 64, 75, 86.
25. J. Kane-Berman (ed.), *South Africa Survey 2004/2005* (Johannesburg: South African Institute of Race Relations, 2006), pp. 371, 384.
26. Ibid., pp. 198, 199, 248.
27. Ibid., pp. 205, 207.
28. Ibid., p. 191.

7
Mediation and the Ending of Conflicts

Christopher Mitchell

Progress towards the settlement of protracted and violent social conflicts usually takes one of two basic forms. In one, the adversaries manage to arrive at some solution through direct, interparty discussion of the issues in contention. They then bargain towards an accommodation of their competing goals that, at the very least, satisfies enough of their underlying interests to make the resultant settlement acceptable to leaders and rank and file followers, and thus durable over time. This process of *negotiation* is usually an extremely complex one, subject to many vicissitudes, and liable, because of its fragility, to break down frequently and disastrously, as in the Basque country and in Sri Lanka. Perhaps for this last reason, a directly negotiated bilateral settlement is something of a rarity.

Far more usually, the adversaries in any protracted conflict find themselves in need of the assistance of others to begin, conduct, and conclude successfully what has fashionably become known as a 'peace process'. Hence, what is often seen as a bilateral negotiating process becomes trilateral, with the introduction of some third party as a 'go-between', 'facilitator', or 'mediator'. Again, the actual mediation of historic protracted conflicts usually turns out, on examination, to be a much more complex process than a simple interaction between two clearly defined and well-articulated adversaries plus one mediating party. In many kinds of conflict, the term 'mediation' has come to be used far from precisely, and to cover a wide variety of activities otherwise labelled informal contacts, conciliation, good offices, brokering, or intermediary initiatives. This seems especially to be the case in violent and protracted conflicts that take place between communities or ethnicities within the formal boundaries of so-called 'nation states' – the Somalias, Sri Lankas and Colombias of today's world. It is possibly for this reason that sure and systematic knowledge about the nature and dynamics of 'mediation processes' in protracted social conflicts is relatively scarce, compared with, for example, our understanding of the work of mediators in other fields, such as industrial or intra-family conflicts. What follows is a brief discussion of some of the issues in the current debate about appropriate and effective mediation practices in protracted social conflicts[1] – otherwise somewhat loosely described as 'civil strife', 'intra-state conflicts', or 'ethnopolitical conflict'.

Mediation: the dominant model

Much current thinking about mediation processes in protracted social conflicts remains strongly influenced by the kind of mediation that has, throughout history, been practised in violent conflicts *between* formally independent 'sovereign' societies. In these, leaders from other societies 'outside' the conflict offer intermediary services to help bring the adversaries together with the aim of concluding an acceptable agreement to end the violence and to compromise on the issues. In the world of Classical Greece, leading city states such as Sparta, Athens, and Corinth frequently acted as powerful intermediaries in conflict between their lesser neighbours, thus providing a classical model for mediators with considerable leverage on the adversaries – 'outsider' intermediaries whose offer of services could not easily be rebuffed, whose advice could not easily be ignored, and whose blueprints for a settlement could not simply be rejected or amended. The model of the 'Great Power' mediator was thus first constructed in the world of the Greek city states.

Similar types of mediator and mediatory processes can be seen operating in the world of separate and formally equal states that came into being in Europe and elsewhere following the end of the 30 Years War, although the reality of the powerful and influential mediator tended to be politely masked on many occasions. The best known of these was Bismarck's use of the concept of the 'honest broker' to describe Germany's role at the Congress of Berlin in 1878, and his claim of disinterested activity for the good of Europe – against which one can set the more cynical but probably more accurate comment of Nikita Krushchev that 'There are no neutral men!'

The world of nineteenth and twentieth-century diplomacy, however, saw the development of other mediatory models than that of the Great Power 'intermediary with leverage'. Intermediary action by a group of governments – what might be termed the multi-government model – can be traced to the post-Napoleonic conception of 'the Concert of Europe' and be most recently exemplified by the successful activities of the Contadora Group in Central America and the less successful efforts of the Western Contact Group in attempting to assist the search for a solution in the conflict over Namibia.[2] Similarly, the same period has seen the frequent use of major international figures as intermediaries, utilizing reputation and prestige to accomplish ceasefires and settlements in violent and volatile situations – Theodore Roosevelt helping to end the Russo–Japanese War in 1905, the Emperor of Ethiopia presiding over the process resulting in the 1972 agreement ending the First Sudanese Civil War, Presidents Nyerere and Mandela brokering an agreement between antagonistic factions in Burundi at the very end of the twentieth century. The 'eminent persons' model is another variant of the theme of outside mediation developed to deal with wars and even – on occasions – with civil wars.

However, while it is clearly the case that both thinking about and practice of mediation in protracted social conflicts has been much influenced by the various models of appropriate mediator activity derived from international practice, questions have been raised in recent years about the utility of any of these models or approaches. This is especially so when the conflict in question takes place within the formal boundaries of one of the 'members of the international community' (i.e., a territorial state); when it involves the formal government of the state as one of the parties to the conflict opposed by ethnic or other types of insurgent; and when the issues in conflict revolve around the preservation of the unity of the state as opposed to its division or disintegration. In such circumstances, it becomes even more difficult to discover an appropriate government as 'honest broker', given the tendency of the governments of existing states – and those international organizations such as the United Nations, the Organization of African Unity (OAU) or the Organization of American States (OAS), that consist of the representatives of the governments of existing states – to be somewhat biased in favour of the principles of continuing territorial integrity and of non-interference in the internal affairs of any other country, *unless genocide clearly threatens*. Both these principles raise major barriers to intermediary action even in situations where the effects of protracted social conflicts spill over borders and disrupt neighbours through raids, refugees, reinforcements, routes for arms, and general mayhem.

Much of the current intellectual and practical debate about the role of mediation in protracted social conflicts thus revolves around the question of who – or more accurately, what type of entity – might be most appropriate to perform mediatory tasks in conflict that are violent, protracted, and dangerous to a region, but which takes place within the confines of an existing state or country, no matter how collapsed the former or disintegrated the latter. Three aspects of this debate currently predominate, and the next sections of this paper will briefly discuss each of these in turn. They are the debates about (1) the timing of mediation (2) 'external neutrals' vs 'insider-partials' as effective intermediaries, and (3) appropriate forms of intermediary activity and their relation to various stages of a 'peace process'.

When can mediation help?

Since William Zartman wrote his pioneering work on the timing of interventions into protracted social conflicts,[3] the issues of timing or a conflict's 'ripeness' for resolution have been much discussed and written about. One focus for debate has naturally taken the form of asking when there exist appropriate conditions for successful intermediary actions, and much of the writing of Ron Fisher and Loraleigh Keashley has concentrated on developing a contingency approach to peacemaking interventions.[4] They argue that the type of initiative (whether from benevolently inclined outsiders or indirectly involved insiders) most likely to have a positive impact on a conflict depends on the stage that particular conflict has reached. For example, Fisher and Keashley suggest that once conflicts have crossed the threshold from hostility and threats to direct violence, only low-key efforts to dampen the violence and – perhaps – restore non-provocative communications between the adversaries are likely to be effective, although in another work on the issue of timing, Jeff Rubin takes a more hopeful view of what might be attempted.[5]

In spite of this body of work, the dominant concepts about 'ripeness' and when third parties might best intervene remain firmly those initially proposed and later elaborated by Zartman[6] himself and his colleague Stephen Stedman.[7] Mediators and other types of third-party intermediaries should best await the development of a 'hurting stalemate' for both adversaries, perhaps accompanied by an approaching mutual catastrophe. Such circumstances offer the best context for mediatory activity, as they will have set leaders on at least the intellectual course of considering alternatives and searching for a way out. In such circumstances, mediators are less likely to encounter a discouraging – if conceptually ambiguous – 'lack of will' on the part of the adversaries and are more likely to be able to move the conflict nearer a solution.

There seem to have been many protracted social conflicts that bear out Zartman's contentions that only mutual pain and a sense of 'no end in sight' will make parties in violent conflict open to the possibilities of mediation and a brokered solution. However, there are clearly other cases that do not fit this model and where mediators have been able to move adversaries towards an alternative process to continuing mutual coercion and harm. In another paper, I have suggested alternative ideas about 'ripe moments', arguing that circumstances that enable leaders to abandon entrapping commitments or to envisage creative alternatives may also provide openings for well-crafted intermediary initiatives.[8]

More generally, it might be that while a situation of stalemate and cost may bring about a change of mind on the part of the leaders of embattled adversaries, other external forms of change can also produce rethinking and reconsideration so that those leaders thus become more receptive to offers of mediation, conciliation, good offices, or facilitation. Now, there seems to be very little systematic examination of the relationship between contextual changes affecting a conflict system and reconsiderations on the part of decision makers therein. However, both anecdotal evidence and some theoretical formulations suggest that such a link does exist and should be explored. Change does beget change, as the old saying has it, and it seems only commonsensical to argue that major alterations in circumstances can become the occasion for leaders locked in a conflict to ask whether alternative courses of action – perhaps involving help from third parties – might exist.

For example, it seems clearly to have been the case that the ending of the Cold War and the collapse of the Soviet Union had a not unimportant effect on British strategic thinking about the conflict in Northern Ireland, while the growing importance of the European Union and the progressive integration of Western Europe did much to affect nationalist thinking about the whole set of relationships involving north western Europe's off-shore islands. We need to know more about the dynamics of this kind of linked change.

Elsewhere, I have argued that three levels or types of change can have a profound effect upon the thinking of both leaders and constituents of parties in conflict.[9] Changes at the systemic, structural, and tactical levels a conflict system can all bring about a situation in which leaders jerk themselves out of an *incremental continuation* mode of decision making and into a *comprehensive reconsideration* mode. The latter is not unlikely to involve a search for alternatives and a potential opportunity for mediators to become involved in a search for such alternatives. At the moment, unfortunately, we know too little about the types of contextual change which lead towards the search for new ideas about solutions and those which lead to decisions about 'more of the same' and an intensification of struggle. However, the idea that change can provide mediators with an opening does seem to offer an interesting alternative to the idea that openings only open when parties recognize hurt.

Appropriate mediators

A second major intellectual puzzle currently being faced is the whole issue about whether it is more appropriate that mediatory tasks are carried out by outsiders, rather on the 'classical' model of international mediation discussed above, or whether success is more likely when insiders – individuals and organization that are themselves part of the society or community within which the conflict is being fought out – act as intermediaries between warring factions. The 'outsider-neutral' vs 'insider-partial' debate is too frequently carried out as though the existence of these two types of intermediary presented an 'either-or' choice, at least in those situations where choice is possible. More fruitfully, enquiry might well start with the assumption that there are circumstances in which one rather than the other is more likely to be successful, while the reverse is true in other circumstances.

Of course, a preliminary question ought to be whether the distinction is as clear-cut as the ongoing debate implies. Where is the dividing line between those who are genuinely 'insiders' and those who, for some unambiguous reason, can be regarded as 'outside' the conflict, in the sense that they are not even a 'peripheral' as opposed to a 'core' party to that conflict? For example, it is clearly the case that the US government is not exactly 'neutral' in the protracted Israeli/ Palestinian conflict, but is it even 'outside' that conflict, given the substantial influence on domestic US politics wielded by the Jewish community in the United States of America and by the number of Florida registered voters that appear to reside normally in Tel Aviv and its environs?

A similar definitional dilemma arises from the intermediary activities of many successful third parties. For example, Kare Loder reports on the successful mediatory role played by Norwegian Church Aid (NCA) in helping to end the civil war in Mali in 1996.[10] He notes that NCA had been working in northern Mali on drought relief since 1984 had 'saved the various communities in the area from disintegration and the nomads in particular from extinction'[11] and had made a point of using Malians rather than Norwegian expatriates in senior positions. Thus, the 'NCA team' that began to act as facilitators of a traditional peacemaking dialogue in the autumn of 1995 consisted of four individuals, three of whom were respected Malians and only one a Norwegian. Was this a case of an outsider-neutral or an insider-partial initiative? On the other hand, might it have been a hybrid case of an insider-neutral? Similar questions might even be asked about the Norwegian team from The Institute for Applied Social Sciences (FAFO) that had been working in the Gaza Strip for over ten years before some of its members launched the informal talks that made up the Oslo Process and led, in 1993, to the tragically undermined Oslo Accords.[12]

Nevertheless, the issue of what kind of mediators are most appropriate for what circumstances remains a baffling and contentious one. Outsiders have problems obtaining access to intra-state conflicts, although the doctrine of non-interference in the internal affairs of an independent state is beginning to fray at the edges, especially when it is hard to argue that a state still exists, as in the cases of Somalia, Rwanda, or parts of former-Yugoslavia. Still, the steadfast refusal of the Madrid government to allow outsiders to act as intermediaries in the Spanish–Basque conflict indicates that in many situations only insiders (or, at the most, relatively powerless and unofficial 'Track Two' intermediaries) can even obtain access to the parties involved in a protracted intra-state conflict. The continuing insulation of the Sri Lankan conflict from external mediation – mainly at the behest of the Colombo government rather than the Liberation Tigers of Tamil Eelam (LTTE) – also indicates the tenacity of this 'domestic jurisdiction' obstacle.[13]

Wehr and Lederach[14] have argued persuasively that in many protracted conflicts, only intermediaries that understand the cultural nuances of the society and who enjoy the *confianza* (something more than simply 'trust') of the antagonists can hope to carry out intermediary roles successfully. Certainly, experiences of the success of local intermediaries in developing peace at least at the local level in parts of north eastern Kenya,[15] in northern Ghana, and in the Atlantic provinces of Nicaragua[16] back up the claim that insider-partials have advantages that are denied to outsiders. On the other hand, there are enough cases of outsiders – usually outsiders who do not conform to the classical model of an 'outsider with leverage' – playing a successful part in processes achieving peace at the national level to raise again the question of what circumstances do favour one type of mediator over the other. Obvious examples of effective outsider mediation range from the work of the San Egidio Community in helping to bring about the Mozambique peace accords[17] to the Vatican's role in helping to arrange an agreement between Argentina and Chile over their disputed boundary in the Beagle Channel.[18] However, the examples are many, the overall picture is a confusing one, and any precise matching of type of intermediary to set of circumstances so that success is likely seems a long way off, even at the theoretical level.

Mediator roles and functions

The final puzzle for students and practitioners of mediation is a variant of the traditional query: What do mediators actually do? In this connection, it has been clear for some considerable time that the answer to this apparently simple query is that it depends on *when* a mediator chooses to take an initiative – that is, that there are clearly appropriate roles and functions – tasks to be undertaken, in plain language – depending upon what stage a peace process has achieved.

Even 30 years ago the then sparse literature on mediation recognized that mediators would be called upon to do different things for the conflicting parties, depending on the recent history of their conflict. If negotiations had taken place but had broken down then the task of an effective intermediary was to restore communications between the adversaries and explore the conditions each was imposing for the resumption of talks. If the antagonists had yet to explore even the possibility of conversations, then the task of the mediator was to sound out both sides to see if there might be any readiness to engage in talks – if the elusive 'will' existed on both sides, and if it did what conditions for meeting might be imposed.

At this time, and subsequently, the vast preponderance of attention was paid to the tasks of mediators once representatives of the parties in conflict were 'at the table' and much time and effort was spent in delineating what skills a mediator required in the role of chairperson or moderator of the actual face-to-face talks. Issues over the appropriate place for third-party 'power' or 'leverage' developed out of these analyses and still occupy a central place in today's diverse and controversial literature about what makes a successful mediator, and whether adroitness and creativity can make up for the absence of resources to be promised or withheld as ways of inducing agreement between rivals. The debates over 'pure' vs 'power' mediation have been well summarized by Ron Fisher,[19] while Marieke Kleiboer has proposed a sophisticated explanation of why different analysts take up very different positions on this and other debates on the nature of appropriate and successful mediation practices.[20]

The publication of Hal Saunders's[21] seminal article on pre-negotiation and of James Wall's[22] analyses of mediation systems derived from his studies of industrial and organization mediation further complicated ideas about mediators' tasks and roles from the early 1980s. Both analyses suggested that mediators could and do carry out a far wider range of tasks than merely acting as a go-between for parties unwilling – perhaps temporarily – to meet face-to-face or moderating face-to-face exchanges when these became a possibility. Wall's analysis suggested strongly that one of the tasks facing many mediators involved dealing not merely with the relationships between negotiators or between negotiators and their own decision makers 'back home' but also between negotiators, their leaders and their constituents, so that this became a further complicating task for mediators aiming for success in ending a conflict. Saunders, in turn, raised questions of what mediators needed to do in the pre-negotiation stages of any peace process, and how various types of intermediary might best prepare parties to be ready to conduct a fruitful negotiation by bringing the most appropriate attitudes, expectations, and skills to any formal, official 'table'.

Finally, some of the recent literature on conflict transformation and the aftermath of achieving an agreement have added a list of still further roles for third parties. Mediators' tasks now do not end with the signing of the agreement or a set of accords. Part of the result of all this has been the suggestion that it might be helpful to think of a mediator less as a single person or organization and more as a set of roles to be fulfilled or tasks to be performed. Furthermore, these necessary tasks may actually be carried out by a variety of individuals or organizations, acting – one hopes – in concert with one another, a hope that Susan Allen Nan has characterized as involving *complementarity* of intermediary initiatives.[23]

All these writings clearly support the suggestion that answering questions about what mediators do depends very much on the answer to a prior question: When do mediators become involved? The answer to the first question is complicated enough, even simply focussing on the traditional view that a mediator's main tasks occur during face-to-face meetings between the adversaries. However, even at this stage of a conflict there are likely to be a variety of very different circumstances calling forth a very different set of mediatory tasks. How do mediator roles differ during smoothly proceeding talks from those needed during a tough but (hopefully) temporary impasse? What do mediators do – apart from shoulder the blame – in the aftermath of a complete breakdown of negotiations and a threatened return to violence?

The picture becomes even more complex when we consider other stages and sub-stages of a protracted conflict. Recent literature on conflict prevention suggests the need for mediator involvement in the development of long-term conflict-avoidance strategies, in times of developing tensions, at points of imminent crisis, and even following the actual outbreak of violence. Possible work at the height of conflict involves efforts to diminish reactive violence or to arrange ceasefires or humanitarian pauses while searching for opportunities for 'talks about talk', especially when stalemate has led to a search for face saving, non-violent alternatives, a stage often marked by face-saving bluster. As noted previously, mediators can also be deeply involved in post-agreement tasks, some concerned with overcoming immediate problems of implementation, others with longer-term reconciliation processes that try to avoid a repetition of the same conflict by future generations.

Hence, the list of appropriate mediator activities grows as our understanding of the dynamics of conflict grows. My own summary list (below) clearly contains some tasks that would not have been regarded as proper for classical mediators even 20 years ago, but I would argue that all have an important impact on the likely success of mediation in moving a conflict towards a resolution. Moreover, this list has become somewhat less startling with the recognition – again brought about by recent work on peacebuilding at the grass roots and opinion leader levels – of the importance of multi-level intermediary tasks that need to be carried out so as to improve the chances of a lasting and generally accepted resolution of a conflict.

Core mediator tasks in conflict resolution[24]

Pre-negotiation

Explorer Determines adversaries' readiness for contacts; sketches range of possible solutions.

Reassurer Reassures adversaries that other not wholly bent on 'victory'.

Decoupler Assists external patrons to withdraw from core conflict; enlists patrons in other positive tasks.

Unifier Repairs intra-party cleavages and encourages consensus on interests, core values, concessions.

Enskiller Develops skills and competencies needed to enable adversaries to reach a durable solution.

Convener Initiates process of talks, provides venue, and legitimizes contacts and meetings.

During talks or negotiations

Facilitator Fulfils functions within meetings to enable a fruitful exchange of versions, aims, and visions.

Envisioner Provides new data, ideas, theories, and options for adversaries to adapt; creates fresh thinking.

Enhancer Provides additional resources to assist in search for positive sum solution.

Guarantor Provides insurance against talks breaking down and offers to guarantee any durable solution.

Legitimizer Adds prestige and legitimacy to any agreed solution.

Post-agreement

Verifier Reassures adversaries that terms of agreement are being fulfilled.

Implementer Imposes sanctions for non-performance of agreement.

Reconciler Assists in long-term actions to build new relationships among and within adversaries.

Conclusion

The list of mediator tasks – what mediators do and when – will undoubtedly soon be modified and extended as we analyse more examples of successful and unsuccessful initiatives, and then draw some general lessons from the wealth of case material currently becoming available. This book is clearly part of this necessary consolidation of knowledge about mediators and mediation, and equally clearly will contribute to our obtaining a better understanding of the nature of mediation work and its role in resolving protracted and dangerous social conflicts. I can only hope that this present paper contributes to the task of understanding what we know and, more importantly, what we still need to know about these issues.

Notes

1. E.E. Azar, *The Management of Protracted Social Conflict* (Aldershot: Dartmouth Publishing, 1990).
2. V. Jabri, *Mediating Conflict: Decision Making and Western Intervention in Namibia* (Manchester NH: Manchester University Press, 1990).
3. I.W. Zartman, *Ripe for Resolution: Conflict and Intervention in Africa* (New York: Oxford University Press, 1985).
4. R.J. Fisher & L. Keashley, 'The potential complimentarity of mediation and consultation within a contingency model of third party consultation', *Journal of Peace Research*, 28, 1 (1991) pp. 21–42.
5. J.Z. Rubin, 'The Timing of Ripeness and the Ripeness of Timing', in L. Kriesberg & S.J. Thornson (eds), *Timing the De-escalation of International Conflicts* (New York: Syracuse University Press, 1991).
6. Zartman (1985), op. cit.
7. S.J. Stedman, *Peacemaking in Civil Wars: International Mediation in Zimbabwe, 1974–1980* (Boulder CO: Lynne Rienner, 1991).
8. C. Mitchell, 'The right moments: Notes on four models of "ripeness"', *Paradigms*, 9, 2 (Winter 1995) pp. 38–52.

9. C. Mitchell, *Gestures of Conciliation* (London: Macmillan, 2000).

10. K. Loder, 'The Peace process in Mali', *Security Dialogue*, 28, 4 (1997) pp. 409–424.

11. Ibid., p. 416.

12. J. Corbin, *The Norway Channel* (New York: Atlantic Monthly Press, 1994).

13. P. Saravanamuttu, 'Sri Lanka: The Intractability of Ethnic Conflict', in J. Darby & R. Mac Ginty (eds), *The Management of Peace Processes* (London: Macmillan, 2000), pp. 195–227.

14. P. Wehr & J.P. Lederach, 'Mediating conflict in central America', *Journal of Peace Research*, 28, 1 (February 1991).

15. D. Ibrahim & J. Jenner, 'Breaking the Cycle of Violence in Wajir', chapter. 10 in R. Herr & J.Z. Herr (eds), *Transforming Violence* (Scottdale PA: Herald Press, 1998).

16. Wehr & Lederach (1991), op. cit., pp. 85–98.

17. C. Hume, *Mozambique's War: The Role of Mediation and Good Offices* (Washington DC: USIP Press, 1994).

18. T. Princen, 'Mediation by a Transnational Organization: The Case of the Vatican', chapter. 7 in J. Bercovitch & J.Z. Rubin (eds), *Mediation in International Relations* (New York: St. Martin's Press, 1992), pp. 149–175.

19. R. Fisher, *Inter-Active Conflict Resolution* (New York: Syracuse University Press, 1997).

20. M. Kleiboer, *International Mediation: The Multiple Realities of Third Party Intervention* (Boulder CO: Lynne Rienner, 1997) and M. Kleiboer & P. t'Hart, 'Time to talk? Multiple perspectives on timing of international mediation', *Cooperation and Conflict*, 30 (1995) pp. 307–348.

21. H.H. Saunders, 'We need a larger theory of negotiation: The importance of the pre-negotiation phase', *Negotiation Journal*, 1, 1 (July 1985) pp. 249–262.

22. J.A. Wall, 'Mediation: An analysis, review and proposed research', *Journal of Conflict Studies*, 25, 1 (March 1981) pp. 157–180 and J.A. Wall & A. Lynn, 'Mediation: A current review', *Journal of Conflict Resolution*, 37, 1 (March 1993) pp. 160–194.

23. S. Allen-Nan, Complementarity and Coordination of Conflict Resolution Efforts in the Conflicts in Abkhazia, South Ossetia and TransDniestria (PhD Dissertation, George Mason University, 1999).

24. Adapted from C. Mitchell, 'The Process and Stages of Mediation: Two Sudanese Cases', chapter. 6 in D. R. Smock (ed.), *Making War and Waging Peace* (Washington DC: USIP Press, 1993), pp. 128–141.

8
Women, Gender and Peacemaking in Civil Wars[*]

Antonia Potter

Introduction

While this chapter is located in Part II (Negotiations) of this book, the issues it addresses are cross cutting, therefore it will briefly scan the spectrum of the broadly defined peace process 'stages', namely violence, pre-negotiations, negotiations, peace accords, and peacebuilding. Across these it examines two strands: first, the presence or representation of women as actors in these stages from conflict to peace; second, the approaches to addressing gender issues and perspectives that are employed by those that have a hand in peace processes, together with successes and failures in implementing them.

It draws attention to changed perceptions of women's roles in these phases, and to the special challenges and opportunities which armed conflict and its resolution can present for women. It suggests where there are gaps in research, literature, and actual practice arguing that much of this is due to ongoing problems of women's exclusion from agency and decision making at certain levels (especially the more senior or official ones) of peacemaking and peace-building, and a continuing failure of those at the highest levels to understand properly and take seriously the implications of that exclusion. Throughout, it draws on recent or contemporary examples[1] of peace agreements and proc-esses including Afghanistan, Cambodia, Eritrea, Guatemala, Kosovo, Nepal, Northern Ireland, Somalia, Sudan, and Timor–Leste.

The chapter concludes by reiterating that reality lags far behind rhetoric on women's involvement in peace processes, to the great detriment of both. It argues that the process and substance of peace negotiations and agreements would be richer, subtler, stronger, and more firmly rooted in the societies whose problems they aim to solve with increased participation of women and the issues which are important to them; but that until those that organize these processes actually make this happen, it will be obviously be hard to make this case with empirical evidence. Thus it calls for political leaders, especially the most visible and powerful, to stop talking and start acting on this issue. Finally, it stresses the basic but often forgotten fact that gender is a concept which embraces both women and men, and exhorts more men to swell the ranks of those working at all levels of peacemaking in the causes of equality and practical sensitivity to gender issues.

Instruments and resources on women in peace and security

Despite the massive violence, bloodshed, and atrocity which characterized so much of its history, the twentieth century and the early years of this century have seen enormous strides made in terms of legal and normative frameworks to address issues of discrimination against women across many dimensions of life. This progress has not excluded the key questions of concern in this chapter – those of women's representation, agency, and victim-hood in conflict, peace, and security issues in civil wars.

Of these documents, there are perhaps three that stand out as key, being intergovernmental, widely adopted, and having an explicit focus on women. These are the 1979 Convention on the Elimination of All Forms of Discrimination against Women (CEDAW), the 1995 Beijing Declaration and Platform of Action, and the 2000 UN Security Council Resolution 1325 (SCR 1325) on Women, Peace, and Security (although there are many more relevant official documents).[2]

The CEDAW provides a basis in international law for realizing equality between women and men through ensuring women's equal access to, and equal opportunities in, political and public life and is the only human rights treaty which targets culture and tradition as influential forces shaping gender roles and family relations. Given that conflict and its aftermath can have a seismic impact on tradition and culture – and indeed that conflict can be at least partially caused by tensions resulting from them – this is very valuable.

The Beijing Declaration states that 'Local, national, regional and global peace is attainable and is inextricably linked with the advancement of women, who are a fundamental force for leadership, conflict resolution and the promotion of lasting peace at all levels'[3] and insists that peace is necessary for the advancement of women, committing itself to disarmament; its associated Platform of Action has a specific, practically oriented section on women in armed conflict.

The most recent of the three, Security Council resolution (SCR) 1325, was one of the most popular SCRs in that body's history, garnering unprecedented support[4] and providing clear language on improving the representation of women and the treatment of their issues which has been copiously deployed by advocates. Three of the key actions it calls for are:

1. to promote equal participation of women and equal opportunities for women to participate in all forums and peace activities at all levels, particularly at the decision-making level;
2. to integrate a gender perspective in the resolution of armed or other conflicts and foreign occupation and aim for gender balance when nominating or promoting candidates for judicial and other positions in all relevant international bodies; and
3. to ensure that these bodies are able to address gender issues properly by providing appropriate training.[5]

Indeed, all three documents are rich in deployable language, but time has shown that the internalization and implementation of norms is a long-term process requiring a sustained effort of 'knowledge creation, dissemination and validation',[6] not to mention dedicated leadership and resources. It might not then be surprising that changes on the ground have been slower than might have been hoped; but, even if we recognize that this is a difficult and long-term venture, it might not be unreasonable to worry that the slow pace of change implies that misogynist or bigoted views continue to hold a certain amount of sway in the most progressive and liberal of societies, even if unconsciously.

Flowing from these documents, a plethora of toolkits and guidelines for practical action on how to implement them has emerged.[7] These cover a gamut of issues from how to assess conflict situations with a gendered perspective,[8] to planning peacekeeping operations,[9] reforming constitutions, and setting up structures within governments to monitor and oversee the implementation of gender-focussed legislation and policy.[10] A review of the literature and case studies on post-conflict situations reveals, however, a depressing paucity of examples of implementation, and in particular strategic or holistic implementation – albeit that the examples themselves, some of which are discussed under 'post-conflict implementation' below are inspiring.

To give an anecdotal example of prevailing attitudes, and both the positive and negative implications we can draw from them, the then United Nations Secretary General (UNSG) Kofi Annan made his first visit to Timor–Leste after the popular consultation of 1999 and its violent aftermath in February 2000. He was accompanied by his wife, for whom as usual, a special programme was planned. This included a meeting with the leading Timorese women's organization, the Organização da Mulher Timor (OMT), for many years a clandestine movement which had played an important role in the struggle for independence. The leaders of the OMT protested that, with all due respect, they were not prepared to meet the wife of the UNSG; they insisted on meeting the official himself, in order to express their own concerns and priorities about the future of their country. Not without some embarrassment amongst the international civil servants, their demand was met. A more recent example comes from the peace process in Nepal, where the Maoists made a vocal show of their intention to 'destroy the patriarchy' and then appointed a team of three men to be their negotiators – a move which drew an outcry, apparently futile, from their supporters.

One might expect the peacekeeping missions of the United Nations – the world's most experienced organization in peacekeeping and post-conflict reconstruction and development – to lead the way with regard to putting into practice the many available guidelines. In their influential report for the United Nations Development Fund for Women (UNIFEM), however, Ellen Johnson Sirleaf and Elizabeth Rehn note that still 'to the best of our knowledge, gender expertise has not been utilized during assessment missions or technical surveys conducted prior to the design or establishment of UN peacekeeping operations nor, most importantly, in the blueprint for action, the concept of operation or the budget'.[11]

Perhaps the area where the most progress has been noted is in constitutional reform, and in women's parliamentary representation in which several war-torn countries far outperform even their most progressive developed world colleagues (e.g., Rwanda at the top of the global list with 48.8 per cent, Mozambique with 34.8 per cent, and Burundi with 30.5 per cent[12] all of whom have 30 per cent quotas for women's representation).[13] A fruitful focus for future research could be the extent to which this post-conflict upswing in women's representation can be shown to have positive impacts in two critical areas: first, the sustainability of peace, and second the extent to which constructive attention is actually paid to women's issues within the peacebuilding period. It should be noted, however, that in several post-conflict cases (e.g., Bosnia–Herzegovina, Cambodia, and Guatemala) women's parliamentary representation has decreased from pre-war levels.[14]

Gendered roles

A place where sustained progress has been made, at least from the point of view of the international community, is on the subtlety of the understanding of women's roles in peacemaking and peacebuilding. Victim-hood has often been highlighted (e.g., women as casualties, victims of sexual crimes especially rape,[15] refugees, internally displaced persons etc.) – and especially the fact that post-conflict periods can often expose women to similar and often worse levels of violence than a conflict period; but, in addition, we can now access useful research and guidelines for conducting such analysis of women as rights-holders, combatants (in state and non-state military groups), mothers/wives/daughters (single) heads of household and economic actors, community and organization members/leaders, and mediators both at grassroots and more official levels.[16] These distinctions are important, not just because they paint a more honest picture of reality but also because of the particular burdens a post-conflict period may place upon women: 'In many cases women are the only segment of society remaining that are able to pick up the pieces and rebuild, if the ranks of male contributors have been drastically thinned by violent death, psychological trauma and other debilitating results of prolonged violence.'[17]

Furthermore, this discussion of women's gendered roles has opened up the question of how conflict can alter those roles, exposing how the post-conflict period can bring a complex time in which society (including women themselves) tries to adapt to women's newfound identities and roles, or, more commonly, tries to put women back into their pre-conflict gendered roles. As a European Parliament Committee has observed, 'The inegalitarian structures of our societies confine women to traditional roles or keep them in subordinate positions. War and conflicts, paradoxically, provide a way for women to affirm their equality.'[18] Both Eritrea and Somalia (which is not yet a post-conflict situation) provide interesting examples of highly traditional and culturally conservative societies where women have become extraordinarily emancipated during conflict (e.g., participating in combat including in leadership positions, and taking on unprecedently powerful roles in terms of family, commerce, and peace process participation), but have experienced great challenges holding onto those gains.[19]

In relation to this, it is interesting to track the growing but still disproportionately small literature and practitioner focus on the issue of men's gendered roles in conflict, particularly around the issue of male identities pre-conflict, during and post-conflict, and especially in relation to violence.[20] We have become more familiar with the phenomenon of women's vulnerability in conflict and post-conflict periods to increased domestic violence; this relates to male reactions to conflict and its aftermath, to gender-based and other violence linked to the conflict itself, and to post-conflict-associated criminality and lawlessness. There is a prevailing tendency to take gender issues in conflict (and perhaps in other areas too) to mean women's issues alone and this case is no exception: in fact, of those who are victims of armed violence, the vast majority is in fact men, particularly young men.[21] The point here is that peace process actors need to recognize that the consideration of women's gendered roles in conflict and its aftermath is incomplete without the consideration of the gendered roles of the men with whom they share and must rebuild their societies.

Peace negotiations

On the question of peace negotiations themselves, there have been very few cases where women have played a formal role – either as representatives of conflict parties, or as third-party mediators. Burundi, Guatemala, and Northern Ireland provide positive examples, and to some extent the much unfinished business of Somalia. The Somalia and Northern Ireland examples[22] are particularly interesting in terms of how they show women organizing across party, political, and clan lines to ensure that their voices are heard. In Guatemala, the Civil Society Assembly included a specific sector on women, one of the few such sectors which continues its work today; however, the failure to enshrine women's political participation and to include broader political reforms in the peace accords themselves has led to disappointing levels of women's public and political participation in the post-conflict period.[23] During the Oslo process, Hanan Ashrawi was indeed a senior female presence on the negotiating team; however, some analysts argue that she was sidelined and relegated to a 'soft' role in liaising with the media.

There is also some argument that male leaders encourage the creation and promotion of women's organizations 'in a moment of political opportunism'[24] during negotiations, as this can provide a powerful media tool which is felt to be very effective especially with important actors in the international community. Nevertheless, as anyone who has been responsible for gender-focussed programming in a post-conflict situation will attest, 'the categorization of women's participation as an "international priority" does not guarantee the sense of ownership for social transformation at the local level'.[25] On the subject of the media, it has also been suggested that the tendency to contrast the image 'women of peace' with 'men of violence' has the effect of excluding women from the 'hard' conflict resolution process[26] which is conceived of as a male political domain. If women tend not to be the ones with guns (and therefore, it is assumed, power or political aspirations), why discuss decommissioning with them? This underlines a continued lack of appreciation of what is often described as a crucial contribution of a female perspective: the awareness of the value of process and dynamic *as well as* substantive political content.[27]

An interesting question poses itself in relation to this issue of participation in negotiations: do women get ignored if they do not organize themselves into a specific constituency which needs managing? Or in other words, do women get ignored because they tend not to act as spoilers and thus do not require management or neutralization as such? This question should not be taken as a literal call to arms for women, but as a reflection on who gets to have a say at the peace table and why. Third-party mediators taking a longer or deeper view of conflict resolution may benefit from a more profound reflection on who really constitutes the drivers of power and change in society and how to build on the most constructive elements of that.

As with all questions of representation at the peace table, those who put the table together need to consider how such actors are selected, to what extent and of whom they are legitimately representative, and the costs and benefits of their inclusion or exclusion. A well-recognized problem of women organizing *qua* women rather than on a specific political platform is that they can be seen to lack political direction and credibility and end up being seen exactly as what they do not want to be seen as – the 'token' women at the table – whose exclusion might not seem to carry a heavy cost for the process. More work needs to be done on the power of these kinds of coalitions (e.g., as above Somalia and Northern Ireland). Women are no more a homogenous group than men are, and differences of ethnicity, religion, social and economic class can create vast gulfs between them. Yet men have tended not to organize across these gulfs in conflict the way that women have, even men from more marginalized groups. This indicates that we do not yet understand how best to optimize the constructive power that kind of political organizing can have – another area which might benefit from more rigorous analysis.

There is an almost complete lack of international third-party conflict mediators who are women.[28] The lack of examples makes it hard to develop a powerful empirical case for the missed opportunities this represents – apart from the obvious *a priori* case that missing half the talent pool or the perspective of half of those who have suffered the scourges of war is senseless. Parallels with women's roles in other fields suggest that women's presence in these kind of leadership positions can provide positive role modelling for women and men from within conflict-affected societies (and indeed within the international community). Their presence may offer other possibilities for conflict resolution through different communication styles and approaches to issue prioritization, and even through the psychological effect that a female presence can have in a male-dominated physical space (perhaps especially one where tensions or animosity are high).

As discussed below, there is striking concordance across peace processes on the kind of issues that women want to see enshrined in peace agreements; it is hard to imagine that those issues might not benefit from a woman's perspective at the head of the negotiation table. This is not, however, to say that all women will instinctively understand the needs and aspirations of women in a conflict situation any more than all men might of men or women; there is no substitute for a sensitive understanding of the politics, culture, and history of a given situation.

Peace accords

The trend in recent years has been towards peace agreements, or at least the approach to their implementation, becoming increasingly holistic, aiming not merely to end violence but to address the causes of conflict by setting in motion the process of transforming society. Guatemala is perhaps the text-book case of a peace agreement[29] which aims to set out what some would say was an idealistically comprehensive vision of a future society. It includes a whole section dedicated to women's role in strengthening civilian power; but major areas of the agreement remain unimplemented, including many which affect women's war-related health, economic security, and political access issues. A counterexample to this trend is Aceh, whose matter of fact 2005 Memorandum of Understanding with the Republic of Indonesia contains no gender references, and very few pointers to possible societal transformation.

This is not the place to get down to the detailed arguments about how deep or shallow a peace agreement should be; however, it would be to miss the point of peace negotiations and accords to suggest that their principal aim should be to address issues of gender inequality. This is not to say, however, that the peace process cannot be seen as a critical strategic opportunity in this regard, as it brings with it possibilities for international support and protection as well as internal restructuring (conceptual, political, and administrative), which might never otherwise present themselves.

Perhaps the most comprehensive work on how language and mechanisms in peace accords can promote gender equality has been undertaken by Christine Chinkin for the UN Division for the Advancement of Women.[30] Her search for 'model clauses' led her to the following conclusion:

> the reality is that there is no peace agreement that provides an overall model for appropriate provisions for ensuring that the needs of women within the conflict zone are served alongside those of men. Nor are there even many provisions that relate specifically or even indirectly to women. Typically, peace agreements are framed in gender-neutral language, assumed to be equally applicable to, and equally appropriate for, the needs of both women and men within the society in question.[31]

Arguing that a gender-neutral approach is proven to be insufficient in addressing women's conflict-related issues, she also points out that, as gender activists across all walks of life are aware, if gender concerns are not included in the peace agreement, any attention to them tends to rely tenuously upon the personal commitment of individual(s) whose tenure is never assured.

In processes where women's priorities and needs for special attention have been expressed either in an agreement (e.g., Burundi, Guatemala, Northern Ireland, Sierra Leone) or in other ways after it (e.g., Afghanistan, Timor–Leste), a striking concordance is found. This covers issues such as women's rights as human rights, women's equal participation in public and political life (often demanding quotas for representation), justice, the protection of women and girls especially in relation to violent sexual crimes, accountability in relation to this, and women's access and rights to land, health, education, and livelihood and employment opportunities. There is a tendency for 'family issues' and 'women's issues' to be conflated, presumably because of the role women play in families, and especially because the phenomenon of the single-female-headed household is such a familiar one in conflict-stricken societies. It is often women, as well, who are most strident in calling for special attention to rural areas which are frequently discriminated against pre- and post-conflict in terms of the provision of infrastructure, social services, and so forth. All of these concerns, it can be argued, have a strong bias towards societal reconstruction and reconciliation.

While there are high levels of activity in organizing women to present their priorities, it clearly remains a challenge to get those taken seriously, or to normalize an approach which routinely checks (and then has an opportunity to revise) how an agreement will affect women post-conflict.[32] As Chinkin trenchantly observes 'if training on gender awareness/sensitivity/the needs of women is mandated within the peace agreement, international bodies offering such training will not be able to dismiss the appropriateness of raising these issues in the particular context, as sometimes occurs'.[33] The same point could of course be made of national authorities.

Post-conflict implementation

As in the peacemaking process, and for very similar reasons, women continue to be at their most active and represented at community level.[34] However, as discussed above, this is at a time when their security in a range of dimensions may be more fragile than ever, including increased vulnerability from abuse by peacekeepers themselves.[35]

In general, practitioners and analysts of peace agreement implementation agree that deep-rooted, sustainable reconciliation requires the rebuilding of social capital, involving organizations, networks, and social codes. It is interesting to note then, that some of the leading texts on this fail to mention or expand on the particular, and perhaps extremely obvious, roles women can play here.[36]

There are examples of women who have been prominent in fighting corruption, campaigning for democracy, or who have been victims (e.g., of imprisonment and torture) during conflict who have made it into leadership positions, such as Ellen Johnson Sirleaf of Liberia or Michelle Bachelet of Chile.[37] Many post-conflict countries now have women in ministerial positions (Burundi, Cambodia, Timor–Leste, Sudan) and not merely as ministers for Women's Affairs. While this is a positive development, it remains rare. Role modelling is important not only for providing women with a vision for change and for their own potential agency but also for correcting the vision of both men and women which tends automatically to picture men, even men of a certain kind, in leadership positions.

There are a number of other examples of positive progress for and by women in peacebuilding periods. As noted above, these have included increases in parliamentary representation; also, contributions to reforming security sector policies and strategies. In South Africa, for example,[38] women parliamentarians' involvement in the 1996–1998 defence review led to a holistic defence policy which recognized the need for community reconstruction and regeneration post-conflict, and which has institutionalized gender training for personnel in peacekeeping and peace support organizations; women were also appointed to senior positions in the Ministry of Defence. Kosovo is able to boast a 13.75 per cent representation of women in its police service, as compared to the UN Civilian Police's (CIVPOL) 5.4 per cent. Teresa Quintos-Deles, a former Presidential Advisor on the Peace Process in the Philippines, describes the strong roles played by women in phases of the ongoing process between the Philippine Government and the Moro Islamic Liberation Front (MILF), including her own efforts to 'promote the ascendance of a new breed of soldier-peacemakers in Muslim Mindanao'.[39]

Humanitarian, reconstruction, and rehabilitation programmes have also seen great strides in beneficiary participation (e.g., in assessment, implementation, monitoring, and evaluation), which has included a focus on identifying the special needs of women and girls – although it should be noted that this kind of 'beneficiary-of-services' – related progress is much easier to achieve than political progress. Gender Units, Officers or Advisors, focussing on issues such as providing training, raising awareness, undertaking analysis of policy and legislation, and institutionalizing national machinery for the promotion of women's rights have been established in a variety of UN missions including in Afghanistan, the Democratic Republic of Congo (DRC), Kosovo, Sierra Leone, and Timor–Leste. Regrettably their resource capacities, both human and financial, and in terms of political clout to see through challenging changes, have normally fallen far short of the grand scope of their mandates.[40]

International donors are another important part of the implementation mix, the policies of whose political/foreign policy arms and development/assistance arms may not always see eye to eye on the issue of attention to women's special post-conflict needs. The former will tend to focus on what is politically practical in terms of ending violence, ensuring security and settling political power struggles in ways which are not detrimental to the donor's own national interest; the second will tend to be more, though not exclusively, driven by policy based on 'best practice' research.

Debate continues to rage about what it is appropriate to 'require' of highly traditional, socially conservative countries emerging from violent conflict in these terms, and to what extent donors should or can adapt their policies in relation to the promotion of women's enjoyment of their human rights. It cannot be assumed that being in favour of increased female representation in the public sphere is a global given; nor can we assume that progressive aid policies in this regard will be the key to transforming attitudes and practices in all societies. Requiring the official removal of burqa as a part of aid conditionality was, for a short time, under discussion in Afghanistan post 9/11, a move which it was soon seen would threaten Afghan women's security much more than it would enhance their freedom or equality at that stage. Kvinna til Kvinna's research in Bosnia–Herzogovina[41] suggests that international organizations still fail to consult adequately with women's organizations in the assessment and planning of programmes, and that, even when they do, they fail to enter into what is perceived as real dialogue or to provide meaningful feedback on what was discussed or eventually decided. This points to the often neglected importance of the messaging and communications of new provisions and strategies which affect women, both to women and to the population at large. Most analysis of peace operations suggests that communications have been under-prioritized, insufficiently imaginative, or simply confusing.[42]

While there are more examples of progress that could undoubtedly be cited at macro and micro level, this discussion indicates that progress has been uneven, and unstrategic, and certainly that the plethora of toolkits and guidelines available have not been systematically in use. This may suggest that more time is needed or more money, or more training. Or perhaps it suggests that better leadership and commitment is needed from the highest levels, and that attitudes at those altitudes have not yet progressed as much as some of the aspirational language used in speeches and declarations might imply.

Conclusion

Perhaps the clearest point demonstrated by this brief survey of issues and literature is not that existing experience of women's involvement, or the employment of gendered perspectives requires significant further analysis; rather, it shows the imbalance between normative frameworks, tools and guidelines and actual experience. By this I mean that women and their perspectives continue to be massively under-represented and considered. The literature shows a staggering imbalance of recommendations over examples of positive practice. We do have some positive examples, but many more are needed to make a significant impact. Now as ever, actions speak louder than words.

This requires the energy, initiative, and commitment of those inside conflict situations as well as those from the outside who play important roles within. And perhaps it can never be stressed too much that leadership by example counts: how can the rich, developed countries who offer their assistance, and who often believe so passionately in the issue of women's equality, expect to be taken seriously when they do not themselves routinely practice what they preach? The difficulties which plague the democracy evangelists today may well be those which also beset crusaders for equality, laying them open to charges of hypocrisy. How can they, it could be asked, require fragile, conflict-devastated states to undertake challenges which they themselves may not have completed or even attempted?

If equality is to be the final word of this chapter, let us not forget that the whole point of the gender concept is to understand women and men in relation to each other and their societal contexts; perhaps, then, one of the factors that could make a real difference to building peace processes which produce sustainable, equitable results would be to see more men among the ranks of activists, strategists, programmers, and implementers for equality and gendered perspectives in peace and security issues.

Notes

* I am particularly grateful to my husband Jonathan Prentice, and my colleagues at the Centre for Humanitarian Dialogue for their comments and advice on this chapter; all mistakes and misjudgements remain of course entirely my own. I hope the chapter can be read as a work in progress.

1. Analysis and reflections are also drawn directly from author's humanitarian and development field experience in Afghanistan, Cambodia, and Timor–Leste.
2. For example, though far from exhaustively, the 1948 Universal Declaration of Human Rights, the 1949 Geneva Conventions and the Additional Protocols thereto, the 1993 Vienna Declaration and Platform of Action on Human Rights, the 1998 Rome Statue of the International Criminal Court, the 2000 European Parliament Resolution On the Participation of Women in Peaceful Conflict Resolution.
3. 1995 Beijing Declaration and Platform of Action, Article 18.
4. N. Hayzer, 'Women, War and Peace: Mobilizing for Peace and Security in the 21st Century', The 2004 Dag Hammarskjøld Lecture (Stockholm: Dag Hammarskjøld Foundation, 2004), p. 19.
5. 2000 Security Council Resolution 1325, Article 142.
6. F. Hill, 'How and When Has Security Council Resolution 1325 (2000) on Women, Peace and Security Issues Impacted Negotiations outside the Security Council', Master Thesis, Uppsala University Programme of International Studies 2004–2005. Note the focus of the argument in this paper is particularly in relation to security and disarmament issues.
7. To name but a few, S. N. Anderlini, *Women at the Peace Table: Making a Difference* (New York: UNIFEM, 2000); *Getting It Right, Doing It Right: Gender and Disarmament, Demobilization and Rehabilitation* (New York: UNIFEM, 2004); C. Chinkin, 'Peace Agreements as a Means for Promoting Gender Equality and Ensuring Participation of Women – a Framework of Model Provisions', *UNDAW, OSAGI, DPA EGM/PEACE/2003/ REPORT*, 10 December 2003; 'Inclusive Security, Sustainable Peace: A Toolkit for Advocacy and Action', International Alert and Women Waging Peace, 2004; J. El Bushra with A. Adrian-Paul & M. Olson, *Women Building Peace: Sharing Know-How Assessing Impact: Planning for Miracles* (International Alert, 2005); P. Harris & B. Reilly (eds), *Democracy and Deep Rooted Conflict : Options for Negotiators* (IDEA, 2003); 'Gendering Human Security: from Marginalization to the Integration of Women in Peace-Building, Recommendations for Policy and Practice', Norwegian Institute of

International Affairs and Fafo Programme for International Co-operation and Conflict Resolution, 2001 and in policy documents by various governments including Canada, Denmark, the UK, and Norway, and by the UN Department of Peace Keeping Operations.

8. This might include asking questions such as whether there is understanding of differential experiences of conflict between men and women and among different groups of women, or what the differential gender divisions in the conflict situation are of for example labour, access to and control of resources etc.

9. This could include considering mechanisms which support women's role in peacebuilding and institutional capacity for this; consideration of individual, public, and state security issues, of women's involvement in political and state structures, or in economic reconstruction etc.

10. These might include women's budgets and associated monitoring mechanisms, special committees in the national legislature, women's multi-party caucuses, a requirement that a certain number of women are present in legislature before a bill is passed, ensuring gender issue representation on every parliamentary committee etc.

11. E. Rehn & E. Johnson Sirleaf, *Women, War, and Peace: The Independent Experts' Assessment on the Impact of Armed Conflict on Women and Women's Role in Peace-Building* (New York: UNIFEM, 2002), p. 64.

12. Interparliamentary Union. Available at http://www.ipu.org/wmn-e/classif.htm (Accessed on 21 March 2007).

13. Global Database of Quotas for Women, International IDEA and University of Stockholm. Available at http://www.quotaproject.org/country.cfm (Accessed on 21 March 2007). Note that quotas may be enshrined in constitutional, electoral law or political party policy, and may have compliance conditions attached.

14. S. Nakaya, 'Women and gender equality in peace processes: From women at the negotiating table to post-war structural reforms in Guatemala and Somalia', *Global Governance*, 9, 4 (October–December 2003), pp. 459–476.

15. For example *Broken Bodies, Broken Dreams: Violence against Women Exposed* (OCHA, 2005), in which numerous statistics of rape in war are cited as proof that it continues to be used as a weapon of war. The report calls for peace agreements and mechanisms of international law to focus on stopping this.

16. For example *Rethink! A handbook for sustainable peace* (Stockholm: Kvinna Til Kvinna Foundation, 2004); On female members of armed groups, D. Mazurana, 'Women in Armed Opposition Groups Speak on War, Protection and Obligations under International Humanitarian and Human Rights Law', Report of Geneva Call and Program for the Study of International Organizations Workshop, Geneva (August 2004); D. Mazurana, 'Women in Armed Opposition Groups in Africa and the Promotion of International Humanitarian Law and Human Rights', Report of Geneva Call and Program for the Study of International Organizations Workshop, Geneva (November 2005).

17. A. Galama & P. van Tongeren (eds), *Towards Better Peacebuilding Practice: On Lessons Learned, Evaluation Practices and Aid and Conflict* (Den Haag, Netherlands: European Centre for Conflict Prevention, 2002), p. 221.

18. 'Report on the Situation of Women in Armed Conflicts and Their Role in the Reconstruction and Democratic Process in Post-Conflict Countries (2005/2215(INI))', *Committee on Women's Rights and Gender Equality, European Parliament Session Document*, reference A6–0159/2006 or RR\370262EN.doc, (3 May 2006), p. 15.

19. J. El Bushra & J. Gardner (eds), *Somalia: The Untold Story – the War through the Eyes of Somali Women* (London: Pluto Press, 2004); S. Hale, 'The Soldier and the State;

Post-Liberation Women: The Case of Eritrea', in M.R. Waller & J. Rzcenga (eds), *Frontline Feminisms: Women, War and Resistance* (New York: Routledge, 2000).

20. For example G. Barker, *Dying to Be Men: Youth, Masculinity and Social Exclusion* (London: Routledge, 2005); D. Smith, 'Women, War and Peace' (chapter Three), in I. Breines, D. Gierycz & B. Reardon (eds), *Towards a Women's Agenda for a Culture of Peace* (Paris: UNESCO, 1999), p. 65.

21. 'Hitting the Target: Men and Guns', Review Conference Policy Brief, Centre for Humanitarian Dialogue, June 2006 (for The United Nations Conference to Review Progress Made in the Implementation of the Programme of Action to Prevent, Combat and Eradicate the Illicit Trade in Small Arms and Light Weapons in All Its aspects).

22. The Northern Ireland Women's Coalition was a non-sectarian political party formed in 1996 expressly to ensure that women's voices were heard at the multi-party talks at which it was able to field two elected delegates. Somali women organized a 'sixth clan', a cross clan grouping of women, to gain access to the first Somali Peace and Reconciliation conference in 2002.

23. Nakaya (October–December 2003), op. cit.

24. Nakaya (October–December 2003), op. cit., p. 470.

25. Nakaya (October–December 2003), op. cit., p. 471.

26. G. Spencer, 'Reporting inclusivity: The Northern Ireland women's coalition, the news media and the Northern Ireland peace process', *Irish Journal of Sociology*, 13, 2 (2004), pp. 43–65.

27. Spencer (2004), op. cit., p. 57.

28. A. Potter, *We the Women: Why Conflict Mediation Is Not Just a Job for Men* (Geneva: Centre for Humanitarian Dialogue, 2005).

29. In fact a set of agreements, dating from 1994 to 1996. Available at http://www.usip.org/library/pa/guatemala/pa_guatemala.html (Accessed on 21 March 2007).

30. Chinkin (10 December 2003), op. cit. Another valuable related resource is C. Bell, *Peace Agreements and Human Rights* (Oxford: Oxford University Press, 2004).

31. Chinkin (10 December 2003), op. cit., p. 2.

32. One such checklist of questions is available in I. Skjelsboek, 'Gendered Battlefields: A Gender Analysis of Peace and Conflict', Peace Research Institute (Oslo) Report 1997.

33. Chinkin (10 December 2003), op. cit., p. 22.

34. E. Rehn & E. Johnson Sirleaf, *Women, War and Peace (Progress of the World's Women)*, Volume 1 (UNIFEM, 2002).

35. Ibid., p. 61.

36. S. Woodward, 'Economic Priorities for Successful Peace Implementation', in S.J. Stedman, D. Rothchild, & E. M. Cousens (eds), *Ending Civil Wars: The Implementation of Peace Agreements* (Boulder CO: Lynne Rienner, 2002).

37. Both recently elected heads of state at the time of writing.

38. S.N. Anderlini 'Negotiating the Transition to Democracy and Reforming the Security Sector: the Vital Contributions of South African Women', Women Waging Peace Policy Commission (August 2004).

39. T. Quintos-Deles, 'Corridors of Peace in the Corridors of Power: Bridging Spaces for Women in Governance for Peace', Speech to International Center for Innovation, Transformation and Excellence in Governance (February 2006), p. 9.

40. Rehn & Johnson Sirleaf (2002), op. cit., p. 66.

41. 'To make room for change – Peace Strategies from women's organizations in Bosnia and Herzegovina', Kvinna Til Kvinna, 2006. Available on the Web site of the United States Institute of Peace, Washington DC, USA.
42. For example S. Chesterman, *You the People: The United Nations, Transitional Administration and Statebuilding* (Oxford: Oxford University Press, 2004); A. Potter, *Assistance to Justice and the Rule of Law in Afghanistan* (Geneva: Centre for Humanitarian Dialogue Report, February 2004).

9
Traditional and Indigenous Approaches to Peacemaking

Roger Mac Ginty

Introduction

Critical accounts of the limitations of internationally supported peace interventions in civil wars often point to strikingly similar failures in peace processes and peace accords. Whether in relation to Bosnia, Bougainville, or elsewhere, critics suggest that peace interventions are often top-down, techno-cratic, fail to deal with the affective dimensions of conflict (such as trust, rec-onciliation, and intergroup perceptions), fail to deliver a broadly shared peace dividend and lack sustainability. In response to the perceived failings of a number of peace processes, some NGOs, international organizations, and com-munities in various contexts are paying attention to indigenous, traditional, or customary approaches to peacebuilding. Such approaches, according to their advocates, offer the potential of peacemaking that is participative, culturally appropriate, low-cost, and sustainable. In other words, traditional and indig-enous peacemaking may be precisely the remedy to complement the apparent failings of the more 'conventional' approaches to peacemaking championed by leading states, international organizations, and international financial institu-tions since 1990. As a result, there has been increased interest in traditional and indigenous peacemaking.

This chapter seeks to clarify what is meant by traditional and indigenous approaches to peacemaking before reviewing the potential advantages they might offer. But caution is required lest traditional and indigenous approaches to peacemaking are regarded as the elixir that can cure all the problems of conventional peacemaking. First, the dislocation associated with civil war has often made traditional and indigenous social patterns unsustainable. Indeed, the descent into civil war may have been facilitated by the failure of traditional and indigenous restraints on conflict. Second, some literature has a tendency to over-romanticize traditional and indigenous practices (and similarly overlook the advantages of conventional approaches to peacemaking). It is important to note that some traditional and indigenous practices can be deeply conservative and exclusionary. For example, they may only be open to men or may emphasize social conformity and the importance of power remaining in the hands of the chiefly classes. Third, there is some evidence that leading states and international organizations, attracted by the apparent advantages offered by traditional and indigenous approaches to peacemaking, are funding and facilitating it. This leads to a fundamental question: can such methods be regarded as 'traditional' or 'indigenous' anymore if they have been co-opted by international organizations?

What is traditional and indigenous peacemaking?

Although often used interchangeably, the terms 'traditional' and 'indigenous' have overlapping but not precisely similar meanings. 'Traditional' denotes a practice or norm that has a heritage of considerable duration. 'Indigenous' suggests that an activity or norm is locally inspired. Crucially, indigenous norms and activities need not be traditional. Indigenous communities, like any other human community, are capable of social adaptation and may embrace (or be compelled to embrace) new forms of social, economic, or political practice. The penetration of mobile phones in relatively remote areas of the globe is a good example of how communities that emphasize customary practice are capable of taking new practices on board.

Traditional and indigenous dispute resolution methods might involve consensus decision making, a restoration of the human/resource ecological balance, and compensation or gift exchange designed to ensure reciprocal and ongoing harmonious relations between groups. Examples include the *Mato-Oput* ceremony among the Acholi in northern Uganda or the *Kgotla* in Botswana. The *Mato-Oput* is a clan-based reconciliation ceremony involving an admission of wrong-doing, an offer of recompense and the sharing of a symbolic drink between disputants. The *Kgotla* takes the form of a community meeting in which everyone has a right to uninterrupted speech and decisions are reached on a consensus basis.[1] Both the *Mato-Oput* and *Kgotla* operate at community level, conform to prevailing cultural norms and aspirations, and require few resources to operate.

Three misconceptions are common to commentary on traditional and indigenous approaches to peacemaking: that they are simplistic; that they are necessarily a good thing; and that they can be regarded as a discrete category quite separate from Western approaches to peacemaking. By dispelling these notions we can reach a greater understanding of the potential and limitations of traditional and indigenous approaches to dispute resolution. To some extent, it is understandable why traditional and indigenous approaches to peacemaking may be regarded as somehow 'simplistic'. Away from the complexity of

Western and apparently 'modern' politics, political practice based on tradition and customary norms may seem in some way primitive, slow-paced, and unsophisticated. They do not draw on Western legalistic notions of sovereignty and constitutionalism, nor use the technocratic language beloved by bilateral and NGO donors. Their use of ritual and symbolism may seem anachronistic and other-worldly. Yet, many traditional and indigenous approaches to dispute resolution depend on highly sophisticated mechanisms that are finely calibrated to suit local norms and expectations. They may be able to accommodate multiple-actors, may be adaptable to changing circumstances, and may rest on sophisticated and complex definitions of 'peace'. Historically, for example, Maori definitions of peace ranged from a temporary tactical peace aimed at securing short-term advantage to more long-lasting varieties of peace with structural safeguards to ensure sustainability.

The second misconception, that indigenous and traditional approaches to peacemaking are automatically superior to alternatives, requires caution. As will be discussed in the next section, many indigenous and traditional approaches offer potential advantages. Yet, some literature has a tendency to inflate these advantages. The *Gacaca* judicial system in Rwanda, for example, has attracted immense commentary, much of it wildly positive.[2] More circumspect commentators, however, have identified problems with the *Gacaca* system, particularly how it may detract from the uniformity and transparency which may be necessary to establish a nation-wide post-peace accord judicial system, and how it may help 'perpetuate a culture of impunity' in a society with high levels of violence in its recent past.[3]

A key problem facing traditional and indigenous approaches to dispute resolution is that the socio-cultural environment upon which they depend may be swept away by civil war and broader global social change to the extent that they can no longer operate (let alone be recreated). Thus, for example, rural-urban migration, a decline in respect for traditional sources of counsel and power, monetization of economic exchange, and the introduction of modern weaponry to disputes that were previously localized and low scale, may create an environment in which traditional and indigenous approaches to dispute resolution have little purchase.[4] As Briggs notes in relation to Inuit dispute resolution practices, 'These ways of managing conflict worked very well in the tightly interdependent world of a hunting camp or small homogenous settlement.'[5] But as Inuit settlements have become larger and more ethnically, linguistically, and economically diverse such methods have limited resonance. A further problem facing traditional and indigenous approaches to peacemaking may be the tendency of some approaches to stamp on social activism and innovation, and to reinforce existing power-holders and conservative practices. Al-Krenawi and Graham note the 'hidden power' of rituals to coax participants into adherence to social order.[6] The conservatism of traditional and indigenous approaches may be antithetical to some of the principles that underpin Western-sponsored peace-support programmes or projects such as the inclusion of women or equity for all ethnic groups. An additional limitation to traditional and indigenous approaches to peacemaking is that they may only function at the very local level, thus restricting their national relevance. While a certain customary dispute resolution practice may be widespread across a broad geographical region, closer examination may reveal local variations. As a result, caution is required when discussing the applicability of traditional and indigenous prescriptions.

Just as important as the need to resist deifying traditional and indigenous approaches to conflict management is the need to resist automatically criticising all Western approaches to peacemaking. The criticisms to such approaches are well known (overly technocratic, top-down, culturally inappropriate etc.), and are covered by many of the chapters in this volume. Yet, in a number of civil war situations (e.g., the Solomon Islands of Haiti), only external powers have had the political will and capacity to intervene in support of peacemaking. In such contexts, traditional and indigenous resources may have been so severely eroded as to be unable to offer anything but the most basic peacemaking or reconstruction assistance.

The third misconception, that traditional and indigenous approaches to peacemaking can be regarded as a discrete category separate from Western approaches to peacemaking, is contradicted by the immense evidence of hybridized peacemaking in which a mix of traditional and Western approaches to peacemaking co-exist. The 'lending and borrowing' between peace processes described by John Darby in Chapter 24 in this book attests to the extent to which social systems are the product of exchange with, and adaptation to, other social systems. As Carolyn Nordstrom makes clear in Chapter 20, civil war contexts are peculiarly penetrated by transnational and international networks. As a result, it is unrealistic to conceive of societies – even remote societies with many traditional aspects – as somehow hermetically sealed to external influences. All peacemaking occurs in contested contexts in which overly homogenized categories such as 'traditional', 'indigenous', or 'western' deserve caution.

The attraction of traditional and indigenous peacemaking

In recent years, ideas of traditional and indigenous peacemaking and dispute resolution in civil war contexts have benefited from an upsurge of interest. This has mirrored a more general increase in interest in indigenous issues as evidenced by the designation of 1995–2004 as the United Nations 'International Decade of the World's Indigenous Peoples'. Although the United

Nations (UN) General Assembly failed to adopt the Declaration on the Rights of Indigenous Peoples, debates and policy concern on the rights, plight, and capacities of indigenous peoples spread far beyond the UN, with the United Kingdom's Department for International Development, the Inter-American Development Bank, the International Labour Organization, the World Bank, and International Non Government Organizations (INGOs) such as Oxfam all showing an interest (rhetorically at least) in indigenous issues, especially in relation to development and poverty reduction.[7]

Three factors help explain the increased interest in traditional and indigenous approaches to peacemaking specifically, and development more generally. The first factor has been the growing understanding of the complexity of conflict by many bilateral donor states, international organizations, international financial institutions, and NGOs. A more sophisticated understanding of conflict, its links with development and the long-term nature of recovery has been internalized in many quarters. This has been aided by conscious lesson-learning by many peace-intervening parties (e.g., through the establishment of the United Nations Peacebuilding Commission or the establishment of the multi-agency Stabilisation Unit by the British government). The growing understanding of the complexity of conflict has been matched by a growing understanding that responses to conflict must also be multi-dimensional, long-term, and flexible. Implicit in this is a recognition that blunt and poorly thought-through interventions by third parties over the past decade and a half have been ineffectual and, at times, counter-productive. There has been an increasing understanding that purely top-down approaches to peacemaking and peace accord implementation risk overlooking (or alienating) local constituencies and that efforts are required to connect elites (national and local) with broader communities and their needs. In this context of multi-dimensional peacemaking, indigenous and traditional approaches to peacemaking may be regarded as one element in a broader suite of peacebuilding techniques. The balance and weighting between these different approaches may differ from context to context and, as will be discussed later, there are concerns about the co-option and subversion of traditional and indigenous approaches by international organizations. The key point though is that a growing number of international actors are positively disposed (rhetorically at least) towards indigenous and traditional dispute resolution and regard it as complementary to more orthodox peace-support interventions.

The other two (interrelated) factors explaining the increased interest in indigenous and traditional approaches to peacemaking are the popularity of the notions of local participation and sustainability in the field of development practice. Both ideas have become cardinal points of development programmes and are increasingly regarded as the means to address perceived failings of previous approaches to under-development. According to proponents of local participation and sustainability, a development programme's chances of success will be improved by maximizing local ownership of the programme (whether a micro-credit scheme or a project to improve school attendance etc.). In order to discourage dependency on external assistance, development interventions may focus on recognizing and utilizing existing local capacities and building new capacities. More far-sighted development interventions have recognized that local participation must move beyond the mere co-option of a handful of (often well-educated, English-speaking, and metropolitan) locals in the implementation of a project or programme to involve broader constituencies of local voices in the conception as well as the implementation of interventions.[8] The perceived advantages of development programming that draws on local sources are that it will be culturally appropriate, will have lower overheads (in the absence of costly expatriate personnel), and will meet with the acceptance of its intended beneficiaries. Ideas of sustainability in development programming are particularly popular among donor states and organizations who are anxious to demonstrate to their primary constituencies (political elites and electorates in Western states) that development assistance will be time-limited and resources are well-spent if they encourage self-reliance.

According to advocates, the key to local participation and sustainability is to tap into existing local resources, coping mechanisms, and understandings of development. Thus, notions of indigenous and traditional peacemaking chime with prevailing best practice (and/or rhetoric) in development. The already mentioned more sophisticated understanding of conflict by some states, international organizations, and NGOs entails an integrated response to conflict in which development issues are dealt with in tandem with conflict issues. Thus it makes sense – for many intervening parties – to apply thinking on development programming (with its emphasis on local participation and sustainability) to peacebuilding. Advocates suggest that by drawing on customary norms, traditional practices and local communities, peace-support initiatives are more likely to gain local acceptance, achieve success, and become self-sustaining. They point to the failings of Western-influenced, top-down, technocratic approaches to peacebuilding and suggest that indigenous and traditional methodologies can reach constituencies and deal with issues often overlooked by international peace-support operations.

A persistent criticism of Western approaches to peacemaking is that they overlook the affective dimension to conflict and its management.[9] Critics argue that such orthodox approaches to peacebuilding emphasize the state, institutions, and technical aspects of post-war recovery such as reform of the bureaucracy or the reconstruction of infrastructure to the exclusion of people. Peace, in this view, risks being reduced to a series of technocratic tasks that are introduced according to a New York, Washington, or Geneva-designed template and with limited reference to local needs or cultural sensitivities. What is missing from many such internationally supported peacebuilding programmes is the thorny, but essential, affective dimension such as intergroup perceptions, trust-building (beyond handshakes between elites), and reconciliation (beyond high-profile truth-recovery events). Critics continue that if raw emotions such as hatred or revenge are not addressed, then Western-inspired peace-support programmes risk restricting themselves to conflict manifestations. By contrast, many local and indigenous approaches to dispute resolution and peacebuilding operate in the affective realm; they are human and community-centric rather than state and institution-centric. Proponents of traditional and indigenous approaches argue that by addressing issues of perceived slights and injured honour these methodologies are able to connect with issues that are local, have very real purchase with communities, and must be dealt with to stave off a resumption of hostilities. The cliché that 'peace is a process rather than an event' is borne out by many traditional and indigenous peacemaking practices that emphasize ongoing relationships, reciprocity, and the fact that territory and resources are shared.

Complementary or co-option?

A number of states, international organizations, and NGOs have championed traditional and indigenous approaches to peacemaking, believing them to hold advantages not on offer from international peacebuilding sources. Thus some international actors have funded, facilitated, and even recreated traditional and indigenous approaches to dispute resolution. The extent of the international involvement raises questions about the degree to which traditional and indigenous practices retain their integrity or trueness to their indigenous and traditional roots. Over-zealous international involvement risks 'contaminating' the process and possibly diminishing its local ownership, cultural appropriateness, and sustainability – the very factors that attract international support in the first place. The examples below suggest a continuum stretching from minimal (if any) external involvement in traditional and indigenous dispute resolution techniques to more intrusive and directive interventions.

The 'purer' forms of indigenous and traditional peacemaking are often found in geographically marginal and resource poor areas in which external actors have little interest. Thus, for example, local communities in remote areas of northern Kenya deploy traditional dispute resolution techniques to regulate pastoralist cattle-raiding. Although these conflicts have been extremely costly in terms of dislocation and lives lost (especially following the introduction of modern weapons), they often occur in areas in which the Kenyan state has little power (or interest) and in areas marginal to geo-political concerns.[10] As a result, traditional dispute resolution techniques, such as the *miss* intertribal peace pacts brokered between elders, are the default response.[11] While such pacts place strong emphasis on ritual performed by elders (with the slaughter of livestock and the burying of weapons), community members have a practical input through donating food, livestock, and weapons for the peace ceremony. The *miss* ceremonies rely heavily on the moral power of community elders and resources from local communities. External interference would be likely to erode their popular legitimacy and ability to effect peace.

A second example, further along the continuum towards greater external involvement in indigenous and traditional peacemaking, comes in the form of the *Nahe Biti* ('laying out the mat') customary mediation process in East Timor.[12] The process operates at the village level and involves the 'victim' bringing a complaint to a traditional leader who facilitates a meeting between the disputants. Following an opening ritual, the disputants present their cases and the traditional leader makes a judgement, imposing a penalty or offering advice where appropriate. The ceremony may end with a statement by the 'guilty' party and a ritual in which the disputants share food and drink. The process is voluntary, only operates in relation to civil or minor cases, and places an emphasis on reconciliation between the disputants and the wider community. Crucially, elements of the international community who have been heavily involved in statebuilding in East Timor, and the East Timorese state itself, have become interested in the *Nahe Biti* process. They have recognized its potential to contribute to post-independence reconciliation and to complement a badly strained criminal justice system.

A Truth and Reconciliation Commission was established in 2002 shortly after independence. While much of the Commission's energies were devoted to investigations of large-scale human rights abuses (largely perpetrated by the Indonesian regime and its proxies), the adoption of the *Nahe Biti* methodology by the Commission allowed it to operate at the community level.[13] Rather than being overly legalistic, or interested in political matters, the *Nahe Biti* mediation process was able to address local grievances, foster community reconciliation, and smooth the re-entry of deponents back into the community. Crucially, the mechanisms of 'confession, contrition and compensation' conformed to public expectations of conflict management and were administered by local communities.[14]

In this case it can be argued that local dispute resolution practices and Western peace-supported peacebuilding were – to a certain extent – complementary. Newly independent East Timor's fledgling judicial system was unable to cope with its case-load and the *Nahe Biti* process proved to be a culturally intuitive, flexible, and widely accepted method of effecting local-level recompense for relatively minor crimes. It did not require the construction of a new system (and the attendant training of personnel and provision of buildings) and so did not raise questions about long-term sustainability. While many international organizations and donors were in favour of the *Nahe Biti* process (to the extent of funding its extension and subjecting it to Western-style evaluations), local actors seemed to be the primary motors behind the system.

A more interventionist and Western-sponsored example of indigenous or traditional peacemaking comes in the form of the Afghan *Loya Jirga* (Grand Council) convened in June 2002 following the defeat of the Taliban regime by the United States and its Northern Alliance warlord allies. *Loya Jirgas* were a traditional consensus decision-making forum whereby tribal chiefs from multi-ethnic Afghanistan could agree on matters of national importance.[15] The unique circumstances of post-Taliban Afghanistan (with the absence of electoral roles or state capacity to organize an election) meant that the *Loya Jirga* mechanism presented itself as an emergency means to legitimize the transitional govern-ment and, in 2003, the draft constitution. The United Nations and INGO com-munity enthusiastically embraced the emergency *Loya Jirga* idea.

A close inspection of the *Loya Jirga* mechanism, and particularly the circum-stances through which it was deployed, raises fundamental questions about the extent to which it can be regarded as traditional or indigenous. The deci-sion to hold the 2002 *Loya Jirga* was taken in Bonn. The last *Loya Jirga* had been held in 1964, with the result that relatively few Afghans had direct experience or knowledge of this form of intergroup dispute resolution. The 2002 *Loya Jirga* was very much a recreation according to the norms that govern Western delib-erative forums. The size of the gathering was increased to 1500 participants in an attempt to achieve multi-ethnic representation and the inclusion of women (the latter being very much a novelty). The sheer scale of the event meant that many delegates did not have an opportunity to speak. To assuage Western concerns, delegates were compelled to sign an affidavit attesting that they had not taken part in crime and human rights abuses. Given that Afghanistan did not have a functioning criminal justice system for decades this was nonsense. The final Western distortion of the *Loya Jirga* came in the venue for the 2002 forum: it was a tented city built by the North Atlantic Treaty Organization (NATO). Yet, from its sponsors' point of view, the emergency *Loya Jirga* was the best that could be envisaged given Afghanistan's unique circumstances and afforded some legitimacy to its post-Taliban transition.

Concluding discussion

As the three examples show, traditional and indigenous approaches to peace-making are informed by the context in which they operate. The East Timorese example shows how international actors can exhibit a light touch in their sup-port of indigenous and traditional dispute resolution without corrupting the essence of such approaches. Indigenous and traditional approaches to peace-making have the potential to address two persistent failings of more orthodox Western approaches to peacemaking. First, they may be able to connect with the often overlooked affective dimension of peacemaking. Western interventions are often required for the 'heavy-lifting' aspects of ending civil wars and implementing peace accords such as providing security, humanitarian assistance, or kick-starting infrastructural reconstruction. The technocratic bias displayed in many Western-inspired peacemaking processes may be insensitive to the affective dimension of peacebuilding such as trust-building or reconciliation. Intergroup attitudes are more likely to change in positive ways if messages are conveyed in a manner that is culturally appropriate (as is the case in traditional and indigenous approaches to peacemaking). Second, Western approaches to peacemaking are often criticized for their top-down nature whereby the peace process is restricted to national and local elites but makes little connection to broader constituencies. Indigenous and traditional approaches to peacemaking, with their emphasis on localism and – in some cases – popular participation, may be able to address this short coming and help connect bottom-up and top-down peacemaking.

Clearly, traditional and indigenous approaches to peacemaking are not applicable to all conflict situations. To be effective, they require a number of precipitants including a secure environment and community acceptance. Such conditions may not prevail in civil war and post-civil war contexts. Indeed, conflicting communities may differ so much in terms of ethnicity, language, and cultural practice that it may be difficult to find a shared basis upon which peace may be built. Yet in other societies where there is basic security, relative cultural homogeneity, and community respect for customary norms, then it may be possible for traditional and indigenous approaches to peacemaking to make a positive contribution to ending civil war and managing tension. The identification of precipitants, or factors that might facilitate the deployment of traditional and indigenous approaches, may in turn help with the identification of types of conflicts to which these approaches can be applied. Such an exercise (beyond the scope of the current chapter) would have the advantage of matching the conflict with the conflict management tool, an approach not always in evidence.

Notes

1. The Lutheran World Federation, 'Inter-Faith Peace Summit: Rediscovering Indigenous Conflict-Resolution Practices', *The Lutheran World Federation: Lutheran World Information* (23 October 2002).
2. This is a traditional village level approach to justice, which – like many forms of restorative justice – brings together perpetrators and victims.
3. S.O. Ilesanmi, 'So that peace may reign: A study of just peacemaking experiments in Africa', *Journal of the Society of Christian Ethics*, 23 (2002) pp. 213–226, at 222.
4. Some of these issues are discussed in M. Fleischer, 'Cattle raiding and its correlates: The cultural-ecological consequences of market-oriented cattle raiding among the Kuria of Tanzania', *Human Ecology*, 26, 2 (1998) pp. 547–572.

5. J.L. Briggs, 'Conflict Management in a Modern Inuit Community', in P. Schweitzer, M. Biesele, & R. Hitchcock (eds), *Hunters and Gatherers in the Modern World* (New York: Berghahn, 2000), pp. 110–124, at 113.

6. A. Al-Krenawi & J.R. Graham, 'Conflict resolution through a traditional ritual among the Bedouin Arabs of the Negev', *Ethnology*, 38, 2 (1999) pp. 163–174 at 170.

7. Foreign and Commonwealth Office, 'UK Priorities: Human Rights – Indigenous Peoples', Available at www.fco.gov.uk (Accessed on 4 January 2007); K. Bhattachan & S. Webster, *Indigenous Peoples, Poverty Reduction and Conflict in Nepal* (Geneva: International Labour Organization, 2005); World Bank, *'Building Social Capital through Peacemaking Circles'* (Washington DC: The World Bank, 2004); Oxfam International, *Towards Global Equity: Strategic Plan, 2001–2004* (London: Oxfam International, 2001).

8. W. Cooke & U. Kothari (eds), *Participation: The New Tyranny?* (London: Zed, 2004); S. Hickey & G. Moran, 'Participation: From Tyranny to Transformation?' Briefing Paper presented at the Development Studies Association conference (London: November 2004) and J. Chopra & T. Hohe, 'Participatory intervention', *Global Governance*, 10, 3 (2004) pp. 289–304.

9. R. Mac Ginty, *No War, No Peace: The Rejuvenation of Stalled Peace Processes and Peace Accords* (Basingstoke: Palgrave, 2006).

10. R. Pkalya, M. Adan, & I. Masinde, *Conflict in Northern Kenya: A Focus on the Internally Displaced Victims of Conflict in Northern Kenya* (Eastern Africa: Intermediate Technology Development Group, 2003), pp. 10–11 and Fleischer (1998), op. cit.

11. R. Pkalya, M. Adan & I. Masinde, *Indigenous Democracy: Traditional Conflict Resolution Mechanisms: Pokot, Turkana, Samburu and Marakwet* (Eastern Africa: Intermediate Technology Development Group, 2004), pp. 35–40.

12. Peace and Democracy Foundation, *Report about Research on Customary Dispute Resolution and Proposed Mediation Model for the Democratic Republic of Timor–Leste* (Dili: Peace and Democracy Foundation, 2004).

13. K.R.X. Gusmão, 'Challenges for Peace and Stability', The Vice Chancellor's Human Rights Lecture by His Excellency President Gusmão at the University of Melbourne (7 April 2003), p. 2 and M. Byrne, *Roads to Reconciliation*, UNIYA-Jesuit Social Justice Centre Occasional Paper 9 (New South Wales: UNIYA, 2005), p. 2.

14. C. Schenk, 'Fostering the Past and Reconciliation in Southeast Asia and the Pacific – A Comparison between Timor–Leste and Bougainville'. Paper Presented at 'From Dealing with the Past to Future Cooperation: Regional and Global Challenges to Reconciliation' conference (Berlin: 31 January–2 February 2005), pp. 6–7.

15. H. Kazem, 'Emergency Loya Jirga: Strength in numbers', *Eurasianet* (5 June 2002). Accessed at <www.eurasianet.org> on 6 March 2006.

10
The Role of the News Media in Peace Negotiations: Variations over Time and Circumstance

Gadi Wolfsfeld

Introduction

One of the most common premises of all peace negotiations is that it is imperative to keep the news media out. The greater the level of media involvement, it is claimed, the more likely the talks will fail. This assumption is, for the most part, correct. It is much more difficult to conduct negotiations within the glare of a spotlight than behind closed doors. It is important however for researchers and policy makers to move beyond this truism and look deeper into the issue.

The role the news media play in negotiations, it turns out, is only one piece in a more complicated puzzle.[1] One cannot separate between the influences the press will have on peace talks from what is happening outside of the negotiating room. When the news media are playing a generally constructive role in the process, and the talks are being held in a mostly supportive environment, press coverage is less likely to have a negative influence on the negotiations. If, on the other hand, the news media are playing a more negative role in the overall process, they are also more likely to have a negative influence on talks. Policy makers who focus exclusively on the more technical issue of how to keep the talks secret are in danger of missing the bigger picture.

The relationship between the press and government can be described as a 'competitive symbiosis'.[2] On the one hand, each side depends on the other to achieve certain goals. The government depends on the news media to pass on information to a variety of audiences, and the press depends on the government to provide it with information and events that can be turned into interesting news stories. Nevertheless, each would like to obtain the most services for the smallest price. The government would like to have total control over the information the press receives and to have it transmitted without criticism or analysis. The media want to have access to all information from as many sources as possible and to process that data as it sees fit. The relationship between governments and the media is an ongoing struggle over who tells the story.

The outcome of this struggle will determine the role the news media play in any political process including a peace process. It is helpful to think of that role in terms of a continuum of independence. On the one side of that continuum would be those situations in which the news media become *government tools* that simply pass on whatever they are told. The opposite extreme would be devoted to those cases in which the news media were *unwelcome intruders* in the process. Here the media become major obstacles as government leaders find themselves constantly reacting to stories either uncovered by the press or planted by others. In the middle of the continuum one finds those cases in which the press plays the role of *informative intermediary* whereby it provides relatively helpful information about the process. In these situations – that many would consider an ideal role for the news media – the media provide independent reports and analyses about what is going on. The news media combine information from a variety of sources that allows them to construct more balanced and sophisticated stories about what is happening.

The key goal for researchers is to better identify those factors that have the greatest influence on the role the media will play both inside and outside the negotiating room. The ideas that will be presented are based on research that I have conducted concerning the role of the news media in political conflicts and peace processes. The Political Contest model[3] attempts to explain how and why the role of the news media in political conflicts varies. The more recent studies have focused specifically on the role of the news media in peace processes.[4]

The empirical research centred on the peace process between the Israel and the Palestinians, between Israel and Jordan and the peace process in Northern Ireland that is based on the Good Friday Agreement. The methodology in each of these cases included in-depth interviews with leaders, advisors, and journalists as well as content analyses of media coverage. The varied circumstances surrounding each of these processes provide important insights about how the role of the media can change.

The political environment and media independence

Political control leads to media control. While this relationship is most obvious concerning non-democratic countries, it can also be applied to those enjoying democratic rule. The most important factor determining a government's level of control over the news media is the extent to which it is able to take control over the political environment. The political environment can be defined as the aggregate of private and public beliefs, discourse, and behaviours concerning political matters within a particular setting and time. It is a 'macro' concept referring to the political situation that confronts political actors attempting to promote their own agenda. What is the distribution of opinions on a particular issue? Who are the major groups and institutions working for and against the government on this topic? What are the most important events that can be linked to the issue? Government leaders and the opposition are in a constant battle to take control over the political environment. The struggle over the news media should be seen as simply one element within this more general competition for political control.[5]

One reason why it is so important to first look at the state of the political environment is because this is exactly what journalists do. The press is much more likely to *react* to political developments than to *initiate* them. A useful way to understand the role of the news media in any political process is to start by looking at the political context, attempt to understand how political actors and journalists interact within the situation, and then examine how the resulting news stories influence the process itself. This idea has been labelled the Politics-Media-Politics (PMP) principle. Changes in the political environment lead to changes in the role of the news media that then lead to further changes in the political environment.[6] This approach differs from others by placing more weight on the political dimension and by arguing that the influence of the news media becomes important in the second stage of the process.

There are two major indicators of governments' level of control over the political environment surrounding a peace process: (1) their ability to mobilize consensus among elites in support of the process; (2) the ability to take control over events and the flow of information associated with the process. The first factor shapes the general political context in which journalists are operating while the second determines the nature of the inputs journalists will use to construct news stories. The greater the leaders' success in each of these areas, the more likely the news media will do their bidding. If they fail in these tasks, the news media have the potential of becoming serious obstacles. As always, it is best to think of success and failure in terms of a continuum rather than a dichotomy.

By far the most important challenge is to mobilize as many elites as possible in support of the peace process. This sets the stage for everything that follows. Journalists depend on their elite sources to give them a sense about which policies are controversial and which are not.[7] They not only reflect those beliefs but they also advance them. They often become advocates for the cause and help define the boarders of legitimacy by treating dissenters as deviants.

The role of the news media in two different wars helps demonstrate this principle. Hallin's work on the Vietnam War shows how in the early years of that conflict, the American news media were extremely supportive of government efforts to 'stop communism'.[8] Anti-war protesters were framed as either crazy or dangerous. Only when respectable elites began to raise questions about the war did the role of the media begin to change, which (I would argue) increased the rate of political change. There was a reverse trend in the Gulf War, albeit in a much shorter time frame.[9] The debate in the Senate over the decision to use force was extremely intensive and the news media reflected that level of dissent and division. Once the hostilities began, however, most elites decided to come together in support of the war effort and the resulting coverage would best be described as celebratory. These are both good examples of the Politics-Media Cycle (PMC).

There is good reason to believe that the level of consensus has a similar influence on the role of the news media in a peace process. When there are deep divisions over the process the news media will (justifiably) focus on these divisions and thus play a more critical and independent role. In those cases in which the opposition to a peace process is relatively small, on the other hand, the news media will feel obligated to run with the tide and become part of the consensus. As noted, this may involve marginalizing those who disagree.

The high level of consensus should also have an influence on the role the news media play in negotiations. First, journalists may be less aggressive looking for stories that raise serious questions about the process. Once a story line has been established, journalists search for information that fits and either ignore or underplay information that run in a different direction.[10] Second, even when journalists do publish negative stories about the negotiations, the damage is likely to be much less. Without a serious challenger able to exploit such information to achieve political advantage, such stories are unlikely to resonate with the general public. Finally, leaders enjoying a high level of political support are in a much better position to take some flak and move on. While negative coverage can completely undermine a weak government, its effects on a powerful government will be considerably less significant.

A second goal for leaders is to take control over events and the flow of information. When governments are in a position to *initiate* events it provides them with important advantages in their relations with the news media. It allows them to carefully orchestrate what happens in the field and to prepare the accompanying spin. When, on the other hand, governments either lose control over events or are forced to react to the actions of others, they find it more difficult to control media coverage. Journalists become less dependent on official sources when they find stories elsewhere.

The control over events and the flow of information can be especially important with regard to the negotiations. Governments must keep the negotiations moving smoothly so that both parties have interest in working together. They also must keep a tight lid on information coming out of the talks. The greater the friction between the two sides the more each will turn to the news media in an attempt to mobilize outside support for its position. The news media are seen as weapons that can be used against the other side.

There is an important lesson here. The path of influence between the level of media involvement and the success of the negotiations runs in *both directions*. Not only does increased media involvement decrease the likelihood of success but also the lower the level of success, the more the media are likely to become involved. When this does take place, the resulting coverage has the potential of making matters even worse. This is another example of the PMP cycle that was mentioned earlier: difficulties in the negotiations lead to damaging press leaks that make it even more difficult to move forward in the negotiations.

When people think about the role of the news media in negotiations they usually focus exclusively on the flow of information. The fact that this topic comes as relatively late in this discussion places this issue within the proper perspective. The struggle for control over information takes place on many fronts, not only in negotiations. News about the peace process is also based on what journalists gather from opposition leaders, from alternative sources within the government, and from the other side, from movement leaders, and from public opinion polls. Whoever provides the best news stories is in the best position to compete for the public agenda.

Here too one must also take into account the level of elite consensus. The greater the level of support for a peace process the less likely there will be massive protests that cast a negative light on the situation and place the government on the defensive. Even more importantly when things do go wrong the media will emphasize the need to get the process back on track. A crisis will probably be framed very differently however when a peace process is considered controversial. There will be an intensive debate over the meaning of the crisis and more critical and pessimistic story lines will emerge.[11]

Every government that is involved in peace talks, however, must inevitably cope with the tradeoff between the need for secrecy and the need for transparency. If all negotiations are kept completely secret, it violates the public's right to know. It also limits the ability of governments to prepare people for the types of concessions that will have to be made in order to move the process forward. If on the other hand, there is no secrecy, the talks have very little chance of succeeding.

Why is secrecy such an essential element in such negotiations? The most important reason has to do with leaders' needs for public posturing. The public wants to achieve peace by paying the smallest price possible. Political leaders interested in moving forward must continually try to convince the public that they are 'winning'. When speaking to their constituencies, leaders stress the need to remain firm and often place their messages within a colourful wrap of patriotic myths and symbols. Above all, they will avoid any appearance of weakness that would play into the opposition's hands. Premature leaks of concessions will severely undermine this strategy.

When both sides begin playing to their constituencies it sours the atmosphere surrounding the talks. Valuable time can be wasted in dealing with public declarations that are offensive to the other side. Negotiators will also find themselves severely limited in their ability to compromise when leaders have promised to remain firm. The type of communication required within the negotiating room is in many ways the exact opposite of what is needed when speaking to the public. Genuine negotiations demand flexibility and at least a minimal amount of empathy. Messages tailored for the public usually entail steadfastness and ethnic loyalty.

The struggle for control over events and the flow of information concerning a peace process is in many ways a microcosm of the more general conflict between officials and journalists. The most important commodity that governments have to offer the press is newsworthy information. When leaders are able to maintain a monopoly on that information, it provides them with tremendous power over the media. When, on the other hand, journalists are in a position to cultivate alternative sources of information it increases their ability to play an independent role. The government loses its power to dictate story lines. This is, for the most part, a healthy development for it provides citizens with a more balanced picture of what is happening. Nevertheless, when governments lose all control over the flow of information media coverage can become a serious obstacle to moving forward.

From the Middle East to Northern Ireland

The three cases alluded to earlier will be used to illustrate the theoretical arguments. One of the most important differences among the three cases was the governments' level of control over the political environment. The Oslo peace process represents a case in which the Israeli government had the least control. That same government, on the other and, had a tremendous amount of control over the environment surrounding the peace process with Jordan. The level of control in the Northern Ireland peace process appears to fall between the other two, but not quite in the middle. For reasons detailed below, I will argue that the situation facing leaders in that part of the world falls closer to the Jordanian case than to Oslo. The goal of the analysis is to demonstrate the close relationship between control over the political environment and the role the news media play in a peace process.

The Rabin Government did have quite a bit of control over the environment during the initial negotiations in Oslo. The talks in Oslo, it will be remembered, were kept completely secret until the breakthrough was announced in August of 1993. One of the intriguing elements in that process was that there were also 'talks' going on in Washington at the same time. The news media were all covering these meaningless talks in the United States, which allowed the actual negotiations to be carried out in complete privacy. There can be little doubt that the fact that the negotiators were kept completely isolated contributed to the success of the talks.[12]

There was also quite a bit of enthusiasm among the public and the press when the initial agreements were announced.[13] The government had a complete monopoly on all of the information about the talks and was able to exploit the complete surprise to their advantage. This short period came to be known as the 'peace festival'; the Israeli news media were filled with euphoric stories about massive economic growth and predictions that a final settlement was just around the corner. The government was also able to initiate a number of grand peace ceremonies that provided wonderful vehicles for promoting peace to the news media and the public. The opposition was caught completely off guard during these first few weeks, and appeared to be running against the political stream.

It was not to last, however. The negotiations that followed were carried out within a very different political environment from what they began. The government was never able to mobilize a broad level of elite consensus is support of the process, had very little control over the flow of events and information about the process. All of these factors led to the news media playing an extremely problematic role in the process. Based on the interviews and content analyses that were carried out, it is fair to conclude that the role of the news media fell closest to the 'unwelcome intruders' at the end of the continuum.[14]

The lack of elite consensus was not surprising. The dispute over how to deal with the occupied territories represents the key division between right and left in Israel. For many years the Israeli public and the Knesset was split completely down the middle over whether or not the country should be willing to make territorial concessions in the West Bank and Gaza. The decision to recognize the Palestine Liberation Organization (PLO) as the legitimate representative of the Palestinian people was also an extremely controversial decision. Arafat was still seen by many in Israel as the leader of a terrorist organizations and Rabin himself had expressed similar views before the elections. The Knesset was split completely down the middle and Rabin found it extremely difficult to mobilize a majority in favour of the interim agreements that were eventually signed.

The atmosphere became even-more negative because of terrorism. The government's inability to take control over these events was its greatest failure. The Israeli news media, which had been so enthusiastic at the start, turned hostile. The coverage of the attacks was nothing short of hysterical and the various news media appeared to competing with one another over who could produce the most shocking coverage. These terrorist attacks provided tremendous advantages to Oslo opponents, especially given the way they were covered. The Rabin government was continually on the defensive trying to justify the process.

The level of control over the flow of information coming from the negotiations themselves tended to vary. There were two different sets of negotiations in the initial years of Oslo and it is interesting to compare them. The first set ended with the signing of the Cairo agreement in May 1994. The media were very involved in these negotiations with both the Israelis and the Palestinians providing journalists with leaks and continual briefings. Both sides agreed that this was a mistake; they decided to keep the press out during the talks that led to the Oslo B agreement that was signed in September 1995. In this case, none of the details of the negotiations was revealed and all agreed that this was a more effective mode of operation.

Once again however, these problems should be understood within the larger context. The government's problems with the flow of information from the negotiations were relatively small compared to what was going on everywhere else. Most of the negative information about the peace process came from members of the opposition, the extremely active and vocal movements working against Oslo, and the terrorist attacks being carried out by Hamas and the Islamic Jihad. The fact that the press became too involved in certain aspects of the negotiations may have made things worst, but it was relatively unimportant in the total scheme of things.

The political environment surrounding the negotiations with Jordan was completely different and so was the role of the news media. The most important feature was the extremely high level of consensus surrounding the agreement. In direct contrast to the other accords, the peace agreement with Jordan received an overwhelming majority in the Knesset: 91 to 3. There were also no major protests against the agreement and no violence during either the negotiations or the final signing. It is hard to imagine a more problem-free peace process between two 'enemies'.

The generally positive relationship between Israel and Jordan was also reflected in the way the negotiations were conducted. The press was informed about where and when the talks would take place but almost nothing about their substance. Some issues, such as the amount of water that was to be given to Jordan, could have proven quite controversial if they had been leaked to the press. Both sides however had a genuine interest in keeping these issues out of the news until they were completed. These talks provide a wonderful illustration of how the causal relationship between media involvement and the success of negotiations runs in both directions. The negotiations went extremely well which meant that neither Israel nor Jordan had any interest in leaking stories to the news media that contributed to the fact that the talks continued to go well.

This case also provides a good example of how political success leads to media success. The Israeli press not only reflected the high level of consensus but it also reinforced it. News stories about the agreement and the numerous ceremonies that followed were tales of celebration. A content analysis of newspaper articles that appeared in the final weeks of that process found that a remarkable 74 per cent of the items were positive and only 5 per cent were negative. Governments rarely enjoy this level of support, especially in peacetime.

The role of the news media in this process falls as close as one can get to the 'government tools' end of the continuum. A particularly revealing incident concerns the major signing ceremony held in the Arava dessert on 17 October 1994.[15] The master of ceremonies for the event was Haim Yavin, the most respected anchor in Israeli television. The fact that a journalist would take an active part in such a ceremony says it all. Any journalist who would have participated in the ceremonies connected with Oslo would have been tainted with political bias. Nevertheless, when 'everyone' agrees, the news media has no need even to feign objectivity.[16]

The final case is the Northern Ireland peace process. The authorities had a fair amount of control over the political environment surrounding the process, especially after the signing of the Good Friday agreement in April 1998. The international commission headed by George Mitchell worked for over two years on the agreement. His efforts eventually proved successful and the agreement received more support across the political spectrum than any previous attempt. Not only was the agreement supported by the major parties from each camp (the Ulster Unionist Party and the Social Democratic and Labour Party) but it was also endorsed by the political parties associated with paramilitary groups (Sinn Féin, The Progressive Unionist Party, and the Ulster Democratic Party). The only major groups to oppose the accord were the Democratic Unionist Party (DUP) and the United Kingdom Unionist Party (UKUP). The level of political consensus was reinforced by the decision to carry out a national referendum on the Good Friday agreement in both Northern Ireland and Ireland. The accord received 71 per cent support in the North and 94 per cent in the South.

The relatively high level of consensus also provided the authorities with a good deal of control over both events and the flow of information. The fact that the paramilitary groups were part of that consensus insured that the level of violence would be kept relatively low. There were also very few public protests against the agreement. This sense of common purpose was also felt in the negotiating room and from all accounts Mitchell was able to keep a fairly tight lid on the discussions.

The news media in Northern Ireland became an enthusiastic supporter of the Good Friday Agreement. This was especially notable in the newspapers that are identified with the different communities. One of the most significant examples of this change was when the unionist newspaper the *Belfast News Letter* and the nationalist *Irish News* published a series of common editorials in favour of the peace process. As the political camps began to move closer on the peace process, so did the newspapers. The culmination of this cooperation was the fact that both newspapers asked the readers to vote 'yes' in the referendum.

The interviews reveal that this is another example of the PMP cycle. Previous agreements, such as the Anglo–Irish agreement of 1985, were much more controversial, especially among Protestants. The *Belfast News Letter* constantly criticized the agreement, while the *Irish news* was much more positive. As the major political parties moved together so did the news media and there is good reason to believe that this made it easier for the government to mobilize public support.

It was argued earlier that the level of consensus sets the stage for everything that follows. One of the most telling demonstrations of this point concerns the manner in which the Northern Ireland press dealt with the terrorist bombing at Omagh that took place in August of 1998. The goal of that attack was to derail the peace process. However, examining the news coverage of that incident and listening to the interviews that were carried out, it seems that the bomb had exactly the opposite effect. The major lesson for the news media was the need to *speed up the process* so that such tragedies would never happen again. This was very different from what happened in Israel, where terrorist attacks led the press to raise serious questions about the wisdom of the peace process.

Thus, the fact that the news media played a relatively supportive role for the peace process in Northern Ireland can be related to the fact that those journalists were working in a very conducive atmosphere. This does not mean that they played an ideal role. Interviews with those who were opposed to the Good Friday Accord are replete with charges of pro-government bias. When the news media move closer to the 'government tools' end of the continuum they are more likely to either ignore or discredit opponents. One would need more evidence before deciding that this is what happened in Northern Ireland. However, there is good reason to suspect that the pro-peace enthusiasm of the media may have made it more difficult for the 30 per cent who opposed the accord to express their opinion.[17]

Conclusion

The major point of this essay was to encourage peace scholars and practitioners to adopt a broader perspective when looking at the role of the news media in negotiations. The optimal approach is to start by looking at the surrounding political environment concerning the peace process, then attempt to understand how this influences the production of news, and only then examine the more specific influences on the process. Governments who are able to mobilize a good deal of political consensus in support of their efforts and to exert a fair amount of control over events and information have little to fear from the news media.

There is both good and bad news here for those interested in the promotion of peace. The good news is that the media can, in some circumstances, play an extremely constructive role in a peace process. In the Jordanian peace process and the one in Northern Ireland, the news media were important agents in creating a conducive atmosphere for reconciliation. The bad news is that there is no simple means of mobilizing the news media to one's cause. The hard work of politics comes first. Only when leaders have been successful on the political front can they expect to get much help from the news media.

One could argue that from a normative point of view this is as it should be. The story lines adopted by the press *should* reflect the distribution of opinions and beliefs in the more general society. An agreement that enjoys a good deal of political support should receive much more positive coverage than one that is marred by controversy. There is something to that point.

It is not that simple, however. A fuller understanding of the issue must also look at the role the news media play before leaders can even consider a peace process. The news media are much more interested in conflict than in peace. They are much more likely to deal with threats than opportunities especially in coverage of the enemy. It can be argued that one cannot really understand the role of the news media in attempts at reconciliation without first looking closely at the extensive damage they do in wartime. The news media are more likely to raise the flames of hatred than to lower them. Therefore, the local news media make it more difficult for leaders even to begin a peace process. Perhaps this might be one reason why there are so many international conflicts and so few peace processes.

Thus, the fact that the news media played a positive role in two out of the three cases is misleading. First, one must think about all of the instances in which the news media make it more difficult even to *initiate* a serious peace process. Such cases are automatically excluded from the study. Second, one must bear in mind the role of the media in the many years leading up to these breakthroughs. There is good reason to believe, for example, that the news media played a much more inflammatory role in the previous attempts to bring peace to Northern Ireland.

The news media then are best thought of as fair-weather friends. In times of trouble, when they could do the most good, they only make things more difficult. When the sun is shining and everything is going well they are all too happy to participate in the celebration. The news media can make a positive contribution to a peace process. However, they only do so when most of the really difficult work has already been completed.

Notes

1. There is relatively little written on the topic of media and peace, especially compared to what has been written on the role of the media in conflict and war. Notable exceptions include G.F. Adam & R. Thamotheram, The Media's Role in

Conflict: Report Reviewing International Experience in the Use of Mass-Media for Promoting Conflict Prevention, Peace and Reconciliation (Geneva: Media Action International, 1996); P.A. Bruck & C. Roach, 'Dealing with Reality: The News Media and the Promotion of Peace', in C. Roach (ed.), *Communication and Culture in War and Peace* (Newbury Park CA: Sage, 1993); J. Galtung, 'High road, low road: Charting the course for peace journalism', *Track Two*, 7 (1998) pp. 7–10; S. Gutierrez-Villalobos, 'The Media and Reconciliation in Central America', in E. Gilboa (ed.), *Media and Conflict: Framing Issues, Making Policy, Shaping Opinions* (Ardsley: Transnational Publishers, 2002), pp. 295–309; S. Himmelfarb, 'Impact is the mantra: The "common ground" approach to the media', *Track Two*, 7 (1998) pp. 38–40; S. Jaeger, 'Reconciliation and the mass media: The coverage of the French-German peace process after World War II', *Conflict and Communication Online*, 2, 2 (2003); J. Lynch, Findings of the conflict and peace journalism Forum, Unpublished manuscript (Buckinghamshire: Tablow Court, 1998); R. Manoff, 'Role plays: Potential media roles in conflict prevention and management', *Track Two* ,7 (1998) pp. 11–16; R. Manoff, 'The media's role in preventing and moderating conflict', *Crossroads Global Report* (March/April 1997) pp. 24–27; R. Manoff, The mass media and social violence: Is there a role for the media in preventing and moderating ethnic, national, and religious conflict? Unpublished Paper (New York: Center for War, Peace, and the News Media, New York University, 1996); C. Roach, 'Information and Culture in War and Peace: Overview', in C. Roach (ed.), *Communication and Culture in War and Peace* (Newbury Park CA: Sage, 1993); D. Shinar, 'The Peace process in cultural conflict: The role of the media', *Conflict and Communication Online* 2 (2003) pp. 1–10; C. Spurk, *Media and Peacebuilding: Concepts, Actors and Challenges* (Bern: Swisspeace Center for Peacebuilding, 2002); G. Wolfsfeld, *Media and the Path to Peace* (Cambridge: Cambridge University Press, 2004). There are a number of studies that deal with such topics as the role of the media in foreign policy and diplomacy: R. Cohen, *Theatre of Power: The Art of Diplomatic Signalling* (London: Longman, 1987); Y. Cohen, *Media Diplomacy: The Foreign Office in the Mass Communications Age* (London: Frank Cass, 1986); J. Fromm, M. Gart, T.L. Hughes, P. Rodman & L. Tanzer, 'The Media Impact on Foreign Policy', in H. Smith (ed.), *The Media and the Gulf War* (Washington DC: Seven Locks Press, 1992); E. Giboa, 'Mass communication and diplomacy: A theoretical framework', *Communication Theory*, 10 (2000) pp. 275–309; E. Gilboa, 'Media diplomacy: Conceptual divergence and applications', *Harvard International Journal of Press/Politics*, 3 (1998) pp. 56–75; N. Gowing, Media Coverage: Help or Hindrance in Conflict Prevention? Unpublished paper (New York: Carnegie Commission on Preventing Deadly Conflicts, 1996); G. Henderson (ed.), *Public Diplomacy and Political Change: Four Case Studies, Okinawa, Peru, Czechoslovakia, Guinea* (New York: Praeger, 1973); P. O'Heffernan, 'Mass Media and US Foreign Policy: A Mutual Exploitation Model of Media Influence in U.S. Foreign Policy', in R.J. Spitzer (ed.), *Media and Public Policy* (Westport CT: Praeger, 1993); P. O'Heffernan, *Mass Media and American Foreign Policy* (Norwich NJ: Ablex, 1991); P. Robinson, 'Theorizing the influence of media on world politics: Models of media influence on foreign policy', *European Journal of Media on World Politics*, 16 (2001) pp. 523–544; S. Serfaty (ed.), *The Mass Media and Foreign Policy* (New York: St. Martin's Press, 1991) and W.P. Strobel, *Late Breaking Foreign Policy: The News Media's Influence on Peace Operations* (Washington DC: United States Institute of Peace, 1997). Several works relate to the problems peace movements face in attempting to mobilize the news media: T. Gitlin, *The Whole World Is Watching*

(Berkeley CA: University of California Press, 1980); Glasgow University Media Group, *War and Peace News* (Philadelphia PA: Open University Press, 1985); R. Hackett, *News and Dissent: The Press and Politics of Peace in Canada* (Norwood NJ: Ablex Publishing Co., 1991); C. Ryan, *Prime Time Activism: Media Strategies for Grassroots Organizing* (Boston MA: South End Press, 1991) and M. Small, 'Influencing the decision-makers: The Vietnam experience', *Journal of Peace Research*, 24 (1987) pp. 185–198. A few articles and chapters deal with the role of the news media in disarmament and international cooperation: P.A. Bruck & C. Roach, 'Dealing with Reality: The News Media and the Promotion of Peace', in C. Roach (ed.), *Communication and Culture in War and Peace* (Newbury Park CA: Sage, 1993); P.A. Bruck, 'Strategies for peace, strategies for news research', *Journal of communication*, 39 (1989) pp. 108–129; W. Dorman, R.K. Manoff & J. Weeks, *American Press Coverage of U.S.–Soviet Relations, the Soviet Union, Nuclear Weapons, Arms Control, and National Security: A Bibliography* (New York: Center for War Peace and the News Media, 1988) and W.A. Gamson & D. Stuart, 'Media discourse as a symbolic contest: The bomb in political cartoons', *Sociological Forum*, 7 (1992) pp. 55–86. Several publications are concerned with images of the enemy: R.W. Ayres, 'Mediating international conflicts: Is image change necessary?', *Journal of Peace Research*, 34 (1997) pp. 431–447; J.A. Becker, 'A disappearing enemy: The image of the United States in Soviet political cartoons', *Journalism and Mass Communication Quarterly*, 73 (1996) pp. 609–619; W. Eckhardt, 'Making and breaking enemy images', *Bulletin of Peace Proposals*, 22 (1991) pp. 87–95; R. Ottosen, 'Enemy images and the journalistic process', *Journal of Peace Research*, 32 (1995).

2. G. Wolfsfeld, *Media and Political Conflict: News from the Middle East* (Cambridge: Cambridge University Press, 1997).
3. G. Wolfsfeld, 'Promoting peace through the news media: Some initial lessons from the Oslo peace process', *Harvard International Journal of Press/Politics*, 2 (1997) pp. 52–70.
4. Wolfsfeld (2004), op. cit.
5. Ibid.
6. Ibid.
7. W.L. Bennett, 'Toward a theory of press-state relations in the United States', *Journal of Communication*, 40 (1990) pp. 103–125.
8. D. Hallin, *The Uncensored War* (New York: Oxford University Press, 1986).
9. G. Wolfsfeld, *Media and Political Conflict: News from the Middle East* (Cambridge: Cambridge University Press, 1997).
10. H. Brosius & P. Epp, 'Prototyping through key events: News selection in the case of violence against aliens and asylum seekers in Germany', *European Journal of Communication*, 10 (1995) pp. 391–412; H.M. Kepplinger & J. Habermeir, 'The impact of key events on the presentation of reality', *European Journal of Communication*, 10 (1995) pp. 371–390; J. Lederman, *Battle Lines: The American Media and the Intifada* (New York: Henry Holt and Company, 1992) and Wolfsfeld (2004), op. cit.
11. Wolfsfeld (2004), op. cit.
12. D. Makovsky, *Making Peace with the PLO: The Rabin Government's Road to the Oslo Process* (Boulder CO: Westview Press, 1995) and U. Savir, *The Process* (New York: Random House, 1998).
13. Wolfsfeld (2004), op. cit.
14. It is worth noting that this conclusion runs completely against conventional wisdom in Israel. The assumption is that because many Israeli journalists are thought to identify with the political left they make a concerted effort to provide positive

coverage. However, when professional considerations compete with ideological considerations, the former will normally win out. See Wolfsfeld (2004), op. cit.

15. An interesting side note concerns the timing of the event. It was held in the middle of the afternoon – despite the predictably oppressive heat – so that the ceremony (and President Clinton) could be shown live on 'Good Morning America'.

16. It is worth noting that the role of the news media in the peace building stage that occurred in the years after the signing of the agreement was much less positive. Studies of the role of both the Jordanian and Israeli press during these years reveals that the Jordanian media published massive amounts of negative coverage of Israel while the Israeli press mostly ignored Jordan, in part because that country was no longer a threat (Wolfsfeld, Khouri, and Peri, 2002). Here too the best explanation for these patterns can be found in the changing political environment surrounding the relations between the two countries.

17. A content analysis of editorials appearing in a number of newspapers provides support for this proposition (Wolfsfeld, 2004). A study of editorials that were written in the wake of twenty-two key events found 126 editorials in favour of the process, twenty-three expressing a more ambivalent attitude, and only two that were opposed.

Part III

Violence and Peace Processes: An Introduction

John Darby and Roger Mac Ginty

Long-running conflicts are often characterized by the structural nature of violence. Whether from state or non-state sources, many forms of violence are subtle and embedded in political and social dynamics. Peace initiatives can be interpreted as a threat and spark an increase in violence. An ending of major violence from the main militant groups is almost always a prerequisite for their inclusion in peace negotiations. The state will be expected to tone down its security measures too. But parties and militants in peace processes are rarely the homogenous blocs they might seem to outsiders. Peace initiatives place participants under enormous strain and can prompt dissent and breakaways.

Armed spoilers, dedicated to derailing any peace initiative, have become a feature in many peace processes. Popularly derided as 'wreckers', they are often sophisticated in the targeting of their violence. The purpose is to shock public and political opinion, through deliberately gratuitous acts of violence, into applying pressure on participants to withdraw from talks. Beyond that, the spoiler's agenda may reflect vested interests in the continuation of the conflict or a manoeuvring for power within a bloc. Neutralizing spoiler violence is often dependent on the spoiler's military capability and popular support, and the ability of the negotiators to build a process capable of withstanding the spoiler's assault.

The legacy of violence stretches from human costs and opportunity costs such as lives lost or devoted to an armed struggle, to criminality fuelled by former combatants or farmland wasted through landmines or pollution. The solutions to these problems tend to be expensive, politically sensitive, and longterm, but failure to address them can jeopardize the survival of a peace accord.

11
Peace Processes and the Challenges of Violence

Stephen John Stedman

Violence poses fundamental challenges to peace settlements. Peace processes are often rife with strategic and tactical deception, and even those who sign peace agreements may cultivate violence in order to undermine their new 'partners' in peace. Multiple actors in civil wars rarely simultaneously choose peace; those who seek to end a violent conflict will often face opposition from parties who are excluded or who exclude themselves from peacemaking. Such spoilers – leaders and factions who view a particular peace as opposed to their interests and who are willing to use violence to undermine it – pose a grave threat to those who risk making peace.[1] Beyond strategic and tactical uses of violence, there is the obvious need to convince those with the guns to lay them down and reconstruct their lives in a peaceful manner. War may end, but if former combatants lack jobs and skills and if weapons are easily available, then violent crime may increase and rob citizens of their security and their hopes for a robust peace dividend. Finally, there are the effects of past violence: addressing the needs of victims and examining issues of accountability and culpability for atrocity and murder.

Not all peace processes, however, are equally vulnerable to violence. Just as there are cases where analysts assert that violence destroyed incipient coalitions for peace, there are others where scholars assert that violence pushed hesitant elites to full settlement.[2] This then is the puzzle identified by Tim Sisk and John Darby, among others: when and why does violence sometimes act as a catalyst for making peace, and when and why does violence destroy potentially promising peace processes? Possible answers include environmental variables such as number of parties, issues at stake, and economic interdependence; the strategies of elites in the face of violence; and attitudes and support for peace among followers.

In this chapter, I approach this question with an emphasis on the short-term implementation of peace agreements. I do so for two reasons. First, I approach the question of violence and peace processes from a belief that peace is most vulnerable in the short term. When countries emerging from civil war revert to large-scale bloodshed, it is usually within the first five years of reaching a peace agreement. Second, I think that we know more about protecting peace in the short term than we know about healing societies in the long term. It is not that longer-term processes associated with peacebuilding, such as establishing a culture of accountability, reconciling former enemies, consolidating democracy, and fostering human rights, are unimportant. However, precisely because they are long-term processes, our ability at any given time to have a large effect on the success or failure of such processes as reconciliation is limited. Moreover, we certainly do not want our evaluation of short-term implementation held hostage to the achievement of processes that likely take decades.

I argue that peace processes differ in their vulnerability to violence; the presence of spoilers, spoils, and hostile neighbours pose the gravest threats to fledgling peace processes. These threats tend to be more manageable by local parties when there is a high degree of economic interdependence, a local tradition of formal democratic politics, and a lively civil society. When such factors are absent, the role of international actors in combating spoilers becomes paramount. Based on research on successful peace implementation I argue that there are clear priorities to sustaining peace processes. The first is to overcome or minimize the threat of spoilers; the second is to demobilize soldiers and reintegrate them into civilian life; and the third is to sow the seeds for future long-term peacebuilding by assisting the reform of police and judiciaries, supporting wider disarmament in society, and building local capacity for human rights and reconciliation. These priorities address the problems of violence that I mention in my opening paragraph: the strategic and tactical use of violence to undermine peace, the potential rise in criminal violence that can rob peace of its value, and finally, undoing the psychological and physical traumas of violence.

I begin by reviewing several strands of literature on implementing peace agreements. I first discuss what we know about environmental factors that make the realization of peace more or less difficult in war-torn societies. I then turn to the key tasks of implementing peace agreements and briefly review insights from three different literatures: spoilers in peace processes, demobilization of combatants, and peacebuilding. Finally, I present a new avenue of research on peace implementation that focuses on how different constituencies view the meaning of implementing peace agreements.

The conflict environment and the effect of violence on peace settlements

Early research on peacemaking in civil wars viewed conflicts in a differentiated manner and hypothesized that efficacy of mediation was related systematically to the presence or absence of important variables endogenous to the conflict. The pioneering work in this regard was I. William Zartman's work on ripeness, which posited that all things being equal, civil wars were more amenable to mediation when the parties had reached a hurting stalemate – where no party sensed it could win, but where all parties sensed that they would be dramatically worse off if conflict continued.[3] My own early work on peacemaking in civil wars took a different tack, but, like Zartman, hypothesized that civil wars differed in terms of likelihood of settlement. My first book focused on group dynamics within warring parties, as well as the presence or absence of leaders who either suffered from decision-making pathologies or simply saw the conflict in all-or-nothing terms and were unable to make necessary concessions to settle.[4]

Beginning in the mid-1990s a second wave of scholarship in civil war termination rejected the insights of the ripeness approach and approached civil war in an undifferentiated manner: El Salvador was Angola was Northern Ireland was Rwanda. The challenges of making peace were generic – overcoming the security dilemma and related commitment problems, building trust and confidence among adversaries, and problem solving to address the security needs of the warring parties. The most potent weapons for overcoming those challenges were provided by outsiders in the form of attention, resources, and guarantees.[5] The problem for this research is that given an undifferentiated treatment of the problem, prescribed solutions tend to be open-ended. That is, more resources, more attention, and stronger guarantees are always suggested, with a resulting danger of tautology: if international actors are willing to do all it takes to make peace, then peace will be made.

Recent work has made great progress in identifying attributes of civil wars that make them more or less amenable to peacemaking. The implication for those concerned with violence and peace processes is that some peace settlements are more vulnerable to extremist violence than others. A study of international implementation of peace agreements in civil wars finds that successful ending of civil wars is much more difficult when there are more than two warring parties; when at least one of the parties is fighting for secession; when coercion has played a large role in producing the peace agreement; when there are more than 50,000 soldiers; when the state has collapsed; when there are easily identifiable spoilers; when there are neighbouring states that oppose the peace settlement; and when there are valuable, easily marketed commodities such as diamonds or timber.[6] The study found that the last three variables – spoilers, spoils, and hostile neighbours – often found in tandem, posed the greatest dangers to peace settlements. Spoilers are more likely to oppose peace when they are assured of support from neighbouring states and if they can grab valuable spoils that can enable them to continue their fight.

A new exciting line of research asks the question in a different way: what variables might provide some peace settlements with greater immunization against extremist violence? Elizabeth Wood, for example, argues that economic interdependence between or among warring parties provides a powerful incentive for them to cooperate in the face of spoilers.[7] Wood contrasts South Africa where the well-developed industrial economy created incentives for the parties to work together for a mutually beneficial outcome with Angola where the lack of economic development and the economy's reliance on oil and diamond exports forged a winner-take-all, zero-sum approach to the conflict. The lack of economic interdependence and an end game that will likely produce separation help to explain why the parties in the Israeli-Palestinian conflict are unable to sustain cooperation against spoilers and collapse into mutual recrimination in the face of extremist violence.[8]

Another contextual variable that may help parties overcome spoiler threats is the provision of international resources. Usually, scholars do not treat international attention and commitment as a contextual variable and by defining it as international will make the error of treating it as completely voluntary. Yet research shows that cases will vary predictably in the amount of international resources and attention they receive.[9] To the extent that the case engages the national interests of a major or regional power, the more likely the case will receive adequate attention and resources. The United States and Europe have provided more than $16 billion to peace implementation in Bosnia since 1995, which by 2001 translates into more than $4200 a person in that war-torn country. In contrast, international actors provided about $35 million to implementing the Arusha Accords in Rwanda during 1993–1994, or about $4 a Rwandan.

It may be possible that when international actors do too much, and play too great of a role in implementing peace, as in Bosnia, it creates perverse incentives for local parties not to take cooperative steps in making peace themselves: an excess of international involvement can deter local ownership of a peace settlement.[10] The international role in implementation should be fine-tuned to the difficulty of the implementation environment. As Doyle and Sambanis argue, where difficulty is high, and local capacities are weak, international actors must increase the resources allotted to making and building peace.[11]

Priorities in peace implementation

Peace agreements often involve multiple pledges, which then translate into implementation sub-goals: demobilization, disarmament, elections, human rights, refugee repatriation, economic reconstruction, reforming police, and establishing accountability. Given a world of limited resources and time, what tasks in peace implementation should receive priority? To protect an incipient peace against the threat of violence, priorities must be given to overcoming spoilers, demobilizing soldiers, providing civilian security, and building up local capacity for peace.

Priority 1: overcoming the threat of spoilers

In previous works I have called attention to the role of spoilers as destroyers of peace agreements and have put forth a typology of spoilers based on their position in the peace process, number of spoilers, type based on intent, and whether the locus of spoiling behaviour lies with the leader or followers of the party. Of crucial importance is the motivation and intent of the spoiler. Does it have limited demands that can be met through inducements? Is it a total spoiler, who sees power as indivisible, and will use any inducement to its strategic advantage? Or is the spoiler greedy, that is possessing goals that expand based on the prospect of appeasement?[12]

Several articles have taken issue with or attempted to refine the spoilers' concept. In particular, four aspects of the original formulation have come under criticism. First, it is said that since it is impossible to identify *ex ante* what type of spoiler one faces, the concept has little predictive or prescriptive value.[13] Second, it is argued that the definition of total spoiler type as immutable is problematic, given the propensity of what are described as total spoilers at one time to change.[14] Third, it is argued that too much attention to spoiler motivation detracts from the much more important considerations of capability and opportunity to spoil.[15] Fourth, some have questioned my emphasis on the role of international actors in overcoming spoiler problems; that attention needs to be paid to strategies that local peacemakers can pursue to moderate spoiler threats.[16]

Marie-Joëlle Zahar calls into question the usefulness of the typology by arguing that ex ante it is impossible to know what kind of spoiler one is confronting.[17] This seems to me an academic criticism distant from the realities of peacemaking, deception, and violence. Indeed, if I understand the criticism correctly it is that the spoiler concept does not eliminate the possibility of strategic deception in peace negotiations. After all, if there was a magic indicator of type, then no party could act to deceive; they would all wear Ts, Ls, or Gs on their chest.[18]

It is impossible to know any type that is based on intention: we are not mind readers. Given that fact, the search for scientific indicators of type misses the point: if we are uncertain about intention, we need to look for intelligence (not indicators) about intention; and then we must update our prior assessments on new intelligence. Intelligence will always be fallible; if it were not the case, intelligence failures would be outdated and the world would be a safer place.

Let me walk through this step by step. We need to enter into peace implementation with an appreciation of uncertainty and incomplete information. This seems to me superior to blithely assuming that all parties that sign peace agreements do so in good faith, or are equally trustworthy. In some cases, we will want to be particularly vigilant to greater likelihood of spoiler behaviour, for instance when a rebel group such as the Revolutionary United Front in

Sierra Leone hacks off the arms and legs of non-combatants, including children and infants, as a standard tactic, or for instance, when a rebel group such as the Khmer Rouge is responsible for millions of deaths by implementing an economic development policy based on forced evacuation of cities and the killing of people who wear eye-glasses. We will also want to be aware that rebel leaders who spend decades in the bush, surrounded by sycophants who assure them that the world revolves around them, may not be able to conceive of power as divisible.

But since the goal at the beginning of implementation is to keep an open mind to the possibility of insincere signatories to an agreement, even where we have good reason to doubt that sincerity, mediators need to try to move forward by including the party. We then judge compliance, and assess motives for non-compliance, best accomplished through intelligence – informants, surveillance, reading of documents and the like. For instance, if an informant comes to a peace implementer and describes in detail arms caches, militias, and lists of ethnic opponents who are to be killed at a rate of 50,000 a week, we should probably update our prior assessment about spoiler likelihood and type. This, of course, happened in Rwanda in January 1994, and the failure of the United Nations to update its belief in the commitment of the Rwandan government to peace contributed to the ensuing genocide.

Nevertheless, can some total spoilers change? Zahar and Darby argue that there are examples of factions who are labelled total spoilers at one time, who then years later are willing to negotiate a settlement. Accordingly, they call into question whether there is such a thing as a total spoiler that holds immutable preferences for total power. Several issues here deserve discussion. The mere fact that some analysts describe a faction as a total spoiler at a given time seems irrelevant for two reasons best referenced through the examples that Zahar provides: the Palestine Liberation Organization (PLO) in the 1970s and 1980s and the Irish Republican Army (IRA), or the Ulster Defence Association (UDA) in Northern Ireland. First, my article went to great lengths to insist that spoilers can only be defined in relationship to a given peace agreement. In the absence of an agreement, the concept of spoiler should not apply. Second, the main fact of abhorrent behaviour and totalistic rhetoric in the past does not create a total spoiler in and of itself. Again, as I pointed out, most parties in civil wars engage in atrocities and many use total rhetoric; the early dismissal of a faction as totalistic is usually done for political reasons to delegitimize it rather than to provide any objective sense of whether there is a compromise to which it might agree. Third, in each of these examples, just as there were critics who portrayed the PLO, IRA, and UDA as irreconcilable, totalistic factions, there were those who were sympathetic with them and characterized them as reasonable, justice-seeking, parties capable of weighing costs and benefits of war, and concessions.

In my article, I did point out a route whereby a party that is a total spoiler can change. When the locus of the spoiler problem lies with a single leader who, for whatever reason, sees a war in an all-or-nothing fashion, there is the potential for the party to change type when the leader changes.

A third criticism holds that intent may not be as important in determining threat as capability and the opportunity structure available to would-be spoilers. This I think is an important refinement of the concept; it calls attention to aspects of the conflict environment that make spoilers a greater threat in some cases than others. Where spoilers have access to easily tradable, valuable commodities, and where they can rely on the support of neighbouring countries who oppose peace, then spoilers are more likely and a greater threat to peace.

Finally, a fourth criticism holds that my article placed too great of an emphasis on the role of international actors in overcoming spoiler threats. Cetinyan and Stein, citing evidence from the Middle East and Northern Ireland, note that if peacemakers anticipate challenges from spoilers, then they can create strategies to isolate them and prevent them from destroying agreements. Zahar argues that since there are a few agreements that have been implemented without international custodians, they are neither necessary nor sufficient to marginalize spoilers.

The fact that there are two to three peace processes where domestic peacemakers were able to marginalize spoilers does not mean that in the great majority of cases international custodians are irrelevant. Again, taking a differentiated view of civil wars is needed. The examples that are cited of self-implementing agreements are usually South Africa, Northern Ireland, and the Middle East. We will disregard the problematic evaluation of the latter two as processes in motion, difficult to measure as successful. These examples suggest that spoilers have different origins and pose different threats to peace depending on the level of development; in a war-torn country where there is a history of democracy and some democratic accountability to constituents, where there is a baseline minimum of industrialization, and where there exists a thriving civil society, the threat of spoilers is very different than where none of these variables obtain. Where power and resources seem indivisible, where leaders lack democratic constraints, and where there are few groups who are independent of the men with guns, spoilers pose a greater threat.

Priority 2: demobilization of soldiers

Beyond overcoming the threat from spoilers, the demobilization of soldiers and their reintegration into civilian life is the *single most* important sub-goal of peace implementation.[19] The ending of a civil war hinges on the willingness of competing armies to relinquish self-help solutions to their insecurity, to demobilize their soldiers, and in most circumstances, to create a new, integrated army. These are processes, however, that are fraught with risks for antagonists.

International implementers can reduce such risks by acting as guarantors – by deterring any party from taking advantage of their adversary's vulnerability, and by protecting any party that is taken advantage of during demobilization. Such guarantees, however, are seldom forthcoming from implementers. With the exceptions of the North Atlantic Treaty Organization (NATO) in Bosnia, Syria in Lebanon, and the Economic Community of West African States (ECOWAS) (on occasion) in Liberia and Sierra Leone, implementers have not committed to such guarantees. Most implementers of peace agreements limit their role to monitoring, verifying, and facilitating demobilization.

Such monitoring has been flawed by the lack of an intelligence capacity to assess the motives behind violations of demobilization agreements and by the unwillingness of implementers to set and maintain strict standards of compliance. An assessment of motives is important because cheating is pervasive in the demobilization of soldiers. There are different motives for cheating – motives that have important implications for the prospects of successful war termination. Starting with the most benign among them, warring parties may hold troops back from demobilization as a form of insurance against adversary attack. Less benignly, parties may keep troops in reserve in order to gain a potential advantage in elections, even deploying them for the purpose of electoral intimidation. Finally, the most malignant motive for cheating is a deliberate effort to sucker an opponent or take military advantage of a rival who, already having complied with demobilization accords, is strategically vulnerable.

Since motives are important for outcomes, a premium should be placed on the robust monitoring and verification of demobilization. The greatest danger stems from implementers who are lax in acknowledging, reporting, or responding to violations of demobilization agreements. In Angola, implementers did not call the parties to account for such violations for fear that condemnation would hinder the implementers' ability to act as impartial brokers. Worse, the implementers would later falsely verify the National Union for Total Independence of Angola's (UNITA) demobilization in order to claim the mission as a success. In Rwanda, the UN Department of Peacekeeping Operations (DPKO) prohibited its peacekeepers from aggressively investigating reports of hidden arms caches for fear that such investigation might provoke violence by extremists.

Priority 3: sow the seeds of long-term peacebuilding

Implementers of peace agreements can make important contributions in the short term and with relatively low costs that can prove to have large payoffs for longer-term peacebuilding: the reform of civilian police and judiciaries, reduction of light weapons, and the strengthening of local civil society organizations. The former two contributions address the problem of increased violent crime that is often found in the aftermath of negotiated settlements; the latter contribution goes to the heart of building local capacity to address the lingering psychological, institutional, and physical affects of war-related violence.

Reform of police and judiciaries

For good reasons, international implementers of peace agreements focus on assuring the security of ex-combatants. However, research has found that assuring the security of the general population is a neglected aspect of peace implementation.[20] This is problematic, however, given that many civil war settlements are based on liberal norms and institutions which depend on citizens' foregoing group-based protections and accepting individual assurances of security by the newly reformed state. In the absence of a police force which can effectively provide those assurances, new post-war arrangements seem unjust and in violation of group rights. In an insecure environment, political entrepreneurs can engage in protection racketeering that undermines the credibility and authority of the new state.

As Charles Call and William Stanley observe, 'virtually all post-1989 cases of negotiated civil war termination experienced perceptions of heightened public insecurity, often as a result of documented increases in violent crime'.[21] As they point out, civil war settlements offer unique opportunities for redesigning and reforming civilian security institutions. The inclusion of civilian security reform into peace agreements provides implementers with clear guidelines for assistance programmes. Their work suggests important lessons for such programmes: the need to design and implement judicial, penal, and police reforms in tandem; and the importance of creating specialized police units, especially Criminal Investigative units and oversight offices (e.g., Internal Affairs, Inspectors-General, and Civilian Commissions).

Societal disarmament

Countries that emerge from civil wars are usually awash in light weapons. The availability of such weapons contributes to crime, lawlessness, and civilian insecurity. When such crime becomes oppressive, citizens question the value and legitimacy of peace. While disarmament of soldiers and police and judicial reform are necessary to reduce the overall supply of weapons in a country, they are not enough. As Virginia Gamba explains in her Chapter 13 in this volume, governments, citizens, and international organizations must make special efforts specifically to reduce the numbers and availability of weapons.[22]

Local capacity building: civil society organizations

At a relatively low cost, implementers can support local civil society organizations that can play key roles in sustaining peace after the implementers leave.[23] Civil society organizations can help to sustain peace agreements by working at the grassroots level to legitimize peace and make it more than an elite concern. Local organizations can address key issues such as reconciliation, justice, and human rights – issues that go to the heart of what many consider to be the root causes of civil wars. Moreover, local organizations tend to have a longer time horizon and are more adept at sustaining long-term processes that are integral to peacebuilding.

New research direction: the meanings of peace implementation

I would like to conclude this chapter with some thoughts about the different connotations of peace implementation; in particular, the very different lenses that people in war-torn societies bring to bear on the question of putting peace into practice. When enemies in civil wars sign peace agreements, leaders, supporters, and people caught in the middle often view implementation as three distinct things: compliance, process, or peacebuilding.

Peace is extremely fragile during implementation of agreements. After the immediate euphoria of agreement and high expectations for what the agreement will bring, comes the basic political reality that putting peace into practice requires cooperation among former enemies; that leaders must still bring followers with them; that disaffected groups may attack those who would make peace; that those who have the guns must be persuaded to lay them down. Inevitably, peace takes time; inevitably, frustrations rise, expectations are not met; and paradoxically, a sense of loss may arise in key constituencies: loss of status, control, identity, and meaning. If such perceptions are not addressed, the likelihood of violence triumphing again persists.

For some people implementation is compliance, nothing more, nothing less: whether or not the parties to an agreement put into practice what they promised in the agreement. Emphasis is placed on the legalistic fulfilment of obligation. Disputes may arise in interpretation of what was promised, but nonetheless implementation is judged on the benchmark of how much that is written and mutually agreed to is carried through.

For others implementation is not about compliance *per se*, but rather about commitment to a process of continuous negotiation of differences. Those who emphasize process insist that peace agreements are often vague, incomplete, and expedient and that they are often built on purposive ambiguity. Such ambiguity, derisively described by some as 'fudging', is included in agreements in order for leaders to protect their positions within constituencies, to buy time to bring supporters along, or simply to kick difficult issues ahead in the hopes that tackling smaller issues and building confidence will someday allow them to revisit their largest sources of disputes. Proponents of implementation as process insist that differences of opinion will always arise about the content of agreement; indeed, some go further to insist that agreements themselves are context-bound and when contexts change, leaders should be willing to revisit their original promises. Adaptation and flexibility are hallmarks of this vision of implementation; enemies are judged by their willingness to discuss their positions, learn their adversaries' needs, and commit themselves to ongoing, non-violent negotiation.

Finally, there are those who see implementation as peacebuilding; that is, the forging of meaningful long-term relationships between former enemies. Those who judge implementation through the lens of peacebuilding are seldom satisfied with compliance with a peace agreement; indeed, the demands and expectations of peace tend to be far greater than clauses in a written agreement. Indeed, in so far as peace agreements silence issues of truth, reconciliation, justice, and accountability, many hope that during implementation moral and ethical values of peace may trump narrow fixation on compliance. The standards for judging successful implementation are broad and long term: will efforts at making peace create the conditions that will allow new identities and relationships to prosper?

My purpose here is not to argue for one perspective over another. It is simply to acknowledge that in conflict-ridden societies, people will disagree about what implementation entails, and to suggest that when such disagreement exists we ignore progress on all three dimensions at our peril. Narrow compliance without process or relationship building runs the risk of medium to longer-term instability and fails to address underlying senses of loss and fear among citizens. Process without compliance runs the risk of severe alienation of constituents from the peace agreement as they see elite political deals without tangible actions behind them. In the worst of conditions, people fear that process trumps substance, and any hopes for a peace dividend are perpetually postponed and unattainable. Relationship building without process or compliance subjects those who would make peace in society to attack from their own groups who label them traitors.

Notes

1. S.J. Stedman, 'Spoiler problems in peace processes', *International Security*, 22, 2 (Fall 1997) pp. 5–53.
2. See the pioneering works of T. Sisk, 'The Violence-negotiation Nexus: South Africa in Transition and the Politics of Uncertainty', *Negotiation Journal*, 9, 1 (1993) and J. Darby, *The Effects of Violence on Peace Processes* (Washington DC: United States Institute of Peace Press, 2001).
3. I.W. Zartman, *Ripe for Resolution* (New York: Oxford University Press, 1985). For Zartman's history of the concept and his reflections on its strengths and weaknesses, see I.W. Zartman, 'Ripeness: The Hurting Stalemate and Beyond', in Paul C. Stern & Daniel Druckman (eds), *International Conflict Resolution after the Cold War* (Washington DC: National Resource Council, 2000), pp. 225–250.

4. S.J. Stedman, *Peacemaking in Civil Wars: International Mediation in Zimbabwe, 1974–1980* (Boulder CO: Lynne Rienner, 1991). For a comparison of South Africa and the Middle East that argues for the importance of group dynamics in conflict resolution, see D. Lieberfeld, 'Conflict "ripeness" revisited: The South African and Israeli/Palestinian cases', *Negotiation Journal*, 15, 1 (1999) pp. 63–82.

5. See for example, F.O. Hampson, *Nurturing Peace* (Washington DC: USIP, 1996) and B. Walter, 'The critical barrier to civil war settlement', *International Organization* (Summer 1997) pp. 335–365.

6. S.J. Stedman, 'Implementing Peace Agreements in Civil Wars: Lessons and Recommendations for Policymakers', IPA Policy Paper on Peace Implementation (New York: International Peace Academy, May 2001).

7. E.J. Wood, 'Civil War Settlement: Modeling the Bases of Compromise', paper presented at the 1999 Annual Meeting of the American Political Science Association (2–5 September 1999).

8. J. Lewis, 'Peace Processes and the Challenge of Credible Commitments: South Africa and Israel/Palestine', Stanford University, Senior Honors Thesis (May 2000).

9. Stedman (2001), op. cit.

10. S. Woodward, 'Avoiding another Cyprus or Israel', *Brookings Review* (Winter 1998) pp. 45–48.

11. M. Doyle & N. Sambanis, 'International peacebuilding: A theoretical and quantitative analysis', *American Political Science Review*, 94, 4 (December 2000) pp. 779–802.

12. Stedman (1997), op. cit.

13. See Marie Joelle Zahar's chapter (Chapter 12) in this volume.

14. Ibid., and Darby (2001), op. cit.

15. G. Downs & S.J. Stedman, 'Evaluation Issues in Peace Implementation', paper presented at the annual meetings of the American Political Science Association (Washington DC, 30 August 2000).

16. R. Cetinyan & A. Stein, 'Assassins of Peace?: Spoilers and the Peace Process in the Middle East', Paper presented at the Annual Meeting of the American Political Science Association (Atlanta GA: 3 September 1999)

17. Zahar (Chapter 12 in this volume), op. cit.

18. That is, total, limited, or greedy spoilers.

19. J. Spear, 'Demobilization and Disarmament: Key Implementation Issues', in S.J. Stedman, D. Rothchild, & E.M. Cousens (eds), *Ending Civil Wars: Volume II.* (Princeton NJ: Princeton University Press, 2004).

20. C. Call & W. Stanley, 'A Sacrifice for Peace? Security for the General Public during Implementation of Peace Agreements', *Ending Civil Wars: Volume II.* (New York: International Peace Academy, 2001).

21. Ibid.

22. See Virginia Gamba's chapter (Chapter 13) in this volume.

23. J. Prendergast & E. Plumb, 'Civil Society Organizations and Peace Agreement Implementation', *Ending Civil Wars: Volume II.* (New York: International Peace Academy, 2001).

12
Reframing the Spoiler Debate in Peace Processes

Marie-Joëlle Zahar[1]

Why do some peace agreements end civil conflict while others break down? Empirical evidence underscores the importance of sustainability: the Rwandan genocide succeeded the 1992 Arusha peace agreement; likewise, some of the worst violence in Angola, Sri Lanka, and Cambodia (among others) followed the breakdown of peace accords.

To date, the most powerful answer to the failure of many a peace settlement points to the emergence of actors who decide to spoil the peace process. Spoilers are leaders who believe that peace 'threatens their power, worldview, and interests, and use violence to undermine attempts to achieve it'.[2] This chapter reviews current research on violence in peace processes, and proposes to reframe the debate in two ways: (1) by moving away from the notion of spoiling and concentrating instead on the adoption of violent strategies and (2) by suggesting a theoretical framework to address the twin notions of capability and opportunity which, I argue, provide the context in which decisions to use violence are taken.

Diagnosing spoilers

When peace agreements collapse, analysts and practitioners point a finger at spoilers. The typical spoiler acts in one of two ways: either systematically refusing to negotiate or, alternatively, entering into agreements and then reneging on promises.[3] There are spoilers galore in civil war settings as the behaviour of the National Union for Total Independence of Angola (UNITA) in Angola and of the Revolutionary United Front (RUF) in Sierra Leone, among others, amply demonstrates. Building sustainable peace requires bringing the parties threatening to peace into the negotiation process (thus managing outside spoilers) and preventing them from developing incentives to renege during the implementation stage (or managing inside spoilers).

Stedman's pioneering study on the topic argues that international custodians of peace are the decisive factor in the success or failure of a spoiler's attempt to derail peace. Where international custodians have created and implemented efficient strategies for protecting peace and managing spoilers, damage has been limited and peace has triumphed. Where international custodians have failed to develop and implement such strategies, spoilers have succeeded.[4]

Critics suggest that research on spoilers fails to determine spoiler types ex ante.[5] While the criticism may be read as a purely academic concern with the predictive power of theories, it is also prompted by practical concerns for the sustainability of peace. Indeed, as per Stedman's own argument, information and *a correct diagnosis of the type of spoiler* are crucial for the choice of an appropriate strategy of spoiler management. In reality, however, most parties to a civil war both desire peace (as war is costly) and want to get away with as much as they can in the event of an agreement (they have incentives to defect for unilateral gains).[6] How can we then tell spoilers from peacemakers? When a spoiler emerges, how can we tell what strategy to adopt? These issues are consequential for the success of peace agreements and they deserve further elaboration.

Critics further note that the typology is problematic as a diagnostic tool. Indeed, two supposedly different types of spoilers share the same characteristics (cell 1); moreover, the same spoiler types often span two cells of the typology (cells 1 & 3 and 1 & 2). This, they contend, derives from the fact that some spoiler types are defined according to their preferences over actions while others are defined according to their preferences over outcomes.[7] Of the three types, only total spoilers exhibit fixed preferences over both outcomes and actions. Is it inconceivable, nevertheless, to induce total spoilers to become peacemakers? Although total spoilers are seemingly willing to incur higher risks and bear heavier costs than most in pursuit of their objectives, the question remains whether this attitude holds regardless of the content of peace proposals. Empirical evidence suggests otherwise. A study of the Palestine Liberation Organization's (PLO) attitude regarding peace with Israel is illustrative. The same PLO, which was the Palestinian cornerstone of peace negotiations with Israel, was accused between 2001 and 2005 (albeit by some, not all) of acting as a total spoiler. Since the January 2006 elections that brought the

Table 12.1   Stedman's typology of spoilers

	Limited goals	Total goals
Low commitment	1 Greedy or limited spoilers	2 Greedy spoilers
High commitment	3 Limited spoilers	4 Total spoilers

Islamist Hamas movement to power, it is once again held as the linchpin of the peace process. Should we accept the premise that the PLO acted as a total spoiler between 2001 and 2005, how do we account for this change in attitude towards the Oslo Process? Some analysts suggest that Yasir Arafat was never interested in peace. His death and replacement by moderate Mahmoud Abbas would provide the key to understanding the PLO's fluctuating attitude towards peace. Others argue that the Israeli-Palestinian peace process was particularly unstable in view of the lack of interdependence of the parties and of an end-game which would produce separation. They point to Abbas's failure to stem violence against Israel and Israelis as evidence in support of such an explanation. Both explanations can be countered convincingly leaving the initial question unanswered.[8] In short, empirical evidence demonstrates that actors do go back on (or revert to) extreme positions under (admittedly often exceptional) circumstances.

Winners, losers, and spoilers

To address the problems identified above, one must first start with the recognition that peace implementation is at heart a political process. While most settlements attempt to create incentives for all factions to support peace, they are bound to create winners and losers. Foremost among losers are those parties that were not invited to the negotiating table (outside spoilers). Little analysis has focused on the differences between inside and outside spoilers. Yet they differ, not only in their motives to spoil but also in their evaluation of the costs and benefits associated with spoiling.

Inside spoilers, outside spoilers, and incentives to spoil

Why do spoilers emerge? Are they attempting to overturn a peace process or to register dissatisfaction? We can sketch a preliminary answer by probing the differences between inside and outside spoilers.

Warring factions that were left out of the peace negotiations may see peace as a threat. Ideologically, their survival may be premised on the continuation of strife. For a movement like the Palestinian Hamas, for example, peace with Israel would undermine the very bases of its existence. If we accept that political actors are ultimately interested in remaining politically relevant,[9] such groups see compromise as a political suicide. Financially, warring factions that benefit from fighting have no interest in a peace that may unravel the war economy.[10] In Sierra Leone, for example, the RUF opposed agreements that would have decreased the group's control over diamond mining and ultimately secured the nomination of its leader to the post of Minister of Natural Resources. Finally, groups that are sidelined for strategic considerations (either because they are considered relatively insignificant or because their presence at the table may prevent the inclusion of other factions) fear negotiations, the result of which may disregard their demands. Conflict provides even the most marginal organizations with the potential to gain power and influence.[11] For these groups, peace holds the prospect of losing whatever marginal influence and power they yielded during the course of the conflict.

In contrast, parties to the talks have a venue to express their demands and they are usually ensured some sort of political representation in the post-agreement phase. Peace settlements are in essence elite pacts.[12] Actors who are involved in these pacts negotiate terms that allow them to maximize their gains in light of the conditions under which they are negotiating. In other words, peace negotiations occur at a time when both sides, for whatever reason, agree to accept the military outcome be it symmetrical or asymmetrical as the basis for determining the political pay offs accruing to each.[13] It is indeed possible for the parties to reach stable peace settlements in which the leaders of warring factions develop vested interests.[14] If these actors fear the post-agreement phase, it is for different reasons. One reason that is frequently invoked is the problem of credible commitment,[15] when parties are genuinely interested in peace but cannot trust each other to keep promises.[16] Custodians are supposed to help the parties overcome this issue but, as will be discussed further below, there are analytical and empirical problems associated with current conceptualizations of the role of custodians.

Reframing the spoiler debate: voice, exit, and violence in peace processes

Many have read into the definition of spoilers a necessary correspondence between opposition to peace and resort to violence. I have argued elsewhere that this correspondence is neither necessary nor theoretically sound: 'As the most extreme manifestation of opposition to peace, the violence perpetrated by militants and ex-militants has been granted primacy in research on the phenomenon of spoiling, contributing in the process to a conflation between violence, spoiling and opposition to peace.'[17]

This conflation limits the usefulness of the notions of insider and outsider as analytical categories to understand spoiling. Stedman rightly argues that one must not 'blithely [assume] that all parties that sign peace agreements do so in good faith, or are equally trustworthy'.[18] No theoretical a-priori underpins a correspondence between insiders and peacemakers; nor can the analyst assume strategic deception. Insiders and outsiders can equally be favourable or opposed to a specific peace agreement.

Insiders may sign peace agreements for strategic considerations – to buy time and secure a lull in the fighting in order to improve their position on the battlefield. If and when they use violence, these actors clearly intend to spoil the peace process. Others intend to live up to their commitments but end up facing a security dilemma – when either their opponents (or the third-party implementer of the agreement) attempt to use the peace to eliminate them. If they elect to use violence, these actors are likely to express their disagreement with implementation. Outsiders can also resort to violence for a variety of reasons. Some – such as opposition to peace on principle or for greed – qualify as spoiling. Others, such as the desire to be noticed and included at the negotiating table, are more aptly described as attempts to secure voice and inclusion.

Insiders and outsiders seek voice in diametrically differing ways. For insiders, voice translates into participation; outsiders may use it to signal an interest in inclusion. Likewise, violence is deployed to differing ends by parties favourable and opposed to a given peace settlement. Parties favourable to peace may resort to violence to express discontent with implementation failures. Parties opposed to peace use violence to overturn the tables on the agreement. To simply say that an actor resorted to violence tells us very little about their attitude towards peace.

Decisions in context: understanding the likelihood of violence

Not all would-be spoilers resort to violence in their opposition to the negotiation or implementation of a given peace process. Nor are all violent actors necessarily spoilers. How then should we understand decisions to use violence? Below, I propose two sets of answers.

A cost-benefit analysis of the violence of insiders and outsiders

One avenue starts with the distinction between insider and outsider. Not only do insiders and outsiders have different reasons to use violence, they also have different assessments of the costs and benefits associated with such a decision. Though information is at best partial and incomplete and the rationality of such a cost-benefit calculus is naturally bounded, there are standard categories of costs and benefits that actors consider.[19]

The benefits associated with a return to violence depend in large part on whether this strategy is used to gain voice or signify exit. Violence may be used to gain access to state resources and to secure a voice in the conduct of state affairs. In post-conflict elections, hardliners have often used the threat of a return to fighting in order to secure gains at the ballot box. Rational choice analyses suggest that voter uncertainty about the threshold at which hardliners may fall back onto violence explains in great part the consecutive electoral victories of such groups in places like Bosnia.[20] Additional benefits from violence include, among others, a return to the war economy and the disruption of a settlement unfavourable to the party that decides to spoil (the use of the term spoiling is justifiable here because the ultimate purpose of the violence is indeed the disruption of the peace process).

Less systematically addressed are the costs associated with such a decision, costs that often loom large especially where the spoils are negligible. The Palestinian and Northern Irish cases come to mind. What do actors stand to gain from using violence and derailing such processes? Are their potential gains larger than the losses associated with such a decision? I argue that there are 'standard' categories of costs and benefits that an analyst or a policy maker ought to consider in any assessment of the likelihood of violence. Costs can be regrouped in two categories. The first category is costs associated with the resumption of fighting; the second category is costs associated with the loss of peace dividends. I especially draw attention to the role of third parties and intra-factional politics as potential sources of constraints on the decision to use violence.

The costs of a new round of fighting. Fighting is a costly decision. In a post-conflict situation, the cost of fighting includes international audience costs and straightforward military costs. An actor who reneges on his commitment to peace runs the risk that international interlocutors will question his reliability as a partner in future talks. His credibility and legitimacy are at stake. Thus, in Sierra Leone, RUF leader Foday Sankoh damaged his credibility by repeatedly 'spoiling' agreements. If such an actor uses violence and fails to achieve its stated objective (whether to modify or interrupt the course of peace implementation), it runs serious risks of being sidelined in future peace talks. In other words, the group's political survival may be at stake. The military strength of the custodians and their willingness to use force determine the military costs associated with a decision to resort to violence. It is more difficult to challenge a custodian who shows resolve to militarily enforce peace if need be. As important as this factor may be, few implementers are willing to commit to do so. The deterrent effect of the willingness to use force has been invoked in understanding the Bosnian Serb compliance with the Dayton Peace Agreement (the resolve of the Implementation Force (IFOR), and the Stabilization Force (SFOR) having been opposed to the 'irresolute' attitude of the United Nations (UN) forces in Bosnia). Time is another important factor. The earlier the decision to use violence, the less likely implementers of the agreement will have had the opportunity to carry out full demobilization and disarmament. The longer an actor waits, the higher the military costs associated with the resumption of fighting.

The loss of peace dividends. Peace agreements are in essence elite pacts; those pacts include a range of benefits for signatories. Power-sharing agreements guarantee that actors will exert political influence in the post-conflict polity.

They also guarantee access to funds and other financial assets through control of, or privileged access to, the resources of the state. This aspect was paramount in the Bosnian Serb decision to go with the Dayton Peace Agreement. Republika Srpska was the means through which the Bosnian Serb leadership amassed power and riches. The Darfur Peace Agreement (DPA) guaranteed the survival of the entity and the continued inflow to Bosnian Serb leaders of material advantages resulting from their control over the institutions of Republika Srpska.[21] Likewise, there are political and financial gains for the PLO from staying within the peace process with Israel. Indeed, not only did the position of insider give the PLO recognition as a political actor, it also provided the organization's leadership with control over international aid flowing into the occupied territories.[22]

The role of intra-factional politics. It has often been argued that conditions of civil war dispense leaders from seeking democratic approval from their would-be constituencies. Thus, most of our analyses of leaders' choices have focused on interfaction negotiations to the expense of intra-factional politics. However, intra-factional politics remain important[23] especially in a peace implementation setting when democratic norms of accountability are likely to be fostered by custodians. Domestic audience costs depend on the specifics of a given situation. However, a leader whose incumbency depends on popular support (or on preventing an internal coup that would remove him from power) is likely to be especially sensitive to internal audience costs, especially on the eve of an electoral deadline. If the leaders' constituency perceives peace to be a net benefit, they will not take lightly to a decision to use violence. If, on the other hand, they believe that they are being wronged, the leader might be putting his political survival at stake if he fails to respond to their grievances. The tightrope that the late Palestinian Authority President, Yasir Arafat, had to walk during the tenure of former Israeli Prime Minister Benjamin Netanyahu and his dilemma after the election of Prime Minister Sharon vividly illustrate this dilemma.

Cost, benefits, and decisions. As noted in Stedman's contribution to this volume, not all peace agreements are equally vulnerable to spoiling. When the implementation of peace agreements proceeds as planned, insiders are given voice – or the means to express their concerns and the access necessary to redress grievances. The longer peace lasts, the more likely that insiders will develop loyalty to the institutions of the negotiated peace pact. The dividends of peace deepen and the cost of violent strategies increases accordingly. If the negotiation process achieves a stable outcome, the leaders' exit options become 'costly and disadvantageous'. Decision-makers find that 'just as they were once trapped in a cycle of conflict, now the structure of incentives works to trap them in the politics of moderation'.[24] Insiders who consider violence have to assess their options not only by considering the cost of fighting but also by factoring in the loss of peace dividends. In counter-distinction, actors who are left out of the negotiated settlements have no stakes in peace and may have extensive stakes associated with the continuation of the conflict. From their perspective, the cost of peace is extremely high and its benefits low. Should they demobilize, these actors are ensured that they will lose the military power that (1) underpins whatever benefits they were gaining from the conflict, and (2) would provide them with the only bargaining edge to secure benefits from peace. For them, the cost of peace is the potential loss of all benefits from war added to the prospect of demobilization. Violence, on the other hand, does not really cost them much. Actors who are excluded from the negotiations process do not have to worry about international audience costs (incurred when reneging on one's commitment to peace). The imminence of peace negotiations constitutes a finite horizon against which they assess their choices and strategies. If several other factions enter into peace negotiations, an excluded party will ultimately either have the choice to take the agreement or leave it. In all likelihood, these actors do not have to concern themselves with domestic audience costs either. Since the actor's exclusion is usually an outside decision, his or her domestic constituency will not fault the actor for not participating in the peace talks. A decision to resort to violence might even be interpreted as standing up to outsiders who fail to acknowledge the actor as a legitimate part of the conflict, and therefore of the peace process.[25] For excluded parties, or outsiders, the only cost to consider is that of a military escalation.

This discussion echoes the fundamental lessons of research on mediation and intervention. The narrower the basis of a peace agreement the more difficult it will be to sustain. Likewise, the clearer the benefits to various factions from the peace deal and the stronger the commitment of third parties to providing the factions with security guarantees, the greater the chances that these factions will be deterred from resorting to violence. However, the cost-benefit calculations are fundamentally different for insiders and outsiders. For insiders, the use of violence raises the spectre of military costs related to the level of demobilization and disarmament already achieved, audience costs – both domestic and international, as well as the loss of whatever peace dividends had accrued to these actors from their participation in the peace agreement. For outsiders, however, violence is only costly militarily. In other words, ceteris paribus, *the use of violence by insiders is expected to be more costly than the use of violence by outsiders.*

A contextual analysis: conflict environments and actor strategies

The costs and benefits of a return to fighting can be constrained or offset by contextual factors. In the rest of this chapter, I discuss two such factors: capability – or the resources available to the groups and individuals, and opportunity – or the constraints on violence posed by the presence and commitment of foreign interveners and by the commitment of other actors to the peace process.

While they might want to use violence in a graduated way, the bluntness of the instrument forces actors to consider that they might not be able to steer the course of violence when unleashed. Actors considering the use of violence thus need to assess whether they can sustain a return to fighting. The answer depends on a host of variables, which may differ from one case to the other.[26] However, two broad categories of factors systematically recur in analyses of post-conflict violence. The capability to resume fighting depends on the availability of resources. These, in turn, can come from two sources: (1) valuable tradable commodities and a regional underground network to produce, ship, and trade these commodities, and (2) foreign patrons.

'The ending of a civil war hinges on the willingness of competing armies to relinquish self-help solutions to their insecurity, to demobilize their soldiers, and in most circumstances, to create a new, integrated army.'[27] Disarmament and demobilization are necessary to consolidate the peace.[28] Regional war economies provide actors with the financial resources necessary to skirt demobilization and disarmament programmes.[29] Regional economic linkages often predate conflicts; in the context of civil wars, warlords instrumentalize these networks to finance their military activities.[30]

> When peace implementation disregards or fails to notice the existence of regional economic linkages and of a regional infrastructure for economic exchanges, the post-agreement experience of many countries including Sierra Leone, Afghanistan and Bosnia – to name only a few – shows that these regional complexes survive and provide actors with the means to finance a return to violence.[31]

Where actors can count on the support of outside patrons for weapons, disarmament and demobilization are equally likely to fail. Taken together, the existence of a regional economic complex and the presence of foreign patrons combine to create particularly unstable conflict environments. Both make it particularly arduous to achieve what Stedman and Spear identify as 'the *single* most important sub-goal of peace implementation',[32] the demobilization of soldiers. Both also decrease the costs associated with a return to violence.

Managing spoilers: the role of third parties

Current research on spoilers places excessive weight on the role of third parties in spoiler management. Most analyses of failed peace settlements determine that third parties are critical to the success of peace settlements and the management of spoilers.[33]

Where Stedman focused on spoilers' beliefs that peace is contrary to their interests, a variation on the theme has framed spoiling in the context of the security dilemma. According to proponents of this approach, civil wars reproduce the anarchy of the international system where self-help is the only logical course of action.[34] The greatest problem that civil war opponents encounter is 'how to write an enforcement contract under conditions of extreme risk'. Negotiations would succeed in designing peaceful transitions if the participants could be protected during the implementation period.[35] Demobilization is an especially thorny issue. Even adversaries who truly wish to resolve their wars remain wary of disarmament as weapons are their only means of protection against the unilateral defection of others. Hence, the emergence of spoilers is less an act of malevolence vis-à-vis the peace process and more a function of the rules of the game in an anarchic context. In this framework, outside intervention can serve the purpose of enforcing the terms of the contract.[36]

The security dilemma is a potentially important obstacle to civil conflict resolution. However, there are problems with the approach as well as with proposed solutions. The problems with the approach are aptly summarized in Stedman's contribution to this volume. Security dilemmas and commitment problems offer an undifferentiated analysis of civil wars. They also offer undifferentiated solutions. Third parties are not sufficient and may not even be necessary to prevent the emergence of spoilers. The involvement of external actors may go a long way to reassure former enemies; nevertheless, the strategic situation of actors continues to matter for decision making even with the presence of custodians. Angola is a case in point. Following the 1994 Lusaka Protocol, sustained UN presence on the ground was not sufficient to allay the fears of Jonas Savimbi and to ensure his continued commitment to the peace process. There have also been cases – albeit few – of self-enforcing peace agreements that succeeded, cases in which one cannot invoke the presence of an external enforcer as the solution to the commitment problems faced by the factions. South Africa is probably the clearest illustration of such success. This suggests that some peace agreements may be more vulnerable to spoiling than others. It also suggests that it is not international presence per se that may be determining but what third parties do on the ground. 'Scholars do not treat international attention and commitment as a contextual variable, and by defining it as international will make the error of treating it as completely voluntarist.' Yet, third parties can do too much or too little and their actions will affect the opportunity structure available to would-be spoilers. In other words, implementers need to be attuned to the context in which they are operating.[37]

This brings up an otherwise neglected aspect of third-party involvement in the implementation process. It can directly contribute to the decision by some actors (insiders and outsiders alike) to resort to violence. Most analytical frameworks of outside implementation take 'neutral' UN missions as their frame of reference. However, a number of peace settlements have been implemented by regional powers such as Syria in Lebanon, India in Sri Lanka, or Nigeria in Liberia. These actors are not only often partial to one faction but they are also less philosophically opposed to the use of force in implementation. This sort of custodianship may heighten the insecurity of some actors who do not see the third party as a custodian but as a hostile neighbour. In Lebanon, for example, the presence of some 35,000 Syrian troops was central to General Awn's rejection of the Ta'if accord. It also played a central role in the Lebanese forces' hesitation to comply with the demobilization and disarmament clauses of the Ta'if Accord and can be largely blamed for troubles in Summer 2001.[38] In brief, the mere presence of third parties is not sufficient for overcoming the commitment problem faced by factions to the peace process. External implementation may, in some cases, directly contribute to the consequent security dilemma. This variation in the role of custodians should be investigated further.

Capability and opportunity: custodians of peace and post-conflict violence

Assuming a benign custodian, and given the difficulties inherent in the assessment of actors' intentions, a correct assessment of capability – an accurate evaluation of the conflict environment – is key to custodians' efforts to manage the implementation of peace. Where regional war economies and outside patrons facilitate the resort to violence, foreigners will need more muscle, political will, and financial resources to see to it that peace is maintained. This violence need not be directed at the peace process to have repercussions on the extent and success of peace implementation. Afghanistan provides a good case in point as tribal violence between warlords has little to do with the Bonn peace process and a lot to do with struggles to control resources and smuggling routes, as well as a number of regional or local rivalries. Yet, this violence is partly to blame for implementation hurdles experienced by the International Security Assistance Force and by the nascent Afghani army as they attempt to restore state monopoly over violence.

Whereas capability refers to the resources available to actors considering the use of violence, opportunity refers to the barriers that can increase the costs associated with violence. The commitment of foreign actors to oversee the implementation of the peace process and decisively deal with would-be spoilers is the most obvious such barrier. Less obvious are those strategies that custodians of peace deploy to generate loyalty to the peace process.

Military options: deterring the use of violence

'In the absence of a functioning central state capable of claiming the monopoly of the use of legitimate violence, it is incumbent upon the custodians to secure the peace'.[39] As argued above, violence management requires the successful implementation of disarmament and demobilization schemes. The strategies to this effect need to be calibrated to the volatility of the conflict environment. Where the risks of violence are high, custodians will need not only to commit sufficient troops but also to be willing to use them and incur casualties to keep the peace.

> In certain limited situations, strategies that derive from traditional peace-keeping (with its underlying emphasis on confidence-building) can be effective. In more challenging situations, however, when predation coexists with fear, confidence-building will prove inadequate, and implementers will need to compel and deter to ensure compliance with a peace agreement.[40]

Volatile conflict environments are 'difficult implementation environments'. They require more resources, greater involvement, and more coercive strategies; however, these are not forthcoming 'because no major or regional power perceives peace in a given country to be in its own vital strategic interest'.[41] 'Where major or regional powers have defined peace implementation as a vital strategic interest – as Syria did in Lebanon or the North Atlantic Treaty Organization (NATO) in Bosnia – custodian commitment has acted as a barrier against the use of widespread violence by insiders and outsiders alike.'[42]

Non-military options: loyalty as a barrier against exit

Securing the peace requires an active deterrence of violent strategies and a simultaneous effort to secure the loyalty of insiders. This reflects empirical evidence that peace need not be challenged violently; in Bosnia–Herzegovina, to cite but one example, it was the inaction of parties to the process that threatened the Dayton Peace Agreement most.[43]

In Hirschman's Exit-Voice-Loyalty framework, loyalty is an exogenous factor that operates to incite dissatisfied customers to exercise voice and exert pressures to reverse the decline in a given organization.[44] There are different reasons that might incite an actor to remain 'loyal' to an organization: to retain the material advantages provided by membership or not to incur the costs of exit if barriers to such an exit are perceived to be substantial.[45]

Discussions of loyalty parallel debates on the meaning of peace implementation. Implementation can mean three distinct things to different actors and observers: compliance, process, or peacebuilding.[46] Compliance emphasizes a legalistic fulfilment of obligations spelt out in the peace agreement; process underscores the commitment to a continuous negotiation of differences; peacebuilding values the forging of meaningful long-term relationships between former enemies. 'Compliance is a necessary but not sufficient condition for the transformation of process into peacebuilding with voice representing the new state's contribution to this transformation by making available channels for participation and the incentives to use these channels.'[47] Each of these understandings corresponds to a different strand in the literature on peacebuilding. Compliance usually evokes a minimalist definition of peace as ending the fighting. Process calls to mind institution building with the intent of securing voice to all parties to the peace process, usually through some form of power sharing.[48] Peacebuilding suggests an 'organic' approach to reconciliation whose proponents seek to establish foundations that reach through to society.[49]

Custodian strategies and the sustainability of peace

At the minimum, peace agreements elicit compliance. Peace agreements represent pacts between unwilling partners often forced to compromise because they could not prevail on the battleground.[50] During peace negotiations, actors will seek to maximize their gains in light of the conditions under which they are negotiating.[51] Compliance-based agreements are particularly vulnerable to insider violence; attachment to the agreement is a function of expected gains from membership. If these gains do not materialize or when gains from a return to war supersede the benefits derived from peace, insiders will exercise their exit option. The decision by Jonas Savimbi of UNITA to walk out on the Lusaka Accords because of his failure to secure election to the presidency of the republic is paradigmatic in this respect.[52] Even though 'Savimbi and UNITA received more from the Angolan settlement than any of the losing parties in El Salvador, Mozambique, Nicaragua, and Zimbabwe received in theirs,'[53] Savimbi calculated that electoral results were 'too meager a prize to persuade [him] from trying his luck at winning power through war'.[54]

Even where military considerations militate in favour of compromise, incentives are still needed to entice the various factions to the negotiating table. In Bosnia–Herzegovina, the Serb leadership, its military power clipped by a joint Bosnian-Croat offensive and NATO bombings, demanded (and secured) the recognition of Republika Srpska. Incentives are not sufficient to secure commitment to peace. Institutionalized channels for voice, often in the form of power sharing, are the most common solution to curtail credible commitment problems. Though analysts question their ability to secure long-lasting peace and democracy,[55] it is hoped that power sharing will be conducive to continuous negotiation of differences eliciting thus a process-based loyalty to the agreement.

'Only when the powersharing formula is tampered with either by a state bent on excluding one of the political actors (Lebanon and the exclusion of Christian opposition forces) or by a custodian seeking to fundamentally reinterpret the bases of powersharing (Bosnia and current attempts by the Office of the High Representative (OHR) to centralize the state)' can we expect insiders to use violence to protest perceived implementation failures.[56]

The politics of peace implementation are particularly vulnerable to the pressures of 'early exit'. These translate into custodian strategies focused on the short- rather than the long-term. That is, I surmise, the reason why custodians tend to privilege compliance and process over peacebuilding and why organic approaches to peace remain cantoned in the realm of NGO action. This is detrimental to stability and to the sustainability of peace efforts. Custodian obsessions with exit strategies further aggravate the problem because they increase the likelihood that custodians will rely on 'force' when faced with bottlenecks. Increasingly, analysts and practitioners alike stress the need for 'resolve' in the face of would-be spoilers.[57] Such methods are unlikely to forge meaningful long-term relationships between former adversaries and create a strong belief amongst them in the goals and values of conflict resolution. Military and political resolve can be credited for progress in peace implementation; these methods also raise the thorny issue of ownership of the peace process. To quote Darby and Mac Ginty, 'Some peace processes are largely creatures of the international community. They reflect the desired outcome of key states in the international community rather than the wishes of local communities.'[58] The Bosnian peace process is a case in point. While the OHR can be credited for breaking a number of logjams in Bosnia, a decade after the Dayton peace agreement, observers question the loyalty of all Bosnians to a united Bosnia–Herzegovina.

Charting future research

These observations chart new directions for research on violence in peace processes. A thorough understanding of violence requires better answers than we now have to two fundamental questions. Why do actors want to use violence? How do they assess the costs and benefits of this strategy? Initial findings pointed to the importance of the distinction between inside and outside spoilers. Further research highlighted the importance of the environment of peace. This environment provides both capabilities and opportunities that constrain or facilitate the recourse to violence. All else being equal, access to tradable commodities and the support of patrons determined the ability of protagonists to skirt disarmament and demobilization. The chapter argues that custodians must therefore calibrate their implementation strategies as a function of the volatility of a given conflict environment. Custodian strategies are also key in shaping the opportunity structure of would-be spoilers. When third parties offer credible guarantees to the factions, they increase the costs of violence and thus decrease its likelihood. But third parties not only shape the opportunity structure of would-be spoilers but they also affect the incentives of factions. Peace implementation involves an intricate exercise in sequencing. Implementation is not limited to compliance with the terms of a given document; it is also about fostering commitment to a negotiating process and ultimately laying the foundations for peacebuilding. However, lack of compliance in the short term will undoubtedly affect the actors' medium to long-term commitment to the process as well as the chances for peace to take root. Likewise, third-party decisions to privilege one aspect of peace implementation at the expense of others is a consequential element that deserves further analysis in relation to the resumption of violence.

Notes

1. The author would like to thank Lynn Eden, Page Fortna, Barry O'Neill, and Steve Stedman for many useful discussions. Thanks are also due to John Darby and to participants in the Research Initiative on the Resolution of Ethnic Conflict for comments and suggestions. The financial assistance of the Social Science and Humanities Research Council of Canada is gratefully acknowledged.
2. S.J. Stedman, 'Spoiler problems in peace processes', *International Security*, 22, 2 (Fall 1997), p. 5.
3. This 'tactical acceptance' thesis is mostly promoted by D. Horowitz, *Ethnic Groups in Conflict* (Berkeley CA: University of California Press, 1985).
4. Custodians have pursued three major strategies to manage spoilers: (1) inducement – entails giving the spoiler what he wants (default mode); (2) socialization – requires the establishment of a set of norms for acceptable behaviour by which to judge the demands and the behaviour of parties; involves material and intellectual components to elicit normatively acceptable behavior, and (3) coercion – that relies on the use or threat of punishment to deter or alter unacceptable behaviour or reduce the capability of spoilers to disrupt the peace process.
5. In his path-breaking study, Stedman introduced three types of spoilers who vary on two dimensions: their goals (limited or total) and their commitment to the achievement of these goals (high, and low). Total spoilers pursue total power and exclusive recognition of authority and hold immutable preferences. Limited spoilers have limited goals – for example, recognition and redress of a grievance, a share of power or the exercise of power constrained by a constitution and opposition, and basic security of followers. Limited goals do not imply limited commitment to achieving those goals, however. Finally, greedy spoilers lie between the limited spoiler and the total spoiler. The greedy spoiler holds goals that expand or contract based on calculations of cost and risk. A greedy spoiler may have limited goals that expand when faced with low costs and risks; alternatively, it may have total goals that contract when faced with high costs and risks.
6. I owe this observation to Page Fortna.
7. See N. Sambanis, 'Conflict Resolution Ripeness and Spoiler Problems in Cyprus: From the Intercommunal Talks (1968–1974) to the Present', Paper presented to the American Political Science Association (25 September 1998).
8. For a rebuttal of the thesis that Arafat has never been interested in peace see D. Sontag, 'Quest for Mideast Peace: How and Why It Failed', *New York Times* (6 July 2001); See also H. Agha & R. Malley, 'Camp David: The tragedy of errors', *The New York Review of Books* (9 August 2001). While separation is indeed the end-game on paper, the territorial reality of the zones A, B, and C created under Oslo belies such

separation. The Palestinian economy is also highly dependent on Israel in terms of both labour and trade. Although the Palestinians are much less important to the Israeli economy, Israel still exports $2 billion/year to the West Bank and Gaza. See R. Brynen, *A Very Political Economy Peacebuilding and Foreign Aid in the West Bank and Gaza* (Boulder CO: Lynne Rienner, 2000), p. 40; See also 'Downsizing amid the Uprising', *The Economist* (10 August 2001).

9. This assumption is common in game theoretic analyses of decision-making. It is also eminently reasonable, as no leader should be expected to sign on his demise. See R. Putnam, 'Diplomacy and domestic politics: The logic of two-level games', *International Organization*, 42, 3 (Summer 1998).

10. This holds especially true if they have not negotiated side agreements that allow them to partake in the financial benefits of peacetime. The financial rewards gleaned by the Khmer Rouge in the ruby-mining business, by UNITA in the diamond trade, and by the Shan United Army in the opium trade illustrate the importance of the war economy. For a discussion of this phenomenon see M. Berdal & D. Keen, 'Violence and economic agendas in civil wars: Some policy implications,' *Millennium*, 26, 3 (1988); S.W.R. de a Samarasinghe & R. Coughlan (eds), *Economic Dimensions of Ethnic Conflict* (London: Pinter Publishers, 1991), p. 184.

11. This holds especially true for organizations that would have otherwise been side-lined from politics.

12. T.D. Sisk, *Power Sharing and International Mediation in Ethnic Conflicts* (Washington DC: United States Institute of Peace, 1996), especially. Chapter 5; C. Hartzell & D. Rothchild, 'Political pacts as negotiated agreements: Comparing ethnic and non-ethnic cases', *International Negotiation*, 2 (1997) pp. 147–171; E.J. Wood, 'Civil War Settlement: Modeling the Bases of Compromise', Paper presented to the Annual Meeting of the American Political Science Association (Atlanta GA: 2–5 September 1999).

13. P. Kecskemeti, 'Political Rationality in Ending War', in W.T.R. Fox (ed.), *How Wars End* (Philadelphia PA: The Annals of the American Academy of Political and Social Science, 1970), pp. 105–115.

14. See M.J. Zahar, Fanatics, Mercenaries, Brigands ... and Politicians: Militia Decision-Making and Civil Conflict Resolution (PhD Dissertation, Canada: McGill University, 2000). See also E.J. Wood, 'Civil War Settlement: Modeling the Bases of Compromise', Paper presented at the 1999 Annual Meeting of the American Political Science Association (2–5 September 1999) and Sisk (1996), op. cit.

15. B. Walter, *Designing Transitions from Violent Civil War*, IGCC Policy Paper 31 (San Diego CA: UC Institute on Global Conflict and Cooperation, 1998); M.J. Zahar, 'The Problem of Commitment to Peace: Actors, Incentives and Choice in Peace Implementation', Paper presented to the Annual Meeting of the American Political Science Association (Washington DC: 31 August, 3 September 2000).

16. J. Fearon, 'Commitment Problems and the Spread of Ethnic Conflict', in D. Lake & D. Rothchild (eds), *The International Spread of Ethnic Conflict: Fear, Diffusion, and Escalation* (Princeton NJ: Princeton University Press, 1998), pp. 107–126.

17. M.J. Zahar, 'Political Violence in Peace Processes: Voice, Exit and Loyalty in the Post-Accord Period', in J. Darby (ed.), *Violence and Reconstruction* (Southbend IL: Notre Dame University Press, 2006).

18. S. Stedman, 'Peace Processes and the Challenges of Violence', in J. Darby & R. Mac Ginty (eds), *Contemporary Peacemaking: Conflict, Violence and Peace Processes* (Basingstoke: Palgrave, 2003), pp. 103–113 at p. 107.

19. For a detailed discussion of these costs and benefits see Zahar, 'Reframing the Spoiler Debate', in J. Darby & R. Mac Ginty (eds), *Contemporary Peacemaking* (Basingstoke: Palgrave, 2003), pp. 119–121.
20. For a detailed account of the rationale behind this argument see L. Wantchekon, 'On the nature of first democratic elections', *Journal of Conflict Resolution* 43, 2 (1999) pp. 245–268.
21. See Zahar (2000), op. cit.
22. See Brynen (2000), op. cit.
23. In my dissertation research, I established the importance of intra-factional politics for leaders' decisions to accept or reject peace settlements. See also S. Stedman, *Peacemaking in Civil Wars: International Mediation in Zimbabwe, 1974–1980* (Boulder CO: Lynne Rienner, 1991).
24. Sisk (1996), op. cit.
25. For a discussion of similar dynamics in international crises see J. Fearon, 'Domestic political audiences and the escalation of international disputes', *American Political Science Review*, 88, 3 (September 1994) pp. 579–581.
26. What follows is thus intended as an indicative rather than exhaustive set of variables to consider in making this assessment.
27. Stedman (2003), op. cit., p. 109.
28. Spear, 'Disarmament and Demobilization', pp. 141–182.
29. The regional dimension of war economies has until recently been downplayed in analyses of peace implementation. In an important addition to the literature, M. Pugh & N. Cooper document the existence of regional dynamics that underpin the political economy of conflict; they further argue that the neglect of such dynamics has detrimental effects on our understanding of conflict dynamics and on the ability to design workable solutions for transition to peace. See M. Pugh & N. Cooper with J. Goodhand, *War Economies in Regional Context: The Challenges of Transformation* (Boulder CO: Lynne Rienner, 2004).
30. This is an important corrective to the literature on war economies not least of all because it also demonstrates that greed and grievance are not polar opposites but often parallel, if not overlapping, tracks.
31. Zahar (2006), op. cit.
32. Stedman (2003), op. cit., p. 109.
33. See especially B.F. Walter, 'The critical barrier to civil war settlement', *International Organization* 51, 3 (Summer 1997).
34. For a discussion of the security dilemma in civil wars see B. Posen, 'The Security Dilemma and Ethnic Conflict', in M. Brown (ed.), *Ethnic Conflict and International Security* (Princeton NJ: Princeton University Press, 1993).
35. B.F. Walter, *Designing Transitions from Violent Civil War*, IGCC Policy Paper 31 (San Diego CA: UC Institute on Global Conflict and Cooperation, 1998). Available at http://www-igcc.ucsd.edu/igcc2/PolicyPapers/pp31.html (Accessed on 12 February 2007); Internet. A modified version of the argument was subsequently published in *International Security* 24, 1 (1999).
36. Walter (1997), op. cit. See also F.O. Hampson, *Nurturing Peace* (Washington DC: USIP, 1996). This argument is very similar to the standard IR argument about the role of institutions or regimes in fostering cooperation under anarchy.
37. On the differentiated role of implementers see particularly the conclusions of the Stedman et al. study. S.J. Stedman, 'Implementing Peace Agreements in Civil Wars: Lessons and Recommendations for Policymakers', IPA Policy Paper on Peace Implementation (New York: International Peace Academy, May 2001).

38. M.J. Zahar, 'The Problem of Commitment to Peace: Lessons from Bosnia and Lebanon', Paper presented to the Annual Meeting of the American Political Science Association (Atlanta GA: 2–5 September 1999).

39. Zahar (2006), op. cit. On the role of custodians see Stedman (1997), op. cit.

40. S.J. Stedman, 'Policy Implications', in S.J. Stedman, D. Rothchild, & E.M. Cousens (eds), *Ending Civil Wars: The Implementation of Peace Agreements* (Boulder CO: Reinner, 2002), p. 664.

41. Ibid.

42. Zahar (2006), op. cit.

43. M.J. Zahar, 'The Dichotomy of International Mediation and Leader Intransigence: The Case of Bosnia and Herzegovina', in I. O'Flynn & D. Russell (eds), *New Challenges for Power-Sharing: Institutional and Social Reform in Divided Societies* (London: Pluto Press, 2005).

44. However, loyalty is not a necessary prelude to voice. See B. Barry, 'Exit, Voice, and Loyalty', in B. Barry (ed.), *Democracy and Power: Essays in Political Theory, I* (Oxford: Clarendon Press, 1991), pp. 187–221.

45. See K. Cannings, 'The voice of the loyal manager: Distinguishing attachment from commitment', *Employee Responsibilities and Rights Journal* 5, 3 (1992) p. 262.

46. For a detailed discussion of the three meanings of peace implementation see Stedman (2003), op. cit., pp. 111–112.

47. M.J. Zahar, 'Understanding the Violence of Insiders: Loyalty, Custodians of Peace, and the Sustainability of Conflict Settlement', in E. Newman & O. Richmond (eds), *Spoilers and Peace Processes: Conflict Settlement and Devious Objectives* (Tokyo: United Nations University Press, 2006).

48. A. Lijphart, 'Consociational democracy', *World Politics* 21 (1969), pp. 207–225; A. Lijphart, *Democracy in Plural Societies* (New Haven CT: Yale University Press, 1977); and A. Lijphart, 'The Power-Sharing Approach', in J.V. Montville (ed.), *Conflict and Peacemaking in Multiethnic Societies* (New York: Lexington Books, 1991), pp. 491–509.

49. J.P. Lederach, *Building Peace: Sustainable Reconciliation in Divided Societies* (Washington DC: United States Institute of Peace Press, 1997).

50. Peace settlements are in essence elite pacts established as a transitional strategy towards democratic regimes or outcomes. See T.D. Sisk, *Power Sharing and International Mediation in Ethnic Conflicts* (Washington DC: United States Institute of Peace, 1996), especially chapter 5; C. Hartzell & D. Rothchild, 'Political pacts as negotiated agreements: Comparing ethnic and non-ethnic cases', *International Negotiation* 2 (1997) pp. 147–171; and E. Wood, 'Civil War Settlement: Modeling the Bases of Compromise', Paper presented to the Annual Meeting of the American Political Science Association (Atlanta GA: 2–5 September 1999).

51. P. Kecskemeti, 'Political Rationality in Ending War', in W.T.R. Fox (ed.), *How Wars End* (Philadelphia PA: The Annals of the American Academy of Political and Social Science, 1970), pp. 105–115.

52. T. Lyons, 'The Role of Postsettlement Elections', in S.J. Stedman, D. Rothchild, & E.M. Cousens (eds), *Ending Civil Wars: The Implementation of Peace Agreements* (Boulder CO: Reinner, 2002), p. 222.

53. S.J. Stedman, 'Negotiation and Mediation in Internal Conflict', in M. Brown (ed.), *The International Dimensions of Internal Conflict* (Cambridge: MIT Press, 1996), p. 370.

54. T. Ohlson & S.J. Stedman, *The New is Not Yet Born: Conflict Resolution in Southern Africa* (Washington DC: Brookings Institution, 1994), p. 193.

55. D. Rothchild & P. Roeder (eds), *Sustainable Peace: Power and Democracy after Civil Wars* (Ithaca NY: Cornell University Press, 2005).
56. Zahar (2006), op. cit. See also M.J. Zahar, 'Power Sharing in Lebanon: Foreign Protectors, Domestic Peace, and Democratic Failure', in D. Rothchild & P. Roeder (eds), *Sustainable Peace* (Ithica: Cornell University Press, 2005), pp. 219–240.
57. This plays itself out in debates over armed humanitarianism and political conditionality. M. O'Hanlon, *Saving Lives with Force: Military Criteria for Humanitarian Intervention* (Washington DC: The Brookings Institution Press, 1997).
58. J. Darby & R. Mac Ginty, 'What Peace, What Process', in J. Darby & R. Mac Ginty (eds), *Contemporary Peacemaking* (Palgrave Macmillan, 2003), p. 4.

13
Post-Agreement Demobilization, Disarmament, and Reconstruction: Towards a New Approach

Virginia Gamba

Introduction

The thawing of the Cold War in the late eighties led the United Nations Security Council and a series of like-minded states acting multilaterally to explore the possibilities open for collective management of conflict resolution in regions affected by war or emerging from violent conflict. Not all of the ensuing peace support operations were successful in promoting or defending peace but, taken as a whole, their analysis assists in determining the challenges that any transition from conflict to peace faces in the contemporary environment. Control over warring parties, ensuring a peaceful transition to the establishment of a democratically elected government, managing demobilization processes, reviewing defence and security structures to serve the needs of peace time, and establishing law, order, and infrastructures to ensure sustainable development of affected countries are all seen – or should be seen – as part of a continuum. The comprehensive nature of a peace engagement is not today disputed. The early strategies of massively engaging on the ground in order to bring peace and then seeking an early exit without focusing on the consolidation of peace and security in the emerging state are now being replaced by a long-haul process which is unpopular but unavoidable.

This chapter does not seek to provide a historic analysis of what went wrong, where, and why. There is abundant literature to provide this background[1] rather it seeks to unpack the Demobilization, Disarmament, and Reconstruction (DDR) elements that are fundamental to the comprehensive development of sustainable peace and security in conflict-affected states and their immediate regions. Each one of these elements will then be developed with particular reference to the experience of Southern Africa since 1994. Finally, the chapter will focus on the corrective mechanisms that the region itself has proposed to ensure sustainability in the provision of peace and security and will analyse what chances the region has, if any, in achieving its goals. By focusing on the case study of Southern Africa the chapter hopes to produce a set of recommendations on how to implement policies that will empower DDR initiatives to genuinely assist the prevention and management of violence today.

The making and consolidation of peace: a DDR continuum

Key objectives of a peace process are to secure peace, to ensure demobilization, to ensure disarmament, and to assist post-conflict reconstruction and development. If these objectives are not realized, peace cannot be consolidated. Since 1989, almost all cases of multinational peacemaking and peace support operations have not fully realized the above mentioned objectives.

In the study of these peacemaking and peace consolidating initiatives, it is possible to identify two principal problems that, unless addressed early and corrected, will compromise the mission itself and the sustainability of lasting peace. These two key problems are: (1) those associated with the establishment and maintenance of a security environment early on; and (2) problems concerned with a lack of coordination of efforts among the regional and international communities, the various groups involved in a peace mission, the peace mission itself, and the post-conflict reconstruction effort.[2]

The establishment of security must come first to ensure stability which requires clear political authority and policy guidelines. The provision of reasonable security to belligerent parties has a direct impact on their willingness to demobilize and disarm. Many failures of the 1980s and 1990s were directly related to this issue as seen in Angola, Somalia, the former Yugoslavia, Liberia, Sierra Leone to name a few.

Similarly, the importance of comprehensive coordination ensures unity of command to sustain security during the peacekeeping phase; the cost effectiveness of emergency sustainability of the population in transition; and influences the ability of sustainable development through the coordinated efforts of the international and regional communities. Lack of coordination impacted almost all the peace support missions since the late 1980s although more effort in this regard can be seen in relatively successful transitions such as Mozambique, Cambodia, Namibia, East Timor, and Haiti.

The truth is that insecurity during the peace process will delay or break the effort as happened in Angola and Somalia. Likewise, lack of coordination will not only endanger the mission and expose it at the time but, more importantly, will slow down or scuttle the post-conflict reconstruction phase where the emphasis lies in the provision of law and order, the creation of infrastructure, the demilitarization of society, and sustainable development.

Ultimately conflict and peace are interrelated. Nowhere is this more evident than on the complex environment of DDR. Weapons enter a conflict area as if sucked in, often leaching across porous borders in a conflict-affected region. The accumulation of weapons over many years, without a clear policy of disarmament and destruction at the end of each cycle of violence, means that they will be available to any new emerging conflict. The porosity of borders, the weakness of transitional states, the corruption of officials, and the emergence of a more organized network of criminals in and across borders allow for the trafficking of weapons with relative ease. New weapons, illicit weapons from neighbouring communities and regions, and the inability to guard and protect legal weapons in possession of the state from negligence or theft make up the majority of arms that find their way to conflict areas. For civilian populations weapons also become a survival tool. These weapons enter civilian hands either through direct issuance by warring parties themselves or through the illicit markets that cash in on the insecurity of peoples living in an environment where they are not assured law and order.

Countries in conflict require a large number of military or paramilitary personnel and the ability to replenish this pool of people on a constant basis. Many countries in conflict do not have professional armies and not all of insurgent forces are trained professionally. The phenomenon of conscription of men and women occurs on the one hand, and that of forced recruitment of men, women, and children to feed insurgent movements is also common. The wartime skills of people are very different from those that will be needed in post-conflict reconstruction processes. People who have survived through the use or the threat of use of armed violence will find themselves operating in a changed environment where those skills are neither rewarded nor replaced. They often turn to crime to ensure some survivability in the changed environment. The type of crime associated with post-conflict reconstruction is of two types for the unemployed at the end of a war: common armed banditry; and organized crime. For the under-employed (with a salary that comes intermittently), the ability to exert power and influence through their standing and their arms and skills will lead to corruption, blackmail, and robbery. In both cases the main victim is the development potential of the country for without security, there is no investment and with no investment no development is possible.

The civilian population and national infrastructures in conflict areas are more often than not the first victims of directed violence. Aside from the normal suffering that civilians always incur in a war, they are also used often as tools for war: the displacement of communities will place an onus on the warring faction that must sustain them; the burning of crops will destroy the sustainability of opponents as well as villagers; the mining of land will ensure tactical demilitarized zones but will become the single most difficult post-conflict reconstruction challenge in rural areas; the issuance of arms to civilian populations will complicate the military operations of an enemy but will create a massive problem with crime and violence in post-conflict reconstruction, and so forth. The destruction of infrastructure will not only complicate and slow down military operations but it will also ensure time for warring factions to muster, arm, and train people. The destruction of natural resource extraction and transport infrastructure will deny its profit to a warring faction but will harm the ability of the nation to rebuild itself in the future. Perhaps the worst damage to infrastructure that happens in a country affected by conflict is the destruction of governance and oversight procedures of which the legislative and the judicial are the first victims, followed closely by provincial authorities, the media, and civil service in general, and the police and armed forces, in particular.

The DDR is therefore a single entity that affects both the chances of peace and the chances of recreating a secure and safe environment for countries emerging from conflict. In the manner in which these three issues are tackled early on – in the grey period between war and peace – lie the roots of a successful transition or the making of a failed state. It is one issue that needs to be taken seriously, if not for humanitarian reasons, at least for strategic consideration. Here it is important to emphasize that our understanding of what makes a failed state is not conclusive. In this era of deep impact globalization, it is difficult even to define what a failed state is. Nevertheless, it is possible to say that the process leading to a state being categorized as such is necessarily a slow one. Today, as Haas indicates, we also view it in strategic terms:

> A state that no longer has control over its territory, that no longer has credible, unifying institutions, is a threat to its people, its neighbors, and the international community. Diagnosing state failure as both a strategic and a humanitarian problem has implications for how we address it. Strengthening or reforming the institutions of weak states is a priority. And ensuring that new states are born with viable institutions – be it East Timor or Palestine – is a serious responsibility. Those of us who long distinguished between hard and soft areas of security studies need to think again.[3]

Taking stock

Between 1990 and 1998 a series of dramatic events in Southern Africa led to an internal analysis process in the region that ultimately led to massive policy changes in Africa, the latest of which is the creation of the Africa Union (Durban 2002), the consensus on a common policy guideline in the New African Partnership for Development (NEPAD; Lusaka 2001), the establishment of a single African Union (AU)/NEPAD agenda for Peace and Security

(Addis, February 2003), and the signature of the AU Framework Document on Post Conflict Reconstruction and Development (PCD; Banjul, 29 June 2006). The internal analysis process and the emerging corrective policies attest to the belief that disarmament and demobilization were never adequately conducted during peace processes in the region.

During the 1990s the region saw the emergence of South Africa as a fully democratic country operating in a changed economic, military, and social environment. It further saw the end of colonialism in South West Africa with the independence and consolidation of the Namibian Republic; the achievement of peace in Mozambique after more than 25 years of civil war; the achievement of peace (twice) in Angola; and the changed status of the situation in the Democratic Republic of Congo (DRC) with the ousting of Mobutu Sese-Seko and the unstable and violent emergence of the Kabila government in Kinshasa in the wake of the Great Lakes crisis that captured the world's attention with the Rwanda genocide of 1994.

Despite setbacks such as renewed war in Angola, the sub-region felt confident that the new found processes in Southern Africa would allow for regional development and the creation of peace structures. Peace and political transition in Zimbabwe, Namibia, and South Africa and the end of two hot wars (Mozambique and temporarily Angola) allowed for regional structures of like-minded states to form and consolidate. This generated the emergence of the Southern African Development Community (SADC) and, associated to it, the emergence of the Southern Africa Regional Police Chiefs Coordinating Committee (SARPCCO) and the InterState Defence and Security Committee (of military forces in the region; ISDSC). These structures, although new, and sometimes *ad-hoc* provided for exchange of information and discussion among member states of the sub-region.

Although these structures had emerged with a vision of post-conflict reconstruction and development as their primary focus, they quickly became involved in regional debate on stability and post-conflict reconstruction. The repeated discussions at the fora, allowed for the exchange of information on factors that were impinging growth and development at national levels. By 1997, there were three issues that kept emerging in regional debates:

- the exponential increase in armed and violent crime (both by individuals and organized criminal groups) in major capitals, and the increase in violent conflict resolution dynamics at community level – often involving illicit arms;
- displaced, repatriated, badly demobilized ex-combatants, and refugee communities in the region were perceived as being vehicles for the barter of illegal arms and the increase in criminal activities and political instability;
- rebel groups were still in existence in several areas of Southern Africa.

It was clear to all that the increased availability of small arms that had become redundant or surplus to the political needs of combatants tended to find their way to civil society and to criminal organizations. Civil society utilized them either to protect itself or to trade and barter in exchange of economic gain – this was particularly true of demobilized but not disarmed soldiers – invariably these arms ended up in the hands of criminals.

Implementing disarmament

The results of these exchanges led to substantive action on the need for the control of the illicit trade in Small Arms And Light Weapons (SALW) in the region. The analysis of the impact of badly conducted disarmament operations during peace processes served to focus attention on a massive mopping up operation that would be regional in character but national in execution. The engine for change on this issue was South Africa.

South Africa, with reduced deterrence capacity due to transitional reintegration and restructuring of its law enforcement capacity, and with increased free flow of people from its immediate sub-region, bore the brunt of peace without disarmament in Mozambique. After 1993, with peace in Mozambique, small arms collected and not destroyed began to escape state control through corruption. Furthermore, there had not been a systematic collection of arms in Mozambique and South Africa then became the prime end-destination and transit point of illicit small arms in the region. Crime fuelled by illegal arms also spread to Swaziland, Malawi, Zimbabwe, and eventually to the emerging military conflict in the Great Lakes region.

The 1998 Annual General Meeting of the Police Chiefs of Southern Africa called the attention of their governments to the need to prioritize a regional strategy for combating illicit small arms proliferation. The general call for action led by the Southern Africa police was based on a simple tenet: without arms, the dynamics of conflict could not be served, but without arms reduction and control the dynamics of peace could not be served. Having identified regional cooperation and coordination as essential for action, governments started to focus on the capacity to implement and the priority afforded such an implementation process at national levels. Disagreements emerged quickly and seemed to depend on how the value system of each of the participating actors affected individual perceptions of the threat posed by light weapons proliferation. Thus, for example, some countries were a 'source' of weapons, others were seen as 'end users', and a third type of country was merely important as 'transit' countries. Consensus was finally reached regionally through the legally binding SADC Protocol for the Control of Firearms, Ammunition, and Related Materials of 2001 which inspired a Common African Approach on how to deal with the illicit trade in arms at the Organization of African Unity (OAU) level, and the African position in the United Nations Programme of Action on the Illicit trade of SALW in All its Aspects in July 2001.

The efforts of the Southern African States on the issue of disarmament have yielded important benefits to the region, not least in setting the tone for the minimum standards required for law enforcement agencies to control and reduce the illicit trafficking in arms as well as for regulating their firearms. The SADC Protocol also paved the way for a similar Protocol on Small Arms developed in the Great Lakes Region and the Horn of Africa (The Nairobi Protocol). The existence of two legally binding protocols in force in 25 States of Africa have also served to influence the Africa Union's continental processes leading to the Windhoek Common Position of December 2005 that was further reaffirmed by the Executive Decision of the AU Ministers signed in Khartoum on January 2006.[4] Perhaps more important than the fact that disarmament is now well recognized as a consolidated position affecting more and more African States is the fact that its links with human security and post-conflict reconstruction are now perceived much more clearly than ever before. For example, the Windhoek Common Position requests the Africa Union Commission to

> ensure that illicit trade in small arms and light weapons issues and this African Common Position be mainstreamed into relevant African processes and documents in all peace and security policies and actions of the Peace and Security Council, and in particular, as needed in the development of an African PCRD policy including its DDR components.[5]

Implementing demobilization

Although most energy was spent on legal frameworks and the enhancement of police activity, the issue of improving reintegration schemes of demobilized soldiers was not forgotten. Foremost on the mind of the regional analysts was the case study of Angola where two peacekeeping operations had been already scuttled largely due to lack of serious disarmament and demobilization. Indeed United Nations Angola Verification Mission (UNAVEM) II and UNAVEM III were classic cases of a failure in procedures and commitment that would eventually threaten the regional stability of Southern Africa in the late 1990s. UNAVEM I demobilized foreign troops based on Angolan soil, namely South African and Cuban troops and did not address any weapons issues or caches of weapons left behind. Still, given its limited mandate it was successful. UNAVEM II focused on the cantonment and not on demobilization of Angolan warring parties, was poorly managed, did not include disarmament, and was neither comprehensive nor sustainable.

Lack of concerted demobilization and disarmament in the practical cases where it was attempted in Southern Africa led to (1) either the continuation of war or (2) the rise of armed bandit groups. In the case of Angola – even in the years of 'peace' entire combatant units that should have been demobilized and disarmed started to operate methodically in armed robbery of humanitarian convoys or in attacks against tourists crossing the border into Namibia and Zambia. Even when demobilization was more effective as in the case of Mozambique, ex-combatants were paid past wages with guns that were then recycled into the illegal market. In the worst cases, those demobilized intelligence and logistics operators that were not re-skilled quickly activated the old smuggling channels that had kept insurgency fed in the past and re-tooled these pipelines to serve the international criminal organizations moving goods and people between borders and continents.

Meanwhile, already active in its own reintegration, restructuring, and downsizing of military forces, South Africa commenced an appreciation of manners in which demobilization could be undertaken without destabilizing transitional societies. But South Africa had not been in open war as had been the case in Mozambique or Angola. The emphasis taken in South Africa was focused on the legal and constitutional framework of military reform and the effort at consolidating a single, smaller, and integrated armed force that would serve the interests of the new South Africa. South Africa then focused on manners in which the reform of institutions with particular reference to Security Sector Transformation could assist in the consolidation of post-conflict societies and help to prevent the emergence of conflict situations in the future.

While countries like South Africa experimented with security reform and improvements in the entire criminal justice system as a key to development and reconstruction, they and other governments in the region such as Botswana and Mozambique focused their attention on prevention as well as management and resolution of conflict. It was clear that a general policy that would look at disarmament, demobilization, and economic development seriously was needed. It took three long years to obtain consensus of all Heads of State of Africa but plans for the reconstruction of Africa finally emerged in consolidated form as the NEPAD agenda agreed in Lusaka in 2001.

Towards an integrated approach to DDR: Africa's NEPAD initiative and the present structures and mechanisms of the Africa union

Evolution of the AU/NEPAD peace and security agendas 2001–2003: the making of a common African peace and security agenda (APSA)

There has been a significant effort by African leaders to develop a road-map for the regeneration of the continent in view of the enormous challenges that face Africa. This initiative has taken the form of the launching of the AU in 2002, and the delineation of a blueprint for reconstruction of the continent in the form of the New Partnership of Africa's Development of 2001. Key in this blueprint is the acknowledgement that peace and security are essential preconditions for accelerated, sustainable growth and development. To drive the process, a NEPAD Heads of State Implementation Committee (HSIC) and its Sub-Committee on Peace and Security, chaired by South Africa (in October 2001) were created. Since then enormous strides have been achieved in the establishment of an institutional framework and cultivation of political will to promote peace, security, and stability in Africa, as a basis for the implementation of other NEPAD programmes. Since the beginning of 2002, a concrete AU-NEPAD framework, that is continually being refined, has emerged for addressing matters of peace and security in and for Africa.

In March 2002, the NEPAD's HSIC tasked South Africa, the Chair of NEPAD's Sub-Committee on Peace and Security, to develop concrete steps for policy and programme development in six areas identified as NEPAD priorities in the peace and security area. These were: (1) improvement of early warning capacity; (2) improvement of the capacity for, and coordination of, early action for conflict prevention, management, and resolution; (3) promotion of post-conflict reconstruction and development with a special focus on disarmament, demobilization, reintegration, and rehabilitation; (4) curbing of the illicit proliferation, circulation, and trafficking of SALW on the continent; (5) promotion of democracy, good governance, and respect for human rights; and (6) assisting in resource mobilization for peace and security intervention in Africa.

In May 2002, the NEPAD Steering Committee endorsed these recommendations. These were presented to the HSIC, which crystallized them into the *NEPAD Initial Action Plan* in their meeting in Rome in June 2002. This plan formed the basis for *G8–Africa Action Plan* adopted later that month in Kananaskas, Canada that eventually led to eight APSA priority areas: (1) developing mechanisms, institution building processes, and support instruments for achieving peace and security in Africa; (2) improving capacity for, and coordination of, early action for conflict prevention, management, and resolution; (3) improving early warning capacity in Africa through strategic analysis and support; (4) prioritizing strategic security issues such as Disarmament, Demobilization, Reintegration, Reconciliation, and Reconstruction (commonly called in Africa DDRR), and coordinating and ensuring effective implementation of African efforts aimed at preventing and combating terrorism; (5) ensuring efficient and consolidated action for preventing, combating, and eradicating the problem of the illicit proliferation, circulation, and trafficking of SALW; (6) improving the security sector and the capacity for good governance as related to peace and security; (7) generating minimum standards for application in the exploitation and management of Africa's resources (including non-renewable resources) in areas affected by conflict; and (8) assisting in resource mobilization for the AU Peace Fund and for regional initiatives aimed at preventing, managing, and resolving conflicts on the continent.[6] The AU-NEPAD consultation also considered the need to adopt a common approach to international peace and security partnership and developed proposals on how to approach such partnerships.

Challenges to the consolidation of the African initiative

Developing a common African agenda for peace and security has not been an easy process; neither has it been easy to convince all African Heads of State that African structures needed a new vision and a new structure for direct action. It is therefore important to reflect on the challenges and the modes for the creation of consensus in Africa around these issues and to note the evolution of these perceptions. The principal internal challenges could be reduced to three: the NEPAD initiative was considered a top-down initiative; it was a Southern African-led initiative; and it generated competition between existing agreed African coordination structures and new NEPAD structures.

The harshest criticism of NEPAD in Africa was that it was a top-down initiative and does not have the buy-in of the African peoples, civil society, or regional organizations. Ultimately, the strategy that originated the NEPAD initiative was led by a cluster of governments under the strong leadership of South Africa. Whatever the original criticisms internally and externally to the idea of a process of renaissance in the continent, the truth is that the idea of re-inventing oneself struck a very strong chord on a tired continent that was unable to step out of its internal problems to look at itself holistically.

The perception that NEPAD was a South African initiative was misplaced but continued to make the rounds, particularly in the academic circuits of Africa, well up to 2004. Rather than engaging NEPAD as a South African initiative, it can be said that initially, competition on the ownership of both the AU and NEPAD ideas was evident particularly between Northern and Sub-Saharan Africa rather than between South Africa and the rest. There also were divisions between East, West, and Southern Africa in the process. Although NEPAD was not presented as a hard and fast plan, it was a hard and fast idea. It is a framework for cooperation based on the principle of all independent states of Africa visualizing a common minimum standard that can push the continent together to peace and prosperity.

The third challenge or misperception relating to the NEPAD initiative was that it threatens the normal run of existing African structures and competes with them. Academics, civil society, NGOs, and the private sector were all suspicious of the initiative. The truth is that since the NEPAD initiative was still to be developed in substance *after* it was agreed on paper, the margins for interpretation as to what it ultimately would entail were very wide and different sectors saw it under different hopes and fears. The signature of NEPAD occurred at the same time that a decision was made to change the structure of the OAU – working towards an Africa Union. This also was seen as threatening by existing bureaucracies who felt that they would be declared irrelevant and new bureaucracies set up in their stead. But these perceptions have changed and NEPAD and the AU have gained greater acceptance, particularly as a result of consultations.

The external challenges to NEPAD were ultimately resolved in a similar manner. Initially, the donor and the international community saw in NEPAD and the AU only a change of name rather than a change in direction. Effectively, the fear abroad was that this was a new political ploy to generate donor interest but that no real reform would come of it. The fact that the NEPAD initiative was able to advance so quickly into the development of operational guidelines for action surprised the international community. African countries have promised and delivered a number of key policies such as the creation of a Common African Defence and Security Policy, the AU Peace and Security Council Protocol, the common agenda for AU/NEPAD peace and security action, the Common Position on SALW, and the Post Conflict Reconstruction Policy Framework among others. Furthermore, individually and collectively, efforts at brokering peace in Africa by Africans also took a turn for the better with relative successes in Angola, Ethiopia, Eritrea, Sierra Leone, DRC, Burundi, Rwanda, Uganda, and Cote D'Ivoire.

Ultimately the biggest challenge remained that of coordinating and harmonizing the guidelines of the NEPAD agenda with the realities of an emerging functional AU Commission. As attested by the record of the peace and security policy formulation of the Africa Union since 2003, the NEPAD initiative has now been successfully unpacked across its key policies; and the AU Commission has the structural operational guidelines to be able to use the new policies to good effect. The challenge continues to be to keep momentum and to implement action, on the one hand, and to revitalize and strengthen the sub-regional organizations that need to prevent, manage, and reduce conflict in Africa.

Putting it to the test: the relationship between the NEPAD agenda and the emerging AU policies

The NEPAD asserts that peace, security, democracy, good governance, human rights, and sound economic management as conditions for sustainable development. As regards peace and security, there is one single over-arching priority – that of preventing, managing, and resolving violent conflict in Africa. The following principles underpin the NEPAD Peace and Security Programme:

- the peace and security programme must be led by Africans;
- the international community must support peace and security efforts in Africa;

- the AU and the Regional Economic Communities (RECs) such as SADC, EAC, IGAD, ECOWAS, and ECCAS[7], must form a single continental architecture for peace and security;
- prevention of conflict is preferable to its management and resolution;
- active participation and involvement of AU Member States in peace and security matters is key.

Conflict prevention, management, and resolution will entail a long-term process focused on enhancing the capacity of sub-regional and regional organizations to reduce the incidence of, and mitigate the effects of, conflict on the continent. For these reasons, the focus of action across the initial six priority areas of the AU/NEPAD Peace and Security Programme revolved around the concept of improved information and analysis; ensuring that early warning leads to early and effective action; and promoting sustainable disarmament, demobilization, and post-conflict reconstruction initiatives that promote a culture of peace and justice in and for Africa. Fundamental to all of these issues was the urgent need to improve the administration, capacity, coordination, and information exchange between and among Africans behind a single objective. Resource mobilization was also important as it impacted independence and sustainability of long-term efforts.

For the NEPAD system first and later for the AU/NEPAD APSA agenda (African Peace and Security Agenda), peace and security was about people. For this reason, post-conflict DDRR must not be conceived of as a process focused solely on implementation in the military context. Issues of reconciliation and development must also be taken into consideration by DDRR.

As NEPAD focused on the issue of the DDR, it was perhaps unavoidable that a concept that was considered as serving more the needs of multinational agencies in temporarily addressing peace building and post-conflict assistance to affected regions rather than in a sustainable addressing of the real needs of the emerging countries themselves, would emerge. The original debates of donor and relief agencies, including the United Nation's (UN) system, about the need to focus on demobilization, disarmament, and reintegration of ex-combatants and to tie these elements to post-conflict reconstruction was perceived to be connected with conflict resolution measures: ultimately an exit point at the end of a peace process. As the discussion of post-conflict reconstruction emerged in Africa, the nature of the problem *for* Africa and *not about* Africa began to change the perception of what classical DDR stands for. Here, the APSA priorities are beginning to identify African DDR needs as being much more complex than those visualized by the international community: it is not just about demobilization of warring parties and their disarmament and reintegration, it really should reach out to the demilitarization and disarmament of the mind of a population and an infrastructure that had been mobilized and prepared to sustain war for decades. In order to generate post-conflict constructs, elements of national reconciliation and economic reconstruction had to be added. Finally, due to the extent of psychological and physical trauma on warring parties and civilians at the end of conflict, the problem of rehabilitation had to be considered and addressed. This is why in the APSA priorities of the AU/ NEPAD agenda the concept of DDR has been changed to that of DDRR with the last 'R' representing all its variables, such as Reintegration, Rehabilitation, Reconciliation, and national Reconstruction.

NEPAD aspirations have met with considerable success in terms of being operationalized by the AU. Indeed, African thinking on DDR has influenced the UN system and the international community. The participating governments and international agencies in the March 2006 Stockholm Initiative on DDR (SIDDR) noted that

> the SIDDR has also closely followed other international initiatives that focus on DDR. Some examples of such initiatives are the African Union's policy framework for post conflict reconstruction and development, the conference on DDR and stability in Africa ... and the multi country demobilisation and reintegration programmed managed by the World Bank for the Central African region.[8]

Conclusion

Post-agreement demobilization, disarmament, and reintegration is one of the major pillars upon which conflict-affected states can organize themselves and generate sustainable post-conflict reconstruction. Most of the lessons learnt on these three items have come from foreign literature based on information gathered by international peace support agencies, international relief agencies, or the donor community. Seldom has the information come from the people that were affected by imperfect demobilization, disarmament, and reintegration. There is great need to be able to look at these three elements from the point of view of the directly impacted and his/her society as a whole.

What we have seen in Africa is a total change of the paradigm of DDR. In Africa, the concept has not only been enlarged but it also has shifted focus. Whereas the international community considered DDR as a *conflict resolution mechanism* at the end of a process; Africa considers DDR as a *conflict prevention mechanism* at the beginning of a process. This naturally requires a different approach to its implementation.

Fundamental in this new vision is a great truth that lies at the bottom of all effective DDR: understanding that the chances for success of peacemaking and post-conflict reconstruction are exponentially increased if there is a regional umbrella immediately surrounding the affected state that speaks with one voice and is willing to take part in a constructive manner in the construct of peace. There is also the need to consider DDR in a broader and more long-term light than what has been the case up to now. In Africa, DDR itself is now unpacked differently, comprising not just ex-combatants but the whole process of reconciliation, rehabilitation, and reintegration as well as reconstruction presented in this component affecting not just warriors but the victims of violence and society in general. This is an important variation since traditional DDR only focuses on weapons in possession of a legal combatant and not on the hands of civilians, bandits, or criminals that operate in and out of borders.

The DDR should also be seen as only one component of a longer and more comprehensive process. By ensuring a broader definition of DDR, providing a regional umbrella to support its implementation, and balancing DDR with other key elements in post-conflict reconstruction an effective road-map for sustainable peace can be developed and conflict prevention be applied. The beauty of this approach is that, if it is taken early enough, it can also form part of the terms and conditions that warring parties must sign off in the pursuit of a lasting peace agreement in the first place. They will then be effectively contributing to the prevention of renewed conflict and would secure sustainable development.

Notes

1. UNIDIR produced 11 publications with case studies on the nature of peacekeeping operations since 1989 (the DRC series 1996–1998); The United Nations has also published all the material related to their peacekeeping operations in their blue book series, and extensive publications worldwide have analysed the nature of success or failure in multinational peace support operations.
2. Disarmament and Conflict Resolution Project, *Managing Arms in Peace Processes: The Issues* (Geneva: UNIDIR, 1996), p. 211.
3. Ambassador Richard Haas, 'Reflections on US policy one year on', Opening speech at the IISS Global Strategic Review (London: 13–15 September 2002), p. 4.
4. *Compendium of Small Arms and Light Weapons Initiatives Applicable to Africa*, Joint publication of the Africa Union and SaferAfrica (June 2006), p. 302.
5. Ibid., p. 303.
6. For a comprehensive discussion refer to the Report of the AU-NEPAD Consultations on Peace and Security.
7. Southern African Development Community, East African Community, Intergovernmental Authority on Development, Economic Community of West African States, Economic Community of Central African States.
8. Stockholm Initiative on Disarmament, Demobilisation and Reintegration, *Final Report* (Stockholm: Ministry for Foreign Affairs Sweden, March 2006) para. 6, p. 11.

Part IV

Peace Accords: An Introduction

John Darby and Roger Mac Ginty

At one level a peace accord is a technical document, often negotiated by lawyers and signed by elites. It is also a political document with the capacity to have a real impact on people's lives. Its success or failure depends on the seriousness of negotiators to sell any accord to their constituents and to deliver on any concessions or reforms.

The extent of any agreement is important, particularly in terms of the degree to which it deals with the constitutional, territorial, and security issues that lie at the core of a conflict or is merely concerned with the manifestations of the conflict. There has been a tendency in recent years to stretch the remit of peace accords to issues of cultural and economic inclusion that define the developmental aspect of conflicts.

One doughty problem is the inflexibility of state sovereignty. The fixity of state boundaries in the face of demands for separation steers states towards the granting of limited autonomy and provision for minorities within established boundaries. This leads to the questions of 'how much autonomy is enough' and whether or not it satisfies or encourages demands for devolution and independence from the centre. A number of workable powersharing formats have been designed over the past few decades, although many have the side effect of perpetuating rather than challenging ethnic politics. The electoral validation of a peace accord conforms to wider international trends towards democratization. Yet electoral mechanisms may complicate a delicate situation, especially if organized prematurely. Although the counting of heads is important, more important is the broadening and deepening of democracy and participation.

14
Power Sharing after Civil Wars: Matching Problems to Solutions

Timothy D. Sisk

Introduction

The trend towards negotiated settlements in civil wars in the 1990s and 2000s, as opposed to military victories, has now become clear. In 2000, Wallensteen and Sollenberg reported that of the 108 conflicts since 1989, 75 have ended by 1998. 'Of these', they write, '21 were ended by peace agreements, whereas 24 ended in victory for one of the sides and 30 had other outcomes (cease-fire agreements or activity below the level for inclusion). Many new peace agreements were signed in the middle and late parts of the period, particularly 1995–1996.'[1] The trend of conflicts ending in peace agreements rather than on the battlefield persisted into the 2000s such that by 2006 the Uppsala project reported that 34 per cent of the conflicts in the post-Cold War period (1990–2005) as a whole ended in negotiated settlement, double the historical average; between 2000 and 2005 there were nearly quadruple the number of conflicts ending in negotiation than by military victories (16 to 4). Starkly, in the 1990s, *more* conflicts (41) ended in negotiated settlements than through outright military victory (23).[2]

This trend in war termination – which represents a dramatic shift over previous trends in the twentieth century, which saw more military victories than negotiated settlements – has profound effects in considering the issue of power sharing: wars that end at the peace table tend to feature power-sharing outcomes, either in the form of interim governments (as in Afghanistan, South Africa, or Liberia) or as seemingly permanent features of politics (as in Lebanon, Bosnia, and Burundi). Ostensibly, power-sharing solutions are designed to marry principles of democracy with the need for conflict management in deeply divided societies. Power sharing involves a wide array of political arrangements – usually embodied in constitutional terms – in which the principal elements of society are guaranteed a place, and influence, in governance. Indeed, the gist of international mediation in such conflicts is to encourage parties to adopt power sharing in exchange for waging war. Why would parties to such wars concede at the bargaining table – or in post-war elections – what they had not lost on the battlefield?

The problem is that, as described below, power-sharing systems are sometimes prone to failure. If power sharing is necessary, but unlikely to endure, how can sustainable peace evolve in post-war situations? This chapter assesses recent experience with power sharing as a means of living together after deadly wars. It describes how new political institutions are a critical element of negotiated settlements, it offers a typology of power-sharing models, and it includes examples of various approaches in practice. The chapter critically evaluates the common proposition that power sharing is a long-term solution to wars that at the negotiating table. While power sharing may be desirable, and necessary, as an *immediate* exit to deadly ethnic wars, power sharing is not a viable *long-term* solution to managing uncertainty in divided societies, including those characterized by sharp ethnic divisions.

The problem with power sharing

Sadly, there is a serious problem with power sharing as the outcome to deadly ethnic conflicts. In sum, the long-term political guarantees inherent in many power-sharing systems sometimes contain the seeds of their own destruction. They are not very durable solutions.[3] A key feature of power sharing – the mutual veto, whereby decisions are only taken with the widest possible consent and only with a near consensus – often leads to the use of 'political blackmail'. Unable to get consensus, governance stagnates and policy making drifts; the result is a 'cold peace', in which the parties do not continue to employ violence but neither have they embarked on a serious process of reconciliation. When power-sharing agreements lead to such political *immobilism* (the inability to make or implement policy due to protracted disagreement), frustration emerges and tensions rise; one or more parties defect from the accord. Eventually war can erupt anew. The outbreak of civil wars in Angola, Cyprus, Lebanon, Sierra Leone, and Sudan have all been the result of broken power-sharing agreements that led to renewed violence.

Power-sharing solutions make for good transitional devices, but in the long run, the best outcome may well be a much more fluid form of democracy that allows for the creation of flexible coalitions that bridge the ethnic divided. *A central question that has yet to be fully explored is the terms under which power-sharing, consensus-oriented forms of democracy can evolve into more flexible institutions that can foster reconciliation and a broader national identity.* If sustainable peace comes through 'conflict transformation', as argued by John Paul Ledearch, power sharing is often a too-rigid system of governances to allow for the social and political changes necessary for addressing the underlying causes of conflict that give rise to war.[4]

How can the rigid structures of political power sharing wither over time to the point where the guarantees for group security they contain are no longer required? This is not a purely academic question. In Bosnia, for example, the ability of North Atlantic Treaty Organization's (NATO) international peacekeepers to end their occupation is premised on the ability of the power-sharing institutions forged in the 1995 Dayton Agreement – now dominated by nationalists – to melt into more moderate and ethnically mixed political institutions.[5]

If power sharing is at best a transitional device, this conclusion begs the question of what types of political institutions can be expected to allow democratic decision-making to prosper in post-war environments in which politics remains deeply divided. How can we match problems inherent in certain types of civil war situations? The remainder of this chapter highlights a broad range of political institutions which, if tailored to the specific conditions they are meant to serve, can move beyond formalized power sharing to foster inclusive multiethnic coalitions that amount to an informal system of sharing power while ensuring equity and distributive justice among contending groups. How can power sharing wither away, leading to a more normal system of liberal democracy?

Negotiating peace: partition or power sharing

Parties in internal conflicts face essentially two choices for the settlement of underlying disputes: 'separation', that is partition, and power sharing, or creating the structures for living together.[6] In very rare and special circumstances, contemporary civil wars end in partition that rearranges international frontiers. Outcomes to civil wars that feature total separation have been seen recently only in Eritrea and East Timor, and both of these instances involved historical claims to self-determination that go back to what was essentially botched efforts of decolonization.[7] Other instances of total political separation are also *sui generis*: the former Soviet Union and the former Yugoslavia were dissolving federations, and the Israeli-Palestinian dispute is also a matter of unresolved, colonial-era self-determination claims.

Partition refers to the creation of an entirely new state that enjoys full sovereignty and international recognition. As noted above, secession remains a strong taboo in the international system. Some question the prevailing policies of the international community that systematically works to keep troubled states together. Chaim Kaufman writes that

> Stable resolutions of ethnic civil wars are possible, but only when the opposing groups are demographically separated into defensible enclaves. Separation reduces both incentives and opportunity for further combat,

and largely eliminates both reasons and chances for ethnic cleansing of civilians. While ethnic fighting can be stopped by other means, such as peace enforcers by international forces or by a conquering empire, such peaces last only as long as the enforcers remain. This means to save lives threatened by genocide, the international community must abandon attempts to save war-torn multiethnic states.[8]

Others disagree with the Kaufman thesis, citing the need to defend the principle of tolerant, multiethnic diversity and the importance of not rewarding disputants with territorial ambitions who may have committed war crimes; these are the principal reasons why the international community insisted upon the maintenance of Bosnia's territorial integrity at the Dayton talks.[9]

In all other wars today, partition – despite being sometimes advocated by secessionist forces – is simply unlikely and improbable. The bias against partition by all the major world powers, and particularly the five Permanent Members of the United Nations Security Council – remains incredibly strong. The stark consequence of this basic reality of the international system is clear: in most civil wars, the terms of settlement will involve living together and some kind of agreement to share political power. Even after civil war, antagonists are destined to live together.

The purpose of a substantive settlement is to reconstitute 'normal' politics in a society after war and to create new, mutually beneficial rules of the political game. Ultimately, parties in a negotiation process to resolve deep-seated conflict arrive at institutional solutions: rules and procedures through which to arbitrate their differences peacefully in parliament rather than violently on the street. These institutional solutions may be augmented with agreements to undertake more long-term socioeconomic change, as has been the case in South Africa and El Salvador. Negotiated settlements as power-sharing agreements have certain common features.

First, they are the product of negotiation. Settlements in internal conflicts reflect the convergence point of the parties at the negotiating table among their preferences for new rules structures, or institutions, to constitute the post-war peace. Waterman argues that 'civil wars are conflicts over political order', and settlements in them entail the 're-creation of the conditions for a viable, common political order'.[10] Importantly, settlements do not end conflict; they are simply agreements to continue bargaining under consensually defined rules of interaction. The aim of power sharing in peace agreements is clearly conflict management not conflict resolution. Perhaps the best example today is the way in which power sharing has been seen as the solution to the wrenching ethnic conflicts in the Great Lakes region of Africa (especially, in Burundi and the Democratic Republic of Congo), where ethnic differences have has necessitated complex 'consociational' deals to share power along ethnic lines.[11]

Not surprisingly, settlements in internal conflicts often take the form of new constitutions or significant packages of amendments to existing constitutions. As constitutional laws, however, the settlement may 'freeze' in time the balance of power among the parties, which may have shifted dramatically during the subsequent phases of a peace process. Even though parties may have entered negotiation because of a perception of relative parity in power, subsequent events may have strengthened or weakened one side or another. This change in fortunes may well be reflected in the terms of a settlement. The settlement reflects the new constellation of forces and codifies and institutionalizes the relative bargaining power of the disputants.

Second, power-sharing settlements reflect the interests and expectations of the parties. In formal substantive negotiations, parties formulate their positions based on their expectations of how the structure of the new institutions will serve their interests, the exercise 'analytical imagination' about the costs and benefits of alternative institutions, such as the electoral system.[12] Therefore, settlements do not end conflicts; they are *promises* to end conflicts by creating new rules of the game to which all parties at the table can agree.

Third, power-sharing settlements in internal conflicts can be either 'interim' or 'final'. In interim settlements, parties are able to arrive at some basis for reconstituting normal politics but cannot agree on, or prefer to defer, highly sensitive or unresolved issues. The best example of an interim agreement, which has not seen a happy period of implementation, is the October 1993 Oslo Accord in the Israeli-Palestinian dispute. Interim settlements are usually partial agreements, whereas final settlements purport to be comprehensive in scope. For example, in recent efforts to end the war in Liberia in 2003, international mediators pushed for an interim government based on power sharing but at the end of the day, following transitional elections there in 2005, power sharing was not a feature of the permanent settlement. In the parliamentary elections of 2005, however, a range of former rebel and government of Liberia commanders were elected to office. Thus, there is informal power sharing today. Thus, the Liberian outcome is similar to Afghanistan's following elections there in 2005: the inclusion through the legislative arena of a number of factions involved in the war who have either emerged as 'warlord' figures or whose hands are not clean in terms of the widespread atrocities that occurred.

Fourth, power-sharing institutions establish systems of incentives. All settlements seek to formalize patterns of interaction and in this respect they seek to establish new incentive structures in their own right, resolving some of the uncertainty about the new rules of the game that characterize earlier phases of the peace process. In many cases, they are package proposals that resolve multiple issues simultaneously by linking them. Similarly, many of the more celebrated settlements in recent years have featured 'democratization as conflict resolution', explicitly marrying the goals of conflict amelioration with the introduction of competitive, multiparty politics. These features of power sharing are illustrated well by the three 'strands' in the Northern Ireland peace process that led to the 1998 Good Friday Agreement. With linked issues and complex decision-making rules, this accord has created a power-sharing system, which seeks to provide incentives for bargaining in several arenas on a wide range of issues.

Settlements are attractive for all parties when they contain the likelihood of greater benefits for parties than they would achieve by abrogating negotiations and returning to the battlefield. Successful settlements are a formula of positive sum gain for all parties. Many suggest that it is the genius of the April 1998 Good Friday Agreement in Northern Ireland that all parties could defend the agreement as containing the elements of what they had fought for all along. Moderate Republicans could claim that the agreement represents the first step towards accession to Ireland; moderate Loyalists could claim that the agreement preserves British sovereignty.[13] These elements of power sharing help us understand the key components of such agreements. In sum, negotiated settlements that create power-sharing institutions

- create political institutions that are broadly inclusive of all major mobilized groups in society, and decisions are made through negotiating, issue trading, and the search for consensus or near-consensus decision-making.
- the key elements of power-sharing institutions are (1) inclusion of all major mobilized actors; (2) influence in decision-making, not just representation in governing institutions; (3) moderation, and the search for common ground; and (4) ongoing bargaining or negotiation within the new rules of the game that the peace agreement has established.

Options for settling ethnic conflicts

A long-standing misconception of power-sharing institutions is that they are all of a specific type, which for many years has been called 'consociationalism'.[14] The elements of this approach to power sharing are well known: grand coalitions, proportional representation, cultural autonomy or federalism, and the mutual veto. Yet this prototype of power sharing is but one of what is in fact a very broad range of political options for settling ethnic conflicts, the gist of which can be exceptionally different in terms of aims, structures, and effects on promoting intergroup moderation and compromise. What are the principal options for sharing power?[15]

Autonomy

For many conflicts today, such as Azerbaijan (Karabagh), Sudan, or Sri Lanka, autonomy is often seen as a reasonable way to balance the claims of states for territorial integrity and the claims of rebel forces for secession. Autonomy, as eminent scholar Yash Ghai suggests, is not a term on which there is a consensus definition.[16] Nonetheless, his best effort at one is useful: 'Autonomy is a device to allow an ethnic group or other groups claiming a distinct identity to exercise direct control over important affairs of concern to them while allowing the larger entity to exercise those powers which are the common interests of both sections.' Among the forms of autonomy include symmetrical federalism in which all units enjoy similar powers, and asymmetrical federalism which might provide enhanced powers to a particular region.[17]

Probably the most appealing candidate for autonomy as a solution is the Kosovo imbroglio. United Nations and Organization for Security and Cooperation in Europe proposals for the solution of the Kosovo problem are examples of potential autonomy solutions in ethnic conflicts in which territory and ethnicity largely overlap. United Nations Security Council Resolution 1244, of 10 June 1999, clearly defines the mandate of the United Nations Interim Administration Mission in Kosovo (UNMIK) as promoting autonomy and self-government within the limits of territorial integrity for Yugoslavia. The resolution authorizes UNMIK to

> establish an international civil presence in Kosovo in order to provide an interim administration for Kosovo under which the people of Kosovo can enjoy substantial autonomy within the Federal Republic of Yugoslavia, and which will provide transitional administration while establishing and overseeing the development of provisional democratic self-governing institutions to ensure conditions for a peaceful and normal life for all inhabitants of Kosovo.

Yet as the continuing tensions and as yet unresolved status of Kosovo demonstrates, the idea of autonomy as a solution is more common than its actual acceptance by the parties in conflict. Autonomy is a difficult option for power sharing precisely because it fails to satisfy the preferences of either side: states, which fear a 'slippery slope' towards disintegration of territory, and secessionist groups, which demand nothing less than full sovereignty and independence. While autonomy must remain on the table as an option, it has in practice seen little success as a means of resolving the issues on the table in settlement negotiations. For example, in Sri Lanka, the ceasefire of 2003 has come under strain as a result of the inability to make progress on the specifics of reaching an autonomy agreement.[18]

Power sharing: group building block approach

Another possible option is a looser form of autonomy, not always explicitly territorial, termed consociationalism. The option is in essence a *group building block approach* that relies on accommodation by ethnic group leaders at the political centre and guarantees for group autonomy and minority rights; in essence, this approach is 'consociational' in that it encourages collaborative decision-making by parties in conflict. The key institutions are federalism and the devolution of power to ethnic groups in territory that they control; minority vetoes on issues of particular importance to them; grand coalition cabinets in a parliamentary framework; and proportionality in all spheres of public life (e.g., budgeting and civil service appointments).[19]

Like Bosnia, Lebanon has a political system in which representation and autonomy for the country's main religious groups is guaranteed in the constitution. Systems of communal representation have been attempted in many setting over the years, as described by scholar Arend Lijphart, an advocate of this approach, in his seminal book *Democracy in Plural Societies* (1977). Some criticize an approach that structures the political system around ethnic identities, arguing that mechanisms such as communal representation 'reify' and help harden ethnic differences, and the use of the mutual veto will lead to gridlock in decision-making. Table 14.1 summarizes the consociational model.

Power sharing: integrative approach

In contrast, the integrative approach eschews ethnic groups as the building blocks of a common society. As a distinct set of options for power sharing, it eschews groups as the building blocks of society and purposefully seeks to

Table 14.1   Consociational power sharing

Principles	Practices	Problems
Broad-based coalitions among ethnic political parties	Grand coalition governments	Elites may initiate conflict to bolster their power at the centre
Minority or mutual veto on matters of importance to the group	Group rights defined in constitutional terms for named ethnic, racial, religious, or cultural groups	Can reify ethnicity, reinforcing the divisions in society rather than promoting cross-cultural understanding
Proportionality	Proportional representation electoral system and the proposal allocation of jobs, spending, representation, and participation by ethnic group leaders	Proportional representation may reflect well the divisions in society but does not provide incentives for building bridges across community lines
Group autonomy	Federalism, territorial, or 'corporate'	May contain disincentives for contending groups to live peacefully together

integrate society along the lines of division. In South Africa's 1993 interim constitution, for example, ethnic group representation was explicitly rejected in favour of institutions and policies that deliberately promote social integration across group lines. Election laws (in combination with the delimitation of provincial boundaries) have had the effect of encouraging political parties to put up candidate slates – if they want to maximize the votes they get – that reflect South Africa's highly diverse society. In addition, the federal provinces were created so as not to overlap with ethnic group boundaries (South Africa's groups are more widely dispersed in any event). In Ben Reilly's chapter on 'Democratic Validation' (Chapter 16) in this volume, he outlines further how the key to such integrative approaches (or 'centripetalism', because it tries to engineer a centre-oriented spin to political dynamics) is the electoral system; its strongest possible effect is to engender the development of multiethnic political parties.

The integrative approach seeks to build multiethnic political coalitions (again, usually political parties), to create incentives for political leaders to be moderate on divisive ethnic themes, and to enhance minority influence in majority decision-making.[20] The elements of an integrative approach include electoral systems that encourage pre-election pacts across ethnic lines, non-ethnic federalism that diffuses points of power, and public policies that promote political allegiances that transcend groups. Some suggest that integrative power sharing is superior in theory, in that it seeks to foster ethnic accommodation by promoting cross-cutting interests. Others, however, argue that the use of incentives to promote conciliation will run aground when faced with deep-seated enmities that underlie ethnic disputes and that are hardened during the course of a brutal civil war. Table 14.2 summarizes this option and its related practices and problems.

The group building block and integrative approaches can be fruitfully viewed as opposite poles in a spectrum of power-sharing institutions and practices. Which approach is best? To make such a determination, it is useful to consider power-sharing practices in terms of three dimensions that apply to both approaches: territorial division of power, decision rules, and public policies that define relations between the government and the ethnic groups.

Power-sharing practices: an overview

Consociational

1. Granting territorial autonomy to ethnic groups and creating confederal arrangements.
2. Adopting constitutional provisions that ensure a minimum level of group representation (quotas) at all levels of government.

3. Adopting group proportional representation in administrative appointments, including consensus-oriented decision rules in the executive.
4. Adopting a highly proportional electoral system in a parliamentary framework.
5. Acknowledging group rights or corporate (non-territorial) federalism (e.g., own-language schools) in law and practice.

Integrative

1. Creating a mixed, or non-ethnic, federal structure with boundaries drawn on other criteria such as natural features or economic development zones.
2. Establishing an inclusive, centralized unitary state without further subdividing territory.
3. Adopting winner-take-all but ethnically diverse executive, legislative, and administrative decision-making bodies (e.g., a purposefully diverse language board to set policies on language use).
4. Adopting a semi-majoritarian or semi-proportional electoral system that encourages the formation of pre-election coalitions (vote pooling) across ethnic divides.
5. Devising 'ethnicity-blind' public policies and laws to ensure non-discrimination based on identity or religious affiliation.

Although this typology presents two conceptually distinct approaches, it is clear power-sharing options can be pieced together in a number of ways. Power sharing can also include measures to divide power, and can have many

Table 14.2   Integrative power sharing

Principles	Practices	Problems
Incentives for elite and mass moderation on divisive ethnic or racial themes	A president who stands for all groups and who emphasizes moderation and reconciliation (like a Mandela)	Leaders who can rise above the fray of intergroup enmity are hard to find; they cannot be simply invented
Intra-group contestation and intergroup moderation in electoral contests	The use of vote-pooling electoral systems, such as the Single Transferable Vote or the Alternative Vote	People may be unwilling to vote for candidates which are not from their community
Minority influence, not just representation	Federalism is a way to give all minority groups access to power in various regions; the regions serve as a training ground for national-level moderates	Political leaders and key publics may not be willing to respond to the incentives for moderation, preferring that minority representation will remain token or symbolic

manifestations; there is a debate, however, as to whether the power-sharing options on the table should include those of the 'power dividing' variety, precisely because it seems difficult to see how dividing power after war can contain fissiparous tendencies within war-torn societies.[21] Like any menu, levers of democratic influence can be combined to suit individual tastes. In deciding which power-sharing institutions and practices might work, there is no substitute for intimate knowledge of any given country. In multiethnic Fiji, for example, a four-year expert review of the country's political system produced a set of recommendations for a recently adopted constitution that combines measures to guarantee a minimum level of traditional Fijian (as opposed to Indo-Fijian) representation in parliament (a group building block option) with measures to promote the formation of political alliances across group lines (an integrative option). The Fiji experience points to how a well-conceived process, featuring a balanced panel of experts with firm political support, can arrive at creative solutions specifically tailored to a unique set of problems.[22] The Fiji case is instructive precisely because the efforts of spoilers (see Chapter 11 on 'Peace Processes and the Challenges of Violence' by Stephen Stedman in this volume) to disrupt integration along ethnic lines was only temporarily successful; as Fiji recovers from the attempted coup d'etat of 2000, it has returned to an integrationist formula for resolving its ethnic tensions.

Conclusion: matching problems to solutions

The practical differences among various types of power-sharing systems, and their implications for managing conflict in divided societies, could easily be lost on even the most interested observer. Most complicated are the issues of electoral system choice and the implications of various alternatives for potentially lessening ethnic tensions and buttressing moderate forces against the cries of betrayal to ethnic solidarity inevitably mounted by ethnic hardliners.[23] However, the differences are important, even pivotal, in determining whether some societies will progress beyond negotiated settlements to sustainable peace.

The underlying differences between the consociational approach and the integrative approach to living together are essential for post-settlement peace. The differences revolve around these questions:

- What are the fundamental building blocks of the political system, homogenous, powerful ethnic parties or fluid, issue-based political parties and movements that crosscut ethnic divisions?
- In governance, how are coalitions formed? Are coalitions forged between or among ethnic parties after elections, or does multiethnic coalescence occur before elections in the creation of multiethnic political parties.

- Most important, is it possible to forge sustainable political institutions that induce moderation and empower tolerant political leaders, effectively penalizing ethnonationalist politicians by marginalizing them in the pursuit of political power?

In sum, consociational power-sharing solutions see ethnic groups as the building blocks of society; in integrative systems, ethnicity is recognized, but it is not the basis of post-war politics.

There is no way to say *prima facie* which type of power-sharing system – consociational or integrative – is inherently best. Moreover, it should be acknowledged that in the most desperate cases, partition should not be abandoned as a viable option to end the violence of an ethnic civil war (as in Sudan). The challenge of all observers of a particular conflict must be to match problems to solutions. What might be possible in South Africa as a settlement to that country's transition from apartheid to democracy (which did away with ethnic representation, state sanctioned racial differentiation, and ethnic title to territory), is not possible to transplant in a complex arena like Bosnia in which it has been virtually impossible to induce the parties to accept a more integrative approach.

In matching options to solutions, much depends on the level of enmity between the contending groups, the trajectory of the war (e.g., the extent of ethnic separation that occurred) and whether or not in their negotiations, they can accept any degree of uncertainty or vulnerability to political loss. Critical to analysis of the problems is a coherent assessment of the role that ethnicity plays in the turn to violence and the salience of identity as a cause of conflict.[24] At some point, it becomes impossible to live together in broad, tolerant, multiethnic coalitions; in such cases, perhaps consociational democracy is the best alternative to violence. When consociationalism cannot work, autonomy might be a solution. When even autonomy is not possible, the time may be ripe to consider partition.

Ideally, power sharing will work best when it can wither away over time. Whether in South Africa, Afghanistan, or Liberia, in the immediate post-war period, formal power sharing has been a necessary confidence-building device to ensure that all groups with the capacity to spoil a peace settlement should be included in the institutions and given influence in decision-making. Perhaps the exclusion of the Taliban in Afghanistan from power-sharing arrangements explains, in part, the renewed violent armed conflict there. Over time, however, post-war societies need to move beyond the mutual hostage taking that a guaranteed place at the decision-making table implies, the *immobilism* it inevitably creates, and the construction of post-war societies around the fixed and unyielding social boundaries of ethnicity. Integrative power-sharing solutions have an inherent advantage, if they can be achieved. Simply put, when successful, they engineer a moderation-seeking, centripetal spin to the political system, one that allows for ethnicity but promotes fluid coalitions that transcend the cleavages of conflict in war-torn societies.

One method for achieving a subtle but steady move towards more integrative power-sharing goal is to keep the process of constitution-making going well into the post-war order. Peace agreements cannot freeze in time the conditions that pertain at the end of the war. Peace settlements need to resolve the war with certainty, but they also need to be imbued with a certain set of provisions for flexibility, continued bargaining, and opportunity for amendment. They need an incentive structure that encourages ongoing bargaining, moderation, and ethnic conflict management.[25] A practical way to begin is to purposefully manipulate the electoral system to provide new incentives to moderate and coalesce across group lines, as suggested above. Electoral systems should be designed to give politicians real incentives to motivate, moving beyond a perhaps natural instinct to play the communal card to attain power.[26] Yet a third is to engender cooperation by designing multiethnic territorial divisions of power within a country, eschewing practices of 'ethnic federalism'.

None of these methods will ensure success. Institutional choice and design, no matter how careful, cannot resolve some of the inherent commitment problems that occur in post-war societies; rules on paper cannot address the deep-seated fear that opponents will win in elections or in parliament what they had not won on the battlefield or in the streets. Nevertheless, with willingness to escape from violence, the right set of power-sharing institutions – one that carefully matches problems to solutions – can provide incentives to tip the balance from war to peace, from rigid ethnic bargaining to a more fluid democracy in which moderation trumps extremism.

Notes

1. P. Wallensteen & M. Sollenberg, 'Armed conflict 1989–1998', *Journal of Peace Research*, 36, 5 (1999) pp. 593–606.
2. See L. Harbom, S. Högbladh & P. Wallensteen, 'Armed conflict and peace agreements', *Journal of Peace Research*, 43, 5 (2006) pp. 617–31 and A. Mack, *Human Security Brief 2006* (Vancouver WA: University of British Columbia Liu Centre for Human Security, 2006). Available at www.humansecuritycentre.org (Accessed on 21 November 2006).
3. Military victories are arguable more unstable than negotiated settlements because they leave grievances among the vanquished unresolved, only to re-erupt at the first opportunity when strength has been re-gathered. For the argument that military victories are more durable than peace agreements, see R. Harrison Wagner, 'The Causes of Peace', in R. Licklider (ed.), *Stopping the Killing: How Civil Wars End* (New York: New York University Press, 1993).
4. J.P. Lederach, *Building Peace: Sustainable Reconciliation in Divided Societies* (Washington DC: United States Institute of Peace Press, 1993).

5. For example of the practical policy challenges, see 'Turning Strife to Advantage: A Blueprint to Integrate the Croats in Bosnia and Herzegovina', an International Crisis Group Report (15 March 2001). Available at www. intl-crisis-group.org (Accessed on 21 November 2006); See also S. Bose, *Bosnia after Dayton: Nationalist Partition and International Intervention* (Oxford: Oxford University Press, 2002).

6. T. Sisk, *Power Sharing and International Mediation in Ethnic Conflicts* (Washington DC: Carnegie Commission on Preventing Deadly Conflict and the United States Institute of Peace Press, 1996).

7. See S. Chesterman, T. Farer, & T. Sisk, 'Competing Claims: Self-Determination and Security at the United Nations', an International Peace Academy *Policy Brief* (May 2001).

8. C. Kaufman, 'Possible and impossible solutions to ethnic conflict', *International Security*, 20, 4 (Spring 1996), pp. 136–175 at 137.

9. For example, S. Burg, 'The International Community and the Yugoslav Crisis', in M. Esman & S. Telhami (eds), *International Organizations and Ethnic Conflict* (Ithaca NY: Cornell University Press, 1995).

10. H. Waterman, *The Political Geography of Peace and Conflict* (New York: John Wiley, 1991), p. 292.

11. R. Lemarchand, 'Consociationalism and power sharing in Africa: Rwanda, Burundi, and the Democratic Republic of Congo', *African Affairs*, 106, 422 (2006) pp. 1–20.

12. For further on this approach to analyzing the origins of power-sharing agreements, see T. Sisk, *Democratization in South Africa: The Elusive Social Contract* (Princeton NJ: Princeton University Press, 1995). For a more recent assessment that includes an emphasis on the importance of strategic interaction, see P. du Toit, *South Africa's Brittle Peace* (Basingstoke: Palgrave, 2001).

13. See J. Darby & R. Mac Ginty, 'Northern Ireland: Long, Cold Peace', in J. Darby & R. Mac Ginty (eds), *The Management of Peace Processes* (Basingstoke: Macmillan, 2000), especially pp. 78–79.

14. A. Lijphart, *Democracy in Plural Societies* (New Haven CT: Yale University Press, 1977).

15. For a more thorough overview of power-sharing options, see T. Sisk, *Power Sharing and International Mediation in Ethnic Conflicts* (Washington DC: United States Institute of Peace Press, 1995); P. Harris & B. Reilly (eds), *Democracy and Deep-Rooted Conflict: Options for Negotiators* (Stockholm: IDEA, 1998); and P. Roeder & D. Rothchild (eds), *Sustainable Peace: Power and Democracy after Civil Wars* (Ithaca NY: Cornell University Press, 2005).

16. Y. Ghai, 'Autonomy as a Strategy for Diffusing Conflict', in P. Stern & D. Druckman (eds), *International Conflict Resolution after the Cold War* (Washington DC: National Research Council, 2000). See also R. Lapidoth, *Autonomy: Flexible Solutions to Ethnic Conflicts* (Washington DC: USIP Press, 1997); H. Hannum, *Autonomy, Sovereignty, and Self-Determination: The Accommodation of Conflicting Rights* (Philadelphia PA: Philadelphia University Press, 1990) and H. Hannum & E. Babbitt (eds), *Negotiating Self Determination* (Lanham MD: Lexington Books, 2006).

17. J. Coakley (ed.), *The Territorial Management of Ethnic Conflict* (London: Frank Cass, 1993).

18. For an analysis of power sharing in the Sri Lanka case, see M. Chadda, 'Between Consociationalism and Control: Sri Lanka', in U. Schneckener & S. Wolff (eds), *Managing and Settling Ethnic Conflicts* (London: C. Hurst & Co, 2004).

19. For an assessment of consociational power sharing in Europe, see U. Schneckener, 'Making Power Sharing Work: Lessons from Successes and Failures in Ethnic Conflict Regulation', *Institut für Interkultrelle und Internationale Studien*, University of Bremen (Working Paper Nr. 19/2000).

20. D. Horowitz, *Ethnic Groups in Conflict* (Los Angeles and Berkeley: University of California Press, 1985).

21. P. Roeder & D. Rothchild (eds), *Sustainable Peace: Power and Democracy after Civil War* (Ithaca NY: Cornell University Press, 2005).

22. See the report of the Constitutional Review Commission, *The Fiji Islands: Toward a United Future* (Suva: CRC, 1996).

23. For details on the importance of electoral system choice for conflict management, see B. Reilly & A. Reynolds, *Electoral Systems and Conflict in Divided Societies* (Washington DC: National Academy Press, 1999).

24. M. Esman, *Ethnic Politics* (Ithaca NY: Cornell University Press, 1994).

25. D. Rothchild, *Managing Ethnic Conflict in Africa: Pressures and Incentives for Cooperation* (Washington DC: Brookings Institution Press, 1997).

26. Human Rights Watch, *Playing the Communal Card: Communal Violence and Human Rights* (New York City: Human Rights Watch, 1995) and B. Reilly, *Electoral Engineering for Conflict Management* (Oxford: Oxford University Press, 2001).

15
Negotiating Human Rights

Christine Bell

Human rights instruments articulate a relationship between justice and peace. The UN Charter itself opens with the objective of avoiding war and immediately references the concept of human rights. The Universal Declaration on Human Rights makes a 'just peace' thesis more explicit. It claims that 'it is essential, if man is not to be compelled to have resources, as a last resort, to rebellion against tyranny and oppression, that human rights should be protected by the rule of law'.[1] More recently, the Council of Europe's Framework Convention notes that 'the upheavals of European history have shown that the protection of national minorities is essential to stability, democratic security and peace in this continent'.[2] While a connection between human rights and peace may seem obvious and is acknowledged in human rights instruments, the attempt to base negotiated settlements to conflicts within a normative understanding of human rights law has often been seen as problematic and controversial.

The context

The controversy has to be seen in the context of negotiated settlements that have emerged over the past 17 years. Post the end of the Cold War, there was a dramatic increase in the use of negotiated settlements to end conflict occurring primarily within state borders.[3] The 1990s appeared to see a process of 'peace escalation' as peace processes took off in conflicts that had seemed intractable. The emergence of ethnic conflicts in former communist states also seemed to demand international efforts at negotiation, contributing to the rise of the negotiated settlement. As a result, since 1990, peace agreements have been signed in over 73 conflicts, each situation typically having many agreements, making over 441 peace agreements all aimed at securing ends to violent conflict.[4] Most of these agreements took place in conflicts that, while having international dimensions, were not interstate conflicts as traditionally defined but conflicts originating from within existing state borders. These conflicts were twofold in nature, conflicts involving a transition from an authoritarian regime to a democratic one, and conflicts involving self-determination challenges to the state by ethnic or indigenous groups, although some conflicts, such as in Guatemala, contained both these dynamics.[5] The post-9/11 'war on terrorism' might have been expected to reduce the number of negotiated settlements. The increased move towards emergency law regimes could be expected to enforce a presumption of state legitimacy and non-state legitimacy that would militate against seeing them as equal negotiating actors. On a more pragmatic level, laws such as those requiring proscription of terrorists simply make face-to-face talks more difficult. Surprisingly perhaps the peace agreement phenomenon shows no sign of abating. This may be due to the self-perpetuation of the international machinery that has grown up around peacemaking (peacekeeping developments, election-monitoring developments, and the new mediation machinery of individual states and international organizations). However, it also signals that the war on terrorism has left some room for political understandings of conflict that underlie acceptance of negotiations. This can be seen in the links articulated between internal conflict and 'failed states' and global terrorism, that point (however problematically) to a 'war on terrorism' rationale to work towards resolving internal conflict in terms of the rule of law.[6]

The conflict and mediation dynamics across these multiple peace processes have been very different. However, it can be argued that the peace agreement patterns demonstrate common elements to the efforts to end conflict. All used processes of negotiations between the main political and military protagonists. All worked towards the production of a common text or peace agreement in which the obligations of the parties and international actors were documented. The resultant peace agreements contain commitments that aimed simultaneously to sustain a ceasefire and effect a more permanent move from violent conflict by providing a blueprint for government and an agenda for future institutional development and agreement.

The controversy

The difficulty is that these settlements involve compromises between those who have been fighting, and their views of what the conflict 'was about'. Settlement terms therefore sit uneasily with justice claims. The argument of a tension between these agreements and human rights has revolved primarily around the issue of accountability for past human rights abuses and violations. Human rights law would appear to be the main normative framework governing the settlement regime, and this framework requires accountability for human rights violations.[7] However, pushing for accountability would seem to have capacity to undo inclusive deals between military protagonists, aimed at ending the conflict. Often presented as a debate between 'peace and justice', principled and pragmatic arguments are involved on either side. Those who argue for a 'peace first' approach that would prioritize securing negotiated settlement over accountability, often view the silencing of guns as a necessary precursor to any efforts to build the rule of law. They make a principled claim for their pragmatic approach. Those who push for accountability or 'justice first' view it as important to establishing the rule of law. The rule of law is argued to be vital to conflict resolution efforts – particularly as the agreed frameworks contemplate ongoing constitutionalized democracy as the mechanism of long-term conflict resolution. This is a pragmatic argument for respecting the principles articulated in human rights norms. This can be viewed therefore as primarily a debate over which means will more effectively lead to the ends of both peace and human rights, rather than a debate over what the desirable ends are.[8]

More recently, however, a second set of challenges to viewing human rights measures as synthetic to peacemaking efforts have begun to emerge. These challenges more fundamentally question the ends of peace processes. The apparent optimism of the early 1990s has been replaced with the clear evidence that obtaining an agreement between opposing groups – itself difficult – is only a first stage in a process that may or may not lead to reduced conflict. The UN documents now claim that nearly half of all peace agreements break down within five years, and more within a ten-year period, while many of the remainder enter a 'no war, no peace' limbo whose evaluation is difficult.[9] Research has begun to grapple with the question of what it is that makes peace agreements succeed or fail, and one answer has been that an emphasis on 'liberal internationalist' modes of peacemaking in the form of frameworks that attempt to inaugurate democratic constitutional government characterized by elections, rights frameworks, and capitalist economic regimes, are inappropriate to inaugurating the type of liberal internationalist polities that they aspire to achieve.[10]

This chapter addresses both of these challenges by examining when and how human rights come to be negotiated in peace agreements. I argue that understanding how peace negotiations reach compromise points to the tension between human rights and peacemaking as based on 'inevitable dilemmas' as regards the process of moving from violent conflict.

Peace agreement practice

At first glance, peace agreement patterns appear to be based around a move towards democratic constitutional blueprints as a 'cure' for conflict. Central to many of the resulting peace agreements is the language of human rights. The agreements of Central America and South Africa, for example, provided for a transition to democracy. They were characterized by constitutionalism designed to define, protect, and enforce rights, and to replace the arbitrary use of power with its legal regulation through checks and balances. In conflicts involving a self-determination claim by ethnonational groups, as in Northern Ireland or Bosnia–Herzegovina (BiH), peace agreements also typically attempted to re-define the access of the groups to power and to state institutions. This was then coupled with the enforced protection of individual rights, aimed at creating a working polity out of a divided society, and at reassuring all citizens that they would not be penalized based on their ethnicity. These patterns are replicated in recent agreements, such as the 2006 agreements in Sudan and Nepal.[11]

A review of peace agreements indicates that the typical peace blueprint involves three elements. First, a central deal on democratic access to power; this can be a fairly straightforward transfer of power, as in South Africa, or also include provisions to ensure the effective participation of minorities, who in divided societies are often locked permanently out of power by majoritarian frameworks. Such measures can include consociational political arrangements or autonomous areas where minority groups enjoy a degree of self-government. Second, peace agreements typically include human rights institutions with measures such as bills of rights, constitutional courts, human rights commissions, or other national institutions for protecting rights, and rights-based reform of policing and criminal justice. These aim to ensure the protection of rights and prevention of past human rights abuses in the future. Third, peace agreements often include some mechanisms to address past human rights violations, from prisoner release provisions, to provisions aimed at enabling refugees to return, through truth and reconciliation commissions which aim to account for the worst abuses in the conflict.

Despite the commonality between agreements that points to an apparent 'liberal internationalist' blueprinting, peace agreement provisions must also be understood as localized 'meta-bargain' as to the causes and solutions to conflicts. As political scientists have pointed out, violent conflict is often characterized by 'multiple disagreements over what kind of conflict it is, and about whether it is "one" or "many"'.[12] That is, there is a 'meta conflict' or 'conflict about what the conflict is about'. The different positions as to what the conflict is 'about' leads to different prescriptions for its resolution. If the conflict is about lack of democracy, for example, that leads to one set of solutions; if it is about intergroup ethnic hatred, then that leads to others.[13] Any attempt to resolve the conflict based on negotiations (rather than victory) must involve an attempt to 'meta-bargain', that is bargain over the nature of the conflict. Peace agreements can be argued to arise from a meta-bargain that is complicated rather than obliterated, by the presence of international actors with their own interests and blueprints. From this point of view, their human rights provisions can be understood as having a 'pre-political' constructivist conflict resolution role, rather than standing as a 'prior' part of a pre-existing social contract that is typical of Western liberal conceptions of rights frameworks.

I have suggested in an earlier work that peace agreements can usefully be thought of as in three categories, which correlate with three different stages of any process, and the point can be demonstrated by tracing how and why human rights commitments emerge at each stage of the process.[14]

Pre-negotiation agreements

The pre-negotiation stage of a peace process typically revolves around who is going to negotiate and with what status.[15] For face-to-face or proximity negotiations to take place each party must be assured that their attempts to engage in dialogue will not be used by the other side to gain military advantage. In order to get everyone to the negotiating table, agreement needs to be reached on matters such as: the return of negotiators from exile, or their release from prison; safeguards as to future physical integrity and freedom from imprisonment; and limits on how the war is to be waged while negotiations take place. Pre-negotiation peace agreements therefore typically include mechanisms such as: amnesties for negotiators; temporary ceasefire agreements; human rights protections; and monitoring of violations both of ceasefires and human rights. Pre-negotiation agreements also typically begin to set the agenda for talks as the parties begin to bargain, and sound out each other's positions on substantive issues. Often this takes the form of attempts to set preconditions on the negotiating agenda. Such agreements often do not include all the parties to the conflict, but are bilateral agreements between several parties; they are often not published but remain secret until a later date. Examples of pre-negotiation agreements from the South African process include: the Groote Schuur Minute, 4 May 1990, between the then South African Government (SAG) and African National Congress (ANC); the Pretoria Minute, 6 August 1990, between SAG and ANC; the Royal Hotel Minute, 29 January 1991, between ANC and Inkatha Freedom Party (IFP); the D.F. Malan Accord, 12 February 1991, between ANC and SAG; and the National Peace Accord, 14 September 1991, between a broad range of political parties including ANC, SAG and IFP, and civic society groups.

Where international mediation takes place while conflict is ongoing, the pre-negotiation agreements can be understood as including the various blueprints and attempts to structure ceasefires which precede any agreement eventually assented to by all the relevant parties. This trial and error settlement process takes place simultaneously with the war in which the parties continue to strive for military victory. Ongoing attempts to find possible frameworks for a settlement are engaged in by all parties in the shadow of their prospects for military victory. Examples of such agreements include the peace blueprints brokered by the international community, which were put on the table during the conflict in former Yugoslavia between 1992 and 1995.[16]

In pre-negotiation agreements, human rights provisions usually enter as a result of principled demands based on the experience of past human rights abuses. The pressure for a human rights component within a peace agreement typically comes from one side's analysis of the causes of the conflict. Human rights therefore necessarily require to be addressed in any attempt to resolve the conflict. Given that many conflicts are asymmetrical, the demand for human rights protections is usually initiated by the weaker party, such as Irish nationalists, Palestinians, or Bosniacs, which sees human rights as addressing a status quo against which they are battling. For both practical and philosophical reasons where the non-state group commits to a ceasefire, the state commits to human rights measures. This is because the state by its very definition claims a 'monopoly on the legitimate use of force' and therefore distinguishing legitimate from illegitimate force, requires a notion of human rights that will ground a distinction between the two.

However, because human rights issues often go to the substance of a conflict, addressing them comprehensively is usually not possible at a pre-negotiation stage. The human rights issues which come to be addressed tend to be confined to discrete issues which impinge on the negotiating context itself, such as measures to limit the waging of violent conflict (see Box 15.1). Any further agreement requires a package of issues to be addressed, and some agreement on what human rights are, and on what the conflict was about, and this is not possible at the pre-negotiation stage.

Framework/substantive agreements

The second type of peace agreement can be termed as 'framework' or 'substantive' agreements. These agreements tend to be more inclusive of the main groups involved in waging the war by military means, and usually are public. Their emergence is often marked by a 'handshake moment', signifying a

---

Box 15.1: Typical pre-negotiation agreement provisions relating to human rights

Provisions to limit the conflict:

- ceasefires
- scaling back emergency legislation
- compliance with humanitarian and human rights standards
- monitoring of compliance

Humanitarian relief to victims of conflict

Ad hoc addressing of the past:

- partial prisoner release
- partial amnesties
- independent commissions to investigate alleged abuses
- return of bodies of disappeared

'historical compromise' between enemies. Those who stay outside the process are often those who choose to do so, so as to 'outbid' those within the process, such as the Democratic Unionist Party in Northern Ireland.

Framework/substantive agreements begin to set out a framework for resolving the substantive issues of the dispute. The agreement usually reaffirms a commitment to non-violent means for resolving the conflict; acknowledges the status of the parties in the negotiations; begins to address some of the consequences of the conflict (such as prisoners, emergency legislation, and ongoing human rights violations); provides for interim arrangements as to how power is to be held and exercised; and sets an agenda, and possibly a timetable, for reaching a more permanent resolution of substantive issues such as self-determination, democratization, armed forces/policing, rights protection, and reconstruction. Examples of framework agreements include the Belfast Agreement in Northern Ireland,[17] the Dayton Peace Agreement (DPA) in Bosnia–Herzegovina,[18] the Interim Constitution in South Africa[19], and possibly the Declaration of Principles and some of the following Interim Agreements in the Middle East,[20] although these increasingly are moving towards breakdown and possible renegotiation, and in the future may even be regarded as pre-negotiation agreements akin to the failed constitutional frameworks attempted during the war in former Yugoslavia.

Box 15.2:   Typical framework agreement provisions relating to human rights

Arrangements for access to power and territory

Provision of a human rights agenda:

- bill of rights
- human rights commission
- other commissions
- reform of policing
- reform of criminal justice
- reform of judiciary

Provision of an agenda for undoing the past:

- return of refugees
- return of land

Ad hoc measures addressed at the past:

- amnesties
- prisoner release
- measures for reconciliation
- measures addressed at helping 'victims'
- embryonic and partial truth processes

Provision for civic society to become involved in implementation

Unlike the pre-negotiation agreement, human rights rhetoric only takes hold in a framework agreement if it serves the interests of all sides for it to do so. Inclusion largely depends on some type of meta-bargain having been reached. While human rights arguments may initially emanate from the less powerful, the fact that human rights standards are framed in general, abstract, and impartial terms as internationally applicable means that both sides may come to frame their claims using human rights language as the process progresses. At the framework or substantive agreement stage, an arrangement regarding access to government and territory aims to address the self-determination issues at the heart of the deal. At this point, the language of human rights can provide a vital negotiating tool by helping to carve out win-win solutions from zero-sum demands (see Box 15.2). Individualized human rights protections can address fears of annihilation, domination, and discrimination that motivate claims to territory and statehood, potentially diluting such claims. Institutions for protecting human rights can soften a power allocation at the centre of the deal by providing protections or safeguards against its abuses. Human rights frameworks at this stage therefore emerge not as 'add-ons' or 'sweeteners' to the political arrangements (although some parties to the agreement might view them as such) but as an integral part of how power is to be exercised and controlled. Interestingly, this link between political power and human rights is underwritten by current directions in international self-determination law, which is moving away from an emphasis on irreconcilable commitments to territorial integrity and representative government for 'peoples' to consideration of what peoples substantively get in terms of access to the power, equality, and resources they need to exercise free choice over their future.[21]

The interrelationship of human rights institutions and political institutions can be illustrated by the cases of South Africa, Northern Ireland, Bosnia–Herzegovina and Israel/Palestine. In South Africa, the deal most obviously provided for one person one vote and democratic constitutionalism.[22] While consociational mechanisms with power sharing provided a measure of group protection for the whites who were relinquishing power, these were all limited to five years, after which time straightforward majoritarian democracy was contemplated. In this democracy, it was clear that the main mechanism to ensure protection for whites would be not consociational tools of vetoes and balancing but human rights protections. Therefore, for example, a Bill of Rights took on increasing importance for the white minority as it became clear that the deal was moving towards majority rule without minority vetoes. For the ANC, human rights protections were also important as signalling a new regime which unlike its predecessor would be democratically legitimate and respectful of human rights. This is not to say that there was consensus on what should be in the Bill of Rights. While the generality of many core rights were accepted by both the ANC and the South African Government/National Party (SAG/NP) as necessary, the meta-conflict re-emerged with regards to whether certain rights, such as a right to property, should be protected and if so what the content of that right should be. However, the mutual self-interest in ensuring protecting of human rights meant that agreement was reached in the Interim Constitution on a Bill of Rights with supremacy over other laws, a new Constitutional Court with new selection procedures to ensure independence of the judiciary; and a number of national human rights institutions – a public protector office, a Commission on Gender Equality, and a Human Rights Commission. The Constitution also addressed criminal justice (through the Bill of Rights) and the restructuring and accountability of police and defence forces.

In Northern Ireland, the deal was classically consociational with an additional 'cross-border' element. This meant that future political institutions were to be shared between Irish nationalists and British unionists. As the deal moved towards this arrangement, human rights began to take a central place. What became known as 'the equality agenda' came to form an area of common ground between Sinn Féin and the various fringe loyalist parties, especially the Progressive Unionist Party (PUP) who particularly emphasized social inclusion. This was supported by pluralist parties such as the Women's Coalition, and by civic society operating in parallel outside the talks process. As McCrudden writes, for Sinn Féin and the PUP

> a failure to address human rights and equality issues of importance to their communities would make it much more difficult to 'sell' any agreement. Once human rights was identified as an area that was important, particularly to Sinn Féin, it then became important for those who wanted to keep Sinn Féin 'on board' to include it for reasons of strategy as well as for reasons of principle in the final Agreement.[23]

Ulster unionists, who were traditionally suspicious of human rights claims, did not tend to frame their own demands in such language. However, when negotiations intensified it became clear that human rights and equality issues could often be conceded more easily than areas that implicated sovereignty, such as cross-border bodies. They could even be traded against these bigger concessions. Furthermore, 'rights for nationalists' could be sold to constituents as a concession necessary to underwriting the international legitimacy of Northern Ireland within its present borders. As a result, the Belfast Agreement has a strong rights emphasis, although it masks disagreement by avoiding substance and instead setting out principles and associated procedures for developing the rights framework – a task which is left to the post-agreement phase. The Agreement provides for incorporation of the European Convention on Human Rights, provision for 'mainstreaming' of equality in public decision making, and other policy measures to target social need, a Human Rights

Commission which among other things is to 'consult and advise' on a Bill of Rights for Northern Ireland, an Equality Commission and commissions to examine criminal justice and policing, with agreed remits which include human rights issues. Interestingly, the agreement also provides for Republic of Ireland reciprocity in human rights, including the establishment of a Republic of Ireland Human Rights Commission and further attention to incorporation of the European Convention on Human Rights. It also provides for a joint committee of the two new Human Rights Commissions to examine the possibility of an all-Ireland Charter of Rights which would provide a rights framework for the island as a whole.

In contrast, in the Oslo Accords of the Israeli/Palestinian conflict[24] the focus of all parties on a 'separation' solution aimed at accommodating Palestinian claims for external self-determination with Israeli demands for security meant that, unlike the other examples, there was no reciprocal interest to see human rights protections instituted as part of the deal. The peace agreements in Israel/Palestine set up a form of autonomy for Palestinians. All difficult issues were postponed to final status negotiations – Jerusalem, refugees, settlements, security arrangements, borders, relations, and cooperation with other neighbours. Palestinian autonomy was limited geographically – only certain areas; it was limited personally – only Palestinians; and limited jurisdictionally – only certain spheres of operation.

What is interesting for this discussion is that the 'separation' nature of the deal undermined any mutuality in seeing human rights protections built into the deal. The focus on separation provided a distinct disincentive to incorporate human rights protections within the text of the deal. With Israelis excluded from the ambit of Palestinian authority, there was no Israeli self-interest to protect human rights. Rather, the granting of a measure of autonomy to Palestinians brought with it Israeli security concerns as to whether autonomy would facilitate or decrease Palestinian attacks on Israelis. Conversely, for the Palestinian Liberation Organization (PLO), although building-in human rights institutions could have provided the Palestinian Authority with a buffer against unreasonable Israeli security demands, there were clear disincentives to do this. Having failed to secure international standards, such as the Fourth Geneva Convention providing humanitarian standards for civilian persons in times of war (and during occupation), as governing the interim period, there was no reason to further limit Palestinian autonomy by conditioning it on human rights as policed by Israel. Not only would this have been offensive to underlying claims of Palestinian statehood but it would also have reinforced Israeli arguments that Israel no longer had responsibility for human rights violations in the occupied territories. Provision for human rights in the Israeli–Palestinian Agreements is therefore virtually non-existent. No overarching 'constitutional' framework for protecting or enforcing rights is provided. Criminal justice and policing are dealt with only so as to divide functions and powers between Israel and Palestinian authorities.

In Bosnia–Herzegovina, the deal itself must be understood as a compromise between opposing demands of separation (of ethnic groups) and sharing (pluralist approaches). The text of the DPA affirms Bosnia–Herzegovina as a unitary international state with legal continuity – thus the international community appeared to get their key demand triumphing over the secessionist demands of Croatians and Serbians.[25] However, the detail of the DPA reveals a compromise. The unitary state is to be comprised of two entities: (1) a Federation of cantons comprising mostly Croats and Bosniacs (themselves further separated through a cantonal structure); and (2) the Republika Srpska – a Serb-dominated entity. The detail of the devolution of powers reveals the entities to be, in effect, ethnic mini-states with the unitary state structure left with very limited competencies. However, a number of human rights institutions are set up to operate at the state level and control the use and abuse of power at the entity level. Thus, the DPA purports to incorporate a large number of international conventions into domestic law, including the European Convention on Human Rights. It provides for a Constitutional Court to stand superior to the governments of the entities and the unitary governmental structures, a Human Rights Commission comprising an adjudicative Human Rights Chamber and an Office of the Ombudsman, and a Commission for Displaced Persons and Refugees.

These human rights institutions are set up not just to police the entities but also to proactively attempt to reverse the ethnic cleansing which resulted in the entity division in the first place. Most notably this is to happen through provision for a right of return for refugees and displaced persons to pre-war locations which is provided for in detail in Annex 7 of the DPA. Interestingly, the human rights institutions all have provision for international membership giving the international community an ongoing role in implementation.

However, in practice the territorial concessions underlined by the deal through the devolution of power to the entities mean that they can often frustrate the implementation and effectiveness of the human rights institutions and negate mechanisms for protection of rights. Five years after Dayton, only 7 out of 37 decisions of the Human Rights Chamber had been fully implemented. Only 27 out of 57 final reports of the Ombudsperson had been complied with.[26] The United Nations High Commission on Refugees estimated that only 340, 919 refugees and 270, 001 displaced persons, out of an estimated 2 million plus displaced by the conflict, had returned, and of those most returns were to the Federation, with less than 0.7 per cent comprising non-Serbs returning to Republika Srpska. Out of 60, 000 certificates in housing cases, less than 3 per cent had led to a change over in land,[27] and the International Crisis Group calculated the number of 'minority returns', that is people returning to home areas where they would now constitute a minority, at less than 5 per cent of all refugees and persons displaced by the war.[28]

In summary, the case studies illustrate that if the deal is one where political institutions and a unified territory are to be shared between different groups, then both sides may have an interest in seeing rights language used, despite radically different notions of what human rights are, and of what their implementation will lead to in practice. In the text of a peace agreement, such differences can often be masked and postponed by the general and universal language of rights. More cynically, the language of rights may be rhetorically useful to those who do not contemplate conceding the human rights demands of the other side. Those who have not framed their demands in human rights language during the conflict will often come to do so during the peace process, recognizing it as an internationally endorsed language. Rights language may signal the satisfaction of human rights claims at the heart of the conflict, even where substance has not been conceded. Human rights institutions may stamp an agreement with the badge of democracy, giving it international legitimacy. In other words, human rights mechanisms can be conceded as the universally recognized chic language in which to write peace agreements. Bosnia–Herzegovina and arguably Northern Ireland provide two very different cases where human rights language was conceded by those who had not traditionally subscribed to such language, for some of these reasons.

Conversely, where the emphasis of the deal is on territorial separation of ethnically distinct groups then rights protections may be resisted or viewed by the parties as irrelevant, as Israel/Palestine and to some extent Bosnia–Herzegovina illustrate. The role of the international community in driving these deals and the lack of a 'mutually perceived hurting stalemate'[29] between local parties also clearly contributes to the difficulties faced.

Implementation agreements

The final category of peace agreements is implementation agreements. These begin to take forward and develop aspects of the framework, fleshing out their detail. The Israel–Palestinian Interim Agreement (Oslo II) filled out and partially implemented the framework in Oslo I; the South African Final Constitution[30] filled out and implemented the Interim Constitution. By their nature, implementation agreements involve new negotiations and in practice often see a measure of renegotiation as parties test whether they can claw back concessions made at an earlier stage. Implementation agreements typically include all of the parties to the framework agreement. Sometimes implementation agreements are not documented, and sometimes agreement takes other forms, such as agreed legislation.

Agreements do not, of course, fit neatly into the above classification; however, it does provide a basis for loosely identifying appropriate comparators across complex documentary trails of peace agreements, enabling comparison of the types of human rights provision they contain. When the texts of peace agreements are examined, a different role for human rights in each stage of agreement can be observed, leading to different types of human rights provision as responsive to the parties' positions.

At the implementation stage of a peace process, a measure of renegotiation often takes place, as parties explicitly renege on earlier commitments or more subtly try to reshape the agreement in their own image (see Box 15.3). Depending on how the agreement holds, the human rights institutions will continue to be implemented and begin their functions. Often this is the point at which civic society can become more involved in a more structural way in the peace process, through engagement with the new institutions established through the peace agreement. However, the nature of the 'deal' also helps to predict some of the difficulties that will arise at the implementation stage.

As has already been noted, conflicts in divided societies are characterized by 'meta-conflict' (the conflict as to what the conflict is about), and the need for a meta-bargain (some level of agreement as to 'what the conflict was about'). Implementation of the human rights component of a peace agreement is largely dependent on some type of resolution of this conflict – a meta-bargain – having been reached. Without such a meta-bargain, as Horowitz notes, 'the antagonists will see the choice as being merely to dominate or to be dominated and so will engage in behavior that aims at hegemony'.[31] The human rights component of

---

Box 15.3: Typical implementation-negotiation agreement provisions relating to human rights

Refinement/clarification/renegotiation of central deal

If agreement continues to move forward:

- demilitarization
- monitoring

Taking forward of human rights commitments:

- establishment of institutions
- institutions engage with society and continue to define human rights and implement HR agenda
- Increased involvement of civic society in human rights agenda (and process generally)
- More measures to deal with past human rights abuses, including perhaps a unified holistic mechanism

the agreement is just as likely to be a site for such conflict as within political institutions of government. Disagreements over what 'human rights' mean, who are the 'real' human rights abusers, and what is necessary to securing or enforcing rights, are all likely to impede and delay coherent implementation, as the examples below illustrate.

In Bosnia–Herzegovina, it is clear from the text of the DPA that the human rights institutions which aim to cement the unitary state stand at odds with the powers of the entities and the scope of their autonomy. Given the lack of ethnonational consent to the unitary structure, it is not surprising that there is resistance to implementing the decisions of the human rights institutions, as the implementation figures bear out. In Northern Ireland, the Belfast Agreement documents a partial meta-bargain. There is agreement on political and other institutions that will give both nationalists and unionists access to power. There is also agreement on mutual recognition of citizenship rights and national identities, and on how the border could be changed in the future. However, there is no agreement on a common national identity or on the final borders or issue of sovereignty, rather there is 'agreement to disagree'. The agreement's language is deliberately ambiguous as to sovereign aspirations and self-determination futures. The implementation of the human rights measures rapidly exposed the lack of agreement in the Belfast Agreement, as the example of policing demonstrates. While the Belfast Agreement contained agreed general statements regarding principles for policing, these principles masked disagreement over whether the pre-agreement Royal Ulster Constabulary (RUC) did or could comply with those principles. While Irish nationalists signed up to the principles as a precursor to radical reform, or even replacement of the RUC, British unionists later claimed that they had signed up on the basis that the RUC already largely complied. When the Patten Commission established as a result finally made its recommendations, it was the recommendation to rename the RUC, thus providing a symbolic break both with the past and a British ethos, which proved the most difficult for unionists to accept. A similar tussle developed with regard for the need, or not, for a Bill of Rights, despite the fact that, unlike the controversy that surrounded policing, prior to the negotiations all the political parties were on record as agreeing that a Bill of Rights for Northern Ireland would be desirable.

What these struggles represent is not just ongoing negotiation around implementing the human rights dimension, but a more fundamental struggle over the meaning of the Belfast Agreement, and the type of transition it establishes. Does the agreement re-define the relationship of nationalists and unionists to the state? Does it herald a 'new beginning' or a reworked former order? Does it mark a creative attempt to transcend the conflict of the past and an innovative solution to a self-determination conundrum? Or does it represent devolution with a few 'tweaks', marking limited reform within a traditional British constitutional framework? Both the implementation and non-implementation of the human rights measures not only indicate the type of transition, but also determine it.

In South Africa, where a meta-bargain can be identified involving, in essence, a clear transfer of power with human rights constraints, implementation of the human rights provisions of the Interim and Final Constitutions has confirmed the nature of the transition. It is a transition from minority rule and human rights abuses to majoritarian democracy constrained by a rights-based legal order. This is all evidenced by the functioning of the Constitutional Court, the primacy given to the Bill of Rights within the Constitution, and the signing of international human rights conventions. However, the failure of the new regime to deliver decisive movement towards socio-economic equality, and the accompanying high crime rate, indicate that while the conflict has been transformed, it has not been eliminated. The pressure for economic justice affects the work of human rights institutions and also on government policy, paradoxically at times resulting in calls for the limitations of human rights in the name of economic and social stability. Again, remaining ambiguities in the 'deal', such as whether political power was traded by the white minority for retention of economic power, continue to be worked out but in significant part, although not exclusively, through the human rights institutions.

Conclusions: tensions and complementarity revisited

This brief account of the place and role of human rights institutions within a peace agreement indicates that human rights provision cannot be separated from the proposed role and scope of the political institutions. Rather than the 'pre-political' conception of rights that underwrites bills of rights in Western constitutional discourse, human rights in peace agreements emerge as an integral part of the political landscape. Individual and group rights, political and legal institutions, mesh together to form complex constitutional arrangements. These form, in essence, a contract between competing groups regarding access to power and, depending on the conflict, territorially based control. Individual human rights provisions (both forward- and backward-looking) are crucially shaped by the deal at the heart of the peace agreement. The central deal on access to territory and power controls whether human rights protections are addressed at all. Where the deal essentially moves towards a complete 'divorce' between peoples and partition of territory, as in the case of Israel/Palestine and to some extent Bosnia–Herzegovina, then the political elites of both sides may not have an interest in seeing human rights protections written into the text of that divorce agreement and the stance of mediators may be determinative. Conversely, where complete territorial separation is not contemplated, as in South Africa and Northern Ireland, human rights institutions may be crucial to enabling agreement on access to government. Human rights protections can address past allegations of lack of legitimacy. They can also provide for future safeguards against abuse of power under the new governmental or territorial arrangements.

The protection and promotion of individual human rights is part of a bigger constitutional picture. Similarly, the political arrangements which form the other dimension of that picture are equally addressed to remedying past human rights abuses such as exclusion and domination. The overlap between law and politics does not evidence a lack of principle. Rather it indicates that peacemaking is often in fact, constitution making, and that peace agreements at the framework stage are often distinctively 'transitional' constitutions.[32]

Understanding the role that human rights protections have in conflict resolution informs both the challenges to viewing the relationship between human rights and conflict resolution as synthetic. As regards the asserted tension between issues of accountability and deal making, the difficulty is that a new dispensation based on protection and promotion of human rights requires some response to the human rights violations of the conflict. While amnesties may be asserted as crucial to achieving an agreement, some level of accountability is likely to be just as crucial to sustaining it. The tension between amnesty and accountability can perhaps best be reframed as a tension not between principle and pragmatism but between short- and long-term peacemaking imperatives. This does not eliminate the dilemmas, but can inform them. The question is changed from either amnesty or accountability, to a question of when and how accountability can best be provided for.[33] The task for mediators accordingly becomes re-shaped around a task of creative drafting aimed at securing agreement, while leaving open a range of accountability possibilities in the future.

The discussion also informs arguments about the difficulties of 'liberal internationalist' peacemaking. To the extent that this is a critique of economic liberalization, then it is convincing. However, it is also worth noting that human rights measures may help to provide a bulwark against privatization and public spending cuts. The December 2006 agreement in Nepal, for example, uses socio-economic rights, to address socio-economic marginalization, and includes provision such as nationalizing all the properties received by King Gyanendra in his capacity as the king.[34] As regards any broader criticism, the description in this chapter has aimed to illustrate that that peace agreements involve a complex meshing of the international language of democratic constitutionalism with local bargains between the primary parties to the conflict in ways that cannot easily be explained solely in terms of the preferences of international actors. Peace agreement provisions are best viewed as locally crafted 'meta-bargains' as to the nature and causes of the conflict, riven with compromise and constructive ambiguity, that are overlain by international blueprinting. To view them as inappropriate international liberal blueprints, can miss the ways in which the peace agreement sow their own implementation difficulties in a set of paradoxes that cannot be simply overcome by 'tweaking' the supposed blueprint. The paradoxes of implementation are truly profound, defying easy 'cures'. Arguments, such as Paris's, that the international community should move more slowly towards elections, would seem to entrench a trusteeship notion of international actors that can easily solidify and fundamentally undermine any attempt to promote democratic institutions as effective and legitimate.[35] Chesterman, in critiquing international transitional administrations, argues very effectively that they use means that are inadequate to the ends (i.e., they lack the necessary commitment and resources), that are inconsistent to the ends (have self-defeating mechanisms), and that are irrelevant to the ends (because they are ineffective).[36] Nevertheless, these difficulties are perhaps more difficult to escape than he suggests. Inadequacy to ends would seem to require increased international presences for longer periods of time. Yet, this would seem to increase the difficulty of the inconsistency of the means to the ends because the international role, in practice, undermines rather than builds domestic political responsibility, in what easily looks like neo-colonization. Finding a way out of this conundrum would seem to be more complicated than what more 'clarity' about the strategic objectives of international community or the relationship between international and local actors, and the justifications for 'temporary assumption of autocratic powers' by international administrations, can offer.[37] To use the example of Kosovo, the difficulty is not one of lack of clarity but rather it is the difficulty of getting agreement between all the relevant parties (local and international) as to what strategic objectives are both desirable and obtainable. The strategic objectives lack clarity because it is difficult to reconcile the competing interests and realities.

Peace agreements must be viewed as establishing a new battlefield in which the conflict over 'ownership' of the state, over inclusion and equality, or domination, continue to be worked out in the peace agreement's implementation, and through all the compromises that characterize its institutional design. This is a battle in which the local parties and international actors all have their own 'meta-conflict' positions, and which it is not preordained that any party (including international organizations) will win. It is a battle in which questions of legitimacy are paramount. It may not service easy specific policy prescriptions, but it is suggested that viewing the connection between international actors and domestic constitutionalization of disputes, and between human rights and peacemaking, as inherently paradoxical, is vitally important to moving beyond the paradoxes. Understanding the depth of the dilemma provides a surer starting pointing than articulating a set of tensions between 'justice' and 'peace' as a precursor to asserting policy options justified in terms of the dominance of either as 'separate' values.

Notes

I would like to thank Catherine O'Rourke for her research assistance.

1. Preamble, Universal Declaration of Human Rights 1948.
2. Preamble, Framework Convention on the Rights of National Minorities, 1995, ETS No. 148.
3. T.D. Sisk, *Peacemaking in Civil Wars: Obstacles, Options and Opportunities* (Joan B. Kroc Institute for International Peace Studies, Occasional Paper Series 20, 2, 2001). Available at http://www.nd.edu/~krocinst/ocpapers/abs_20_2.htm (Accessed on 6 February 2007). See also *A More Secure World: Our Shared Responsibility, Report of the High-level Panel on Threats, Challenges and Change*, UN GAOR Council, 59th Session., Agenda Item 55, para. 85, UN Document. A/59/565 (2004); *In Larger Freedom: Towards Development, Security and Human Rights for All, Report of the Secretary-General*, UN GAOR Council, 59th Session., Agenda Items 45, 55, para. 108, UN Document. A/59/2005 (2005) (hereafter Larger Freedom Document); cf. P. Wallensteen & M. Sollenberg, 'Armed conflicts, conflict termination and peace agreements, 1989–1996', *Journal of Peace Research*, 34 (1997) pp. 339–358.
4. For an incomplete list see C. Bell, *Peace Agreements and Human Rights* (Oxford: Oxford University Press, 2000), pp. 323–374; See also the peace agreement collections at Conciliation Resources. Available at http://www.c-r.org/our-work/accord (Accessed on 6 February 2007); INCORE, University of Ulster. Available at http://www.incore.ulst.ac.uk/services/cds/agreements (Accessed on 6 February 2007); United States Institute of Peace. Available at http://www.usip.org/library/pa.html (Accessed on 14 March 2007); UN Peacemaker. Available at http://peacemaker.unlb.org (Accessed on 14 March 2007); Uppsala Conflict Data Program. Available at http://www.pcr.uu.se/database/index.php (Accessed on 14 March 2007).
5. M.E. Mulvihill & G.A. Lopez, 'The Human Rights Dimensions of Peace Accords in Internal Conflicts: Insights for a Research Design', paper prepared for the panel of Do Good Things Go Together? Rights and Resolution at the 43rd Annual Meetings of the International Studies Association (New Orleans LA: March 24–27, 2002). See also Integrated Network for Societal Conflict Research, State Failure Project: Internal Wars and Failures of Governance 1954–1996, Centre for International Development and Conflict Management, 2003. Available at http://www.cidcm.umd.edu/inscr/stfail/sfdata.htm (Accessed on 14 March 2007) (categorising revolutionary wars and ethnic wars), and I.W. Zartman (1995), Elusive Peace: Negotiating an End to Civil Wars (Washington DC: The Brooking Institution) (categorising centralist and regionalist types of internal conflict).
6. See *The National Security Strategy of the United States of America* (2006), p. 15, dealing with 'failed states'. Available at http://www.whitehouse.gov/nsc/nss/2006.pdf (Accessed on 14 March 2007).
7. For the difficulties of the appropriate international legal regime governing transitions from conflict, see C. Stahn, ' "Ius ad bellum", "jus in bello" ... "jus post bellum"? – Rethinking the conception of the law of armed force', *European Journal of International Law*, 17 (2007), pp. 921–943.
8. Although it can be argued that this understates deeper theoretical differences over the definition of 'peace'.
9. Larger Freedom Document; D.A. Bekoe, 'Toward a theory of peace agreement implementation: The case of Liberia', *Journal of Asian & African Studies*, 38 (2003), pp. 256–294; R. Licklider, 'The consequences of negotiated settlements in civil wars, 1945–1993', *American Political Science Review*, 89 (1995), pp. 681–690.

10. R. Paris, *At War's End: Building Peace after Civil Conflict* (Cambridge: Cambridge University Press, 2004) and 'The perils of liberal international peacebuilding', *International Security*, 22 (1997), pp.54–89 (does not question the ends of liberal internationalism but rather argues that the implementation needs to be phased in differently). See also R. Mac Ginty, *No War, No Peace: The Rejuvenation of Stalled Peace Processes and Peace Accords* and S. Chesterman, *You, The People: The United Nations, Transitional Administration, and State-Building* (Oxford: Oxford University Press, 2004) (arguing that the peacebuilding efforts of international interim administrations are 'inconsistent with the ends', inadequate to the ends, and irrelevant to the ends); cf. also E. Mansfield & J. Snyder, 'Democratisation and the danger of war', *International Security*, 20 (1995), pp. 5–38 (arguing that in the transitional phase of democratization, countries become more aggressive and war-prone and not less).

11. Darfur Peace Agreement, 5 May 2006 (hereafter Darfur Agreement) and the Eastern Sudan Peace Agreement between the Government of Sudan and the Eastern Front, 14 October 2006 (hereafter Eastern Sudan Agreement). Available at http://www.c-r. org/our-work/accord/sudan/key-texts-index.php (Accessed on 14 March 2007); Comprehensive Peace Agreement concluded between the Government of Nepal and the Communist Party of Nepal (Maoist), 21 November 2006 (hereafter Nepal Peace Agreement). Available at http://peacemaker.unlb.org (Accessed on 14 March 2007).

12. J. McGarry & B. O'Leary, *Explaining Northern Ireland: Broken Images* (Oxford: Blackwell, 1995), p. 1.

13. Ibid., see J. McGarry & B. O'Leary, *The Politics of Ethnic Conflict Regulation* (New York: Routledge, 1993); D. Horowitz, *Ethnic Groups in Conflict* (Berkeley CA: University of California Press, 1985) and *A Democratic South Africa? Constitutional Engineering in a Divided Society* (Berkeley CA: University of California Press, 1991), pp. 1–41.

14. Bell (2000), op. cit., pp. 19–32. See also C. Mitchell, *The Structure of International Conflict* (London: Macmillan, 1981), p. 207, and T. du Toit, 'Bargaining about bargaining: Inducing the self-negating prediction in deeply divided societies: The case of South Africa', *Journal of Conflict Resolution*, 33 (1989), pp. 210–233.

15. Mitchell (1981), op. cit., pp. 206–216.

16. Bell (2000), op. cit., pp. 108, 110–111, 112–114.

17. Agreement Reached in Multi-party Negotiations, 10 April 1998 (hereafter Belfast Agreement).

18. The General Framework Agreement for Peace in Bosnia and Herzegovina, 4 December 1995 (hereafter Dayton Peace Agreement).

19. Constitution of the Republic of South Africa, 1993 (200 of 1993) (hereafter Interim Constitution).

20. Declaration of Principles, 13 September 1993, see also Interim Agreement between Israel and the Palestinians, 28 September 1995 (hereafter Interim Agreement).

21. See A. Cassese, *Self Determination of Peoples: A Legal Reappraisal* (Cambridge: Cambridge University Press, 1998); A. Eide, *New Approaches to Minority Protection*, Minority Rights Group International Report 93/4, (London: MRG International, 1995); And 1999 Lund Recommendations on the Effective Participation of National Minorities in Public Life. Available at www.osce.org/henm/documents/lund.htm (Accessed on 14 March 2007).

22. Interim Constitution (1993), op. cit.

23. C. McCrudden, 'Mainstreaming equality in the governance of Northern Ireland', *Fordham International Law Journal*, 22 (1999), pp. 1696–1775 at 1724–1727.

24. See Declaration of Principles on Interim Self-Government Arrangements, 13 September 1993, Isr.-PLO, 32 ILM 1525, and other agreements. Available at http://www.mfa.gov.il/MFA/Peace+Process/Reference+Documents (Accessed on 14 March 2007).
25. Dayton Peace Agreement (4 December 1995), op. cit., Article I.
26. Figures supplied by the Office of the High Representative Human Rights Department, September 1999.
27. Figures supplied by the Office of the High Representative Human Rights Department, September 1999.
28. International Crisis Group, *Is Dayton Failing? Bosnia Four Years after the Peace Agreement* (Sarajevo: International Crisis Group, 1999), p. 32.
29. I.W. Zartman, 'The Timing of Peace Initiatives: Hurting Stalemates and Ripe Moments', in J. Darby & R. Mac Ginty (eds), *Contemporary Peacemaking: Conflict, Violence and Peace Processes* (Basingstoke: Palgrave, 2003) pp. 19–29.
30. Constitution of the Republic of South Africa 108 of 1996.
31. Horowitz (1991), op. cit., p. 34.
32. See Bell (2000), op. cit., pp. 293–321. On transitional constitutions, see R. Teitel, 'Transitional jurisprudence: The role of law in political transformation', *Yale Law Journal*, 106 (1997), pp. 2009–2080 and *Transitional Justice* (New York: Oxford University Press, 2000).
33. See further International Council on Human Rights Policy, *Negotiating Justice? Human Rights and Peace Agreements* (Geneva: ICHRP, 2006), pp. 75–98.
34. Nepal Peace Agreement (21 November 2006), op. cit., section 3. cf. also Comprehensive Agreement (21 November 2006), op. cit., chapter. 3; Eastern Sudan Agreement (14 October 2006), op. cit., chapter. 2; And Darfur Agreement (5 May 2006), op. cit., chapter 2.
35. Paris (2004), op. cit.
36. Chesterman (2004), op. cit.
37. Ibid.

16
Democratic Validation

Ben Reilly

Introduction

In any transition from conflict to peace, the creation or restoration of some form of legitimate governing authority is paramount. While there are relatively few cases of peace deals themselves being put directly to a national vote for acceptance or rejection, at some time in the process of moving from conflict to peace, the support of the citizenry must be tested and obtained. In some form and at some point during every relatively successful process, and sometimes at more than one, the negotiators must seek public approval.

Post-conflict elections or referendums are a common, but not the only, vehicle for achieving this aim. But they are also fraught with problems which, if not appreciated, can easily undermine the foundations of any peace deal. Understanding the complex relationship between peace negotiations and the broader process of mass elections is thus a key step in crafting a lasting peace.

There is an inescapable linkage between the forging of peace deals and the process of democratic legitimation. For example, almost all peace treaties between formerly warring parties involve some changes to the apparatus of the state via revised arrangements for representative bodies, distribution of powers, territorial structure, and the like.[1] States need governments, and governments need some form of validating mechanism to prove their democratic credentials – not least to the international community and its donors, for whom this has become an essential condition for post-conflict assistance.

The most important reason for some kind of democratic exercise, however, is to ensure that the new regime can derive some claim to legitimacy on behalf of the citizens it will represent and the polity it will govern. Indeed, the consent of the electorate, and the legitimacy of a new, post-conflict dispensation is a key – and under-appreciated – variable in determining whether a peace deal will succeed or fail. How that consent can be obtained in the highly fraught atmosphere which characterizes most peace processes is the subject of this chapter.

'Legitimacy' is a difficult concept at the best of times, but in post-conflict situations it can be particularly thorny. Almost by definition, post-conflict societies are torn between competing conceptions of authority, and riven by deep societal cleavages and barely masked hostilities. Particularly in ethnically divided societies, competing visions of the state and the ideal makeup of its citizenry abound. These are often encapsulated in ethnically exclusive visions: Kosovo for the Kosovars, Fiji for the Fijians, and so on.[2] Validating or legitimizing a peace deal under such conditions is thus both an unavoidable issue that must be confronted in any transition from war to peace, and an extremely fragile high-wire act that can easily derail a nascent peace.

Democratic legitimation in such circumstances usually requires some kind of election – be it a public plebiscite on a peace deal, the selection of some kind of constituent assembly, or a full-fledged national election for a new government. And this is often where the problems of democracy in severely divided societies begin. Take, for example, the dilemma faced by United Nation's (UN) peacekeeping operations, be they in Europe (Bosnia and Kosovo), Africa (Democratic Republic of Congo), Asia (East Timor), or Central Asia (Afghanistan). In all of these cases, while the immediate focus of peacekeeping operations is, understandably, on the application of credible military force and the restoration of governing authority, the *political* dimension of peacekeeping missions quickly came to the fore once a basic peace is achieved. After all, the purpose of such missions is to create a viable state apparatus that has the capacity to function without external assistance. A primary task of promoting international security is thus the establishment of domestic political order.

Not least because so many of today's conflicts take place within states, the overarching challenge of peacebuilding is to construct a sustainable democratic state that can function without direct international involvement. To achieve this, critical choices need to be made about how the internal politics of fragile states can be stabilized, how moderate and multi-ethnic political parties can be encouraged, and how the rhythm of democratic politics can be developed and made sustainable. Post-conflict elections in high-profile cases of international intervention such as Iraq, for instance, are not just means of choosing a government but also important symbolic events signalling a new political order. In cases such as East Timor, post-conflict elections have even marked the assumption of a new nation into the family of international statehood.

Over the past decade, international peacekeeping missions appear to have developed a kind of standard operating procedure in such contexts. Once a minimum level of peace has been obtained (which does not necessarily mean a full ceasefire agreement), and a basic level of infrastructure is in place, the next step is usually to hold some sort of elections – often within a year or two of the start of the mission – followed by a rapid hand over to the newly elected authorities, and an even more rapid departure of UN troops and personnel.

All of this places considerable timing pressure on the post-conflict election timetable, and frequently leads to elections being held as early as possible in the life of a peacekeeping mission in order to create some kind of legitimate government – a pressure which in Iraq led to elections being held in 2005 in the absence of popular security and despite a boycott from one of the country's main ethnic groups, the Sunni. Such 'premature elections' can create ongoing repercussions for the development of peacetime politics in deeply divided societies even years after the war has ended – as demonstrated by the regular re-election of hardline nationalist leaders in post-conflict Bosnia, where nationalist parties and elites have not only continued to be elected by the voters but also used the democratic political process to press their sectarian aims. In most cases, the early application of elections immediately following a conflict almost guarantees that the contest will become a *de facto* contest between the former warring armies masquerading as political parties.

Undoubtedly, difficult policy challenges are involved in such circumstances. In many cases, the push towards holding rapid elections has been fuelled as much as anything by a desire to remedy the perceived lack of local political legitimacy inherent in international administrations. Elections also provide a clear point of departure for the international community – an 'exit strategy' for their involvement in a particular country. But what the 'as quickly as possible' approach to the exercise of the democratic process often fails to take account of is the stark reality that, if held too early, elections in fragile situations can easily undermine the longer-term challenge of building a sustainable democracy.

There are several reasons for this. First, elections in conflictual situations can catalyze the development of parties and other organizations which are primarily (and often solely) vehicles to assist local elites gain access to governing power. These parties are not, in most cases, broad-based vehicles for presenting competing policy and ideological platforms, but rather narrowly based elite cartels. In other cases – exemplified by the transformation of liberation movements such as East Timor's Fretilin or the Kosovo Liberation Army – political parties are merely thinly disguised variants of the armies which fought in the original conflicts. Either way, holding elections too early in the transition period can have the perverse effect of stymieing the development of more aggregative and programmatic political parties – institutions which are now widely accepted to be important facilitating agents for successful democratisation.

Second, because of the underdeveloped and deeply divided nature of most post-conflict societies, elections often have the effect of highlighting societal fault lines and hence laying bare very deep social divisions. In such circumstances, the easiest way to mobilize voter support at election time is to appeal to the very same insecurities that generated the original conflict. This means that parties have a strong incentive to 'play the ethnic card' or to take hard-line positions on key identity-related issues, with predictable consequences for the wider process of democratization. The 1993 elections in Burundi, for example, which were supposed to elect a power-sharing government, instead mobilized population groups along ethnic lines and served as a catalyst for ethnic genocide. Bosnia's 1996 and 1998 elections effectively served as ethnic censuses, with parties campaigning on ethnic lines and voters reacting to heightened perceptions of ethnic insecurity by re-electing hardline national-ists to power.[3]

This tendency towards vote radicalization has been seen in a number of post-peace accord elections and has important implications for the internation-ally supported strategy of promoting democratization. The victory of Hamas, which the United States considers a terrorist organization, at the January 2006 elections to the Palestinian Authority is a case in point. Other exam-ples include the ongoing successes for Sinn Féin and the Democratic Unionists in Northern Ireland, the inclusion of the hardline People's Liberation Front, Janatha Vimukti Peramuna (JVP) in the alliance government in Sri Lanka, and even the continued presence of Hezbollah in Lebanon. In one respect, the international champions of democracy should applaud this, since these actors are 'in the system' and their contestation of elections can be taken as a sign of moderation. But particularly in relation to the Middle East, there has been little acceptance of elections which produce the 'wrong' results – highlighting not only the hypocrisy of some Western democracy rhetoric in many cases but also the severe challenge the elections of radical movements can pose to the pluralistic, liberal notions of democracy that are typically promoted by inter-national peace-support operations.[4]

A final reason for caution about elections in post-conflict situations is more economic than political. The key problem here is the distorted economic base that most societies emerging from a protracted period of armed struggle inherit. In almost all post-conflict situations, but particularly in developing countries, local economies have been shattered by the conflict. There is often an enor-mous and highly visible disparity between the financial and other resources of local actors compared to that of the international community. In addition, handsome international development aid commitments and other potential financial rewards await the new, localized government administration. Local elites therefore tend to conclude – rightly, in many cases – that access to the state itself is a primary means for gaining economic advancement. One con-sequence of this is that, as well as being highly charged *politically*, elections in such circumstances also function as highly contested forms of *economic* com-petition, in which access to the resources of the state is the real prize. It is no surprise that two of the most successful examples of conflict transformation in the 1990s – South Africa and Northern Ireland – took place in more economically developed countries which offered real alternatives to politics as a means of economic advancement for local elites.

Taken together, all of these factors have the effect, when an election is held, of heightening tensions and undermining broader prospects for the institutionalization of democratic politics. In addition, a more immediate problem often comes not from the domestic realm but from the approach taken by the international community itself. International policymakers, not least at the UN, have tended to view elections as a convenient punctuation point in a peacekeeping mission, which can usher in not just a new government but also provide an exit strategy for international involvement. Thus Cambodia's 1993 election, the culmination of one of the biggest UN peacekeeping missions to date, was followed by a rapid departure of international forces – a departure which did little to translate results of an exemplary electoral process into solidifying a fragile new polity.

The wider obsession in the 1990s with elections as a form of conflict resolution is perhaps the most obvious manifestation of this 'quick-fix' mentality. The world is littered with elections, often conducted at the behest of the international community, which only served to inflame and politicize the root causes of conflict. Given this, it is not surprising that elections held too early in the process of state rebuilding often have the opposite results to those intended. The December 1991 Algerian elections, which were aborted after the fundamentalist Islamic Salvation Front clearly won the first round of voting, and which led to the suspension of the constitution and the strengthening of military rule, were one case in point. Another was the return to war in Angola by Jonas Savimbi after he too looked likely to lose the 1992 presidential elections. Iraq's 2005 elections, which marginalized the Sunni minority and polarized the electoral along communal lines, may be a third. In all cases, early and ill thought-through elections appeared to undermine the broader path of democratic development.

There are, however, powerful pressures, both domestically and internationally, for early elections to occur as part of the process of rebuilding in postconflict societies. For one thing, given the risk-averse nature of the international community when it comes to peacekeeping commitments, such elections can (as noted above) provide a clear exit point for international involvement. But supporting the difficult process of transforming a poor, traumatized, and war-ravaged society into a well-functioning democracy requires more than the presence of a UN mission for 18 months, with an election at the end. It means, quite simply, being prepared to invest substantial time and money in an open-ended process of social and political development. With the exception of the Balkans, which benefits from its location in Europe, there are few post-conflict societies anywhere in the world where international actors have the inclination to pursue such a long-term commitment. In most cases, the roving eye of the international media and major donors move on to other, more fashionable, causes.

A second-best alternative to this (admittedly, in most cases, unrealistic) kind of open-ended commitment is not to rush into immediate elections following a peace deal, but rather to encourage local involvement for a few years until some of the basic elements of a pluralistic party system and a functioning state have been established. This was the approach taken by recent UN missions in East Timor, Kosovo, and Afghanistan, where the establishment of local-level democratization and security took precedence over the holding of a national poll, and where national consultative bodies of local leaders were initially introduced *without* an electoral process. In East Timor, for example, the UN established a National Consultative Council, made up of representatives of East Timor's government-in-waiting, into a form of unelected legislature. In early 2001, in the lead-up to the country's first-ever national elections, the Council's membership was increased to include representatives of outer districts, women, youth, and the church. In Kosovo, similarly, municipal elections deliberately preceded nationwide ones. In Afghanistan, presidential elections were held in 2004, almost three years after the fall of the Taliban, while the parliamentary poll was further postponed until September 2005. As these examples suggest, there are some signs of an international 'best practice' or lesson-learning emerging. By contrast in Iraq, national elections to a constituent assembly were pushed through within a year of the conflict being declared over by the US president.

The problem, of course, is that an extended period of non-elected administration cannot be carried on indefinitely, and even with many years of international tutelage there are no guarantees that a democratic society will emerge. But the same can be said of too many opportunities for popular consultation as well. One criticism of the democratic principle of popular consent becoming a prerequisite for progress in peace talks is that it is open to abuse: every little step in the way can become an opportunity for procrastination or reworking by opponents. Thus in Northern Ireland, critics contend that the rolling series of elections held in the lead-up to the Good Friday Agreement merely kept unresolved issues alive, giving losers the hope that they may achieve their aims 'next time', and that fundamental principles which had apparently been agreed upon were, in fact, open to revision indefinitely.

In addition, the problem in war-torn societies of political parties often being little more than thinly disguised former armies, who may view electoral politics as a vehicle for the continuation of their previous struggles, is difficult to wish away even over a longer-term period. Simmering ethnic conflicts can be transformed into competition between new, ethnically based political parties. In such contexts, holding an election before the norms of civic peacetime politics have taken hold almost inevitably results in increased support for extremist parties. This has been a recurring feature of elections in Bosnia, for example, and is one reason why the Organization for Security and Cooperation in Europe (OSCE) in Kosovo devoted substantial resources to establishing a network of 'political party service centres', intended to support the territory's nascent political groupings and provide them with logistical and material assistance and, by implication, move them towards becoming functioning, policy-oriented parties, rather than the narrow and personalized vehicles for ethnic extremists that were evident in Bosnia.

Lest all this be taken as a counsel of despair, it is important to emphasize that under some circumstances, well-timed and designed elections and other devices for public consultation in the midst of peace negotiations can do much good. The 1998 Northern Ireland Assembly elections ushered in a power-sharing executive of predominantly pro-peace members drawn from both sides of the communal divide. It succeeded not only because its timing capitalized on the weariness with the conflict and the moderate sentiment in a significant section of the Northern Irish community but also because the 'rules of the game' were structured in such a way so as to promote moderate voices over extremist ones, and to facilitate intra-group as well as intergroup competition.[5] Similarly, the breakthrough 1994 South African election was a crucial step on the road to peace. In both cases, several years of bargaining and negotiation between rival elites preceded the electoral contests, which thus came to be viewed less as zero-sum, either/or choices than as devices by which the public could approve, or reject, a new multi-ethnic vision for the country that had been the subject of painstaking debate and many years of conflict.

Importantly, in both cases political leaders eschewed what is clearly the most damaging form of democratic legitimation – a yes or no vote on the peace deal in a plebiscite or referendum.[6] Rather, in both South Africa and Northern Ireland, early referendums were rejected in favour of a patient, carefully calibrated series of negotiations that brought extremist elements from both sides together. In each case, only after a basic package of territorial and constitutional issues had been agreed upon was a national vote held – not as a yes/no referendum but in the form of a general election that asked voters to decide on a range of issues aimed at building peace, not just on self-determination. In both cases, the result was a victory for compromise, for the moderate forces in those societies and, in a wider sense, victory for the democratic process as well.

By contrast, one of the starkest lessons of all is the danger of using 'all-or-nothing' mechanisms such as plebiscites or referendums to solve conflicts over statehood. The terrible violence which followed the announcement of results of the 1999 East Timor referendum, for example, gives a graphic illustration of the possible consequences of holding a ballot *before* basic issues of politics have been aired and discussed. In effect, such one-off plebiscites can serve to short circuit any nascent routines of political dialogue that may be emerging, and funnel all issues down into a single for or against choice. Such an exercise represents not the triumph of democracy but, more often, the rejection of politics as a means for reconciling divergent views.

Because of this, many referendums have the effect of heightening tensions, forcing both voters and politicians to adopt fixed positions and pushing rhetoric towards extreme positions. This is compounded by the highly charged nature of plebiscites on territorial disputes or self-determination, in which those with the minority view tend to see the result as a threat to their security and, sometimes, their continued existence. With no other options, minority groups often view extra-constitutional avenues, including violence, as their only recourse. In some cases, the logic of ordinary elections can work the same way. The slide into civil war in Sri Lanka, for example, was stimulated by the increasing inability of the Tamil population to achieve their objectives via constitutional and democratic means, as they always formed the parliamentary opposition to the Sinhalese majority. War became a more promising option than democratic politics for achieving political change: exit, not voice, to borrow Hirschman's typology.[7]

Despite hollow claims that the 'will of the people' must prevail, it is only the most obtuse interpretation that would recommend building peace in this way. Majoritarian devices like plebiscites are typically blunt instruments that obscure as much as they reveal. As a device for resolving deep-rooted sociopolitical conflicts, they are a particularly poor choice for one simple reason: *in a yes/no vote, one side will always lose.* Unlike in ordinary elections, in which an issue may be debated and reconsidered every few years, plebiscites – particularly on highly charged issues such as self-determination or statehood – tend to be one-offs. There are no second chances, no face-saving ways to sugar-coat the pill and no creative options such as power-sharing arrangements that build in some voice for the losers. Losers, in such circumstances, often perceive themselves to be losers forever.

Despite all this, the 1990s saw a plethora of plebiscites in sticky situations around the world. In the Balkans alone, a total of five referendums on autonomy or independence were held between 1990 and 1991 in Slovenia, Croatia, and Bosnia. Each one pushed the region closer towards war. Votes for independence not only fragmented Yugoslavia but they also radicalized the anti-independence Serb minorities, particularly in Croatia and Bosnia. In East Timor, what the UN referred to as a 'popular consultation' process was a choice between ongoing integration with Indonesia or independence. Yes or no. Under such circumstances, it was inevitable that the referendum itself would become the cause of intense conflict. Even the overwhelming vote for East Timor's independence that followed the August 1999 plebiscite, with 78.5 per cent voting in favour, left a significant proportion of the electorate – 21.5 per cent – who favoured remaining part of Indonesia. Following the announcement of the election result, this group was a fissionable, angry, and insecure minority that, with the active encouragement of the Indonesian military, acted accordingly.

Finally, because they are usually based on the most simple interpretation of majority rule, referendums almost always disadvantage minorities. This is not just because they are majoritarian in terms of assessing victory but also because they do not enable voters to express their strengths or gradations of opinion on an issue. Another reason is that, in ethnically divided societies, referendums have an alarming tendency to turn into an ethnic census, a head count of rival groups, and to encourage the mobilization of voters around stark, all-or-nothing positions which are tailor-made for extremist voices to gain circulation and currency.

Even previously non-divided societies can be polarized by the harsh logic of referendums on contentious issues. Possibly the best example of this comes from the small Pacific island state of Palau, a former US Trust Territory which separated from the Federated States of Micronesia (FSM) in 1978 as a result of referendum. Since then, Palau held no less than eight subsequent referendums, as pro- and anti-independence forces became further divided over a 'non-nuclear' clause in the new country's constitution, which was opposed by the United States, with which Palau, like other former members of the FSM, has a 'compact of association'. These eight referendums bitterly polarized the polity of a small and fragile new democracy, leading to the assassination of one president and the apparent suicide of another.[8]

Most national governments show much greater awareness of this dilemma than the international community. For example, successive Indian governments since 1947 have rejected UN resolutions which would allow a plebiscite on self-determination in Kashmir because of the likelihood that it would trigger a bloody war for independence.[9] Indeed, it is difficult to point to one successful use of referendums to resolve a deeply contentious issue such as self-determination. Even in relatively successful cases such as Eritrea, which voted overwhelmingly for independence in 1993, referendums typically serve to legitimize choices that have already been decided on the battlefield.

In the Western Sahara, successive attempts to hold a self-determination plebiscite in the Moroccan-claimed territory to determine whether the region should remain part of Morocco or become an independent state have been repeatedly postponed, with the Moroccan government accused by the pro-independence Polisario front of manipulating the voters' list. Most observers do not believe that Morocco will allow a referendum to take place until they are absolutely confident that the result will be in their favour. Such an exercise undermines the legitimating function of the democratic process, rendering the referendum itself an empty symbolic activity.

There are clear democratic alternatives to plebiscites in most cases, but they involve taking a longer-term approach to decision-making than most international actors are willing to consider. One that deserves greater attention is the French approach to dealing with democratization and decolonization in New Caledonia. In the 1980s, New Caledonia was brewing into a potentially very violent and irreconcilable conflict between the indigenous Kanak peoples and the French-origin *caldouch* settlers. The former wanted independence, the latter continued integration with France. Violence between these groups, which required the intervention of French armed forces, resulted in a 1988 peace agreement, the Matignon Accord, which guaranteed a referendum on sovereignty after ten years of increased educational and infrastructural aid to the marginalized Kanak peoples.

This ten-year period gave the space for two things to occur: genuine economic and political development on the one hand; and increasing space for alternatives to full independence to be discussed on the other. By the time the date for the referendums had arrived, a consensual agreement had been negotiated between leaders of both sides (and those of metropolitan France). The new agreement outlined a period of phased devolution of control from Paris, such that by 2015 only the overarching issues of security, defence, and foreign affairs will still be in French hands. The agreement has received overwhelming support within New Caledonia and seems to have set the territory on a more peaceful path which meets many of the concerns of both communities. As in other successful peace processes, the issue was put to a vote only *after* fundamental agreement on most contentious issues had been reached.[10]

The key issue here is one that is consistently overlooked by the international community: the *temporal dimension* of democracy and peacebuilding. By lengthening the process of negotiation in New Caledonia, the agreements provided the space for new political alliances to be forged, and for disputants to move away from fixed and artificial non-negotiable positions towards a more fluid and nuanced view of their conflict. The result was that an issue that could easily have been degenerated into a nasty civil war has instead, by skilful political handling and creative institutional approaches, apparently led to a much more benign outcome instead.

A clear indication of the danger of referendums is that, while the international community may encourage such devices to solve thorny issues in the developing world, they are used rarely and with great caution in most Western states. Major democracies such as the United States, Japan, India, and Germany have *never* held a national referendum in the post-war period, even on contentious territorial issues such as the expansion of the union in the United States or the presence of American military bases in Japan. In Germany following the fall of the Berlin Wall, a national referendum on reintegration was rejected in favour of an early national election in which parties supporting rapid reunification triumphed. In Canada, since Quebec's divisive and inconclusive 1995 referendum which rejected independence by the barest of margins (50.6% to 49.4%), and the earlier rejection of the Charlottetown accords in 1992, the national government has avoided putting the issue to a nationwide vote and now favours handling such questions without recourse to yes or no referendums.

While referendums are unavoidable in some cases, they should not be used in divided societies which are being asked to make stark choices about their future. In such cases, where a bare majority of '50 per cent plus one' is the threshold for victory or defeat, the plebiscite is a zero-sum game that rarely defuses conflict. In fact a threat of a referendum in such circumstances will often play into the hands of hardliners, who know how easy it is to mobilize mass support around nationhood issues. Thus the promise in 1999 by former Israeli Prime Minister Ehud Barak to hold a referendum on the final shape of the Israeli-Palestinian peace accords was part of a series of steps which played into the familiar cycle of escalating conflict and increasing polarization in both Israel and Palestine.

The wider lesson is clear: in any transition from conflict to peace, elections and other types of ballot need to be viewed as the beginning of a long-term process of democratization, not the end-point. Ill-considered polls are sometimes worse for long-term democratization than no elections at all. They need to be carefully designed to promote moderate sentiment, and carefully timed to avoid the perils of a too-early stimulation of competitive politics. Most importantly, they need to be seen as just one step in a much more complex and lengthy process of building a genuine sometimes-win, sometimes-lose, democracy.

Notes

1. For a survey of these see P. Harris & B. Reilly (eds), *Democracy and Deep-Rooted Conflict: Options for Negotiators* (Stockholm: International Institute for Democracy and Electoral Assistance, 1998).
2. For the best discussion of the structural patterns of ethnic conflict, see D. Horowitz, *Ethnic Groups in Conflict* (Berkeley CA: University of California Press, 1985).
3. For more on such cases, see B. Reilly & A. Reynolds, 'Electoral Systems and Conflict in Divided Societies', in P. Stern & D. Druckman (eds), *International Conflict Resolution after the Cold War* (Washington DC: National Academy Press, 2000).
4. My thanks to the editors of this volume for their insights on this issue.
5. B. Reilly, *Democracy in Divided Societies: Electoral Engineering for Conflict Management* (Cambridge: Cambridge University Press, 2001).
6. Although the South African peace process gained early impetus from a 'whites-only' plebiscite held in March 1992.
7. A. Hirschman, *Exit, Voice, and Loyalty: Responses to Decline in Firms, Organizations, and States* (Cambridge MA: Harvard University Press, 1970).

8. A. Leibowitz, *Embattled Island: Palau's Struggle for Independence* (Westport CT: Praeger, 1996).

9. For a good discussion of this and related issues, see T. Sisk, *Power Sharing and International Mediation in Ethnic Conflicts* (Washington DC: United States Institute of Peace Press, 1996).

10. D. Chappell, 'The Noumea accord: Decolonization without independence in New Caledonia?', *Pacific Affairs*, 72, 3 (1999) pp. 373–391.

17
Territorial Options

Yash Ghai

Introduction

A great deal of conflict, in ancient as well as modern times, has concerned territory. Most interstate wars have been about territory and sovereignty over it. Today most internal conflicts are over the territorial organization or partition of the state. Land and territory are emotive subjects, revered as the cradle of history, legends, and myths of communities. They are also the source of material wealth and physical security. Self-rule, jurisdiction, national security, rights of citizens, mobility, employment, and resources hinge on territory and sovereignty. It is the artefact of sovereignty with its connotations of control that give territory its political and even emotional significance.

When territory is the source of conflict, various territorial options – none of them easy – may be available to solve it. In the mid-twentieth century, major reorganizations of territory took place with decolonization, with massive withdrawals of foreign sovereignty, and the redrawing of boundaries or the partition of former colonies. The redrawing of boundaries (as the securing of independence) is seldom easy. African colonies were carved out without any regard to geography or demography, and their emergence into statehood raised acute ethnic conflicts about boundaries, cutting as they did across indigenous communities, cultures, and institutions. Such was the desire of minorities for territorial reconfiguration and such was the resistance of majorities, that Julius Nyerere urged the new states to learn to live with colonially endowed boundaries, precisely because they were so absurd – and this became the official policy of the Organization of African States. India has tried to solve its problems with China and Pakistan by redrawing boundaries – with little success. Solutions to the Israeli–Palestine conflict have foundered over precise boundaries that should separate their territories, compounded by Israeli claims to the sacredness to Jews of lands, in 'Judea and Samaria', which also constitute the heartland of the Palestinian West Bank. Boundaries, even when they are redrawn, frequently leave bitter legacies, as in Ireland and India/Pakistan/Bangladesh. It is not therefore surprising that the redrawing of boundaries has usually taken place under the hegemony of a dominant power or by the victorious after a war.

Some times when the redrawing of boundaries cannot be achieved, sovereignty over the disputed territory may be shared. In history, condomiums represent this sharing, as over the Sudan (between the British and the Egyptians) or the New Hebrides (between the British and the French). Sometimes sovereignty over disputed territory may be exercised by the international community – at least for temporary periods, as with the United Nation's (UN) administrations of South West Africa (Namibia) and East Timor, or as has frequently been proposed for Jerusalem.

Solutions to today's problems frequently involve territory in some sense, even if it is to make territory and sovereignty less salient, as in the European Union (EU) by diminishing the significance of borders among member states through mobility of their nationals, provision of common currency, direct access of groups to Brussels, resource transfers, common policies, and institutions. This may be regarded as a species of merger of territory, more clear-cut cases of which lie in classical federations, or the integration of princely states in post-independence India, or the union of Eritrea with Ethiopia.

At other times, the solution is seen to lie in making territory and sovereignty more salient, as in the disintegration of the Soviet Union and the former Yugoslavia, or the dismemberment of Czechoslovakia along ethnic fault lines. Occasionally the normal consequences of territory are obliterated or minimized by quirks of sovereignty – denials of citizenship or franchise or exclusion from land or other economic rights negate in part or wholly the constitutional status of lawful residents, and thus, in an important sense, delink them from the territory. South Africa did this by stripping Africans of citizenship rights, and eventually of citizenship itself (with the establishment of Bantustans). Israel, by conferring limited, second-class citizenship on Israeli Arabs, has maintained itself essentially as an ethnic state. More drastic versions of this approach are represented by ethnic cleansing or forced expulsions or transfers of population, for which India/Pakistan, Cyprus, Israel, and Yugoslavia provide contemporary examples. The converse of this approach is to flood territory inhabited by one group with members of another community, to dilute the claims of the original community, as with transmigration policies of Indonesia which has seen, for example, the Javanese become the majority community in West Irian, or white settlers in Australia, and North and South Americas. In Sri Lanka, one cause of the resentment of Tamils against the Sinhala is that successive governments have established settlements of the Sinhala in Tamil 'homelands'.

Because most of the approaches above are fraught with difficulties (tending mostly to sharpen conflicts), and some may indeed be outdated in this age, today the solution to territorial disputes are sought through the territorial reorganization of the state. The purpose of this chapter is to examine future prospects for some form of the spatial distribution of power, whether it is federation, devolution, or autonomy. To achieve a federal state, with its clear understanding of divided sovereignty, through the disaggregation of a previously unitary state is the hardest of the three options, while devolution seems to assume the ultimate undivided sovereignty at the centre, the protection of self-government being the restraint of the central authorities (as with the Scottish devolution). Autonomy frequently refers to an asymmetrical relationship of a part of the state to the central authorities (such as Puerto Rico with Washington, Åland with Helsinki, or Hong Kong with Beijing), with legal guarantees that can span the range between federalism and devolution. Thus while there are legal and political differences between these terms, in practice the distinctions are not always clear-cut. As limitations of space do not permit explorations of differences, I use the term autonomy throughout the paper to refer to all three forms of spatial distribution of power.

The importance of autonomy in contemporary world

Autonomy has a special fascination for politicians and political movements. It serves as a device both to bring states together in regional associations (the EU being the most outstanding example) and to keep states intact by accommodating and diffusing secessionist claims. The latter issue is particularly acute in multi-ethnic states; in many states political stability, social peace and their very future as sovereign entities depend on a satisfactory resolution of ethnically based claims for autonomy (as in Indonesia, Sri Lanka, India, the Philippines, Russia, Papua New Guinea (PNG), Canada, Yugoslavia, etc.). Some states have fragmented due to the failure to handle autonomy effectively (Pakistan with the loss of Bangladesh and Indonesia with the loss of East Timor). It is no exaggeration to say that today the very future of some states, like Russia and India, depend on how disputes about autonomy are resolved. Autonomy could be a staging post for full integration (Hong Kong–China) or for complete separation (Palestine–Israel or Cook Island–New Zealand). But autonomy also serves other purposes, examples of which are provided by the EU concept of subsidiarity, to ensure efficiency and accountability, and China's strategy for the unification with Hong Kong, Macau, and Taiwan through the policy of 'one country, two systems'.[1]

Autonomy has acquired new importance today, because of the value which is being placed on identity rooted in the culture and other traditions of a group. There are many ways in which identity can be nurtured (e.g., through recognition of linguistic, religious, and cultural rights), but autonomy is the preferred choice of groups for the possibilities it offers also of political power or self-government to protect their culture and other interests, a particularly important consideration for groups with distinct but vulnerable cultures, such as indigenous peoples. There are currently three forms of self-government: territorial/regional autonomy, cultural/group autonomy, and independence. The appeal of territorial autonomy is partly that it is an alternative to both, which for different reasons are deemed less acceptable than territorial autonomy. A particular advantage of autonomy, based on territory, is that it enables ethnic problems to be solved without 'entrenching' ethnicity, although some forms of autonomy may indeed entrench ethnicity, as with reservations where the cultural dimensions and the need to preserve the identity of the group, may serve to sharpen boundaries against outsiders, or the claims of the francophones in Quebec. Autonomy often provides a basis for a compromise as it is a mid-point of competing claims; that of a separate statehood/sovereignty, and a unitary state (as in Kosovo's relationship with Serbia; devolution proposals in Sri Lanka; current negotiations between China and Taiwan; Russia and Chechnya; current negotiations in Sudan). Autonomy can thus fudge the thorny issue of sovereignty, which has been so troublesome in several conflicts. Self-government and self-determination can be accommodated within the confines of autonomy (with substantial devolution of powers, and the paraphernalia of 'statehood' such as a flag, postal stamps, and even an anthem) while retaining intact the boundaries of the state. Various forms of autonomy are also linked to consociationalism, which, as a political form of power sharing, has been gaining popularity in recent years (Bosnia, Belgium).

Autonomy enables a region to exercise substantial self-government without assuming all functions of a state or losing the benefits of metropolitan nationality; it has been used as a form of decolonization (as with associated states such as the Cook Islands which opted for a link with New Zealand after decolonization, but assumed most functions of self-government; and as in the case with several British territories in the Caribbean). In a somewhat related way, autonomy has been used when a region of a state does not want to join a bigger union (e.g., Greenland and Faroe when Denmark joined EU; and special provisions could be negotiated for Åland when Finland joined the EU because of its pre-existing autonomy). This observation illustrates the flexibility of autonomy, which can comprise a wide variety of arrangements regarding structure and powers. Consequently, it allows considerable flexibility in negotiations and permits a gradual transfer of powers, giving time for adjustment to both sides.

While there is no consensus on the effect of autonomy on diffusing conflicts, the promise of autonomy (or the concession to renounce separation in favour of autonomy) can bring parties round a table and start the process of negotiations, even if the overall agenda is wider (Bougainville and Papua New Guinea; the Sudanese; Spain and Catalonia, and the Basque Country etc.). Sometimes merely the commitment to consider autonomy can serve to diffuse tensions, as in South Africa where the agreement to consider a 'white homeland' secured the participation of hardline Afrikaner to the interim constitution. Even if autonomy does not or cannot solve all problems, it can serve as a holding operation, allowing a 'cooling off' period and facilitating further negotiations (Palestine–Israel, New Caledonia–France).

Territorial autonomy can increase the political integration of ethnic groups with the rest of the country by accentuating intra-group differences and leading to the fragmentation of previously monolithic ethnic parties. The proliferation of parties enables coalitions of similarly situated ethnic parties (Nigeria, India) across the state. Local problems which might otherwise have created a national crisis are dealt with by the locality itself. Territorial asymmetrical arrangements encourage demands for similar arrangements by other groups (India, Nigeria, Papua New Guinea (PNG), China). The proliferation of these arrangements increases the prospects of national unity as it diffuses state power and enables central authorities to balance regional with national interests.

Autonomy arrangements, because they divide power, also contribute to constitutionalism. The guarantees for autonomy and the modalities for their enforcement emphasize the rule of law and the role of independent institutions. The operation of the arrangements, particularly those parts governing the relationship between the centre and the region, being dependent on discussions, mutual respect and compromise, frequently serve to strengthen these qualities.

The legal basis for autonomy

The presence or absence of an entitlement in either international or national law to autonomy, as well as provisions limiting its scope, can play an important role in the conduct of negotiations and the relative bargaining position of parties, especially when there is international or third-party mediation. While there is no general right to autonomy under domestic or international law, there is an increasing recognition internationally and regionally that in some circumstances there is at least a strong moral case for autonomy.[2] There is also growing political support for autonomy internationally and regionally, as well as in certain national constitutional laws. In various conflicts where the international community or foreign states have become involved, autonomy has been adopted as a solution (League of Nations in Finland and Åland; Southern Philippines; Bosnia; Kosovo; Crimea).

General principles

For a long time the principal provision for minorities was Art. 27 of the International Covenant of Civil and Political Rights. It was drafted to exclude collective rights, as it was addressed to the right of individual members of a minority, and it has been narrowly interpreted. However, in recent years the UN Human Rights Committee (which supervises the implementation of the Covenant) has adopted some interpretations of Art. 27 which recognizes that a measure of autonomy and group rights may be necessary for the protection of cultural rights of minorities. This broader approach is reflected in a UN Declaration on the Rights of Minorities adopted by the General Assembly in 1992. Unlike the International Covenant on Civil and Political Rights (ICCPR), it places positive obligations on the state to protect the identity of minorities and encourage 'conditions for the promotion of that identity' (Art. 1).

Regional instruments in Europe as well as policies towards ethnic groups place increasing importance on the identity of the minorities and consequently support a measure of self-government. The European Community used conformity with these norms as a pre-condition for the recognition of new states in Europe. The ability of existing states (which is relatively unregulated by international law) to confer recognition on entities, especially breakaway entities, can be a powerful weapon to influence their constitutional structure.

Indigenous peoples

Another source of support for autonomy is international instruments for the rights of indigenous peoples. The Convention on Indigenous Peoples adopted in 1991 and representing a reversal of the approach followed in the 1959 Convention recognized the 'aspirations of these peoples to exercise control over their own institutions, ways of life and economic development and to maintain and develop their identities, languages and religions, within the framework of the States in which they live'. The Draft UN Declaration on the Rights of Indigenous Peoples (submitted by the UN Sub-Commission on Minorities, August 1994) goes even further and proclaims their right to self-determination, under which they may 'freely determine their political status and freely pursue their economic, social and cultural development' (Art. 3). The principle of self-determination gives them the 'right to autonomy or self-government in matters relating to their internal and local affairs', which include social, cultural, and economic activities, and the right to control the entry of non-members (Art. 31).

Self-determination

The third and broadest basis is self-determination, in itself a difficult and controversial concept, but which is increasingly being analysed in terms of the internal, democratic organization of a state rather than in terms of secession or independence. The UN General Assembly resolved many years ago that autonomy is a manifestation of self-determination. The greater involvement of the UN or consortia of states in the settlement of internal conflicts have also helped to develop the concept of self-determination as implying autonomy in appropriate circumstances.

Such a view of self-determination has some support in certain national constitutions. Often constitutional provisions for autonomy are adopted during periods of social and political transformation, when an autocratic regime is overthrown (when there is considerable agitation and legitimacy for autonomy), or a crisis is reached in minority-majority conflicts, or there is intense international pressure (in which case autonomy is granted rather grudgingly). Propelled by these factors, a number of constitutions now recognize some entitlement to self-government.

The resistance to autonomy

Despite the theoretical advantages of autonomy and developing norms, there has been considerable resistance to it on part of governments. Even when granted, it may not survive, due to continuing questioning of its legitimacy by the state, or due to difficulties of managing it. In numerous cases, a settlement on autonomy has eluded negotiators, or one party has escalated its demands beyond autonomy (Sudan and Sri Lanka are obvious examples). Questions of territory can arouse deep emotions, motherland versus homeland, and other historical associations. There can also be disputes about the precise boundaries of the territory in question, as in Palestine, Sri Lanka, India (in relation to the division of the Punjab in the 1960s), and the Philippines.

Occasionally a minority may reject autonomy because it is seen as compromising the fundamental goal of separate statehood, such as Turks in Cyprus and Tamil Tigers in Sri Lanka. In such cases, a solution may be to make autonomy a temporary expedience, pending further negotiations or a referendum after a specified period allowing for time to see if autonomy provides an acceptable measure of self-government (such as in the Israel–Palestine agreement or the agreement between France and the Kanaks in New Caledonia); similar procedure was successfully adopted in the September 2001 agreement between Bougainvilleans and the national government in PNG, which brought the civil war and the attempted secession to an end. The parties not only agreed on a high degree of autonomy for Bougainville now but also agreed to hold a referendum 'no sooner than 10 years and no later than 15 years' which would include the option of full independence.

The establishment of autonomy involves a major or at least a significant reorganization of the state. For a long time autonomy was seen to clash with the project of 'nation' and 'state' building which underlay much modernization theory – and with the ambitions of 'nationalist' leaders. It upsets long-held views of the sacredness of territory and the unity of 'motherland'. It necessitates a significant reallocation of resources, including that of political power.

The leaders of the majority community may be reluctant to concede autonomy fearing the loss of electoral support among its own community (a problem that has bedevilled Sri Lanka). Majority leaders, even if well disposed to autonomy, may not have the confidence that they would be able to implement the autonomy agreement, especially if it requires an amendment of the constitution, a referendum, or even merely fresh legislation. There may be fears that autonomy will be merely a springboard to secession. This is seen to be a serious problem when the group demanding autonomy is related, and contiguous, to a neighbouring kin state. Autonomy granted to a minority in its 'homeland' may in turn create new minorities (as with Muslims in the Eastern District of Sri Lanka which the Tamil Tigers want under their control, or Christians in Mindanao, the reorganization of states in Nigeria and India, or the fear that Malaysian Borneo states may get too close to Indonesia). This may trigger demands for autonomy by the 'new minorities' and lead to further fragmentation of the state. There are of course ways to deal with these new minorities through special representation in the region, special consultative councils, local government, and by vesting special responsibilities in the central institutions for their welfare and protection (e.g., in Canada, minorities in any province can appeal to the centre against provincial discrimination, or constitutions of states which emerged out of the former Yugoslavia, or in the 2000 constitutional proposals of the Sri Lanka government). Nevertheless, these methods have seldom been effective. Connected with the preceding point is the fear that if autonomy can be justified on ethnic grounds, the rationalization and rules justifying the grant of autonomy (identity, a sense of discrimination, or injustice) may encourage the mobilization of other communities along ethnic lines, indeed to manufacture 'ethnic communities'. Autonomy may be resisted for another reason – the unpredictability of its consequences. The adoption of the federal device changes the context of ethnic relations. Territorial or corporate federal arrangements are not purely instrumental. Merely by providing a framework for interethnic relations, they affect and shape these relations. They may fashion new forms of identity or reinforce old identities. They may enhance or decrease the capacity of particular groups to extract resources from the state. They may provide new forms of contention and dispute. Equally, autonomy may break-up the internal unity of a community, leading to intra-community conflicts (Mindanao, Sri Lanka, Bougainville), and jeopardize autonomy.

The agreement between Southern Sudan and Khartoum in 2002 carries this approach farther by providing for a compulsory and binding referendum in Southern Sudan after six years from the coming into force of the agreement on secession. The Northern Ireland agreement gives the majority of the people of Northern Ireland the right to choose between continued union with Great Britain or sovereign united Ireland. Perhaps the broadest basis for secession is established by the Canadian Supreme Court which says that if any part of Canada (the case arose in reference to Quebec's desire to secede) wishes to secede, and negotiations to keep it within Canada do not succeed, the federal government must enter into further negotiations for the terms of secession.

There may also be a concern with economic and administrative efficiency which is frequently seen to be jeopardized by complex autonomy arrangements, both upwards in relations to the centre and downwards to local authorities. Because autonomy arrangements are frequently negotiated, involving different political parties, ministries, and so on, rather than planned, there may be a mismatch between powers, institutions, and resources. Autonomy inevitably adds to the costs of government (even if there are in fact efficiency gains, as much theory of decentralization claims). Autonomy also effects the operation of the economy, especially as there may be regional taxes and restrictions on the mobility of labour or preferences for local capital or labour. A related difficulty can arise from the unequal regional distribution of resources, giving a particularly sharp edge to ethnic differences. Autonomy may be interpreted merely as a way to ensure for the richer region (and community) the unequal share of that wealth; if it is a minority which resides in the rich region, it may produce resentment (and possible retaliation) by the majority group, and if it is the majority group which lives in the richer region, it may lead to the ghettoization of the other. Secessionist groups or those demanding internal autonomy are frequently accused of greed and unwillingness to share their resources with others, as in Katanga, Biafra, Bougainville, and so on.

A further limitation, connected to the need for habits of tolerance and compromise, is that federalism may be unable to accommodate communities with very different ideas, beliefs, and practices. There is sometimes fear that the fundamental values of the state may be compromised by the recognition through autonomy of different cultural or religious values. A classic, although simplified case of this, was the civil war in America (when Abraham Lincoln justified the stance of the northern states by saying that 'This country cannot endure permanently half slave and half free'). In more modern times, this was one (although not the fundamental) reason for the rejection of a federal solution to the Jewish–Arab problem in Palestine under the mandate or the UN schemes.[3] The Muslim League in colonial India rejected a federal solution for Muslims for the same reason, and the position of the French in Quebec is not dissimilar.

A specific objection to autonomy regimes comes from those who espouse an individual-oriented view of human rights. The notion of group rights that is the basis of some, even if a minority of autonomy regimes, is considered problematic from that point of view. However, even those who are less committed to an individualist conception of rights have problems with some kinds of autonomy systems. Steiner, valuing the diversity and richness of ethnic groups, has cautioned against autonomy regimes which hermetically divide one community from another. He writes, 'Rights given ethnic minorities by human rights law to internal self-determination though autonomy regimes could amount to authorisation to them to exclude "others".'[4] 'Enforced ethnic separation both inhibits intercourse among groups, and creative development within the isolated communities themselves. It impoverishes cultures and peoples.'[5]

The reluctance about autonomy may be reinforced by a sense that autonomy arrangements for the purposes of ethnic coexistence have not worked; there are certainly many examples of failure, abandonment of autonomy, and attempted and even successful secession on the back of autonomy (as was demonstrated by the break-up of the former Yugoslavia). Even if such drastic consequences are not envisaged, there may be reluctance on the basis that the relevant political culture is alien to habits of consultation and compromise necessary for success.

The future of autonomies: a framework

From the preceding analysis, it would be clear that there is no easy way to forecast the future of autonomies. I have already noted some paradoxes of autonomy: it (1) seeks to solve problem of territory, and yet may aggravate it; (2) is intended to solve the problem of identity, yet it may accentuate identity and stimulate the 'manufacture' of new communities; (3) seeks to increase pluralism, yet depends for its own success on pre-existing traditions of pluralism; and (4) aims to resolve conflict, yet aggravates disputes. It is in part around the resolution of these contradictions that the future of autonomies will depend.

It seems certain that the claims for autonomy will continue and multiply. There is now strong support for autonomy, politically, morally, and legally. These include new international norms, the concern with stability and the search for regional peace, regional and international interventions in disputes regarding autonomy, and the ability of groups to mobilize domestic and international support for autonomy or external involvement in internal affairs. There is also resistance to autonomy from the international community, states, or regional associations (as in The Association of Southeast Asian Nations (ASEAN)), arising from the commitment to integrity of states. More importantly, the majority community is usually opposed to autonomy of minorities. The future of autonomies will depend on how these competing forces are balanced.

In part, it will depend on attitudes to and the use of violence. Since the birth of or the struggle for autonomy is so often tied to violence, the dialectics of violence will be a determining factor. Will the community seeking or defending autonomy be able to mobilize violence – certainly the purchase of arms, often with the financial and logistical support of the diaspora, is easy enough? Will the state retaliate in kind, and if it does, would the citizenry tolerate high levels of violence? If the Canadian Supreme Court's decision on the unilateral right of Quebec to secede is any guide, Canada has low tolerance for violence, and pressures will build for a political settlement, which would normally favour autonomy. In India too there are limits to the use of violence, although in Punjab and Kashmir the scale of violence has been very high. Russia has shown propensity for high levels of violence, at least in Chechnya. Limits to the use of violence may also be dictated by economic costs; in some countries almost a third of the national budget is spent on armaments and armies, investments dry up, and there is a massive brain drain. Sri Lankan governments have repeatedly resorted to negotiations with the Tamil Tigers because the cost of violence and disruption is too high. Limits on the use of armed force may also emanate from foreign pressures, the effectiveness of which in turn depends on dependence on external funds. For example, PNG has been under considerable pressure from Australia and New Zealand to moderate the use of arms in Bougainville and to consider instead the grant of autonomy.

The future of autonomy may depend on how compelling or fashionable the concept of 'identity' remains. The political recognition of identities involves asymmetries in the constitutional and political systems, and is hard to justify in the face of 'universalising' values. There could be a swing back to a more 'ordered' and 'manageable' society. Identity has fewer resonances in Asia and Africa than in Europe and Canada.

Predictions about autonomies have also to be alert to other distinctions. We may need to distinguish between the fortunes of existing autonomies from prospects of establishment of new autonomies. Established autonomies are likely to survive for the costs of dismantling are high, and known to be high. Even suspensions of autonomous governments can entail severe costs, as India has discovered in Kashmir or Uganda under Obote when he dismantled Buganda's autonomy or Milosevic when he removed Kosovo's autonomy.

Another distinction that might be mentioned is the differences in political systems within which autonomy is located. The more democratic and pluralistic a state is, the better the chances that autonomy may be successfully negotiated and operated. It is thus not surprising that the more successful examples are to be found in Europe and Canada, even though more autonomies have been formed or agitated for in Asia and Africa. Relatively few autonomies have been withdrawn or suspended in Europe than in Africa. The Soviet Union and the former Yugoslavia had many formal provisions for autonomy, but in reality, the communist party dominated all public institutions and allowed little autonomy, an observation which applies to China today. Post-colonial states in Asia and Africa, engaged on the project of modernization and 'nation-building', had little patience with autonomists, and even where formal provisions exist for autonomy, they are hedged with qualifications, and permit extensive central interventions.[6] With this complexity and diversity of political systems and traditions, and socio-economic circumstances, which have a fundamental effect on the future of autonomies, it is hard to make firm predictions. Nevertheless, one statement can be made with some certainty – questions of and controversies on autonomy will remain key political issues for the near future.

Notes

1. See Y. Ghai, *Hong Kong's New Constitutional Order: The Transfer of Sovereignty and the Basic Law* (Hong Kong: HU Press, 1997).
2. For more details and references see, Y. Ghai, 'Autonomy as a Strategy for Diffusing Conflict', in P. Stern & D. Druckman (eds), *International Conflict Resolution After the Cold War* (Washington DC: National Academy Press, 2000).
3. C. Cruise O'Brien, *The Siege: The Saga of Israel and Zionism* (New York: Simon & Schuster, 1986) p. 228.
4. H. Steiner, 'Ideal sand counter-ideals in the struggle over autonomy regimes', *Notre Dame Law Review*, 66 (1991), pp. 1539–1568 at 1551.
5. Ibid., 1554.
6. Y. Ghai, 'Decentralisation and the Accommodation of Ethnic Diversity', in C. Young (ed.), *Ethnic Diversity and Public Policy: A Comparative Inquiry* (Basingstoke: Macmillan, 1998).

Part V

Peace Accord Implementation and Post-war Reconstruction: An Introduction

John Darby and Roger Mac Ginty

Peacebuilding is often associated with schemes to reinforce peace after a peace accord has been reached. The term presupposes that there is peace to build upon. In practice, peacebuilding can occur at almost any stage in a peace process and can, for example, take the form of confidence-building measures in advance of a ceasefire and negotiations. The implementation of any peace accord is highly dependent on political will and the ability of the accord to maintain a relevance to changing circumstances. In a sense, the post-accord dispensation needs to develop a life of its own. Ultimately, it needs to regularize the transfer of power and facilitate the transition from a peace agreement to a lasting peace settlement.

A key part of any process of institutionalization is the need to reform those institutions linked with security and the judiciary. These institutions may be powerful stakeholders in the 'old order', often necessitating a long and delicate reform process. Matters are often complicated by an increase in crime rates, which in turn are linked with the failure of the post-war economy to fulfil public expectations.

Barring partition, which is rarely the 'clean break' its proponents suggest, the former conflicting groups in an ethnonational conflict will be destined to share the same territory and polity. While powersharing and other technical mechanisms can be used to ease certain functional relationships, the wider issue of reconciliation is dealt with less easily. Truth recovery schemes have been employed in various locations, and often encounter the same difficulties over amnesties, partial involvement of former combatants, and compensation. In approaching this and other problems of peacemaking, there has been an active search for parallels between peace processes, and substantial lending and borrowing between cases. It is becoming increasingly clear that post-war reconstruction is as much about the reconstruction of fractured relationships (political, social, cultural, and economic) as it is about the reconstruction of infrastructure, housing, and industry. Just as civil wars are marked by peculiar economic dynamics, post-war reconstruction programmes are often accompanied by specific economic circumstances that require careful management lest public expectations become disillusioned with a poor quality or unevenly shared peace dividend.

18
The UN and Liberal Peacebuilding: Consensus and Challenges

Oliver Richmond

Introduction

The elite level, top-down, processes that have developed in order to construct the liberal peace in conflict and post-conflict zones via the United Nations (UN) and an alliance of associated actors, represent a loose, liberal 'peacebuilding consensus'. This is reflected in much of the UN, agency, donor, and NGO documentation since the 1990s,[1] as well as in much of the key contributions to the literature, both supportive and critical.[2] Yet, what does the 'peace' that is being installed in post-conflict zones through UN peace operations entail?

Through peacekeeping, peacemaking, and peacebuilding, and often under the umbrella of transitional administrations run by the UN in association with the World Bank, the United Nations Development Programme (UNDP), and many other agencies and NGOs, it is assumed that UN peace operations contribute to the construction of universally accepted liberal peace.[3] This is conceptualized through a problem-solving model that initially aims to stabilize the existing disorder through peace treaties and UN Security Council resolutions, and then endeavours to restructure it through liberal institution building.[4] The UN family, ranging from the Secretariat, Departments dealing with Peacekeeping, Political Affairs, Humanitarian Affairs International Law, the Security Council, or agencies such as UNDP or the United Nations High Commission for Refugees (UNHCR), aims to provide security, administration, and government at political levels if necessary in the context of democratization, along with development strategies, creating a rule of law, humanitarian aid, and facilitating 'Demobilization, Disarmament and Reintegration' (DDR).[5] It also plays the role of coordinator for the many other peacebuilding actors, their strategies, and resources, based upon a foundational UN Security Council resolution and mandate, where possible. These roles are often supported by regional organizations, be they politically oriented (such as the European Union (EU), the North Atlantic Treaty Organization (NATO), or the African Union (AU)) or security oriented (NATO). The World Bank and the International Monetary Fund (IMF) provide assistance and direction in the realms of marketization and economic governance. In addition an enormous range of local and international NGOs are used to subcontract human rights monitoring, local government institutional building, local development, education, reconciliation projects. These are regulated through conditional relationships between major donors such as the US, UK, Norwegian, Swedish, Canadian, or Japanese governments, foreign ministries, or development and peacebuilding organizations. Such major donors often form 'friends of' groups or contact groups whose role is to advise and guide peacebuilding in post-conflict states, often within a 'Track II' peacemaking context.

In practice, this ambitious liberal peacebuilding project has often resulted in a 'virtual peace' based upon contested attempts to import liberal democratic models via military intervention, and political, social, and economic institution building, reconstruction, and social engineering.[6] What this represents in the eyes of some is a form of limited and voluntary empire, embodied in the assistance programmes of the World Bank or the IMF, or the various forms of UN 'trusteeship', with their light or heavy 'footprints' as in Cambodia, Bosnia, Kosovo, East Timor, and Afghanistan.[7] Its purpose is to provide a 'breathing space' in which international assistance can facilitate the construction of a democratic process, a rule of law, a free market, development, nurturing security for the state, and stimulating a more active civil society. This breathing space reflects an illiberal peacebuilding interval where governance is controlled by external actors until they deem it to be sustainably constituted, whereupon governance is returned to local institutions and populations. Its voluntary nature provides it with legitimacy,[8] in which one of the most important norms of the modern era – self-determination – is deferred.[9] However, this is far from being accepted by all local actors in conflict and post-conflict zones, as 'Kosovanisation', 'Timorisation' campaigns, and spoiling violence in Afghanistan and Iraq recently illustrate. Throughout the Balkans, the liberal peace has so far generally failed to supplant ethnic nationalism.

This chapter examines the role of the UN in building and coordinating the liberal peacebuilding project in conflict zones around the world, and outlines the problems that are faced by this ambitious project.

Theorizing the role of the UN in peacebuilding

The construction of the liberal peace through the creation of new modes of social, economic, and political governance in conflict zones associated with the liberal peace is very dependent upon high levels of local and international consent and consensus as well as material support. It is often based upon an initial peace agreement, backed by the UN in many cases. It is here that the historic role and experience of the UN and its family of institutions, agencies, and networks of related NGOs, is crucial in peacekeeping and peace-support operations, peacebuilding, holding elections, providing humanitarian support, and effectively taking over governance. From the elite, top-down level, and operating from the outside-in, institutions, organizations and NGOs cooperate to a large extent on constructing the liberal peace, though of course there are the usual bureaucratic disagreements over how democratization, development, economic reform, and civil society capacity building should be conducted, by whom, and with what resources, and for which objectives. Yet this represents a consent-based governance approach, as can be seen as these practices have evolved in the UN peace operations in Namibia, Cambodia, Angola, Bosnia, and Kosovo, Sierra Leone, and East Timor.

Furthermore, the UN itself (more specifically the Secretariat, agencies, and institutions) has accepted that the 'ends' provided by the liberal, humanitarian, developmental, and democratic conception of peace are often more pressing than allowing the arguments for or against humanitarian intervention to impede the establishment of peace operations, humanitarian missions, advisory missions, democratization processes, and political reform under its auspices. The reluctance to accept the US and UK attempts[10] to renegotiate the norm of non-intervention for reasons related to humanitarianism or the dangers of weapons of mass destruction on the part of some Security Council members (such as Russian and China), the Secretariat, and members of the General Assembly on account of their stance against unilateralism in the cases of Iraq, Afghanistan, or Kosovo, has not diminished the resolve of the UN that it should be involved in post-conflict peacebuilding in line with its Charter.[11] This can be seen in the implicit symbiosis now seen between peacekeeping and peacebuilding, as laid out in a Department of Peacekeeping Operations Report of 1999, among others,[12] and in the recent creation of a Peacebuilding Commission as laid out in the *High Level Panel Report* of 2004. In some cases the UN and the broader peacebuilding community now become involved even where there has not been a formal agreement, and some-times their work is underpinned by military or humanitarian intervention, as occurred in later on in Bosnia, in Kosovo, and Afghanistan.

The UN is now expected to provide a basis for peacebuilding and the reconstruction of war-torn societies. This complex installation of peace represents a liberal-institutionalist approach based on the experience gained from the reconstruction of Germany and Japan after 1945, democratic peace theory, humanitarianism and human security, and neo-liberal development and economic reform discourses. The emergence of a peacebuilding consensus[13] can be seen in the evolution of peace interventions from Cambodia in the early 1990s to Kosovo in the late 1990s.[14] This has also led to the privatization or subcontracting of many of these tasks to the humanitarian community through the UN system or more directly by major state donors.[15] These dynamics have led to far more complicated multi-dimensional processes first theorized in the peacebuilding literatures. This evolution into peacebuilding approaches, institutionalized in the work of the UN and international agencies, International Financial Institutions (IFIs), NGOs, and the many actors engaged in conflict environments, has effectively both reopened the debate on the plausibility of outside forms of governance to mitigate and stabilize conflict, and neo-imperial critiques of the liberal bodies engaged in such activities.

These developments are outlined clearly in UN documentation.[16] *Agenda for Peace* was an attempt to improve the peace that was to be supplanted into conflict zones, based on the universal ideals supposedly encapsulated within the UN Charter, through early warning systems, preventative diplomacy, peacemaking, peacekeeping, peacebuilding, as well as peace-enforcement operations. Implicit in *Agenda* was a general commitment to the liberal peace, thus denoting responses to disarmament issues, refugees, the restoration of order, election monitoring, the protection of human rights, reforming and strengthening governmental institutions, and 'promoting formal and informal processes of political participation'.[17] This clearly required deep intervention into the social, political, and economic functions of a society if the liberal peace was to be installed. As a result, the issue of consent become a key problem, dealt with by Kofi Annan through a combination of 'coercive inducement' and 'induced' consent.[18] Yet, the UN's role in democratization is a crucial part in the construction of the liberal peace,[19] implying high levels of local legitimacy and consent are required. The democratization processes from El Salvador to Angola, Mozambique and Cambodia have been seen as integral to the creation of long-term sustainable conditions of peace. As in Bosnia, Kosovo, and East Timor transitional administrations have taken a firmer grip of this democratization. Of course this type of short-cut to the 'democratic peace' may well just lead to the creation of nationalist and ethnic 'pseudodemocracies' rather than what Snyder calls 'well-institutionalised' civic democracies.[20] Democratic elections do not necessarily prevent the re-emergence of violence, as happened in Angola after the holding of what were described as 'free and fair' elections in 1992,[21] or recently in East Timor. The UN's experience in organizing elections has seen mixed results: democratically elected representatives may be internationally recognized but not actually be locally recognized, and vice versa[22] or there may be little connection between representatives and constituencies.

Both Kofi Annan and Boutros Boutros Ghali have articulated a notion of a 'sustainable peace' – essentially a liberal peace – in their various writings on peacekeeping, peacebuilding, and humanitarian assistance. The UN embodies the historical experience of this project, mainly derived from its peacekeeping and peacemaking functions not only as an international organization in itself but also an as 'actor'. This reflects what ultimately was the post-Cold War settlement,[23] requiring strategies involving traditional military and diplomatic tasks, and deep intervention into the social, economic, and governmental institutions of that region in question. The sustainable resolution of conflict therefore implies deep and multi-dimensional forms of intervention, and a liberal and cosmopolitan faith on the part of the interveners on the infallibility of their approach. This has occurred, as Paris points out, through four key top-down and elite level mechanisms: the insertion of political and economic liberalism into peace settlements; providing expert advice during implementation; conditionality attached to economic assistance; and proxy governance.[24]

This has created practices in which states and organizations that profess to understand peace are able to intervene in conflict in order to educate others in their ways of peace, without necessarily renegotiating the peace frameworks that have arisen from the recipients' experience, culture, identity, or geopolitical location. The question of what peace might be expected to look like from the *inside* (from within the conflict environment) is given less credence than the way the agents of intervention desire to see it from the *outside,* and moderates searching for peace from within the conflict environment almost universally endeavour to expropriate Western models in their search for a solution. This resembles a quasi-colonial framework,[25] which Ignatieff describes this as 'Empire Lite' – a temporary imperial tutelage required to install peace.[26] Indeed, some commentators argue that there is no real alternative to a 'quasi-permanent, quasi colonial relationship between the "beneficiary" country and the international community'.[27] Where this exists it is normally very indirect, however, and is expressed in the conditionalities that major donors, the UN, the World Bank, and other actors impose upon the organizations that they subcontract many peacebuilding activities to, and of course on local counterparts in recipient countries. There has been resistance to these conditionalities, particularly on the part of local elites, or civil society actors concerned about their impact on local culture and identity, leading to an attempt to soften the ideological imprint of liberal peacebuilding (particularly its neo-liberal components) through devolution of responsibility, and through local participation and local ownership strategies.

UN peace operations in practice

The UN peace operations in Central America provided early examples of what was to develop more generally. These operations took their cue from previous US interventions in the region which had focused upon establishing a basis for democratic elections.[28] In Nicaragua from 1989, El Salvador from 1992, and Guatemala from 1996, solutions were reached which were then implemented by UN and joint peace operations. In Nicaragua, the UN's efforts led to the voluntary demobilization of the resistance movement, and in 1990, a UN mission observed

Nicaragua's elections. This was the first time the UN had observed elections in an independent country.[29] In El Salvador, mediation by the Secretary-General ended 12 years of fighting and a UN peacekeeping mission verified the implementation of the resultant agreements.[30] In Guatemala, UN-assisted negotiations ended a 35-year civil war, though the ensuing UN Verification Mission continues to work in the implementation of the comprehensive peace agreements.[31] In Haiti, an attempt to install the liberal peace soon faltered, despite its emphasis on democratization, human rights, consensus-building, and civil society.[32] Such operations have generally been regarded as successful in implementing the terms of the relevant peace settlements, and in starting the process of constructing a liberal peace. Yet, while democratization may have been effective in the case of Nicaragua and El Salvador, economic liberalization may have recreated some of the dire socio-economic conditions that gave rise to the conflict in the first place.[33] In Guatemala, it has been well documented that land reform has failed to occur as expected since the peace settlement in late 1996, despite progress in other areas. The major weakness of the peacebuilding experiment in these cases has been that democratization can be undermined by a failure to address socio-economic issues, and effectively that neo-liberal marketization may not complement democratization, at least in early stages.[34]

The UN operation in Namibia from 1989–1990 also focused on democratization[35] and subsequently the Electoral Assistance Division was established in 1992 to guide states making a transition to democracy.[36] The UNDP also followed suit in its attempts to promote good governance as well as the eradication of poverty.[37] The Organization for Security and Cooperation in Europe (OSCE), the EU, and the World Bank as well as many other organizations (and national development agencies such as United States Agency for International Development (USAID) or Department for International Development (DFID)) followed similar paths. Problems soon emerged, however. In Angola, the comprehensive peace accord signed in 1991 between National Union for Total Independence of Angola (UNITA) and the Popular Movement for the Liberation of Angola (MPLA) followed a pattern of democratization and elections, respect for civil liberties, and the integration of the opposing armies, to be verified by a UN verification mission.[38] Yet, elections held the following year led to prolonged fighting over a contested result. The UN eventually withdrew in 1999 and a ceasefire between UNITA and the MPLA was not signed until 2002. This failure stemmed from an inability to disarm the warring factions, or to respond to civil society voices' warnings that elections might lead the disputants into conflict. The United States and UN experience in Somalia provides another indication of the problems that were emerging. Though the UN Secretary-General was given the opportunity to apply the framework developed in *Agenda for Peace,* and the United States continued the attempt to translate its state-building experiences partially learnt through the occupation of Germany and Japan, state building in Somalia[39] led to a violent response by local warlords and militias.[40]

In the context of Rwanda, a similar picture emerged. There is a strong argument that the Arusha Accords, signed in 1993, led to violence even though they followed a familiar pattern in the creation of a transitional government, the return of refugees, and the holding of multi-party elections in 1995. This was to be supervised by a UN force.[41] The Hutu president, Habyarimana, was reluctant to sign or implement the accords but was forced to do so by international and donor pressure (especially from the World Bank).[42] This undermining of Hutu privileges probably contributed to their attempt to over-turn the Arusha Accords and to the genocide of 1994,[43] during which the UN and the international community infamously failed to respond.

In order to take a more direct control of peace processes, the practice of establishing of limited UN administrations has also emerged[44] as in Cambodia, Eastern Slavonia, Bosnia, Kosovo, and East Timor. In Cambodia during 1991–1993 the UN Transitional Authority in Cambodia (UNTAC) implemented the terms of the Paris Peace Agreements, which involved assuming responsibility for foreign affairs, defence, security, finance, communications, and civilian affairs.[45] This was effectively a transitional government even though its powers were delegated from the Cambodian Supreme National Council in which sovereign powers had been vested as a result of the preceding Paris Peace Agreements. As in Rwanda, however, the democratization process exacerbated tensions in the period running up to national elections in both 1993 and 1998 as different factions manoeu-vred for more influence.[46] In Liberia, Economic Community of West African States (ECOWAS) and the UN were involved in establishing a process whereby democratic elections could be held in May 1997. This seemed merely to exacer-bate the then President Taylor's reliance on security forces rather than a plural, democratic discourse.[47]

This form of governance intervention is reinforced by the activities of a concert of actors, including the UN and an 'alphabet soup' of international agencies, regional organizations, (IFI's), and NGOs. Their tasks involve pro-moting civil and political rights, democratization and election administration, drafting constitutions, establishing police forces and legal institutions, estab-lishing civil society, political parties, and free market economies.[48] This was and is exemplified in post-Dayton Bosnia (replicated to a large degree in Kosovo), which was to be pacified explicitly through its transformation into a liberal democracy, through the involvement of NATO's Stabilization Force, the United Nations Mission on Bosnia–Herzegovina (UNMIBH), UNHCR, International Committee of the Red Cross (ICRC), UNDP, OSCE, Council of Europe, UN Commission on Human Rights, European Court of Human Rights, and the World Bank. These actors were and are partly coordinated by an international 'high representative', an intergovernmental Peace Implementation Council, and a Five Nation Contact Group.[49] They have comprehensively taken control of governance in an effort to establish a liberal peace,[50] reinforced by the Office of High Representative's 'Bonn powers' established in December 1997, which have allowed him to issue binding decisions where agreement was not forthcoming, and to remove individuals from public office if they were undermining the implementation of the Dayton Accords.[51] Yet, local actors' responses to the attempt to construct a liberal peace in Bosnia–Herzegovina, for example, betray marked continuities with the pre-Dayton situation.[52] What is more, the construction of the liberal peace has 'paid little attention to the social and human consequences of the liberal peace'[53] and UN officials made frequent reference to 'national pathologies' and the need for 'radical surgery'.[54] Consequently, peacebuilding, despite being couched in the language of a liberal peace, overlooked the social and human consequences of the process of constructing that peace.[55] This has meant that peace in Bosnia is at best a bitter peace.[56]

Similar problems have been prominent in post-intervention Kosovo.[57] After the 11-week NATO bombing campaign in 1999, when Kosovo became a governance vacuum after the withdrawal of the Yugoslav authorities, UN Security Council Resolution 1244 created the UN Interim Administration in Kosovo (UNMIK) which was to be closely coordinated with the NATO force Kosovo Force (KFOR) by a Special Representative of the Secretary General.

(SRSG), who would also be responsible for Kosovo's administration.[58] The role of the SRSG was to oversee the replacement of Yugoslav authority and assume an interim role of governance. However, the UN, UNHCR, OSCE, and the EU struggled to coordinate themselves when the scale of the operation became clear.[59] Outside of this framework KFOR was to provide security while UNMIK's role was to perform basic civilian administrative functions, promote autonomous self-government, and reach an agreement on the future status of the region, coordinate humanitarian aid and reconstruction, maintain law, order, human rights, and assure the return of refugees. Add to these roles are a broad swathe of further responsibilities including education, health, banking and finance, post, and telecommunications. UNMIK organized elections in November 2001, but essentially governs Kosovo. There have been the usual complaints from the local communities that UNMIK did not consult with them sufficiently and ignored the local and increasingly vibrant NGO community.[60]

Similar difficulties can be observed during the UN Transitional Administration in East Timor (UNTAET), deployed in October 1999 to administer East Timor during its transition to independence in 2002.[61] The UN was mandated to establish an effective administration, to support capacity building for self-government, to assist in the development of civil and social services, coordinate and deliver of humanitarian, rehabilitation and development assistance, and establish the required conditions for sustainable development. The governance of East Timor was representative of a coalescence of the different actors and roles engaged in UN peace operations. It faced three main challenges including the creation of a sustainable budget, staffing, and gaining legitimacy in the eyes of the local population (or 'Timorisation').[62] Along with UNDP and many other agencies, the World Bank was also involved in the peace operation in East Timor in developing a number of projects in the areas of community empowerment and local government, as well as in development planning.[63] Its involvement ranged from the training of ministers, micro-loans, anti-corruption programmes, and promoting an independent media.[64] Effectively it also became indirectly involved in the establishment of democratic institutions.[65] The main criticisms levelled at the institution focused upon its elitist and enclosed bureaucracy and lack of accessibility for local actors.[66] Broader criticisms of liberal peacebuilding argued that too little was being done, generally too late, being wasteful, excessively bureaucratic, and erecting barriers to local participation. A common complaint has been that locals cannot contribute to the state-building exercise meaningfully because of their lack of capacity while internationals tend to ignore what local capacity there is.[67] There has been little effort to initiate peacebuilding to deal with social justice and welfare issues.[68] The operation in East Timor emphasized top-down peacebuilding and governance at the expense of bottom up peacebuilding, social justice, and welfare. It represented a conservative version of the liberal peace but, as the violent events of summer 2006 illustrated, has not created a self-sustaining peace.

In Afghanistan there has been a focus on advisory functions, reconstruction, and reconciliation, through the work of the United Nations Assistance Mission in Afghanistan (UNAMA) and UNDP. The UN has still effectively operated as a parallel administration, despite the resistance of the Afghan government (and its own stated intentions). The UN operation has, however, been based not on international administration, but on promoting local Afghan capacity though this has clearly been overshadowed by the sheer weight and capacity of the internationals present. This has become known in the context of state-building debates as the 'light footprint' approach.[69] The UN documentation on this assistance has been very careful to defer to the lead role of the local transitional administration, but even so the mandate of UNAMA includes national reconciliation, the tasks entrusted to the UN in the Bonn Agreement, human rights, the rule of law, gender issues, and the management of all UN humanitarian, relief, recovery, and reconstruction activities.[70] Given the fragmented nature of politics, and the presence of foreign troops engaged in providing security, perhaps the most that can be achieved in the medium term is to collude with regional fiefdoms in order to construct what Ignatieff describes as a 'rough and ready peace' rather than a fully fledged liberal peace.[71] This is also what may transpire in the context of the attempt to construct the liberal peace in Iraq after the intervention of 2003.[72]

These different versions of the peacebuilding consensus have been constructed through a globalized hybridization of approaches to the creation of the liberal peace. During transitional periods at least, this project rests on an illiberal precursor to liberal peace. This involves security forces, peacekeepers, sometimes the use of force (as seen in Bosnia and Kosovo), officials working on democratization, IFIs and development agencies, humanitarian agencies and NGOs, and a plethora of international and regional institutions and organizations working in *ad hoc* manner, though attempting to coordinate their activities where possible, while also protecting their own epistemic control of specific issue areas.[73] This complex network of actors comprise and contribute to this peacebuilding consensus, creating a perception that ever-broadening attempts to intervene, reconstruct, liberalize, and democratize failed states is a liberal imperative bounded only by strategic imperatives. The problem here is while there may be international consent in theory for such processes; gaining broad consent from factions on the ground is extremely difficult. This can be seen in the tendency for nationalists to regain power through elections, or for corruption and black markets surviving development and marketization, for local resistance to international transitional authority, and even outright violence aimed at international security forces and peacebuilders (most notably in Afghanistan).

Conclusion

It has been suggested that the first task of top-down approaches to peacebuilding and the construction of the liberal peace would be to return the monopoly over the use of violence to the state (initially in the hands of external actors), and that peacebuilders must be prepared to remain *in situ* for lengthy periods of time, regardless of the problems of creating a culture of dependency or neocolonialism.[74] Recent attempts to create a centralized UN peacebuilding agency with a much more structured approach to the full range of peacebuilding powers, rather than the ad hoc approaches generally applied,[75] imply a centralized model of peace to be implanted by the UN Peacebuilding Commission with marginal differentiation according to specific locales, but focussing essentially on the same elements of the liberal peace. A mark of how problematic this experiment has been in practice was the UN Secretary General's realization that 'participatory governance' was required for there to be a sustainable peace.[76]

Governance has become the 'new vocabulary' of the top-down version of the liberal peace and the associated peacebuilding consensus, defined as a multi-level, 'multilayered' process incorporating aspects of civil society, state and global politics, operating with public as well as private instruments. Some have described this as a rehabilitation of imperial duty,[77] while others see it as a liberal imperative. Chesterman, for example, ridicules the claim that transitional authority belongs to local communities and depends on their views.[78] The unspoken bargain is that governance will be devolved to local inhabitants once a sustainable outcome can be expected. But this might never happen. Thus, the peacebuilding consensus might lead to permanent 'peace-as-governance' – a form of 'empire lite' as described above by Ignatieff or as 'UN protectorates' by Caplan, which risk administrative and donor dependency.[79] Much has been achieved, but there are also many flaws in the liberal peacebuilding project. As ever, what little that can be done is regarded as necessary by international peacebuilders and the UN bodies involved, which are also increasing mindful of the dangers of the unintended consequences of such broad-ranging interventions.

Notes

1. Necla Tschirgi has argued that this has occurred since 9/11. This agenda appeared as early as the UN operation in Cambodia, however. See N Tschirgi, 'Post-conflict peacebuilding revisited', *IPA Peacebuilding Forum*, 7 October 2004 (New York: IPA, 2004) p. 17.
2. See in particular, K. Annan, 'Democracy as an international issue', *Global Governance*, 8, 2 (April–June 2002) pp. 134–142; A. Bellamy & P. Williams, 'Peace operations and global order', special issue of *International Peacekeeping*, 10, 4 (2004); R. Caplan, *A New Trusteeship? The International Administration of War-torn Territories* (The Adelphi Papers, Oxford: Oxford University Press, 2002); D. Chandler, 'The responsibility to protect: Imposing the "liberal peace"', *International Peacekeeping*, 11, 1 (2004); D. Chandler, *From Kosovo to Kabul: Human Rights and International Intervention* (London: Pluto, 2002); J. Chopra & T. Hohe, 'Participatory intervention', *Global Governance*, 10 (2004); E. Cousens & C. Kumar, *Peacebuilding as Politics* (Boulder CO: Lynne Rienner, 2001); M. Duffield, *Global Governance and the New Wars* (London: Zed Books, 2001); F. Fukuyama, *State Building: Governance and Order in the Twenty First Century* (London: Profile, 2004); International Commission on Intervention and State Sovereignty, *The Responsibility to Protect* (Ottawa: International Development Research Centre, 2001); R. Paris, *At War's End* (Cambridge: Cambridge University Press, 2004); Report of the Secretary-General's High Level Panel on Threats, Challenges, and Change (New York: United Nations, 2004); D. Rieff, *A Bed for the Night* (London: Vintage, 2002).
3. For an elaboration of this point see O. Richmond, *Maintaining Order, Making Peace* (London: Palgrave, 2002) especially chapter. VI.
4. M. Pugh, 'Peacekeeping and Critical Theory', BISA, LSE (18–21 December 2002) p. 1. Pugh argues that 'modern versions of peacekeeping can be considered as forms of riot control directed against unruly parts of the world'.
5. The UN Peacebuilding Commission is envisioned to take up a crucial role in these areas.
6. See, among many others, Annan (April–June 2002) op. cit., p. 135.
7. R. Cooper, *The Breaking of Nations* (London: Atlantic Books, 2003) pp. 70–71.
8. Ibid., p. 71.
9. D. Harland, 'Legitimacy and effectiveness in international administration', *Global Governance*, 10, 1 (2004) p. 15.
10. See for example, British Prime Minister Tony Blair, *Doctrine of the International Community*, Speech to the Chicago Economic Club (22 April 1999) and US President Bill Clinton, *Address to the Nation* (24 March 1999).

11. See also Bill Clinton, 'Address to the 54th Session of the United Nations General Assembly', *US-UN Press Release, No. 59 (99) 21 September 1999*.
12. DPKO, *Multidisciplinary Peacekeeping: Lessons from Recent Experience* (April 1999). See also *Report of the Secretary-General's High Level Panel on Threats, Challenges, and Change* (New York: United Nations, 2004).
13. Pugh has also described what he calls the 'New York consensus'. See M. Pugh (18–21 December 2002), op. cit., pp. 6–9. These conceptions are similar to, and perhaps familiar as the 'Washington Consensus', which has often come to be used as a synonym for neo-liberalism and 'market fundamentalism'. See J. Williamson, 'What Should The Bank Think About The Washington Consensus?', Paper prepared as a background to the World Bank's *World Development Report 2000* (July 1999), Available at www.worldbank.org/research/journals/wbro/obsaug00/pdf/(6)Williamson.pdf (Accessed on 18 August 2006), p. 1. For a critique, see G. Soros, *The Crisis of Global Capitalism* (London: Little Brown, 1998).
14. N. Wheeler, 'The Political and Moral Limits of Western Military Intervention to Protect Civilians in Danger', in C. MacInnes & N. Wheeler (eds), *Dimensions of Western Military Intervention* (London: Frank Cass, 2002) p. 3.
15. See in particular, M. Duffield, *Global Governance and the New Wars: The Merging of Development and Security* (London: Zed Books, 2001).
16. See B. Boutros Ghali, *An Agenda for Peace: Preventive Diplomacy, Peacemaking and Peace-Keeping*, A/47/277-S/24111 (17 June 1992); *An Agenda for Development: Report of the Secretary-General*, A/48/935 (6 May 1994); *An Agenda for Democratization*, A/50/332 AND A/51/512 (17 December 1996).
17. *Agenda for Peace* (17 June 1992), op. cit., para. 55.
18. K. Annan, cited by P. Wilkinson, 'Sharpening the Weapons of Peace: Peace Support Operations and Complex Emergencies', in T. Woodhouse & O. Ramsbotham, *Peacekeeping and Conflict Resolution* (London: Frank Cass, 2000) p. 63.
19. Annan (April–June 2002), op. cit., p. 135.
20. J. Snyder, *From Voting to Violence* (London: W.W. Norton, 2000) p. 43.
21. Annan (April–June 2002), op. cit., p. 136.
22. Chopra & Hohe (2004), op. cit., p. 292.
23. I. Clarke, 'Another double movement: The great transformation after the Cold War?', *Review of International Studies*, 27 (2001) p. 248.
24. Paris (2004), op. cit., pp. 642–645.
25. M. Shaw, 'Post-imperial and quasi-imperial: State and empire in the global era', *Millennium*, 31, 2 (2002) pp. 327–336.
26. Michael Ignatieff, Empire Lite: Nation-Building in Bosnia, Kosovo and Afghanistan, Vintage, 2003, p. vii. Indeed, he argues that this 'humanitarian empire is the new face of an old figure: The democratic free world, the Christian west', p. 17.
27. Fukuyama (2004), op. cit., p. 141.
28. K. von Hippel, *Democracy by Force* (Cambridge: Cambridge University Press, 1999).
29. See *UN Security Council Resolution 644* (7 November 1989).
30. See UN *Security Council resolution 693* (20 May 1991).
31. See UN *Security Council Resolution 1094* (20 January 1997).
32. See among many other UN resolutions on Haiti, *UN Security Council Resolution 975* (30 January 1995).
33. Paris (2004), op. cit., pp. 121, 124.
34. Ibid., p. 134.
35. *UN Security Council Resolution 632* (16 February 1989).
36. See *General Assembly Resolution A/RES/46/137* (9 March 1992).

37. *UNDP Mission Statement.* Available at http://www.pcpafg.org/Organizations/undp/ UNDP%20Mission%20Statement.htmcheck web. Accessed on 1 November 2004.
38. *UN Security Council Resolution 696* (30 May 1991).
39. *UN Security Council Resolution 814* (26 March 1993).
40. For an excellent analysis of this see von Hippel (1999), op.cit., pp. 80–90.
41. *UN Security Council Resolution 872* (5 October 1993).
42. Paris (2004), op. cit., p. 71.
43. Ibid., p. 74.
44. Ibid., p. 18.
45. *UN Security Council Resolution 745* (28 February, 1992).
46. Paris (2004), op. cit., p. 87.
47. For more on this see *Liberia Unravelling*, ICG Africa Briefing Paper (19 August 2002). Available at http://www.icg.org/library/documents/report_archive/A400741_1908 2002.pdf. Accessed 1 November 2004.
48. See Paris (2004), op. cit., pp. 18–20 for an excellent overview of this.
49. For a fascinating evaluation of this complex operation see Cousens, E. 'Building Peace in Bosnia', in Cousens & Kumar, op. cit., pp. 113–152.
50. R. Caplan, 'International authority and state building: The case of Bosnia and Herzegovina', *Global Governance,* 10, 1 (2004) p. 15.
51. Ibid., p. 14. See also Peace Implementation Council, *Bosnia and Herzegovina 1998: Self-sustaining Structures* (Bonn: 10 December 1997).
52. M. Pugh, 'Bosnia and Herzegovina in South-East Europe', *War Economies in Their Regional Context: The Challenge of Transformation* (Boulder CO: Lynne Rienner, 2003) pp. 235–236.
53. Ibid., p. 267.
54. UNDP Resident Representative, cited by Pugh, Ibid., p. 256.
55. Ibid., p. 267.
56. This was the assessment of DFID personnel in Sarajevo. Personal Interview, Unattributable Official Source, DFID, Sarajevo (17 January 2005).
57. For example, see Independent Commission for Kosovo *Kosovo Report: Conflict, International Response, Lessons Learned* (Oxford: Independent Commission for Kosovo/Oxford University Press, 2000).
58. *Security Council Resolution 1244* (10 June 1999) mandated UNMIK to perform basic civilian administrative functions; promote the establishment of substantial autonomy and self-government in Kosovo; facilitate a political process to determine Kosovo's future status; coordinate humanitarian and disaster relief of all international agencies; support the reconstruction of key infrastructure; maintain civil law and order; promote human rights; and assure the safe and unimpeded return of all refugees and displaced persons to their homes in Kosovo. It was to work closely with Kosovo's leaders and people. It brought together four pillars under its leadership: Pillar I – Police and Justice, under the direct leadership of the United Nations; Pillar II – Civil Administration, under the direct leadership of the United Nations; Pillar III – Democratization and Institution Building, led by the Organization for Security and Co-operation in Europe; and Pillar IV – Reconstruction and Economic Development, led by the European Union.
59. For an excellent account of this see W. O'Neill, *Kosovo: An Unfinished Peace* (Boulder CO: Lynne Rienner, 2002) pp. 37–40.
60. O'Neill (2002), op. cit., p. 129.
61. See *UN Security Council Resolution 1272* (25 October 1999).
62. M. Smith, *Peacekeeping in East Timor* (Boulder CO: Lynne Rienner, 2003) p. 63.
63. Ibid., p. 88.

64. P. Chandran, Personal Interview, Public Relations, World Bank, Dili (10 November 2004).
65. A member of the World Bank team in Dili admitted to me that this role was not openly referred to because of the sensitivity of the Timorese government, and because the bank is not supposed to have a political agenda.
66. See among many others, 'The World Bank in East Timor', *The La'o Hamutuk Bulletin*, 1, 4 (December 2000).
67. S. Frietas, Personal Interview, Programme Manager, Democracy and Governance Programme, USAID (11 November 2004).
68. O. Ofstad, Personal Interview, Head of Delegation, International Federation of Red Cross and Red Crescent Societies (Dili: 11 November 2004).
69. See for example, 'Speech of the Special Representative of the Secretary-General for Afghanistan', Opening of 55th Annual DPI/NGO conference, *Rebuilding Societies Emerging from Confect: A Shared Responsibility* (New York: 9 September 2002).
70. See *UN Security Council Resolution 1401* (28 March 2002).
71. Michael Ignatieff, Empire Lite: Nation-Building in Bosnia, Kosovo and Afghanistan, Vintage, 2003, p. 92.
72. Graham Day & Christopher Freeman have argued that what is required in this case is 'policekeeping', an approach based upon 'chapter VII and a half' of the UN Charter in which the responsibilities of 'cosmopolitan humanitarianism' leads to military intervention followed by regional policing and reconstruction along the lines suggested by the peacebuilding concensus. See G. Day & C. Freeman, 'Policekeeping is the key: Rebuilding the international security architecture of postwar Iraq', *International Affairs*, 79, 29 (2003), p. 301.
73. Chopra points out that the subculture of the UN is rooted in 'talking to a minority elite'. Ibid., p. 290.
74. Paris (2004), op. cit., p. 207.
75. See *Report of the Secretary-General's High Level Panel on Threats, Challenges, and Change*, A/59/565 (2 December 2004), p. 69; Paris (2004), op. cit., pp. 228–233.
76. UN Secretary General Report, 'No Exit Without Strategy', *UN Doc. S/2001/394* (20 April 2001) p. 2.
77. Chandler (2002), op. cit., p. 190.
78. Chesterman Simon, *You, the People: The United Nations, Transitional Administration, and State-Building* (Oxford: Oxford University Press, 2004), p. 5.
79. Caplan (2004), op. cit., pp. 7, 11.

19

From Peace to Democratization: Lessons from Central America

Cynthia J. Arnson and Dinorah Azpuru

> The transition from war to peace does not come spontaneously or easily ... years of strife inevitably leave deep scars, bitter memories and rancour. Peace is won only by effort and resolve. There must therefore be a change in attitudes, a change in mentalities. Reconciliation must be the new challenge; social justice and the struggle against poverty, the new goals.
>
> (UN Secretary-General Boutros Boutros-Ghali, on the occasion of the final demobilization of El Salvador's Farabundo Martí National Liberation Front (FMLN), December 1992[1])

Introduction

In 1999, at a seminar on peacemaking and preventive diplomacy sponsored by the UN Institute for Training and Research, a participant identified two types of peace: the 'no more shooting type', and the 'no need for more shooting type'.[2] The remark captured an essential distinction governing the resolution of conflicts, between ensuring the minimal conditions for peace – ending the fighting between armed factions or between insurgents and the state – and building peace over the long term, by establishing stable polities that process and deal with conflict without recourse to violence. This latter effort involves an attempt to address at least some of the conditions that led to conflict in the first place.[3]

This chapter attempts to explore not only how the shooting stopped in two Central American republics, El Salvador and Guatemala, but also how and why peace has endured. El Salvador's 12-year war between 1980 and 1992 claimed some 75,000 lives; Guatemala's 36-year conflict ended in 1996, after 200,000 deaths. At the time of this writing, El Salvador had traversed 15 years since the signing of the peace accord and Guatemala, 10. In neither country had the ceasefire been breached. Our principal task in this chapter is to explain the durability of the settlements in Central America, in sharp contrast to other parts of the world where they have fallen apart in relatively short order. In other words, rather than focusing on the shortcomings of implementation – the part of the glass that is half empty – we will focus on the part that is half full.

In spite of their differences, both countries share several characteristics that make a comparison useful. These include: a history of exclusionary authoritarian rule involving many decades of direct rule by the military and marked by pervasive human rights abuse; socioeconomic systems characterized by high levels of poverty and inequality; weak democratic institutions, persistent impunity, and limited adherence to the rule of law. Decades of political exclusion fostered the development of guerrilla insurgencies of Marxist inspiration committed to the overthrow of the existing political and economic system. These insurgent/counter-insurgent wars evolved within the dominant framework of the Cold War.

While conditions that led to negotiated settlements in each country differed, as did the dynamics of the negotiations, the post-accord phase in El Salvador and Guatemala was also marked by similarities: an extended UN presence, the successful demobilization of combatants (and their less successful reintegration into productive life), the transformation of guerrilla organizations into political parties, reform of greater or lesser degree of the armed forces, and the establishment of truth commissions to grapple with the legacy of human rights violations. The conclusion of peace agreements overcame much skepticism that negotiated settlements were possible at all, and the accords themselves have had an important impact on political democratization in both countries.[4]

El Salvador and Guatemala differ in many respects from other international experiences with peacemaking and peacebuilding in that the state, while institutionally weak, had not collapsed either before or during the conflict, and foreign troops played no central role in re-establishing the functions of a central government.[5] The distinction is important, as it focuses attention less on the role of the international community in preserving a settlement than on what states do or do not do to build a stable peace. To be sure, the international and domestic factors cannot be considered in isolation, and much of the story of peace consolidation in Central America lies in the creative tension between the two.

In explaining the durability of peace in El Salvador and Guatemala, we stress four elements. The first and most important is that the stability of the peace is intimately related to those factors – internal and external – that led to the settlements in the first place. That is, the confluence of circumstances that made the conflicts in El Salvador and Guatemala 'ripe for resolution'[6] signified a fundamental realignment in the interests of major actors, such that key goals came to be seen as more attainable through peace than through war.[7]

Second, peace as an absence of armed confrontation has been sustained over time to a great extent because the peace accords represented a conscious effort to address at least some of the root causes of conflict, even if implementation has been incomplete and highly problematic in some areas. Attention to root causes stemmed not only from the effort of the parties to the conflict to use the peace talks to advance their own core interests but also from a recognition by the UN officials and the parties involved that a stable peace would have to address at least some of the issues that gave rise to conflict in the first place. At the end of this chapter we discuss the limitations of the accords in seriously impacting on poverty and inequality, factors that helped fuel conflict in both countries. While we do not argue that peace accords can or even should serve as alternative models for overcoming centuries of poverty and underdevelopment, we do note that the durability of peace is all the more remarkable in Central America given the shortcomings in the socioeconomic arena.

Third, we explore the complex and at times contradictory relationship between peace processes and democratization: the liberalization of authoritarian regimes during the war provided an incipient institutional framework for transforming conflict from the military to the political sphere; the peace process furthered democratization by expanding the representativity of the political system and by channelling resources to institutional strengthening; at the same time the very existence of the peace process reflected the limitations of democratization, in that the process became a venue for discussing and attempting to resolve issues that the democratic transition had failed to address.[8]

Finally, we stress the critical role of the international community in settling the Central American wars, first in observing and mediating peace talks amid high levels of distrust, then in establishing human rights verification missions that began operations long before the armed conflict ended, and in verifying the implementation of the accords through sizable missions, and finally, in renegotiating aspects of the accords through high-level diplomacy when implementation faltered. In both El Salvador and Guatemala, the principal outside role was played by the UN, although other countries from the region as well as the United States and countries of Western Europe provided important additional support.[9] Furthermore, international financial institutions and foreign governments marshaled significant monetary resources to support the accords' various commitments. Third parties, particularly the UN, helped diminish (but did not eliminate) the elements of risk and uncertainty that are present in any post-conflict phase, and exerted significant although at times uneven political pressure in favour of accord compliance.[10]

Critical issues in the achievement and maintenance of peace

Changes in the international and domestic political context

Common to both conflicts was a changed international environment occasioned only in part by the end of the Cold War. Beginning in 1987, an agreement signed by the presidents of Central American known as Esquipulas II called for an end to outside intervention in the region's wars, favouring instead internal dialogues between governments and insurgent groups throughout the region. Under the umbrella of Esquipulas II, and before the fall of the Berlin Wall, the 'contra' war in Nicaragua ended, leftist exiles returned to El Salvador, and Guatemala's small guerrilla movement had begun to breach its political isolation by a dialogue abroad with a Church-led National Reconciliation Commission.

The end of the Cold War removed the principal ideological underpinning of the insurgent movements (the FMLN in El Salvador and the Guatemalan National Revolutionary Unity (URNG) in Guatemala), as well as diminishing an alternative socialist model of political and economic development. To the extent that the insurgent movements were partially financed by external sources, that too disappeared. Just as important, the end of the Cold War reduced the stakes that the dominant external actor – the United States – saw in the Central American conflicts.

The waning influence of the United States contributed to another change critical to the settlements in El Salvador and Guatemala: an expanded, and unprecedented, role for the UN. El Salvador's peace talks represented the first time the UN had attempted to mediate an internal armed conflict. And the launching of the human rights observer mission in El Salvador in 1991 marked the first time that the UN had monitored (as opposed to reported on) human rights in a member state, let alone the first time such an effort was undertaken during war-time.

Despite the common external environment that contributed to peace, internal conditions in El Salvador and Guatemala differed dramatically in one central aspect: in El Salvador, the FMLN by 1989 had fought the Salvadorean government to a battlefield stalemate; in Guatemala, the guerrillas, while retaining a minimal capacity for skirmishing, were basically a defeated military force. Thus, the stalemates that emerged from both situations were different, as were the insurgents' capacity to wrest concessions at the bargaining table. In El Salvador there were classic manifestations of a 'hurting stalemate', in that both sides saw the impossibility of attaining their goals through military victory.[11] In Guatemala, by contrast, the stalemate was more political in nature. In both cases however, the war prevented political, military, and economic elites from realizing key goals, be they democratization, professionalization, international legitimacy, or the ability to compete in a new globalized world.

The content of the settlement package

The scope of the issues addressed in the agreements contributed decisively to the maintenance of peace in Central America.[12] We highlight four issues in this regard: demobilization of combatants, the creation of power-sharing mechanisms, institutional reform to the armed forces, and mechanisms to address accountability for, and knowledge of human rights violations.

Demobilization

Quite apart from any structural change attempted through a peace agreement, the importance of properly addressing the needs of ex-combatants on all sides of the conflict, both as they demobilize and then as they reintegrate into society, appears as minimum conditions of a peaceful transition. The laying down of arms signifies acceptance of the terms of the settlement package by insurgents, removes their principal source of pressure and bargaining power, and involves an assumption of risk that, once disarmed, ex-combatants will not be targeted for elimination by their former enemies. Demobilization and reintegration thus mean attending to the physical safety, food security, access to land and credit, employment and other needs of ex-combatants, even if none of these things can be guaranteed in the strictest sense.[13] Both El Salvador and Guatemala achieved much greater success with demobilization than with reintegration, because of the specificity of the agreements, the presence of the UN, and the financial support of the international community.[14]

In El Salvador, the phased demobilization of the FMLN was to last between February and October 1992, and the accord itself contained 'an intricately designed and carefully negotiated mechanism'[15] linking demobilization with the fulfillment of key government obligations.[16] The UN officials interceded twice to reschedule the parties' mutual commitments, and the demobilization of the last of the FMLN's 12,362 troops took place on 15 December 1992.[17] The armed forces also underwent significant reductions, and by mid-1993, official estimates were that it had just over half (54.4 per cent) of its personnel during war-time. Civil defence and other paramilitary bodies such as the Territorial Service were also disbanded, bringing to approximately 66,000 the total number of demobilized combatants in the post-war period. Economic and social reintegration programmes, however, had only 'mixed results' according to the UN, and failure to address the needs of ex-combatants, particularly former government soldiers, led to several outbreaks of violence in the mid-1990s.[18]

The demobilization of insurgents in Guatemala was easier than in El Salvador, given the small number of URNG combatants; the official number came to 2950. The entire process of demobilization lasted between March and May 1997, ending only a few months after the signing of the peace accords. Supervised by the UN, the process took place without major incident.[19] Despite some initial success, the process of economic reinsertion has also been incomplete. A survey of ex-combatants carried out in 2000 revealed concerns over the lack of stable jobs, adequate housing, and sufficient economic resources to sustain a family. These problems are common to the majority of the Guatemalan population but appear to have been more acute for ex-combatants.[20]

Guatemala also faced violence from former members of government security forces dismantled by the peace accords. Early in the post-conflict period, the Ambulatory Military Police (PMA), for example, staged what one former government official called a 'near riot' in order to press demands for severance pay and assistance in returning to civilian life.[21] Former members of the Patrullas de Autodefensa Civil (PAC), civil defence patrols widely cited for human rights abuses during the conflict, also demanded compensation. In the context of the November 2003 presidential elections, President Alfonso Portillo of the Guatemalan Republican Front (FRG) attempted to exploit the issue, offering monetary compensation to those who had served as civil patrollers (*patrulleros civiles*). The bid to win votes ultimately failed, and the FRG lost to the Great National Alliance (GANA) candidate Oscar Berger, who took office in 2004.

The failure to adequately reabsorb ex-combatants has, by most accounts, contributed to a spiraling crime wave in both countries.[22] Even if demobilized fighters from both sides in El Salvador and Guatemala have not become 'spoilers' in the classic sense of the term, their apparent participation in diverse forms of violent crime does constitute a threat to the long-term viability of the democratic transition linked to the peace process.

Power-sharing

Fen Osler Hampson recalls that an agreement must create instruments for participation that allow for the parties to work as equal partners during both the negotiation and the implementation phases.[23] Overall, the peace accords in El Salvador and Guatemala were more successful in ensuring a role for former insurgents in verification and implementation mechanisms than they were in incorporating and sustaining the interest of other social actors. The according of special power and status to former guerrillas during an implementation phase, independent of and prior to any expression of popular will, was identified by UN moderator for Guatemala Jean Arnault as one of the undemocratic but necessary features of a peace settlement.[24]

In El Salvador, a supervisory body known as the National Commission for the Consolidation of Peace (COPAZ) was given responsibility 'for overseeing the implementation of all the political agreements reached by the Parties' and consisted of two members each of the FMLN and the government (including a military representative), as well as one representative from each political party or coalition in the Legislative Assembly. (The archbishop of San Salvador and United Nations Mission in El Salvador (ONUSAL) were designated as observers.) In practice, the formula allowed for the guerrillas as well as the political parties to have a voice in verification. Gridlock developed, however, reflecting divisions among the parties, the lack of technical expertise, and the relatively lower stake of the political parties in a successful outcome, given their virtual exclusion from the negotiations process.[25] Ultimately, many of the issues discussed within COPAZ were taken up by the legislature as the FMLN became one of the major political parties in the country.

In Guatemala, an Accompaniment Commission (*Comisión de Acompañamiento*) consisted of equal numbers of government and URNG representatives (a proportion far outweighing the URNG's military or political strength), as well as four prominent citizens agreed to by the parties, one representative of Congress, and the chief of mission of MINUGUA (UN Verification in Guatemala) who had voice but no vote. Unlike El Salvador's COPAZ, the Guatemalan follow-up commission envisioned little role for the political parties represented in Congress. This led to their disengagement from the process of implementing the accords and contributed to the failure to approve constitutional reforms contemplated in the agreements. By contrast, civil society participation was stronger in Guatemala than in El Salvador, channelled through 15 newly established multisectoral commissions charged with making recommendations in several key areas. The consultative mechanisms in the Guatemalan peace agreement highlight one of its principal features: that it is an accord on *processes* for discussing change, rather than an accord on specific results.[26] In the end, the follow-up commissions served as initial power-sharing mechanisms that helped foster national debate over key social and political issues.

Security force reform

The settlement packages in Central America also gave priority to institutional and, especially military reform, given the armed forces' dominance in the political life of both countries and the military's role in extensive human rights violations during the war. The attention to military issues reflected not only the role of the armed forces as a key root cause of conflict but also the practical necessity of moulding a security environment in which former combatants would not simply be murdered when they laid down their arms. The accords in Guatemala and El Salvador differed substantially, however, in the extent and specificity of measures aimed at armed forces reform, a difference rooted principally in the weakness or strength of the guerrillas' bargaining position.

The Salvadorean agreement was detailed and sweeping in its overhaul of the Salvadorean security apparatus. The accord redefined the armed forces' mission in terms of external, not internal security, abolished rapid-reaction counter-insurgency battalions that had participated in some of the worst atrocities of the war, established a civilian Ad Hoc Commission to purge the officer corps of corrupt and abusive members, abolished the National Intelligence Department, and set up a new intelligence agency under civilian control, disbanded the National Guard and Treasury Police, two internal security bodies notorious for their abuses, and established a new National Civilian Police (PNC) open to former members of the FMLN as well as the National Police.

Despite numerous delays in implementing provisions regarding the military, five years after the peace agreement, the UN stated that 'the armed forces have been reduced and have respected the profound changes in their nature and role called for by the peace accords'.[27] Overall, the army went from 63,175 soldiers at the height of the war in 1990 to 15,500 by 2003.[28] The transformation of the police represented a significant achievement that nonetheless was subject to repeated political efforts to sabotage the reform process.[29] Problems involved the lack of experienced personnel and financial resources, weak mechanisms of internal discipline and accountability, and the creation of parallel security structures out of sync with the PNC's new and democratic doctrine.[30] The UN's five-year assessment of the peace process concluded that the PNC represented an 'unprecedented' and 'qualitative change in the institutional structure of the country', but one that had 'not been consolidated without the occurrence of distortions'.[31] In 2002, ten years after the signing of the peace accords, former FMLN guerrilla leader Salvador Samayoa described the PNC as 'a more consolidated, healthy and efficient institution. Its deficiencies and current problems are of a different nature. They are normal problems of institutional development. Far behind are the deformities of the old security forces that were a structural part of a perverse political model'.[32]

For its part, Guatemala also experienced a notable reduction in levels of militarization. Counter-insurgency campaigns beginning in the 1960s saw a proliferation of military bases throughout the country, as well as the creation of military and paramilitary structures especially in rural areas to combat and defeat the insurgency. Civilians armed by the military often acted autonomously from the army and were involved in numerous human rights violations.

Some security force reforms began taking place before the final peace agreement was signed, including the partial demobilization of civil defence forces, and the elimination of *fuero militar* (military court jurisdiction over common crimes committed by the military) and of tax privileges enjoyed by the armed forces. Ultimately, as a result of the Agreement on the Strengthening of Civilian Power and the Role of the Army, more than 275,000 mostly indigenous members of the civil defence patrols were completely demobilized. All 2421 members of the PMA, which performed police functions and also served as a para-state security company for banks and other companies, were also demobilized on schedule. The Presidential General Staff (*Estado Mayor Presidencial*), which controlled security issues, was disbanded and reorganized under civilian control. A law passed in 2003 made social service an option in place of military service and a new human rights-based military doctrine was unveiled in July 2004.

In the UN's final report on the Guatemalan peace accords in 2004, the UN Secretary-General reported that although implementation of the commitments to demilitarize the state had been 'slow and difficult', important progress had been achieved.[33] The UN credited the Berger government with trimming the army from 27,000 to 15,500 and capping the military budget at 0.33 per cent of GDP, 'the boldest such actions taken in may years'.[34] Changes envisioned in the peace accords that would have limited the armed forces' role to external and not internal defence, however, were compromised by the failure of a constitutional referendum that included military as well as other reform measures.[35]

As in El Salvador, the Guatemalan peace accords called for the establishment of a new PNC. By 2004, the new police force had 20,000 agents nationwide. But according to MINUGUA, 'neglect, constant turnover in leadership and corruption' had put the police on a downward spiral since 2000. The UN's final report noted a lack of resources and infrastructure, but blamed the PNC's problems primarily on the infiltration of a large number of former members of the 'corrupt and militarized police force' of the pre-accord era.[36] As in El Salvador, the new police has been unable to successfully fight the post-war increase in common crime. In both countries, the army has been called in several times to assist in fighting crime, a contradiction of the peace accords.

Truth and justice

Intimately related to questions of military reform in both countries were issues of truth and justice, given the scale and intensity of human rights abuses during the conflict. Drawing on the examples of transitions from authoritarian to civilian rule in Latin America's Southern Cone, the peace accords in Guatemala and El Salvador established truth commissions, this time under UN auspices, to investigate and report on human rights abuses committed by both sides.[37] Although invested with different powers and mandates, the truth commissions in El Salvador and Guatemala produced comprehensive reports that stunned many observers. The issue of punishment for those responsible for violations has constituted a major setback in both countries because the peace accords were accompanied by amnesties. And it remains to be seen whether an official acknowledgment of the truth may over time help in the process of political healing at the societal level, especially if most recommendations of the commissions remain unfulfilled.

The UN Commission on the Truth for El Salvador, composed entirely of international representatives, issued its report on 15 March 1993, ascribing 85 per cent of abuses to state agents, paramilitary groups, or death squads allied with official forces, and 5 per cent of abuses to the FMLN. In a novel and controversial step, it named the names of over 40 military officers and 11 members of the FMLN responsible for ordering, committing, or covering up abuses, and called for the resignation of the entire Supreme Court given the judiciary's role in fostering impunity. Although the commission's findings were vehemently denounced by the Salvadorean government and armed forces, they contributed to a process by which senior military officers, including the Minister of Defence, were ultimately purged from the Salvadorean army, as previously recommended by the Ad Hoc Commission.

The mandate of Guatemala's Historical Clarification Commission (CEH) was weaker than El Salvador's, containing specific provisions that it will have no 'judicial aim or effect' and that it will not name individual names of perpetrators.[38] Partly as a result of its limited powers and restrictions of the length of its investigation, the Catholic Archdiocese's Human Rights Office established a parallel, non-governmental effort (the Recovery of Historical Memory, or REMHI Project), to assist in gathering documentary evidence of abuses during the conflict.[39] The CEH issued its report in February 1999, attributing 93 per cent of violations to state or state-supported agents, and 3 per cent to guerrilla forces. The report accused agents of the state of 'acts of genocide' against the Mayan indigenous population during counter-insurgency operations in the early 1980s.[40]

In spite of unmistakable advances in the knowledge of human rights violations during the Central American conflicts, there has been no explicit acknowledgement of responsibility by the armed forces of either side, despite their involvement in the majority of abuses.[41]

In both countries, those with the most to lose from a broader sense of accountability have defined post-war reconciliation in terms of forgetting the past and moving on, leaving unaddressed the material and psychological needs of thousands of civilian victims. Guatemala has made somewhat more progress than El Salvador regarding reparations to victims and their communities, and continual exhumations of massacre sites in rural areas have kept the issue of war-time atrocities before the public. But the task of a deeper reconciliation within society and between individuals remains unfinished and may never be accomplished.

The link between democratization and peace: the importance of political opening

Political exclusion, direct military rule, and fraudulent elections were key root causes of conflict in Central America, therefore post-conflict political openings constitute another central element in the maintenance of peace. Post-war elections in both El Salvador and Guatemala were heavily influenced by the limited democratic openings that began during the conflict, which constricted the political spectrum to the centre and right. In both countries, moderate, centrist parties held the formal reins of power in the mid-1980s, subsequently to be displaced by right-or centre-right parties close to business elites.

El Salvador's 'elections of the century' took place in June 1994, two and a half years after the signing of the peace accords. Despite what the UN deemed 'deficiencies' in the electoral system – and despite a troubling upsurge of political violence and targeted assassinations of former guerrilla – the FMLN emerged as the second strongest political force in the country. Over the course of five legislative elections, the FMLN steadily increased its share of seats, winning more than the National Republican Alliance (ARENA) in 2000 and 2003, but not in 2006, when the two parties tied. The FMLN also initally increased its share of mayoralties at ARENA's expense, only to suffer reversals in 2006. Nationally, however, ARENA remained dominant, in part because of bitter infighting and splits within the FMLN.[42]

In Guatemala, the first general election of the post-war era was held in October 1999, also two and a half years after the signing of the peace agreement. The URNG, allied with the New Nation Alliance (ANN), won nine congressional seats and took third place in those elections, although its showing was far behind the two dominant parties on the right. By the 2003 elections, support for the left had dwindled. The URNG and the ANN participated as separate parties, each obtaining less than 5 per cent of the vote, with the URNG obtaining only two seats in the legislature.

At the national level, the outcome of the 1999 elections was not particularly promising for the peace process: the elections were won by the conservative FRG party, which was reluctant to accept the peace accords as a commitment of the state, rather than of the previous administration. After President Alfonso Portillo of the FRG took office in January 2000, implementation of the accords notably slowed, although publicly the peace accords remained a central element of the President's discourse.

In both countries, less quantifiable but nonetheless appreciable is the impact of political openings on political discourse. In sharp contrast to the conflict era, it is now possible to openly debate a broad range of once taboo issues: the role of the military in national life, human rights, intelligence reform, the role of the state in the economy, and, in the case of Guatemala, the issue of indigenous rights and discrimination against the indigenous population. The forums for intersectoral dialogue have also multiplied. There are notable exceptions to the general aura of tolerance – increased threats against human rights workers in Guatemala among them – but measured against the past, the importance of the broadening of civil discourse should not be underestimated.

A related change involves greater freedom of association and growing participation by diverse groups in civil society, involving many that openly oppose government policy, including on military issues.

The key role of third parties and support from the international community

Most observers would agree that without international presence and pressure, the negotiation and maintenance of peace in Central America might have never been possible. Some have gone so far as to conclude that the international role in the Central American peace processes was *the* key ingredient of their success.[43] The processes of negotiation involved phases of observation, moderation, and mediation and the final accords in both countries gave specific responsibilities to UN verification missions (ONUSAL and MINUGUA) to oversee the peacebuilding process over a period of years.

The accords gave wide latitude to the UN missions, including the capacity to identify, monitor, manage, and resolve major conflicts, as well as the power to issue public reports and statements; this latter aspect enabled the missions, through criticism, to marshal international pressure in favour of compliance. Active verification included at times deploying senior UN officials from headquarters in New York in order to overcome crises in implementation.[44]

Once the agreements were in place, the efforts of the UN missions were complemented by the work and financial contributions of other UN agencies, foreign governments, and non-governmental organizations in providing development assistance, repatriating refugees, monitoring elections, and other activities. Bilateral and multilateral contributions in the hundreds of millions of dollars allowed both countries to finance commitments made in the accords, and constituted the international community's most important source of leverage in favour of accord compliance.

However critical the role of the international community in negotiating and maintaining peace, we underscore the UN's own recognition that durable peace, while it can be shaped by outsiders, can only be secured by the parties themselves.[45]

The need for deeper democratization and social development

Most analysts view as remote any resumption of civil war in El Salvador and Guatemala, at least the kind of civil war that took place in the late twentieth century. Yet many scholars note that both countries face the potential for future social unrest if key problems are not addressed. These problems centre on the need for a deeper democratization that widens and makes more meaningful citizens' participation in political life, and the need for social development, to reduce the high levels of poverty and flagrant socioeconomic inequality in both countries.[46]

To be fair, the political and social challenges faced by El Salvador and Guatemala mirror those faced by other countries in Latin America and the developing world. However, the legacy of war makes progress in these areas both more urgent and more difficult. As previously noted, major advances in political democratization have contributed significantly to the maintenance of peace. But achievements in the social arena have been modest and accompanied by dramatic rises in the rates of crime, dashing expectations that life would improve significantly in the post-conflict period.

Socioeconomic issues

Despite improvements during the 1990s, for example, levels of poverty in Guatemala and El Salvador are still striking. By 2001, 60.4 per cent of Guatemalans and 49.9 per cent of Salvadoreans lived below the poverty line, although poverty rates in rural areas are significantly higher in both countries.[47] Inequality is also pronounced: by 2002 the wealthiest 20 per cent of the population in Guatemala held 60 per cent of national income; in El Salvador, the top 20 per cent held 56 per cent of wealth.[48]

The peace accords in Guatemala and El Salvador differed in the extent to which they considered socioeconomic issues. The lack of specificity in the Salvadorean accord on social and economic issues led to the establishment of several commissions and forums. These initiatives – most of them undertaken in the first five years after the signing of the accords – failed to establish concrete goals, or to forge consensus over the direction of economic policy at the end of the twentieth century.[49]

Guatemala's accords did establish sweeping goals for improving social development and expanding opportunity, calling for increased social investment by the state, greater access to land and credit, reform of labour legislation, a more progressive and modern tax structure, and the modernization and decentralization of social services.[50] The implementation of Guatemala's socioeconomic accord has been sluggish, and has faced numerous obstacles unforeseen by the parties. Increased social spending goals for education and health have been achieved, but one of the cornerstones of the socioeconomic accord, the tax issue, remains highly contentious. Despite significant international pressure, the goal of raising tax revenues to 12 per cent of GDP remains unmet.[51]

Political issues

Although progress on the political front has been more tangible than in the socioeconomic arena, both Guatemala and El Salvador are far from consolidated democracies. Key political institutions in Central America, particularly legislatures and political parties, have low levels of legitimacy among the population.[52] Despite an increase in federal budgets devoted to the judiciary, and measures to enhance the political independence of judges, judicial systems in both countries remain weak, inefficient, underfunded, and subject to corruption.[53]

The shortcomings of the justice system, combined with the inefficiency of law-enforcement institutions such as the National Police, are more acute given rampant common crime in the post-war period. El Salvador and Guatemala have some of the highest homicide rates in Latin America, and indeed, the world, and some of the highest rates of crime victimization. Most significant for the long-term viability of the peace process is the high cor-relation between crime and diminished support for the democratic process overall.

Electoral turnout in both countries remains low, although recent elections show some improvement.[54] In addition, civil society remains highly frag-mented, with little capacity to articulate interests and little connection to political parties that traditionally mediate demands.

Conclusion

An analysis of the post-settlement era in El Salvador and Guatemala leads us to reaffirm that peace accords are not panaceas, ushering in new golden eras of democracy, freedom, and development. Rather, they are significant and unprecedented stages in both countries' transition from authoritarianism to democracy, creating, as conflict resolution specialist Robert Rothstein has put it, 'a new set of opportunities that can be grasped or thrown away'.[55] Peace accords in both countries resolved historic crises of political exclusion that had spawned decades of violence and war, and the settlements launched sig-nificant processes of institutional reform. That the societies emerging from peace processes are still highly imperfect should not detract from the accords' significance: the agreements should not be blamed for the limits of democrati-zation or for the failure of market-oriented economies to overcome centuries of poverty and underdevelopment.

That being said, accords can be judged not only by degrees of compliance or non-compliance but also by the extent to which they address root causes of war and satisfy short- and long-term post-war needs for demobilization, secu-rity, participation, recovery, and justice. On all of these counts, the glass has been both half empty and half full, and the role of the international com-munity in pushing the line upward cannot be underestimated. Peace in both countries reflected the establishment of a coalition of social forces that defined or fulfilled its interests along lines of compromise rather than conflict.[56] An ongoing task of the post-war period in El Salvador and Guatemala is to solidify and expand that coalition, through the provision of concrete benefits and an ongoing commitment to democratic reform.

Notes

The authors would like to thank Woodrow Wilson Center Latin American Program interns Craig Fagan and Audrey Yao for their invaluable research assistance for the first edition, and Program Assistant Kelly Albinak and intern Sarah Walker for research assistance for the second edition.

1. United Nations, *The United Nations and El Salvador 1990–1995*, Blue Book Series, Volume IV (New York: United Nations Department of Public Information, 1995) (hereinafter cited as United Nations Blue Book), p. 283.
2. United Nations Institute for Training and Research, 'The Challenge of Democratic Transitions in Post Conflict Situations: Applying Lessons from the Past to Future UN Peacemaking and Peacebuilding', Final Report, Seminar, 26–29 March 1999, mimeographed, p. 1.
3. See M. Doyle & N. Sambanis, 'International peacebuilding: A theoretical and quantitative analysis', *American Political Science Review*, 94, 4 (December 2000), pp. 779–801; C. Arnson, 'Introduction', in C. Arnson (ed.), *Comparative Peace Processes in Latin America* (Stanford CA: Woodrow Wilson Center Press and Stanford University Press, 1999), pp. 1–28 and Á. de Soto, 'Reflections', in C. Arnson (ed.), Ibid., pp. 385–387.
4. For a detailed account of the contributions of the peace process to political democratization in El Salvador and Guatemala, see D. Azpuru, L. Blanco, R. Córdova, C. Ramos, & A. Zapata., *Construyendo la democracia en sociedades posconflicto: Guatemala y El Salvador en perspectiva comparada* (Ottawa and Guatemala City: IDRC Publishers and F&G Editores, 2007).
5. B. Walter, 'Designing Transitions from Violent Civil War', University of California Institute on Global Conflict and Cooperation, Policy Paper No. 31 (December 1997).
6. The phrase is from I.W. Zartman, 'Ripening Conflict, Ripe Moment, Formula, and Mediation', in D. Bendahmane & J. McDonald, Jr. (eds), *Perspectives on Negotiation: Four Case Studies and Interpretations* (Washington DC: Center for the Study of Foreign Affairs, Foreign Service Institute, 1986). Elisabeth Wood has emphasized that the structural basis of compromise is in place when the expected returns from conflict are less than the expected returns from compromise. See E. Wood, *Forging Democracy from Below: Insurgent Transitions in South Africa and El Salvador* (Cambridge UK: Cambridge University Press, 2001), p. 205.
7. Authors' interview, former Deputy Secretary for Peace Ricardo Stein, Guatemala City (24 October 2000); C. Call, 'Assessing El Salvador's Transition from Civil War to Peace', in S.J. Stedman, D. Rothchild, & E.M. Cousens (eds), *Ending Civil Wars: The Implementation of Peace Agreements* (Boulder CO: Lynne Rienner Publishers, 2002), p. 384.
8. D. Azpuru, 'Peace and Democratization in Guatemala: Two Parallel Processes', in Arnson (ed.), op. cit., pp. 97–125; J. Arnault, 'The Case of Guatemala', paper presented to the seminar on Peace Settlement and Democratic Transition, Geneva, Switzerland (April 1999), mimeographed, pp. 1–2.
9. D. Azpuru, L. Blanco, C. Mendoza, & E. Blank, 'Democracy Assistance to Post-Conflict Guatemala: Finding a Balance between Details and Determinants', Working Paper No. 30 (The Hague, Netherlands: Netherlands Institute for International Relations, 2004).
10. Walter (1997), op. cit.; F. Osler Hampson, *Nurturing Peace: Why Peace Settlements Succeed or Fail* (Washington DC: United States Institute of Peace Press, 1996); and D. Holiday & W. Stanley, 'Broad Participation, Diffuse Responsibility: Peace Implementation in Guatemala', in Stedman et al., op. cit., pp. 421–462; and T. Whitfield, 'The Role of

the United Nations in El Salvador and Guatemala: A Preliminary Comparison', in Arnson (ed.), op. cit., pp. 257–290.

11. R. Córdova Macias, *El Salvador: Las negociaciones de paz y los retos de la postguerra* (San Salvador: IDELA, 1993); T. Lynn Karl, 'El Salvador's negotiated revolution', *Foreign Affairs*, 71, 2 (Spring 1992), pp. 147–164.

12. Although the agreements were similar in many respects, there were also important differences. The Salvadorean accords, for example, went into greater detail about military reform and the creation of a new police force, while the Guatemalan accords touched on a broader range of issues, including socioeconomic reform and ethnic discrimination. See, for example, L. Pásara, *Paz ,ilusión y cambio en Guatemala: el proceso de paz, sus actores, logros y límites* (Guatemala City: Universidad Rafael Landívar, Instituto de Investigaciones Jurídicas, 2003).

13. See United Nations Institute for Training and Research (26–29 March 1999), op. cit., p. 4.

14. For an evaluation of the programmes of reintegration of former guerillas in Guatemala see ASIES, Unión Europea, and Cruz Roja Española, *El Programa de Incorporación para los Ex-combatientes, 1997–2001* (Guatemala City: Artgrafic de Guatemala, 2001).

15. United Nations Blue Book (1995), op. cit., p. 245.

16. These included obligations regarding the FMLN's political status, the transfer of land to ex-combatants, and security reform.

17. The numbers included 8876 combatants and 3,486 war-injured members. United Nations Blue Book (1995), op. cit., Annex II, p. 285.

18. See P. Williams and K. Walter, *Militarization and Demilitarization in El Salvador's Transition to Democracy* (Pittsburgh PA: University of Pittsburgh Press, 1997), pp. 151–163, 180–181.

19. S. Jonas, *Of Centaurs and Doves, Guatemala's Peace Process*, (Boulder CO: Westview Press, 2000); and Holiday & Stanley, in Stedman et al., op. cit.

20. ASIES, Unión Europea, Cruz Roja Española (2001), op. cit.

21. Authors' interview, Ricardo Stein, Guatemala City (24 October 2000). As in El Salvador, the episode revealed the danger of privileging the demobilization of those who had taken up arms against the state over the needs of ex-government forces, including some who participated in the repressive apparatus of the state.

22. Numerous studies of crime in the post-war period cite the failure to economically reintegrate ex-combatants, as well as general conditions of poverty, unemployment, and the proliferation of weapons, as principal explanations for the rise in common crime. However, hard data about the participation of former combatants in crime is difficult to come by. See J. M. Cruz, 'Violencia y democratización en Centroamérica: El impacto del crimen en los regímenes de posguerra', in United Nations Development Programme, *Aportes para la convivencia y la seguridad ciudadana* (San Salvador: United Nations Development Programme, 2004); and J. M. Cruz & R. Fernández de Castro, 'Youth Gangs and Violence in Central America and Mexico', Paper presented at the conference 'Comparative Peace Processes in Latin America: A Second Look' (Woodrow Wilson International Center for Scholars, Washington DC: 3–4 April 2006).

23. See Hampson (1996), op. cit., p. 222.

24. Arnault (1999), op. cit., p. 2.

25. D. Holiday & W. Stanley, 'Building the peace: preliminary lessons from El Salvador', *Journal of International Affairs*, 46, 2 (Winter 1993), pp. 427–429.

26. J. Arnault, 'Visión General de Implementación', in Woodrow Wilson Center Latin American Program, *El Proceso de Paz en Guatemala: Logros y Desafíos*, Abril de 1999, pp. 19–20. In such an atmosphere, one former government official

involved in implementation lamented that 'everyone participates, but no one takes responsibility'. Authors' interview, Stein (24 October 2000), op. cit.

27. United Nations, A/51/917, 1 July 1997, p. 16. See also, R. Córdova Macias, *El Salvador: Reforma Militar y Relaciones Cívico-Militares* (San Salvador: FUNDAUNGO, 1999).

28. Data from H. Corado Figueroa, 'Los procesos de desmovilización de las Fuerzas Armadas', in F. Aguilar Urbina (ed.), *Desmovilización, desmilitarización y democratización en Centroamérica* (San José, Costa Rica: Fundación Arias para la Paz y el Progreso Humanos y Centro Internacional para los Derechos Humanos y el Desarrollo Democrático, 1994); and The International Institute for Strategic Studies, *The Military Balance, 2003–2004* (London: Oxford University Press, 2003).

29. G. Costa, 'Demilitarizing Public Security: Lessons from El Salvador', in M. Studemeister (ed.), *El Salvador: Implementation of the Peace Accords* (Washington DC: United States Institute of Peace Press, 2001), pp. 20–26; and G. Costa, *La Policía Nacional Civil de El Salvador (1990–1997)* (San Salvador: UCA Editores, 1999). For four years, Costa was the ONUSAL official responsible for liaison to the PNC.

30. W. Stanley, *Protectors or Perpetrators? The Institutional Crisis of the Civilian Police* (Washington DC: Washington Office on Latin America and Hemisphere Initiatives, 1996).

31. United Nations, A/51/917 (1 July 1997), op. cit., p. 3.

32. S. Samayoa, *El Salvador: La Reforma Pactada* (San Salvador: UCA Editores, 2002), p. 652.

33. United Nations Verification Mission in Guatemala (MINUGUA), 'Report of the Secretary-General', United Nations General Assembly, A/59/307, 30 August 2004, p. 11. This was MINUGUA'S ninth and final report on the fulfillment of the peace accords. For an analysis of the shortcomings of the military reform process before 2004, see J. Mark Ruhl, 'The Guatemalan military since the peace accords: The fate of reform under Arzú and Portillo', *Latin American Politics and Society*, 46, 4 (Spring 2005), pp. 55–85.

34. Ibid., p. 11.

35. On the tenth anniversary of the Guatemalan peace accords, President Berger announced that his government would present the pending constitutional reforms to Congress in February 2007. If approved by the legislature, the reforms would have to be ratified in a national referendum.

36. Ibid., p. 12.

37. For a discussion of truth commissions worldwide, see P. Hayner, *Unspeakable Truths: Confronting State Terror and Atrocity* (New York: Routledge, 2001).

38. The Guatemalan Commission was formed by one international member and two prominent Guatemalans.

39. Authors' interview, Oficina de Derechos Humanos del Arzobizpado (25 October 2000). In April 1998, REMHI's four-volume report on political violence, *Nunca Más*, was published. Two days later, the senior church official overseeing the project, Bishop Juan Gerardi, was murdered. In June 2001, a Guatemalan tribunal found three military men, including a former chief of intelligence, as well as a priest guilty of Gerardi's murder.

40. *Guatemala: Memoria del Silencio, Conclusiones y Recomendaciones de la Comisión para el Esclarecimiento Histórico*, 2nd edn (Guatemala: Servigráficos, SA, 1999), p. 22.

41. In Guatemala, several civilian government officials (including former President Álvaro Arzú in 1996 and President Oscar Berger in 2006) have asked for forgiveness on behalf of the government.

42. See Spence, J., M. Lanchin, & G. Thale, *From Elections to Earthquakes: Reform and Participation in Post-War El Salvador* (Cambridge MA: Hemisphere Initiatives, 2001),

pp. 4–10; and M. Allison, 'The transition from armed opposition to electoral opposition in Central America', *Latin American Politics and Society*, 48, 4 (Winter 2006), pp. 137–162.

43. According to Fen Osler Hampson, where there has been unified and sustained third-party involvement in both the negotiation and implementation of the agreement, settlements were more durable than in those cases where settlements were 'orphaned' and third-party intervention was sporadic.

44. In the autumn of 1992, for example, the FMLN refused to demobilize on schedule in response to the military's failure to carry out a purge mandated by the peace accords. UN Secretary-General Boutros-Ghali dispatched Under-Secretary-General for Peacekeeping Operations Marrack Goulding and Assistant Secretary-General for Political Affairs Álvaro de Soto to El Salvador to work out a compromise. Special envoys of the Secretary-General also visited Guatemala several times to monitor progress in implementation.

45. United Nations Institute for Training and Research (26–29 March 1999), op. cit., p. 4.

46. See R. Córdova & G. Maihold, 'Democracia y ciudadanía en Centroamérica', in R. Córdova Macias, G. Maihold, & S. Kurtenback (eds), *Pasos Hacia una Nueva Convivencia: Democracia y Participación en Centroamérica* (San Salvador: Imprenta Criterio, 2001).

47. United Nations Development Programme, *La Democracia en América Latina: Hacia una democracia de ciudadanos y ciudadanas* (Buenos Aires: Aguilar, Altea, Taurus, Alfaguara, 2004), p. 135.

48. World Bank, World Development Indicators, cited in US Agency for International Development, Bureau for Latin America and the Caribbean, *Latin America and the Caribbean: Selected Economic and Social Data* (Washington DC: USAID, 2006).

49. R. Córdova Macias, 'Demilitarizing and Democratizing Salvadoran Politics', in Studemeister (ed.), op. cit., pp. 30–32.

50. Jonas (2000), op. cit., p. 188.

51. Some reform measures have advanced, including most notably the creation of the Superintendency of Tax Administration (SAT) and increases in personal income tax.

52. See D. Azpuru, 'Resumen Ejecutivo', in *Construyendo la democracia en sociedades posconflicto: un enfoque compardo entre Guatemala y El Salvador* (Guatemala City: ASIES, IDRC, FUNDAUNGO, 2006).

53. See Call (2002), op. cit., p. 408; M. Popkin, *Peace without Justice* (University Park PA: Pennsylvania State University Press, 2000); and H. Byrne, 'Trials and tribulations of justice reform in Guatemala', in *LASA Forum*, XXXI, 1 (Spring 2000), p. 10.

54. In El Salvador, turnout in the presidential elections went from 47.3 per cent (1999) to 57.5 per cent (2004). In Guatemala, turnout went from 46.8 per cent in the 1995 elections to 58 per cent in the 2004 elections. See D. Azpuru et al. (2007), op. cit. Emigration from El Salvador and Guatemala (largely to the United States) may depress the levels of voter turnout, in that the names of those who leave the country remain in the electoral registry.

55. R. Rothstein, *After the Peace: Resistance and Reconciliation* (Boulder CO: Lynne Rienner, 1999), p. 224.

56. The fact that the FMLN organized its own commemoration of the tenth anniversary of the Salvadoran peace accords, refusing to participate in the government's ceremony, and that the URNG did not participate in Guatemala's ten-year celebration of its peace agreement, demonstrates that much remains to be done to foster consensus and post-war reconciliation.

20
Casting Long Shadows: War, Peace, and Extra-Legal Economies

Carolyn Nordstrom

Introduction

This is an ethnography of the shadows.[1] The term shadows as I use it here refers to systems of association and exchange that occur outside the law. Ethnography underscores the fact that the data presented here comes from live fieldwork conducted in epicentres of political violence and apart from formal state systems – in the poorly illuminated yet powerful realm of the extra-legal.[2]

In the frontier realities that mark political upheaval, the people, goods and services that move along shadow lines are often closely and visibly linked to the most fundamental politics of power and survival. Large amounts of arms, actors, and supplies flow into a country at war as valuable resources flow out of a country to pay for these items and alliances. A good deal of this takes place outside formal state institutions and international law. In fact, shadow transactions can equal a third to more than a half of a country's entire Gross National Product in many locations in the world.[3] For countries embroiled in war economies, the figure can rise even higher. The end of political hostilities does not herald a reduction in extra-legal activities. In fact, in many cases, post-war economies can show both a rise and an institutionalization of illegal activity.

Globally, taken in total, shadow economies involve trillions of dollars annually, and this brokers significant political power. My interest here is with vast, international networks – those residing in the shadows – whose economic and political power can match, even exceed, that of some states.

Defining the shadows

'How many businesses do you think cross the lines of legality?' I asked one of the world's largest drug smugglers.

> *One hundred percent, he said.*
>
> *'How many of the legal enterprises in the West do you think cross the lines of legality in some way in the course of their business?' I asked.*
>
> *One hundred percent, replied the detective at Scotland Yard, London.*[4]

A person can stand at the epicentre of practically any war in the world and watch an extensive assortment of international actors pass through. If a person works in different war-zones, even ones located on different continents, he/she will begin to recognize the same actors moving from one zone of political violence to another. Arms vendors, military 'advisors', merchants of survival, diplomats, profiteers, non-governmental organizations, and a host of others ultimately make war and peace possible. This international cast of characters moves substantial amounts of commodities, influence, and services across the countries of the world. A significant portion of these exchanges take place outside formally recognized state channels: some moving along brown and grey market routes, some along incontestably illicit and black market pathways.

Given that all wars rely on the vast array of technologies and alliances produced throughout the world, war today, by definition, is constructed internationally.[5] We may speak of internal wars, but they are set in vast global arenas. We may speak of contests within or between states, but a considerable part of war and post-conflict development takes place along extra-state lines. War and peace, unfold as much according to these extra-state realities as they do according to state-based ones. Thinking only in discrete and bounded states and their legal systems cannot come close to approximating the reality of states today.

The phenomena I am dealing with here are not simply (shadow) markets or economies; they are a compilation of political, economic, and socio-cultural forces. Shadow associations are characterized by several core features. First, in configuration, these are networks, not formal state structures. Second, they are transnational. Third, they are transactional; they are networks that function not only by exchange and alliance but also by internalized norms and cultures of exchange and alliance. As with all human social endeavours, people follow codes of conduct and rules of behaviour when engaging in illicit transactions. People must know with whom they can and cannot engage, how these patterns of association must evolve, and where they can take place. At each step of the way illicit, grey, and legal institutions intersect.[6]

While these shadow networks are not comprised by states themselves, they work both through and around states. For example, corruption, by definition, exploits the junctures between the legal and illegal; and illicit profiteering must make use of legal production, transport, and monetary institutions. This point is an important one. Extra-legal networks form a different kind of power formation than the state does. For this reason, I refer to these powers as 'extra-state', denoting that while they may partake of state structures, they are not modelled on state systems. Chingono, writing on Mozambique, observes:

> *The International Labour Organization (ILO), the agency that has formalized the term 'informal economy', characterized the informal economy as 'a sector of the poor' in which 'the motive for entry into the sector is essentially survival rather than profit making'...On the contrary, not all of those who participated in the grass-roots economy were poor nor were their motives for entry merely to survive. Corrupt bureaucrats and professionals used their office, influence or contacts to acquire via the grass-roots war economy, through for instance, smuggling, fraudulent export, barter, speculation, bribery, and embezzlement, and invest in building houses, hotels/restaurants, or in transport. Similarly corrupt commercial elites, religious leaders, international agency personnel, as well as international racketeers and their middle-men, smugglers, money-dealers, pirates, and slavers and abductors, not to mention soldiers in the warring armies and foreign troops, were among those who yielded substantial benefits, and in many cases, became obscenely rich, by participating in the grass-roots war economy.*[7]

Shadow networks, then, are not marginal to the world's economies and politics, but central. They fashion economic possibilities, and they execute political power. If we do not yet know the exact financial and personnel strength of the non-formal sectors of the world, perhaps more dangerously, we do not know how these vast sums affect global (stock) markets, economic (non) health, and political power configurations. What we can surmise is that these extensive transnational transactions comprise a significant section of the world's economy, and thus of the world's power grids.

In the midst of war

> *In 1990, at the height of the war in Mozambique, I traveled to a remote town in the middle of the country. It was remote, but it was of strategic importance: it was the site of gem mines. This location, largely forgotten in the sweep of nation-wide war atrocities and power-war development history, captures the deep linkages between shadows and war. As I conducted interviews, I came across scores of stories from civilian and military locals about the foreign white men and troops who passed through to collect large quantities of precious gems. I also collected photographs of solider-drawn graffiti on the barren walls poking up from the bombed out buildings. The graffiti chronicled the war from the young bush soldier's perspective. There were pictures of battle plans; of helicopters strafing villages and villagers; of soldiers proudly holding the latest in automatic weapons. There were*

> *pictures of the human tragedies of war: soldiers raping women, and old grandmothers carrying the wounded on their backs.*[8] *The drawings held a deeper truth: these soldiers were not merely villagers fighting a local bush war – these were people trained in the latest international technologies, both technological and ideological. Soldiers in tattered uniforms wield the latest superpower arms. The pilots flying the helicopters have been trained in cosmopolitan military centers. The methods of the rapes are enactments of the latest pornographic magazines that are yet one more military currency in battle-zones. The political slogans inscribed in the drawings are battle cries forged in distant nations and other wars and carried across time and continents by military allies, mercenaries, gem and arms runners, military texts, and the latest fads in the Rambo genre. In this graffiti and in these gem mines I saw perhaps as clearly as anywhere the powerful intersections of local and transnational, the legal and the illegal, and of the curious ways the power of these realities insinuates itself into the fabric of living and dying.*[9]

Consider the complex ways these international transfers blur the boundaries of legal and illegal. Gems, ivory, oil, and other goods and resources brought out of rebel areas to pay for military supplies cannot be said to fit the description of legal or illegal: international law applies to formal states not to rebel-held regions. On the other side: what layers of legality apply to governments and militaries who sell off national resources for military gain and buy sanctioned commodities? The economic answer is in part supplied by recognizing the fact that a wartime economy can yield considerable riches for the canny and the powerful, and these riches move far beyond war supplies. They also move beyond the military.

The links between the shadows and the formal sector should be evident by now: profiteers assist the transfer of military goods and payments in precious resources; these profits fuel formal businesses, and these profits – both material and political – can be converted into political power.

Military, business, and politics intersect in these transactions, and public policies are often in actuality crafted in the shadows. This is not merely the movement of goods around a country. Consider the fact that the parallel economy sets the black, or street, exchange rate for currency, and that this street rate is considered by many, including the banks, the International Monetary Fund (IMF), and governmental agencies, as the accurate one. The official bank rate is often more a political than a factual rendering. The more successful business people (those who set up and control both legal and illicit wartime economic enterprises, and dictate economic policy on the ground) are also the people who set the daily street currency exchange rates. Not the government, not formal international governmental economic alliances. The true value of currency, in these instances, is set in the shadows. It is set according to transactions that partake of formal and shadow economic and political realities. And it is this that under-girds the foundations of economy.

Post-war development

> We've always run goods and people across these borders. We do it, our fathers did it, our grandfathers did it, back to the time when these stupid senseless borders didn't divide us all.
>
> Honestly, how would we survive otherwise? It's not like the government is knocking on our door with baskets of plenty. And this trade keeps us linked into larger communities, with international goods and markets. Food, clothing, electronics, petrol, machinery, you name it.
>
> So, you know, when the war heats up, we are tapped to carry arms as well. And now we have to navigate all kinds of political divisions and threats. And it gets deeper: the commanders begin to control areas of trade, and to get permits, transport, permission, a person has to grease the palms of the commanders. Now it's like we are working for them in a way. And the damn war now sits on our doorstep
>
> How are we going to get this thing off our doorsteps? Those commanders who control 'business' [both legal and illegal] in the extremes of war. Are they going to let go of this with the end of the war? I doubt it.[10]

An irony in this analysis is that the very extra-state activities I have been discussing are also those by which a significant amount of development and more stable transitional peacetime economies are created. It is not a question that classical economic and development theories easily address: traditional wisdom posits conflict transformation and development succeeding through the strengthening of societies' formal infrastructures. Thus aid and development monies go to existing state institutions to instigate formal programmes. My fieldwork suggests this model little matches the actual dynamics of reconstruction.

Consider the conditions that characterize wartime and greet most post-war societies. In addition to militarized and decimated infrastructure, agricultural lands lay fallow, and water sources may be polluted. Old currencies may have collapsed, and with them, banking systems. New currencies may be only as valuable as the paper they are printed on in international markets. Even the most legal of companies – those that haven't been bombed, looted, raided, or taken over – find that they have to exchange monies, and possibly goods, on the black market. Currency exchange rates often fluctuate to extreme levels, making formal business transactions virtually impossible: who can buy goods one day not knowing if they will sell them for a profit or a loss the next day depending on the vicissitudes of a powerful, but formally uncontrolled, financial market? In 1996 in Angola, I exchanged US dollars variously for 120,000; 200,000; and 270,000 kwanza in the space of a week: a rollercoaster of currency valuations. When I bought at 120,000 and the prices soared to 270,000, I paid over two times the amount for goods as those who had changed at more auspicious times. By 1998, I received nearly half a million kwanza for a US dollar, and with the war's end in 2002, the currency was completely revalued. What industry can function in such financial uncertainty? But of course, who takes kwanza anyway? Most goods must be networked across numerous international borders: war-devastated countries often are unable to produce many of the basics, much less the luxury items, they need. To buy internationally requires 'hard currency' from dollars and marks to gold and guns. To gain access to these goods frequently entails having to resort to grey (informal or illicit) or black market (illegal) local resources. The bread and meat industries – and by that I mean the basic industries of everyday life from bakeries through clothing manufacturers to equipment plants – do not survive easily in these conditions (of course adding to this landmines, roving militias, severe corruption, and destroyed trade routes), and pack up to leave for greener pastures.

Who then thrives in such economies? From urban centres to remote rural communities there are those who do well in such conditions, who profit from the political instability or social chaos that reduces normative and legal restraints. Informal markets surface to provide the daily requirements to the broad spectrum of citizens. Non-formal banking systems emerge to transfer funds and provide loans. Grey market economies function on the borders between government regulations and practical survival, between formal international systems and the realities of daily life.

These are the conditions of a frontier: the perilous transport of daily necessities to the millions who need them; the wildcatting of vast fortunes; and the systems of protection, usury, and domination that see these various ventures to fruition. From kindly women trading tomatoes for medicines, through mafias trading in gems, drugs, and high-tech computers, to violent gun runners selling post-war weapons to urban criminals, the non-formal sector steps into the limelight in these transitional times.

Such people will be unlikely to give up their network alliances, or their reliance on the shadows, when they enter a formal state role. The development of many war-afflicted economies is largely jump-started along non-formal economic lines – far from the laws and taxes of failed government institutions. The final irony in this is that virtually all aid and loan dollars go through government channels. The government that controls only a portion of the economy; the government where military spending, failed institutions, and corruption have taken a lasting toll.

A question evolved from this research, a question that I incorporated into my ethnography of the shadows:

> If the formal sector is largely inoperational; if what is operational largely assists the fortunes of very few and for the most part barely affects the daily life of the population as a whole; and if the massive informal market (including gray, brown, and black) largely sustains the population as a whole: *Where does actual political and economic (post-war) rebuilding power come from?*

Classical theory states that as these countries settle down in the course of normal state development, their economies will become increasingly defined by state-regulated institutions. In this view, while illegal goods (i.e., drugs and weapons) and service rings (i.e., mercenaries and prostitution) will always exist in the countries of the world, they comprise a marginal part of the world's real economy.

My research to date suggests we need to rethink these assumptions. As Chingono writes, 'the informal economy seems here to stay, and may even become the mainstay of the economy'.[11] On a larger scale, local non-formal economies link with worldwide economic and political concerns: I can stand in the most remote war-zones of the world and watch a veritable super market of goods move in and out of the country. Tracing the supply routes of these goods takes one through both major and minor economic centres of the world. The sanctions-regulated lap top, satellite-linked computer I see on the battle-fields of Africa was made in a major cosmopolitan centre of the world, and the gold, diamonds, ivory, and seafood that pay for these commodities move along the same channels back to those cosmopolitan centres. These international transactions are not comprised solely of such luxury goods. Clothing, watches, industrial components, VCRs, books, and medical supplies travel these same routes. At the bottom line, it would appear non-formal economies play a formidable role in countries like Japan, Germany, and the United States of America as well as in areas of more rapid economic and political change and development – when the gems and oil of Angola and Sierra Leone and Burma and Colombia buy computers and armaments (or clothing, medicines, and VCRs) from cosmopolitan centres, the money helps define the financial realities of these centres, regardless of whether it arrives through formal or shadow means. All these factor into corporate sales, bank (laundered) revenues, stock market prices, cost of living indices, and so on, whether these facts are recognized in formal analyses or not.

These realities are belied in development programmes: virtually all aid and development organizations deal directly, and generally exclusively, through the formal sector. The formal sector deals almost not at all with the vast majority of people in countries like Angola. So most of the development monies coming into the country are going into the formal sector that, to a large extent, is taking money out of the country, either in agreements like large weapon and foreign goods purchases, or in corruption. The last issue is critical: the corruption that is currently a prime topic of concern in development circles has its main font in the formal sector – the formal sector that intergovernmental loans and aid monies are channelled through. In addition, aid may well be channelled into the very structures that are most likely to foment continuing conflicts.

Peace

> *Now a Peace Accord is signed and someone says it is all over – do you expect this all to end? You expect these smuggling routes to suddenly close up and these people return home hungry and empty-handed?*[12]

Wartime economic relationships follow markets into peace. Wartime profiteers emerge as peacetime economic and political leaders. Markets are not as free as democratic ideals would have them.

The end of war often finds rich resource and land concessions, industrial locales, patronage systems, and control of key aspects of trade consolidated into the hands of exclusive elite – political, business, and military leaders who extended domains of personal control during the war. Once such gains have been institutionalized in the frontier-like conditions of war, the owners may now find that the stability of peace allows them better profits. But the fact remains that the systems were honed in exploitative conditions, some of which continue with peace in the form of unfair hiring, work, and pay practices, and restricted legal recourse. In these conditions, access to political, economic, and military power continues to rest in the hands of a few.

Even the people dedicated to business ethics can find post-war conditions hinder their best attempts to formalize their enterprises. Consider the conditions many post-war societies face: in addition to militarized and decimated infrastructure, old currencies may have collapsed, and with them, banking systems. On the international market, new currencies may be no more valuable than the paper on which they are printed. Currency exchange rates often fluctuate to extreme levels. National production is likely to be severely curtailed, resulting in a heavy reliance on import goods that requires foreign currency. Antiquated and militarized laws, corruption, and onerous taxes, levies, and tariffs can plague all levels of business endeavour. Even the most legal of companies may find that they have to exchange monies, goods, and services extra-legally. As one successful businessman, a man noted for integrity in business, noted: 'If I followed the letter of the law in every case, I'd be out of business. Period.'

While national economic and political systems may remain militarized, the military and political leaders are not the only profiteers. Militarization benefits global vendors. It benefits international wildcatters. It benefits legitimate vendors of information, services, and technology in the urban centres of the world who sell their goods for the hard currency oil, drugs and precious gems buy. An extensive network of people has grown wealthy on these extra-state exchanges; they are not easily convinced to give them up for less lucrative pursuits.

Postscript

Considering post-agreement reconstruction

We can't really talk about it, but it is right there in the center of everything.

The informal economy.

And we can't explain it, because we don't deal in the informal economy formally.

(Regional Head of World Bank, who asked to remain anonymous)

Two uncomfortable truths emerge in considering post-agreement reconstruction. The first is that abusive profiteering has to some extent become institutionalized into the formal economy. The second is that average people survive the economic crises of the twenty-first century in part through the extra-legal. To condone the first is dangerous, to deny the second can be lethal.

Classical economics and modernist development philosophies do not offer tools to effectively deal with these realities.[13] In any scientific investigation, it would be unthinkable to render analyses and policies based on a data set that was missing a significant portion of its data. But that is precisely what is taking place when classical economics is applied to the world, and disregards non-legal and non-transparent economic activity and the political power it encompasses.

And herein rests one of the key aspects of the intersections of illicit power. Angolans, for example, are familiar with the paths regulated and unregulated commodities take around the world. They have seen international wildcatters amass considerable fortunes from the ashes of war and political turmoil. Fortunes are made on these illegal sales, and political power stems from these fortunes. Industries are forged on these profits, and industries merge into transnational corporations with the power to influence world markets and international law.

Yet these relationships are not as highlighted – or even apparent in many cases – in Western political and economic theories. The 'politics of invisibility' is no accident: it is created, and it is created for a reason. It would appear that the modern state is as dependent on shadow economies and war-zone profits as it is on keeping these dependencies invisible to formal reckoning. Jean-François

Bayart captures these complexities when he writes, 'The matrices of disorder are frequently the same as those for order.'[14]

The challenge facing twenty-first century economics, and by extension, all reconstruction work, is for formal economy theory and practice to catch up with the truth of extant economies. One solution is to continue to develop the research questions and methodologies presented here. We need to ask how extra-legal networks operate in contrast to, and in liaison with, state systems. How is authority managed? How resources are procured and used; and how are proceeds laundering? How is power expressed? How do extra-legal networks link internationally? What determines belonging, recruitment, loyalty in any group? How are commodities, monies, and people moved and managed?

These are not idle questions. A new era of power contestations is forming in the twenty-first century. Looking at the history of extra-state groups defeating the colonial world and of extra-legal networks toppling governing systems, people have learnt that the extra-state is the most powerful way of challenging the state, or of controlling it. Yet our understanding is embryonic. To leave it here is to condemn people and their governments to post-war solutions that, at best, can only be partially useful, and at worst leave abusive power unchecked.

Anthropologists have long worked with multiple nodes and trajectories of power defining any given site. Heuristically, the state represents one such model. Concurrent systems, such as the extra-legal powers I discuss here, operate coexistentially across time and space. The relationships holding between different formulations of power do not stay constant. In the same way that international networks of traders during the time of *king*doms helped pre-configure the modern state, and their market tribunals presaged contemporary international law – extra-legal networks today may foreshadow new power formulations barely emergent on the horizons of political and economic possibility. Perhaps the most important question facing us today is who is shaping these outcomes?

Notes

1. An ethnography, in anthropology, is a long-term, in-site field study, usually where the anthropologist learns the language, customs, and cultures of the people among whom they are working. The research here is based on 12 years of in-site ethnographic research in Africa, Asia, Europe, and Latin America.
2. The term extra-legal refers to all activities that fall outside legality as it is formally defined and used in law and law enforcement. This includes illegal, illicit, informal, and undeclared, unregistered, and unregulated actions. For example, informal transactions, say trading food for services, are not technically illegal in themselves, but violate the letter of the law in not being responsible to systems of declaration and taxation. They are clearly a different arena of behaviour than illegal transactions such as narcotics and trafficking, the province of cartels; or corruption, the province of elites. All are extra-legal.

Extra-state refers to all activities that take place outside of formal state ruling systems. In this book, those of most interest constitute economic and/or political forces. Like extra-legal activities, these are diverse: rebel groups are extra-state players quite different from mafias and cartels, and both these differ significantly from extra-state activities done by state actors (corruption). Yet as a whole, these can be an invisible part of the way states function, and they can also challenge the supremacy of the state as the twenty-first century form of governance and community. Extra-legal networks often grow in economic sophistication and political authority to constitute serious extra-state forces.

3. See C. Nordstrom, *Global Outlaws: Crime, Money and Power in the Contemporary World* (Berkeley CA: University of California Press, 2007).
4. Field notes, 2002. See also Nordstrom (2007), op. cit.
5. See C. Nordstrom, *A Different Kind of War Story* (Philadelphia PA: University of Pennsylvania Press, 1997) and Nordstrom (2007), op. cit.
6. See R.T., Naylor, *Wages of Crime: Black Markets, Illegal Finance, and The Underworld Economy* (Ithaca NY: Cornell University Press, 2005); W. van Schendel & I. Abraham (eds), *Illicit Flows and Criminal Things: States, Borders, and the Other Side of Globalization* (Bloomington IN: Indiana University Press, 2005) and J. MacGaffey & R. Bazanguissa-Ganga, *Congo-Paris: Transnational Traders on the Margins of the Law* (Bloomington IN: Indiana University Press, 2000); W.T. Ngugi, *Moving the Centre: The Struggle for Cultural Freedoms* (London: James Currey, 1993); K. Maier, *Angola: Promises and Lies* (Rivonia UK: William Waterman, 1996) and J. MacGaffey, *The Real Economy of Zaire: The Contributions of Smuggling and Other Unofficial Activities to National Wealth* (Philadelphia PA: University of Pennsylvania Press, 1991) .
7. M. Chingono, *The State, Violence and Development* (Brookfield: Avebury, 1996), p. 101.
8. I took photos of these pictures, and some have been published: see C. Nordstrom, 'A war dossier', *Public Culture*, 10, 2 (Winter 1998) and *A Different Kind of War Story*. (Philadelphia PA: University of Pennsylvania Press, 1997).
9. Nordstrom, field notes, Mozambique, 1990.
10. Nordstrom, field notes, Angola, 2001.
11. Chingono (1996), op. cit., p. 115.
12. Author interview with David Hesketh (2002). Hesketh heads the International Assistance Branch of Her Majesty's Customs and Excise, United Kingdom.
13. C. Nordstrom, *Shadows of War: Violence, Power, and International Profiteering in the Twenty-first Century* (Berkeley CA: University of California Press, 2004).
14. J.F. Bayart, *The State in Africa: the Politics of the Belly* (London: Longman, 1993), p. 209.

21
Military and Police Reform after Civil Wars

William D. Stanley and Charles T. Call

Armed institutions and civil war settlements

A basic goal of any civil war settlement is to reestablish a legitimate state monopoly over the use of force in society, under terms agreeable to the parties in conflict. For all parties, the composition and control of state forces will shape post-war security. Whatever party expects to gain control of the government must consider whether post-war military and police will remain unitary and loyal to the new order. Groups that expect minority representation or limited power sharing within the post-war order must consider their risk of persecution and violence at the hands of the new government forces. In addition to the particular interests of the former civil war adversaries, the long-term stability of post-civil war regimes, particularly those based on liberal democratic models, depends on institutional arrangements that minimize the likelihood that organized coercive forces of any kind will intervene in politics.

To address these concerns, most peace settlements envision some degree of reform of military and police forces. Although the type and extent of reforms differ dramatically from case to case, a common element in most settlements is the creation of some kind of counterbalance of political and institutional forces that makes it less likely that one group will be in a position to intervene forcefully in politics.[1] Here we discuss two widely drawn upon models, which we will call 'military merger' and 'demilitarization and police reform'. These two paths are not mutually exclusive in theory but have generally proven so in practice. 'Military merger' refers to the notion that integrating former enemy armies into one another (usually into the government armed forces) is necessary to establish security guarantees (and overcome the domestic security dilemma) among parties to conflict. This has been most common in African settlements, including Zimbabwe, South Africa, Mozambique, and Sierra Leone. Such power sharing provides all sides with, at a minimum, eyes and ears within the post-war armed institutions. Presence in the military gives the parties early warning of any effort by their former adversaries to carry out repressive actions.

The second path, 'demilitarization and police reform', postulates that the best means of establishing security guarantees among former enemies is to try to demobilize or reduce the power of combatant armies, shifting the bulk of interior security responsibilities to a reformed civilian police force. This option usually involves reducing the budget and size of armed forces, demobilizing rebel armies, and confining the military to external defence missions. Demilitarization is accompanied by significant institutional development and reform to the civilian police, which may include former enemies in its ranks. This model was followed in El Salvador, Guatemala, and Namibia.[2] Other models exist, including the presence of international monitors or the complete elimination of the armed forces. Political conditions constrain what models are possible in any given case. The demilitarization and police reform model appears to be feasible only in cases where there is a low probability of renewed military conflict.

In this chapter, we argue that no single model for post-conflict security should be followed in all circumstances, as local conditions should be the departure point for developing effective and accountable security guarantees. However, we find that the path of demilitarization and police reform holds advantages over military merger. Strong civilian police can serve, among other things, as a counterweight to the military. Moreover, civilian police with appropriate training, doctrine, personnel selection, civilian oversight, and mechanisms of internal control are likely to be more respectful of the rule of law and individual rights, and are likely to use force more selectively. At the same time,

Table 21.1 Security arrangements and peace-plan implementation[a]

Security guarantees in peace accord	Accords implemented	Accords partially implemented	Accords collapsed/not implemented
Demilitarization and police reform	El Salvador Namibia	Guatemala	Haiti Kosovo
Integration of opposing forces within military	Mozambique South Africa Zimbabwe	Bosnia	Angola Liberia Rwanda Sierra Leone
Temporary external guarantees only	Nicaragua	Cambodia	

[a] The categories in the table are simply characteristics that are really shades of grey. Tables 21.1 and 21.2 are included as heuristics. Categorizations are based heavily upon case chapters prepared for the Stanford University/International Peace Academy project on Implementing Peace Agreements after Civil Wars (August 2000).

militaries that are less involved in internal security have fewer opportunities and pretexts for intervention, and are less likely to abuse or threaten members of the public.

Military reform

There is little consensus regarding the best approach to military institutional development after civil wars, and few peace processes provide detailed plans for redesign of military doctrine, conduct, or organizational structure. Policy makers associated with defence establishments in Western countries have tended to advocate efforts to develop new roles, missions, equipment, and capabilities for post-civil war militaries.[3] They argue that militaries that are engaged in higher levels of professional development are less likely to get involved in politics. The historical record, particularly in Latin America, appears to contradict this argument, as the more highly institutionalized and 'professional' militaries in the region, especially in the Southern Cone, committed some of the worst atrocities during military authoritarian regimes of the 1970s and 1980s. Human rights advocates have generally argued for reduced military roles, force size, and budgets, arguing that weaker militaries are less likely to threaten democracy.[4] Western powers and intergovernmental organizations such as the UN, NATO and the OSCE, have pursued a variety of strategies in different contexts – seeking demilitarization in some cases and supporting military development in others. Western powers deliberately took sides during some recent civil conflicts, bolstering one side militarily.[5]

Military mergers

In several cases, international actors have supported military mergers as part of peace processes. These efforts have usually entailed limited efforts to build smaller national militaries that integrate former civil war adversaries, while developing a somewhat higher level of professionalism. Mozambique's peace process required the demobilization of 70,000 government and rebel troops, combined with a simultaneous effort to form a new national army that would receive international training and general assistance. The new army was to include roughly equal representation (at the officer level) of the two opposing sides. In practice, it proved difficult to recruit troops for the new army, and as of early 2001, force levels remain at around 12,000, well below the 30,000 called for in the peace accord. Although there have been complaints from the Mozambican National Resistance (RENAMO) that its representatives in the new army have less influence than officers originally from the ruling Front for the Liberation of Mozambique (FRELIMO) party, the integration of the two sides into a single military force has generally been successful.[6] Peace processes in Zimbabwe and South Africa similarly involved successful integration of former adversaries, although Zimbabwe's successful military merger at independence in 1980 experienced serious problems in 2000.

While these successes show the potential feasibility of integrating former enemies, in Angola, Liberia, Rwanda, and Sierra Leone, similar military merger schemes proved impossible to implement. These failures may reflect these particularly difficult contexts, rather indicating an inherent flaw with idea of sharing power within the military. All four of the failure cases were ones with determined spoilers, where very little confidence had been built between the adversaries.[7] Integration of opposing forces into the military is primarily a way of providing security guarantees for the more vulnerable parties in an accord. Determined spoilers such as Jonas Savimbi of the National Union for the Total Independence of Angola (UNITA), the Hutu-dominated government forces in Rwanda before 1994, Charles Taylor in Liberia, or the Revolutionary United Front in Sierra Leone proved to be more interested in relative gains than in security. Where spoilers don't win, but don't settle either (as in Angola and Sierra Leone), the government has no incentive to permit integration of national forces until such time as the spoiler makes a credible commitment to stop fighting. Where the spoiler wins, as did Taylor in Liberia, the planned integration simply never happens, and former opponents are in no position to enforce the original agreement. Where the spoiler loses (Rwanda after the genocide), the winner has little incentive to permit extensive integration of forces.

Military reform deferred

In some cases, peace plans make no detailed provisions regarding post-war military institutional arrangements. In Cambodia, for example, the agreement authorized the UN mission (UNTAC) to help canton existing forces, oversee the demobilization of 70 per cent of each faction's forces, and fully disarm militia forces. What kind of military force would exist thereafter would depend on the outcome of the election and the preferences of the new government. In practice, demobilization did not take place, largely because the Khmer Rouge defected from the process. The May 1993 elections produced a victory for the Front for an Independent, Neutral, Peaceful, and Cooperative Cambodia (FUNCINPEC), but the militarily more powerful State of Cambodia (SOC) faction rebelled and forced FUNCINPEC to accept a power-sharing agreement under which the heads of each faction would be co-prime ministers. The UNTAC then brokered a hasty deal among the military leaders of the three factions (excluding Khmer Rouge) to form a unified military command.[8] In practice, the various factional forces were not integrated down to the unit level, and the dominant SOC units later backed SOC leader Hun Sen in seizing *de facto* power. The lack of institutional reforms to reduce the likely political use of military force clearly contributed to the overturn of democratic process in Cambodia. This was one of several ways in which the formula for ending Cambodia's civil war lacked adequate planning for institutional reforms beyond the elections.

The unsuccessful experience of Cambodia and other cases illustrate the importance of institutional security reforms after wars. Cambodia's disappointing post-electoral democratic performance has unfolded with a security apparatus still firmly in the hands of only one party of the earlier conflict. In Angola, Rwanda, and Sierra Leone, peace processes faltered before planned military mergers – or any effective security guarantees – could be put into place. Where military mergers have occurred, they appear to have helped prevent renewed conflict and found useful employment for thousands of combatants who might otherwise turn to illicit activities. In Zimbabwe, South Africa, and Mozambique, the integration of enemy military officers and soldiers into a single armed force represented an important component of successful peace processes. We now turn to an alternative path, more prevalent in recent years.

Police reform and democratic consolidation

While successful military mergers and other military reforms can have an important impact on short-term stabilization of a peace process, police reforms, and accompanying steps towards reduced military power and prerogatives arguably have more impact on the prospects for long-run consolidation of peaceful, democratic systems. Societies recovering from civil war often suffer high rates of violent crime due to factors such as the prevalence of military weaponry, the lack of employment opportunities for former combatants, and the ease with which clandestine military structures can be adapted to become self-sustaining criminal enterprises. Ironically, in places like El Salvador and South Africa, civilians faced greater risk of violent death or serious injury after the end of the conflict than during it.[9] Political violence may be concealed amidst such generalized violence, and the public may perceive more political violence than is actually occurring. Overall, public confidence in the post-war government can depend heavily on the government's ability to provide general public security. Moreover, in the absence of open combat, citizens are more likely, on a daily basis, to deal with police than with military forces. The tenor of those interactions, particularly the fairness of police conduct with respect to both individual and group rights, and the police's moderation in use of force, will have a significant effect on whether the public trusts and supports the new order. As police scholar David Bayley puts it, 'The police are to government as the edge is to the knife.'[10] Abusive, corrupt, or neglectful police conduct can quickly undercut public commitment to a post-war order and can lead to a variety of damaging reactions such as re-constitution of ethnically or ideologically based militias.

Unfortunately, a huge gap exists between the importance of police reform and the international community's ability to deliver assistance to police institutional development. While donor states and international organizations have ample ability to provide military training and development, few resources are available to help post-civil war governments build efficient and humane police forces. Moreover, efforts to build civilian police institutions are beset by multiple dilemmas: peace-plan implementers must, for example, choose between incorporating personnel from old security forces versus starting fresh with new people. Measures that may help new governments deal effectively with typical immediate post-war crime problems can be damaging to the long-term development of more democratic policing models. New policing models may be needed to replace inhumane, repressive, or politicized policing traditions, yet foreign models may not be well adapted to local cultures and conditions.

Not only does the international community have limited capacity to implement police reform but also it has not generally made a priority of security for the general public during peace negotiations. This chapter turns now to a more detailed discussion of the challenges of long-term police institution building after civil wars. We believe that the international community will need to devote substantially more resources to post-civil war policing issues if it hopes to deal effectively with the various dilemmas that arise regarding these crucial public services and institutions.

Police reform

Of 18 recent agreements to settle civil wars, 12 included some provisions for police reform. Table 21.2 below categorizes peace implementation cases according to whether minimal police reforms were included in peace accords, and whether reforms have been implemented to date. In many cases, agreed-upon police reforms were limited to brief references to incorporating former enemies into the police, to enhanced training or professionalization, and to conformity with international human rights standards. Croatia's Erdut Peace Agreement (1995), for example, provides only that a transitional administration in Eastern Slavonia will 'help establish and train temporary police forces, to build professionalism among the police and confidence among all ethnic communities'.

In other cases, lengthy provisions called not only for incorporating former enemies but also for fundamental reorientation of policing along new models emphasizing citizen service. Northern Ireland's 'Good Friday' agreement (1998) and Angola's Lusaka Protocol (1994) stipulated that post-war policing would be impartial, non-partisan, committed to the rule of law and human rights, representative of diverse communities, and professional. Peace agreements in El Salvador and Guatemala, as well as international interventions in the non-negotiated cases of Haiti and Kosovo, resulted in the replacement of

Table 21.2   Post-civil war police reforms

Police reform included in peace accord?	Police reform implemented?	
	Yes	No
Yes	El Salvador, Namibia	Angola (Lusaka)
	Guatemala, N. Ireland	Rwanda
	South Africa, Bosnia	Somalia
	East. Slavonia	Sierra Leone I (Abidjan)
	Mozambique	
No	Haiti, Kosovo[a]	
	Cambodia	Liberia
	Nicaragua	Western Sahara
		Sri Lanka
		Sierra Leone II (Conakry)

[a] Though not cases of civil war settlement, Haiti and Kosovo are included because of their importance in shaping international approaches to police reform and because prior peace agreements (for Haiti the 1993 Governor's Island accord, and for Kosovo the 1999 Rambouillet Accord) included significant police reform provisions. Although the Haitian government and the Yugoslav government, respectively, failed to observe (or sign) these agreements, in each case the accords served as roadmaps for subsequent international implementation of police reforms.

old security forces with new police forces trained in new academies under new doctrines. In Bosnia, agreed-upon 'advisory' roles for the International Police Task Force opened the door to downsizing, retraining, purging, inclusion of ethnic minorities, and acceptance of 'democratic principles' among Federation and Republika Srpska police forces.

Significant police restructuring is rare in peace agreements, and rarer still in implementation. Of the 12 cases of police reforms in peace agreements, in only 8 cases was any reform really implemented.[11] Only in the cases of El Salvador, Namibia, and South Africa were most of the provisions and international expectations regarding police reform realized in practice (it remains too early to draw conclusions about Northern Ireland). In two cases (Cambodia and Nicaragua), police reforms occurred although they were omitted from peace accords; however, these reform processes were less profound than those written into peace agreements.

These cases suggest three broad propositions: first, police reform matters for medium- and long-term public security and democratization. In more successful cases, police reforms helped improve human rights performance and the public's expectations for and understanding of how police should protect citizens. Second, far-reaching public security reforms are unlikely to be implemented if not written directly into peace agreements. Where authorities eventually implemented reforms without any prior agreement to do so, the outcome was more limited than in cases of agreement. Given the difficulties of getting civil war adversaries to focus on less pressing public-interest issues during nego-tiations, international actors need to be prepared to provide agenda-setting leadership on this issue. In El Salvador, for instance, the UN drafted a new police law and insisted on the inclusion of non-combatants so that the new civilian police would benefit the public as a whole as well as helping to protect the disarming guerrillas.

Third, recent experiences with public security reforms point to a series of tensions or trade-offs that confront local and international decision-makers regarding longer-term public security issues. Coping with these tensions requires planning, realistic assessment of public security threats and available resources, and institutional engineering to minimize the costs to the public of implementing peace accords. Drawing mainly upon the cases where signa-tories both agreed to and implemented public security reforms, the following sub-sections address the choices and tensions encountered.

Transitional security

In most peace processes, some kind of transitional arrangement is included, if for no other reason than that most peace plans require the various factions' armed forces to be separated from one another, cantoned, and at least partially demobilized. Transitional arrangements may well shape subsequent institu-tional developments. Unfortunately, neither national nor current international capabilities are usually able to provide transitional security in a manner that is effective and acceptable to local populations. Existing public security forces are the most obvious resource for providing interim security. However, these often include large numbers of individuals with histories of political violence, provo-cation, and extensive human rights violations. Sometimes a degree of vetting is done to remove the most egregious offenders, but such screening is generally done hastily, superficially, and without adequate information. Under these cir-cumstances, existing forces can pose a threat to the security of disarmed rebels, their supporters, returning refugees, or minority ethnic groups. They are also likely to violate human rights more generally, and may pose a threat to nascent democratic institutions.

The most common approach to dealing with these drawbacks of existing forces is for the United Nations (UN) or another international body to deploy civilian police observers (CIVPOL) to monitor the local cops and attempt to prevent abuses. While CIVPOL can be quite effective in this monitoring role, they do face a number of limitations. CIVPOL officers do not always speak the local language, are cobbled together from disparate cultures and back-grounds, often with little international experience, are generally deployed for short tours (typically six months), and most important, are not available in the numbers required around the world. Donor countries can ill afford to lose their police officers, and thus international cops cannot be counted upon to serve as the administrative and investigative police for entire countries.[12] Using international military troops as interim police is another option, as occurred in Somalia and Bosnia. However, many countries, especially the United States, are deeply reluctant to expose their troops to the potential dangers and costs of extended policing tasks. In addition, military forces are not appropriate for most public security tasks, since their training, equipment, and doctrine emphasize use of overwhelming force, rather than the controlled application of force necessary for police work.[13]

Consequently, the provision of interim security remains a challenge for almost every peace process. The international community could do more to relieve the public security pressures on governments after civil wars by increased public safety training for military peacekeeping forces, increased use of military police capabilities already available, and wider use of gendarme-type support units. In addition, the UN should continue its efforts to improve the availability, quality, consistency, and management of CIVPOL. Until these measures occur, however, transitional security dilemmas will persist.

Models of policing

Those peace agreements that do address public security reforms have often granted wide latitude to implementers, especially international actors, in designing, training, and equipping new police forces. What model should be adopted? Adoption of foreign models means that policing may not respond to the realities of the society. In particular, foreign models may fail to address particular security problems that contributed to conflict in the first place. Yet, reliance upon local structural and doctrinal models may simply recreate exclusionary structures and recruitment patterns, reinforce doctrines that might sow the seeds of future conflict, or leave some sectors of the civilian population unprotected.

Perhaps the most important consideration for international technical assistance donors is that they make the effort to familiarize themselves with local conditions, and seek input, rather than attempting to transplant complete policing systems without adaptation.[14] In situations where several bilateral donors are involved in developing new or reformed police institutions, there is potential for confusion as different national contingents provide distinct and sometimes contradictory advice. This can be dealt with in part by having different nationalities focus on different specializations – one on general policing, another on investigations, and so on. Where multiple nationalities participate in training, as has occurred where CIVPOL missions have provided training, confusion and contradictions can be minimized if the mission prepares a common field-training syllabus. The development over the past decade of international norms regarding basic standards for police conduct, and especially for police use of force, helps provide guidance to different training contingents.[15]

Police force composition

A core interest of some armed opposition parties is that their combatants have the possibility of participating in state military or police forces. This participation is one guarantee that their members will not suffer persecution from state forces once they lay down arms. Even relatively small representation generates greater transparency and greater confidence on the part of former rebels or their supporters. Thus, incorporation of previously disenfranchised political and social groups into the police can be both a means of political reconciliation as well as a source of legitimacy for the new police among some popular sectors.

Although some international peacekeeping personnel recognize the importance of including former enemies in new or reformed police forces, other international personnel (especially military and police) can equate attention to composition with politicization. The CIVPOL missions and police advisors from bilateral donors have often pressed these issues only tentatively, even where failure to incorporate opposition or distinct ethnic groups into the police represents a serious violation of a peace accord. In Bosnia, most international police officers were more comfortable enhancing police skills and capabilities than enforcing agreements to incorporate minority ethnic groups into cantonal police forces.[16] Similarly, in Guatemala a European Union (EU) project implemented by the Spanish Civil Guard tended to accept the *ladino*-dominated government's low priority on recruiting Mayans into the police.[17]

Some peace agreements have established educational and other personnel standards for admission to reformed police forces. Higher standards are likely to produce more effective police, as well as improved conduct vis-à-vis the public. But there are costs as well. High educational standards may exclude historically oppressed groups from participating in the police. Waiving some educational standards, or providing remedial training, may be needed to make a reformed police adequately inclusive. Other exclusionary standards, such as stature requirements, could often be lowered to accommodate groups such as Mayan Guatemalans, without in any way compromising the future professionalism of the police.

Finding the right international cops for the job

The international community is not well organized to deploy specialists in training and developing police forces. Because CIVPOL are recruited mainly to monitor transitional public security forces, they are not well prepared to advise and support institutional development.[18] The tasks of creating new police academies, drafting doctrine, restructuring police forces, and establishing specialized police units require experienced senior police managers and supervisors. Bilateral programs such as that of the US Justice Department may be properly structured to do this kind of work, but are few in number, and limited in capacity.

Moreover, no bilateral effort possesses the capacity to deploy field trainers to supervise and build upon classroom training. The Spanish Civil Guard (GCE) has played a crucial role in countries such as Guatemala and Mozambique, but has sometimes made unfortunate choices of personnel and exhibited a tendency to transplant Spanish models with little adaptation to local conditions.[19] Commonwealth countries have provided assistance in Sierra Leone and South Africa, but these programs are relatively small. The EU, though increasingly supportive of police development projects, depends on national agencies such as the GCE to implement projects.

The emergence of new multilateral programmes has done little to expand the pool of qualified technical assistance personnel, or improve the coherence and rationality of their deployment. It has also failed to contribute to improved continuity across missions. The OSCE, for example, took over police development efforts from the UN in the Eastern Slavonia region of Croatia, and is responsible for training in Kosovo. Yet very few 'lessons learned' are retained from mission to mission, and fresh senior police officers, new to international police development, continue to dominate police missions, reinventing the wheel with each new operation. A key problem with many of the cases examined is that police development was an afterthought not integrated into peace implementation. This reflects the absence of an institutional home for police development within the UN bureaucracy. As already noted, CIVPOL is not organized to plan and implement police development. The UNDP, though it has growing experience in this area, lies outside DPKO and coordination has sometimes been poor between UNDP and peace missions.

Conclusion

Reconfiguration of military and police forces after civil wars is central to the stability of any negotiated settlement, as well as to the prospects for long-term consolidation of a democratic framework of government. Our review of cases showed marked differences in the success rates of different approaches to military reform. Reduction in the size and authority of militaries, combined with strengthened civilian police institutions, has enjoyed moderate success in all cases it was introduced, and seems to correlate with successful overall peace implementation. Military mergers have also been important components of successful peace processes but are alone insufficient to prevent a reversion to war. These varied outcomes may reflect the political contexts shaping the overall peace process. The contexts where it was possible to negotiate total disarmament of opposition groups in exchange for partial demilitarization of the state were ones in which both parties were highly motivated to stop fighting, and fairly confident of their opponent's commitment to peace.[20] Contexts where the parties insisted on power-sharing agreements were more often ones where one or more parties were not fully committed to peace, where perceived risks of bolt-from-the-blue attacks were high, and where all sides insisted therefore on power sharing within the military. From a normative point of view, we concur with Donald Rothchild that settlements that lock in group powers, rights, and prerogatives (as is typically the case in military power-sharing approaches) are less likely in the long run to produce consolidated peace than are settlements that establish national institutions designed to protect individual rights across the board.[21]

In the absence of renewed combat, police are more likely to affect average citizens than are military troops. The effects of reconstituting police after civil war depend heavily on institutional features of the new or reformed police: who is allowed to join the police, who commands, how police are held accountable for their conduct, how they are trained, and what doctrines they follow. These qualities, in turn, are heavily affected by how peace implementers handle transitional security arrangements, as well as what resources they can bring to bear to build new policing institutions. Unfortunately, despite the importance of police reform and public security issues, the international community has little capacity to assist in this area. The UN, regional organizations, and member states need to undertake a major effort in institution building of their own, so as to have the capacity to provide or help provide transitional security, and to have the ability to assist in the construction of military and especially police forces that conform to democratic norms.

Notes

1. See J. Frazer, 'Sustaining Civilian Control: Armed Counterweights in Regime Stability in Africa', PhD Dissertation in political science (Stanford University: 1994).
2. The Guatemalan military reforms have not been fully implemented. Military force levels and budget were cut substantially as required, but reforms to the constitutional and legal status of the military stalled following defeat in a public referendum. Nonetheless, there has been no overt breakdown of the process, rebel forces disarmed ahead of schedule, and there has been one successful cycle of legislative and presidential elections.
3. S.P. Huntington, *The Third Wave: Democratization in the Late Twentieth Century* (Norman OK: University of Oklahoma Press, 1991).
4. L. Diamond, 'Democracy in Latin America', in T. Farer (ed.), *Beyond Sovereignty: Collectively Defending Democracy in the Americas* (Baltimore MD: Johns Hopkins University Press, 1996), p. 87.
5. Such intervention has occurred in the midst of faltering peace processes. After the apparent failure of peace processes, for instance, the United States intervened in Haiti in 1994, NATO bombed Yugoslav forces in Kosovo in 1999, and the British backed the government in Sierra Leone in 2000.
6. P. Chabal, 'Mozambique: Prospects for Stability', London: King's College and UNHCR Center for Documentation and Research; WriteNet Paper No. 11/2000. Available at http://www.unhcr.ch/refworld/country/writenet/wn11_00.pdf. Last accessed on 22 May 2001.

7. S.J. Stedman, 'Spoiler problems in peace processes', *International Security*, 22, 2 (Fall 1997) pp. 5–53.
8. J. Shear, 'Riding the Tiger: The UN and Cambodia', in W.J. Durch, (ed.), *UN Peacekeeping, American Policy, and the Uncivil Wars of the 1990s*, (New York: Saint Martin's Press, 1996) pp. 170–172.
9. C.T. Call. 'Why the World's Most Successful Peace Processes Produce the World's Most Violent Countries', Paper delivered at International Studies Association conference (Chicago: March 1999).
10. D. Bayley, *Patterns of Policing: A Comparative International Analysis* (New Brunswick NJ: Rutgers University Press, 1985) p. 189.
11. In the other four cases of agreed-upon reforms, renewed combat precluded implementation of institutional reforms.
12. For more on CIVPOL, see T. Tanke Holm & E. Barth Eide, *Peacekeeping and Police Reform* (Boulder CO: Lynne Rienner, 2000); C.T. Call & W.D. Stanley, 'Protecting the people: Public security choices after civil wars', *Global Governance*, 7, 2 (Spring 2001); and C. Call & M. Barnett, 'Looking for a few good cops: Peacekeeping, peacebuilding and UN civilian police', *International Peacekeeping*, 6, 4 (Winter 1999).
13. Military reluctance to undertake public security tasks in a growing number of transitional settings has led to experiments in Bosnia and Kosovo with the use of constabulary or gendarme-type police units who combine police training and military capabilities, yet the need for gendarme-type forces in peace operations abroad outstrips the available supply.
14. One illustration of this problem is the work of the Spanish Civil Guard (GCE) in Guatemala, who wrote a disciplinary code for the new Guatemalan civilian police that is a near replica of the GCE code and, in practice, far too complex and cumbersome to work effectively given the low level of education of most Guatemalan police officers and commanders.
15. United Nations, *Compendium of United Nations Standards and Norms in Crime Prevention and Criminal Justice* (UN Document ST/CSDHA/16).
16. Author interviews with several UNCIVPOL officers, Sarajevo, March 1999.
17. The term 'ladino' is used in Guatemala to refer to people who identify themselves as belonging to the dominant Hispanic culture, as distinct from the various (mainly Mayan) indigenous cultures.
18. Call & Barnett (Winter 1999), op. cit.
19. W. Stanley, 'Building new police forces in El Salvador and Guatemala: Learning and counterlearning' and M. Malan, 'Peace-building in Southern Africa: Police reform in Mozambique and South Africa', both in *International Peacekeeping*, 6, 4 (Winter 1999).
20. See M. Peceny & W. Stanley, 'Liberal social reconstruction and the resolution of civil wars in Central America', *International Organization*, 55, 1 (Winter 2001) pp. 149–182.
21. D. Rothchild, 'Implementation and Its Effects on Building and Sustaining Peace: The Effects of Changing Structures of Incentives', Paper prepared for Stanford University/ International Peace Academy project on Implementing Peace Agreements after Civil Wars (October 1999).

22
Refugees and IDPs in Peacemaking Processes

Karen Jacobsen, Helen Young, and Abdalmonim Osman

Introduction

Refugees and Internally Displaced Persons (IDPs)[1] in camps are the most directly affected by war and protracted conflict (after those who are killed or hospitalized) but with the exception of the Palestinians, refugees' role in peacemaking processes has not received much academic attention nor has the impact of these processes on refugees and IDPs in camps been much studied. The reason for this neglect is probably because refugees and IDPs have rarely been consulted by the protagonists involved in peace processes, and have been viewed as passive recipients of outcomes that are negotiated in distant arenas of power. Yet there are significant potential linkages between peace processes and refugees and IDPs. This chapter explores the role of refugees and IDPs in peacemaking processes, and suggests that contemporary changes, including advances in communications technologies, are giving refugees a more salient role.

Peace has traditionally been negotiated by the combatants of warring sides, and non-combatants have had little role in peace processes. As the editors of this volume point out in the Introduction: 'Those who held the guns or the dominant position on the battlefield when a ceasefire was called become negotiating partners regardless of their ability to represent their community. Other voices, often those without firepower, tend to go unheard.' This helps explain why peace processes tend to be overwhelmingly male-dominated, and it also explains why refugees and IDPs are so often sidelined from negotiations. However, Timothy Sisk argues that the past decade of the twentieth century saw a change in the way civil wars are terminated. Sisk shows that from 1990–2000, about half of the world's armed conflicts ended as a result of a negotiated agreement, compared with only about one-fifth of conflicts in the preceding 90 years of the twentieth century. Sisk attributes this change to the more assertive role of the international community in peacemaking: 'Greater consensus among the great powers enabled more vigorous United Nations and regional peacemaking (or mediation), leading to a higher proportion of negotiated settlements.'[2] This more vigorous and assertive role of the international community (i.e., the UN, international human rights and humanitarian organizations, and donor governments) has meant that other actors, including non-state ones, also become actors in peacemaking processes. Just as wars have become more globalized, with stakes and actors that go well beyond the territory under conflict, so it is that peacemaking processes are becoming more globalized, incorporating a greater number of actors.[3] Scholarship on peacemaking now includes analysis of the roles of warlords, NGOs, diasporas, and individual UN agencies. Sisk argues that despite the many obstacles and constraints, the peacemaking experience of the 1990s has revealed new *opportunities* for innovation in promoting sustainable settlements in civil wars.[4]

Why focus on refugees in peace processes?

The growing number of actors seeking and playing a role in peacemaking processes suggests that peacemaking has become a matter that goes beyond the signing of high profile, internationally sponsored agreements. Such agreements are embedded in a wider context of international and more regional political and economic interests, and the success or failure of the peace agreement depends on how it addresses these wider interests. Those actors with stakes in the continuation of conflict, or who believe that their interests have not been adequately addressed, will work on the sidelines to undermine peace agreements and their accompanying peace processes. Refugees and IDPs clearly have a stake in peace agreements. For most of them, peace – or even security without peace – will enable them to leave the camps, and perhaps return home, reclaim their land, and re-establish their livelihoods. Others will have economic or ideological interests in continuing the conflict and undermining the peace process.

Refugees and IDPs are widely seen as a marginalized and disempowered group, with little power and importance in the resolution of conflict. Their concerns – widely seen as humanitarian rather than political – have not been seen as having relevance for peace agreements or peace processes. If refugees and IDPs were indeed passive and powerless observers, unable to influence outcomes and therefore obliged to accept them even when such outcomes did not meet their needs, the role of refugees in peace processes would have only academic interest. However, in recent years a number of international peace agreements have included clauses that addressed IDP and refugee situations. Annex 7 of the Dayton Peace Agreement grants refugees and displaced persons the right to safely return home and regain lost property, or to obtain just compensation.[5] Another example is the 1991 Paris Peace Agreement that ended the war in Cambodia. This agreement included a stipulation that the UN would organize and implement the voluntary repatriation of Cambodians then residing in the seven border camps in Thailand and from other countries of the region.[6]

To what extent have refugees and IDPs themselves been a force in pushing their own agenda? We argue that it is possible to discern a growing trend in which refugees and IDPs are able to influence conflict and peace outcomes. This gain in influence has occurred both in the camp context, that is where refugees and IDPs reside in camps close to the conflict zone, and in the diaspora context, that is where refugees have left their country of origin and the conflict zone and are trying to influence the peace or conflict while based in third countries. Both the camp and the diaspora contexts are important for peace outcomes, but in this chapter, we focus only on camps, and try to show how and why the voice of refugees and IDPs in camps has gained power. We do not address the refugee diaspora because this is a well-researched area with a large literature on among others, the Palestinian, Eritrean, Northern Irish, Afghan, and Iraqi diaporas.[7]

How do camps become politicized? Jonathan Goodhand and David Hulme argue that 'conflict is a social process in which the original structural tensions are themselves profoundly reshaped by the massive disruption of complex political emergencies'.[8] When conflict is protracted, power relations in the conflict zones are reshaped in part by the resultant war economies. New leaders and political structures emerge, creating countervailing forces both for peace and for the continuation of conflict. Refugee camps are one such new political structure. Created to serve humanitarian purposes, over time as the conflict and displacement becomes protracted, camps transcend their humanitarian *raison d'etre* and economic and political activities emerge. This chapter explores the implications of these activities for peace processes, peacemaking, and conflict reduction, and the extent to which the political forces in camps support or undermine these processes. We do this by exploring the relationship between peace processes and three political aspects of camps: political solidarity and cohesion, leadership, and the kinds of political activities that appear, including militarization. The chapter draws on a range of examples, but we focus on the Darfur conflict that began in 2003 and the Darfur Peace Agreement (DPA) signed in May 2006. The conflict in Darfur did not end with the DPA, rather it got worse, and we do not know at the time of writing this (May 2007) how or when it will end. Nevertheless, we offer some preliminary observations about how the Darfurian refugees and IDPs might affect the outcome of the conflict. These observations are based on our fieldwork there from 2004 to 2007.

Refugee and IDPs in camps

At the end of 2005, the population of concern to UN High Commission for Refugees (UNHCR), the UN agency responsible for both the world's refugees and an increasing number (but not all) of the world's IDPs, was 20.8 million people, of whom refugees constituted 40 per cent or 8.5 million; IDPs protected or assisted by UNHCR constituted 32 per cent, and stateless persons were 11 per cent.[9] Global estimates of the IDP population in 2005 amounted to 23.7 million.[10] The IDPs are the responsibility of their national governments, but in most cases these governments have been unable or unwilling to provide protection and assistance.[11] The international response has been similarly weak, and there is no international agency with designated responsibility for the protection and assistance of IDPs, that is no UNHCR equivalent. Instead IDPs are assisted by a range of organizations, often on an ad hoc basis. The main intergovernmental agencies are UNHCR, which assisted approximately 6.6 million or 28 per cent in 2005, and International Organization for Migration (IOM), which assisted IDPs in Iraq, Timor–Leste, Colombia, Uganda, and elsewhere. Over seven million IDPs, almost a third of the global total, did not receive any UN assistance at all, although many are assisted by international NGOs and local organizations.

Most refugees and IDPs reside in urban or rural areas amongst the host population, but a substantial number are in camps. At the end of 2005, UNHCR assisted over 3.6 million people living in camps and organized settlements. The host country with the largest number of refugees in camps was Pakistan, where UNHCR assisted over a million Afghans,[12] followed by Tanzania with almost 348,000 refugees from Burundi and the Democratic Republic of Congo (DRC) in camps, Uganda, with over 257,000 mainly from Sudan, Chad with approximately 243,500 from Darfur (Sudan) and Central African Republic., and Kenya with almost 235,000 from Somalia, Sudan, and Ethiopia (see Table 22.1).

The number of IDPs housed in camps, under the care of their own governments, is difficult to calculate, but camps tend to be the way in which governments seek to manage their IDP populations. Most countries with large IDP populations have camps, including Uganda, Sudan, Colombia, and Afghanistan (see Table 22.2). Like refugees, many IDPs choose to avoid camps and official assistance and try to blend in amongst the local population in the areas to which they have fled.

Table 22.1 Top five refugee camp populations in 2005

Host country	Pop. in camps	Countries of origin
Pakistan	1,084,208	Afghanistan
Tanzania	347,927	Burundi; DRC
Uganda	257,256	Sudan (south); Rwanda; DRC
Chad	243,512	Sudan (Darfur); Cent. Afr. Rep.
Kenya	234,611	Somalia; Sudan (south); Ethiopia

Table 22.2 Top five IDP populations assisted by UNHCR, 2005

Origin	IDPs	IDP camps
Colombia	2,000,000	–
Iraq	1,200,000	–
Sudan	841,946	95,569
Azerbaijan	578,545	33,161
Somalia	400,000	–
Sri Lanka	324,699	67,949

Political activity in camps

There is a long history of political mobilization and organization in camps, beginning with the displaced persons of Europe after World War II.[13] This political activity sometimes organized by local NGOs, and more prevalent where educated and urban displaced people are gathered, is usually aimed at the improvement of the livelihoods and rights of the displaced persons. Thus, refugees protest at the lack of sufficient assistance, resist being re-located or settled elsewhere, speak out about their living conditions, or demand more resettlement to third countries.[14] The IDPs also protest their treatment, lack of rights, and the problems afflicting them once they became IDPs. In Georgia, for example, IDP organizations have publicized and protested against collective centre degradation and psychosocial trauma.[15]

The active political involvement of refugees and IDPs in either the conflict generating their displacement or the peace agreements seeking to resolve those conflict is less well documented. The exception is the case of the Palestinians, which boasts a substantial literature on conflict and peacemaking in the post-World War II era.[16] Research and writing on the role of non-Palestinian refugees and IDPs in contemporary peacemaking is less developed, although recent writing and case studies are beginning to emerge, as are NGOs seeking to support the cause of IDPs and refugees in peacemaking.[17]

The most obvious and extreme way in which refugee camps undermine peace processes is when camps become militarized, that is, they become sites of organized military activity including military recruitment, housing of combatants, and the conduct of activities such as training and arms smuggling that directly feed into the conflict. The mixing of militants and refugees in the same camp was common during the Cold War era, and the cases of Afghan 'refugee-warriors' in Pakistan, and the Interahamwe militias' control of the Goma camps after the Rwandan genocide[18] are well documented.[19] Less well-known cases include the Sahrawi camps in Algeria.[20]

The militarization of camps and the phenomenon of 'refugee warriors' (a term first coined by Ari Zolberg et al., in 1989)[21] has been well researched. Stephen J. Stedman and Fred Tanner argue that militarization is

> part of a larger strategy of warring parties to manipulate refugees and the entire refugee regime established for their protection. Hence some refugee camps become a breeding ground for refugee warriors: disaffected individuals, who – with the assistance of overseas diasporas, host governments, and interested states – equip themselves for battle to retrieve an idealized, mythical lost community.[22]

However, most refugee and IDP camps are civilian entities, as required by international refugee law and (usually) the host government, and the full-blown militarization of camps has been the exception rather than the rule. One estimate suggests that about 15 per cent of refugee crises become militarized.[23] In most cases, militias are based in military camps, well separated from refugee camps. However, since combatants use the refugee camps for rest and recuperation or to shelter their families, refugee camps can operate in conjunction with military camps, as was the situation with the Khmer Rouge fighting the Vietnamese in Cambodia during the 1980s. Militias also raid refugee camps for supplies and resources like vehicles and radios as has been reported in numerous border camps, including the Sudanese refugee camps in northern Uganda. When camps are used by militias to sustain or support their armed struggle, refugees are seen as security threats – either by the host government (when it has not acquiesced to this activity) or by the opposing forces in the sending country, who then conduct punitive raids across the border against the refugee camps. Examples of the latter during the 1980s include the Guatemalan army's attack on refugee camps in Mexico and the Salvadoran army against camps in Honduras; in 1996, the Rwandan army shelled the Goma camps to drive out the Interahamwe rebels. The existence of militarized camps clearly constitute a problem for peace processes, but the political activities that occur in non-militarized camps are more common and it is on these that we now focus.

The growth of the political influence of refugee and IDP camps

We argue that in the past ten years, the voice of refugees and IDPs has become louder and more insistent, with more effect on peace processes and security, not all of which has been positive. There are two reasons for this. First, refugees' experience in camps is itself politicizing – in camps, they are exposed to a variety of political forces and forms of organization that increase their political awareness and willingness to mobilize. Thus, even if refugees and IDPs were not aware, before they were displaced, of the causes of the conflict that led to their displacement, in camps they are likely to acquire political information and experience political mobilization. The politicization of camp refugees is evident from studies of returnees, who, carrying the legacy of political mobilization in camps, also play a role in peacemaking and peace processes when they return home.[24]

This process of politicization in camps is helped by the increasing availability of modern communications technologies, now widely available in the world's remote and isolated places, including refugee and IDP camps. Cell phones, satellite phones, and radios serve to draw refugee camps into the global communications grid, enabling camp residents to keep informed of developments both in the conflict and in peacemaking efforts. This communications technology also enables camp leaders to make their voices heard, whether to advocate for their constituents, the refugees, or to influence the peace process and peacemaking outcomes by communicating with the diaspora or with rebel groups outside the camp.

Political solidarity and cohesion

Displaced people (whether refugees or IDPs) living in the same community have much in common: they share the experience of violence, flight, and prolonged displacement, they are often of similar ethnicity, religion, and language, and usually stand against a common enemy – either the government or rebel militias (sometimes both). However, these commonalities do not necessarily mean that refugee communities are characterized by a high degree of political cohesion and solidarity. Scholars have shown that they are often riven by internal political conflict – with detrimental consequences for their ability to obtain their socio-economic and political rights. Writing about Guatemalan refugees who returned from Mexico in the 1990s, Roman Krznaric shows that there was a high degree of internal political conflict among the returnees. He attributes this to the effects of political organization and consciousness-raising in the refugee camps in Mexico in the 1980s and early 1990s, which led to political power struggles in the communities.[25]

Political leadership in camps

Another factor that contributes to the lack of political cohesion in camps is the diversity of political leadership that evolves over time. Political leadership in camps is of two types. One type comprises those who were leaders in their communities before they became displaced. Many refugees and IDPs leave their homes in aggregate communities, led by their village or community heads or sheikhs or chiefs. In the camps, they re-assemble themselves in similar political and living arrangements, falling in behind their traditional leaders who speak on their behalf, manage dispute resolution, and make decisions about such issues as repatriation and whether or not their community members should support peace processes.

A second type of leadership arises when new leaders emerge in the camps. This occurs when traditional leaders are absent or dead and new leaders emerge from the refugees, or when other political players, such as rebel leaders, enter and use the camps as a base of political support. The deliberate killing of community leaders is linked to 'targeted ethnic cleansing', where men, and especially older men, suffer a higher risk of death from war related trauma than women.[26] According to Spiegel and Salama, in Kosovo this tactic served 'to weaken the social and cultural integrity of the Kosovar Albanian society and to encourage abandonment by the family of their land, or to decrease the likelihood of relatives returning from neighbouring countries to care for them when the conflict ended'. In Darfur, men were more likely to be killed than women by Janjaweed militias, who also deliberately killed tribal leaders, as a tactic to undermine local governance and the cohesion of local communities. The IDPs in the Geneina camps of Western Darfur were left leaderless as their sheikhs fled across the border to the refugee camps in Chad.

The way in which relief camps form and are managed can either actively support traditional leadership structures or promote new forms of leadership. In Darfur in 2003, the International Committee of the Red Cross (ICRC) was one of the first agencies to assist internally displaced people in urban centres. In Abu Shouk camp near El Fasher, (ICRC) prioritized identifying the existing traditional leadership and keeping displaced communities intact as far as possible by settling them in an adjacent area and not leaving it to chance, that is spontaneous settlement. By contrast, in some IDP areas in Darfur, registration and camp management were handled by logisticians with little understanding of the importance of verifying the authority of self-identified leaders, and who paid little attention to the validity of the lists of people in need. Subsequently, these contexts were prone to manipulation by new local leaders, often self-appointed, who abused their positions by operating 'sheikh cartels' who controlled the distribution of aid to their own advantage. For example, these new leaders controlled the selling of ration cards or prevented registration of certain groups or individuals.

The lack of cohesion and diversity of leadership in the camp mean that leaders can assume the role of either 'spoilers' or enablers of peace agreements. New leaders can emerge as a challenge to traditional ones in the camps, basing their competing platforms on grievances shared by a specific group of refugees. Leaders often mobilize followings around complaints and grievances specific to camp life, but they also reflect political responses to the conflict or to peace processes. For example in Darfur, the leaders of the rebel insurgency (particularly the Sudan Liberation Movement (SLM)) were principally young intellectuals and military leaders – rather than the older traditional tribal leadership – and therefore appealed to a new younger constituency. New leaders can include the 'conflict entrepreneurs and political opportunists' who seek to mobilize and manipulate refugees and IDPs in order to prolong the conflict in which these entrepreneurs have vested interests.[27] As a war economy develops with prolonged conflict, the predatory elements that benefit from the war economy also appear in camps – in part linked with the trade in aid resources. The difficulty is determining whether the leaders that assume power are indeed representatives of the refugee community, or rather, which elements in that community they represent. Suzanne Jaspars argues that it is essential for humanitarian actors to assess the presence or absence of a political contract between leadership and a particular group of people. A political analysis of conflict, she suggests, should explore the political or economic interests represented by local leadership or institutions, and which entities represent a threat to the legitimacy of local leadership. She also argues that where the political contract is absent an external agency is justified in trying to establish new independent structures for the distribution of relief in order to prevent manipulation and abuse by local leaders.[28]

In the Introduction, the authors argued for the importance of local level reconciliation as 'opportunities for local interchange'. It is these often-humdrum interactions that will make or break a peace process, the authors argue, 'rather than the hubris of signing ceremonies in the corridors of power'. However, organizing for peace during conflict is a potentially risky business, and for this reason it is not widespread. In her discussion of peace organizations in Sri Lanka, Camila Orjuela says that there is no massive mobilization for peace or against the war, and most peace activities draw relatively small numbers of participants.[29]

> In the war zones ... showing support for peace can have dangerous consequences. Tamils who engage politically are viewed with suspicion by both the government (in whose eyes they are potential terrorists) and the LTTE (which claims the sovereign right to express the will of 'the Tamil people') has made the peace organizations Sinhalese-dominated.

For IDPs and refugees in camps, this risk is greater, as their activities are more visible. However, there are cases where refugees and IDPs have engaged in activities that promote peace, and initiated their own responses to the conflict. The best example of this is the Colombian peace communities, where local people and IDPs engage in 'citizen-based peacemaking', which refers to the unarmed efforts of war-torn communities to stop military activity within their territories.

Refugee camps also offer opportunities for building peace. Camps can contain indigenous organizations and forms of customary mediation that were in place before the conflict and displacement. Julie Flint shows that in North Darfur and in the Darfurian refugee camps in Chad, *Judiyya* mediation – a system of customary mediation in northern Sudan that developed over hundreds of years persists during the current conflict:

> Even in the middle of the present war, although under strain and unable to address complex problems and conflicts, it remains in wide use for managing and resolving grassroots conflict in all tribes – including among refugees in Chad. The Fur, the Masalit, the Zaghawa and the Ta'aisha have a reciprocal arrangement to settle disputes, a council called *rakuba* or *dirbo* in Fur which reaches settlements according to customary law.[30]

Flint says that traditionally the package agreements reached through *judiyya* mediation included a reduction in the number of arms, but 'agreements on all but the most trivial disputes are seldom implemented today because of the absence of durable solutions to the conflict'.[31] In other words, the traditional forms of conflict resolution in Darfur are intended to deal with localized intertribal conflict, and not with the much more profound effects of government counter-insurgency operations. This indicates the importance of distinguishing between levels and causes of conflict, and between local enmities and grievances that require locally specific reconciliation and peace processes, and nationally driven agendas that may require the support of international peacemaking initiatives. In the case of Darfur, the international community has clearly prioritized the latter (by actively supporting the talks in Abuja) while largely ignoring the former. In part this was because it was assumed that the 'Darfur-Darfur Dialogue and Consultation'[ok] planned to take place after the agreement was signed would ensure popular ownership and support of those not present at the negotiations. This particular omission and failure to adequately integrate local voices into the Abuja peace processes[32] partly accounts for the localized rejection of the DPA.

The impact of peace processes on refugees

In considering some of the problems created by formal peace processes, the Introduction suggested that 'peace processes, once institutionalised, stymie opportunities for real political change, and instead channel energies in pre-ordained directions that often reflect international rather than local opinion'. While media attention is focused on the international actors, activities that can support or undermine peace processes being played out at the level of civil society by less public actors who have been sidelined from the peace process are discounted or ignored. Refugees and IDPs are good examples of 'less public actors' and many of the problems and shortcomings associated with peace processes identified in the Introduction become the source of political organizing and mobilization by refugees. Two in particular are worth mentioning. The first relates to the ways in which peace processes and their associated activities sometimes allow the 'macro-level dynamics' of the conflict to survive unchanged, so that grievances that underlay the conflict persist. Such grievances can include patterns of land ownership, or ingrained perceptions that the law operates to benefit some groups against others. For refugees and IDPs, these omissions have immediate consequences. For example, refugees are less likely to return to their homes when a peace agreement does not adequately address the issue of land ownership or the ability to reclaim land from which people were forcibly displaced. In many cases, peace agreements fail to resolve land problems and they fail to address problems of economic development underlying deeply divided societies. These divisions are often aggravated during the conflict – as when war economies take hold and increase poverty and inequality in conflict zones. Land and economic problems are at the root of the needs of displaced populations.

In Darfur, the various rounds of the internationally mediated peace talks in Abuja, Nigeria, were accompanied by increased tensions and localized security incidents, usually instigated by groups wanting to send a message to their representatives in Abuja, or by those not represented at the Peace Talks wanting to draw attention to their situation. Protests against the international peace processes and the peace agreement itself reached a head following the partial signing of the Darfur Peace Accords on 5 May 2006 between Minni Minawi's faction of the Sudan Liberation Movement (SLM/MM) and the Government of Sudan, while the two other rebel groups refrained from signing. This split polarized the movements along tribal lines. The DPA was rejected by the Fur, the majority tribe in the Darfur region who generally support the SLM faction led by Abdul Wahid Nur, which was not a signatory to the DPA. Local protests to the DPA led to rioting by the Fur in Kalma camp and in Zalingei (with deaths of IDPs and relief workers). It subsequently became increasingly difficult for Minnawi, the fourth-ranking member in the Presidency of Sudan, to even travel safely in Darfur because of the factionalism of the non-signatory groups and continued insurgency and government counter-insurgency activity. Thus, the failure of the peace talks served to further politicize and polarize IDP communities in Darfur, leading to mistrust, tensions, and then spiralling violence.

Humanitarian aid intended to assist displaced people can aggravate these divisions. There are many cases of food aid being diverted to support warlords, as in the case of Somalia, or refugee camps being used by militias to support their war efforts, as in the case of Goma in 1994. But, the withdrawal of food aid and other humanitarian assistance can lead to an uptick of political activity in camps. When refugees and IDPs are stuck in camps for protracted periods and are unable to pursue their normal livelihoods, humanitarian assistance can lead to reliance on aid, and the loss or erosion of livelihoods. In the transition from the conflict phase, when peace processes are in progress, food aid and in-kind assistance to refugees in camps are reduced and return packages substituted in an effort to encourage refugees to return home. These changes are seldom welcomed by refugees who have their own preferences about when and how they would like to return home. These dislocations and disruptions can be blamed on or associated with the peace process, especially if the refugees believe their voice has been excluded. Instead of the peace process being associated with tangible benefits, refugees may see it associated with loss of assistance, disruption, and further marginalization.

Conclusion

The ways in which refugees and IDPs enable or inhibit both formal and informal peacemaking processes is one component of the logic of war and peace, and what Sisk calls the 'powerful set of incentives that prevent parties from taking the usually very risky steps toward a negotiated end to their struggle'.[33] Understanding this logic and the incentives motivating the actors involved in peace processes can engender new ways to support pro-peace movements. There is growing evidence, we suggest, that refugees and IDPs are becoming more actively involved in both the undermining and the support of peace processes. In analysing the evolution of conflict and peace, it is important to recognize their voices and try to understand their message and the potential power they wield. There is significant emotional power associated with displacement and links with 'home'. When displacement issues become sticking points in peace negotiations, this affective power can prove to be a serious obstacle, as we have seen with the Palestinians. The international community has developed sophisticated methods for dealing with displacement as a technical issue (camps, reducing mortality repatriation, etc.) but it is less well able to deal with this thorny affective issue. The efforts of refugees and IDPs to engage in traditional conflict mediation and citizen-based peacemaking should be complemented by active efforts on the part of negotiators to include them in formal peacemaking activities. Displaced people have a right to be involved and a strong interest in peace negotiations, but they have not been actively sought out by negotiators and engaged in high-level negotiations. An opportunity awaits.

Notes

1. Both refugees and IDPs are people who have been forced to leave their homes for reasons of persecution, conflict, or violence; the difference is that refugees have crossed an international border.
2. T. Sisk, 'Peacemaking in Civil Wars: Obstacles, Options, and Opportunities', in *Kroc Institute Occasional Paper 20: OP:2* (2001), p. 2.

3. There is now an extensive literature on the nature of contemporary war and complex political emergencies, ranging from ethnographic accounts such as C. Nordstrom, *Shadows of War: Violence, Power, and International Profiteering in the Twenty-First Century* (California: University of California Press, 2004) to conflict analyses such as J. Goodhand & D. Hulme, 'Understanding conflict and peace-building in the new world disorder', *Third World Quarterly*, 20, 1 (1999) pp. 13–26.
4. Sisk (2001), op. cit., p. 3.
5. See the Summary of the Dayton Peace Agreement on Bosnia–Herzegovina, released by the US Department of State (30 November 1995). Available at http://www.pbs.org/newshour/bb/bosnia/dayton_peace.html (Accessed on 7 May 2007).
6. B. Ballard, 'Reintegration Programmes for Refugees in South-East Asia. Lessons Learned from UNHCR's Experience', UNHCR EPAU/2002/01 (2002). According to Ballard (pp. 1–2), the agreement, which was signed by several Western and regional governments and the four political parties involved in the conflict, also established the UN Transition Authority in Cambodia (UNTAC). Under UNTAC, UNHCR was designated as the lead agency to oversee and coordinate the repatriation and reintegration process. A Memorandum of Understanding (MOU) between Thailand, Cambodia, and UNHCR, signed in November 1992, governed the repatriation operation. Both the Paris Peace Agreement and the tri-partite MOU called for the voluntary return of all Cambodians in safety and dignity in time for them to participate in the national elections scheduled for May 1993.
7. See, for example, B. Blitz, 'Serbia's War Lobby: Diaspora Groups and Western Elites', in S. Mestrovic & T. Cushman (ed.), *This Time We Knew. Western Responses to Genocide in Bosnia* (New York: New York University Press, 1996) pp. 187–243; G. Kent, 'Diaspora Power: Network Contributions to Peacebuilding and the Transformation of War Economies', Paper presented at the 'Transforming War Economies' seminar, Plymouth, (16–18 June 2005); A. Mohamoud, 'African Diaspora and Post-Conflict: Reconstruction in Africa', in Danish Institute For International Studies (Copenhagen: Danish Institute for International Studies, 2006), H. Lindholm Schulz, *The Palestinian Diaspora: Formation of Identities and Politics of Homeland* (London & New York: Routledge, 2003), and J. Brinkerhoff, 'Contributions of Digital Diasporas to Governance Reconstruction in Post-Conflict and Fragile States: Potential and Promise', Paper presented at the 'Rebuilding Governance in Post-Conflict Societies: What's New, What's Not' conference (2005).
8. Goodhand & Hulme (1999), op. cit., p. 18.
9. UNHCR, *Global Refugee Trends* (2005), Available at http://www.unhcr.org/statistics (Accessed on 29 March 2007).
10. The global number of IDPs in the past five years has ranged between an estimated 22–26 million people. The main source of figures for this population, the Internal Displacement Monitoring Center (IDMC), identified a decrease of 1.6 million IDPs to an estimated population of 23.7 million at the end of 2005. See IDMC, *Internal Displacement: Global Overview of Trends and Developments in 2005* (Geneva: Internal Displacement Monitoring Centre, 2006).
11. For a fuller discussion of national and international responses to IDPs, beyond the scope of this chapter, see IDMC, Ibid., pp. 15–21.
12. According to UNHCR, a 2005 government census of Afghans in Pakistan indicated there are an additional 1.5 million Afghans living outside camps, some of whom may be refugees. Afghans living outside camps in Pakistan receive no UNHCR assistance except access to UNHCR-facilitated voluntary repatriation. See UNHCR (2005), op. cit., table 13.

13. See the account by R. Somers, *Jewish Displaced Persons in Camp Bergen–Belsen 1945–1950: The Unique Photo Album of Zippy Orlin* (Seattle WA: University of Washington Press in association with Netherlands Institute for War Documentation, 2004).

14. For studies of these kinds of activities see E. Kauffer Michel, 'Leadership and social organization: The integration of the Guatemalan refugees in Campeche, Mexico', *Journal of Refugee Studies*, 15, 4 (2002) pp. 359–387, A. Oliver-Smith, 'Involuntary resettlement, resistance and political empowerment', *Journal of Refugee Studies*, 4, 2 (1991) pp. 132–149, and G. Verdirame, 'Human rights and refugees: the case of Kenya', *Journal of Refugee Studies* 12 (1999) pp. 54–77.

15. IDMC (2006), op. cit., p. 41.

16. See, for example, D. Forsythe, 'Unrwa, the Palestine refugees, and world politics: 1949–1969', *International Organization*, 25, 1 (1971) pp. 26–45.

17. See, for example, S. Utterwulghe, 'Conflict management in complex humanitarian situations: peacemaking and peacebuilding work with Angolan IDPs', *Journal of Refugee Studies*, 17, 2 (2004) pp. 222–242.

18. See H. Adelman & G. Rao, *War and Peace in Zaire/Congo: Analyzing and Evaluating Intervention, 1996–1997* (Trenton NJ & Asmara: Africa World Press, 2004).

19. F. Terry, *Condemned to Repeat?: The Paradox of Humanitarian Action* (Ithaca NY: Cornell University Press, 2002). There is an extensive sub-literature on the militarization of refugee camps, see, for example, S. Kenyon Lischer, *Dangerous Sanctuaries: Refugee Camps, Civil War, and the Dilemmas of Humanitarian Aid* (Ithaca NY: Cornell University Press, 2005). Early examples were the mixing of refugees and guerilla fighters in Mozambique and Zambia during the Rhodesian war in the 1970s. See M. Preston, 'Stalemate and the termination of civil war: Rhodesia reassessed', *Journal of Peace Research*, 41, 1 (2004) pp. 65–83.

20. D. Chatty, G. Crivello, & G. Lewando Hundt, 'Theoretical and methodological challenges of studying refugee children in the Middle East and North Africa: Young Palestinian, Afghan and Sahrawi refugees', *Journal of Refugee Studies*, 18, 4 (2005) pp. 387–409.

21. A. Zolberg, A. Suhrke, & S. Aguayo, *Escape from Violence: Conflict and the Refugee Crisis in the Developing World* (Oxford: Oxford University Press, 1989).

22. S. Stedman & F. Tanner (eds), *Refugee Manipulation: War, Politics, and the Abuse of Human Suffering* (Washington DC: Brookings Institution Press, 2003) p. 3.

23. Ibid.

24. Such analysis has been conducted in the case of Guatemalan returnees, see R. Krznaric, 'Guatemalan returnees and the dilemma of political mobilization', *Journal of Refugee Studies*, 10, 1 (1997).

25. Ibid. Lack of political cohesion amongst refugees is not unique to camps. In her study of Somali refugee organizations in London and Toronto, Gail Hopkins has shown how 'exclusionary dynamics', including the persistent clan rivalry among Somalis, inhibited the development of a united, collaborative Somali voice and the ability of community organizations to build a sense of community and a setting that enabled integration within the receiving society. See G. Hopkins, 'Somali community organizations in London and Toronto: Collaboration and effectiveness', *Journal of Refugee Studies*, 19, 3 (2006) pp. 361–380.

26. In Kosovo mortality rates among Kosovar Albanians peaked in April 1999, which coincided with an intensification of the Serbian campaign of ethnic cleansing. Men older than 50 years were three times more likely to die of war related trauma than men between 15 and 49 years of age, and nearly 10 times more likely to die than

older women. P. Spiegel & P. Salama, 'War and mortality in Kosovo, 1998–99: An epidemiological testimony', *The Lancet*, 355 (2000) pp. 2204–2249.

27. Goodhand & Hulme (1999), op. cit., p.17.
28. S. Jaspars, 'Solidarity and Soup Kitchens: A Review of Principles and Practice for Food Distribution in Conflict', Humanitarian Policy Group, Overseas Development Institute & Nutrition Works, Public Nutrition Resource Group, 2000.
29. C. Orjuela, 'Building peace in Sri Lanka: A role for civil society?', *Journal Of Peace Research*, 40, 2 (2003) pp. 195–212.
30. J. Flint, 'Local Security Arrangements – Darfur', *Draft*, (2006).
31. Ibid., p. 18.
32. According to L. Nathan, the pressurized timeline of 'deadline diplomacy' and exclusion from Abuja of local groups 'creates the risk that the process will fail to meet popular expectations, generating resentment and conflict'. L. Nathan, 'No Ownership, No Peace: the Darfur Peace Agreement', Crisis States Research Centre, Working Paper No. 5 (London Crisis States Research Centre, London School of Economics, 2006).
33. Sisk (2001), op. cit., p. 10.

23
Negotiating Justice: The Challenge of Addressing Past Human Rights Violations

Priscilla Hayner[1]

Introduction

Addressing questions of justice for massive past human abuses is often cited as one of the most difficult challenges of any peace negotiations. Almost by definition, those persons sitting at the peace table would have had command responsibility for combatants responsible for any atrocities that may have taken place. Those negotiating terms of a peace deal may be at the greatest risk of facing justice if serious accountability measures are put in place.

Despite this apparent quandary, many peace agreements have included a variety of measures for accounting for past abuses. While these have not often included an explicit commitment to prosecutions and punishment for wrongdoers, many have left open that possibility, avoiding a blanket amnesty, while also committing to non-judicial measures such as a truth commission, reparations for victims, and screening the security forces for those implicated in past abuses. All of these policy options have received greater attention in recent years as the field of 'transitional justice' has rapidly developed and become part of the lexicon of international relations, and of peacemaking more generally.[2]

Transitional justice

Accountability for past human rights abuses might be incorporated into a peace agreement in a number of different ways. There are a range of mechanisms and policy options that may be considered, both judicial and non-judicial. While the question of amnesty versus prosecutions has attracted the most attention, certainly the justice challenges reach far beyond the question of whether perpetrators will be tried for their crimes. The tension that is often cited between the desires for peace and the demands for justice only captures only one element of the transitional justice challenge.

The field of transitional justice refers to a range of possible policies and approaches that may be engaged, following a civil war or authoritarian regime, to respond to a history of massive human rights abuses or war crimes. These include the following:

Non-judicial truth-seeking. Many peace agreements since the early 1990s have included an agreement to establish a truth commission – a temporary, non-judicial body that investigates the patterns of rights abuses over a period of time, finishing with a public report that includes recommendations for policy and institutional reforms. The over 30 truth commissions to date have differed considerably, as each must be crafted to fit the circumstances of each country.[3] Truth commissions that have emerged from peace agreements include those in El Salvador, Guatemala, Sierra Leone, and Liberia. The most well-known such body, the Truth and Reconciliation Commission (TRC) of South Africa, was unique in its amnesty-granting powers, but the attention it attracted helped to inspire many truth commissions that followed.

Reparations. Whether through financial, symbolic, or community measures, reparations or compensation for past abuses may be an important element of national and individual healing. Many peace accords include an agreement for a reparations programme, although implementation is often a challenge. The most broad-reaching reparations programme in recent years has been implemented in Peru, following recommendations by that truth commission.

International, hybrid, and national courts. The establishment of a hybrid or international court is not likely to be included as part of a peace agreement, but may arise out of a request from the national government to the United Nations (UN), for example. Meanwhile, the strengthening of national courts is usually critical for justice in the long term – and often necessary for a stable and lasting peace – and has received scant attention in peace agreements. The Special Court for Sierra Leone is an example of a hybrid court – with both national and international judges and prosecutors – that was proposed and created many months after the 1999 peace agreement was signed.

Vetting and reform of the armed forces. Accounting for past human rights crimes, with the aim of preventing such crimes from being repeated in the future, should affect the selection of post-war military, police, and other security forces. Members should be vetted so that anyone involved in human rights abuses is excluded, with appropriate due process procedures in place. In Liberia, for example, the peace agreement specifically makes provisions for vetting of the army based on each individual's record of past human rights violations.

There are now a number of organizations working to advance best practice in the area of transitional justice.[4] However, while it is not unusual for today's peace agreements to incorporate some of these elements, this has typically been done with limited knowledge of the policy options available or the international legal obligations that pertain. There are also important questions of the interrelationship between these various measures, and whether they can or should be usefully sequenced over time.

Constraints and obligations of international law

Legal experts describe a rapidly developing field of law that, at least under strict legal terms, limits the options for immunity that can be granted at the peace table.

There are many crimes that can rightly be amnestied without violating international human rights commitments. The crimes of treason, sedition, or illegally transporting arms, for example, are uncontroversial. Other crimes such as murder (in very limited circumstances), mayhem, or arson might also be legitimately amnestied, under the obligations of international law, presuming they do not rise to the level of being an 'international crime'. This is determined, in brief, by their severity, context, and circumstance. In contrast, genocide, serious war crimes, crimes against humanity, and gross violations of human rights are generally not acceptably amnestied under international law.[5]

The source of this law is in part treaty-based, which requires an analysis in each country-specific context of which treaties a country has ratified. However, most major human rights treaties have now been ratified by a good majority of nations. Second, these norms depend on customary international law, which reflects general acceptance and practice of states and applies to all nations irrespective of any treaty. Customary international law disfavours amnesties for serious violations of human rights and international humanitarian law.[6]

Those countries that may choose to incorporate a sweeping amnesty into a peace agreement, regardless of such international legal constraints, could find the amnesty challenged and overturned based on the international legal commitments that the country has undertaken. Such an amnesty also may not have any force outside of that country, leaving the beneficiaries of the amnesty at risk if they travel.

International bodies have also taken the position that non-judicial mechanisms such as truth commissions do not lessen the requirement for judicial action in response to serious crimes.

As international organizations such as the UN are holding increasingly closely to these international norms, the pressures on the negotiators, and on the parties to an agreement, will grow.

Negotiating justice

The experience of several recent peace negotiations highlights the difficulties faced in incorporating justice policies into peace agreements. The lack of strong justice components is sometimes due to the strength of the perpetrators at the negotiating table, and their insistence on impunity. But the dynamics are rarely so simple or straightforward. Opportunities are sometimes missed due to ignorance or misunderstanding of the justice mechanisms and policies that are available, a lack of time or effort to detail such provisions, a failure to be creative in considering limitations or conditionalities to any amnesties, and a basic lack of clarity about the international legal standards or obligations that pertain.

The following cases demonstrate some of these dynamics that shape peace talks and the varied approaches to justice and accountability that may result.

Liberia

Over a dozen peace agreements were signed between 1990 and 1996 to end civil conflict in Liberia. These agreements resulted in transitional governments, internationally monitored elections, and international peacekeeping forces. But they did not result in permanent peace. In most cases, the agreements were signed with no apparent intention on the part of the warring parties to abide by the accord, and fighting usually continued very shortly thereafter.[7] Only one of these agreements promised an amnesty, although this was understood not to apply to serious crimes.[8]

After rebel leader Charles Taylor was elected president in 1997, fighting subsided. But Taylor's repressive governance sparked new rebel movements, putting the country back in war from 1999. A peace conference was finally called in 2003 in Accra, Ghana, under the auspices of the Economic Community of West African States (ECOWAS), and brought together the Government of Liberia and both rebel factions.

President Charles Taylor flew to Accra to attend the opening ceremony. Taylor had long been accused of serious rights abuses, but he and others were caught by surprise when the Special Court for Sierra Leone unsealed an indictment against him just before the opening ceremony of the peace talks. Rather than arresting him, the Ghanaian authorities provided their presidential plane for Taylor's free passage back to Monrovia. It was another two months before Taylor departed from Liberia for exile in Nigeria, where he remained until he was arrested and transferred to the court in 2006.

The effect of the indictment was to greatly strengthen the peace talks, as the indictment made it clear that Taylor would play no part in a future government in Liberia. Many people involved in the talks credit the indictment for making a peace deal possible. Without it, it was fully expected that Taylor would insist on continuing in power or taking part in any new elections.

The talks lasted 76 days in Ghana. The discussion about whether an amnesty would be granted for the warring factions, and whether to have a truth commission, lasted less than four days. The final wording in the peace accord indicates that the transitional government 'shall give consideration to a recommendation for general amnesty'.[9] Despite this open language, many came away from the talks believing that an amnesty had been awarded to the warring parties, perhaps based on informal discussions and a general spirit between the parties that made clear that 'witch-hunting' was in no one's interest. Some believed that an amnesty would be granted conditionally, based on participation in the TRC, following the South African model.

It is possible that the warring factions felt no need for an amnesty, since the national courts barely function and they apparently have little fear of prosecution. In the three years after the accord was signed, many persons well-known for specific and horrific atrocities continued to live freely in Monrovia, and no legal action has been taken against any of them. Furthermore, the former rebel leaders may have some mixed feelings on a blanket amnesty. While the rebels were involved in serious abuses themselves, some of their leadership today continue to insist that those involved in the most notorious atrocities should be held to account. But overall, relatively little attention was given to these issues at the peace talks.

The agreement calls for a truth commission, but provides only general guidance on its structure, membership, and form, leaving a more detailed discussion for intensive consultation and drafting that took place over the following eighteen months. The final language, as stipulated in the TRC Act of 2005, grants the TRC the power to recommend amnesty for individuals, but explicitly prohibits amnesty for serious crimes. The Comprehensive Peace Accord also explicitly calls for vetting of the new army and police on human rights grounds.

There is no mention of reparations in the agreement. Those delegates that gave consideration to the idea quickly decided that it was unrealistic, given that virtually every Liberian was directly affected by the war. A Law Reform Commission was also proposed but rejected.

The majority of the time was taken up with debates about power sharing. More precisely, the crux of the negotiations was whether the factions would occupy key positions in a transitional government, how long this transitional government would last, and who would occupy what positions. Many have noted that the rebel factions ended up with those ministries where grand corruption could result in the greatest wealth. An ECOWAS audit in 2005 documented widespread corruption and stealing at all levels of the transitional government.

Sierra Leone

After nine years of war, the final peace talks for Sierra Leone opened only four months after Freetown, the capital of Sierra Leone, was attacked and virtually destroyed by rebel forces, leaving several thousand killed and many more mutilated or raped. The government barely had a functioning army, the majority of its soldiers having joined with the rebels two years earlier, and the international forces fighting on its behalf were expected to be withdrawn very shortly.[10] In short, the government was negotiating from a position of considerable weakness.

The rebels, now fighting in tandem with dissident soldiers, had made clear their destructive powers and intentions, and it was clear to all that considerable violence would follow if the peace talks were to fail. The atrocities by the Sierra Leone rebels, the Revolutionary United Front (RUF), have been widely documented, most notably the practice of cutting off limbs of civilians as a form of terror, leaving behind many 'amputees'; high incidents of rape by rebel soldiers; and the forced conscription of children into the rebel army.

The rebels also had an incentive to negotiate a peace agreement. A number of people associated with the armed opposition sat on death row in Freetown's main prison.[11] The RUF leader, Foday Sankoh, had himself recently been convicted and sentenced to death; his case was on appeal when the peace talks began, and the government agreed to release him provisionally so that he could travel to the talks in Togo.[12] The threat of execution was very real: 24 persons had been hanged only months earlier, after a military court-martial and without the right of appeal.[13]

Some members of the international community were outraged when the final peace accord, signed in July 1999, granted a full and unconditional amnesty to all parties to the conflict. The Sierra Leone public also reacted very angrily, but their anger was focused on the power-sharing elements of the accord: the accord granted four ministerial posts to the RUF, and awarded Foday Sankoh the status of vice president, as well as chairman of a new commission on mineral resources.

Most participants in the 1999 talks insist that a peace deal would not have been possible without an amnesty; even most rights advocates who were then lobbying against a blanket amnesty agree that this is true.[14] Agreement on the amnesty clause was reached fairly quickly, discussed and agreed within a sub-committee handling political issues. Indeed, many of the official delegates who attended the talks, including key international representatives, arrived at the talks assuming that a broad amnesty had been tacitly agreed. This was in part because the delegates relied on a prior peace agreement, a 1996 peace agreement signed in Abidjan, as the basis for the 1999 talks. A similar amnesty was included in this 1996 accord, although this received little attention from the international community at the time.[15]

The difference in the international reaction to the 1999 amnesty agreement, as compared to a similar agreement in 1996, reflects the rapid development in the international attention given to the issue of impunity for serious human rights crimes. With the advancement of the human rights field as a whole, and with a number of critical judicial decisions by international courts, a crystallization of the international legal standards and obligations has taken form. Only weeks before the signing of the Lome peace accord for Sierra Leone in 1999, the UN released new guidelines for its representatives which explicitly disallowed their signing on to any immunity agreements for genocide, crimes against humanity, or war crimes.[16] These guidelines did not receive proper attention from the senior UN representative at the talks until a day or two prior to the scheduled signing. To keep within the bounds of UN policy, the UN representative added a written disclaimer next to his signature during the signing ceremony, stating that the UN understood the amnesty not to apply to international crimes. Foday Sankoh was unhappy with this addition, according to participants, and was unsure what the implication of such a unilateral addendum might be, but he made no formal protest and allowed the signing ceremony to continue. It was partly on the basis on this disclaimer that the Special Court for Sierra Leone was later created through an agreement between the UN and the Government of Sierra Leone.

Other components on transitional justice were incorporated into the 1999 Lome agreement. A TRC was agreed to, partly at the suggestion and persuasion of civil society representatives. There was a stipulation for a war victim's fund, although little detail was discussed as to how this would be funded or implemented.[17]

The agreement called for the demobilization of the rebel forces and the incorporation of some of them into the army, but there is no indication that individuals' past human rights records should be taken into account. This issue of vetting was not seriously contemplated at the talks, as those handling the security aspects of the agreement considered this to be a violation of the amnesty aspect of the accord.[18]

Ten months later, Foday Sankoh was arrested after his security guards shot into a crowd of demonstrators, killing a number of people, and evidence showed an intention of further fighting. Several hundred other RUF members were also arrested, many kept in prison without charge for close to six years. It was with Sankoh's arrest, under a new RUF leadership, that the peace implementation process began to take hold.

Amnesty, prosecutions, and peace

Some have suggested that a peace agreement built around an amnesty for serious crimes is unlikely to hold, and will instead always lead to further violence – the idea perhaps being that the amnesty encourages the perpetrators to believe they can easily get away with further crimes. This precise proposition does not appear to hold up, as such. For example, in Sierra Leone, it is not the amnesty that is blamed for the breach of the peace in 2000; rather, Sierra Leoneans cite the slow deployment and insufficiently robust mandate of international peacekeeping forces, the composition of those forces, a delayed disarmament process, and a questionable commitment on the part of the rebel forces to implementing the peace agreement.[19] In fact, the amnesty was reaffirmed later in 2000 when the Lome accord was re-engaged, and it is still considered to be in full force on the national level.[20]

However, there does appear to be a link between prosecutions and stable peace in some contexts. Where specific individuals have played a critical and continuous role in fomenting conflict, the indictment, arrest, and prosecution of those individuals has been a critical factor in solidifying the peace. But these individuals usually play a central role in any negotiations – since peace cannot be reached without their agreement – so it would be unusual for the peace agreement itself to include any provision for their arrest.

Despite these practical constraints, there are several recent examples that demonstrate this link. As described above, the arrest of Foday Sankoh in Sierra Leone in May 2000 changed the dynamics and made a real peace process possible under new RUF leadership. In Liberia, the indictment of Charles Taylor changed the dynamics of the peace negotiations, making a more durable agreement possible after many earlier failures; Taylor's arrest two years later further calmed things down, removing lingering concerns that he might yet again foment instability in the region. And in northern Uganda, while the situation is still developing as of this writing, it is generally believed that the indictment of the leadership of the rebel Lord's Resistance Army helped push the rebel group to take part in the most serious peace talks yet after 20 years of war.

The challenges presented by the peace talks for northern Uganda have perhaps brought the greatest international attention to the dilemmas that may arise with overlapping initiatives towards justice and peacemaking. As efforts towards peace negotiations were apparently stalling in late 2005, the International Criminal Court (ICC) unsealed arrest warrants for five senior members of the Lord's Resistance Army. This has raised questions and concerns about how and whether the rebel leaders might ultimately agree to a peace deal. There are however, several possibilities that might resolve this legal quandary pertaining to the ICC warrants.[21] The development of this situation – and the relationship more generally between the ICC and ongoing peace negotiations elsewhere around the world – should command our attention for some time to come.[22]

Conclusion

The question of how and whether elements of justice are incorporated into a peace agreement, in these and other cases, has been dependent on a number of factors: the inclination of the lead negotiator, the involvement of independent civil society groups, and the relative power of warring factions sitting at the peace table, for example. Many aspects of justice have been uncontroversially incorporated into peace accords in numerous contexts. However, criminal justice for senior perpetrators may be more likely outside of the context of the peace negotiations, as opportunities develop over time.

As the field of transitional justice matures, considerable wisdom and expertise is being developed that may be of use to those grappling with the challenge of addressing accountability while negotiating peace. The common presumption that there will always be an unresolvable tension between these two interests is proving to, not always, be true. Working for both peace and justice requires a broader and more holistic view of how both of these aims are achieved, and the important connection between them. It requires a long-term view that preserves the possibility of criminal justice in the future, and an emphasis on building a lasting foundation for the full respect for the rule of law in contexts where this has often been lacking. It also requires a fair appreciation for the complexities of peacemaking that avoids short-term, maximalist demands that may simply be impossible to achieve in some contexts. A holistic approach to these interlinked interests of justice and peace may open up possibilities that ultimately strengthen the likelihood of achieving both ends.

Notes

1. This chapter is based on extensive primary research done by the author in 2006, with research support provided by the US Institute of Peace. Please see future publications by the author for more in-depth descriptions of additional cases. The Liberia and Sierra Leone sections are based on extensive in-country interviews of participants in the peace talks, undertaken in July, August, and September 2006.
2. 'Transitional justice' was first used as a term of art to describe this field in the early 1990s, but the term was not more widely used until 2001 or later. Despite the name, the approaches and lessons offered by this field are equally applicable to non-transitional contexts, such as the United States, Canada, and Spain. For further information, please see www.ictj.org.
3. See P. Hayner, *Unspeakable Truths: Confronting the Challenge of Truth Commissions* (New York and London: Routledge, 2001).
4. For example, the International Center for Transitional Justice, with headquarters in New York and offices in a number of other countries, provides technical assistance to governments, intergovernmental organizations, and NGOs. Available at www.ictj.org (Accessed on 4 April 2007).
5. Naomi Roht-Arriaza, an expert on international human rights law, describes the possibilities for an acceptable amnesty as follows:

   What, then, would be permissible under the current state of the law? While the answers are quite murky, as a first cut, crimes solely against national law might be amnestied. This might include murder, mayhem, arson and the like if not committed (1) by state-related forces or (2) during conflict or (3) widespread or systematic enough to be considered a crime against humanity. Second, perhaps, individual war crimes that were neither grave breaches nor, in the case of civil conflict, violations of Article 3 of the 1949 Conventions might be amnestiable so long as they did not at the same time constitute crimes against humanity. Finally, it might be possible to argue in cases where an alternative accountability mechanism involving the rights of victims to obtain information and the imposition of some sanction exists, that the requirements of general human rights treaties are met, but only if the crimes involved did not involve the treaty obligations of the state with respect to war crimes, genocide, torture, or disappearance.

See N. Roht-Arriaza, *Transitional Justice and Peace Agreements*, 2005 conference paper made available by the International Council on Human Rights Policy at ichrp.org. See also C. Bell, *Negotiating Justice? Human Rights and Peace Agreements* (International Council on Human Rights Policy, 2006), pp. 83–94.

6. The Special Court for Sierra Leone found in 1994 that an amnesty for serious international crimes is 'contrary to the direction in which customary international law is developing.' See Prosecutor *v.* Morris Kallon, Brima Bazzy Kamara, SCSL-04-15-PT-060-II, Decision on Challenge to Jurisdiction: Lome Accord Amnesty, 13 March 2004, para. 84. For an authoritative description of the current state of the law on amnesties and other aspects of accountability, including the legal principles accepted by the United Nations, see Diane Orentlicher, *Independent study on best practices, including recommendations, to assist States in strengthening their domestic capacity to combat all aspects of impunity*, UN Document. E/CN.4/2004/88; and *Updated Set of principles for the protection and promotion of human rights through action to combat impunity*, UN Doc. E/CN.4/2005/102/Add.1.

7. For a detailed description of 14 peace agreements between 1990 and 1996, and a useful analysis of why most of these failed, see A. Adebajo, 'Liberia: A Warlord's Peace', in S.J. Stedman, D. Rothchild, & E.M. Cousens (eds), *Ending Civil Wars: The Implementation of Peace Agreements* (Boulder CO & London: Lynne Rienner, 2002) pp. 599–630. For further background on the Liberian conflict, see P. Dennis, 'A Brief History of Liberia', International Center for Transitional Justice, May 2006 (Available at www.ictj.org); S. Ellis, *The Mask of Anarchy: The Destruction of Liberia and the Religious Dimension of an African Civil War* (New York: New York University Press, 1999); and report on the Liberia peace negotiations by P. Hayner, 2007 from the Humanitarian Dialogue Centre, Geneva (Available at www.hdcentre.org) (Accessed on 4 April 2007).

8. The Cotonou Agreement, 25 July 1993. Interviews by author of participants in the Cotonou talks, July 2006, Monrovia.

9. *Peace Agreement between the Government of Liberia (GOL), the Liberians United for Reconciliation and Democracy (LURD), the Movement for Democracy in Liberia (MODEL) and the Political Parties*, signed in Accra, Ghana, 18 August 2003, Article XXXIV.

10. Nigeria provided the bulk of the international forces. After years of losses in Nigerian lives and expense, all the leading candidates for the imminent elections in Nigeria were promising to withdraw its forces from Sierra Leone. For further background on the Sierra Leone conflict and its peace processes, see L. Gberie, *A Dirty War in West Africa: The RUF and the Destruction of Sierra Leone* (Bloomington IN: Indiana University Press, 2005); D. Lord (ed.), *Paying the Price: The Sierra Leone Peace Process* (Conciliation Resources, September 2000) Available at www.c-r.org; J.L. Hirsch, *Sierra Leone: Diamonds and the Struggle for Democracy* (Boulder & London: Lynne Rienner, 2001); and report on the Sierra Leone peace negotiations by P. Hayner, forthcoming from the Humanitarian Dialogue Centre (Available at www.hdcentre.org) (Accessed on 4 April 2007).

11. Those on death row were primarily persons involved in the government of the Armed Forces Revolutionary Council, which took power in a 1997 coup (and then invited the rebel RUF to join the government).
12. Sankoh was arrested on charges of illegal possession of arms while travelling in Nigeria in 1997. He was transferred to Sierra Leone to be tried for treason in 1998.
13. Again, those executed were all former military officers, some of these claiming they had no choice but to continue service under the coup government of the AFRC.
14. Some observers however suggest that some sort of limitation or condition may have been possible to amend to the agreement, such as conditioning the amnesty on future behaviour that complied with the peace deal, or making the amnesty conditional on truth-telling. Interviews by author, August 2006, Freetown.
15. See J.L. Hirsch (2001), op. cit., p. 52, where he describes the amnesty granted in 1996 as the 'least controversial' of all issues discussed during those negotiations.
16. These guidelines are not public, but the basic principles have been reiterated in public documents. See, for example, *Report of the Secretary-General on the rule of law and transitional justice in conflict and post-conflict societies,* UN Document. S/2004/616, para. 10.
17. The TRC made explicit recommendations on the war victim's fund. And in 2006, human rights groups were pushing the government to establish a fund for war amputees. A broader fund or program for victims remains outstanding.
18. Interviews by author, August 2006, Freetown.
19. Interviews by author, August 2006, Freetown.
20. 'Ceasefire Agreement between Government and RUF' (10 November 2000) signed in Abuja, Nigeria.
21. For further information, see International Crisis Group, 'Peace in Northern Uganda?' Africa Briefing 41 (13 September 2006) Available at www.crisisgroup.org
22. For further information on the role of the ICC in contexts of peacemaking, see P. Seils & M. Wierda, 'The International Criminal Court and Conflict Mediation', International Center for Transitional Justice Occasional Paper, June 2005, Available at www.ictj.org (Accessed on 4 April 2007).

24
Borrowing and Lending in Peace Processes

John Darby

In 1998, Herri Batasuna, the political party closest to the Euskadi ta Askatasuna/ Basque Homeland and Freedom's (ETA) aims, invited all the main Basque political parties and other movements to participate in an 'Ireland Forum' in order to explore the relevance of the Northern Ireland process to the Basque Country. The development was inspired by the 'pan-nationalist' front in Northern Ireland which brought together the main interests favouring a broad nationalist position – Sinn Féin, the Social Democratic and Labour Party (SDLP), the government of the Irish Republic, and Irish-American interests. The 'Ireland Forum' led directly to the Lizarra Agreement. Four days later ETA declared a ceasefire. Mees argues that the Basque peace process was almost unimaginable 'without the domino effect of the Northern Irish model'.[1] Herri Batasuna's leader Arnaldo Otegi confessed that 'Ireland was a mirror for us, and so was the republican movement'.[2]

The open adoption of the Northern Ireland model by the Basques was not exceptional, except in degree. There has been a high level of deliberate 'borrowing' between contemporary peace processes, inspired and stimulated by the proliferation and perceived success of other processes during the 1990s. 'If the Arabs and the Israelis can do it,' the Irish Taoiseach Albert Reynolds wrote to John Major the UK Prime Minister in 1993, 'why can't we?'[3] Eight years later Senator George Mitchell, chairman of the Northern Ireland talks and leader of a fact-finding commission on the Israeli-Palestinian violence, reversed the advice: 'I regularly say to the political leaders in the Middle East ... if they can do it in Northern Ireland, you can do it in the Middle East.'[4] Some negotiators, notably the South Africans, were more proactive and became evangelists for peace. Nelson Mandela as an individual became a significant incentive for budding negotiations, particularly in Africa. The use of 'famous people' to lend support and advice in crisis areas was institutionalized by the Carter Center at Emory University. Visits between those engaged in peace negotiations in different countries became commonplace. A shared language evolved, referring to 'hurting stalemates', 'respect for cultural diversity', 'confidence-building measures', 'a conflict-resolution situation', even the term 'peace process' itself.

By the late 1990s, the interdependence between peacemaking initiatives in different parts of the world was widely visible and acknowledged. In the midst of the mounting crisis in December 2000, the Israeli Prime Minister Ehud Barak had time to reflect that 'if we don't make an agreement and drift, God forbid, into a situation of deterioration, there will be cracks in other peace deals'.[5]

Why so much borrowing?

The search for models in peace negotiations is scarcely new. International diplomacy has drawn from a common pool of approaches stretching back beyond the 1648 treaty of Westphalia. The incentives are evident in recent and contemporary peace processes. Negotiators can benefit from contact with sympathisers from more developed peace processes and learn from their experiences. The lessons learnt can significantly reduce both economic and political start-up costs and accelerate the process. International organizations involved in encouraging peace processes increasingly find parallels with their own experiences in humanitarian and development intervention; indeed, by the late 1990s, many governments and international organizations had deliberately cultivated a holistic relationship between their interests in conflict and development, and developed a corpus of common expertise. Some governments, including South Africa, became evangelical in supporting other peace processes and pointing to lessons between them. The experience of the Norwegian Foreign Ministry in Latin America, for example, encouraged and instructed its facilitation of the Oslo Process in the Middle East and its intervention in Sri Lanka.

Another trigger for the recent surge in borrowing was a change in how contemporary peace processes are negotiated. Before the early 1990s, many peace processes either depended on friendly external support[6] or followed on the heels of military intervention by the United Nations (UN). Since the ending of the Cold War, not only has the number of negotiated accords risen steadily but the proportion of them negotiated by the parties primarily engaged in the conflict also has increased. The absence of an external custodian shifted the driving force from military sanctions to evolving joint procedures for talks. Consider the 38 formal peace agreements signed between 1988 and 1998. In the first five years, from 1988 to 1992, six of the ten peace agreements (60 per cent) were brokered with the direct involvement of the UN. But the UN was involved in only 10 of the 28 agreements signed between 1993 and late 1998 (35.7 per cent).[7] Since 1998, however, the involvement of the UN and regional organizations in peace processes has revived, especially in Africa. The emergence of hybrid peace processes, involving closer cooperation between local and international initiatives, seems likely to remain the dominant pattern for some time.

The cascade

The increasingly internal nature of peace processes since the 1990s has increased the search for new approaches and guidelines. Historical models, especially those preceding the end of the Cold War, were often dismissed as irrelevant. Instead guidance and support were sought from contemporary processes. As a consequence, a cascade of borrowing developed during the 1990s. The fountainhead was South Africa, where a raft of innovative approaches to negotiations was developed: 'the channel'; sufficient consensus; bush summits; transitional institutions;[8] the imaginative use of symbols to encourage national unity; most of all, the fact that the process was accomplished through negotiation and compromise rather than force. These seemed to offer a new way forward to others, including Israel–Palestine and Northern Ireland, and a secondary set of models emerged.

The cascade effect might be best illustrated by following a specific flow path, from South Africa to Northern Ireland and thence to the Basque Country. The connection between South Africa and Northern Ireland pre-dated the Irish peace process, to links between Sinn Féin and the ANC during the years of violence, links strongly emphasized in republican rhetoric and iconography.[9] The ANC leaders made a number of visits to Northern Ireland at strategic stages during the peace process, most notably in the week following the Good Friday Agreement when they met republican prisoners and advised a Sinn Féin gathering that 'the Belfast Agreement was a major step forward'.[10] The 'ideological sympathy'[11] between the two revolutionary organizations was a key factor in persuading recalcitrant members of Sinn Féin to back the Agreement. The influence of South Africa on Northern Ireland was not confined to militant parties. A number of cross-party groupings from Northern Ireland visited South Africa.[12] A conference in 1992 brought together leading political players in Northern Ireland and South Africa across a wide range of parties, and follow-up meetings were held in Boston (1995), Belfast (1997), and South Africa (1997).[13] The South African connection continued during the post-Accord implementation stage. The South African human rights lawyer Brian Curran helped to oversee the early release of paramilitary prisoners and in 2000 was appointed as independent mediator in the dispute over Orange marches at Drumcree. Cyril Ramaphosa of the ANC acted as an independent inspector of the Irish Republican Army (IRA) arms dumps in order to overcome the decommissioning impasse. In addition to this comradely support, Northern Ireland adopted a number of negotiation approaches pioneered during the South African process, notably the use of 'sufficient consensus' to ensure that the process continued if relatively minor groups disagreed with the majority view.

The Good Friday Agreement in April 1998 promoted Northern Ireland as another model of a successful peace process. The Agreement was greeted with almost universal enthusiasm internationally. A survey of 30 reports from 20 countries was unanimously supportive, although some urged caution. A few pundits dwelt on perceived similarities and differences between Northern Ireland and their own regions. The Calcutta *Ananda Bazar Patrika* called for 'the same policy of peaceful dialogue' to be adopted in Kashmir. Israel's *Maariv*, under the headline 'The Irish Model' contrasted Irish peace with a peace that 'is increasingly becoming more remote in this region'.[14] The enthusiasm was nowhere greater than in the Basque Country. Interest there was partly rooted in ideological empathy. Contacts between the IRA and ETA stretched back into the Troubles, and Sinn Féin had developed a close association with Herri Batasuna. A number of republican strategies were borrowed, most notably the use of strategic ceasefires and the determination to forge a broad alliance of constitutional nationalists. The 'pan-nationalist front' combining Sinn Féin, the SDLP, the Irish government, and Irish America inspired the 'third space', which performed a similar function for Basque constitutional and revolutionary nationalists. Any shift within a militant revolutionary movement towards a broader accommodation including constitutional nationalists is a strong indicator of ripeness for negotiations. Indeed, the broad nationalist front in Northern Ireland influenced not only ETA but also the Corsican independence group the Front de Libération Nationale de la Corse (FLNC), who carried it a step further into dialogue with 'non- and even anti-nationalist groups such as elements within the French centre-right or sections of the socialist party'.[15]

The flow from South Africa through Northern Ireland to the Basque Country and beyond is, of course, merely illustrative of the cascade. Other examples can be cited. The South Africans 'studied with great deliberation the Latin American examples before setting up its own Truth and Reconciliation Commission'.[16] The South African Truth and Reconciliation Commission (TRC) in turn was followed with great attention in Latin America, especially for its innovative public hearings, and for its power to grant amnesty to individuals. So far, despite considerable interest, and envy at the resources applied to the problem in South Africa, there has been little evidence that the South African model has been taken on board.[17]

What is borrowed?

Borrowing has taken a variety of forms since the early 1990s. Before considering these in more detail, it is important to emphasize that they operated within an international context conducive to peace processes. The great increase in the number of peace accords since the end of the Cold War in itself created an ambience which encouraged protagonists to imitate their example. During the early 1990s, it sometimes appeared that delegations from the former Soviet Union and Yugoslavia were randomly scouring the world for models for democratic transformation. As time passed, the traffic became more specific and strategic, and began to fall into recognizable categories.

Constitutional models

In detailing 12 reasons for South Africa's success, Roelf Meyer, the National Party negotiator, began by highlighting two: first, that they 'made a fresh start in 1990 – a clean slate'; and second, that they dared to do it by themselves, without any 'formal external intervention'. The ANC present a similar view. 'We designed an individual process,' claimed Pravin Gordhan. 'There is no model that I am aware of.'

Despite the indisputably innovative features of the South African agreement, few major decisions were taken without at least reviewing comparative alternatives. Gordhan continued:

> But at the same time we were very aware in designing our constitution that there were many models available to us in many parts of the world – Canada, United States, Nigeria, India, Australia etc. We looked at all of them and chose what we thought was appropriate to our own situation.[18]

Germany became the main constitutional model, especially for the upper house. The distinctiveness of the South African approach was its refusal to adopt constitutional and institutional structures *en bloc*, but its willingness to adopt specific elements from other constitutions and then to adapt them to local needs.

This sensitivity did not go unnoticed. Other constitution builders, notably the Fiji Constitution Reform Commission, launched a systematic search for constitutional models appropriate to Fiji's tense and stratified conflict between native Fijians and Indians, including solicited papers and hearings in London and Suva.[19] The resulting constitution was a modified consociational democracy, which soon came under challenge during an attempted coup.

This selective approach to constitutional change was also a feature of the Northern Ireland accord. The joint role of the British and Irish governments as guardians of the process, with prime responsibility for agenda and deadline setting, drafting key papers and enforcing ground rules, was an innovative approach to reassure all negotiating parties that the proceedings would be even-handed.

Approaches to negotiations

Modern peace processes are more often multi-party than bilateral. This raises the problem that, if relatively small parties carry the same weight as major actors, they have a potential veto on progress. The South Africans came up with a device to forestall this eventuality.[20] The 'sufficient consensus' rule ensured that the process should continue, despite the dissent of smaller parties, if the two major parties agreed. 'Disagreement would be recorded; dissenters could remain in the process, await its outcome, and then decide whether to support it.'[21] The 'steamroller effect'[22] of this rule raised charges that the two largest parties had formed a conspiracy of bullies, but it emphasized the common commitment to a solution and the recognition that the maintenance of momentum was critical. The formula reached in South Africa has been widely adopted and adapted. It was interpreted in Northern Ireland as 'the requirement that substantive decisions should have the support of majorities of both Unionists and nationalists',[23] and was incorporated into the Agreement.

Borrowings from other negotiations were sometimes quite casual and serendipitous. In 1996, the introduction of proximity talks in Northern Ireland to deal with the Unionists' refusal to communicate directly with Sinn Féin was suggested by Irish Foreign Minister Dick Spring, who had apparently read about its use in the Dayton talks in a morning newspaper.[24]

Dealing with violence

As most peace processes follow periods of violence, they must deal with fears that ex-militants would seek to influence the negotiations by the use of tactical violence. In Northern Ireland, the Mitchell Principles were introduced in 1996 to address these fears. Before participants were admitted to multi-party negotiations they were required to agree to six principles, including their commitment:

- to democratic and exclusively peaceful means of resolving political issues;
- to the total disarmament of all paramilitaries;
- to agree that such disarmament must be verifiable by an independent commission; to renounce and oppose any effort to use force or the threat of force; to influence the course of the outcome of all-party negotiations;
- to abide by the letter of any agreement reached in all-party negotiations; and
- to resort to democratic and exclusively peaceful methods in trying to alter any aspect of that outcome with which they may disagree;
- to take effective steps to end 'punishment' killings and beatings.[25]

The insistence that all participants in multi-party talks sign up to the Mitchell Principles was a useful device for regulating political violence. The suspension of Sinn Féin and the departure of the Ulster Democratic Party for breaches of the principles, however temporarily, were necessary to sustain credibility in the Mitchell principles. Their acceptance of the suspension, however truculently, indicated their determination to remain within the peace process.[26]

A second threat posed by violence to the Northern Ireland peace process was the issue of decommissioning. 'No guns, no government' summarized unionist refusal to allow government to function until paramilitary weapons had been handed over. The IRA refusal to decommission led to the suspension of the power-sharing executive in February 2000. In the end the compromise which allowed the Ulster Unionists to return to government in May was an IRA declaration that they would 'initiate a process that will completely and verifiably put IRA guns beyond use'.[27] The key move was the IRA's agreement to permit inspection of its arms dumps by two independent inspectors, Martti Ahtisaari, the former Finnish President, and Cyril Ramaphosa, the former ANC leader. After their first inspection in June 2000, the inspectors reported that the armaments they had seen could not be used 'without our detection'.[28] The device they installed was described as a dual-key system, similar to a bank deposit box with two keys held by the IRA and the inspectors. The dual-key system was borrowed from El Salvador, where the UN had successfully applied it in the early 1990s.

> UN inspectors held one of two keys that had to be turned simultaneously to open arms caches belonging to the left-wing FMLN guerrilla movement...Tonnes of weapons and explosives belonging to the FMLN were locked in secure dumps as part of peace negotiations between the Marxist guerrillas and the pro-American government in San Salvador.[29]

In Northern Ireland this approach bypassed the decommissioning dispute and allowed the peace process to continue, although it did not resolve the issue. On 26 July 2005, however, an IRA statement appeared to bring decommissioning closer to resolution. 'The leadership of Oglaigh na hEireann (the IRA) has formally ordered an end to the armed campaign... All IRA units have been ordered to dump arms.'[30] Three months later the Independent International Commission on Decommissioning (IICD) confirmed that the IRA had completed the decommissioning of all of its arms. In 2007 Northern Ireland's two main political parties, the Democratic Unionist Party and Sinn Féin, agreed to lead a power-sharing executive.

Institutional modelling

New forms of peace processes require new institutions, so it is not surprising that the peace negotiations of the late 1990s should borrow heavily from each other. The 38 comprehensive peace accords between 1988 and 1998 shared many similarities, partly because of bilateral and multilateral influences, but also because they evolved within the same international context. Three themes will be outlined here: approaches to human rights, truth commissions, and policing reform.

International law played an important part in shaping peace agreements and in turn was influenced by them. The shaping was sometimes positive, as in setting minimum standards for compliance in Northern Ireland and South Africa, and sometimes negative, such as the failure to set or enforce such standards in Israel–Palestine and Bosnia–Herzegovina. In any case, international law imposes at least 'a superficial similarity' on peace agreements, including reform of policing and the judicial system, human rights commissions, and compliance with international standards of human rights.[31] The traffic was two way. Peace agreements became an arena for the debate on self-determination. The fact that so many peace accords are 'neither entirely domestic nor entirely international documents' challenged traditional views of statehood. Christine Bell also suggests that international law has other lessons to learn from peace agreements in other fields, including ethnic balance, dealing with the past, and the role of civic society.

The interrelationship between past and future practice is increasingly worked out through truth commissions. It is sometimes forgotten that truth commissions operated in Latin America before the South African model was established. Argentina, aware of the limitations of the case-by-case approach to past crimes, introduced a truth commission to address the broader political and moral responsibility. This was later adopted by Chile, El Salvador, South Africa, and many other countries. Although the approaches varied, the key innovation was that 'truth commissions are meant to function as moral panels, not legal courts'.[32] The South African TRC radically extended the model and by the late 1990s it was rare for a peace accord not to include the intention to establish some approach to addressing past grievances.

Policing reform and training are examples of practical borrowing. The need to reform the police to reflect a new dispensation, and the difficulty in implementing it, is a common feature of peace processes, including those in the Basque Country, South Africa, and Northern Ireland. Since 1993, the Royal Ulster Constabulary (RUC) sought lessons on community policing from various forces in the United States, including the New York Police Department (NYPD) and the Los Angeles Police Department (LAPD), and a close relationship had been established with the South African Police Services, including bilateral meetings. The Patten Commission on the future of policing in Northern Ireland, one of whose members was a South African, drew on examples from South Africa, the United States, Canada, Spain, and Holland. In Latin America, the exemplars were different, but the approach not dissimilar. The UN was involved in guiding through radical reforms of the police in Guatemala and El Salvador, and so was Spain. The Spanish Civil Guard was involved, both as an implied model, but more directly in implementing the transition to a civilian force. They helped to establish training academies in both places: in El Salvador they helped to frame the curriculum and provided instructors, and in Guatemala 'the Spanish Civil Guard contingent was put in charge of overall restructuring, particularly in the operations of the new training academy'.[33]

Negative borrowings

It has been argued that some cases are unsuitable wells from which to draw lessons for other countries. Arend Lijphart has suggested that Northern Ireland, Cyprus, and the Lebanon are all unsuitable models because of their 'complex international dimensions',[34] although this did not prevent him from drawing extensively from Northern Ireland's experience. Approaches from one peace process to another have sometimes been adopted with insufficient consideration of local concerns; Ben Reilly points out that the almost universal rush to hold early elections may merely count heads rather than reflect a deeply entrenched democracy. In another sense too borrowings may have negative as well as positive effects. Those opposed to agreement are as willing to learn by example as those in agreement. Northern Ireland had particular interest for Basque nationalists and there are parallels between the breakdown of the Basque ceasefires in 2000 and the IRA breakdown in 1996. In each case the militants became increasingly frustrated by the failure of the respective governments to advance towards inclusive negotiations after the declaration of a ceasefire. The renewal of tactical violence by the IRA ultimately led to their re-entry into a more accelerated process, and it is unlikely that the lessons escaped the attention of ETA.

The problems caused by decommissioning in Northern Ireland provide another example of the negative potential of borrowings. Although insistence that the IRA hand over its weapons did not feature as a major disagreement in the early negotiations, it became more a line in the sand for Unionists than for republicans, who wanted the issue to disappear. In the three years following the 1998 accord it was the most serious obstacle to progress. Why did it assume such negative force? International experience presents no clear answer. Decommissioning was rarely a major issue during the many peace processes in Latin America since the 1980s, although a number of Colombian guerrilla groups laid down their weapons in exchange for amnesties and other benefits.[35] In Israel, even after the transfer of power to the Palestinian Authority, Yasser Arafat was unable to persuade the leaders in Palestinian refugee camps to hand over their weapons.[36] The 1991 South African National Peace Accord did not ask the African National Congress (ANC) to hand over their arms caches, but required that firearms should not be displayed at public meetings. The retention of weapons by militants was accepted as an unfortunate reality in many other agreements, including the Anglo-Irish war in 1921. In other settlements, however, weapons were decommissioned. As Mac Ginty has pointed out, 'over 850,000 ex-combatants have been disarmed in eight sub-Saharan states: Ethiopia, Angola, Eritrea, Liberia, Mali, Mozambique,

Namibia and Uganda'.[37] Rebel groups in Niger laid down their weapons after the 1996 accord. Even the Kosovo Liberation Army (KLA) handed over its weapons to the North Atlantic Treaty Organization (NATO) peacekeepers within the 90 days deadline agreed under a post-war accord signed in June 1999, although some of the weapons were merely transferred to the Kosovo Corps, a defence force newly created from the KLA. 'We are not going to take off our uniforms and our weapons off,' said one of their commanders. 'We are only changing to new uniforms and a new badge.'[38]

Therefore, recent peace processes include plenty of examples where weapons were decommissioned, and plenty where they were not. Northern Ireland's legacy to other peace processes is that decommissioning is likely to be included in future peace processes.

Lessons learned and missed

The search for comparative models has become a boom industry in recent years for countries entering peace processes, sometimes without sufficient regard to local differences. Despite this caveat, four observations may be made.

À la carte, not table d'hote

Since the early 1990s, the tendency to seek complete constitutional templates for incipient peace processes has been replaced by a more nuanced search for guidelines that might instruct specific aspects of a peace process. This *à la carte* approach also carries its own dangers: it is sometimes too random, determined by casual and chance contacts; it may ignore important cultural differences. Despite these caveats, the more specific the borrowing between peace processes, the more likely it is to succeed. The adoption of proximity talks in Dayton and Belfast allowed talks to start despite deep distrust and distaste. The borrowing of approaches to policing reform, and of human rights clauses from other peace accords, have become commonplace, notably in Latin America. In each case, the merits of the central idea were adopted, but were then adapted to local circumstances.

More trade-offs

Peace processes are typically conducted by a number of parallel negotiating teams, each dealing with a relatively discrete facet of the dispute, such as political structures, demilitarization, and reforms of the police and army. The demands of negotiations probably make this inevitable, but it reduces the potential for trade-offs, even in cases where trade-offs seem natural: decommissioning in exchange for demilitarization; dealing with victims of violence in return for amnesties, or the release of militant prisoners. There have been cases when such reciprocation greatly eased progress, as in Guatemala when the Guatemalan National Revolutionary Unit (URNG) agreed to suspend its 'war taxes' in return to the government's agreement to demobilize its civil defence patrols. It is natural, and proper, that the increased borrowing between peace processes is usually the result of a search for appropriate models and structures. One of the most striking lessons from recent peace processes, however, is the need to encourage borrowing across the entire spectrum of negotiations.

Guidance for borrowing

In the early 1990s, many of those engaged in peacemaking were eager to seek guidance and inspiration from other peace processes, but their models were often selected in a haphazard or serendipitous manner. The creation of a number of new websites has provided much-needed guidance. The United States Institute of Peace (USIP) (www.usip.org/library/diglib.html) runs a digital library on peace agreements and truth commissions and has links to most of the texts of peace accords signed since 1989; Conciliation Resources (www.c-r. org/accord/index.shtml) produces a review of peace initiatives with histories and links to the texts of peace agreements. The ACCORD (www.accord.org. uk) provides useful information on conflicts and peace accords and often gives contextual background as well. The Uppsala Conflict Data Project (UCDP) (www.pcr.uu.se/database/index.php) also has links to material on peace agreements. In 2007 the Kroc Institute at the University of Notre Dame established a joint initiative between its own Peace Accords Matrix and the UCDP to launch the PRIME. Its aim is to provide user-friendly data for practitioners and scholars, with a particular focus on post-agreement implementation and reconstruction, a matter of growing concern. In October 2006, the UN established UN Peacemaker, 'a web-based operational support tool for international peacemaking professionals' (http://peacemaker.unlb.org/index1.php). All these websites reflect both the growing interest in the value of borrowing by both practitioners and scholars, and the need for more systematic approach to selecting appropriate models and approaches.

Lessons missed

Given the success of the South African process, it is perhaps surprising that some of its innovations were not more widely imitated. These include not only South Africa's constitutional court and transitional council but also innovations in negotiations such as the *bosberade* (bush summits), where disputants left the plenary negotiations to resolve bilateral or interparty disputes. Another useful South African device was *the channel*, a deadlock-breaking mechanism representing the main parties, which met daily in secret to review progress and encourage new initiatives. Nor were neglected innovations confined to South Africa. Despite the success of the joint British-Irish direction of the process,

Northern Ireland provides the only contemporary example of its use. Many of these mechanisms would benefit from a dusting-off and re-appraisal.

Notes

1. L. Mees, 'The Basque Peace Process, Nationalism and Political Violence', in J. Darby & R. Mac Ginty (eds), *The Management of Peace Processes* (London: Macmillan, 2000).
2. Ibid., p. 180.
3. A private letter quoted in E. Mallie & D. McKittrick, *The Fight for Peace: The Secret Story behind the Irish peace Process* (London: Heinemann, 1996), p. 187. A similar point was made by the Sinn Féin leader Gerry Adams in his *Selected Writings* (Dingle: Brandon, 1997).
4. D. de Bréadún, 'If they can do it in Northern Ireland you can do it in Middle East', *Irish Times* (24 May 2001).
5. *The Independent* (London: 26 December 2000).
6. For example, the Spanish government convened the first meeting between the Guatemalan government and the URNG (Unidad Revolucionaria Nacional Guatemalteca), and was the only non-regional member of the four-nation innovative Friends of the Secretary General, set up in 1990 to support negotiations in El Salvador.
7. J. Darby & J. Rae, 'Peace processes from 1988–1998: Changing patterns', *Ethnic Studies Report*, XVII, 1 (1999).
8. See P. du Toit, *South Africa's Brittle Peace: The Problem of Post-Settlement Violence* (London: Macmillan, 2001).
9. See A. Guelke, 'Comparatively Peaceful: South Africa, the Middle East and Northern Ireland', in M. Cox, A. Guelke, & F. Stephen (eds), *A Farewell to Arms? from 'Long War' to Long Peace in Northern Ireland* (Manchester: Manchester University Press, 2000).
10. 'ANC applauds participants in agreement', *Irish Times* (30 April 1998).
11. Guelke (2000), op. cit., p. 228.
12. For a representative of one of the loyalist parties the main benefit of visiting South Africa was not his introduction to new approaches to negotiations, but observing 'civilised cooperation' between members of the ANC and National Party (Author interview with UDP member, April 2000).
13. K. Cullen, 'Wise lessons from South Africa nurture peace in North', *Irish Times* (13 May 2000).
14. D. McCaffrey, 'Irish referenda', *USIA Media reaction Daily Digest* (28 May 1998).
15. F. Letamendia & J. Loughlin, 'Peace in the Basque Country and Corsica', in Cox, Guelke, & Stephen (2000), op. cit., p. 246.
16. J. Zalaquett, 'Truth, Justice and reconciliation: Lessons from the International Community', in C. Arnson (ed.), *Comparative Peace Processes in Latin America* (Washington DC: Woodrow Wilson Center, 1999), p. 349.
17. See P. Hayner, 'In Pursuit of Justice and Reconciliation', in Arnson (1999), Ibid, pp. 368–371.
18. P. Gordhan, *Political Leadership in Divided Societies: The Case of South Africa.* Paper presented at Parliament Buildings (Stormont: 10 April 2000).
19. See Sir P. Reeves, T.R. Vakatora, & B.V. Lal, *The Fiji Islands – Towards a United Future: Report of the Fiji Constitution Review Commission* (Fiji: Parliament of Fiji Paper No. 34, 1996). The commissioned papers were published in a separate volume, B.V. Lal & T.R. Vakatora (eds), *Fiji and the World* (Fiji: University of the South Pacific, 1997).

20. For a more detailed discussion of South Africa's innovative negotiating rules, see du Toit (2001), op. cit., especially. pp. 94–97.
21. D. Atkinson, 'Brokering a Miracle? The Multiparty Negotiating Forum', in Friedman and Atkinson (eds), *South African Review 7: The Small Miracle* (Johannesburg: Ravan Press, 1994), p. 22.
22. du Toit (2001), op. cit., p. 96.
23. Guelke (2000), op. cit., p. 230.
24. Mallie & McKittrick (1996), op. cit., p. 363.
25. 'The Mitchell Principles', in Report of the International Body on Decommissioning, *Irish Times* (18 February 1996).
26. K. Fearon pointed out that 'the degree of seriousness with which Sinn Féin treated the indictment indicated precisely how serious they were about the talks process and their desire to be part of it'. See K. Fearon, *Women's Work: The Story of the Northern Ireland Women's Coalition* (Belfast: Blackstaff Press, 1999) p. 100.
27. The IRA statement and the joint statement by the two governments in response are printed in the *Irish Times* (8 May 2000).
28. 'Unionists divided over arms dump visit', *The Times* (27 June 2000).
29. H. McDonald, 'Foolproof "dual-keys" used to seal IRA arsenals', *The Observer* (2 July 2000).
30. Statement from the IRA released through *An Phoblacht* (Republican News: 28 July 2005).
31. C. Bell, *Peace Agreements and Human Rights* (Oxford: Oxford University Press, 2000), p. 313.
32. J. Zalaquett, 'Truth, Justice and Reconciliation', in Arnson (1999), op. cit., p. 356.
33. G. Vickers, 'Renegotiating Internal Security: The Lessons of Central America', in Arnson (1999), op. cit., p. 407.
34. A. Lijphart, 'The framework document on Northern Ireland and the theory of power-sharing', *Government and Opposition*, 31, 3 (Summer 1996) pp. 267–274.
35. M. Chernick, 'Negotiating Peace amid Multiple Forms of Violence: The Protracted Search for Settlement to the Armed Conflicts in Colombia', in Arnson (1999), op. cit., pp. 177–179.
36. *New York Times* (29 September 1999).
37. R. Mac Ginty, 'Biting the Bullet: Decommissioning in the Transition from War to Peace in Northern Ireland', *Irish Studies in International Affairs*, 10 (1999) p. 238.
38. *New York Times* (20 September 1999).

Conclusion: Peace Processes, Present, and Future

John Darby and Roger Mac Ginty

Christine Bell reckons that more than 441 peace agreements have been signed since 1990 in 73 conflicts.[1] Most of these agreements relate to disputes operating within state boundaries and, although the vast majority of them addressed relatively minor segments of the disputes, together they reflect an astonishing number of peace processes. However, if the 1990s was the decade of the peace agreement, there is a growing concern that the 2000s may become the decade of agreements of disillusion. It is true that new peace accords, including innovative agreements in Sudan (2005) and Nepal (2006), were agreed, but the number of uncompleted, stalled, or collapsed agreements – in Sri Lanka, East Timor, Lebanon, the Basque Country, Kosovo, for example – is raising questions about the viability of approaches which were accepted as successful a decade ago.

Sequencing peace processes

The origins of any peace agreement – changes in the international climate, initiatives from civil society, secret meetings, chance encounters between significant actors – are often unrecognized at the time. It is even more difficult to determine when a peace process has succeeded, but it is clearly not the final signature on a peace accord. The function of an accord is to identify general principles and parameters of agreement. Their implementation may prolong the peace process cycle for many years, during which functioning institutions must be established and reforms carried through.

This chapter will follow the cycle of peace processes through four phases: (1) pre-negotiation; (2) the management of the process, including negotiations and violence; (3) peace accords; and (4) post-accord reconstruction and conflict transformation. It is not suggested that these phases are sequential. Peace processes are not strictly linear, and different societies sometimes tackle problems outside the normal sequence. If every peace process had to wait for a complete ending to violence, few would get off the ground. The history and politics of each country account for the distinctive sequencing of its process. Sometimes it is possible to tackle traditional 'post-settlement' tasks such as decommissioning and disarmament early in the process, and the momentum created by this may assist the move towards negotiations. The chapter will conclude by presenting 12 propositions about the nature and problems of contemporary peace processes.

Getting into talks: pre-negotiation

Conflicting parties rarely want to reach a settlement at the same time. During the war in Bosnia during 1993 and 1994, for example, the willingness of Muslims, Serbs, or Croats to engage in negotiation was determined primarily by their fortunes on the field of war and the resulting territorial gains or losses. By definition, these conditions never coincide for all parties. The result is a pendulum-like swing, with ethnic rivals proposing talks in turn, but rarely at the same time. Windows of opportunity, when all parties are simultaneously prepared to negotiate, are rare and of limited duration. Yet it is only during such relatively infrequent opportunities that a settlement may be reached.

The central metaphor in determining these opportunities is Zartman's concept of a 'ripe moment', when the parties' reach a mutually hurting stalemate (MHS) and 'find themselves locked in a conflict from which they cannot escalate to victory and this deadlock is painful to both of them'. The concept has been criticized by some as too passive, although Zartman insists that 'unripeness should not constitute an excuse for second or third parties' inaction'.

When compromise is in the air, other metaphors may be applied. Imagine the set of factors required to end ethnic violence – 'Track-two' approaches (non-governmental contact by such mediators as the business community, academics, or churches), secret talks, a ceasefire, agreement to negotiate, mediation, demilitarization, decommissioning – as a circle of dominoes standing like the stones at Stonehenge. The ending of violent conflict ultimately requires the movement of all the dominoes, but the process can be triggered initially by moving one of them forward, creating a momentum which nudges its neighbour along, and so on to the next one, and the next. The momentum depends on readiness to exploit temporary advantages. The effects of the 2004 tsunami, for example, stimulated peace moves in Aceh and Sri Lanka, but only led to agreement in the former case.

Most often the process requires a combination of more than one of these triggers to create momentum. Then the momentum itself, by providing the opportunity for opponents to work together, can become an agent in the process. The peace processes in South Africa, Northern Ireland, and Israel–Palestine all began with secret talks. These have certain advantages over traditional diplomacy as a preliminary to substantive talks: the formal barriers imposed by protocol are dropped; the temperature of the water and the temper of one's opponents may be tested with limited risk; 'what-if' scenarios can be floated without commitment. Secret talks can be a useful transition process for those who rose to leadership as security or insurgent leaders, and who often have little or no experience of the art of compromise. The exclusion of the media helped to keep the talks in Oslo and Northern Ireland secret. Secret talks are attractive to negotiators because, in du Toit's words, they have 'low exit costs'.[2]

Occasionally, the move from secret to open negotiations is managed by the protagonists themselves. Far more often, as Christopher Mitchell points out, a third party becomes involved. Intermediaries such as the business community, the churches, and academics were active in South Africa and Northern Ireland. Mediators, such as the Norwegian academics who were critical in starting the Oslo talks, often play a more effective role during the preliminaries of a peace process than later.

It is not uncommon for the constitutional and paramilitary opponents of the existing government to form a temporary alliance in advance of negotiation. As John Loughlin demonstrates, the 'pan-nationalist front' in Northern Ireland, the 'third space' in the Basque Country and similar developments in Corsica, forged temporary alliances between constitutional and revolutionary nationalists. Even the Tamil United Liberation Front (TULF) in Sri Lanka insisted that talks could not be confined to constitutional parties but must include the Tamil Tigers. When a militant revolutionary movement shifts towards a broader approach which includes constitutional nationalist parties, it is a strong indicator of ripeness for negotiations. These alliances help to compensate for the asymmetrical nature of negotiations, where the initial advantage leans towards the government side.

In the suspicious climate that accompanies the early stages of pre-negotiation, confidence-building measures can reassure opponents, but they carry high risks. Confidence-building measures are concessions by one side to encourage movement from the other – the declaration of a ceasefire, the inclusion of militants in talks, decommissioning of weapons. The symbolic gestures by Nelson Mandela to white South Africans greatly eased the first stages of negotiations. The danger is that premature concessions may be banked rather than reciprocated by the recipients, as was the case with Andreas Pastrana's territorial concessions to the Revolutionary Armed Forces of Colombia (FARC). The general lesson is that unilateral confidence-building gestures should only be conceded rarely. It is better to negotiate reciprocal gestures, as when significant demobilization by Guatemala's armed forces and by the Farabundo Marti National Liberation Front (FMLN) were carried out, with UN supervision, by 1993. Thus each side can point to mutual concessions to demonstrate momentum towards agreement.

Managing the process: dealing with negotiations and violence

During the years of violence preceding peace negotiations, cross-ethnic communications diminish and hostile stereotypes become entrenched. Opposing aspirations are expressed in mutually exclusive terms. The belief grows that one's opponents are cohesive, devious and successful, while one's own side is divided and frustrated. These are not ideal conditions for negotiations.

How can confidence be built at this stage in the fledgling process, and rules and procedures established to move it forward? Israel's recognition of the Palestine Liberation Organization (PLO) as legitimate representatives of the Palestinian people in Oslo A Accord, coupled with acceptance of the Palestinian right to self-determination, had great symbolic significance. There and elsewhere, the fact that negotiations are taking place at all presumes an acceptance, often implicit, that the representatives of militants have been admitted to negotiations in return for giving up violence. Their inclusion, whatever pressures it imposes on the process, admits militants to the common enterprise and applies a moral pressure on them to preserve the process in the face of violence from dissidents or spoiler groups.

The decision to include militants does not presume that the mechanics of their admission had been agreed. They are often required to surmount a tortuous series of 'good behaviour' tests. Probation periods were set before Sinn Féin was admitted to talks in Northern Ireland, and Sharon's insistence in 2002 that negotiations with Palestinians could not start until violence had ended for two clear weeks created an effective stalemate. Nevertheless, it is necessary to agree to rules to regulate the resumption of violence. The South African process, while not requiring arms decommissioning, insisted that arms should be banned from public meetings. In Northern Ireland the Mitchell Principles were devised, and imposed, as conditions for entry to talks and for punishing breaches by paramilitaries associated with negotiating parties.[3]

As a general rule, secrecy diminishes in importance as negotiations proceed. The need to involve the community in the forthcoming compromises increases. An excess of early publicity entrenches differences before an agreement can be reached. An excess of secrecy not only encourages conspiracy interpretations but also fails to prepare public opinion for the necessary compromises. Of course, secrecy and transparency are not so easily controlled. Gadi Wolfsfeld concludes, in his comparison of the media's role in Israel and Northern Ireland, that the news media are more interested in conflict than in peace and 'are best thought of as fair weather friends'.

The prime responsibility for preparing discussion papers on procedures for negotiation usually falls to government, especially if the talks involve a number of competing parties; the talks in Northern Ireland were eased considerably by the central involvement of two governments. Shuttle diplomacy may be needed to establish the preconditions and ground rules for participants. If these can be agreed, proximity talks are often necessary before the participants are willing to meet in plenary sessions.

The key role in managing the process does not always belong to local negotiators, especially in the early stages. External actors are often essential. The involvement of the British and Irish governments as joint custodians of the talks in Northern Ireland reassured both communities during negotiations and greatly facilitated progress. Neighbouring states and the UN continue to play key parts in certain settings. 'In both El Salvador and Guatemala', Cynthia Arnson and Dinorah Azpuru point out:

> the principal outside role was played by the United Nations, although other countries from the region as well as the United States and countries of Western Europe provided important additional support. Furthermore, international financial institutions and foreign governments marshalled significant monetary resources to support the accords' various commitments.

The issues under negotiation are distinctive to each conflict, but some themes are constant. The early release of prisoners is almost always a *sine qua non* for militants engaged in talks; it is also a highly emotive reminder to victims of violence that their sensibilities have been pushed into the background in the interests of securing peace. Reforms in policing, security, and the administration of justice are also constant features if an accord is agreed. Protection for human rights, and aspirations towards economic reform, are more common in Latin American accords than elsewhere. No clear pattern is discernible on decommissioning; it emerged as a major threat to the process in Northern Ireland but hardly rated as a problem in South Africa.

Pierre du Toit shows how 'rules and procedures provide structure to the process of negotiating for peace'. He describes a number of innovative negotiation devices developed to cope when the South African process stalled: the *'bosberade'* or 'bush summits' designed to smooth out bilateral disagreements; the 'channel', a subcommittee of three which met daily to maintain momentum; and the creation of new institutions such as the Transitional Executive Council and the Independent Electoral Commission to counter the asymmetrical nature of power structures in South Africa. Some of these have been consciously imitated in other places. The concept of 'sufficient consensus', for example, designed to keep dissenters in the process if they were outvoted on a specific issue, was effectively applied in Northern Ireland.

Time frames and deadlines are essential to maintain momentum, and deserve greater attention. The 1994 ceasefires in Northern Ireland were followed by a fatal lack of urgency, which eventually led to the ending of the Irish Republican

Army (IRA) ceasefire. In Israel–Palestine, the 1993 Oslo A Accord set a specific date (May 1999), five years from the start of its implementation, for the transfer of authority and land. Majority rule in South Africa was only implemented five years after the peace agreement was signed. Deadlines may not always be met, but the concept and demands of a timetable provide focus and urgency to negotiations. The deadline for the 1998 agreement in Northern Ireland was Thursday, 9 April. In fact, the accord was finalized on the following day, presenting it with a more memorable name, the Good Friday Agreement.

One by-product of establishing deadlines is that negotiations sometimes advance in surges rather than by gradual increments. This encourages the emergence of a brinkmanship style of negotiation. This approach carries obvious risks but has some incidental benefits. It confirms to a divided community that its leaders are fighting a tough fight, thus helping to prepare them for the compromises to come. The help is often necessary, for the interests of leaders and their supporters may diverge as a deal nears completion. By that time it is often more difficult for the negotiators to leave the process than to stay in it. By the more optimistic reading, their engagement in a common enterprise creates a common bond; more cynically, the failure of the peace process and a return to war places those who initiated the strategy in personal danger from militants within their own community.

The process of making an accord is always played out to a background of violence. It may even be perpetrated by some of those engaged in the negotiations. This includes national governments. A UN report in 2001 found evidence of systematic terror in East Timor 'planned and carried out' by the Indonesian army.[4] The Israeli government has openly admitted using torture since 1999,[5] and has been in breach of international agreements over settlements in the Palestinian Authority. There is little new about governments adopting covert force during wars. More worrying is the apparent willingness to acknowledge this openly, a trend more visible following the post-9/11 emphasis on security and stability.

The debate about spoilers, well treated in chapters by Stephen Stedman and Marie Joëlle Zahar, is important both in helping to clarify terminology and for its policy implications. They agree that the greatest short-term threat to a peace process comes from spoilers. The 'documented increases in violent crime' identified by Charles T. Call and William Stanley in their chapter, usually emerges later; although it clearly has the potential to disrupt fragile post-war states, there is evidence that a rise in conventional crime may have been exaggerated as a threat to peace agreements themselves.[6] More threatening are the issues of demobilization and decommissioning. As Virginia Gamba points out, arms not surrendered during peace processes more often than not end up fuelling other conflicts or armed crime. Alongside Gamba's plea for a greater priority for these issues, it is hard to avoid the conclusion that demobilization and decommissioning, which presented Northern Ireland with its most serious post-accord problem, might be more systematically handled in tandem during negotiations, with simultaneous and reciprocal reduction of the state's and militants' ability to resume hostilities.

Peace accords

Before the point is reached when a peace accord is being negotiated, a fundamental question needs to be addressed. Can the central grievances be resolved within the existing national framework, or do they require secession and autonomy? Yash Ghai underlines the paradoxes of autonomy:

> It (a) seeks to solve problem of territory, and yet may aggravate it; (b) is intended to solve the problem of identity, yet it may accentuate identity and stimulate the 'manufacture' of new communities; (c) seeks to increase pluralism, yet depends for its own success on pre-existing traditions of pluralism; and (d) aims to resolve conflict, yet aggravates disputes.

Given these tensions, many contemporary peace processes concentrate on the constitutional options that occupy the space between secession and conceded reforms. Most of them demand an element of powersharing. As Timothy Sisk points out,

> it is difficult to envisage a post-war political settlement that does not, or would need to, include guarantees to all the major antagonists that they will be assured some permanent political representation, decision-making power, and often autonomous territory in the post-war peace. Indeed, the gist of international mediation in such conflicts is to encourage parties to adopt powersharing in exchange for waging war.

Although this is the central deal in most peace processes, powersharing arrangements rarely survive in the long term. It is best to regard them as a transitional process. 'Ideally,' Sisk continues, 'powersharing will work best when it can, over time, wither away.'

Peace accords have broader aims than political agreement. Bell suggests that most peace accords involve three elements: a central deal on democratic access to power; the establishment of human rights institutions; and some mechanisms to address past human rights violations. Most interest focuses on the first of these, and 'human rights mechanisms can be conceded as the universally recognized chic language in which to write peace agreements'. Future research attention needs to be applied to the substance of the human rights and reconstruction dimensions of peace accords.

Peace accords are not only concerned with the clauses in the agreement. If the peace accord reached through negotiations between elites is to become a settlement accepted by their followers, it must be subjected to democratic validation through referenda or the discipline of elections. The choice is important – the hurried referendum in East Timor increased the level of violence instead of easing it. Ben Reilly's view is that 'the consent of the electorate, and the legitimacy of a new, post-conflict dispensation is the key – and under-appreciated – variable in determining whether a peace deal will succeed or fail'.

Reconstruction and conflict transformation

Despite the avalanche of new peace agreements since the late 1980s, the gilt has become a little tarnished in recent years. Agreements signed in Israel/Palestine (1994), the Philippines (1996), Colombia (1999), Eritrea–Ethiopia (2000), and elsewhere have reverted to violence. Even in South Africa, El Salvador, and Guatemala, often regarded as among the most enduring peace agreements, stability has been undermined by high crime and low economic growth, stemming in part from the preceding violence.

Explanations of why so many peace processes and peace accords fail to survive, mature, or bring about positive peace include:

the weakness of many post-war and post-accord states, many of them poor countries with weak institutions;

flaws in the process, which may not have included all the fundamental issues in dispute, or all the key actors, thereby prolonging and even extending the dispute;

the failure of leaders to carry their followers on the agreement, especially if the benefits expected to flow from an agreement are disappointing or delayed;

failure to implement the agreement, which sets out a broad agenda rather than the difficult details; the 'post-negotiations negotiations', as du Toit described them, are often tortuously slow;

the corrosive effects of post-accord violence;

failure to deliver the economic buttressing necessary for post-war reconstruction;

the emergence of unanticipated (some of them un-anticipatable) developments, such as the War on Terror and the tsunami.

The disappointment, however, mainly arises from a mistaken view that a peace agreement marks the end of a peace process. Certainly, it means that a peace process has passed a significant symbolic milestone on the road to stability, moving the journey on to the different but no less difficult implementation stage. In order to secure the agreement, it is tempting for negotiators to defer some sensitive issues for post-accord attention, laying minefields for the future in the interests of short-term gain. During the Oslo negotiations, for example, five critical issues, including Jerusalem, settlements and refugee return, were 'blackboxed' to enable the two sides to move forward on other less inflexible issues. In Northern Ireland, the post-war years were dogged by the deferred issues of policing and decommissioning. The dismantling of war machines is often a dominant theme. The transfer of ex-militant activists into the police and security forces in the Palestinian Territories and South Africa were tangible acknowledgements of past abuses and an effective way of converting a potentially destabilizing armed threat into support for the new structures. It was also a tangible demonstration of commitment to fair employment practices. The integration of ex-militants into the security forces, of course, is not always possible or even desirable. William Stanley and Charles T. Call warn that 'the path of demilitarization and police reform holds advantages over military merger'.

The need to move smoothly from an elite-driven political settlement towards a more fair and democratic society cannot be exaggerated. In South Africa, the inability to deliver either economic regeneration or greater social equality led to a growing sense of disillusion with peace itself. Similarly, in El Salvador and Guatemala, both relatively successful peace processes, 'achievements in the social arena have been modest and accompanied by dramatic rises in the rates of crime'. The post-settlement task, as Arnson and Azpuru go on to demonstrate, is to solidify past achievements 'through the provision of concrete benefits and an ongoing commitment to democratic reform'.

Apart from having to confront these continuing disputes, post-settlement administrations also inherit the problems left by years of violence and confrontation. Truth commissions have become a common but far from universal approach to confront past misdemeanours, with mixed records of success. Latin American truth commissions and the Truth and Reconciliation Commission in South Africa attempted to address the hurts of victims as a basis for reconciliation. The controversy surrounding these bodies demonstrates that it may take as long to repair community dysfunction as it took to create it – decades rather than years. So the referenda and elections necessary to endorse an agreement should be regarded, in Reilly's words, as 'the beginning of a long-term process of democratization, not the end-point'. They provide a licence to encourage a strengthened and energized civil society in the task of social reconciliation.

Civil society has been rediscovered, or at least redirected, in some recent peace processes, playing a vital role in the reconstruction of South Africa, Guatemala, and El Salvador, and generating energy into the campaigns to endorse the Good Friday Agreement in Northern Ireland. Peace agreements have been typically negotiated by elites, and have focused on the minutiae of disputes. They have paid less attention to the need to transform conflicting communities into stable and sustainable societies. Peace processes since the early 1990s has demonstrated that failure to do this can lead to public disillusionment, and may precipitate the collapse of the agreement itself. The tendency to broaden the nature of peace accords, and to include strategies for reconciliation at every level of society, is often called conflict transformation.

Conflict transformation requires involvement of a much broader range of participants than the political and military leaders who dominated the years of violence and negotiations. Antonia Potter shows how, although women's role in peacemaking is increasingly recognized at every phase of a peace process, they are still often excluded from decision-making at the most senior and official levels. A similar case is made by Karen Jacobsen, Helen Young, and Abdalmonim Osman that the involvement of refugees, who are often regarded as negative or at best 'passive recipients of outcomes that are negotiated in distant arenas of power', could also be utilized as positive forces in peace processes. All of these actors operate within a framework which rarely features officially in conflict transformation, what Carolyn Nordstrom describes as 'vast, international networks – those residing in the shadows – whose economic and political power can match, even exceed, that of some states'. The recognition of this broader framework is essential if conflicts are to be transformed.

The task for academic research is not only to focus on the missing parts of the research jigsaw puzzle: the long-term effects of sustained violence on individuals, families, and communities; how to judge the success of conflict transformation projects; and the appropriate role for the UN. It also needs to step outside traditional disciplines if it is to address the problems of conflict transformation. Among the research interfaces that require bridges are those between the need for peace and the need for justice; between economic reconstruction and economic redistribution; and between peace negotiations and reconciliation. These research interfaces are further tested as the boundary between international relations and individual case studies becomes increasingly fluid. It is no longer possible to understand specific local conflicts and peace processes – Israel–Palestine; the horn of Africa; Sierra Leone – without realizing how they are affected by regional and international developments beyond their control.

Twelve propositions

If peace processes are so shaped by their individual characteristics, is it possible to extract general guidelines for peacemakers? What lessons can be taken from almost 20 years of peace processes? We propose 12 propositions.

Proposition 1

A lasting agreement is impossible unless it actively involves those with the power to bring it down by violence.

Is it possible to make a settlement without including parties with militant associations? The greatest initial obstacle to an inclusive peace process is the unwillingness of constitutional politicians to deal with parties associated with violence. This has altered somewhat since the early 1990s, and the involvement of the 'veto holders' – those who were in a position to prevent a settlement – has become more common, almost a trend. The vehicle for their involvement is invariably secret negotiations through mediators or with political parties representing the gunmen. The unwillingness of successive Spanish governments to treat directly with Basque separatists, however understandable, prevented the development of a sustained peace process. The absence of a political front for Kosovo militants in early 1998 ruled out any possibility of negotiations with the Serbs.

Other peace processes were sparked off by the decision to include militants. The settlement in South Africa started with the release of Nelson Mandela and the African National Congress (ANC) prisoners in 1990. In Northern Ireland, there were seven unsuccessful attempts to reach agreement through negotiation between constitutional politicians, until the inclusion of Sinn Féin and the loyalist parties led to the Good Friday Agreement. Indeed, it is difficult to think of a situation where serious ethnic violence was terminated without either unacceptable repression or the involvement of those perpetrating the violence. The failure of the Colombian government's approach to FARC in 1998, however, is a reminder that the involvement of militants in talks is a necessary condition, but not a sufficient one, for success.

Even when the political representatives of militants are included in negotiations, the question then arises about how to respond when more extreme groups continue or resume campaigns of violence. The relationship between governments and militants presents an uncomfortable moral ambiguity. Having accepted the principle of amnesties for earlier terrorists in order to attract them into negotiation, the negotiators then assume a stern approach to the use of terror in the future. At the same time, they must also keep the door open to the inclusion of late converts. At this point, the creation of a mechanism is necessary to regulate the process – criteria for admission to talks, the conditions for expulsion, and the future inclusion of spoilers. The Mitchell Principles proved to be a useful model in Northern Ireland.

The reality is that total inclusion is never possible. There are always zealots who will not compromise. The more numerous and compromising the moderates, the greater the likelihood that the extremes can be marginalized. Therefore, the demand for inclusive talks is always a qualified one. Just as the principle of 'sufficient consensus'[7] was adopted in South Africa in recognition of the impossibility of progress if all participants had veto powers, it is necessary to apply a principle of 'sufficient inclusion' in relation to militant organizations. This does not mean the inclusion of all parties using or threatening to use violence. The principle of 'sufficient inclusion' is that a peace process includes both all actors who represent a significant proportion of their community and all actors who have the ability to destroy an agreement. The two groups are often coterminous.

Proposition 2

The absence of violence is not a prerequisite for peace. Negotiations are. Successful peace negotiations must anticipate and manage the problem of continuing violence.

Agreement by violent groups to negotiate is never unanimous. It often leads to the formation of splinter groups determined to continue the armed struggle. If they in turn enter the process, further breakaway spoilers emerge. The actions of spoilers move increasingly towards the margins during and after the process of peace negotiations. This traffic raises the question of how spoiler violence will be tackled by a coalition government which includes former militants.

At some point during the process, when all the splinter groups likely to join the process have done so, two rumps may remain – mavericks who are engaged in crime for personal advantage, and ideological zealots. They pose different problems. It is relatively straightforward to criminalize the former and to confront them through a reformed police force and justice system acceptable across the community. It is much more difficult for ex-militants to turn against groups who share their general orientation but have refused to buy the peace process. One key aspect is the size of the spoiler group and the seriousness of its threat to the peace process. If the spoilers carry significant popular support, as Hamas does, the authority of negotiators such as the PLO is seriously circumscribed. The ANC's dominance of political protest in South Africa, on the other hand, made condemnation a lot easier.

A successful peace process is organic and cumulative. The public euphoria following the ending of violence contrasts with the mutual suspicion of the early negotiations. Constitutional politicians are forced to negotiate with people they regard as criminals, often at the risk of alienating their voting support. They overlook the risks facing the militants who have entered negotiations, and whose position is severely undermined if the talks collapse. Tests were imposed in Israel, in Northern Ireland, and in the Basque Country before militants were admitted into talks. These delays may be understandable but can be dangerous, as the breakdown of the IRA and the Euskadi ta Askatasuna/Basque Homeland and Freedom (ETA) ceasefires demonstrate.

If the process survives the first nervous contacts, it tends to strengthen. Sometimes it is reinforced by internal pressure from public opinion, as happened in South Africa when the process faltered in 1992. During the Oslo process, support for violence among Palestinians declined from 57 per cent to 21 per cent between 1994 and 1996, in tandem with suicide bombs by Islamic Jihad and Hamas. This dynamic does not mean that the negotiators have become friends; it is sufficient that they can define a common problem and attempt to negotiate an accommodation. Working relationships often develop between the negotiators as they concentrate on the practical minutiae of negotiations and become better acquainted with the boundaries within which their opponents operate. The process of achieving this position locks those involved in negotiation in an uncomfortable embrace. As negotiations progress, the participants become more attracted to the positive rewards of a historic breakthrough. It becomes increasingly difficult for any of them to contemplate a return to the earlier violence. Failure to make progress would rule out another initiative for the near future. It would also probably mean the end of their political careers and, sometimes, threaten their lives

One of the greatest challenges to this dynamic is continuing violence from dissidents, from rival militant groups, and from militias. Some of the violence may even be sponsored by the negotiators themselves for strategic advantage. Persistent stalemates during the negotiations will strengthen the internal cohesion of competing parties and erode the common ground between them, as happened within both the Israeli and Palestinian communities in late 2000.[8] This underlines the importance of maintaining forward momentum in negotiations, presenting evidence of advantages for all parties.

Generally speaking, the further the process develops, the stronger its shock-absorbent facility and the more capable its ability to withstand the inevitable atrocities designed to undermine it. The policy implication is to focus economic and political support on the initial stages of the process.

Proposition 3

Peace processes are deals: they require trade-offs.

Peace negotiations are complex and multi-faceted, involving a range of teams negotiating across a range of constitutional, political, economic, and cultural issues. This 'disaggregation' – the conduct of negotiations through plenaries and sub-groups, each dealing with a different issue and reporting according to a different time frame – is perhaps unavoidable.[9] In retrospect however, a greater willingness to broaden the negotiation frame, and to encourage reciprocation between and within different issues in dispute is needed. In some cases, of course, this happens. In Northern Ireland, for example, a British–Irish Council was created to provide a balance for the North–South bodies demanded by nationalists, and concessions to encourage use of the Irish language were, somewhat awkwardly at times, balanced by similar advantage to those advocating the use of Ulster-Scots. Other parts of the Good Friday Agreement, and other peace accords, might also have benefited from similar reciprocation.

If a peace accord has terminated a period of political violence, there is a clear reciprocation between the need to demobilize the state security apparatus and the need to decommission paramilitary weapons. In 1992, an impasse in El Salvador, where the government distrusted the FMLN's compliance on demobilization, and the FMLN believed the government was reneging on the purification of the armed forces called for in the Chapultepec Accords, was resolved by UN mediation establishing that 'compliance with specific undertakings by one side would be contingent upon compliance with specific undertakings by the other side'.[10] Nevertheless, many peace accords, while indicating the need for both, does not address decommissioning by militants and demilitarization by the state as related. A peace accord does not banish suspicion and fear within either the security branches and ex-militants, and many will wish to hold their weapons as guarantees against its collapse. A pre-determined agreement to phase in decommissioning and demilitarization in parallel offers a way to approach the problem, and to anticipate either issue becoming a serious obstacle to post-settlement reconstruction.

Proposition 4

During peace negotiations, the primary function of leaders is to deliver their own people. Assisting their opponents in the process is secondary.

Peace accords are negotiated by the elites of both power holders and seekers, who must then persuade their followers to endorse it through an election or referendum. Power seekers who abandon violence and entered talks are always vulnerable to accusations of betrayal; in the emotional atmosphere it is a powerful challenge to their leaders. There are similar constraints on power holders. 'Political leaders', as Berkowitz observed, 'cannot lead where their followers are unwilling to go'.[11] The work needed to prepare their followers for the shift usually starts many years before it becomes public.

The transitional problems facing both power holders and power seekers are superficially similar. In both cases, extremists rather than moderates leaders are more likely to deliver suspicious followers. Reluctant converts, like Buthelezi and Viljoen in South Africa, are more convincing, and more trusted by the extremes. At that point, the similarity ends. The power holders – usually the state – enter negotiation because they recognize the inevitability of change before their followers do; their main difficulty is to convince their supporters that the resulting changes are minimal. The power seekers – usually militant leaders – get into negotiation because they recognize the advantages of negotiation before their followers do; their main difficulty is to convince their supporters that the negotiations are achieving major concessions. If the process moves too slowly, it hurts the power seekers. If it moves too speedily, it hurts the power holders.

In navigating this complex journey, the primary function of leaders is to deliver their own followers. It is true that both sets of leaders are more likely to recognize the difficulties of their opponents as negotiations evolve. They also come to realize that a peace process cannot be completed unless their opponents also have enough to satisfy their followers. This mutual dependency is in tension with the risk that assisting their opponents may alienate their own supporters. The reality is that the loss of their followers is a greater threat to party leaders than the collapse of the process.

Propositions 5 and 6

If a peace agreement is to stick, initiatives are needed to re-integrate members of the security forces and paramilitary groups into normal society. Such initiatives must be integrated with moves to address the needs of the victims of violence.

The problem of re-integrating ex-militants into society is sharpened by their ability to undermine the peace process. In Mozambique and Sierra Leone and elsewhere the problem was partially addressed by transferring ex-guerrillas into the regular army and police force.

There are other options. Prudence demands that those who were engaged in the war must be provided with jobs and training. The ending of violence leaves an inheritance of high risk. The shrinkage of the security industry – army, police, prison officers, private security guards – brings on to the unemployment register people skilled in the use of arms. A similar risk of redundancy faces the militants whose lives have been devoted to armed resistance. Their speedy return to civil society is essential, less because they deserve a reward than because they have the means to destabilize the peace process.

Historically, two distinct approaches have been applied to the victims of violence – what John Groom has called the Nuremberg Tribunal way and the South African way.[12] The punishment of war crimes continues today through the UN's war crimes tribunal in the former Yugoslavia. In South Africa, as in Chile after Pinochet's fall, a new model was created in a Truth and Reconciliation Commission. All these approaches focused on individual victims, but violence also leaves a collective heritage.

If there is need to re-integrate ex-militants and members of the security forces into society, there is also need to anticipate society's response to the provision of preferential treatment for people convicted of murder, bombings, and mutilations. When the Argentine military declared a self-amnesty after the Falklands–Malvinas defeat, the newly elected Argentine parliament, reflecting public outrage, declared it null. In Uruguay, the public reaction to an Impunity law led to a petition by 25 per cent of all registered voters for a plebiscite to repeal it, although the resulting plebiscite was defeated.

The early release of political prisoners is usually a pre-condition to ceasefires, and is often regarded as one of the earliest tasks to be resolved in a peace process. Early prisoner releases often infuriate the families of victims and the community at large. This is, of course, a moral issue, but it is also a pragmatic one. Peace accords require democratic approval through an election or referendum. The creation of an initial injustice may undermine the agreement by alienating voters.

This issue reaches beyond monetary compensation. War memorials, for example, need careful treatment in divided societies if they are to avoid becoming shrines to division rather than to common suffering. Reparations too can provoke rather than ease tensions if the amounts are low or they are unaccompanied by investigations of atrocities. Even after reparations were instituted by law in Chile, and accepted by the victims' relatives, there were few prosecutions against the military, because they were protected by the 1978 Amnesty law. In general, the efficacy of truth and reconciliation commissions is heavily determined by timing and local sensitivities. It may have been appropriate to the needs of Chile and South Africa, but each society must find a form appropriate to its traditions and circumstances. Whatever the circumstances, the needs of victims should be confronted at a much earlier stage than has often been the case in peace processes.

Proposition 7

A peace process does not end with a peace accord.

There are no rules about the best time to reach formal agreement during a peace process. The agreements in Northern Ireland and Israel were only made possible by postponing some contentious issues for later resolution, leaving enormous minefields to traverse in the post-accord period. Even in South Africa, where a remarkably broad range of agreements had been agreed before the 1994 elections, the issues of economic development and truth and reconciliation lingered well into the future.

If negotiators wait until all major issues have been agreed, the process may collapse from mutual distrust or violence before they reach a conclusion. If they defer complex and divisive issues for later resolution, it will be more difficult to contain negotiations as mutual fears and suspicions flourish among the uncertainty. In either case, post-settlement euphoria may be followed by post-agreement *tristesse*, and the all-important momentum lost. As the terms of the 1998 Good Friday Agreement were implemented, Northern Ireland unionists became increasingly disillusioned. In the Middle East, despite Israeli withdrawals from Palestinian territories and the creation of the Palestinian National Authority following the 1993 Israeli–Palestinian Declaration of Principles, the peace process has become bogged down over issues of implementation – full Israeli withdrawal, agreement over Jerusalem and the settlements, and ceasefires.

It is becoming increasingly undeniable that many peace processes fail after apparent political agreement has been reached through an accord. The causes and dynamics are varied and under-studied, but some guidelines are evident. Parties may wish to re-negotiate some provisions in an agreement which they find unpalatable or cannot sell to their supporters. Public expectations, initially raised by any agreement, are often dashed by inability to implement them, compounding the problems during negotiations with added distrust. The problems and challenges which emerge after an accord has been agreed are new, so there are fewer guidelines available for tackling them. They are likely to assume a more urgent research priority in coming years.

Proposition 8

Peace is a development issue.

A formal peace process, negotiated between elites and focussed on constitutional and legal issues, can only go so far. The issues that have the most chance of making an impact on people's lives inhabit the social and economic realm. These issues require serious attention during mainstream political negotiations lest the gap between public expectation and reality remain unfulfilled in the fragile post-accord years. Failure to address these 'bread and butter' issues may lead to a public disenchantment that overshadows political or constitutional compromises. In sum, peace processes must embrace development issues.

According to a popular story, King William of Orange crossed the river Boyne by boat during a famous Irish battle in 1690. The boatman asked him how the battle was progressing. 'What is it to you?' replied the King, 'You'll still be boatman whoever wins.' The lesson for those involved in contemporary peace processes is that poverty, inequality, and social exclusion require serious attention (as part of any peace initiative). Uneven development is a major contributory cause of conflict. If a peace accord replicates serious inequality and provides few routes of economic opportunity then the accord itself may become the first step towards a new cycle of violence.

Notwithstanding complex constitutional transformations, the main problems facing many people in Guatemala, the Solomon Islands, and elsewhere are economic. To speak of 'haves' and 'have nots' may be unfashionable, but when having nothing threatens peace, it becomes salient. In the years after the dissolution of the last minority-rule government in South Africa, *The Economist* summed up the persistence of racial divisions: 'Black children still die of tuberculosis, and increasingly of AIDS; white children are more likely to drown in the swimming pool.'[13]

Just as war affects different sections of society in different ways, peace has a differential impact. Peace will often impact upon men and women, young people and the elderly, urban and rural dwellers in different ways. It is no coincidence that wartime population displacement usually has the greatest impact on the most vulnerable, usually the elderly, infirm, and dependent. Peace processes need to focus on the variations within society and not necessarily minister to those who can shout the loudest, often men and those who retain their arms. On top of structural inequalities within societies, the international economic system has the capacity to undermine peace. While the international community may promise a peace dividend, the reality of currency flows, uneven trade relationships and competition can hamper post-accord development.

Proposition 9

Peace and justice are not always compatible during peace processes.

In 2006 the government of Uganda began negotiations with the Lord's Resistance Army (LRA) in an attempt to end the vicious war there. The LRA leaders insisted that they should be granted amnesty for crimes committed during the war, as a pre-condition for entering negotiations. The government was prepared to grant an amnesty to the leaders in order to secure peace. Further, the Acholi community, which had suffered the worst atrocities from the LRA, also supported the amnesty. The problem was that the International Criminal Court (ICC), on behalf of the international community, had issued arrest warrants against six leaders of the LRA. Morris Ogenga-Latigo, the head of Uganda's parliamentary opposition summed up the dilemma well: 'The ICC has become an impediment to our efforts. Should we sacrifice our peacemaking process here so they can test and develop their criminal-justice procedures there at the ICC? Punishment has to be quite secondary to the goal of resolving this conflict.'[14]

Clearly not every peace process faces such a stark confrontation between peace and justice as Uganda, but all of them have to confront the issue to some degree. It seems important that political elites prepare their constituencies for a peace that involves compromises and an imperfect symmetry between the gains and grievances of each side. The need for flexibility in seeking escape routes from apparently intractable confrontations can be reinforced if public and political opinion is encouraged to have a sense of perspective in which the larger goal of peace is prioritized over subordinate issues.

Proposition 10

The absence of war is not peace.

A significant number of peace processes become stalled after a ceasefire has been reached. The protagonists are able to enjoy the benefits of an end to direct violence, but they lack an impetus to reach a comprehensive peace agreement. The result can be a 'no war, no peace' situation in which the peace process is an empty vessel. International peace support in the form donor conferences or recognition of the legitimacy of militant groups can inadvertently reinforce these 'no war, no peace' situations by removing incentives for parties to enter into serious negotiations on core issues of contention. At certain stages in the Sri Lankan, Colombian, and Oslo peace processes antagonists were content to bank the benefits of an absence of war but saw no advantage in pushing for peace. The danger with 'no war, no peace' situations, as evidenced by the three cases just mentioned, is that violence creeps back into the void left by the absence of a dynamic peace process.

'No war, no peace' situations are also apparent in some post-peace accord societies in which the peace accord fails to address the core issues of the conflict. The Dayton Accords, for example, have had limited effect in dealing with the nationalisms and pejorative intergroup perceptions that have fuelled conflict in the former Yugoslavia. This is despite enormous levels of peace support and reconstruction intervention by the international community. While the peace accord may have success in stanching violence, instituting a new political dispensation, and kick-starting reconstruction, it may fail to deal with underlying grievances and so be prone to a resumption of violence. Flare-ups in violence in Kosovo (2003) and East Timor (2005–2007), for example, reflected a failure to deal with development issues and the perception that some groups were benefiting more than others from the peace.

A final type of 'no war, no peace' situation is visible in situations whereby the conflict is mainly confined to a specific geographic region of a larger state. With the conflict effectively compartmentalized, governments and large sections of the population and economy of the United Kingdom, Spain, India, Colombia, and Sri Lanka have been relatively insulated from the civil war. Therefore, while one part of the population enjoys the 'peace', the other endures the war. Southern Uganda has experienced an economic boom despite the civil war in the north. The obvious danger of such situations is that governments and others can maintain a fiction of peace in the majority of the country and so regard peace initiatives as a lesser priority.

Proposition 11

Indigenous approaches to dispute resolution are often more appropriate than international 'best practice'.

The involvement of external actors in peace processes brings the risk of a standardization of peacemaking techniques and reconstruction programmes. In some cases, international 'best practice' may be culturally inappropriate, unsustainable, and resemble a top-down imposition that makes little connection with the bulk of the population. For example, techniques honed to ameliorate the symptoms of psycho-social trauma among prosperous adolescents in Los Angeles may have little application to child soldiers in West Africa. Yet the transfer of Western ideas and practice is a persistent trend in contemporary peacemaking. It is a trend with potentially serious cultural implications in reshaping how citizens in war-affected states interact with each other, their state, and the market. This is not to deny the very real potential advantages accruing from international practice, expertise, and resources. But while it is useful to look for guidance from comparative examples, no magic template applies to all peace processes. Instead, it seems sensible that local and international actors are open to a wide range of peacemaking techniques and are free to adopt and adapt dispute resolution techniques according to local circumstances.

Proposition 12

Political elites and international organizations must find ways to broaden the appeal of peace processes and peace accords.

Despite the interest of major funding bodies, NGOs, and some international organizations in 'bottom-up' approaches to peacemaking, popular peace movements have a poor record of stimulating peace talks. Demonstrations for peace attracted substantial popular support in Northern Ireland in the 1970s and in the Basque Country and Israel in the 1990s, but failed to generate a sustained political initiative. Indeed, peace initiatives are often restricted to political elites for understandable practical reasons. The reality of many peace processes boils down to elite-level bargaining behind closed doors.

Popular participation may come only at the end of peace talks, when the peace accord is presented as a *fait accompli* in the form of a yes/no referendum. There is an onus on those involved in peace processes to find ways of involving as broad a constituency as possible and of managing popular expectations, especially in relation to post-accord development issues. This might involve consultation and 'peace process education' programmes as occurred in Sudan. The emphasis on technocratic 'solutions' to the problems of civil war societies, favoured by many international organizations and the International Non Government Organizations (INGOS), may be unable to deal with the affective dimension of conflict. Again, participatory mechanisms may help with the management of public opinion, especially in relation to calculations of relative 'winners' and 'losers' in peace.

Notes

1. Other sources, including the University of Uppsala, have suggested even higher numbers of peace agreements.
2. P. du Toit, 'South Africa: In Search of Post-Settlement Peace', in J. Darby & R. Mac Ginty (eds), *The Management of Peace Processes* (London: Macmillan, 2000) p. 19.
3. The 1996 Mitchell Report, named after US Senator George Mitchell, chair of the International Body on Arms Decommissioning, laid down conditions for all negotiators. Before participants were admitted to all-party negotiations they were required to agree to six principles, including their commitment: to democratic and exclusively peaceful means of resolving political issues; to the total disarmament of all paramilitaries; that such disarmament must be verifiable by an independent commission; to renounce and oppose any effort to use force or the threat of force to influence the course of the outcome of all-party negotiations; to abide by the letter of any agreement reached in all-party negotiations and to resort to democratic and exclusively peaceful methods in trying to alter any aspect of that outcome with which they may disagree; and 'to take effective steps' to end 'punishment' killings and beatings.
4. The UN report was leaked by the *Sydney Morning Herald*: 'East Timor Massacre Work of Indonesia's Army' (20 April 2001).

5. See, as examples, reports in the *New York Times* (14 September 1999) and *Los Angeles Times* (4 December 1999).

6. On the issue of crime after peace accords see R. Mac Ginty, 'Post-Accord Crime', in J. Darby (ed.), *Violence and Reconstruction* (Notre Dame IN: Notre Dame University Press, 2006) pp. 101–119 and C.J. Steenkamp, *The Political Implications of Violence after Peace Accords: Civilian Perceptions of Physical Insecurity in Northern Ireland and South Africa*, PhD thesis submitted to the University of York, November 2006.

7. The condition of 'sufficient consensus' is defined by Friedman thus: 'consensus was sufficient if the process could move on the backing of only those who supported a proposal. Disagreement would be recorded; dissenters could remain in the process, await its outcome, and then decide whether to support it' in S. Friedman, 'Afterword: the Brief Miracle', in S. Friedman & D. Atkinson (eds), *South African Review: 7 The Small Miracle – South Africa's Negotiated Settlement* (Johannesburg: Ravan Press, 1994) p. 22.

8. The return to 'us against them' attitudes is described by Deborah Sontag in 'Eye for Eye Once Again', *New York Times* (9 October 2000), and by Vivienne Walt, 'Poverty, Lack of Change Add to Anger in the Street', *USA Today* (9 October 2000).

9. D. Bloomfield, C. Nupen, & P. Harris. 'Negotiation Process', in P. Harris & B. Reilly (eds), *Democracy and Deep-rooted Conflict: Options for Negotiators* (Sweden: Institute for Democracy and Electoral Assistance, 1998).

10. F. Osler Hampson, *Nurturing Peace: Why Peace Settlements Succeed or Fail* (Washington DC: United States Institute of Peace Press, 1996) p. 153.

11. Ibid.

12. J. Groom, 'Coming out of Violence: Ten Troubling Questions', Proceedings of the International Peace Studies Symposium, *Coming Out of War and Ethnic Violence* (Okinawa: Okinawa International University, 1996).

13. 'Survey of South Africa', *The Economist* (20 May 1995).

14. Helena Cobham, 'Uganda: When international justice and international peace are at odds', *Christian Science Monitor* (24 August 2006).

Bibliography

Reports

Adam, G.F. & R. Thamotheram, 'The Media's Role in Conflict: Report Reviewing International Experience in the Use of Mass-Media for Promoting Conflict Prevention, Peace and Reconciliation' (Geneva: Media Action International, 1996).

Adibe, C. *Managing Arms in Peace Processes: Somalia* (UNIDIR's Disarmament and Conflict Resolution Project Series, Geneva: United Nations, 1995).

Adibe, C. *Managing Arms in Peace Processes: Liberia* (UNIDIR's Disarmament and Conflict Resolution Project Series, Geneva: United Nations, 1996).

Anderlini, S.N. *Women at the Peace Table: Making a Difference* (New York: UNIFEM, 2000).

Azpuru, D. 'Resumen Ejecutivo', in *Construyendo la democracia en sociedades posconflicto: un enfoque compardo entre Guatemala y El Salvador* (Guatemala City: ASIES, IDRC, FUNDAUNGO, 2006).

Ballard, B. 'Reintegration Programmes for Refugees in South-East Asia. Lessons Learned from UNHCR's Experience', UNHCR EPAU/2002/01 (2002).

Berman, E. *Managing Arms in Peace Processes: Mozambique* (UNIDIR's Disarmament and Conflict Resolution Project Series, Geneva: United Nations, 1996).

Bhattachan, K. & S. Webster, *Indigenous Peoples, Poverty Reduction and Conflict in Nepal* (Geneva: International Labour Organization, 2005).

Centre for Humanitarian Dialogue, 'Hitting the Target: Men and Guns', Review Conference Policy Brief, Centre for Humanitarian Dialogue, June 2006 (for The United Nations Conference to Review Progress Made in the Implementation of the Programme of Action to Prevent, Combat and Eradicate the Illicit Trade in Small Arms and Light Weapons in All Its Aspects).

Chinkin, C. 'Peace Agreements as a Means for Promoting Gender Equality and Ensuring Participation of Women – A Framework of Model Provisions', *UNDAW, OSAGI, DPA EGM/PEACE/2003/REPORT* (10 December 2003).

Committee on Women's Rights and Gender Equality, 'Report on the situation of women in armed conflicts and their role in the reconstruction and democratic process in post-conflict countries (2005/2215(INI))', European Parliament Session Document, reference A6–0159/2006 or RR\370262EN.doc. (3 May 2006).

Constitutional Review Commission, *The Fiji Islands: Toward a United Future* (Suva: 1996).

Cruz, J. 'Violencia y democratización en Centroamérica: El impacto del crimen en los regímenes de posguerra', in United Nations Development Program, *Aportes para la convivencia y la seguridad ciudadana* (San Salvador: UNDP, 2004).

Eide, A. *New Approaches to Minority Protection*, Minority Rights Group International Report 93/4 (London: MRG International, 1995).

El Bushra, J., A. Adrian-Paul, & M. Olson, *Women Building Peace: Sharing Know-How Assessing Impact: Planning for Miracles* (London: International Alert, 2005).

Foreign and Commonwealth Office, *UK Priorities: Human Rights – Indigenous Peoples*, Available at www.fco.gov.uk (Accessed on 25 February 2007).

Goulding, M. *Enhancing the United Nations' Effectiveness in Peace and Security* (United Nations: Report to the Secretary General, 30 June 1997).

Independent Commission for Kosovo, *Kosovo Report: Conflict, International Response, Lessons Learned* (Oxford: Independent Commission for Kosovo/Oxford University Press, 2000).

IDMC, *Internal Displacement: Global Overview of Trends and Developments in 2005* (Internal Displacement Monitoring Centre, Norwegian Refugee Council, Geneva: 2006).

International Alert, *Inclusive Security, Sustainable Peace: A Toolkit for Advocacy and Action* (London: International Alert and Women Waging Peace, 2004).

International Commission on Intervention and State Sovereignty, 'The Responsibility to Protect' (Ottawa: International Development Research Centre, 2001).

International Crisis Group, *Liberia Unravelling*, ICG Africa Briefing Paper (19 August 2002) Available at http://www.icg.org//library/documents/report_archive/A400741_19082002.pdf (Accessed on 15 May 2007).

International Labour Organisation/JASPA, *Employment in Africa: Some Critical Issues* (Geneva: ILO, 1988).

Jaspars, S. 'Solidarity and Soup Kitchens: A Review of Principles and Practice for Food Distribution in Conflict' (London: Humanitarian Policy Group, Overseas Development Institute & Nutrition Works, Public Nutrition Resource Group, 2000).

Lord, D. (ed.), *Paying the Price: The Sierra Leone Peace Process* (London: Conciliation Resources, September 2000).

Mack, A. *Human Security Brief 2006* (Vancouver WA: University of British Columbia Liu Centre for Human Security, 2006) Available at www.humansecuritycentre.org (Accessed on 23 May 2007).

Managing Arms in Peace Processes: The Issues (UNIDIR's Disarmament and Conflict Resolution Project Series, Geneva: United Nations, 1996).

Mazurana, D. 'Women in Armed Opposition Groups Speak on War, Protection and Obligations under International Humanitarian and Human Rights Law', Report of Geneva Call and Program for the Study of International Organisations Workshop (August 2004 Geneva: Geneva Call and the Program for the Study of International Organization(s)).

Mazurana, D. 'Women in Armed Opposition Groups in Africa and the Promotion of International Humanitarian Law and Human Rights', Report of Geneva Call and Program for the Study of International Organisations Workshop (November 2005 Geneva: Geneva Call and the Program for the Study of International Organization(s)).

Mohamoud, M. *African Diaspora and Post-Conflict: Reconstruction in Africa* (Copenhagen: Danish Institute for International Studies, 2006)

NIIA, 'Gendering Human Security: from Marginalisation to the Integration of Women in Peace-Building, recommendations for policy and practice' (Norwegian Institute of International Affairs and Fafo Programme for International Co-operation and Conflict Resolution, 2001).

Ohlson, T. *Power Politics and Peace Politics* (Uppsala: Uppsala University of Uppsala, Department of Peace and Conflict Research), Report 50.

Oxfam International, *Towards Global Equity: Strategic Plan, 2001–2004* (London: Oxfam International, 2001).

Peace and Democracy Foundation, *Report about Research on Customary Dispute Resolution and Proposed Mediation Model for the Democratic Republic of Timor–Leste* (Dili: Peace and Democracy Foundation, 2004).

Peace Implementation Council, *Bosnia and Herzegovina 1998: Self-sustaining Structures* (Bonn: 10 December 1997).

Pkalya, R., M. Adan, & I. Masinde, *Conflict in Northern Kenya: A Focus on the Internally Displaced Victims of Conflict in Northern Kenya* (Eastern Africa: Intermediate Technology Development Group, 2003).

Pkalya, R., M. Adan, & I. Masinde, *Indigenous Democracy: Traditional Conflict Resolution Mechansims: Pokot, Turkana, Samburu and Marakwet* (Eastern Africa: Intermediate Technology Development Group, 2004).

Potter, A. *Assistance to Justice and the Rule of Law in Afghanistan* (Geneva: Centre for Humanitarian Dialogue Report, February 2004).

Potter, A. *We the Women: Why Conflict Mediation Is Not Just a Job for Men* (Geneva: Centre for Humanitarian Dialogue, 2005).

Raevsky, A. & B. Ekwall-Uebelhardt, *Managing Arms in Peace Processes: Croatia and Bosnia–Herzegovina* (UNIDIR's Disarmament and Conflict Resolution Project Series, Geneva: United Nations, 1996).

Rehn, E. & E. Johnson Sirleaf, *Women, War, Peace: The Independent Experts' Assessment on the Impact of Armed Conflict on Women and Women's Role in Peace-Building* (New York: UNIFEM, 2002).

SaferAfrica, Compendium of Small Arms and Light Weapons Initiatives Applicable to Africa (African Union and SaferAfrica, June 2006).

Seils, P. & M. Wierda, 'The International Criminal Court and Conflict Mediation', International Center for Transitional Justice Occasional Paper (June 2005) Available at www.ictj.org (Accessed on 12 May 2007).

Stockholm Initiative on Disarmament, Demobilisation and Reintegration, *Final Report* (Stockholm: Ministry for Foreign Affairs, March 2006).

'Turning Strife to Advantage: A Blueprint to Integrate the Croats in Bosnia and Herzegovina', an International Crisis Group Report (15 March 2001).

United Nations, Report of the Secretary-General's High Level Panel on Threats, Challenges, and Change (New York: United Nations, 2004).

UNIFEM, *Getting It Right, Doing It Right: Gender and Disarmament, Demobilization and Rehabilitation* (UNIFEM, 2004).

US Agency for International Development, Bureau for Latin America and the Caribbean, *Latin America and the Caribbean: Selected Economic and Social Data* (Washington DC: USAID, 2006).

Wang, J. *Managing Arms in Peace Processes: Cambodia*, UNIDIR's Disarmament and Conflict Resolution Project Series (Geneva: United Nations, 1996).

World Bank, *Building Social Capital through Peacemaking Circles* (Washington DC: The World Bank, 2004).

Conference proceedings, conference papers, and occasional papers

Azpuru, D., L. Blanco, C. Mendoza, & E. Blank, 'Democracy Assistance to Post-Conflict Guatemala: Finding a Balance between Details and Determinants', Working Paper No. 30 (The Hague, Netherlands: Netherlands Institute for International Relations, 2004).

Berman, E.G. 'Re-Armament in Sierra Leone: One Year after the Lome Peace Agreement', Small Arms Survey, Occasional Paper 1 (Geneva: December 2000).

Blair, T. *Doctrine of the International Community*, Speech to the Chicago Economic Club (22 April 1999).

Brinkerhoff, J. 'Contributions of Digital Diasporas to Governance Reconstruction in Post-Conflict and Fragile States: Potential and Promise', Paper presented at the 'Rebuilding Governance in Post-Conflict Societies: What's New, What's Not' Conference (2005).

Byrne, M. *Roads to Reconciliation*, UNIYA-Jesuit Social Justice Centre Occasional Paper 9 (New South Wales: UNIYA, 2005).

Call, C.T. 'Why the World's Most Successful Peace Processes Produce the World's Most Violent Countries', Paper delivered at International Studies Association conference (Chicago: March 1999).

Caplan, R. *A New Trusteeship? The International Administration of War-Torn Territories*, The Adelphi Papers (Oxford: Oxford University Press, 2002).

Cetinyan, R. & A. Stein, 'Assassins of Peace?: Spoilers and the Peace Process in the Middle East', Paper presented at the Annual Meeting of the American Political Science Association (Atlanta GA: 3 September 1999).

Chesterman, S., T. Farer, & T. Sisk, 'Competing Claims: Self-Determination and Security at the United Nations', an International Peace Academy Policy Brief (May 2001).

Clinton, B. 'Address to the 54th Session of the United Nations General Assembly', *US–UN Press Release*, No. 59, 99 (21 September 1999).

Cruz, J. & R. Fernández de Castro, 'Youth Gangs and Violence in Central America and Mexico', Paper presented at the conference 'Comparative Peace Processes in Latin America: A Second Look' (Woodrow Wilson International Center for Scholars, Washington DC: 3–4 April 2006).

Downs, G. & S.J. Stedman, 'Evaluation Issues in Peace Implementation', Paper presented at the annual meetings of the American Political Science Association (Washington DC: 30 August 2000).

Gordhan, P. 'Political Leadership in Divided Societies: The Case of South Africa', Paper presented at Parliament Buildings (Stormont: 10 April 2000).

Groom, J. 'Coming out of Violence: Ten Troubling Questions', Proceedings of the International Peace Studies Symposium (Okinawa: Okinawa International University, 1996).

Gusmão, K.R.X. 'Challenges for Peace and Stability', The Vice Chancellor's Human Right's Lecture by His Excellency President Gusmão at the University of Melbourne (7 April 2003).

Haas, R. 'Reflections on US Policy One Year on', Opening Speech at the IISS Global Strategic Review (13–15 September 2002) London.

Hayzer, N. 'Women, War and Peace: Mobilizing for Peace and Security in the 21st Century', The 2004 Dag Hammarskjøld Lecture (Stockholm: Dag Hammarskjøld Foundation 2004).

Hickey, S. & G. Moran, 'Participation: From Tyranny to Transformation?', Briefing Paper presented at the Development Studies Association conference (London: November 2004).

Kane, A. 'The United Nations and the Maintenance of Peace and Security: Challenges and Choices', in *Proceedings of the Forty-Third Pugwash Conference on Science and World Affairs – Hasseludden, Sweden, 9–15 June 1993 – A World at the Crossroads: New Conflicts, New Solutions* (London: World Scientific, 1994).

Kent, G. 'Diaspora Power: Network Contributions to Peacebuilding and the Transformation of War Economies', Paper presented at the 'Transforming War Economies' Seminar, Plymouth (16–18 June 2005).

Mulvihill, M.E. & G.A. Lopez, 'The Human Rights Dimensions of Peace Accords in Internal Conflicts: Insights for a Research Design', Paper prepared for the panel of Do Good Things Go Together? Rights and Resolution at the 43rd Annual Meetings of the International Studies Association (New Orleans LA: 24–27 March 2002).

Nathan, L. 'No Ownership, No Peace: The Darfur Peace Agreement', Crisis States Research Centre, LSE, Working Paper No. 5. (London: 2006).

Quintos-Deles, T. 'Corridors of Peace in the Corridors of Power: Bridging Spaces for Women in Governance for Peace', Speech to International Center for Innovation, Transformation and Excellence in Governance (February 2006).

Reilly, B. & A. Reynolds, 'Electoral Systems and Conflict in Divided Societies', Papers on International Conflict Resolution (Washington DC: National Academy Press, 1999).

Sambanis, N. 'Conflict Resolution Ripeness and Spoiler Problems in Cyprus: From the Intercommunal Talks (1968–1974) to the Present', Paper presented to the American Political Science Association (25 September 1998).

Schenk, C. 'Fostering the Past and Reconciliation in Southeast Asia and the Pacific – A Comparison between Timor–Leste and Bougainville', Paper Presented at Conference on From Dealing with the Past to Future Cooperation: Regional and Global Challenges to Reconciliation (Berlin: 31 January–2 February 2005).

Schneckener, U. 'Making Power Sharing Work: Lessons from Successes and Failures in Ethnic Conflict Regulation', *Institut for Interkultrelle und Internationale Studien*, University of Bremen (Working Paper Nr. 19/2000).

Sisk, T. 'Peacemaking in Civil Wars: Obstacles, Options, and Opportunities', *Kroc Institute Occasional Paper* 20, 2 (2001).

Stedman, S.J. 'Implementing Peace Agreements in Civil Wars: Lessons and Recommendations for Policymakers', IPA Policy Paper on Peace Implementation (New York: International Peace Academy, May 2001).

Steenkamp, C.J. 'The Political Implications of Violence after Peace Accords: Civilian perceptions of physical insecurity in Northern Ireland and South Africa', PhD thesis submitted to the University of York (November 2006).

Sutterlin, J.S. 'Military Force in the Service of Peace', *Aurora Papers* 18 (1993).

The Lutheran World Federation, 'Inter-Faith Peace Summit: Rediscovering Indigenous Conflict-Resolution Practices', *The Lutheran World Federation: Lutheran World Information* (23 October 2002).

Tschirgi, N. 'Post-Conflict Peacebuilding Revisited', IPA Peacebuilding Forum, New York (7 October 2004).

Walter, B.F. *Designing Transitions from Violent Civil War*, IGCC Policy Paper 31 (San Diego CA: UC Institute on Global Conflict and Cooperation, 1998).

Williamson, J. 'What Should the Bank Think about the Washington Consensus?', Paper prepared as a background to the World Bank's *World Development Report 2000* (July 1999), Available at www.worldbank.org/research/journals/wbro/obsaug00/pdf/ (6)Williamson.pdf (Accessed on 17 December 2006).

Wood, E.J. 'Civil War Settlement: Modeling the Bases of Compromise', Paper presented at the 1999 Annual Meeting of the American Political Science Association (Philadelphia: 2–5 September 1999).

Zahar, M.J. 'The Problem of Commitment to Peace: Actors, Incentives and Choice in Peace Implementation', Paper presented to the Annual Meeting of the American Political Science Association (Washington DC: 31 August, 3 September 2000).

Zartman, I.W. 'Ripeness: The Hurting Stalemate and Beyond', Paper presented to the International Political Science World Congress (Quebec City: August 2000).

Journal articles

Aggestram, K. & C. Jönson, '(Un)ending conflict', *Millennium* XXXVI, 3 (1997) pp. 771–794.

Al-Azm, S. 'The view from Damascus...continued', *New York Review of Books*, XLVII, 13 (10 August 2000).

Al-Krenawi, A. & J.R. Graham, 'Conflict resolution through a traditional ritual among the Bedouin Arabs of the Negev', *Ethnology*, 38, 2 (1999) pp. 163–174.

Annan, K. 'Democracy as an international issue', *Global Governance*, 8, 2 (April–June 2002) pp. 134–142.

Anonymous, 'Human rights in peace negotiations', *Human Rights Quarterly*, 18 (1995) pp. 249–258.

Ayres, R.W. 'Mediating international conflicts: Is image change necessary?', *Journal of Peace Research*, 34 (1997) pp. 431–447.

Becker, J.A. 'A disappearing enemy: The image of the United States in Soviet political cartoons', *Journalism and Mass Communication Quarterly*, 73 (1996) pp. 609–619.

Bekoe, D.A. 'Toward a theory of peace agreement implementation: The case of Liberia', *Journal of Asian & African Studies*, 38 (2003) pp. 256–294

Bellamy, A. & P. Williams, 'Peace operations and global order', special issue of *International Peacekeeping*, 10, 4 (2004).

Bennett, W.L. 'Towards a theory of press-state relations in the United States', *Journal of Communications*, 10 (1990) pp. 103–125.

Berdal, M. & D. Keen, 'Violence and economic agendas in civil wars: Some policy implications', *Millennium*, 26, 3 (1988) pp. 795–821.

Berinsky, A.J. & D.R. Kinder, 'Making sense of issues through media frames: Understanding the Kosovo crisis', *Journal of Politics*, 68 (2006) pp. 640–656.

Breytenbach, B. 'Cuito Cuanavale revisited: Same outcomes, different consequences', *Africa Insight*, 27, 1 (1999) pp. 54–62.

Brosius, H. & P. Epp, 'Prototyping through key events: News selection in the case of violence against aliens and asylum seekers in Germany', *European Journal of Communications*, 10 (1995) pp. 391–412.

Burton, M. & J. Higley, 'Elite settlements', *American Sociological Review*, LII, 2 (1994) pp. 295–307.

Byrne, H. 'Trials and tribulations of justice reform in Guatemala', *LASA Forum*, XXXI, 1 (Spring 2000).

Cannings, K. 'The voice of the loyal manager: Distinguishing attachment from commitment', *Employee Responsibilities and Rights Journal*, 5, 3 (1992) p. 262.

Caplan, R. 'International authority and state building: The case of Bosnia and Herzegovina', *Global Governance* 10, 1 (2004).

Chappell, D.A. 'The Noumea accord: Decolonization without independence in New Caledonia?', *Pacific Affairs*, 72, 3 (1999) pp. 373–391.

Chatty, D., G. Crivello, & G. Lewando Hundt, 'Theoretical and methodological challenges of studying refugee children in the Middle East and North Africa: Young Palestinian, Afghan and Sahrawi refugees', *Journal of Refugee Studies*, 18, 4 (2005) pp. 387–409.

Chopra, J. & T. Hohe, 'Participatory intervention', *Global Governance*, 10, 3 (2004) pp. 289–304.

Clarke, I. 'Another double movement: The great transformation after the Cold War?', *Review of International Studies*, 27 (2001) pp. 237–255.

Darby, J. & J. Rae, 'Peace processes from 1988–1998: Changing patterns', *Ethnic Studies Report*, XVII, 1 (1999).

Day, G. & C. Freeman, 'Policekeeping is the key: Rebuilding the international security architecture of postwar Iraq', *International Affairs*, 79, 2 (2003) pp. 299–313.

Doyle, M. & N. Sambanis, 'International peacebuilding: A theoretical and quantitative analysis', *American Political Science Review*, 94, 4 (December 2000) pp. 779–802.

Fearon, J. 'Domestic political audiences and the escalation of international disputes', *American Political Science Review*, 88, 3 (September 1994) pp. 579–581.

Fisher, R.J. & L. Keashley, 'The potential complimentarity of mediation and consultation within a contingency model of third party consultation', *Journal of Peace Research*, 28, 1 (1991) pp. 21–42.

Fleischer, M. 'Cattle raiding and its correlates: The cultural-ecological consequences of market-oriented cattle raiding among the Kuria of Tanzania', *Human Ecology*, 26, 2 (1998) pp. 547–572.

Forsythe, D. 'Unrwa, the Palestine Refugees, and world politics: 1949–1969', *International Organization*, 25, 1 (1971) pp. 26–45.

Galtung, J. 'High road, low road: Charting the course of peace journalism', *Track Two*, 7 (1998) pp. 7–10.

Ghee-Son Lim, S. & J.K. Murnighan, 'Phases, deadlines and the bargaining process', *Organizational Behaviour and Human Decision Processes*, 58 (1994) pp. 153–171.

Goodby, J. 'When war won out: Bosnian peace plans before Dayton', *International Negotiation*, 3 (1996) pp. 501–523.

Goodhand, J. & D. Hulme, 'Understanding conflict and peace-building in the new world disorder', *Third World Quarterly*, 20, 1 (1999) pp. 13–26.

Gurr, T.R. 'Ethnic warfare on the wane', *Foreign Affairs*, 79, 3 (May/June 2000) pp. 52–64.

Harbom, L., S. Högbladh, & P. Wallensteen, 'Armed conflict and peace agreements', *Journal of Peace Research*, 43, 5 (2006) pp. 617–631.

Harland, D. 'Legitimacy and effectiveness in international administration', *Global Governance*, 10, 1 (2004) pp. 15–20.

Hartzell, C. & D. Rothchild, 'Political pacts as negotiated agreements: Comparing ethnic and non-ethnic cases', *International Negotiation*, 2 (1997) pp. 147–171.

Himmelfarb, S. 'Impact is the mantra: The "common ground" approach to the media', *Track Two*, 7 (1998) pp. 38–40.

Holiday, D. & W. Stanley, 'Building the peace: Preliminary lessons from El Salvador', *Journal of International Affairs*, 46, 2 (Winter 1993) pp. 427–429.

Hopkins, G. 'Somali community organizations in London and Toronto: Collaboration and effectiveness', *Journal of Refugee Studies*, 19, 3 (2006) pp. 361–380.

Ilesanmi, S.O. 'So that peace may reign: A study of Just Peacemaking experiments in Africa', *Journal of the Society of Christian Ethics*, 23 (2002) pp. 213–226.

Jaeger, S. 'Reconciliation and the mass media: The Coverage of the French–German Peace Process after World War II', *Conflict and Communication Online*, 2, 2 (2003).

Kahnerman, D. & A. Tversky, 'Prospect theory: An analysis of decisions under risk', *Econometrica*, IIIL, 3 (1979) pp. 263–291.

Kauffer Michel, E. 'Leadership and social organization: The integration of the Guatemalan refugees in Campeche, Mexico', *Journal of Refugee Studies*, 15, 4 (2002) pp. 359–387.

Kaufman, C. 'Possible and impossible solutions to ethnic civil wars', *International Security*, 20, 4 (1996) pp. 136–175.

Kepplinger, H.M. & J. Habermeir, 'The impact of key events on the presentation of reality', *European Journal of Communications*, 10 (1995) pp. 371–390.

Klatch, R. 'Of meanings and masters: Political symbolism and symbolic action', *Polity*, 21, 1 (Fall 1998) pp. 137–154.

Kleiboer, M. & P. t'Hart, 'Time to talk? Multiple perspectives on timing of international mediation', *Cooperation and Conflict*, 30 (1995) pp. 307–348.

Krznaric, R. 'Guatemalan returnees and the dilemma of political mobilization', *Journal of Refugee Studies*, 10, 1 (1997).

Lieberfeld, D. 'Conflict "ripeness" revisited: The South African and Israeli/Palestinian cases', *Negotiation Journal*, 15, 1 (1999) pp. 63–82.

Lijphart, A. 'Consociational democracy', *World Politics*, 21 (1969) pp. 207–225.

Lijphart, A. 'The framework document on Northern Ireland and the theory of power-sharing', *Government and Opposition*, 31, 3 (Summer 1996) pp. 267–274.

Loder, K. 'The Peace process in Mali', *Security Dialogue*, 28, 4 (1997) pp. 409–424.

Loughlin, J. 'The "Europe of the regions" and the federalization of Europe', *Publius: The Journal of Federalism* (Fall 1996) pp. 141–162.

Loughlin, J. 'Regional autonomy and state paradigm shift in western Europe', *Regional and Federal Studies*, 10, 2 (2000) pp. 10–34.

Loughlin, J. 'The "transformation" of governance: New directions in policy and politics', *Australian Journal of Politics and History*, 50, 1 (March 2004) pp. 8–22.

Loughlin, J. & D.L. Seiler, 'Le comité des Régions et la supranationalité en Europe', *Etudes Internationales* (Décembre 1999).

Lynch, J. Findings of the conflict and peace journalism Forum, Unpublished manuscript (Buckinghamshire: Tablow Court, 1998).

Manoff, R. 'Role plays: Potential media roles in conflict prevention and management', *Track Two*, 7 (1998) pp. 11–16.

Manoff, R. 'The media's role in preventing and moderating conflict', *Crossroads Global Report* (March/April 1997) pp. 24–27.

McCrudden, C. 'Mainstreaming Equality in the Governance of Northern Ireland', *Fordham International Law Journal*, 22 (1999) pp. 1696–1775.

Mac Ginty, R. 'Biting the bullet: Decommissioning in the transition from war to peace in Northern Ireland', *Irish Studies in International Affairs*, 10 (1999) pp. 237–247.

Mitchell, C. 'The right moments: Notes on four models of "ripeness"', *Paradigms*, 9, 2 (Winter 1995) pp. 38–52.

Mooradian, M. & D. Druckman, 'Hurting stalemate or mediation? The conflict over Nagorno-Marabakh, 1990–95', *Journal of Peace Research*, XXXVI, 6 (1999) pp. 709–727.

Nakaya, S. 'Women and gender equality in peace processes: From women at the negotiating table to post-war structural reforms in Guatemala and Somalia', *Global Governance*, 9, 4 (October–December 2003) pp. 459–476.

Nordstrom, C. 'A war dossier', *Public Culture*, 10, 2 (Winter 1998).

Oliver-Smith, A. 'Involuntary resettlement, resistance and political empowerment', *Journal of Refugee Studies*, 4, 2 (1991) pp. 132–49.

Orjuela, C. 'Building peace in Sri Lanka: A role for civil society?', *Journal Of Peace Research*, 40, 2 (2003) pp. 195–212.

Paris, R. 'The perils of liberal international peacebuilding', *International Security*, 22 (1997) pp. 54–89.

Power, S. 'Bystanders to genocide', *Atlantic Monthly*, 288, 2 (September 2001) pp. 84–108.

Preston, M. 'Stalemate and the termination of civil war: Rhodesia reassessed', *Journal of Peace Research*, 41, 1 (2004) pp. 65–88.

Putnam, R. 'Diplomacy and domestic politics: The logic of two-level games', *International Organization*, 42, 3 (Summer 1998) pp. 427–460.

Robinson, P. 'Theorizing the influence of media on world politics: Models of media influence on foreign policy', *European Journal of Media on World Politics*, 16 (2001) pp. 523–544.

Roth, A.E., J. Keith Murnighan, & Francoise Schoumaker, 'The deadline effect in bargaining: Some experimental evidence', *The American Economic Review*, 78 (September 1988) pp. 806–823.

Ruhl, J. 'The Guatemalan military since the peace accords: The fate of reform under Arzú and Portillo', *Latin American Politics and Society*, 46, 4 (Spring 2005), pp. 55–85.

Sala, M. 'Creating the "ripe moment" in the East Timor conflict', *Journal of Peace Research*, XXXIV, 4 (1997) pp. 449–466.

Saunders, C. 'Of treks, transitions and transitology', *South African Historical Journal*, 40 (May 1999).

Saunders, H.H. 'We need a larger theory of negotiation: The importance of the pre-negotiation phase', *Negotiation Journal*, 1, 1 (July 1985) pp. 249–262.

Shaw, M. 'Post-imperial and quasi-imperial: State and empire in the global era', *Millennium*, 31, 2 (2002) pp. 327–336.

Shinar, D. 'Media diplomacy and "peace talk": The Middle East and Northern Ireland', *International Communication Gazette*, 62 (2000) pp. 83–97.

Shinar, D. 'The peace process in cultural conflict: The role of the media', *Conflict and Communication Online*, 2 (2003) pp. 1–10.

Small, M. 'Influencing the decision-makers: The Vietnam experience', *Journal of Peace Research*, 24 (1987) pp. 185–198.

Spencer, G. 'Reporting inclusivity: The Northern Ireland women's coalition, the news media and the Northern Ireland peace process', *Irish Journal of Sociology*, 13, 2 (2004) pp. 43–65.

Spiegel, P. & P. Salama, 'War and mortality in Kosovo, 1998–99: An epidemiological testimony', *The Lancet*, 355 (2000) pp. 2204–2249.

Stedman, S.J. 'Spoiler problems in peace processes', *International Security*, 22, 2 (Fall 1997) pp. 5–53.

Steiner, H. 'Ideals and counter-ideals in the struggle over autonomy regimes', *Notre Dame Law Review*, 66 (1991) pp. 1539–1568.

Teitel, R. 'Transitional jurisprudence: The role of law in political transformation', *Yale Law Journal*, 106 (1997) pp. 2009–2080.

du Toit, T. 'Bargaining about bargaining: Inducing the self-negating prediction in deeply divided societies: The case of South Africa', *Journal of Conflict Resolution*, 33 (1989) pp. 210–233.

Touval, S. 'Coercive mediation on the road to Geneva', *International Negotiation*, 3 (1996) pp. 547–570. Utterwulghe, S. 'Conflict management in complex humanitarian situations: peacemaking and peacebuilding work with Angolan IDPs', *Journal of Refugee Studies*, 17, 2 (2004) pp. 222–242.

Verdirame, G. 'Human rights and refugees: The case of Kenya', *Journal of Refugee Studies*, 12 (1999) pp. 54–77.

Wall, J.A. 'Mediation: An analysis, review and proposed research', *Journal of Conflict Studies*, 25, 1 (March 1981) pp. 157–180.

Wall, J.A. & A. Lynn, 'Mediation: A current review', *Journal of Conflict Resolution*, 37, 1 (March 1993) pp. 160–194.

Wallensteen, P. & M. Sollenberg, 'Armed conflict 1989–1998', *Journal of Peace Research*, 36, 5 (1999) pp. 593–606.

Walter, B. 'The critical barrier to civil war settlement', *International Organization* (Summer 1997), pp. 335–365.

Wantchekon, L. 'On the nature of first democratic elections', *Journal of Conflict Resolution*, 43, 2 (1999) pp. 230–243.

Wehr, P. & J.P. Lederach, 'Mediating conflict in central America', *Journal of Peace Research*, 28, 1 (February 1991) pp. 85–98.

Wolfsfeld, G. 'Promoting peace through the news media: Some initial lessons from the Oslo peace process', *Harvard International Journal of Press/Politics*, 2 (1997) pp. 52–70.

Wolfsfeld, G. 'Fair weather friends: The varying role of the media in the Arab–Israeli peace process', *Political Communication*, 14 (1997) pp. 29–48.

Wolfsfeld, G., R. Khouri, & Y. Peri, 'News about the Other in Jordan and Israel: Does Peace make a Difference?', *Political Communication*, 19 (2002) pp. 89–210.

Woodward, S. 'Avoiding another Cyprus or Israel', *Brookings Review* (Winter 1998) pp. 45–48.

Wright, Q. 'The escalation of conflicts', *Journal of Conflict Resolution*, IX, 4 (1965) pp. 434–449.

Books and chapters in books

Adams, G. *Selected Writings* (Dingle: Brandon Press, 1997).

Adebajo, A. 'Liberia: A Warlord's Peace', in S. Stedman, D. Rothchild, & E. Cousens (eds), *Ending Civil Wars: The Implementation of Peace Agreements* (Boulder CO & London: Lynne Rienner, 2002) pp. 599–630.

Adelman, H. & G. Rao, *War and Peace in Zaire/Congo: Analyzing and Evaluating Intervention, 1996–1997* (Trenton NJ & Asmara: Africa World Press, 2004).

Age, Eknes, Jarat Chopra & Toralv Nordbo, *Fighting for Hope in Somalia* (Oslo: NUPI, 1995).

Allen-Nan, S. Complimentarity and Coordination of Conflict Resolution Efforts in the Conflicts in Abkhazia, South Ossetia and TransDniestria (PhD Dissertation, George Mason University, 1999).

Alter, P. *Nationalism*, 2nd edn (London: Edward Arnold, 1994).

Anderson, B. *Imagined Communities: Reflections on the Origin and Spread of Nationalism* (Cambridge: Cambridge University Press, 1983).

Arnson, C. (ed.), *Comparative Peace Processes in Latin America* (Washington DC: Woodrow Wilson Center, 1999).

Arrow, K. *Social Change and Individual Values* (Yale: Yale University Press, 1963).

Art, R.J. & P.M. Cronin (eds), *The United States and Coercive Diplomacy* (Washington DC: United States Institute of Peace, 2003).

Atkinson, D. 'Brokering a Miracle? The Multiparty Negotiating Forum', in S. Friedman & D. Atkinson (eds), *South African Review: 7 The Small Miracle – South Africa's Negotiated Settlement* (Johannesburg: Ravan Press, 1994) pp. 13–43, at 22.

Azar, E.E. *The Management of Protracted Social Conflict* (Aldershot: Dartmouth Publishing, 1990).

Azpuru, D., L. Blanco, R. Córdova, C. Ramos, & A. Zapata, *Construyendo la democracia en sociedades posconflicto: Guatemala y El Salvador en perspectiva comparada* (Ottawa and Guatemala City: IDRC Publishers and F&G Editores, 2007).

Baker, J. & T. deFrank, *The Politics of Diplomacy* (New York: Putnam, 1995).

Barber, J. & J. Barratt, *South Africa's Foreign Policy – The Search for Status and Security 1945–1988* (Johannesburg: Southern, 1990).

Barker, G. *Dying to Be Men: Youth, Masculinity and Social Exclusion* (London: Routledge, 2005).

Barry, B. 'Exit, Voice, and Loyalty', in B. Barry, *Democracy and Power: Essays in Political Theory, I* (Oxford: Clarendon Press, 1991) pp. 187–221.

Barth, F. (ed.), *Ethnic Groups and Boundaries* (Boston: Little, Brown and Company, 1976).

Bayart, J.F. *The State in Africa: The Politics of the Belly* (London: Longman, 1993).

Bayley, D. *Patterns of Policing: A Comparative International Analysis* (New Brunswick NJ: Rutgers University Press, 1985).

Bell, C. *Peace Agreements and Human Rights* (Oxford: Oxford University Press, 2000).

Bell, C. *Negotiating Justice? Human Rights and Peace Agreements* (New York: International Council on Human Rights Policy, 2006).

Benvenisti, M. 'The Peace Process and Intercommunal Strife', in H. Giliomee & J. Gagiano (eds), *The Elusive Search for Peace: South Africa, Israel and Northern Ireland* (Cape Town: Oxford University Press, 1990).

Bercovitch, J. & J.Z. Rubin (eds), *Mediation in International Relations* (New York: St. Martin's Press, 1992).

Blitz, B. 'Serbia's War Lobby: Diaspora Groups and Western Elites', in S. Mestrovic & T. Cushman (eds), *This Time We Knew. Western Responses to Genocide in Bosnia* (New York: New York University Press, 1996) pp. 187–243.

Bloomfield, D., C. Nupen, & P. Harris, 'Negotiation Process', in P. Harris & B. Reilly (eds), *Democracy and Deep-rooted Conflict: Options for Negotiators* (Sweden: Institute for Democracy and Electoral Assistance, 1998).

Bose, S. *Bosnia after Dayton: Nationalist Partition and International Intervention* (Oxford: Oxford University Press, 2002).

Brams, S. *Negotiation Games* (New York: Routledge, 1990).

Brams, S. *Theory of Moves* (Cambridge: Cambridge University Press, 1994).

Brass, P.R. *Theft of an Idol: Text and Context in the Representation of Collective Violence* (Princeton NJ: Princeton University Press, 1997).

Briggs, J.L. 'Conflict Management in a Modern Inuit Community', in P. Schweitzer, M. Biesele, & R. Hitchcock (eds), *Hunters and Gatherers in the Modern World* (New York: Berghahn, 2000) pp. 110–124.

Brown, M.E. (ed.), 'Internal Conflict and International Action', in M.E. Brown, *The International Dimensions of Internal Conflict* (Cambridge MA: MIT Press, 1996) pp. 235–264.

Brynen, R. *A Very Political Economy Peacebuilding and Foreign Aid in the West Bank and Gaza* (Boulder CO: Lynne Rienner, 2000).

Burg, S. 'The International Community and the Yugoslav Crisis', in M. Esman & S. Telhami (eds), *International Organizations and Ethnic Conflict* (Ithaca NY: Cornell University Press, 1995).

Burton, J. *Deviance, Terrorism and War: The Process of Solving Unsolved Social and Political Problems* (New York: St. Martin's Press, 1979).

Campbell, J. *Successful Negotiation: Trieste* (Princeton NJ: Princeton University Press, 1976).

Cassese, A. *Self Determination of Peoples: A Legal Reappraisal* (Cambridge: Cambridge University Press, 1998).

Chadda, M. 'Between Consociationalism and Control: Sri Lanka', in U. Schneckener & S. Wolff (eds), *Managing and Settling Ethnic Conflicts* (London: C. Hurst & Co, 2004).

Chandler, D. *From Kosovo to Kabul: Human Rights and International Intervention* (London: Pluto, 2002).

Chesterman, S. *You the People: The United Nations, Transitional Administration and Statebuilding* (Oxford: Oxford University Press, 2004).

Chingono, M.F. *The State, Violence and Development* (Brookfield: Avebury, 1996).

Chirot, D. & M.E.P. Seligman (eds), *Ethnopolitical Warfare: Causes, Consequences, and Possible Solutions* (Washington DC: American Psychological Association, 2001).

Cliffe, L. et al., *The Transition to Independence in Namibia* (Boulder CO: Lynne Rienner, 1994).

Coakley, J. (ed.), *The Territorial Management of Ethnic Conflict* (London: Frank Cass, 1993).

Cohen, R. *Theatre of Power: The Art of Diplomatic Signaling* (London: Longman, 1987).

Cohen, Y. *Media Diplomacy: The Foreign Office in the Mass Communications Age* (London: Frank Cass, 1986).

Conversi, D. *The Basques, the Catalans and Spain: Alternative Routes to Nationalist Mobilisation* (London: Hurst, 1997).

Cooke, W. & U. Kothari (eds), *Participation: The New Tyranny?* (London: Zed, 2004).

Cooper, C. et al., *Race Relations Survey 1992/93* (Johannesburg: South African Institute of Race Relations, 1993).

Cooper, R. *The Breaking of Nations* (London: Atlantic Books, 2003).

Corado Figueroa, H. 'Los procesos de desmovilización de las Fuerzas Armadas', in F. Aguilar Urbina (ed.), *Desmovilización, desmilitarización y democratización en Centroamérica* (San José, Costa Rica: Fundación Arias para la Paz y el Progreso Humanos y Centro Internacional para los Derechos Humanos y el Desarrollo Democrático, 1994).

Corbin, J. *The Norway Channel* (New York: Atlantic Monthly Press, 1994).

Cornell, S. & D. Hartmann, *Ethnicity and Race: Making Identities in a Changing World* (Thousand Oaks CA: Pine Forge Press, 1998).

Costa, G. *La Policía Nacional Civil de El Salvador (1990–1997)* (San Salvador: UCA Editores, 1999).

Costa, G. 'Demilitarizing Public Security: Lessons from El Salvador', in M. Studemeister (ed.), *El Salvador: Implementation of the Peace Accords* (Washington DC: United States Institute of Peace, 2001), pp. 20–26.

Cousens, E. & C. Kumar, *Peacebuilding as Politics* (Boulder CO: Lynne Rienner, 2001).

Crocker, C.A. *High Noon in Southern Africa – Making Peace in a Rough Neighborhood* (Johannesburg: Jonathan Ball, 1992).

Crocker, C., Chester, A., Fen Osler Hampson & Pamela Aall (eds), *Herding Cats: The Management of Complex International Mediation* (Washington DC: USIP, 1999).

Cruise O'Brien, C. *The Siege: The Saga of Israel and Zionism* (New York: Simon and Schuster, 1986).

Darby, J. *The Effects of Violence on Peace Processes* (Washington DC: United States Institute of Peace, 2001).

Darby, J. & R. Mac Ginty (eds), *The Management of Peace Processes* (New York: St. Martin's Press, 2000).

de Samarasinghe, S.W.R. & R. Coughlan (eds), *Economic Dimensions of Ethnic Conflict* (London: Pinter Publishers, 1991).

Diamond, L. 'Democracy in Latin America', in T. Farer (ed.), *Beyond Sovereignty: Collectively Defending Democracy in the Americas* (Baltimore MD: Johns Hopkins University Press, 1996).

Doubell, L. 'SWAPO in Office', in C. Leys & J.S. Saul (eds), *Namibia's Liberation Struggle – The Two-Edged Sword* (London: James Currey, 1995) pp. 171–195, at 176.

Duffield, M. *Global Governance and the New Wars* (London: Zed Books, 2001).

Eide, A. *A Democratic South Africa? Constitutional Engineering in a Divided Society* (Berkeley CA: University of California Press, 1991).

El Bushra, J. & J. Gardner (eds), *Somalia: The Untold Story – The War through the Eyes of Somali Women* (London: Pluto Press, 2004).

Ellis, S. *The Mask of Anarchy: The Destruction of Liberia and the Religious Dimension of an African Civil War* (New York: New York University Press, 1999).

Esman, M.J. *Ethnic Politics* (Ithaca NY: Cornell University Press, 1994).

Fearon, K. *Women's Work: The Story of the Northern Ireland Women's Coalition* (Belfast: Blackstaff Press, 1999).

Fisher, R. *Inter-Active Conflict Resolution* (New York: Syracuse University Press, 1997).

Fisher, R. & W. Ury, *Getting to Yes* (New York: Bantam, 1991).

Frazer, J. 'Sustaining Civilian Control: Armed Counterweights in Regime Stability in Africa', (PhD Dissertation in political science, Stanford University, 1994).

Friedman, S. (ed.), *The Long Journey – South Africa's Quest for a Negotiated Settlement* (Johannesburg: Ravan Press, 1993).

Friedman, S. & D. Atkinson (eds), *South African Review: 7 The Small Miracle – South Africa's Negotiated Settlement* (Johannesburg: Ravan Press, 1994).

Friedman, S. & L. Stack, 'The Magic Moment – The 1994 Election', in S. Friedman, & D. Atkinson (eds), *South African Review 7: The Small Miracle – South Africa's Negotiated Settlement* (Johannesburg: Ravan Press, 1994). pp. 301–330.

Fukuyama, F. *State Building: Governance and Order in the Twenty First Century* (London: Profile, 2004).

Galama, A. & P. van Tongeren (eds), *Towards Better Peacebuilding Practice: On Lessons Learned, Evaluation Practices and Aid and Conflict* (European Centre for Conflict Prevention, 2002).

Gamba, V. (ed.), *Society under Siege: Crime, Violence and Illegal Weapons* (Johannesburg: Institute for Security Studies, The Towards Collaborative Peace Series, Volume I, 1997).

Gatti, M. *The Secret Conversations of Henry Kissinger* (New York: Bantham, 1976).

Gberie, L. *A Dirty War in West Africa: The RUF and the Destruction of Sierra Leone* (Bloomington IN: Indiana University Press, 2005).

Geldenhuys, D. *Foreign Political Engagement – Remaking States in the Post-Cold War World* (London: Macmillan, 1998).

Geldenhuys, J. *A General's Story – From an Era of War and Peace* (Johannesburg: Jonathan Ball, 1995).

Ghai, Y. *Hong Kong's New Constitutional Order: The Transfer of Sovereignty and the Basic Law* (Hong Kong: Hong Kong University Press, 1997).

Ghai, Y. 'Decentralisation and the Accommodation of Ethnic Diversity', in C. Young (ed.), *Ethnic Diversity and Public Policy: A Comparative Inquiry* (Basingstoke: Macmillan, 1998).

Ghai, Y. (ed.), *Autonomy and Ethnicity: Negotiating Claims in Multi-ethnic States* (Cambridge: Cambridge University Press, 2000).

Ghai, Y. 'Autonomy as a Strategy for Diffusing Conflict', in P. Stern & D. Druckman (eds), *International Conflict Resolution After the Cold War* (Washington DC: National Academy Press, 2000).

Ghai, Y. 'Autonomy Regimes and Conflict Resolution' (Washington DC: National Research Council, Committee on International Conflict Resolution, 2004).

Giddens, A. *The Third Way: A Renewal of Social Democracy* (Malden MA: Polity Press, 1998).

Glazer, D. & P. Moynihan (eds), *Ethnicity: Theory and Experience* (Cambridge MA: Harvard University Press, 1975).

Gowing, N. *Media Coverage: Help or Hindrance in Conflict Prevention?* (New York: Carnegie Commission on Preventing Deadly Conflicts, 1996).

Greenfeld, L. *Nationalism: Five Roads to Modernity* (Cambridge MA: Harvard University Press, 1992).

Guelke, A. 'Comparatively Peaceful: South Africa, the Middle East and Northern Ireland', in M. Cox, A. Guelke, & F. Stephen (eds), *A Farewell to Arms? From 'Long War' to Long Peace in Northern Ireland* (Manchester: Manchester University Press, 2000).

Gutierrez-Villalobos, S. 'The Media and Reconciliation in Central America', in E. Gilboa (ed.), *Media and Conflict: Framing Issues, Making Policy, Shaping Opinions* (Ardsley: Transnational Publishers, 2002) pp. 295–309.

Haas, R. *Conflicts Unending* (Yale: Yale University Press, 1990).

Hackett, R. *News and Dissent: The Press and Politics of Peace in Canada* (Norwood NJ: Ablex, 1991).

Hale, S. 'The Soldier and the State; Post-Liberation Women: The Case of Eritrea', in M.R. Waller & J. Rzcenga (eds), *Frontline Feminisms: Women, War and Resistance* (New York: Routledge, 2000).

Hallin, D. *The Uncensored War* (New York: Oxford University Press, 1986).

Hampson, F.O. *Nurturing Peace: Why peace Settlements Succeed or Fail* (Washington DC: United States Institute of Peace Press, 1996).

Hannum, H. *Autonomy, Sovereignty and Self-Determination: The Accommodation of Conflicting Rights* (Philadelphia PA: University of Pennsylvania Press, 1990).

Hannum, H. & E. Babbitt (eds), *Negotiating Self-Determination* (Lanham MD: Lexington Books, 2006).

Hardin, R. *One for All: The Logic of Group Conflict* (Princeton NJ: Princeton University Press, 1995).

Harris, P. & B. Reilly (eds), *Democracy and Deep-Rooted Conflict: Options for Negotiators* (Stockholm: International Institute for Democracy and Electoral Assistance, 1998).

Hayner, P. *Unspeakable Truths: Confronting State Terror and Atrocity* (New York: Routledge, 2001).

Héraud, G. *L'Europe des Ethnies* (Paris: Presses d'Europe, 1964).

Hill, F. 'How and When Has Security Council Resolution 1325 (2000) on Women, Peace and Security Issues Impacted Negotiations outside the Security Council' (Masters Thesis, Uppsala University Programme of International Studies, 2004–2005).

Hirsch, J. *Sierra Leone: Diamonds and the Struggle for Democracy* (Boulder CO & London: Lynne Rienner, 2001).

Hirschman, A.O. *Exit, Voice, and Loyalty: Responses to Decline in Firms, Organizations, and States* (Cambridge MA: Harvard University Press, 1970).

Hirshfeld, L.A. *Race in the Making: Cognition, Culture, and the Child's Construction of Human Kinds* (Cambridge MA: MIT Press, 1996).

Hobsbawm, E.J. *Nations and Nationalism since 1780* (Cambridge: Cambridge University Press, 1990).

Hoffman, M. 'Third Party Mediation and Conflict Resolution in the Post-Cold War World', in J. Baylis & N.J. Rengger (eds), *Dilemmas of World Politics* (Oxford: Clarendon Press, 1992).

Holbrooke, R. *To End a War* (New York: Random House, 1998).

Horowitz, D.L. *Ethnic Groups in Conflict* (Berkeley CA: University of California Press, 1985).

Horowitz, D.L. *The Deadly Ethnic Riot* (Berkeley CA: University of California Press, 2001).

Human Rights Watch, *Playing the Communal Card: Communal Violence and Human Rights* (New York City: Human Rights Watch, 1995).

Hume, C. *Mozambique's War: The Role of Mediation and Good Offices* (Washington DC: USIP Press, 1994).

Huntington, S.P. *The Third Wave: Democratization in the Late Twentieth Century* (Norman OK: University of Oklahoma Press, 1991).

Ikle, F. *How Nations Negotiate* (New York: Harper & Row, l964).

International Crisis Group, *Is Dayton Failing? Bosnia Four Years after the Peace Agreement* (Sarajevo: International Crisis Group, 1999).

International Institute for Strategic Studies, *The Military Balance, 2003–2004* (London: Oxford University Press, 2003).

Isaacs, H.R. *Idols of the Tribe: Group Identity and Political Change* (New York: Harper & Row, 1975).

Jabri, V. *Mediating Conflict: Decision-making and Western Intervention in Namibia* (Manchester: Manchester University Press, 1990).

Jeong, H.W. *Peacebuilding in Postconflict Socities* (Boulder CO: Lynne Rienner, 2004).

Jonas, S. *Of Centaurs and Doves, Guatemala's Peace Process* (Boulder CO: Westview Press, 2000).

Kane-Berman, J. (ed.), *South Africa Survey 2004/2005* (Johannesburg: South African Institute of Race Relations, 2006).

Keating, M., J. Loughlin, & K. Deschouwer, *Culture, Institutions and Regional Development: A Study of Eight European Regions* (Cheltenham: Edward Elgar, 2003).

Kecskemeti, P. 'Political Rationality in Ending War', in W.T.R. Fox (ed.), *How Wars End* (Philadelphia PA: The Annals of the American Academy of Political and Social Science, 1970) pp. 105–115.

Kenyon Lischer, S. *Dangerous Sanctuaries: Refugee Camps, Civil War, and the Dilemmas of Humanitarian Aid* (Ithaca NY: Cornell University Press, 2005).

Kissinger, H. *The White House Years* (London: Weidenfeld & Nicolson, 1979).

Kleiboer, M. *International Mediation: The Multiple Realities of Third Party Intervention* (Boulder CO: Lynne Rienner, 1997).

Kriesberg, L. & S.J. Thornson (eds), *Timing the De-escalation of International Conflicts* (Syracuse NY: Syracuse University Press, 1991).

Kruger, B.W. Prenegotiation in South Africa (1985–1993) – A Phaseological Analysis of the Transitional Negotiations, Unpublished MA thesis (University of Stellenbosch, 1998).

Kymlicka, W. *Multicultural Citizenship: A Liberal Theory of Minority Rights* (Oxford: Oxford University Press, 1995).

Lal, B.V. & T.R. Vakatora (eds), *Fiji and the World* (Fiji: University of the South Pacific, 1997).

Lapidoth, R. *Autonomy: Flexible Solutions to Ethnic Conflicts* (Washington DC: United Sates Institute of Peace Press, 1996).

Ledeen, M.A. 'Why Peace Processes Do Not Work: A Machiavellian View', in L.S. Germani & D.R. Kaarthikeyan (eds), *Pathways Out of Terrorism and Insurgency: The Dynamics of Terrorist Violence and Peace Processes* (New Delhi: New Dawn Press, 2005).

Lederach, J.P. *Building Peace: Sustainable Reconciliation in Divided Societies* (Washington DC: United States Institute of Peace, 1997).

Lederach, J.P. 'Qualities of Practice for Reconciliation', in R. Helmick (ed.), *Reconciliation* (New York: Templeton Press, 2001).

Lederman, J. *Battle Lines: The American Media and the Intifada* (New York: Henry Holt, 1992).

Leibowitz, A.H. *Embattled Island: Palau's Struggle for Independence* (Westport CT: Praeger, 1996).

Lemarchand, R. *Burundi: Ethnocide as Discourse and Practice* (Washington DC: Woodrow Wilson Center Press, 1994).

Letamendia, F. & J. Loughlin, 'Peace in the Basque Country and Corsica', in M. Cox, A. Guelke, & F. Stephen (eds), *A Farewell to Arms? From 'Long War' to Long Peace in Northern Ireland* (Manchester: Manchester University Press, 2000).

Leys, C. & J.S. Saul (eds), *Namibia's Liberation Struggle – The Two-Edged Sword* (London: James Currey, 1995).

Lieberfield, D. *Talking with the Enemy: Negotiation and Threat Perception in South Africa and Israel/Palestine* (New York: Praeger, 1999).

Lijphart, A. *Democracy in Plural Societies* (New Haven CT: Yale University Press, 1977).

Lijphart, A. 'The Power-Sharing Approach', in J.V. Montville (ed.), *Conflict and Peacemaking in Multiethnic Societies* (New York: Lexington Books, 1991), pp. 491–509.

Loughlin, J. *Regionalism and Ethnic Nationalism in France: A Case Study of Corsica* (Florence: European University Institute, 1989).

Loughlin, J. *Subnational Democracy in the European Union: Challenges and Opportunities* (Oxford: Oxford University Press, 2001).

Loughlin, J., C. Olivesi, & F. Daftary (eds), *Autonomies Insulaires: vers une politique de différence pour la Corse?* (Ajaccio: Editions Albiana, 1999).

MacGaffey, J. *The Real Economy of Zaire: The Contributions of Smuggling and Other Unofficial Activities to National Wealth* (Philadelphia PA: University of Pennsylvania Press, 1991).

MacGaffey, J. & R. Bazanguissa-Ganga, *Congo–Paris: Transnational Traders on the Margins of the Law* (Bloomington IN: Indiana University Press, 2000).

McGarry, J. & B. O'Leary, *The Politics of Ethnic Conflict Regulation* (New York: Routledge, 1993).

McGarry, J. & B. O'Leary, *Explaining Northern Ireland: Broken Images* (Oxford: Blackwell, 1995).

Mac Ginty, R. *No War, No Peace: The Rejuvenation of Stalled Peace Processes and Peace Accords* (Basingstoke: Palgrave, 2006).

Mac Ginty, R. 'Post-Accord Crime', in J. Darby (ed.), *Violence and Reconstruction* (Notre Dame IN: Notre Dame University Press, 2006) pp. 101–119.

Mac Ginty, R. & J. Darby, *Guns and Government: The Management of the Northern Ireland Peace Process* (London: Palgrave, 2002).

Maier, K. *Angola: Promises and Lies* (Rivonia UK: William Waterman, 1996).

Makovsky, D. *Making peace with the PLO: The Rabin Government's Road to the Oslo Process* (Boulder CO: Westview Press, 1995).

Mallie, E. & D. McKittrick, *The Fight for Peace: The Secret Story behind the Irish Peace Process* (London: Heinemann, 1996).

Manlow, R. *The Mass Media and Social Violence: Is There a Role for the Media in Preventing and Moderating Ethnic, National, and Religious Conflict?* (New York: Center for War, Peace, and the News Media, New York University, 1996).

Manoff, R. The Mass Media and Social Violence: Is There a Role for the Media in Preventing and Moderating Ethnic, National, and Religious Conflict? Unpublished Paper (New York: Center for War, Peace, and the News Media, New York University, 1996).

Marx, A.W. *Making Race and Nation: A Comparison of South Africa, the United States and Brazil* (Cambridge: Cambridge University Press, 1998).

Mees, L. 'The Basque Peace Process, Nationalism and Political Violence', in J. Darby & R. Mac Ginty (eds), *The Management of Peace Processes* (London: Macmillan, 2000).

Miall, H., O. Ramsbotham, & T. Woodhouse, *Contemporary Conflict Resolution* (Cambridge: Polity Press, 2005).

Mitchell, C. *The Structure of International Conflict* (London: Macmillan, 1981).

Mitchell, C. 'External Peace-Making Initiatives and Intranational Conflict', in M.I. Midlarsky (ed.), *The Internationalization of Communal Strife* (New York: Routledge, 1992).

Mitchell, C. 'The Process and Stages of Mediation: Two Sudanese Cases', chapter. 6 in D.R. Smock (ed.), Making War and Waging Peace (Washington DC: USIP Press, 1993) pp. 121–148.

Mitchell, C. *Gestures of Conciliation* (London: Macmillan, 2000).

Mitchell, G. *Making peace* (New York: Knopf, 1999).

Moreno, L. *Federalizing the Spanish State* (London: Frank Cass, 2000).

Moses, R.L. *Freeing the Hostages* (Pittsburgh PA: University of Pittsburgh Press, 1996).

Naylor, R.T. *Wages of Crime: Black Markets, Illegal Finance, and the Underworld Economy* (Ithaca NY: Cornell University Press, 2005).

Ngugi, W.T. *Moving the Centre: The Struggle for Cultural Freedom* (London: James Currey, 1993).

Nordquist, K.J. 'Boundary Disputes: Drawing the Line', in Zartman (ed.), *Preventive Diplomacy: Avoiding Conflict Escalation* (Lanham MD: Rowman & Littlefield, 2000).

Nordstrom, C. *A Different Kind of War Story* (Philadelphia PA: University of Pennsylvania Press, 1997).

Nordstrom, C. *Shadows of War: Violence, Power, and International Profiteering in the Twenty-first Century* (Berkeley CA: University of California Press, 2004).

Nordstrom, C. *Global Outlaws: Crime, Money and Power in the Contemporary World* (Berkeley CA: University of California Press, 2007).

Norlen, T. *A Study of the Ripe Moment for Conflict Resolution and Its Applicability to Two Periods in the Israeli–Palestinian Conflict* (Uppsala: Uppsala University Conflict Resolution Program, 1995).

O'Hanlon, M. *Saving Lives with Force: Military Criteria for Humanitarian Intervention* (Washington DC: The Brookings Institution Press, 1997).

Ohlson, T. & S. Stedman, *The New Is Not Yet Born* (Washington DC: Brookings, 1994).

Olson, M. *The Logical of Collective Action* (New York: Schocken, 1965).

Olzack, S. & J. Nagel (eds), *Competitive Ethnic Relations* (Orlando FL: Academic Press, 1986).

Omi, M. & H. Winant, *Racial Formation in the United States from the 1960s to the 1990s* (New York: Routledge, 1994).

O'Neill, W. *Kosovo: An Unfinished Peace* (Boulder CO: Lynne Rienner, 2002).

Paris, R. 'Wilson's Ghost: The Faulty Assumptions of Postconflict Peacebuilding', in C.A. Crocker, F.O. Hampson, & P. Aall, *Turbulent Peace: The Challenges of Managing International Conflict* (Washington DC: United States Institute of Peace Press, 2001) pp. 765–784.

Paris, R. *At War's End* (Cambridge: Cambridge University Press, 2004).

Pásara, L. *Paz ,ilusión y cambio en Guatemala: el proceso de paz, sus actores, logros y límites* (Guatemala City: Universidad Rafael Landívar, Instituto de Investigaciones Jurídicas, 2003).

Popkin, M. *Peace Without Justice* (University Park PA: Pennsylvania State University Press, 2000).

Posen, B. 'The Security Dilemma and Ethnic Conflict', in Michael Brown (ed.), *Ethnic Conflict and International Security* (Princeton NJ: Princeton University Press, 1993).

Princen, T. 'Mediation by a Transnational Organization: The Case of the Vatican', chapter 7 in J. Bercovitch & J.Z. Rubin (eds), *Mediation in International Relations* (New York: St. Martin's Press, 1992) pp. 149–175.

Pruitt, D. & P. Olczak, 'Approaching to Resolving Seemingly Intractable Conflict', in B. Bunker & J. Rubin (eds), *Conflict, Cooperation and Justice* (New York: Jossey-Bass, 1995).

Prunier, G. *The Rwanda Crisis: History of a Genocide* (New York: Columbia University Press, 1995).

Przeworski, A. *Democracy and the Market* (Cambridge: Cambridge University Press, 1991).

Pugh, M. 'Bosnia and Herzegovina in South-East Europe', in Pugh M. & N. Cooper, & J. Goodhand (eds),*War Economies in Their Regional Context: The Challenge of Transformation* (Boulder CO: Lynne Rienner, 2003).

Pugh, M. & N. Cooper with J. Goodhand, *War Economies in Regional Context: The Challenges of Transformation* (Boulder CO: Lynne Rienner, 2004).

Quandt, W. *Camp David* (Washington DC: Brookings, 1986).

Rabinovich, I. *The Brink of Peace: The Israeli–Syrian Negotiations* (Princeton NJ: Princeton University Press, 1998).

Rabushka, A. & K.A. Shepsle, *Politics in Plural Society: A Theory of Political Instability* (Columbus OH: Charles E. Merrill Publishing Company, 1972).

Reilly, B. *Democracy in Divided Societies: Electoral Engineering for Conflict Management* (Cambridge: Cambridge University Press, 2001).

Reilly, B. & A. Reynolds, 'Electoral Systems and Conflict in Divided Societies', in P. Stern & D. Druckman (eds), *International Conflict Resolution after the Cold War* (Washington DC: National Academy Press, 2000).

Richmond, O.P. *Maintaining Order, Making Peace* (London: Palgrave, 2002).

Rieff, D. *A Bed for the Night* (London: Vintage, 2002).

Roach, C. 'Information and Culture in War and Peace: Overview', in C. Roach (ed.), *Communication and Culture in War and Peace* (Newbury Park CA: Sage, 1993).

Roeder, P. & D. Rothchild (eds), *Sustainable Peace: Power and Democracy after Civil War* (Ithaca NY: Cornell University Press, 2005).

Rothchild, D. *Managing Ethnic Conflict in Africa* (Washington DC: Brookings, 1997).

Rothchild, D. & P. Roeder (eds), *Sustainable Peace: Power and Democracy after Civil Wars* (Ithaca NY: Cornell University Press, 2005).

Rothstein, R. *After the Peace: Resistance and Reconciliation* (Boulder CO: Lynne Rienner, 1999).

Rubin, J.Z. 'The Timing of Ripeness and the Ripeness of Timing', in L. Kriesberg & S.J. Thornson (eds), *Timing the De-escalation of International Conflicts* (New York: Syracuse University Press, 1991).

Ryan, C. *Prime Time Activism: Media Strategies for Grassroots Organizing* (Boston MA: South End Press, 1991).

Said, E.W. *Peace and Its Discontents* (London: Vintage, 1995).

Said, E.W. *The End of the Peace Process* (New York: Pantheon, 2000).

Samuels, R. et al., *Political Generations and Political Development* (Boston: Lexington, 1977).

Saravanamuttu, P. 'Sri Lanka: The Intractability of Ethnic Conflict', in J. Darby & R. Mac Ginty (eds), *The Management of Peace Processes* (London: Macmillan, 2000) pp. 195–227.

Saunders, H. *A Public Peace Process: Sustained Dialogue to Transform Racial and Ethnic Conflicts* (Basingstoke: Palgrave, 2001).

Savir, U. *The Process* (New York: Randon House, 1998).

Schulz, H.L. *The Palestinian Diaspora: Formation of Identities and Politics of Homeland* (London & New York: Routledge, 2003).

Seegers, A. *The Military in the Making of Modern South Africa* (London: I.B.Tauris, 1996).

Sen, A. *Collective Choice and Social Welfare* (San Francisco CA: Holden-Day, 1970).

Serfaty, S. (ed.), *The Mass Media and Foreign Policy* (NewYork.: St. Martin's Press. 1991).

Shaw, R.P. & Y. Wong, *Genetic Seeds of Warfare: Evolution, Nationalism, and Patriotism* (Boston: Unwin Hyman, 1989).

Shear, J. 'Riding the Tiger: The UN and Cambodia', in W.J. Durch (ed.), *UN Peacekeeping, American Policy, and the Uncivil Wars of the 1990s* (New York: St. Martin's Press, 1996) pp. 170–172.

Sisk, T. *Power Sharing and International Mediation in Ethnic Conflicts* (Washington DC: United States Institute of Peace Press, 1995).

Sisk, T.D. *Democratization in South Africa – The Elusive Social Contract* (Princeton NJ: Princeton University Press, 1995).

Smith, A.D. *The Ethnic Origin of Nations* (Oxford: Basil Blackwell, 1986).

Smith, D. 'Women, War and Peace', in I. Breines, D. Gierycz, & B. Reardon (eds), *Towards a Women's Agenda for a Culture of Peace* (Paris: UNESCO, 1999), chapter 3.

Smith, M. *Peacekeeping in East Timor* (Colorado: Lynne Rienner, 2003).

Smock, D.R. (ed.), *Making War and Waging Peace* (Washington DC: USIP Press, 1993).

Snyder, J. *From Voting to Violence* (London: W.W. Norton, 2000).

Somers, R. *Jewish Displaced Persons in Camp Bergen-Belsen 1945–1950: The Unique Photo Album of Zippy Orlin* (Seattle WA: University of Washington Press & Netherlands Institute for War Documentation, 2004).

Soros, G. *The Crisis of Global Capitalism* (London: LittleBrown, 1998).

Spear, J. 'Demobilization and Disarmament: Key Implementation Issues', in S.J. Stedman, D. Rothchild, & E.M. Cousens (eds), *Ending Civil Wars: Volume II.* (Princeton NJ: Princeton University Press, 2004).

Spence, S., M. Lanchin, & G. Thale, *From Elections to Earthquakes: Reform and Participation in Post-War El Salvador* (Cambridge MA: Hemisphere Initiatives, 2001).

Spurk, C. *Media and Peacebuilding: Concepts, Actors and Challenges* (Bern: Swisspeace Center for Peacebuilding, 2002).

Stedman, S.J. *Peacemaking in Civil Wars: International Mediation in Zimbabwe, 1974–1980* (Boulder CO: Lynne Rienner, 1991).

Stedman, S.J. & F. Tanner (eds), *Refugee Manipulation: War, Politics, and the Abuse of Human Suffering* (Washington DC: Brookings Institution Press, 2003).

Stedman, S.J., D. Rothchild, & E.M. Cousens (eds), *Ending Civil Wars: The Implementation of Peace Agreements* (Boulder CO: Reinner, 2002).

Stein, J. & L. Pauly (eds), *Choosing to Cooperate: How States Avoid Loss* (Washington DC: The Johns Hopkins University Press, 1992).

Strobel, S. *Late Breaking Foreign Policy: The News Media's Influence on Peace Operations* (Washington DC: United States Institute of Peace Press, 1997).

Teitel, R. *Transitional Justice* (New York: Oxford University Press, 2000).

Terry, F. *Condemned to Repeat? The Paradox of Humanitarian Action* (Ithaca NY: Cornell University Press, 2002).

du Toit, P. 'South Africa: In Search of Post-Settlement Peace', in J. Darby & R. Mac Ginty (eds), *The Management of Peace Processes* (London: Macmillan, 2000) pp. 16–60, at 29, 30.

du Toit, P. *South Africa's Brittle Peace: The Problem of Post-Settlement Violence* (London: Macmillan, 2001).

Touval, S. *The Peace Brokers* (Princeton NJ: Princeton University Press, 1982).

Touval, S. 'Coercive Mediation on the Road to Geneva', in S. Touval & I.W. Zartman (eds), Negotiations in the Former Soviet Union and Former Yugoslavia, *International Negotiation*, 1, 3 (1996) pp. 547–570.

Touval, S. & I.W. Zartman (eds), *International Mediation in Theory and Practice* (Boulder CO: Westview, 1985).

United Nations, *The United Nations and El Salvador 1990–1995*, Blue Book Series, Volume IV (New York: United Nations Department of Public Information, 1995) (also known as 'United Nations Blue Book').

Urwin, D. 'Territorial Structures and Political Developments in the United Kingdom', in S. Rokkan & D. Urwin (eds), *The Politics of Territorial Identity* (London: Sage Publications, 1982).

van Schendel, W. & I. Abraham (eds), *Illicit Flows and Criminal Things: States, Borders, and the Other Side of Globalization* (Bloomington: Indiana University Press, 2005).

von Hippel, K. *Democracy By Force* (Cambridge: Cambridge University Press, 1999).

Wagner, R.H. 'The Causes of Peace', in R. Licklider (ed.), *Stopping the Killing: How Civil Wars End* (New York: New York University Press, 1993).

Waters, M. *Ethnic Options: Choosing Identities in America* (Cambridge MA: Harvard University Press, 1990).

Wheeler, N. 'The Political and Moral Limits of Western Military Intervention to Protect Civilians in Danger', in C. MacInnes & N. Wheeler (eds), *Dimensions of Western Military Intervention* (London: Frank Cass, 2002).

Wilkinson, P. 'Sharpening the Weapons of Peace: Peace Support Operations and Complex Emergencies', in T. Woodhouse & O. Ramsbotham (eds), *Peacekeeping and Conflict Resolution* (London: Frank Cass, 2000).

Williams, P. & K. Walter, *Militarization and Demilitarization in El Salvador's Transition to Democracy* (Pittsburgh PA: University of Pittsburgh Press, 1997).

Wolfsfeld, G. *Media and Political Conflict: News from the Middle East* (Cambridge: Cambridge University Press, 1997).

Wolfsfeld, G. 'Political Waves and Democratic Discourse: Terrorism Waves during the Oslo Peace Process', in W.L. Bennett & R. Entman (eds), *Mediated Politics: Communication in the Future of Democracy* (NewYork: Cambridge University Press, 2000).

Wolfsfeld, G. *Media and the Path to Peace* (Cambridge: Cambridge University Press, 2004).

Wood, E. *Forging Democracy from Below: Insurgent Transitions in South Africa and El Salvador* (Cambridge: Cambridge University Press, 2001).

Yack, B. 'The Myth of the Civic Nation', in Ronald Beiner (ed.), *Theorizing Nationalism* (Albany: State University of New York Press, 1999) pp. 103–118.

Young, C. *The Politics of Cultural Pluralism* (Madison : University of Wisconsin Press, 1976).

Young, C. (ed.), *The Rising Tide of Cultural Pluralism* (Madison : University of Wisconsin Press, 1993).

Young, C. *The African Colonial State in Comparative Perspective* (New Haven CT: Yale University Press, 1994).

Young, C. (ed.), *Ethnic diversity and Public Policy: A Comparative Inquiry* (Basingstoke: Macmillan, 1998).

Young, C. (ed.), *The Accommodation of Cultural Diversity: Case Studies* (Basingstoke: Macmillan, 1999).

Zahar, M. *Fanatics, Mercenaries, Brigands ... and Politicians: Militia Decision-Making and Civil Conflict Resolution* (PhD Dissertation, Canada, McGill University, 2000).

Zahar, M.J. 'Reframing the Spoiler Debate', in J. Darby & R. Mac Ginty (eds), *Contemporary Peacemaking* (Basingstoke: Palgrave, 2003) pp. 114–124.

Zahar, M.J. 'Power Sharing in Lebanon: Foreign Protectors, Domestic Peace, and Democratic Failure', in D. Rothchild & P. Roeder (eds), *Sustainable Peace* (2005) pp. 219–240.

Zahar, M.J. 'The Dichotomy of International Mediation and Leader Intransigence: The Case of Bosnia and Herzegovina', in I. O'Flynn & D. Russell (eds), *New Challenges for Power-Sharing: Institutional and Social Reform in Divided Societies* (London: Pluto Press, 2005).

Zahar, M.J. 'Political Violence in Peace Processes: Voice, Exit and Loyalty in the Post-Accord Period', in J. Darby (ed.), *Violence and Reconstruction* (Southbend IL: Notre Dame University Press, 2006).

Zahar, M.J. 'Understanding the Violence of Insiders: Loyalty, Custodians of Peace, and the Sustainability of Conflict Settlement', in E. Newman & O. Richmond (eds), *Spoilers and Peace Processes: Conflict Settlement and Devious Objectives* (Tokyo: United Nations University Press, 2006).

Zartman, I.W. 'The Strategy of Preventive Diplomacy in Third World Conflicts', in A. George (ed.), *Managing US-Soviet rivalry* (Boulder CO: Westview, 1983).

Zartman, I.W. *Ripe for Resolution: Conflict and Intervention in Africa* (New York: Oxford University Press, 1985).

Zartman, I.W. 'Ripening Conflict, Ripe Moment, Formula and Mediation', in D. BenDahmane & J. McDonald (eds), *Perspectives on Negotiation* (Washington DC: Government Printing Office, 1986).

Zartman, I.W. 'Ripeness: The Hurting Stalemate and Beyond', in P.C. Stern & D. Druckman (eds), *International Conflict Resolution after the Cold War* (Washington DC: National Academy Press, 2000) pp. 225–250.

Zartman, I.W. & M.R. Berman, *The Practical Negotiator* (New Haven CT: Yale University Press, 1982).

Zartman, I.W. & J. Aurik, 'Power Strategies in De-Escalation', in L. Kriesberg & J. Thornson (eds), *Timing The De-Escalation Of International Conflicts* (Syracuse NY: Syracuse University Press, 1991).

Zolberg, A., A. Suhrke, & S. Aguayo, *Escape from Violence: Conflict and the Refugee Crisis in the Developing World* (Oxford: Oxford University Press, 1989).

Index

9/11, 2, 7, 76, 115, 211, 267n, 357

Abbas, Mahmoud, 161
Aceh, 75, 112
Afghanistan, 7, 114, 115, 199
  Bonn peace process, 169
  elections, 234
  ISAF (International Security Assistance
    Force), 169
  Loya Jirga, 128
  and power-sharing, 206
African Union, 181–2
Agenda for Peace, 260, 263
Ahtisaari, Martti, 345
amnesty, 225, 328–35, 342, 366, 367, 369
ANC (African National Congress), 68, 70,
    81, 84, 89
Angola, 25, 150, 182, 234, 263, 294
  Lusaka Protocol, 168
  National Union for the Total
    Independence of Angola (UNITA),
    80, 154, 159, 171
  Popular Movement for the Liberation of
    Angola (MPLA), 80
  and ripeness, 29
  Tripartite Agreement, 83
Annan, Kofi, 107, 260
Arafat, Yasser, 73, 161, 347
Art, Robert, 64
Arusha, peace accord, 64, 150, 159, 263
Ashrawi, Hanan, 110
autonomy, 201, 242–53
  future of autonomies, 251–3
  importance of, 244–6
  legal basis, 246–8
  resistance to, 248–51

Bachelet, Michelle, 113
Baker, J., 26
Barak, Ehud, 240, 340
Basque Country, 6, 38, 46, 54, 55–6,
    94, 245, 341, 347, 352, 354, 362,
    363, 371
  Herri Batasuna, 339, 342

Paetido Nacionalista Vasco (PNV), 54, 55
Basque separatism, 26
Bayley, David, 304
Beijing Declaration, 106
Belgium, 14, 245
Bell, Christine, 346, 352
Benvenisti, Meron, 69
Berger, Oscar, 276
Blair, Tony, 48, 49, 53, 55
Bosnia, 19, 24, 150, 306
  Dayton Agreement, 67, 71, 170, 197,
    216, 220, 263–4, 314, 344, 348, 370
  elections, 232, 233
  human rights, 220–1
  Office of the High Representative,
    171–2
  power-sharing, 197
  and ripeness, 29
Bougainville, 120, 245, 248, 249, 252
Boutros-Ghali, Boutros, 260, 271
Brass, P., 18
Burton, John, 64, 65
Bush, George, Sr, 26
Bush, George, W., 66

Call, Charles, 155, 357, 360
Cambodia, 234, 263, 314–15
Campbell, J., 22
Canada, 240, 249–51
Catalonia, 55
Chechnya, 251
Chesterman, Simon, 226, 266
Chile, 100, 113, 346, 367
Chinkin, Christine, 112
civil society, 53, 110, 148, 153, 154–6,
    183, 187, 222, 258, 263, 277, 281, 346,
    360, 366
Cliffe, L., et al., 83
Clinton, Bill, 53, 144n
coercion, and negotiations, 64
Conciliation Resources, 349
confidence building measures, 9, 156, 354
conflict prevention, 102
Congress of Berlin, 95

Connor, W., 12
constructive dimension of ethnicity, 17
Contadora Group, 95
Convention on Indigenous Peoples, 247
Convention on the Elimination on all
    forms of Discrimination Against
    Women (CEDAW), 106
corruption, 113, 180, 183, 265, 266, 284,
    290, 294–6, 332
Corsica, 46, 54, 56–7, 342
Croatia, 305, 310
    Krajina offensive, 26
Crocker, C., 25–6, 30–1
Cuba
    and agreement with Angola and South
        Africa, 25–6
    and war in Angola, 81, 82
Curran, Brian, 341
Cyprus, 63, 71–2

Darby, John, 123, 147, 152, 172
Darfur, 64
De Klerk, FW, 84, 86
de Sota, A., 26
Delors, Jacques, 52
demobilization, 153–4, 167, 168, 184–5,
    301
    central America, 275–6
democracy, 2
Democracy in Plural Societies, 202
Democratic Republic of Congo (DRC),
    114, 182
Democratic Unionist Party, 57, 139, 216,
    233
democratisation, 5, 193, 216, 232, 260,
    282–3, 360
    and power-sharing, 199–200
    Spain, 46
DFID (Department for International
    Development), 263
disarmament, 168, 183–4
du Toit, Pierre, 354, 356

East Timor, *see* Timor-Leste
ECOWAS (Economic Community of West
    African States), 263
Egypt, 31
El Salvador, 26, 271–88, 345, 346
    COPAZ (National Commission for the
        Consolidation of Peace), 276

United Nations Commission for Truth
    for El Salvador, 279–80
Eritrea, 108, 197, 238
ETA (Basque Homeland and Freedom), 47,
    56, 57, 339, 347, 363
Ethiopia-Eritrean conflict, 24
ethnic conflict, 9
    dynamic of, 4, 17–18
ethnicity
    analytical approaches, 15–17
    conflict potential, 11–12, 14–15, 19
    constructivist dimension, 17
    instrumental dimension, 16–17
    and nationalism, 12–14
    primordial dimension, 15–16
ethnography, 289, 295, 298n
ethnonationalism, 12
European Commission, 51–2, 53
European Community of West African
    States (ECOWAS), 154, 332
European Convention on Human Rights,
    218, 220
European Round Table of Industrialists,
    52
European Union, 45, 243, 244, 309
    and Cyprus, 71–2
    institutions, 52

FAFO, 99
Falklands-Malvinas, 366
Fiji, 205, 343
Finland, 14
Fisher, Ron, 96, 101
Flint, Julie, 322
FLMC (Front de Libération Nationale de
    la Corse), 47
FMLN (Farabundo Marti National
    Liberation Front), 26, 274, 275–81,
    345, 354, 364
France, 19, 45–6, 48, 51, 81
    and Angola, 82
    and New Caledonia, 238–9, 246, 248

Gamba, Virginia, 155, 357
gender, *see* women
Geneva Protocol, 82
genocide, 11–12, 96
Ghai, Yash, 201, 358
Goodhand, Jonathan, 315
Gordhan, Pravin, 343

Goulding, Marrack, 27
governance, 54, 75, 186, 263, 266–7
Greenfeld, L., 12, 13
Groom, John, 366
Guatemala, 111–12, 271–88, 309, 346
    Accompaniment Commission, 277
    CEH (Historical Clarification
        Commission), 280
Guinea Bissau, 4
Gurr, T., 19

Hamas, 161, 233, 363
Hampson, Fen Olser, 276
Hani, Chris, 89
Hardin, R., 17
Herri Batasuna, 57
Hezbollah, 66, 233
Hobsbawm, E.J., 12
Hoffman, Mark, 65
Holbrooke, R., 26
Horowitz, D., 222
Hulme, David, 315
human rights, 106, 210–29, 279, 330
humanitarianism, 259
Hume, John, 55

Ignatieff, Michael, 261, 265, 267
India, 238, 242, 250
Indonesia, 243
informal economy, 289–99
instrumental dimension of ethnicity,
    16–17
Inter-American Development Bank, 124
international community, 108, 214, 272,
    282
    elections, 232, 234
    political will, 150
    top-down, 5, 124–5, 128, 187, 257, 266
International Court of Justice (ICJ), 80
International Criminal Court, 335, 369
International Crisis Group, 220
International Monetary Fund, 5, 258, 292
IRA (Irish Republican Army), 47, 56, 152,
    341, 345, 347, 363
Iraq, 7
    elections, 232, 234
ISDSC (InterState Defence and Security
    Committee), 182
Isetbegovic, President, 27
Islamic Jihad, 363

Israel, 15, 27, 29, 31, 66, 67, 68, 161, 243
Israel-Palestine, 4, 69, 99, 150, 242
    Declaration of Principles, 73, 216, 367
    human rights, 219–20
Issacs, H., 16

Jaspars, Suzanne, 321
Jordan-Israel Peace Treaty, 29, 141
JVP (Janatha Vimukti Peramuna), 233

Kashmir, 238
Kaufman, Chaim, 197
Keasley, Loraleigh, 96
Kenya, 126
Kissinger, Henry, 3, 22, 31, 64
Kleiboer, Marieke, 101
Korean War, 64
Kosovo, 114, 201, 226, 264, 310, 348, 362
    elections, 232, 234
    refugees, 320
Kroc Institute, 349
Kruschev, Nikita, 95
Krznaric, Roman, 319
Kuhn, T., 48

Lancaster House negotiations, 72
Lebanon, 154, 195, 196, 202, 233, 347, 352
    Taif Accord, 169–71
Lederach, John Paul, 27, 99, 196
Lemarchand, L., 18
liberal peace (liberal internationalism), 5,
    213, 225–6, 256–70
Liberia, 199, 263, 303
Lieberfield, D., 25
Lijphart, Arend, 202, 347
Lincoln, Abraham, 250
local participation, 124–5
Loder, Kare, 99
Lord's Resistance Army, 335, 369
Loughlin, John, 354
Lusaka Manifesto, 68, 305

Mac Ginty, Roger, 172
Madrid peace process on the
    Middle East, 29
Major, John, 339
Mali, 99
Mallon, Seamus, 64
Mandela, Nelson, 84, 89, 90, 96, 204, 339,
    354, 362

Mbeki, Thabo, 90
Media
  Gulf war, 134
  Northern Ireland, 139–40, 141
  Oslo Process, 136–9
  and peace negotiations, 131–44
  Vietnam war, 133
  and women, 110
Mediation
  dominant model, 95–6
  timing of, 22, 69, 97
mediators, 40, 98, 152
  appropriate mediators, 98–100
  insider-partial, 98–100
  outsider-neutral, 98–100
  roles and functions, 100–3
  women, 111
Meyer, Roelf, 343, 345
Mindanao, 4
Miskito/Sandinista negotiations, 37
Mitchell, Christopher, 354
Mitchell, George, 139, 339
Mozambique, 183, 291, 302
Mutually Enticing Opportunities (MEO),
  30–1
Mutually Hurting Stalemate (MHS), 22–3,
  24, 25, 26, 28, 29, 30, 64, 68, 274, 353

Namibia, 79, 80–4, 182
  Brazzaville Accord, 83
  Democratic Turnhalle Alliance, 84
  Geneva Protocol, 83
  Mount Etjo Agreement, 83
  UN Mission, 262
  WGC in, 81, 88, 95
Nan, Susan Allen, 101
nationalism, 12–14, 45–7, 258, 370
NATO (North Atlantic Treaty
  Organisation), 154
  and Afghanistan, 128
  and Bosnia, 26–7, 31, 170, 171, 263
negotiations, 4, 61, 94, 282, 363
  conflict resolution model, 66
  deadlines, 79–80
  endorsement, 72–3
  gender, 108–11
  implementation, 73–4
  innovations, 87
  institutionalization, 73–4
  media, 135–6

multilateral talks, 70–1
  phases of, 68–75
  pre-agreements, 214–15
  pre-talks, 68–70, 101, 353–4
  realpolitik model, 66
  reasons to resist, 66
  and ripeness, 37–9, 96
  rules and procedures, 78
  secret talks, 70, 84
  settlement, 71–2
  and trust, 64, 126
neo-liberal paradigm, 48, 52, 58n
neo-liberalism, 5, 53, 268n
Nepal, 1, 108, 213, 225
New African Partnership for Development
  (NEPAD), 181, 185, 187–9
  HISC (Heads of State Implementation
    Committee), 186
New Caledonia, 239
Nigeria, 16–17
  civil war, 16
'no war, no peace', 6, 212, 369–70
Nordic Council, 56
Nordstrom, Carolyn, 123
Northern Ireland, 4, 38, 46, 56, 69–70,
  98, 249, 347
  Anglo-Irish Agreement, 54, 56, 140
  British-Irish Council, 75
  Civil Rights Movement, 51
  elections, 235, 236
  Good Friday Agreement (or Belfast
    Agreement), 54, 75, 139–40, 200,
    218, 305, 341, 342, 357, 360, 362,
    364, 367
  human rights, 218–19, 223
  Independent International Commission
    on Decommissioning (IICD), 345
  media, 139–40
  Mitchell Principles, 344, 355, 362
  Omagh bombing, 140
  Peace People, 66
Norwegian Church Aid, 99
Nyerere, Julius, 242

ONUSAL (United Nations Mission in El
  Salvador), 277, 282
Organisation for Security and Cooperation
  in Europe (OSCE), 235, 310
Organization of African Unity (OAU), 96,
  183–4

Organization of American States (OAS), 96
Orjuela, Camila, 321
Oslo Process and Accords, 4, 73, 99, 110,
    161, 199, 354, 363
  media coverage, 136–9
Otegi, Arnaldo, 339

Paisley, Ian, 57, 66
Palau, 238
Paris, Roland, 226, 261
Peace accords/agreements
  criteria for success, 3
  enforcement, 72
  failed, 67
  framework/substantive agreements,
    215–21
  gender, 108–13
  implementation, 2, 3, 4, 5, 73–4
  'implementation agreements', 221–4
  pre-negotiation agreements, 214–15
  and war on terror, 211
peace dividend, 7, 89–91, 120, 147, 157,
    164–6, 256, 360, 368
peace implementation, 5, 113–15, 149
  compliance, 156, 170–1
  economics of, 6
  research agenda, 156–7
peace initiatives, timing, 22–35, 37
peace processes, 1, 94
  academic studies, 4
  critical views, 4–6, 120, 124
  definition, 2–3
  gender, 6, 105–19
  lending and borrowing, 1, 255,
    339–51
  pace of, 42
  regional dimensions, 4, 45
  sequencing and stages, 2, 105
  western dominance, 5
peacebuilding, 5, 41, 102, 171, 255
Philippines, 2, 4, 38, 114
PLO (Palestine Liberation Organization),
    69, 152, 160–1, 219, 355
police reform, 154–5
  El Salvador, 284
  Guatemala, 284
  Northern Ireland, 223
Portillo, Alfonso, 276, 281
post-accord crime, 147, 155, 181, 182,
    184–5, 276, 283, 304, 357

post-conflict elections, 230–41, 260,
    280–1
  and economic conditions, 233–4
post-war reconstruction, 4, 180, 189,
    255–6, 297–8, 361
Potter, Antonia, 361
power-sharing, 310–11
  and autonomy, 201
  consociationalism, 202–1, 203–4, 206
  and integration, 202–6
  and partition, 197–8
  problems with, 196–7
pre-negotiation, 3
primordial dimension of ethnicity, 15–16
Prunier, G., 18

Rabinovic, Itamar, 27
Ramaphosa, Cyril, 341
'Real' IRA, 56
reconciliation, 113, 121, 126, 127
refugees, 182
  and peace processes, 314–15
  politicization of refugees, 318–22
Rehn, Elizabeth, 108
Reilly, Ben, 203, 358, 360
religious identity, 18
Revolutionary United Front (RUF), 151, 159
Reynolds, Albert, 339
ripe moments, 22–3, 26
ripeness, 22–3, 24, 27, 29, 36, 64, 96, 149
  alternative metaphors, 41–3
  critique of, 37–9
  cultivation metaphor, 41–2
  in eye of the beholder, 39–40
  as a limited metaphor, 37–40
  as a rear-view mirror, 37–9
  and relationships, 41–2
Rothchild, Donald, 311
Rothstein, Robert, 284
Royal Ulster Constabulary, 223, 346
Rubin, Jeff, 97
Rwanda, 18, 19, 65, 67, 152, 154
  Gacaca, 122

Sadat, Anwar, 67
SADC (Southern African Development
    Community), 182
Said, Edward, 73
Samayoa, Salvador, 278
Sankoh, Foday, 334

SARPCCO (Southern African Regional Police Chiefs Coordinating Committee), 182
Saunders, Harold, 3, 101
Savimbi, Jonas, 168, 171, 234, 303
SDLP (Social Democratic and Labour Party), 55, 64, 139, 339
security dilemma, 149, 163, 168–9, 300, 308
Security Sector Reform, 277–9, 300–12
  military reform, 302–4
  policing, 304–11
  transitional security, 307–8
Sierra Leone, 67, 114, 161, 335
Single European Act, 52–3
Sinn Féin, 51, 56, 57, 69–70, 139, 218, 339, 341, 344, 355
Sirleaf, Ellen Johnson, 108
Sisk, Tim, 147, 313–14, 358
Snyder, Jack, 260
Sollenberg, M., 195
Somalia, 108
South Africa, 4, 28, 79, 81, 150, 168, 182, 214, 216, 243, 347, 357, 362, 367
  and Angola, 25–6
  and autonomy, 245–6
  colonization of Namibia, 80
  Congress of South African Trade Unions (COSATU), 91
  Congress for a Democratic South Africa (CODESA), 84–6, 87
  elections, 236
  human rights, 217–18, 224
  Independent Electoral Commission, 87, 88, 356
  Inkatha Freedom Party, 86, 88
  innovations in negotiations, 87, 341, 349
  international pressure, 85–6
  National Party, 71, 84–6, 342
  negotiations, 64, 343–4
  peace dividend, 89–91, 360, 368
  peace process, 84
  Reconstruction and Development Programme (RDP), 89–90
  Record of Understanding, 86, 88
  and regional disarmament, 183, 185
  South African Communist Party, 91
  Transitional Executive Council, 87, 356
  Truth and Reconciliation Commission, 329, 332, 342, 346, 360

women's representation, 114
South West African People's Organization (SWAPO), 80, 81, 83, 88
Soviet Union, 64, 80, 98
Spain, 46, 51, 346
  civil war, 47
Spear, J., 167
spoilers, 80, 110, 145, 147–58, 159–77
  capability, 167
  cost benefit analysis, 163–5
  incentives, 161–2
  insiders and outsiders, 163–6
  study of, 162, 167–8, 172–3
spoiling, 88
Spring, Dick, 344
Sri Lanka, 17, 201, 233, 237, 321
  and autonomy, 243, 249, 251
Stanley, William, 155, 357, 360
Stedman, Stephen, 25, 97, 160, 162, 165, 167–8, 173n, 205, 319, 357
Sudan, 4
  Darfur peace accord, 315
  government, 64
  north-south peace accord, 213, 249
  refugees, 320–1, 322–3
Sunningdale Agreement, 64
Syria, 27, 67, 169

Tamil Tigers, 17, 99, 354
Tamil United Liberation Front (TULF), 354
Tamils, 17, 243, 321
Tanner, Fred, 319
Taylor, Charles, 303, 331, 335
Thatcher, Margaret, 52
timing, 22–35, 37, 72, 75, 162
Timor-Leste, 107, 114, 127, 197, 357, 358
  Elections, 232, 234, 237–8
  Truth and Reconciliation Commission, 127
Touval, S., 24–5
Track Two, 99, 258, 353
traditional peacemaking, 120–30
  Afghanistan, 128
  case for, 123–6
  definitions, 121–3
  Kenya, 126
  Timor-Leste, 127–8
transitional justice, 328–30
Treaty of Westphalia, 340

Tripartite Agreement, 83
truth recovery, 255, 279–80
  Liberia, 331–2, 335
  Sierra Leone, 333–4, 335
  Special Court for Sierra Leone, 329, 331

UK, 46, 51
  DFID (Department for International
    Development), 124
Ulster Defence Association (UDA), 152
Ulster Democratic Party (UDP), 344
Ulster Unionist Party (UUP), 139, 218,
  345
UNAMA (United Nations Assistance
  Mission to Afghanistan), 265
UNAVEM (United Nations Angola
  Verification Mission), 184
UNDP (United Nations Development
  Programme), 257, 310
UNHCR (United Nations High
  Commission on Refugees), 220, 257,
  315–16
UNIFEM (United Nations Development
  Fund for Women), 108
United Kingdom Unionist Party, 139
United Nations, 96
  and Bosnia, 27
  and Cyprus, 72
  Division for the Advancement of
    Women, 112
  Human Rights Committee, 247
  International Decade of the World's
    Indigenous Peoples, 123
  Peacebuilding Commission, 124, 259
  Resolution on Women, Peace and
    Security, 106
  theorising UN peacebuilding, 258–61
United States Institute of Peace (USIP),
  349
Universal Declaration on Human Rights,
  210
UNMIK (United Nations Interim
  Administration Mission in Kosovo),
  201, 264
UNTAET (United Nations Transitional
  Administration in East Timor), 264–5

UNTAC (United Nations Transitional
  Authority in Cambodia), 263, 303
UNTAG (United Nations Transition
  Assistance Group), 81, 83
Uppsala, 195, 349, 371n
URNG (Guatemalan National
  Revolutionary Movement), 274,
  275–81, 348–9
USA, 4, 19, 64, 67
  and Angola, 81, 82
  and central America, 274
  and Israel-Palestine, 99
USAID (United States Agency for
  International Development), 263

Vietnam, 67, 71, 72–3
violence, 145
  causes of, 67–8
  cycles of, 37, 47, 51
  economics of, 167, 169, 321
  impact on peace settlements, 148–50
  separatist, 47
  by the state, 47, 58n

Wall, James, 101
Wallensteen, P., 195
'war on terror', 2, 7, 76, 211, 357
Waters, M., 15
Western Contact Group, 81–2, 88, 95
Western Sahara, 238
The White House Years, 64
Wolfsfeld, Gadi, 355
women
  gendered roles, 108
  legal instruments and resources,
    106–8
  Wood, Elizabeth, 140
World Bank, 5, 124, 257, 258, 263–5

Yugoslavia, 26

Zahar, M.J., 151, 152, 153, 357
Zartman, I.W., 36, 64, 68, 69, 96–7, 149,
  353
Zimbabwe, 25, 72, 182
Zolberg, Ari, 318